RECENT AMERICA: A HISTORY

Book Two: Since 1933

RECENT AMERICA: A HISTORY

Book One: 1900–1933

Book Two: Since 1933

Book Two: Since 1933

RECENT AMERICA

A History

HENRY BAMFORD PARKES

VINCENT P. CAROSSO

New York University

THOMAS Y. CROWELL COMPANY

New York, Established 1834

COPYRIGHT © 1963 BY THOMAS Y. CROWELL COMPANY
All Rights Reserved

No part of this book may be reproduced in any form,
by mimeograph or any other means, without permission
in writing from the publisher, except by a reviewer,
who may quote brief passages in a review to be
published in a magazine or newspaper.

Library of Congress Catalog Card Number: 63-9192

TYPOGRAPHY BY LAUREL WAGNER
COVER DESIGN BY THOMAS RUZICKA

Manufactured in the United States of America
by Vail-Ballou Press, Inc., Binghamton, N.Y.

Preface

Although any division of history into periods must be some-what arbitrary, there are good reasons for regarding either the Spanish-American War of 1898 or the accession to the Presidency of Theodore Roosevelt in 1901 as the beginning of a new epoch in the development of the United States. American history since these two events has been dominated by many of the same trends, and the people of the United States have been confronted by many of the same basic problems. An equally significant dividing line is the year 1933, when the newly elected administration of Franklin D. Roosevelt assumed the responsibility of alleviating the numerous social and economic problems arising from the grave economic crisis facing the nation. The legislation that followed Roosevelt's inauguration radically altered many previously held conceptions of the proper role of the federal government in promoting the general welfare.

The later nineteenth century was a period of rapid expansion in both agriculture and industry, with little awareness of the consequent growth of economic inequality and insecurity. During the twentieth century the chief factor causing social change has been the continued growth of machine technology and of the large corporation as the characteristic institution of machine civilization; furthermore, the American people have become increasingly concerned about the economic, social, and political problems which this growth has presented. Thus, the main trend in American political history during the twentieth century has been the prolonged attempt of the American people to cope realistically with these problems.

During the nineteenth century the United States enjoyed complete security against any possible attack from abroad and was able to indulge in the luxury of isolation in foreign affairs. The twentieth century, on the

vi   PREFACE

other hand, has witnessed the emergence of the United States as a world power, and its gradual assumption of the responsibilities of leading the free world in defense against Communist aggression.

Both of these twentieth-century trends are of enormous and lasting importance in this era of increasing momentum. History moves more rapidly than at any earlier period. Attitudes and opinions need constant revision, and doctrines firmly established only a decade ago appear already to require change.

Our purpose has been to present a clear and reasonably comprehensive account of recent American history in terms intelligible to both the college student and the general reader. Our central theme has been the political and economic development of American society. We have also given considerable attention to social, cultural, and intellectual changes and have sought to relate these to the main lines of American development. But our central emphasis has been upon political and economic changes at home and on the growth of American interests and responsibilities abroad.

Any historical account that aims to be more than a lifeless chronicle of events must necessarily reflect the point of view of the historian; and while we have sought to achieve strictest factual accuracy and to present opposing interpretations fairly, we have not tried to suppress our own judgment of events. We believe that both the movement toward greater governmental supervision of the economy and the assumption by the United States of international responsibilities, despite numerous errors and failures, have been necessitated by historic trends too powerful to be resisted. And we feel that, with wise statesmanship, they promise a better life not only for Americans but for all mankind.

We should like to express our thanks to Professor John Morton Blum of Yale University and Professor John D. Hicks of the University of California at Berkeley for the care with which they read the entire manuscript and for their many invaluable suggestions. We are indebted also to Mrs. Julanne Arnold and Mr. Philip Winsor of the Thomas Y. Crowell Company for editorial advice and services far beyond the call of duty, and to Mr. Irving Katz, a doctoral candidate at New York University, for assisting us in checking the bibliographies. Rose Carosso helped by typing a large part of the manuscript, and several of our colleagues gave us the benefit of their expert knowledge.

H.B.P.
V.P.C.

New York City
December, 1962

Contents

Preface   v

I   THE ERA OF FRANKLIN D. ROOSEVELT, 1933–1945

1   The New Deal, I, 1933–1934   3

FRANKLIN D. ROOSEVELT   *4*
THE PERSONNEL OF THE NEW DEAL   *10*
THE PURPOSES OF THE NEW DEAL   *12*
THE FIRST "ONE HUNDRED DAYS": THE BANK CRISIS   *16*
THE BEGINNING OF THE NEW DEAL   *18*
THE CONGRESSIONAL ELECTIONS OF 1934   *50*
Suggested Readings   *51*

2   The New Deal, II, 1935–1936   58

OPPOSITION TO THE NEW DEAL   *59*
FROM THE "FIRST" TO THE "SECOND" NEW DEAL   *70*
THE LEGISLATION OF THE SEVENTY-FOURTH CONGRESS   *72*
THE ELECTION OF 1936   *94*
Suggested Readings   *100*

viii CONTENTS

3 The New Deal, III, 1937–1939   104

THE SUPREME COURT FIGHT *105*
THE MEAGER LEGISLATIVE RECORD OF 1937 *113*
THE BUSINESS RECESSION OF 1937–1938 *115*
THE SECOND AGRICULTURAL ADJUSTMENT ACT *116*
THE FAIR LABOR STANDARDS ACT *117*
THE DECLINE OF THE NEW DEAL *120*
THE CONGRESSIONAL ELECTIONS OF 1938 *121*
THE NEW DEAL AND THE FEDERAL BUDGET *123*
THE NEW DEAL AND THE ECONOMIC SYSTEM *126*
Suggested Readings *130*

4 American Foreign Policy and the Coming
of World War II, 1933–1941   133

ISOLATION OR INTERVENTION? *134*
THE HULL TRADE TREATIES *137*
LATIN AMERICA *138*
THE FAR EAST, 1933–1940 *142*
EUROPE, 1933–1940 *144*
THE ELECTION OF 1940 *152*
THE ROAD TO WAR, 1940–1941 *159*
Suggested Readings *181*

5 The United States in World War II, 1941–1945   186

THE ALLIED NATIONS ON THE DEFENSIVE, 1941–1943 *186*
THE ROAD TO VICTORY, 1943–1945 *200*
Suggested Readings *224*

6 Mobilizing the Home Front and
Allied Diplomacy, 1941–1945   229

THE HOME FRONT, 1941–1945 *229*
WARTIME DIPLOMACY *248*
THE DEATH OF FRANKLIN D. ROOSEVELT *270*
Suggested Readings *271*

II THE UNITED STATES AND THE POSTWAR WORLD, 1945–1961

7 The Beginning of the Truman Era, 1945–1947   279

EFFORTS TO ESTABLISH THE PEACE *282*
DEMOBILIZATION *288*
RECONVERSION *291*
LAUNCHING THE "FAIR DEAL" *296*
DEMOCRATIC PARTY DISCORD AND DISUNITY *303*
THE DEVELOPMENT OF A BIPARTISAN FOREIGN POLICY *315*
THE DISINTEGRATION OF THE GRAND ALLIANCE, 1945–1947 *316*
Suggested Readings *328*

8 The Truman Policies, 1947–1952   333

THE FOREIGN POLICY OF "CONTAINMENT" *333*
THE ELECTION OF 1948 *348*
THE FAIR DEAL, 1949–1952 *356*
RUSSIA AND THE UNITED STATES IN THE FAR EAST,
      1945–1952 *364*
Suggested Readings *382*

9 The Fair Deal Yields to Modern Republicanism   387

LOYALTY AND INTERNAL SECURITY, 1949–1953 *387*
THE END OF THE DEMOCRATIC ERA *396*
THE ELECTION OF 1952 *398*
THE BEGINNING OF THE EISENHOWER ERA, 1953–1956 *406*
Suggested Readings *433*

10 The Eisenhower Years   435

FOREIGN POLICY, 1953–1956 *435*
THE ELECTION OF 1956 *451*
DOMESTIC DEVELOPMENTS, 1956–1961 *455*
FOREIGN POLICY, 1956–1961 *473*
Suggested Readings *492*

x CONTENTS

II Social and Cultural Developments 495

RELIGION 496
EDUCATION 499
THE PRESS 502
SOCIAL TRENDS 503
PROBLEMS OF INEQUALITY 507
THE ARTS AND THE SCIENCES 511
Suggested Readings 520

12 The New Frontier of John F. Kennedy 523

THE ELECTION OF 1960 523
JOHN F. KENNEDY 529
Suggested Readings 535

Index 539

PART I THE ERA OF
F.D.R., 1933–1945

I

The New Deal, I

1933-1934

ON MARCH 4, 1933, when Franklin Delano Roosevelt took office as President, most of the banks in the nation were closed, the depression was at its worst, and there was a widespread feeling that possibly democratic government might be abandoned and some form of dictatorship established. Never before, in the whole history of the United States, had pessimism been deeper or more nearly universal. The descent from the heights of the prosperity of 1928 had been precipitous and rapid. By 1933 the realization of what had happened and the fact that no one seemed to know what to do to stem the tide of bankruptcies, foreclosures, and unemployment and their heavy toll of human suffering created an atmosphere of fear and desperation which paralyzed the nation. Roosevelt responded to the challenge at once, and in his inaugural address promised that he would take "direct, vigorous action" against the depression along a broad front. But even more important than the promise to do something immediately was his reassertion of faith in the democratic process and in the ability of the American people to bring about recovery. "This great Nation," he declared, "will endure as it has endured, will revive and will prosper. So, first of all, let me assert my firm belief that the only thing we have to fear is fear itself—nameless, unreasoning, unjustified

4   THE ERA OF F.D.R., 1933–1945

terror which paralyzes needed efforts to convert retreat into advance." Roosevelt's inaugural address revived hope and aroused the spirit of the people. In the midst of a great fear he did not despair. He stood before them, optimistic about the future and confident in the ability of the American people to resolve the economic plight which beset them.

FRANKLIN D. ROOSEVELT

Career to 1933

Franklin Delano Roosevelt came from an old, wealthy, patrician New York family, distantly related to that of President Theodore Roosevelt. Born at Hyde Park on January 30, 1882, the only child of his father's second marriage, F.D.R. grew up in an atmosphere of indulgence, enjoying all of the privileges that go with wealth and social position. Tutored privately at home until he was fourteen years old, he then went on to study at Groton and Harvard. Like his kinsman Theodore Roosevelt, F.D.R. traveled widely in his youth, and while on his numerous European sojourns he also studied abroad. By the time he had graduated from Harvard (1904), he was as much at home in the major European cities as he was in those of his own country. On March 17, 1905, while studying law at Columbia University, he married a sixth cousin, Anna Eleanor Roosevelt. President Theodore Roosevelt, "the lion of the afternoon," according to the bride, gave his niece away in marriage. Admitted to the New York bar in 1907, F.D.R. practiced law on Wall Street until 1910, when, much to everyone's surprise, the Republican stronghold of Dutchess County elected him as a Democrat to the New York State senate.

During the campaign, in which the opposition accused him of being the legal representative of the very trusts which Teddy Roosevelt had fought, he attacked boss rule, aligned himself with the progressive reformers of both parties, and supported the policies of the state's popular Republican Governor Charles Evans Hughes. "I am running," he said again and again, "squarely on the issue of honesty and economy and efficiency in our State Senate . . . ." [1] Elected by a plurality of 1,140 votes, Roosevelt at once indicated that he intended to fulfill his pledge to fight for clean government. He opposed Tammany Hall's choice for United States sen-

[1] Quoted in Frank Freidel, *Franklin D. Roosevelt: The Apprenticeship* (Boston [1952]), p. 93.

ator and, with a group of Democratic insurgents in the legislature, prevented Tammany from dictating who would be the party's choice. His fight with the bosses attracted considerable attention in New York and among progressive leaders in other states. As a result, Roosevelt became associated with "insurgency" and progressivism, both of which were becoming increasingly powerful forces in American politics at this time. F.D.R.'s progressivism at first, however, was largely political. It centered around fighting bossism and promoting more political democracy by endorsing such reforms as the direct primary, the direct election of senators, and, after some hesitation, women's suffrage.

Within the next two years Roosevelt's preoccupation with political reform was to change markedly, as he realized that the social and economic programs which Theodore Roosevelt and Woodrow Wilson were elaborating on the national level confirmed what he was discovering about conditions in his own state. The progressive debate of 1911 and 1912, as well as Roosevelt's own humanitarian instincts, idealism, and sympathy for the plight of the underprivileged, caused him to extend and broaden his own ideas about the need and wisdom of social justice legislation. In 1912, for example, he spoke of the necessity to secure "the liberty of the community" against individual selfishness. The following year, he supported various legislative proposals to benefit the worker, such as a workmen's compensation law, and he fought hard to secure the passage of a bill to limit the labor of sixteen- to twenty-one-year-old youths to fifty-four hours a week. When the New York Factory Investigation Commission recommended a comprehensive program of reforms, he approved and supported all of it. F.D.R.'s concern for labor's welfare did not prevent him from continuing to safeguard and promote the interests of the farmers whom he represented. After his reelection in 1912, he introduced legislation to regulate New York City's commission merchants, to strengthen the state's agricultural cooperatives, and enlarge farm credits, and, along with Republican and Democratic progressives, he supported Governor Hughes's efforts to promote forest conservation and to develop the state's water power resources. By 1913, when Roosevelt left Albany to become Wilson's Assistant Secretary of the Navy, he was a respected leader of the New York Democratic party's progressive wing. Because of this and because he had been an "original Wilson man," wanted the job, and had favorably impressed Josephus Daniels, Wilson's Secretary of the Navy, he received the appointment.

Despite his youth—he was thirty-one years old—Roosevelt fulfilled

THE ERA OF F.D.R., 1933–1945

the many duties of his job with marked ability. While in the New York senate, he had learned much about the many-faceted and useful art of practical politics. The administration of the Navy Department provided him with ample opportunity to exercise his talents in accommodating the many differences which arose between the naval and civilian personnel. Roosevelt's knowledge of ships and the sea and the fact that he was a "big navy" man made him *persona grata* with the career officers, who had little use for Secretary Daniels' plans to reform the Navy Department, while his sympathetic understanding of the civilian workers' interests caused him to win the cooperation of organized labor. Roosevelt proved equally capable in his other duties, which included resolving knotty contract negotiations with businessmen and procurement difficulties with suppliers, and, once the United States was at war, meeting the many pressing problems and decisions involved in expanding the navy and planning its operations with those of the Allies. The Navy Department provided Roosevelt with invaluable experience: he emerged from it an effective political administrator with an enhanced national reputation and influential contacts throughout the country. As the Democratic vice presidential candidate in 1920, he campaigned vigorously across the country, defending Wilson and the League and, with prophetic truth, accusing the indecisive and vacillating Harding of being incapable of governing. Defeated by the landslide which drove the Democrats from power, Roosevelt at thirty-eight prepared to retire from politics, at least temporarily, and to return to his New York law practice.

In August, 1921, while vacationing with his family at Campobello, in New Brunswick, he was stricken with infantile paralysis. For the next three years he battled to regain control of his legs, and though his progress was remarkable, considering the original extent of the paralysis, he was never again able to walk without crutches and braces. Roosevelt refused to be an invalid or succumb to his mother's desire that he live the life of a Hyde Park country squire managing the family estate. By the end of the year, he was already corresponding with Democratic politicos, and with the aid of his wife and Louis McHenry Howe, his close friend and political adviser since 1911, F.D.R. became increasingly involved in his party's affairs. No one worked so hard, so long, or with such unswerving loyalty, dedication, and effectiveness to put Roosevelt in the White House as Howe. Sickly, frail, and likened in appearance to a "medieval gnome" and "a troll out of a Catskill cave," [2] Howe operated efficiently and con-

---

[2] James MacGregor Burns, *Roosevelt: The Lion and the Fox* (New York [1956]), p. 44.

THE NEW DEAL, I (1933-1934)

tinuously on all levels of political activity. He persuaded Eleanor Roosevelt to take an active part in Democratic party affairs and tutored her in the ways of politics. These efforts, along with Roosevelt's own statements to the press, kept his name before the public.

Meanwhile, his convalescence had progressed sufficiently by 1924 for him to accept Alfred E. Smith's offer to deliver the New York governor's nominating address before the Democratic presidential convention of that year. This speech, in which he referred to Smith as the " 'happy warrior' of the political battlefield," was Roosevelt's first important public appearance in four years, and it proved to be an immensely successful one, not only because of the plaudits his address earned from the politicians, but because it marked Roosevelt's return to active politics. Smith lost the nomination to Davis and the latter lost the election to Coolidge, and for the next four years Roosevelt worked to reform and rejuvenate the Democratic party, but with little success. At the 1928 Democratic convention, however, he nominated Smith for the Presidency again, and this time the New Yorker won. Because he wished to assist Smith in his campaign and because the party needed a strong candidate to keep New York State Democratic, Roosevelt agreed to accept the draft for governor, though he had strong misgivings about the political wisdom of his decision, as well as doubts as to whether his health had improved sufficiently to allow him to take on such a responsibility. Elected while Smith went down to defeat, F.D.R. was reelected in 1930 with an even larger majority.

As governor of New York, Roosevelt carried on and extended the liberal programs inaugurated by Smith and introduced others of his own. He was not always successful in achieving all his goals, and often he was forced to accept compromises. He advocated public ownership of power sites, but like his predecessor failed to get the legislature to approve his program; and although public welfare, social security, and labor laws were enacted during his first term, these measures fell far short of what he had recommended.

Roosevelt moved with far greater speed and decisiveness to meet the onslaught of the depression. When it became apparent that private and local charities could not meet the demands of the needy and unemployed, he proposed that the state government provide the necessary relief assistance. "In broad terms I assert," he told the New York legislature on August 28, 1931, "that modern society, acting through its Government, owes the definite obligation to prevent the starvation or the dire want of any of its fellow men and women who try to maintain themselves but cannot . . . . To these unfortunate citizens," he went on to say, "aid must be extended by Government, not as a matter of charity, but as a matter of social duty." Because of the advanced and comprehensive work relief and welfare programs that he proposed and the legislature enacted, New York was the first state to appropriate money for local relief during the depression. Many of these measures, along with the welfare, labor, and farm aid laws which Roosevelt sponsored while at Albany, later served as models for the New Deal program of 1933.

Because of his record, Roosevelt was generally regarded as a liberal and a progressive; yet because he had been vague and contradictory during the campaign, few people expected that as President he would display unusual talents or adopt any very novel policies. When Roosevelt entered the White House, he was, as Walter Johnson has suggested, still "grossly underrated." [3]

Roosevelt as President

The Roosevelt administration sponsored legislation of an importance and a variety equaled by none of its predecessors, and its leader inspired both admiration and hatred of an intensity almost without precedent in American history. For twelve years Roosevelt provided the American people with the leadership required to fight the worst depression and the greatest war in their history. Whatever may be the judgment of posterity concerning the achievements and deficiencies of his administration, his ability to lead and to inspire hope and confidence is indisputable. Above all else, Roosevelt possessed remarkable political competence, as exhibited by his capacity to win popular approval and to understand, express, and respond to popular sentiment. He was an excellent public speaker and, despite his "Hah-vahd accent," unequaled over the radio. When he spoke to the nation in his fireside chats, people everywhere and in all stations of life listened attentively, convinced that he was speaking to each one of them and that he was personally interested and concerned with their individual problems. The radio became a potent weapon in Roosevelt's political arsenal, not only because of his magnificent radio voice or because of the simplicity and clarity of his prose, but because he knew when and how to use it effectively. More important, he learned how to project his personality over it, with all of its warmth, charm, good humor, confidence, and self-assurance.

[3] Walter Johnson, *1600 Pennsylvania Avenue* (Boston, 1960), p. 49.

Throughout his life Roosevelt had a warm sympathy for the under-privileged and a real desire to improve their condition, but neither in his social ideas nor in his political or economic ones was there anything doctrinaire about him. He was an intuitive and pragmatic statesman who displayed courage, persistence, and a willingness to make innovations and to abandon doctrines and practices he believed to be no longer valuable. "The country," he told a preconvention audience in May, 1932, "needs . . . the country demands bold, persistent experimentation. It is common sense to take a method and try it. If it fails admit it frankly and try another. But above all, try something." This was Roosevelt's approach to most problems, and it explains much of the confusion and contradiction which characterized many of his policies and programs. At the same time, however, he showed, as his numerous public addresses reveal, an awareness of national and international problems which was unusual for both its penetration and its comprehensiveness. His friends held that his qualities ranked him among the greatest of American Presidents. His enemies, on the other hand, declared that he was too eager for power, that he made political stability and economic recovery impossible by constant changes in his methods and tactics, and that in the execution of his policies he showed himself a careless and ineffective administrator and a poor judge of men.

There was equal disagreement as to the objectives of the Roosevelt administration. The heir of prewar progressivism, Roosevelt himself wished to preserve and strengthen the American system of political democracy and of private capitalistic enterprise. He believed, however, that it was now necessary for the government to intervene in economic processes and to enforce new methods upon capitalistic industry and finance. He became President at the time when the Nazi dictatorship was being established in Germany; and he was convinced that unless capitalist democracy in the United States could reform itself, it would eventually be either overthrown by revolution or replaced by dictatorship. Roosevelt's enemies, however, insisted that he was bringing about the very thing which he wished to avoid: that in attempting to reform the economic system, he was depriving it of its freedom and subjecting it to bureaucratic control, and that in trying to save democracy by government action, he was laying the foundations of dictatorship.

As head of the Democratic party, Roosevelt endeavored to work in cooperation with the Democratic leaders in Congress. Like Theodore Roosevelt and Woodrow Wilson, both of whom he admired, Roosevelt looked

THE ERA OF F.D.R., 1933–1945

upon the Presidency as "pre-eminently a place of moral leadership." During his tenure he greatly extended presidential authority, and, as with Woodrow Wilson, the most permanent consequences of F.D.R.'s years in the White House may be their effect upon the growth, influence, and prestige of the Executive. Most of the legislation of the New Deal originated in the Executive rather than in the legislative department of the government. Many of the Democrats in Congress, once the immediate crisis of the depression had passed, were unsympathetic to the more liberal aspects of the New Deal. Much of the voting strength of the party came from the South, and while some of the southern Democrats were the spokesmen of workers and tenant farmers, there were a number who represented the interests of landlords and industrialists and were likely to rebel against some of Roosevelt's proposals. In the North, the Democratic organization consisted partly of corrupt city machines, such as those in New York, Chicago, Boston, Jersey City, and Kansas City, and partly of conservative elements with Wall Street connections. While the city machines continued to support the New Deal for purely partisan reasons, many of the conservative Democrats became its outspoken opponents. The most genuine adherents of the New Deal were, for the most part, outside the Democratic party organization. They included the trade unions, the bulk of the farm population, many progressive Republicans who had supported Theodore Roosevelt in 1912 and La Follette in 1924, and a number of young intellectuals, lawyers, and college professors who believed in the need for radical reforms in the economic system. However, although the New Dealers made up a considerable proportion of the voting population, as proved in the elections of 1934 and 1936, they were inadequately represented in Congress. The machinery of the American political system failed to provide a fair representation of the popular will.

THE PERSONNEL OF THE NEW DEAL

The discordance between the Democrats and the New Dealers was reflected in Roosevelt's cabinet and among his advisers. Vice President John Nance Garner of Texas, Secretary of State Cordell Hull of Tennessee, Secretary of War George H. Dern of Utah, Secretary of the Navy Claude A. Swanson of Virginia, Attorney General Homer Cummings of Connecticut, Secretary of Commerce Daniel C. Roper of South Carolina, and Postmaster General James A. Farley of New York were members of the Democratic party. Farley, chairman of the Democratic National Committee, was regarded as one of the ablest political managers in American history because of his role as one of the chief engineers of Roosevelt's nomination and election. The other members of this group had very little influence over the program of the New Deal. Cordell Hull, however, gradually asserted himself as one of the strongest figures in the administration and as its most universally respected member. Of the other members of the cabinet, Secretary of the Interior Harold L. Ickes of Illinois and Secretary of Agriculture Henry A. Wallace of Iowa were progressive Republicans; Secretary of Labor Frances Perkins of New York, the first woman to be appointed to a cabinet position, had been a social worker; and Secretary of the Treasury William H. Woodin of Pennsylvania, the Republican president of the American Car and Foundry Company, was a personal friend of F.D.R.'s. Of this latter group, Ickes and Perkins served throughout Roosevelt's four terms, and Wallace remained in the cabinet until 1940. All three of these officials fulfilled important administrative functions and were responsible for the execution of numerous programs. Ill health forced Woodin to resign, and early in 1934 he was replaced by Henry Morgenthau, Jr., the President's Dutchess County neighbor and publisher of the influential *American Agriculturalist,* who had already served Roosevelt as chairman of the New York State Agricultural Advisory Committee and as Commissioner of Conservation. Morgenthau remained an influential and loyal member of the administration to the very end.

Roosevelt also gathered around him at the White House a group of personal advisers, who had accompanied him from Albany and who became known as the "brain trust" because of their academic backgrounds. The membership of this group changed according to Roosevelt's needs, and as a group they did not survive the first term. Among the original members were Raymond Moley, Rexford G. Tugwell, and Adolf A. Berle, Jr., three Columbia University professors; Arthur E. Morgan, the president of Antioch College; and O. M. W. Sprague, professor of banking and finance at Harvard University. This group had been formed to gather material on current questions, such as banking and corporation and business policy, and to help prepare Roosevelt's speeches during the presidential campaign. During the early period of the New Deal it continued to supply him with information and advice and to recommend policies.

Moley and Hugh S. Johnson, a retired brigadier general with considerable business experience who helped draft and administer much of the early New Deal's business and industrial policy, soon left and became vocal opponents of Roosevelt. Thomas G. Corcoran, a brilliant, politically astute, and enterprising $10,000-a-year lawyer in the Reconstruction Finance Corporation who had assisted the administration in writing and pushing through the security legislation, then took over as F.D.R.'s chief administrative assistant. One of Harvard University law professor Felix Frankfurter's most promising protégés, Corcoran never held an official White House title, but between 1936 and 1940 he was, according to Samuel I. Rosenman, also a long-time presidential assistant, "as intimate and important a part of the Administration as any Cabinet officer or Presidential adviser . . . and much more so than most of them." [4] When "Tommy the Cork," as F.D.R. used to call him, fell from grace, he was replaced by the Iowa-born social worker Harry L. Hopkins, who came to Roosevelt's attention because of his excellent welfare work in New York City and, after the onset of the depression, for his relief work in the state. In 1933 Hopkins went to Washington to head the Federal Emergency Relief Administration. He later became chief of the Works Progress Administration and Secretary of Commerce, and filled other high posts in the defense and war efforts. Hopkins remained Roosevelt's chief adviser and close associate until the President's death.

From the time he was first inaugurated until his death on April 12, 1945, Roosevelt faced a vast and increasing array of complex problems and crises which required expert knowledge and immediate attention. Like Washington, Jackson, and Wilson before him, F.D.R. made use of presidential assistants to facilitate and expedite the many duties which the depression and the war imposed upon him. With but few exceptions, these presidential aides made an impressive contribution to the success of the Roosevelt administrations.

THE PURPOSES OF THE NEW DEAL

The legislation of the early New Deal was enacted to meet specific problems which demanded immediate attention. Because of this, many of its features and some of its purposes were blurred; its long-term objectives were not clearly defined, and many of its immediate programs were not systematically integrated. In retrospect, however, it is possible to distinguish to some extent between measures designed to restore economic activity and bring about recovery, measures designed to reform the eco-

[4] Quoted in Louis W. Koenig, *The Invisible Presidency* (New York [1960]), p. 251.

"THE NEW DEAL'S SEVEN DWARFS"—A WASHINGTON VIEW

President Roosevelt and the New Dealers were strongly criticized by the editorial writers and cartoonists of the conservative press for failing to balance the budget and for squandering government funds on what conservatives considered unsound relief and recovery projects. (Brown Brothers)

nomic system and prevent future depressions, and measures of long-range planning which pointed to the eventual growth of a new kind of economic order. The recovery measures, which predominated during the early months of the New Deal, had the purpose of checking the process of deflation and bankruptcy by generally raising prices and wages and by making an expansion of credit possible. Some of these measures may be regarded as a continuation of the Hoover program, but in a far more drastic and comprehensive form. Meanwhile, federal money was appropriated for unemployment relief, and no real attempt was made to balance the budget. Some of the New Dealers regarded large-scale federal spending for relief as in itself a recovery measure which would stimulate purchasing power. Roosevelt himself, however, does not appear to have accepted this point of view until 1938, and then only hesitantly and as a temporary expedient. If he left the budget unbalanced, it was not from choice but because the resources of the states and municipalities were almost exhausted and there was now no other method of feeding the unemployed.

These recovery measures failed to end the depression, and from this the New Dealers drew the conclusion that more radical changes in the functioning of the economic system were required. Once the crisis had passed, business leaders started to oppose vigorously even the relatively conservative measures of government regulation adopted at the outset of the New Deal. For these and other reasons, such as the demands of labor and other groups who wanted more security, Roosevelt was gradually driven to adopt more radical policies. At this point, reform began to prevail over recovery. Among the measures of reform may be included collective bargaining for labor, raising of wages and shortening of hours, insurance against unemployment and old age, and government regulation of stock exchanges and public utilities. These measures were adopted in the belief that the primary cause of depression was deficiency of purchasing power on the part of workers and farmers. Government action, it was argued, must establish a fairer balance between the different sections of the community. Roosevelt emphasized the conception of balance, which was central to much of his thinking, in a number of his speeches. "What we seek," he declared on March 5, 1934, "is balance in our economic system —balance between agriculture and industry and balance between the wage earner, the employer, and the consumer. We seek also balance that our internal market be kept rich and large, and that our trade with other nations be increased on both sides of the ledger."

Meanwhile the New Deal also adopted certain measures of long-range planning of a kind which progressives had favored for a long time and which probably interested Roosevelt himself more than any other part of his program. These measures included the conservation of natural resources, particularly of the soil, the development of cheap electrical power, and provision for rural communities of the facilities made possible by modern science. In their ultimate effects, these measures of the New Deal may prove to be more important than its program of reform, while its program of reform will probably be considered more significant than its program of recovery.

Although many of the changes made by the New Deal were admitted, even by a number of its opponents, to be necessary and permanent, the New Deal failed conspicuously in its primary task—that of ending unemployment and reviving full economic activity. Opinions differed, however, as to the causes for this failure. While conservatives maintained that the New Deal made recovery impossible by interfering with business and destroying confidence, reformers argued that the New Deal had not gone far enough. Among reformers themselves, moreover, there still prevailed the differences of viewpoint which characterized the progressive movement from the beginning. While one group argued that monopolistic conditions must be accepted and subjected to government control, others continued to favor a trust-busting program which would restore effective competition. Among Roosevelt's advisers, the former of these opinions prevailed in 1933, the latter in 1938.

Friends of the New Deal themselves occasionally declared that it was the equivalent of a revolution; its enemies were convinced that it was a violation of American traditions, that it was destroying democracy and private enterprise, and that it resembled the dictatorships of Germany and Russia. Both of these viewpoints were unjustified. The New Deal was certainly no revolution, since it did not involve any transfer of economic power and privilege from one class to another or disturb the established constitutional order. On the contrary, one of the most legitimate arguments against it was that many of its measures had the effect of making the government a guarantor of the political and economic *status quo*. Nor were the New Deal's interventions in the economic system lacking in precedent in American history. Business had always claimed and received government assistance in the form of the tariff, gifts of public land and natural resources, and—during the Hoover administration—the Reconstruction Finance Corporation. The government as promoter and regulator of economic activity is an old established idea in America. What was novel in the New Deal was that it gave assistance of a similar kind not merely to business but also to agriculture and labor. And although the New Deal undoubtedly involved a great extension of bureaucratic power, it was following examples set not only by the European dictatorships but also by the democracies. Some New Deal measures, such as unemployment and old age insurance, had been adopted by almost every European country at least a generation earlier, and in some cases even before then; others had been instituted in Europe since the outset of the depression. There was not one New Deal measure of which there did not exist parallels in the European democracies, and there was no democratic nation which had not found it necessary to take similar actions. Many students of social development regarded the extension of bureaucratic power as an alarming tendency, but this tendency was worldwide, and no country, either democratic or dictatorial, has yet discovered how to avoid it.

Probably the most justifiable criticisms against the New Deal were those made not against its principles but against their execution and administration. For such practical deficiencies, however, the New Dealers themselves were not wholly to blame. The economic crisis was so great and the demand for action so imperative that there was little time for careful advanced planning; moreover, between 1914 and 1933 there had been little progressive legislation, and the New Dealers were compelled to make up for lost time by carrying out within a single administration reforms which should have taken a generation. Many New Deal measures were therefore adopted with inadequate preliminary study and discussion. In addition, the nature of the American form of government made the enactment of a consistent program singularly difficult. Different pressure groups were able to secure special favors through influence in Congress. The division of responsibility between President and Congress meant that the conservatives in Congress could sometimes block parts of the President's program but were unable to carry out any alternative program of their own. The powers of the Supreme Court meant that measures which were regarded by the administration as essential parts of the recovery program were liable to be declared unconstitutional several years after they had been put into operation. The American federal government had not been designed as an agency for economic planning, and the attempt to use it for this purpose encountered considerable difficulties.

Another handicap of the New Deal was the lack of a sufficiently large body of trained and nonpartisan civil servants. The young lawyers and college professors who filled many of the newly created administrative positions represented an attempt to remedy this deficiency; but unfortunately, as it was frequently declared, their idealism and enthusiasm did not always compensate for their lack of practical wisdom and experience. Some of the New Deal agencies, moreover, were at least partially controlled by old Democratic politicians, who were likely to abuse their new government responsibilities for partisan objectives.

THE FIRST "ONE HUNDRED DAYS": THE BANK CRISIS

On Sunday, March 5, 1933, one day after he was inaugurated, Roosevelt issued a proclamation calling an extraordinary session of Congress to convene at noon on March 9 in order to meet the acute banking crisis which was threatening the financial structure and institutions of the country. Even before taking this action, Roosevelt and his advisers had already prepared another proclamation (issued on March 6) closing all of the country's banks for the next four days. The purpose of the "bank holiday" was to stop the heavy withdrawals and the hoarding of gold, which had assumed nearly panic proportions during the week before the inauguration. Roosevelt found legal justification for his decision to suspend the nation's banks in the war powers granted to the Wilson administration in the Trading with the Enemy Act of October, 1917. This old World War I law had never been repealed, and F.D.R. used the provision authorizing the President "to investigate, regulate, or prohibit, under such rules as he may prescribe . . . any transactions in foreign exchange and the export, hoarding, melting, or earmarkings of gold or silver coin or bullion or currency" to take control of the banking system. The administration was prepared to use scrip in order to permit business to continue while the banks were closed and being investigated by the Federal Reserve and other government agencies to determine their financial condition and whether to permit them to reopen. Since Treasury Secretary Woodin rejected the use of any kind of "stage money," however, none was issued.

On March 9, when Congress convened, Roosevelt attached a message to the administration's emergency bank bill which the Treasury and his advisers had been working upon almost ceaselessly since March 4 but which had just been completed within the hour, urging the "clear necessity for immediate action." Since there was only one copy of the bill and few knew what it contained, it was read to the members of the House by Representative Henry B. Steagall, chairman of the Banking and Currency Committee. In record-breaking speed the House passed the bill unanimously, and less than four hours later the Senate voted 73 to 7 to approve it. That evening the President signed the Emergency Bank Act into law.[5] Besides legalizing all the actions Roosevelt had taken since March 4, the act provided for the issuance of sufficient emergency currency to meet any demands which might arise; permitted the Reconstruction Finance Corporation to acquire the preferred stock of national banks, thereby supplying them with new funds; granted the President additional authority "to control foreign exchange transactions, gold and currency movements, and banking transactions in general"; prohibited the hoarding or exporting of gold; empowered the Secretary of the Treasury to recall all gold bullion, coins, and certificates in circulation; and authorized the Treasury to determine which banks were solvent and should be allowed to reopen. Reconstruction Finance Corporation funds were made available to banks essentially solvent but temporarily in need so

[5] Arthur M. Schlesinger, Jr., *The Coming of the New Deal* (Boston, 1959), pp. 7–8.

18 THE ERA OF F.D.R., 1933–1945

that they too could be reopened as quickly as possible. Those banks found to be insolvent were to remain closed and to be placed under the direction of "conservators" appointed by the Comptroller of the Currency.

On Sunday, March 12, Roosevelt, in his first fireside chat to the American people, explained in simple terms and without a trace of condescension exactly what the government had done and how it proposed to restore normal banking operations. "Confidence and courage," he declared, "are the essentials of success . . . . You people must have faith . . . . We have provided the machinery to restore our financial system; it's up to you to support [it] and make it work." The nation, including most of the banking community, approved wholeheartedly of what the President and Congress had done; the administration's quick response to the crisis inspired hope and allayed fear. The next day the banks began to reopen. Hoarding ceased, and currency and gold started to flow back into the banks. Within three days, 76 per cent of the member banks of the Federal Reserve System (representing some 90 per cent of the nation's deposits) were in operation. Within six weeks nearly 13,000 banks, more than three-fourths of the total number that had survived the depression, were authorized to resume business. The bank crisis had passed, and the nation's financial structure, without fundamental or radical alterations, had been salvaged. Roosevelt's decisive action and his assurance to the people that it was "safer to keep . . . money in a reopened bank rather than under the mattress" explains his success. As Rexford G. Tugwell expressed it, "The first battle with fear was won with talk." [6]

THE BEGINNING OF THE NEW DEAL

The Seventy-third Congress, which convened on March 9, was called for one purpose—to resolve the financial crisis; but once it had come together, Roosevelt decided to take advantage of the goodwill and unprecedented public support created by his forceful action in the bank crisis and the near abdication of congressional authority and initiative to secure enactment of programs he had planned for later. During the next three months, or the so-called hundred days, from March 9 through June 16, Congress enacted at the President's request a series of laws so comprehensive and far-reaching in their implications that in normal times they would have occupied the legislative energies of a generation. Such legis-

[6] Rexford G. Tugwell, *The Democratic Roosevelt* (New York, 1957), p. 273.

THE NEW DEAL, I (1933–1934)

lative achievement would not have been possible without the enthusiastic support of the people, who deluged their congressmen and senators with letters and telegrams instructing them to endorse the President's proposals. Roosevelt knew the nation was overwhelmingly on his side and capitalized upon the fact, employing every technique of presidential leadership to influence the Congress. Patronage to "hungry Democrats" was dispensed skillfully and, when necessary, withheld until the administration's program was enacted. Friendly White House spokesmen on Capitol Hill were called to confer with the President or his advisers in drawing up legislation, and then were entrusted with getting it safely through the Congress. If the legislators disregarded his directives, Roosevelt was prepared to use the veto, but often the mere threat of using it was sufficient to cause Congress to reconsider its action.

In addition to his highly cultivated political sense and his ability to know when to be firm and when to compromise to get Congress to legislate his program, Roosevelt was a master in using the press and the radio to advertise and win popular support for his policies. He revitalized the press conference, which Hoover had allowed to deteriorate, and he used it so frequently (337 times during his first four years) and so effectively that one Washington newsman observed that F.D.R. made the presidential press conference into "a distinctively American device for informing the nation of what the President is contemplating and the President of what the nation is thinking." [7] His further ability with well-timed radio appeals, in which he had no rival, led *The New York Times's* Washington correspondent to conclude that F.D.R. was "the best showman the White House has lodged since modern science made possible such an effective dual performance." [8] The result of Roosevelt's vigorous leadership was that for the time being almost every group in the nation rallied enthusiastically to his support; party and class differences were temporarily forgotten, and men who a few years later became his most bitter opponents acclaimed the President as a great national leader. Whatever the verdict of history on the Roosevelt administration, one achievement will always stand to its credit: during its first hundred days it restored the faith of the American people in democracy and in their future.

Within three weeks of taking office, Roosevelt secured the passage of two of the Democratic party's campaign pledges: the Economy Act (March 20, 1933) and the Beer Act (March 22, 1933). The former aimed

[7] Quoted in James E. Pollard, *The Presidents and the Press* (New York, 1947), p. 781.
[8] Quoted in *ibid.*, p. 785.

THE ERA OF F.D.R., 1933–1945

to balance the "normal budget" of ordinary disbursements, as distinguished from "the extraordinary relief expenditures," by slashing government salaries as much as 15 per cent and cutting the pensions paid to veterans. Provision was also made to allow the President to reorganize or eliminate unnecessary governmental agencies, thus reducing the operating costs of the government further. The economies achieved by this law, nearly $243 million, were some 50 per cent less than anticipated. The Beer Act legalized the manufacture and sale of beer and light wines of an alcoholic content of no more than 4 per cent by volume, and imposed, as Roosevelt recommended, a "substantial tax" upon them, which would provide the government immediately with a new and needed source of revenue. The tax feature of this measure proved disappointing, and its chief effect was to expedite repeal of the Eighteenth Amendment, an action proposed in Congress less than a month before Roosevelt was inaugurated and completed on December 5, 1933, after it was ratified by three-fourths of the state conventions. The only amendment to be ratified by state conventions, the Twenty-first Amendment made the states again responsible for liquor regulation within their boundaries.

Unemployment Relief

When Roosevelt became President, there were about 15 million persons unemployed out of a total working population of about 50 million. During the Hoover administration, the unemployed had been supported by the state and municipal governments, whose financial resources were now almost exhausted, and by private charity. It was therefore necessary for the federal government to assume direct responsibility. There was a distinct break with previous American custom in the recognition that it was the duty of the federal government to protect unemployed persons from starvation and that, when men were unable to find jobs, it should be regarded as their misfortune rather than as their fault. The Roosevelt administration wanted, moreover, to provide the unemployed with work and not merely with a dole; work relief might cost more than a dole, but it would prevent demoralization and it would give the community something in return for its money.

CIVILIAN CONSERVATION CORPS

On March 15 Roosevelt told the press that he was preparing to ask the Congress to consider other legislation of a more "constructive" nature

THE NEW DEAL, I (1933–1934)

than the banking, economy, and beer acts. The first of these proposals was that jobs be provided for the unemployed by putting them to work in the government forests. The Civilian Conservation Corps Reforestation Relief Act, which Congress passed on March 31, 1933, was the first of the New Deal's relief agencies and, because of Roosevelt's interests in forest conservation, the one he was most personally involved in establishing. The CCC was organized under the Department of Labor and placed under the control of Robert Fechner, vice president of the Machinists' Union and an occasional college lecturer on labor and government relations. The responsibility for recruiting, maintaining, and running the CCC was assigned to the Department of Labor, the army, and the Forestry Service. Unemployed young men between the ages of eighteen and twenty-five, a large number of whom had never worked before, were prevented from glutting the crowded labor market by being drafted into the corps. They were sent to camps where they worked on reforestation and soil conservation, constructed dams for checking soil erosion, built firebreaks and lookout towers for checking forest fires, campaigned against tree-destroying diseases and animals, and carried on other useful projects. Payment amounted to $30 a month, of which $25 was sent to the boys' families, thus augmenting the purchasing power of their families. The corps employed from 300,000 to 500,000 youths at a time for periods averaging nine months each. By the end of 1941, six months before Congress allowed the CCC to expire, more than 2 million young men had served in it. Because of both the utility of its work and the physical and moral value to its members, the CCC probably won more widespread approval than any other New Deal agency.

FEDERAL EMERGENCY RELIEF ADMINISTRATION
AND THE CIVIL WORKS ADMINISTRATION

The second of the federal relief agencies was the Federal Emergency Relief Administration, established on May 12, 1933, and placed in the charge of Harry Hopkins. One-half of the FERA's $500 million appropriation was to go to local authorities, who were required to contribute part of the costs of relief themselves. The rest was given to the states to spend on direct relief for the needy and the unemployed. Between 1933 and 1935, the FERA paid 71 per cent of all relief costs. On November 8, 1933, the Civil Works Administration was created. Its purpose was to create jobs, controlled by the federal government, as quickly as possible to ease the economic distress of the winter months. In January, 1934, the

As FERA (1933) and WPA (1935–38) administrator, Secretary of Commerce (1938–40), and lend-lease administrator (1941), Harry L. Hopkins was one of Roosevelt's closest and most trusted advisers. (Brown Brothers)

CWA was giving employment to 4.25 million persons. Much of the work was of a makeshift character, but Hopkins, who administered the program, believed that jobs should be created if none were available so that the unemployed need not depend upon a dole, which he emphatically opposed. The administration of the program was often lax, a result of the fact that it was an emergency measure aimed at providing employment rather than a long-term measure with carefully planned projects. Moreover, the whole program was temporary.

The CWA was dissolved in March, 1934, after having paid out nearly a billion dollars, of which some $750 million was used for payrolls. At the time the CWA was abolished, many of its projects and employees were taken over by the FERA. When it became apparent that more relief would be required, Congress enacted (February 15, 1934) the Civil Works Emergency Relief Act, which provided the FERA with $950 million to pay for its civil works projects and direct relief. The FERA was returned to the local authorities in January, 1935. The federal government undertook more careful supervision of the wage schedules, the conditions of labor, and the persons eligible for employment. Relief rates were increased, the monthly family allowance averaging $15 in May, 1933, and

THE NEW DEAL, I (1933-1934)

$35 in July, 1935. In addition to contributing relief funds to the local authorities, the FERA also built a number of transient camps, which were giving shelter to 300,000 persons by 1935, bought cattle during the drought of 1934 and used them as food for the unemployed, and spent money for health and education. Roosevelt and his advisers hoped that these direct relief measures and make-work programs would meet the immediate needs of the unemployed while the administration's recovery legislation was getting under way.

PUBLIC WORKS ADMINISTRATION

The Public Works Administration was established on June 16, 1933, under Title II of the National Industrial Recovery Act, with Secretary of the Interior Harold L. Ickes as its administrator. Its aim was to stimulate the recovery of the capital goods industry by adopting a program of building public works, and to relieve unemployment by providing new jobs. The $3.3 billion PWA appropriation was to be used to construct public buildings, bridges, dams, sewage systems, housing developments, and comparable projects, and the agency was to loan money to states and

An outspoken progressive, Harold L. Ickes supported Theodore Roosevelt's bid for the Presidency in 1912 and La Follette's in 1924. In 1932 Ickes endorsed Roosevelt, who appointed him Secretary of the Interior and head of the Public Works Administration. (Brown Brothers)

municipalities for similar purposes. A large proportion of the money was to be spent on materials in order to stimulate private industry. Ickes supervised the spending of PWA funds competently and honestly but with what seemed to many people such excessive care that many of the operations were slow in getting under way. Although the PWA projects were generally well chosen and added considerable wealth to the nation, they did little to stimulate early recovery or to provide much immediate relief because, as Henry Morgenthau said, Ickes "was so anxious to keep graft and politics out of the public works program that he practically spent money through a medicine dropper." [9] By 1936 the PWA had spent about $4.25 billion on more than 30,000 projects. Actually, less money was spent on public works under the New Deal than in the 1920's. During the 1920's states and municipalities had spent an average of $3 billion a year on roads and public buildings and had incurred heavy debts in order to do so. The only novel feature of the New Deal policy was that it was now the federal government which spent the money and incurred the debts.

Agriculture

As the administration tackled the problem of unemployment, worked to increase the people's purchasing power, and tried to stimulate economic activity, it was also concerned with the rehabilitation of business and agriculture. On March 16, Roosevelt asked the Congress to meet the crisis on the farms by adopting a far-reaching and comprehensive agricultural bill. "I tell you frankly," he addressed the legislators, "that it is a new and untrod path, but I tell you with equal frankness that an unprecedented condition calls for the trial of new means to rescue agriculture." The chief objective of the New Deal agriculture program was to reduce production and thereby to raise prices and increase farm incomes and purchasing power. That American farmers were producing more than the nation could consume was a fact, and in an epoch of economic nationalism it was unlikely that they could find new foreign markets for their surpluses. The Farm Board set up under Hoover's Agricultural Marketing Act had urged the farmers to plant less, and in 1932 it had recommended that the cotton planters plough under one-third of their crop. But the farmers, unlike the big industrial corporations, could not restrict production by voluntary effort; government assistance was essential. The New

[9] Quoted in John Morton Blum, *From the Morgenthau Diaries: Years of Crisis, 1928–1933* (Boston, 1959), p. 234.

Deal proposed, by government intervention, to extend to agriculture the power to raise prices by limiting production—the same power that was enjoyed by big business. This policy of subsidizing scarcity was regretted by the New Dealers themselves, but under the circumstances no other policy seemed possible.

The personnel of the Department of Agriculture probably typified the spirit of the New Deal more fully than did that of any other branch of the government. Henry A. Wallace of Iowa, the Secretary, was the son of Harding's Secretary of Agriculture and the editor of a farm weekly. He was a scientific student of farm statistics and of genetics, and he had made important improvements in the breeding of corn, hogs, and chickens. He was interested also in religious mysticism and was a friend of George William Russell, the Irish poet, landscape painter, and organizer of the Irish Agricultural Society who signed himself A.E. Associated with Wallace were men like Rexford G. Tugwell, Mordecai Ezekiel, Louis H. Bean, Gardiner C. Means, and Jerome Frank.

The basic principles of the New Deal farm program had been first suggested by Milburn L. Wilson of the Montana State College of Agriculture, and had been adopted by Roosevelt during the presidential campaign after discussion with farm leaders across the country.[10] The Agricultural Adjustment Act passed Congress on May 12, 1933. This act was to apply at first to wheat, cotton, corn, hogs, rice, tobacco, and milk, but subsequent amendments brought other commodities under its provisions. In April, 1934, for example, the Jones-Connally Farm Relief Act provided AAA benefits to cattle ranchers and to barley, peanut, rye, and flax farmers; and the Jones-Costigan Sugar Act of May, 1934, aimed to help the sugar industry "by limiting the marketing of sugar to estimated consumption requirements, and by fixing a quota for each sugar-producing area within the continental United States, its insular possessions, and foreign countries exporting sugar to the United States." Under the AAA a contract was to be made with each farmer who chose to adopt the program in accordance with the "historic base" of his farm, that is, with the acreage he had normally devoted to each crop. The farmer would agree to reduce the acreage by a fixed percentage and to use the surplus land for soil-improving crops or for crops to be consumed by his own family. In return, farmers who entered the program were to receive government payments, which would be financed through excise taxes levied on proc-

[10] Gertrude Almy Slichter, "Franklin D. Roosevelt and the Farm Problem, 1929–1932," *Mississippi Valley Historical Review*, XLIII (September 1956), 238–58.

essors. The excise tax was disliked by some of the New Dealers since it would tend to raise consumers' prices, but it was considered desirable to make the plan self-supporting and to avoid outright government subsidies. Enforcement of the AAA was entrusted as far as possible to local committees of farmers rather than to federal officials in order to prevent bureaucratic regimentation.

The Agricultural Adjustment Administration was headed until December, 1933, by George N. Peek, author of the McNary-Haugen bill, who believed that the solution to the farm problem was in more effective marketing arrangements at home and in expanded sales overseas. Subsequently Wallace, who was convinced that better production controls rather than Peek's marketing approach were the answer to the farm surplus, decided that Peek was allowing consumers' prices to increase too greatly, and he was replaced by Chester C. Davis, a farmer and farm journalist from Montana. The total area taken out of production by the AAA amounted to 10.4 million acres in 1933, 35.7 million acres in 1934, and 30.3 million acres in 1935. The cash income of farmers rose from $4.6 billion in 1932 to $6.8 billion in 1935. Incomes from wheat, cotton, tobacco, corn, and hogs increased by 90 per cent. In terms of the ratio between prices received and prices paid, the farm population was 35 per cent better off in 1935 than in 1932. In 1934 and 1935, when a referendum was taken among certain classes of farmers, 3,707,642 of them, out of a total of 4,288,510, voted for a continuance of the program.

In addition to the AAA, and in the long run far more important for the relief of the farmer, were the New Deal's efforts to refinance the numerous farm mortgages, which in 1933 amounted to about $8.5 billion. The farmers in that year, moreover, also owed about $3.5 billion in short-term debts. On June 16, 1933, Congress created the Farm Credit Administration to assume responsibility over all federal agricultural credits, which previously had been divided among several agencies, and to help the farmers refinance these obligations by making reductions in both the principal and the rate of interest. Subsequent legislation in 1933 and 1934 extended federal farm credit further. On January 30, 1934, the Federal Mortgage Refinancing Act provided for the Federal Farm Mortgage Corporation to issue $2 billion of bonds whose principal and interest were guaranteed by the federal government, thus making additional long-term funds available to the farmers. Because so many farmers needed immediate help to bring their crops to market, the Crop Loan Act of February 23, 1934, which F.D.R. hoped would "be the last of its kind," made available $40 million of FCA funds to farmers who needed short-term loans and could not borrow elsewhere. Under the provisions of the Crop Loan Act, some 445,000 loans, averaging about $85, were negotiated. On June 12, 1934, the Farm Mortgage Foreclosure Act was passed to allow farmers to borrow from the government in order to buy back property they had lost by foreclosure. To reduce the number of foreclosures, Congress enacted the Frazier-Lemke Bankruptcy Act of June 28, 1934, which allowed bankrupt farmers to buy back their land at a "fair and reasonable" price, to be determined by appraisal, and to pay for it within six years in small installments. The interest on these new mortgages was fixed at 1 per cent. Should the mortgagee refuse the new terms, the law permitted the foreclosed farmer to remain on his land for five years, paying only a small rental.

All this farm credit legislation eased the agricultural credit crisis greatly and augmented the amount of government credit available to the farm population. The result was that by the end of 1937, about one-half of the farm mortgages were held by agencies of the federal government; and the debt itself, which had stood at about $11 billion in 1923, was reduced to some $5 billion in 1940.

The New Deal also came to the aid of the farmer by a series of marketing agreements, which fixed prices and rationed sales, with the producers of milk, fruit, and vegetables. On October 18, 1933, F.D.R., by Executive order, established the Commodity Credit Corporation, capitalized at $3 million (increased by RFC capital to $100 million in 1936), for the purpose, as the President declared, of contributing "to the support of farm policies by enabling producers to hold on to their products which might otherwise have been dumped with resulting price declines." The corporation achieved its purposes by storing surplus agricultural commodities under the AAA control program and by allowing farmers to borrow against them. Originally intended to rescue the cotton growers, CCC loans were also made available to producers of other storable commodities.

The administration hoped that the voluntary acreage controls under the AAA would be sufficient to reduce the surplus in the basic staples, but the farmers insisted upon restricting actual production and not only acreage. In May and June, 1934, Congress imposed production quotas on cotton (Bankhead Cotton Control Act) and on tobacco (Kerr-Smith Tobacco Control Act), and taxed farmers who produced more of these commodities than their quotas. These measures were disliked by many of the New Dealers, since they involved too much regimentation of the farmers, and they were passed with the aid of Republican farm votes.

Criticisms of the AAA were numerous. It was attacked in the first place on the ground that it set out to create scarcity. In 1933 the program caused the ploughing under of 10.5 million acres of cotton, which had been planted before the act was passed, and the slaughtering of 6.5 million pigs, which were processed into food for the unemployed. Wallace and the New Dealers replied that the encouragement of scarcity was not an inherent part of the program, and that when the condition of the market warranted it, the government could plan for abundance as easily as for scarcity. In the second place, said AAA critics, its program resulted in a loss of foreign markets, particularly in the case of cotton. The cotton planters and sharecroppers were, in point of fact, caught in a vicious circle. They could hold their export trade only through low prices, but low prices meant a continuance of their low standard of living. In 1938 and 1939 the government was compelled to begin paying export subsidies to exporters of wheat and cotton. Other criticisms of the AAA were that it caused too sharp an increase in prices and that it deprived farmers of their individual freedom and subjected them to bureaucratic regimentation. Opponents of the AAA were unable to suggest any feasible alternative program, however. The basic problem of American farming was that there were too many commercial farmers, and so long as industry was unable to provide jobs for the surplus rural population, the restriction of production by one method or another was unavoidable.

One of the most important criticisms of the AAA—and perhaps the most unfortunate feature of the whole program—was that it benefited chiefly the more prosperous commercial farmers and landowners. Tenant farmers, sharecroppers, and hired laborers derived few benefits from it and were often even worse off than before because of the restriction of production. Not only did the AAA fail to remedy the more serious problems of the tenant farmers and the sharecroppers, but it tended to intensify the already difficult problem of rural unemployment.

Tenant farmers, unlike the more prosperous farmers of the West, were not represented by powerful organizations that could bring pressure on congressmen; and, unlike the landlords of the South, they did not have champions among the leaders of the Democratic party. The attempts of the New Deal to solve the problem of farm tenancy were, judged as experiments, of considerable interest; but by contrast with the magnitude of the evil, their scope was negligible.

In 1933 a Division of Subsistence Homesteads was established, with a fund of $25 million. In May, 1935, this was replaced by the Resettlement Administration under Rexford G. Tugwell. These organizations removed destitute farmers from submarginal lands, resettled them in semirural cooperative communities, loaned them money for tools and seeds, and planned for them to combine part-time work in industry with part-time agriculture. By 1936, 124 such communities had been established. The sponsors of these projects, believing strongly in the moral values of rural life, hoped that this combination of industry and agriculture would become a pattern for the social organization of the future. Critics, on the other hand, declared that in view of existing economic conditions, such expectations were totally impractical. In 1936, at the President's request, Congress appointed a committee to study farm tenancy, and a majority of the committee arrived at the revolutionary conclusion that the traditional public land policy of the American government should be abandoned. Instead of converting public land into private property, the government should retain legal ownership in order to protect farmers from expropriation through mortgage foreclosures, to prevent speculation, and to check soil erosion.

Congress, however, preferred the traditional individualistic policy and distrusted the cooperative ideals of the Resettlement Administration. Moreover, many of the farmers involved disliked being uprooted from their land, poor as it was, and refused to avail themselves of the opportunity of resettlement in other communities. In July, 1937, Congress passed the Bankhead-Jones Farm Tenant Act, creating the Farm Security Administration and appropriating money which tenants could borrow at 3 per cent for the purchase of land. This act enabled tenants to become owners at the rate of only about 5,000 a year, whereas the total number of tenants was nearly 3 million. More successful were the rehabilitation loans, averaging $350 each and numbering about 750,000 in three years, which the Farm Security Administration gave to tenant farmers who could use them profitably. The value of these loans lay chiefly in the careful advice that accompanied them as to how they could best be spent. Despite these efforts, the problem of tenancy remained largely unresolved.

Industrial Recovery

Less than a week after Roosevelt had signed the AAA into law, he recommended that the Congress "provide for the machinery necessary for a great cooperative movement throughout all industry . . . to obtain wide reemployment, to shorten the working week, to pay a decent wage for the shorter week and to prevent unfair competition and dis-

30   THE ERA OF F.D.R., 1933-1945

astrous overproduction." Out of this recommendation came the National Industrial Recovery Act of June 16, 1933, the New Deal's first attempt to reform and regulate industry and, in the process, to bring about its recovery from depression. The NIRA was almost the only New Deal measure which represented an attempt at cooperation with big business. It was notable also because it was both the most extravagantly publicized and the most generally unsuccessful of all the New Deal laws. The Blue Eagle, the symbol of the National Recovery Administration, at first was confidently looked upon as the means through which the United States would regain prosperity; less than two years later it was the object of ridicule and derision.

The principal authors of the NIRA included not only New Dealers like Hugh Johnson and Rexford Tugwell and representatives of labor like Secretary Perkins and William Green of the AFL, but also certain business leaders who wanted the assistance of the federal government in checking cutthroat competition and legalizing the price-fixing practices sponsored by the trade associations of the 1920's. It was suggested that government cooperation would enable business to plan production and maintain price levels, and that this was what was needed to bring about recovery. Proposals to this effect had been made during the Hoover administration by Gerard Swope, president of General Electric, and Henry I. Harriman, and were supported by the United States Chamber of Commerce. But they had been rejected by President Hoover as unconstitutional, though similar informal arrangements had been drawn up in the 1920's when Hoover was Secretary of Commerce. Of the forty-nine principal speakers at the sessions of the Chamber of Commerce in May, 1933, more than half wanted more government regulation of business. Meanwhile liberals were asking that the business community assume greater responsibility for the social consequences of its decisions, and labor leaders were asking for higher wages, shorter hours, and guarantees of collective bargaining. On April 6, 1933, a thirty-hour-week bill, introduced by Senator Hugo Black of Alabama, had passed the Senate.

The administration decided that these various objectives and attitudes, which required cooperation and planning on the part of business, government, and labor, might be achieved at the same time. Industrialists should be given government support in restricting competition. In return, they should be asked to make concessions to labor and to assume part of the burden to help stimulate recovery. The NIRA declared that codes of fair competition, regulating wages and hours and checking price cutting, should be drafted for each industry. Public hearings should be held on the codes, which should be submitted to the President and which, when approved, should have the force of law. Any action permitted under the act should be exempt from prosecution under the antitrust laws. Section 7a of the act declared that employees might join unions and "bargain collectively through representatives of their own choosing." Some of the New Deal economists disapproved of the NIRA, believing that it would tend to raise prices faster than it raised wages. Roosevelt, in signing the law, declared that if it had this effect, it would prove to be futile. It was, however, loudly hailed by many spokesmen of the administration as the measure which would end the depression.

The National Recovery Administration, which was to enforce the NIRA, was headed by General Hugh S. Johnson, the principal author of the draft legislation of 1917 and subsequently a partner of George N. Peek in the Moline Plow Company and a business associate of Bernard M. Baruch. Johnson was a singularly forceful personality gifted with a flair for picturesque language; and he had the confidence of the big industrialists. The codes of fair competition were being drafted throughout the summer of 1933. It was considered desirable to complete them as rapidly as possible in order to stimulate recovery, and many of them were adopted with little study. The trade associations were in general allowed to make their own terms in return for concessions on wages and hours; and, although an advisory board had been appointed to represent consumers, little attention was paid to the latter. Of 557 basic codes, 441 included price-fixing regulations. Child labor was banned, and in a number of codes wages were raised and hours were reduced. These reforms, however, affected mostly the more backward industries, especially in the South. In the more developed industries there were few improvements, and there was a tendency for minimum wages to become also maximum wages. Section 7a was vigorously opposed by certain employers, particularly by Henry Ford and by Ernest T. Weir of National Steel, while others attempted to counteract it by forming company unions. It gave considerable stimulus to a number of trade unions, however, particularly to the United Mine Workers.

On the whole, organized labor appears to have benefited from the NRA, if only because the law virtually outlawed child labor and improved wages, even though moderately. Still, labor was far from pleased with the NRA's results. It did not receive the protection it had hoped would accrue to it under Section 7a, and in some cases, as with the en-

32 THE ERA OF F.D.R., 1933–1945

forcement of the automobile code, F.D.R. proved more friendly and sympathetic to management than to the workers.[11] Almost every other group in the community, moreover, soon became disillusioned with the NRA. Consumers opposed it because its policies resulted in a sharp rise in prices, which the condition of the market did not warrant. Small businessmen disliked it because they felt that the codes had been drafted to serve the interests of big business and because they were often unable to pay even the minimum wages which the codes prescribed. Big industrialists turned against it because they suspected that once the principle of government regulation had been admitted it might eventually be used to limit their powers; they also disliked Section 7a.

In 1934 a number of industrial leaders asked that government regulation be abandoned and that business be allowed to regulate itself. They were willing to accept wage and hour rules, but they made no mention of collective bargaining or of price reductions. The opposition to the NRA was strengthened by the report of the National Recovery Review Board, set up in February, 1934, under the chairmanship of Clarence Darrow, which criticized it because of its encouragement of monopoly. Moreover, many price-fixing regulations in the codes proved to be unenforceable because of opposition from consumers and small businessmen. There was widespread indignation when in New Jersey, which had passed a miniature NRA of its own, a small tailor was sent to jail for pressing a pair of pants at less than the code price.

Johnson left the NRA in 1934 and was succeeded first by Donald Richberg, a railroad and labor attorney who had helped draft the NRA bill, and later by S. Clay Williams, an executive of the Reynolds Tobacco Company. Many of the codes were relaxed, and the price-fixing rules began to be abandoned. Some of the New Dealers hoped that the control over business which the government had acquired through the NRA might be maintained and used for somewhat different purposes, in particular for the reduction of monopoly prices. Such ideas ended, however, on May 27, 1935, when the Supreme Court, in *Schechter Poultry Corporation v. the United States*, unanimously declared the National Industrial Recovery Act unconstitutional on two grounds: that it violated the constitutional principle of the separation of powers by transferring legislative authority to the Executive, and that it called for federal regulation of intrastate commerce.

[11] Sidney Fine, "President Roosevelt and the Automobile Code," *Mississippi Valley Historical Review*, XLIV (June 1958), 23–50.

THE NEW DEAL, I (1933-1934)

According to the government, the NRA had brought about a decrease of average hours of labor from 42.6 a week to 36.2 a week and an increase of average wage rates from 42 cents an hour to 52 cents an hour. Its effect on the economic system was impossible to calculate. The establishment of the NRA gave industry a "shot in the arm," as F.D.R. had hoped it would, and it stimulated employment, if only temporarily. The NRA was followed by an increase in production, but this was not maintained for more than a few months. On the other hand, the dissolution of the NRA was followed by another and more vigorous increase in production. But of far greater significance than the NRA's contribution toward recovery were the many new precedent-breaking social innovations it established on the national level, among them the regulation of hours and wages and the responsibility of the federal government in collective bargaining (Section 7a pertaining to labor), both of which became subjects of subsequent New Deal legislation, and the abolition of child labor and numerous "unfair trade practices." [12]

With the demise of the NRA the administration made no further attempt to regulate industry until after 1937, when it returned to the traditional method of the antitrust laws. The most important problems presented by the industrial system—those of adjusting prices to purchasing power and of expanding production until unemployment disappeared—remained unsolved.

Credit, Currency, and Finance

The growth of debt was one of the most serious problems of the American economic system, particularly during the depression. By 1933 interest payments on long-term debts amounted to nearly one-fifth of the total national income. According to the rules of laissez-faire economics, this problem should have been allowed to adjust itself through bankruptcies. Such a solution might have been beneficial in the long run, but its immediate effects would have been so catastrophic that no government could have tolerated it. The Hoover administration had set out to prevent bankruptcies through the Reconstruction Finance Corporation and through aid to owners of homes and farms. The New Deal continued these policies and extended them in order to assist a larger number of people. Under the chairmanship of Jesse Jones, the RFC continued to loan money to railroads, trust companies, banks, and other institutions. By the end of 1937,

[12] Schlesinger, *op. cit.*, pp. 174-75.

34   THE ERA OF F.D.R., 1933–1945

it had made loans totaling $6.5 billion of which $4.45 billion had been repaid. New legislation included the Municipal Bankruptcy Act (May, 1934) and the Corporate Bankruptcy Act (June, 1934), which allowed cities and corporations, with the consent of their creditors, to readjust their debt structures, thereby easing the burden of payment and adjusting it to the condition of the times.

The railroads, for example, constituted one of the major industries requiring special attention from the federal government. In 1933 they were in need of a large-scale program of replacement and new construction. Their importance in the marketing structure meant that a modernization program would stimulate the demand for capital goods and thus contribute substantially to recovery from the depression. Private enterprise in this case, however, was not able to function successfully without government assistance. The depression had reduced at least one-third of the American railroad system to bankruptcy. Owing to the decrease in the volume of freight, the railroads suffered more directly than any other part of the economic system. They were, moreover, suffering from overcapitalization and from the rise of the automobile, and their debts were exceptionally large. Sixty-two per cent of their securities consisted of bonds, the interest on which amounted to about $500 million a year. The railroads borrowed heavily from the Reconstruction Finance Corporation; and on June 16, 1933, Congress passed the Emergency Railroad Transportation Act, under which Joseph B. Eastman, a long-time member of the Interstate Commerce Commission, was appointed Federal Coordinator of Transportation. Eastman was able to do little, however, to remedy the situation. Reduction of the railroad debt was what seemed to be required, but the bulk of the debt was held by insurance companies, educational and philanthropic bodies, and other institutions which could not be expected to sacrifice it. Purchase of the railroads by the government was felt to be too costly. Although it was generally admitted that the railroads needed to spend large sums on new equipment, no method was devised for making this expenditure possible.

HOME OWNERS REFINANCING ACT

Just as the federal government helped businessmen and farmers to refinance their debts, the New Deal also came to the assistance of mortgaged home owners in the cities. The urban mortgage debt, which amounted in 1932 to about $26 billion, was to be refinanced when necessary by the Home Owners Loan Corporation, established under the Home Owners

Refinancing Act of June 13, 1933. Under the terms of the act, the corporation could give no more loans after 1936 and was to be dissolved in 1951. The HOLC took over more than a million mortgages with a total value of about $3.1 billion, reduced interest payments by $60 million a year, and arranged for repayment within fifteen years of the principal of the debts it assumed. The HOLC also made loans to owners who needed money to pay taxes and to repair or improve their homes. Further reorganization of the urban mortgage debt was undertaken by the Federal Housing Authority, set up under the National Housing Act of June 28, 1934. The FHA created a mortgage-insurance scheme designed to encourage borrowing for new residential construction and for alterations and improvements on older homes by guaranteeing credit institutions against losses and by reducing interest rates. In four years the FHA underwrote over $1.8 billion worth of home mortgages. New loans for improvements and building, on the other hand, amounted to only $775 million.

The reorganization of the debt structure by the New Deal benefited both creditors and debtors. Creditors received repayment from the government instead of being required to foreclose on properties whose immediate value was often far smaller than the sums for which they were mortgaged; debtors kept their properties and paid lower rates of interest. The ratio of debt obligations to the national income continued, nevertheless, to be dangerously high, and the HOLC soon found itself compelled to foreclose on a number of the householders whom it had attempted to rescue.

CURRENCY

In its currency policy the New Deal set out to increase the amount of money in circulation, including both cash and bank credit, in the hope that this would lower interest rates, reduce debt burdens, and assist industrial expansion. It also planned to strengthen government control over the currency in the hope of checking cycles of inflation and deflation and maintaining a stable price level. This program involved a devaluation of the dollar—a step vigorously opposed by conservatives on the ground that it would end in uncontrolled inflation. Every other important country in the world, however, had already devalued its currency, and in each case devaluation appeared to have given a stimulus to economic recovery.

The United States formally abandoned the gold standard on April 19, 1933, and on June 5, by the Gold Repeal Joint Resolution, it was declared that debts were to be paid in legal tender and not in gold. The

36 THE ERA OF F.D.R., 1933–1945

dollar then began to fall in relation to foreign currencies, thus stimulating American exports, and prices began to rise. In June, the World Monetary and Economic Conference, meeting in London, began its deliberations. Both Hoover and Roosevelt had agreed to American participation, and F.D.R. sent Cordell Hull to lead the United States delegation. But since Roosevelt had not yet decided what kind of monetary policy the country should adopt, the delegation left for London with almost no knowledge of the President's ideas. While Hull and the representatives of sixty-five other nations were debating the stabilization of currencies as a step toward promoting international trade and economic recovery, Roosevelt was becoming increasingly dubious about the value of international monetary arrangements as a solution to the economic crisis. For one thing, he believed that stabilization would give an advantage to those countries whose currencies were already devalued more than the American. For another, by tying the United States to an international monetary agreement, it would virtually destroy the administration's efforts to raise prices. Largely for the same reasons, he refused to consider a return to the gold standard, which France, the leader of the gold-bloc powers, was insisting upon. On June 17, he informed Hull by cable that the administration "must retain full freedom of action . . . in order to uphold [the] price level at home"; and two weeks later, he cabled Moley, who had followed Hull to London with further instructions, that "a sufficient interval should be allowed . . . to permit . . . a demonstration of the value of price-lifting efforts which we have well in hand." [13] Finally, on July 3, the President disclosed his views more fully in a wireless message to the conference itself. "I would regard it as a catastrophe amounting to a world tragedy," he said, "if the great Conference of Nations, called to bring about a more real and permanent financial stability and a greater prosperity to the masses of all Nations, should, in advance of any serious effort to consider these broader problems, allow itself to be diverted by the proposal of a purely artificial and temporary experiment affecting the monetary exchange of a few Nations only." With this so-called "bombshell" message denouncing currency stabilization as contrary to American interests, the conference came to naught, and the administration proceeded to try to raise prices and bring about economic recovery by cheap money and other more nationalistic policies. F.D.R.'s message virtually ended the conference, though it is doubtful whether it would have accomplished anything of value even without his intervention.

[13] Quoted in *ibid.*, pp. 215, 221.

Meanwhile, in the United States the demand for outright inflation was growing stronger in many different quarters. Debtors, both agrarian and urban, insisted upon it, and their arguments were forcefully advertised to millions of radio listeners by Father Charles E. Coughlin, who asserted repeatedly that devaluation was "the one practical moral-economic remedy which can destroy the depression." The demands of these traditional advocates of inflation were strengthened further by a number of senators from the silver mining states and by the Committee for the Nation to Rebuild Prices and Purchasing Power, organized in 1932. Its members represented nearly the entire spectrum of inflationist opinion; and while some of them were impractical extremists, many more, like Robert E. Wood, the head of Sears, Roebuck, and Frank A. Vanderlip, the president of the National City Bank of New York, were highly respected businessmen and financiers. Faced by mounting pressures from these groups, Roosevelt decided to accept the Thomas amendment, a clause in the Agricultural Adjustment Act giving him certain limited discretionary powers of inflation, such as devaluation, coinage of silver, or the issuance of paper money.

In October prices began to fall, and Western leaders renewed their demand for inflation. Roosevelt then adopted a gold-purchase plan, proposed by Professor George F. Warren of Cornell and others, by which the government bought gold at increasing prices, thus making the dollar cheaper. The buying of gold caused the dollar to fall in relation to foreign currencies, but it did not have the effect, expected by its sponsors, of raising commodity prices. On January 30, 1934, Congress passed the Gold Reserve Act. The government was allowed to fix the dollar at between 50 and 60 per cent of its former value, and by means of an Exchange Stabilization Fund of $2 billion it could manage its value within these limits. The government could, moreover, impound all gold into the treasury, giving gold certificates to its former owners. The purpose of this nationalization of gold was to prevent it from being hoarded or exported by persons who lacked confidence or hoped for speculative profits. One of its results was a large profit for the Treasury. Roosevelt then stabilized the dollar at 59.06 per cent of its former value; and, being afraid of inflation, he undertook no further monetary experiments. The Treasury continued, however, to buy gold and, until the summer of 1936, to issue gold certificates, which increased bank reserves and contributed to the "easy money" policy of these years. By 1940 the Treasury had about $19 billion worth of gold, nearly three-quarters of the total world supply.

Western senators, faithful to the traditions of Bryan and 1896, demanded that something be done for silver, and on December 21, 1933, in order to prevent more drastic action by the silverites in Congress, F.D.R. employed his authority under the Thomas amendment and instructed the Treasury to buy all silver mined in the United States for the next four years at 64.5 cents an ounce, the current price being 43 cents. This action pleased only a few of the silver senators; most of them, along with a large number of other inflationists, expected and demanded much more. The President was opposed to further silver purchases, but the strength of the silverites in Congress was considerable. Unless they were placated, the administration's entire program would be in jeopardy. Since Roosevelt could neither defeat nor afford to alienate them, he struck the best bargain he could. The result was the Silver Purchase Act of June, 1934. Silver was to be nationalized in the same manner as gold; but instead of the government's being required to purchase a specified amount of silver at a fixed price, which the silverites and bimetallists had called for, Roosevelt succeeded in getting them to accept a provision requiring the Secretary of the Treasury to buy the metal "at such rates, at such times, and upon such terms and conditions as he may deem reasonable and most advantageous to the public interest." The law also provided that 25 per cent of the nation's currency was eventually to be based on silver. By June, 1938, the Treasury had bought 1.7 billion ounces of silver, more than three-quarters of which came from abroad, and the price had risen to 75 cents an ounce. Some silver certificates were put into circulation, but no serious attempt was made to reach the 25 per cent proportion stipulated by Congress. The program, incidentally, brought considerable benefits to Mexico, which produced large quantities of silver, and caused hardships to China, whose currency was based on silver.

The New Deal's efforts to increase commodity prices and bring about recovery by manipulating the currency and the money supply failed because the men who proposed devaluation overstressed the significance of the gold value of the dollar and underestimated the importance of supply and demand in determining prices. The rise registered by the commodity price index (from 60.2 to 71.8) between March and October, 1933, was temporary; by the end of the year most prices were again moving down. On the other hand, by taking the country off the gold standard and devaluating the dollar, the administration found it much easier to experiment with other methods of raising prices. Despite its many shortcomings, the New Deal's monetary policy resulted in at least two important changes:

THE NEW DEAL, I (1933–1934)

it shifted the financial center of the United States from New York City to Washington; and, with the exception of the subsidy to the silver interests, it sought "to make money the instrument of public rather than of private purposes." [14]

THE GLASS-STEAGALL BANKING ACT

One of the most constructive of early New Deal reform measures was the Glass-Steagall Banking Act of June 16, 1933. This law, which was strengthened and broadened by the Banking Act of 1935, was designed to prevent any future panics like the one which faced the country when the Roosevelt administration took over in March, 1933, by providing that bank deposits of individuals would be guaranteed up to $5,000 by a government agency, the Federal Deposit Insurance Corporation. The funds of this corporation were to be contributed partly by the government, partly by the twelve Federal Reserve banks, and partly by those commercial banks which accepted the plan. Provision was also made to allow savings banks to join the Federal Reserve System and for national banks to open branches in states where it was permissible. In addition, deposit and investment banking were separated, and in the hope of bringing about financial and banking stability, the law extended the authority of the Federal Reserve over the credit of its twelve district banks. The Glass-Steagall Act inspired new confidence in the banking system and achieved some long-needed reforms. During the four years from 1934 to 1937, there were only 194 bank failures as contrasted with an average of about 500 a year throughout the 1920's.

REGULATION OF THE SECURITY MARKETS

The New Deal also endeavored to prevent any repetition of the speculative boom of the 1920's by increasing government control over stock exchanges. The public demand for government regulation of the stock market grew by leaps and bounds after the 1929 crash, and the Democratic party, appreciating its significance, incorporated a plank in its 1932 platform which called for federal action to protect the investor against misrepresentation by requiring that all of the facts on new issues be true and made readily available to prospective buyers. Meanwhile, the Senate investigations of 1932, 1933, and the early part of 1934, which were bringing to light the manner in which Wall Street financiers during the boom had unloaded worthless securities upon small investors and had stimulated

[14] *Ibid.*, p. 253.

excessive speculation to profit by it, added to the growing insistence for reform. In explaining the administration's legislative intent to the public, Roosevelt stated in March, 1933, that the proposed law should be one which "changes the ancient doctrine of *caveat emptor* to 'let the seller beware,' and puts the burden on the seller rather than on the buyer." The Federal Securities Act of May 27, 1933, and the Securities Exchange Act of June 6, 1934, were the New Deal's answer to the speculation evils which had characterized so much of the securities market during the 1920's. The act of 1933 incorporated the basic principles which F.D.R. had stated in March when he recommended the bill to Congress. The one of 1934 established the Securities and Exchange Commission. All securities were to be registered with the SEC, which was to require full and accurate information about them. Various forms of stock manipulation prevalent in the 1920's were forbidden, and the Federal Reserve Board was to control the use of credit for brokers' loans and other speculative purposes. Persons buying stocks on margin were required to pay at least 55 per cent of their value. Joseph P. Kennedy, the father of the thirty-fifth President and himself a wealthy financier, was the first chairman of the SEC.

The SEC proved to be one of the most controversial of the New Deal agencies. Supporters of the New Deal argued that the SEC was disliked by Wall Street because it checked unscrupulous speculation by protecting small investors from fraud. Wall Street, on the other hand, declared that the SEC acted as a deterrent to business expansion by surrounding the issuance of new securities with too much red tape, insisting on too much detailed information, imposing too many delays, and charging too heavy registration fees.

Power and the Tennessee Valley Authority

The power industry was also the subject of special attention during the first "one hundred days" of the New Deal. During the 1920's a large part of the industry had been controlled by unscrupulous financiers, who had created public utility empires, controlled by means of holding companies, with inflated capital value upon which dividends had to be earned. The representatives and spokesmen of the power industry had also conducted elaborate propaganda campaigns against government control. During the depression some of these enterprises, particularly the Insull system, had gone into bankruptcy in spite of a relatively low fall in their earnings. The industry had consequently acquired a particularly bad reputation

THE NEW DEAL, I (1933-1934)

The Grand Coulee Dam in central Washington, was one of the major conservation, flood control, and electric power projects of the New Deal. Work on this project, begun in 1933, continued for eight years. (U.S. Information Agency)

among the American public. Roosevelt had for a long time been an enthusiast of cheap power and an enemy of financial manipulation of the industry, and during his campaign for the Presidency he formed an alliance with Senator George Norris and gave his support to Norris' long campaign against the power corporations. Roosevelt was a strong believer in the traditional values of rural life, and one of his most cherished ideals was that of a rural society whose members should enjoy economic security and all the advantages of modern technology. In the achievement of this ideal, cheap electrical power would play an essential part.

The most spectacular efforts of the New Deal to provide cheaper power consisted of the construction of a number of large hydroelectric plants. Among these were Boulder Dam on the Colorado River in the southwest, which had been initiated by the Hoover administration, Grand Coulee Dam and Bonneville Dam on the Columbia River in the Northwest, and

Fort Peck Dam on the Missouri River. These gigantic engineering projects of the democratic government of the United States were far larger than any of the more loudly publicized building achievements of the European communist and fascist dictatorships.

Meanwhile a project had been undertaken on the Tennessee River which involved not only the building of dams but also the forcing down of the electrical rates charged by the power corporations as well as an elaborate scheme of economic and social rehabilitation. Senator Norris' proposal that the government complete and operate the power plant at Muscle Shoals was accepted by Roosevelt and enlarged into a bold and constructive program of social and regional planning which aroused more enthusiasm among progressives than did any other part of the New Deal. The Tennessee Valley Authority was created by Congress in May, 1933. The TVA, "a corporation clothed with the power of government but possessed of the flexibility and initiative of a private enterprise," was to complete the dams at Muscle Shoals and to build other dams along the Tennessee River. It was to build transmission lines for rural districts; generate and sell power, giving preference to public bodies; and fix the resale rates of the power, thus creating a "yardstick" by which the rates charged by private corporations might be measured. It was also to improve navigation, carry out flood control operations, undertake reforestation, manufacture and sell cheap fertilizer, and promote the economic and social welfare of the communities living in the area watered by the Tennessee River. Including parts of seven states and covering about 80,000 square miles with a population of 2 million, this area had previously been one of the most backward and poverty-stricken regions in the United States. The original members of the Tennessee Valley Authority were A. E. Morgan, an engineer and flood control expert who had previously been president of Antioch College; David Lilienthal, a lawyer who had reorganized the public utility commission of the State of Wisconsin; and Harcourt Morgan, president of the University of Tennessee and an agricultural scientist.

The TVA proceeded rapidly with the construction of a series of dams. By 1940 seven were completed, and the Tennessee River floods, which previously had devastated the area, were now brought under control. Further, by the construction of a 650-mile navigation channel from Paducah, Kentucky to Knoxville, Tennessee, the river was made into an avenue of commerce which benefited the whole area. In cooperation with local authorities and citizen groups, the TVA promoted improved farming methods, reforestation, and other conservation measures which

THE NEW DEAL, I (1933–1934)

prevented further soil erosion. By developing many new fertilizers and helping to spread their use, TVA chemical plants thereby increased soil fertility and farm incomes. The TVA also began to reduce rates and campaigned to extend the use of electrical appliances and to attract new industries, thus enormously increasing the consumption of power. By 1940 the inhabitants of the Tennessee Valley were using 1,179 kilowat hours of energy per person per year as contrasted with a national average of 850, and were paying 2.14 cents per kilowatt hour as contrasted with a national average of 4.21. Since then, the area's use of electric power has increased at an even greater rate, so that by 1959 it was nearly three times larger than the national average. Meanwhile, the price per kilowatt hour was continuously reduced. In 1959, the average non-TVA customer paid nearly 2.5 cents per kilowatt hour for his electricity, while residents buying TVA electricity paid less than a cent for theirs.

The growth of the TVA was criticized by conservatives as socialistic and was bitterly opposed by the utility companies. Most of the companies operating in the Tennessee Valley were a part of the Commonwealth and Southern system, headed after 1933 by Wendell L. Willkie. Willkie declared that the TVA yardstick was unfair since the TVA did not make sufficient allowance, in fixing rates, for the fact that it obtained its capital interest-free from the government and was exempt from taxation. A champion of private enterprise and an enemy of socialism, Willkie maintained that the threat of government competition prevented private capital from entering the power industry and thus impeded economic recovery.

The controversy with the utility companies caused disputes among the three members of the TVA, and in 1938 A. E. Morgan, who had supported some of the claims of the companies, was dismissed by Roosevelt and replaced by James P. Pope, former United States senator from Idaho. It was decided finally that the TVA should purchase all private utility plants in the region which it served, and that the price should be a generous one in order not to discourage construction by private corporations in other parts of the country. In 1939 Commonwealth and Southern sold its Tennessee Valley properties to the TVA for $78.6 million, of which $45 million was paid by the TVA itself and the remainder by the local governments. The long fight conducted by the private companies continued up to the outbreak of World War II and prevented any extension of the TVA idea to other parts of the country. In 1937 Roosevelt had proposed the creation of seven other public bodies similar to the TVA for other

44 THE ERA OF F.D.R., 1933-1945

regions of the United States, but Congress failed to take any action on this recommendation.

Conservation

Closely allied to Roosevelt's desire to promote widespread use of cheap power was his belief in the duty of the federal government to conserve the soil and other natural resources. The conservation question was also intimately connected with the agricultural problem of the 1930's. Underlying the economic difficulties of the farmers was the growth of soil erosion, the long-range consequences of which were of incalculable significance. The importance of safeguarding the topsoil was understood as early as the eighteenth century by the great Virginians George Washington and Patrick Henry, and it had been studied scientifically in George Perkins Marsh's *The Earth as Modified by Human Action*, published in 1874. Yet it was not until the 1930's, when irreparable damage had been done, that there was any general recognition of the need for action to prevent it. Earlier administrations, particularly that of Theodore Roosevelt, had campaigned for conservation, but it was not until the New Deal that the federal government undertook a really comprehensive effort to check soil erosion and promote reforestation. In view of the enormous importance of this problem to future generations, Franklin D. Roosevelt's conservation program must be regarded as one of his administration's most valuable achievements.

SOIL EROSION

Before the coming of the white man, topsoil was held in place by forests and grass, which prevented rain and wind from carrying it away. On the American continent the arrival of the European races disturbed this natural economy; and there began a reckless despoliation of timber and grassland with little attempt to replace what was being destroyed. Enormous natural resources, the fruit of tens of thousands of years of slow accumulation, were wasted within a few generations.

There had originally been, within the area of the United States, 800 million acres of virgin forests. By the 1930's 90 per cent of this had been destroyed, and such replanting as had been undertaken was wholly inadequate to repair the damage. During the first 250 years of white colonization, the timber resources of the Northeast were mostly exhausted. In the later decades of the nineteenth century the lumbermen attacked the forests of Michigan, Wisconsin, and Minnesota and moved thence to Louisiana and other southern states, until finally, at the turn of the century, they turned to the last large areas of untouched timber, in Washington, Oregon, and Idaho.

By the 1930's only 60 million acres of forest land existed in the East and only 77 million in the West. The peak of timber production was reached in 1907, after which production declined and prices began to rise in spite of the continued use of timber for building and the rapidly growing demand for paper to supply the needs of the newspapers. The growing scarcity of timber was increased by the prevalence of forest fires, which sometimes consumed as much as 10 million acres in a year. The government began gradually to assume the duty of reforestation, but no obligation was laid upon the lumber companies to replace what they used—an attitude contrasting with that of several European countries, such as Sweden, where the law required a tree to be planted for every one that was cut down. This wholesale exploitation of the forests not only meant that future generations would be confronted by a timber shortage; it also weakened the topsoil and made it easy for rain water to carry it away. The weakening of the topsoil was increased even further by the widespread practice of burning areas where trees had been cut down, the result being the destruction of the humus content in the soil.

Equally harmful was the destruction of grass on sloping land where there was nothing else to hold the soil. Millions of acres which should have been left to grass were made into arable land by American farmers. Whether farm prices were high or low, there was a stimulus to sacrifice the future to the present: during boom times the grass was ploughed to take advantage of prosperity, during slumps to pay debts. The destruction of grass was especially serious on the Great Plains, a region several thousand feet up, whence rain water had an uninterrupted flow down into the Mississippi and the Gulf of Mexico. The grass of the Great Plains was initially damaged in the 1880's by wheat farmers and through overcropping by cattle. By 1885, on land where forty acres per head would have been the correct proportion, the ratio was ten acres per head. The severe winter of 1886, which decimated the cattle, gave a respite to the grass; but during World War I the demand of Europe for wheat caused much of this land to be put under the plough.

The result of this cutting of timber and ploughing under of the grass was that rain water flowed off it and carried the topsoil along instead of sinking into the ground. Soil erosion was most noticeable where it took the form of steadily expanding gullies. More widespread and more dangerous was sheet erosion, the importance of which was first shown in 1903 by Hugh Bennett, then a surveyor for the Department of Agriculture. Land with an 8 per cent slope might lose as much as an inch of soil a year through sheet erosion. On one recorded occasion a farm in California, situated on a heavy slope, lost three inches of soil in a single cloudburst. Careless farming might ruin land irreparably within a generation. The total loss of topsoil through erosion by water has been calculated at 3 billion tons a year; and since it requires 600 years for a single inch of soil to be recreated by the processes of nature, this loss is, for all human purposes, irreplaceable. By 1934, according to the Soil Conservation Service of the federal government, 50 million acres of land in the United States had been totally ruined, another 50 million had been almost ruined, 100 million had been seriously damaged, and another 100 million was losing soil at an alarming rate. Thus, out of the 610 million acres of land where agriculture was possible, the people of the United States in their relatively brief career had already destroyed or damaged nearly half.

The most spectacular consequences of soil erosion were a series of floods and dust storms. These, more than anything else, brought home to the American people the meaning of soil erosion. Since the ground could no longer hold water, it flowed down into the rivers, which then at the end of wet winters would rise far above their normal levels. Floods in the Mississippi valley had grown steadily worse throughout the whole period

Kim, a small Colorado village, is shown here in the midst of a severe dust storm, typical of those storms in the 1930's that made an uninhabitable Dust Bowl of much of the Midwest. (Brown Brothers)

THE NEW DEAL, I (1933-1934)

since the beginning of white settlement, and by the 1920's flood control required large-scale projects of government engineering. By the 1930's great floods on the Ohio and Connecticut rivers were becoming almost as catastrophic as those on the Mississippi. Dust storms, which carried clouds of topsoil for hundreds of miles, were less destructive than water erosion, but the spectacle of the nation's natural wealth being blown out into the ocean dramatized the problem of soil erosion even more vividly. It has been calculated that in the great storm of May 11, 1934, 300 million tons of soil were carried from Texas, Oklahoma, Colorado, and Kansas out into the Atlantic. The storm of this and subsequent years reduced large areas of Western agricultural lands virtually to desert and left their inhabitants destitute. The subsequent migration of thousands of the victims of the Dust Bowl from Kansas and Oklahoma into California and their exploitation by the fruit-growing corporations of that state were the theme of the most widely read novel of the decade, John Steinbeck's *The Grapes of Wrath* (1939). The inescapable meaning of these dust storms and floods was that large areas of the United States were in danger of becoming as barren as the Sahara Desert. Morris Cooke, head of the water section of the National Resources Board, declared in 1936, "As the matter now stands, and with continuance of the manner in which the soil is now being squandered, this country of ours has less than one hundred years of virile national existence."

The solution of this problem—in its long-range effects perhaps the most important of all American problems—required a drastic reorganization of American agriculture and an effective conservation program. The farmers themselves were not entirely to blame for the wastage of the soil, since they were caught in an economic system which did not promise them secure prosperity and which encouraged the wastage of natural resources at the expense of future generations. To guarantee effective soil conservation, several conditions were necessary. The farmers must enjoy prosperity, since otherwise they might be compelled to cut their timber and plough their grass; the drift toward tenancy must be checked, since tenants rarely preserve the soil as carefully as do owners; and farming must be regarded not as a business, in which a man might make money in a few years by mining the soil and then retire or move elsewhere, but as a way of life which farmers would transmit to their descendants. A check was needed, moreover, upon the individualism hitherto characteristic of American life; floods and dust storms often damaged the good farmer as well as the bad, and only cooperative action could prevent this. The question was whether

48   THE ERA OF F.D.R., 1933-1945

the necessary degree of cooperation could be secured by democratic methods, without unduly restricting individual freedom or enlarging the area of government control.

The conservation program of the New Deal interlocked with its recovery program, and a number of measures which were open to justifiable criticisms from the viewpoint of recovery appeared much more commendable when they were regarded in terms of conservation. This was notably true of the AAA. The latter was condemned by many critics of the New Deal because it paid farmers to produce less, but it was also a soil conservation project on a very wide scale. Farmers were required to devote the land withdrawn from production to sorghums, legumes, grasses, and other soil-conserving crops. One of the basic purposes of the AAA was to preserve for the use of future generations the land not immediately needed. Similarly, much of the money spent on work relief was invested in conservation projects, such as the forestry programs carried on by the CCC. The FERA, the CWA, and the WPA also devoted much of their funds to conservation. These agencies worked on the prevention of soil erosion and undertook large-scale engineering projects for the control of floods. Another New Deal agency which combined conservation with other purposes was the TVA.

Government responsibility for soil conservation had first been recognized by Congress in 1929. In that year Congress had authorized the establishment of ten experimental stations for the study of soil erosion. In September, 1933, a Soil Erosion Service was created. In April, 1934, this was changed by the Soil Conservation Act into a Soil Conservation Service and made a bureau of the Department of Agriculture. Headed by Hugh Bennett, who had been studying the subject for thirty years, the Soil Conservation Service employed 13,000 permanent officials and made use of CCC labor. By establishing experimental erosion projects to demonstrate the value of conservation, the officials of the service set out to persuade farmers to accept their cooperation in building terraces on sloping lands and in adopting other devices for checking wind and water erosion. Meanwhile the New Deal speeded up the purchase of forest reserves by the government and urged private timber companies to adopt a policy of cutting no timber in excess of the annual growth. The Resettlement Administration, established in May, 1935, purchased marginal land for reforestation, and the Taylor Grazing Act of 1934 restricted cattle grazing on public land. In 1934, in order to check dust storms, the government began to plant trees along a "shelter belt" one hundred miles broad, east of the Dust Bowl, from Canada to Texas, thereby conserving moisture and breaking the force of the wind. By 1940, 100 million trees had been planted.

One other New Deal measure which may be considered under the heading of conservation was the Indian Reorganization Act of 1934. The previous Indian policy of the government had been to integrate the Indians into white civilization and to break up the Indian common lands into private properties. This policy had been conspicuously unsuccessful, since the Indians refused to accept amalgamation, and the creation of private property in land had meant, in practice, the transfer of Indian land to white ownership at the rate of 2 million acres a year over a forty-five year period. By 1934 the Indians retained only 47 million acres, of which half was desert or semidesert and the remainder was grassland that had been largely ruined by excess grazing. A program of rehabilitation in order to save the Indians from starvation was therefore necessary. John Collier, who became Commissioner of Indian Affairs under the New Deal, believed that there were values in the traditional communal life of the Indians which deserved to be rescued and that the Indians should be encouraged to remain Indian instead of being forcibly transformed into bad imitations of white men. By the Indian Reorganization Act, the land which still belonged to the Indians was to remain as communal tribal property. The Indians were, moreover, given credits and additional land, and were to receive assistance in checking overgrazing.

The legislative record of the special "one hundred day" session of the Seventy-third Congress was, regardless of the merit of the various laws enacted, an impressive performance of responsible democratic government acting through vigorous Executive leadership. Not everything that was done proved wise or beneficial, and many of the programs had to be dropped or revised because they proved ineffective, while others were invalidated by the courts. Still, one fact is indisputable: because of the legislation of this special session, the way of life of the American people was altered considerably. The second session of the Seventy-third Congress (January 3 to June 18, 1934) devoted itself largely to modifying and making more complete the measures adopted during the "hundred day" session. The Securities and Exchange Act of 1934 strengthened the Securities Act of 1933, the Cotton Control Act and the Tobacco Control Act of 1934 augmented the powers of the AAA, the Gold Reserve Act and Silver Purchase Act increased the federal government's control over the currency, and much the same can be said for the other legislation.

On June 28, 1934, ten days after the Seventy-third Congress adjourned,

Roosevelt, in his first fireside chat of 1934, reported to the American people on the legislation of the past session, pointing out that of the "three related steps"—relief, recovery, and reform—the government had of necessity to emphasize relief because "the primary concern of any Government dominated by the humane ideals of democracy is the simple principle that in a land of vast resources no one should be permitted to starve." Insofar as the administration worked to bring about recovery, he suggested that each American ask himself: "Are you better off than you were last year? Are your debts less burdensome? Is your bank account more secure? Are your working conditions better? Is your faith in your own individual future more firmly grounded?" At the same time, he took the opportunity to strike at his critics, most of whom were conservative businessmen who were convinced that the New Deal would lead to fascism, communism, or socialism, and that its "regimentation" would deprive the people of their liberties, threaten democratic government, and undermine the Constitution. F.D.R. countered his opponents by asking his listeners to answer these charges "out of the facts of your life," and he asserted, "I believe that what we are doing . . . is a necessary fulfillment of what Americans have been doing . . . a fulfillment of old and tested American ideals."

THE CONGRESSIONAL ELECTIONS
OF 1934

The administration's leaders were generally convinced that the New Deal had the support of a majority of the population. Roosevelt, for example, believed that most people were, as he told Garner before the 1934 elections, "pretty well satisfied that we are going some place and that they still want action." Postmaster General Farley was more optimistic about the outcome of the elections than Roosevelt, but nonetheless continued to work hard to ensure a Democratic party victory. "The sole question in this election is," he told the voters a few days before they went to the polls, "shall we go on or shall we go bust?" On Tuesday, November 6, the voters made known their decision on what they thought about Roosevelt and the New Deal by a nationwide endorsement of such proportions that it left the Republican party in near collapse. Of the thirty-five Senate races contested, the Democrats won twenty-nine; in the House of Representatives, they picked up an additional twelve seats.

THE NEW DEAL, I (1933–1934)

When all the votes were counted, the make-up of the newly elected Seventy-fourth Congress was 69 Democrats, 24 Republicans, 1 Farmer-Labor, and 1 Progressive in the Senate, and 318 Democrats, 99 Republicans, 4 Farmer-Labor, and 7 Progressives in the House. The Democratic party victory on the state level was also impressive. Only seven Republican governors survived. "The President and his New Deal," commented *The New York Times*'s Arthur Krock, "in its first electoral test . . . won the most overwhelming victory in American politics . . . . By their vote . . . the people of the United States invested the President with the greatest power that has ever been given to a Chief Executive on the submission of his case." The *Herald*, Boston's Republican daily, explained the GOP rout more simply: "The people . . . still trust Roosevelt and distrust the opposition." And as *The New York Times*'s postelection editorial asserted, F.D.R. himself was the issue. His "personality dominated the whole campaign. It was as if he were present in every polling place . . . . Candidates stood or fell according to their attitude toward him . . . . Ancient Republican citadels like Pennsylvania [which went Democratic for the first time since 1874] fell before attackers whose battle cry was the name of Roosevelt."

Suggested Readings

The literature on Franklin D. Roosevelt and the New Deal is immense, and the flow of new books on the man and his epoch shows no signs of diminishing. A most useful guide to the more recent studies is Richard L. Watson, Jr., "F.D.R. in Historical Writing, 1950–1957," *South Atlantic Quarterly*, LVII (Winter 1958), 104–26.

The best of the Roosevelt biographies is the still unfinished multivolume work by Frank Freidel, *Franklin D. Roosevelt* (3 vols., Boston, 1952–   ), which covers the years to his election in 1932. Volume III, subtitled *The Triumph*, is devoted entirely to F.D.R.'s years as governor of New York. On this phase of Roosevelt's career, consult also Bernard Bellush, *Franklin D. Roosevelt as Governor of New York* (New York, 1955).

Among the single-volume biographies, the best one is George MacGregor Burns, *Roosevelt: The Lion and the Fox* (New York [1956]); but see also the able one by Rexford G. Tugwell, *The Democratic Roosevelt* . . . (New York, 1957). Tugwell, as one of the "journeymen" in the brain trust, was involved in much of the early New Deal. His biography adds much that is new and not available elsewhere, thus making it a memoir of a participant as well as the biography of the "master craftsman."

There are numerous other one-volume biographies, some of which, like

52 THE ERA OF F.D.R., 1933–1945

John Gunther, *Roosevelt in Retrospect: A Profile in History* (New York [1950]), are highly favorable; others, such as John T. Flynn, *Country Squire in the White House* (Garden City, N.Y., 1940), are bitterly critical. William S. White, *Majesty and Mischief: A Mixed Tribute to F.D.R.* (New York [1961]) attempts to strike a balance.

Roosevelt on the political stump is expertly analyzed in Harold F. Gosnell, *Champion Campaigner* (New York, 1952). The statistics on F.D.R.'s presidential contests are collected in Edgar Eugene Robinson, *They Voted for Roosevelt . . . 1932–1944* (Stanford, Calif. [1947]).

Daniel R. Fusfield, *The Economic Thought of Franklin D. Roosevelt and the Origins of the New Deal* (New York, 1956) examines F.D.R.'s training and "economic philosophy" and discusses his comprehension of economic affairs, concluding that Roosevelt was more aware of economic considerations and principles than many people thought him to be. Clarke A. Chambers, "F.D.R., Pragmatist-Idealist," *Pacific Northwest Quarterly*, LII (April 1961), 50–55, is brief and perceptive.

Convenient collections of F.D.R.'s letters and writings include Elliott Roosevelt, ed., *F.D.R.: His Personal Letters, 1905–1945* (4 vols., New York, 1947–50) and Samuel T. Rosenman, comp., *The Public Papers of Franklin D. Roosevelt* (13 vols., New York, 1938–50). F.D.R.'s interpretation of the domestic scene when he took office and after one year as President are available in his *Looking Forward* (New York, 1933) and *On Our Way* (New York [1934]).

Just about everyone associated with Roosevelt felt compelled to publish his memoirs, reminiscences, or diary entries. Among those especially helpful in revealing some of the workings of the New Deal, see the following: Tom Connally and Alfred Steinberg, *My Name is Tom Connally* (New York, 1954), which covers the Capitol Hill career of a long-time Texas Democrat, emphasizing the foreign policy developments with which Connally was associated; James A. Farley's two books, *Behind the Ballots*, already cited, which is pro-Roosevelt, and *Jim Farley's Story* (New York, 1948), which reflects the man's views after his break with Roosevelt; William Hassett, *Off the Record with F.D.R., 1942–1945* (New Brunswick, N.J., 1958), containing the wartime reminiscences of Roosevelt's assistant secretary; Cordell Hull, *The Memoirs of Cordell Hull* (2 vols., New York, 1948), primarily concerned with foreign policy, but also good on administration personalities; Harold L. Ickes, *The Autobiography of a Curmudgeon* (New York, 1943), covering to 1932, and *The Secret Diary of Harold L. Ickes* (3 vols., New York, 1953–54), reviewing the period 1933–41; Ross T. McIntire and George Creel, *White House Physician* (New York, 1946); Charles Michelson, *The Ghost Talks* (New York, 1944); Raymond Moley, *After Seven Years* (New York, 1939); John Morton Blum, *From the Morgenthau Diaries: Years of Crisis* (Boston, 1959–), the first of a proposed two-volume digest of the vast Morgenthau diaries, with extensive quotations from that source; Henrietta Nesbitt, *White House Diary* (Garden City, N.Y., 1948), the housekeeper's story; Frances Perkins, *The Roosevelt I Knew* (New York, 1946), an exceptionally valuable statement; Michael F. Reilly, *Reilly of the White House* (New York, 1947), which reveals some interesting

THE NEW DEAL, I (1933–1934)

sidelights; Samuel Rosenman, *Working With Roosevelt* (New York, 1952), an important source; Eleanor Roosevelt, *This Is My Story* (New York, 1937) and its sequel *This I Remember* (New York, 1949); Sara Delano Roosevelt, *My Boy Franklin* (New York, 1933), the revealing narrative of F.D.R.'s mother; James Roosevelt and Sidney Shallett, *Affectionately, F.D.R.: A Son's Story of a Lonely Man* (New York [1959]), which contains much interesting material on Roosevelt in the White House; Henry L. Stimson and McGeorge Bundy, *On Active Service in Peace and War* (New York, 1948), which is very important on the coming of the war; Grace Tully, *F.D.R., My Boss* (New York, 1949); and Francis Biddle, *A Casual Past* (Garden City, N.Y. [1961]), which is somewhat limited but contains new information.

The most recent and comprehensive general appraisal of the New Deal is contained in volumes II and III of Arthur M. Schlesinger, Jr., *The Age of Roosevelt* (3 vols., Boston, 1957–60). Subtitled *The Coming of the New Deal* and the *Politics of Upheaval*, the volumes bring the New Deal through the election of 1936. Older but still satisfactory is Basil Rauch, *The History of the New Deal, 1933–1938* (New York, 1944), and equally useful is Arthur M. Schlesinger, *The New Deal in Action, 1933–1938* (New York, 1940). Shorter, more recent surveys include Denis W. Brogan, *The Era of Franklin D. Roosevelt: A Chronicle of the New Deal and Global War* (New Haven, Conn., 1950) and Dexter Perkins, *The New Age of Franklin D. Roosevelt, 1932–1945* (Chicago, 1957). The first year of the New Deal is appraised in Louis M. Hacker, *A Short History of the New Deal* (New York, 1934) and in the equally contemporary account by Schuyler C. Wallace, *The New Deal in Action* (New York, 1934).

For the general social and economic history of the Roosevelt years to 1941, see Dixon Wecter, *The Age of the Great Depression, 1929–1941* (New York, 1948), the last volume in *The History of American Life* series; Broadus Mitchell, *Depression Decade, 1929–1941* (New York [1947]), the ninth volume in *The Economic History of the United States* series, is general economic history. The social scene is also portrayed in Frederick Lewis Allen, *Since Yesterday* (New York, 1940), but see also Charles A. Beard, *America in Midpassage* (New York, 1939), the last volume in his *Rise of American Civilization.* Two convenient anthologies of miscellaneous readings are Milton Crane, ed., *The Roosevelt Era* (New York, [1947]) and Don Congdon, ed., *The Thirties: A Time to Remember* (New York, 1962).

The New Deal has produced numerous interpretative accounts. Edgar Eugene Robinson, *The Roosevelt Leadership, 1933–1945* (New York, 1956) views the legacy of the Roosevelt years in terms of "a weakened constitutional system . . . imperiled national security . . . diminishing national morale . . . deteriorated political morality, and . . . an overburdened economy." Much more favorable to Roosevelt is Mario Einaudi, *The Roosevelt Revolution* (New York [1957]), which concludes that the New Deal provided America with "a sturdier framework of institutions and of political wisdom. . . ." The views of the editors of the London *Economist* on the New Deal show much understanding in *The New Deal: An Analysis and Appraisal* (New York, 1937).

54   THE ERA OF F.D.R., 1933–1945

For a sampling of some early interpretations, consult Charles A. Beard and George H. E. Smith, *The Future Comes* (New York, 1933) and the same authors' *The Old Deal and the New* (New York, 1940); Stanley High, *Roosevelt—and Then?* (New York, 1937); Ernest K. Lindley, *The Roosevelt Revolution: First Phase* (New York, 1933) and the same author's *Half-way with Roosevelt* (rev. ed., New York, 1937); and Benjamin Stolberg and Warren J. Vinton, *The Economic Consequences of the New Deal* (New York [1935]).

The literature on the personnel of the New Deal and on the men close to F.D.R. is large. Apart from the personal accounts cited above, see Louis W. Koenig's fine chapters on Corcoran and Hopkins in his *The Invisible Presidency* (New York [1960]). On Hopkins' later career, Robert E. Sherwood, *Roosevelt and Hopkins: An Intimate History* (New York, 1948) is indispensable. See also Joseph Alsop and Robert Kintner, *Men around the President* (Garden City, N.Y., 1938) and for contemporary flavor, The Unofficial Observer [John F. Carter], *The New Dealers* (New York, 1934).

Some useful biographies of men around Roosevelt include Bascom N. Timmons, *Garner of Texas: A Personal History* (New York, 1948); Lela Stiles, *The Man behind Roosevelt: The Story of Louis McHenry Howe* (Cleveland, Ohio, 1954); Harold B. Hinton, *Cordell Hull: A Biography* (New York, 1942); and Dwight MacDonald, *Henry Wallace: The Man and the Myth* (New York [1948]).

A contemporary economists' account of the financial emergency when F.D.R. became President is Jules I. Bogen and Marcus Nadler, *The Banking Crisis: The End of an Epoch* (New York, 1933). New Deal financial and monetary policies are discussed in G. Griffith Johnson, *The Treasury and Monetary Policy, 1933–1938* (Cambridge, Mass., 1939); Quincy Wright, *Gold and Monetary Stabilization* (Chicago, 1932); James D. Paris, *Monetary Policies of the United States, 1932–1938* (New York, 1938); Arthur W. Crawford, *Monetary Management under the New Deal: The Evolution of a Managed Currency System, Its Problems and Results* (Washington, D.C., 1940); and Joseph R. Reeve, *Monetary Reform Movements: A Survey of Recent Plans and Panaceas* (Washington, D.C., 1943), a critical account of the changing New Deal policies. The theory behind devaluation is explained in George F. Warren and Francis Pearson, *Gold and Prices* (New York, 1935) and attacked in a pamphlet by Charles O. Hardy, *The Warren-Pearson Price Theory* (Washington, D.C., 1935). The silver legislation of the years 1933–46 is analyzed in Allan S. Everest, *Morgenthau, The New Deal and Silver: A Story of Pressure Politics* (New York, 1950).

Rudolph L. Weissman, *The New Wall Street* (New York, 1939) covers the New Deal's security legislation.

The changes in the Federal Reserve System are analyzed in Rudolph L. Weissman, *The New Federal Reserve System: The Board Assumes Control* (New York, 1936) and autobiographically in Marriner S. Eccles, *Beckoning Frontiers* (New York, 1951). See also the more general work by Charles C. Chapman, *The Development of American Business and Banking Thought, 1913–1936* (New York, 1936).

THE NEW DEAL, I (1933–1934)

General works on recovery include Leonard P. Ayres, *The Economics of Recovery* (New York, 1933), a contemporary view; Adolph A. Berle, *et al.*, *America's Recovery Program* (New York, 1934), which is told by men closely associated with the measures discussed; Brookings Institution, *The Recovery Problem in the United States* (Washington, D.C., 1936); Alvin H. Hansen, *Full Recovery or Stagnation?* (New York [1938]); and Merle Fainsod and Lincoln Gordon, *Government and the American Economy* (New York, 1941).

Specialized studies on the relief program include Harry L. Hopkins, *Spending to Save: The Complete Story of Relief* (New York [1936]), by one of the New Deal's leading participants; Josephine C. Brown, *Public Relief, 1929–1939* (New York [1940]), which compares the pre-New Deal system with the changes brought about by the FERA and WPA; Marie D. Lane and Francis Steegmuller, *America on Relief* (New York [1938]); Harold L. Ickes, *Back to Work: The Story of W.P.A.* (New York, 1935), the account of the director; Jack F. Isakoff, *The Public Works Administration* (Urbana, Ill., 1938); Donald S. Howard, *The W.P.A. and Federal Relief Policy* (New York, 1943); Arthur D. Gayer, *Public Works in Prosperity and Depression* (New York, 1935); William Whitman, *Bread and Circuses* (New York, 1937), which reviews the WPA's theater projects; Kenneth Holland and Frank Ernest Hill, *Youth in the C.C.C.* (Washington, D.C., 1942); and Lewis L. Lorwin, *Youth Work Programs* (Washington, D.C., 1941).

The New Deal's agricultural policies are defended by Henry A. Wallace, *New Frontiers* (New York, 1934) and censured by Joseph S. Davis, *Our Agricultural Policy, 1926–1938* (New York, 1939). The AAA is appraised more objectively in the Brookings Institution's study by Edwin G. Nourse, *et al.*, *Three Years of the Agricultural Administration* (Washington, D.C., 1937). Two other useful studies by Edwin G. Nourse are *Marketing Agreements under the A.A.A.* (Washington, D.C., 1935) and *Government in Relation to Agriculture* (Washington, D.C., 1940). Murray R. Benedict and Oscar C. Stein, *The Agricultural Commodity Programs: Two Decades of Experience* (New York, 1956) is detailed and exhaustive. Arthur L. Moore, *The Farmer and the Rest of Us* (Boston, 1945) gives a newspaperman's viewpoint on farm problems. The official account of the AAA program is in the series of reports issued by the AAA chief; see especially *Agricultural Adjustment: A Report on the Administration of the Agricultural Adjustment Act* (Washington, D.C., 1934–45). Consult also U. S. Department of Agriculture, *Toward Farm Security* (Washington, D.C., 1941). Other works on agricultural policy include Lawrence J. Norton, *Financing Agriculture* (rev. ed., Danville, Ill., 1948); Donald C. Blaisdell, *Government and Agriculture: The Growth of Federal Farm Aid* (New York, 1940); Wesley C. McCune, *The Farm Bloc* (Garden City, N.Y., 1943), on the politics of farm policy; Carey McWilliams, *Ill Fares the Land: Migrants and Migratory Labor in the United States* (Boston, 1942); Wesley Calef, *Private Grazing and Public Land* (Chicago, 1961) which discusses the Taylor Act; and Dean Albertson, *Roosevelt's Farmer: Claude R. Wickard in the New Deal* (New York, 1961), which appraises the role of the successor to Secretary Wallace.

56   THE ERA OF F.D.R., 1933–1945

The NRA and industrial recovery have received considerable attention. Specific studies include Persia S. Campbell, *Consumer Representation in the New Deal* (New York, 1940); Carroll R. Daugherty, *Labor Under the N.R.A.* (New York [1934]); Charles L. Dearing, *et al.*, *The A.B.C. of the N.R.A.* (Washington, D.C., 1934), a Brookings Institution study; George B. Galloway, *Industrial Planning under the Codes* (New York, 1935); Leverett S. Lyon, *et al.*, *The National Recovery Administration* (Washington, D.C., 1935), an analysis by economists; Charles F. Roos, *N.R.A. Economic Planning* (Bloomington, Ind., 1937). Hugh S. Johnson, *The Blue Eagle from Egg to Earth* (New York, 1935) is the story by the first administrator, and his successor, Donald Richberg, tells his experiences in *The Rainbow* (Garden City, N.Y., 1936).

On housing, see Carl Aronovici, *Housing the Masses* (New York, 1939); Michael V. Straus and Talbott Wegg, *Housing Comes of Age* (New York, 1938); Nathan Straus, *The Seven Myths of Housing* (New York, 1944); Langdon W. Post, *The Challenge of Housing* (New York [1938]); William Ebenstein, *The Law of Public Housing* (Madison, Wis., 1940); and Thomas R. Carskadon, *Houses for Tomorrow* (rev. ed., New York, 1944), a brief pamphlet.

Claude M. Fuess, *Joseph B. Eastman: Servant of the People* (New York, 1952) is a full-length study of the Federal Coordinator of Transportation; more specialized is Earl Latham, *The Politics of Railroad Coordination, 1933–1936* (Cambridge, Mass., 1959), which emphasizes Eastman's trials and tribulations. See also Herbert Spero, *Reconstruction Finance Corporation Loans to Railroads, 1932–1937* (Cambridge, Mass., 1939).

On soil conservation, see Stuart Chase, *Rich Land, Poor Land: A Study in the Natural Resources of America* (New York, 1936); Hugh H. Bennett, *Soil Conservation* (New York, 1939); Axel F. Gustafson, *et al.*, *Conservation in the United States* (Ithaca, N.Y., 1939); and the study on the politics of farm organizations and government services in relation to soil conservation by Charles M. Hardin, *The Politics of Agriculture: Soil Conservation and the Struggle for Power in Rural America* (Glencoe, Ill., 1952). Especially interesting on F.D.R.'s concern with conservation is the collection of many of his papers by Edgar B. Nixon, ed., *Franklin D. Roosevelt and Conservation, 1911–1945* (2 vols., Hyde Park, N.Y., 1957).

Among the many useful studies on the TVA, see especially Preston J. Hubbard, *Origins of the T.V.A., The Muscle Shoals Controversy, 1920–1932* (Nashville, Tenn., 1961); Gordon R. Clapp, *The T.V.A.: An Approach to the Development of a Region* (Chicago [1955]), the account of the project's first twenty years by its former general manager and board chairman. The objectives and achievements of TVA are analyzed in David E. Lilienthal, *T.V.A.: Democracy on the March* (enl. ed., New York [1953]). A well-written account of TVA's effect upon the region it serviced is Robert L. Duffus, *The Valley and Its People: A Portrait of T.V.A.* (New York, 1944). Consult also Clarence L. Hodge, *The Tennessee Valley Authority* (Washington, D.C., 1938); John F. Carter, *The Future Is Ours* (New York [1939]); Louis B. Wehle, *Hidden Threads of History: Wilson through Roosevelt* (New York,

THE NEW DEAL, I (1933–1934)

1953); C. Herman Pritchett, *The Tennessee Valley Authority: A Study in Public Administration* (Chapel Hill, N.C., 1943); Philip Selznik, *T.V.A. and Grass Roots* (Berkeley, Calif., 1949); and the views of an Englishman, Julian Huxley, *T.V.A.: Adventure in Planning* (Cheam, England, 1943).

The utilities industry is studied in the expert account by the Twentieth Century Fund, *The Power Industry and the Public Interest* (New York, 1944); James C. Bonbright, *Public Utilities and the National Power Policies* (New York, 1940); and Bernhard Ostrolenk, *Electricity: For Use or for Profit* (New York, 1936).

2

The New Deal, II

1935-1936

THE CENTRAL PURPOSE of Roosevelt's first twenty months in the White House, the period of the so-called "first" New Deal, had been to bring about recovery by "affirmative national planning" on the part of business, government, labor, and agriculture.[1] There was nothing radical in the legislation enacted by the Seventy-third Congress and, with the possible exception of TVA, nothing which involved major alterations in the structure of the economy. The New Dealers of 1933 and 1934, men like Moley, Tugwell, and Johnson, believed that the business cycle could be controlled by government planning, and this is what the administration attempted to do in the industrial and agricultural legislation of 1933. The results, insofar as they were registered by national income and employment statistics, indicated that by the end of 1934 considerable progress had been made in restoring the economy. Recovery, however, was far from complete, even though the fear and the panic conditions of early 1933 had given way to renewed hope and confidence.

The principal beneficiaries of the "first" New Deal were the bankers, whose very existence was saved by the administration's bold and quick

---

[1] Arthur M. Schlesinger, Jr., *The Age of Roosevelt: The Politics of Upheaval* (Boston, 1960), pp. 389, 391.

THE NEW DEAL, II (1935–1936)

decisions in March, 1933; big business, which profited from the NRA's stimulus to industrial recovery and from the privileges which businessmen received from its codes; and large commercial farmers, who benefited by the various provisions of the AAA, especially those intended to raise agricultural prices while paying the growers to restrict production. To be sure, the unemployed and the destitute were helped by the augmented relief programs, just as labor received some benefits from Section 7a, but neither of these groups was especially satisfied with its lot. Nor were many small businessmen content with the state of affairs. The same was true of the impoverished marginal farmers, the millions of unemployed, and the aged, all of whom had few resources of their own. By the summer of 1935, the administration could no longer ignore the demands of these various dissatisfied elements. Nor could it overlook the fact that its middle of the road approach had been invalidated by the Supreme Court in the NRA decision. Alternative solutions had to be found, and without delay. Meanwhile the very groups which the New Dealers had befriended and aided and upon whose cooperation Roosevelt had counted were becoming increasingly vocal in their dissatisfaction with the administration.

OPPOSITION TO THE NEW DEAL

The Attack from the Right

At first there had been little open opposition to the New Deal among any section of the population. Since all classes had been alarmed by the spread of the depression and by its culmination in the closing of the banks, all classes were willing to accept almost any program Roosevelt might recommend. Many conservative Democrats disapproved of a number of the New Deal's objectives and often of its haste, but few of them ventured to oppose it publicly. Many Republicans in Congress also voted for a number of New Deal measures, so that much of the legislative program of 1933 took on a bipartisan character.

In 1934 and 1935, on the other hand, as certain progressive tendencies of the New Deal became more apparent, public opinion began to crystallize. The New Deal ran counter to the traditional party divisions; and while the bulk of the farming and wage-earning groups, both Democratic and Republican, supported the administration, the majority of the business classes opposed it. As in 1800, 1828, and 1896, American opinion, much to Roosevelt's distaste, was becoming divided along class lines. The business classes, however, were by no means unanimous in their sentiments. While the representatives of the capital goods industries were against the New Deal, a number of spokesmen of the consumption goods industries and of retail trade, the prosperity of which depended directly on mass purchasing power, supported Roosevelt. Other businessmen favored the New Deal because they disliked the isolationist tendencies of Republican foreign policy and approved of the New Deal's effort to increase international trade and promote international peace, or because they believed that drastic reform in the American economic system was the only alternative to collapse and revolution.

A very large proportion of the wealthier business families in America, however, soon became the most bitter antagonists of the whole New Deal program. A number of them, at the suggestion of R. R. M. Carpenter, a retired executive of the Du Pont Corporation, and John J. Raskob, a former chairman of the Democratic party's National Committee and a director of the General Motors Corporation, decided to form an "educational organization" which, in Raskob's words, would "protect society from the sufferings which it is bound to endure if we allow communistic elements to lead the people to believe that all businessmen are crooks." [2] On August 22, 1934, Jouett Shouse, a former chairman of the Democratic Executive Committee, announced the formation of the American Liberty League. Its declared purpose was to "teach the necessity of respect for the rights of persons and property as fundamental to every successful form of government . . . ." Besides Shouse, the League's executive committee included two former Democratic party presidential candidates: the 1928 standard-bearer, Alfred E. Smith, who had broken with F.D.R. earlier, and John W. Davis, the party's nominee in 1924 and a corporation lawyer for the House of Morgan. The League's other leaders included Irénée Du Pont, the multimillionaire industrialist; James W. Wadsworth, Jr., a former Republican United States senator from New York and in 1934 a member of the House of Representatives; and Nathan L. Miller, the former GOP governor of New York and a lawyer and director of the United States Steel Corporation. This group, financed principally by the Du Pont and General Motors interests, was reinforced by other influential members it soon attracted to its cause, among them the news-

[2] Quoted in Frederick Rudolph, "The American Liberty League, 1934–1940," *American Historical Review*, LVI (October 1950), 19.

"MOTHER, WILFRED WROTE A BAD WORD!"

Popular with the majority of the American people, President Roosevelt provoked among many members of the upper-income groups an antagonism unparalleled in American political history. (Dorothy McKay; Franklin D. Roosevelt Library)

paper magnate William Randolph Hearst, who had now totally abandoned his semisocialism of a generation earlier.

The League thus joined under its banner the spokesmen of America's wealthiest industrial and financial interests and representatives of the more conservative elements in the Democratic party of the North. These men, the most vigorous opponents of the President, declared that the college professors and young lawyers whom F.D.R. had called to Washington for advice and the labor leaders who supported the New Deal were Communists, or at least leaned in that direction. They declared further that Roosevelt was making himself a dictator, and that he was destroying the American form of government by making Congress into a rubber stamp. They denounced the growth of bureaucracy, the failure to balance the budget, the squandering of public money on unemployment relief, the encouragement given to organized labor, the raising of wages and shortening of hours, and the regulation of the stock exchanges; and they insisted that any economic recovery was impossible as long as a group of impractical theorists in Washington were allowed to destroy business confidence and shackle business expansion with unnecessary regulations. The intensity with which the Liberty League and many of the nation's wealthiest families hated Roosevelt was probably unparalleled in American history. The weakness of the opposition to the New Deal was, however, that it was almost wholly negative. Whatever justification there may have been for specific criticisms of the New Deal, many of its opponents gave the impression that they wanted to return to the days of Harding and Coolidge or McKinley and Mark Hanna, that they were incapable of recognizing that the American system could not survive unless it were reformed, and that they had learned nothing by the depression. Though Roosevelt "twitted" the league, as *The New York Times* put it, for being more concerned with property rights than human rights, he was nonetheless disturbed by the intensity of its attacks, especially since he looked upon them as unfair and unwarranted. But if the President was concerned by criticism from the right, he was made even more aware of the mounting discontent from the left.

The Attack from the Left

The widespread suffering and humiliation caused by the depression gave rise during the 1930's to many prophets with various panaceas, each of whom was convinced that the remedy he proposed would not only cure all the social and economic ills which plagued so many Americans at the time but would lead them to a new promised land of plenty. The voices of these "new messiahs" were especially attractive to those groups which had benefited least from the recovery which had accompanied the first year of the New Deal. Years of privation and degradation had caused many people to lose all hope. These citizens, old and young alike, on farms or in the cities, were so disturbed by the dismal course of events that they became easy prey to the more radical and demagogic movements of the times, many of which were reaching the height of their influence in 1935.

The 1930's, therefore, like the later decades of the nineteenth century, provided excellent conditions for the growth of third party farmer-labor movements. And though these twentieth-century coalitions, like their predecessors, were numerically weak, they attracted much attention and exercised considerable influence upon the administration in Washington, partly because of events in Europe and partly because of the continuing economic malaise at home.

Immediately to the left of the Democratic party were various labor and farmer organizations which sought the gradual transformation of capitalism into some form of democratic socialism but which, on immediate issues, generally supported the New Deal. The oldest of these was the Minnesota Farmer-Labor party. This party, formed in 1918, had elected Henrik Shipstead to the United States Senate in 1922, and it reelected him three times thereafter. From 1932 until 1938, under the leadership first of the state's energetic Governor Floyd B. Olson and after his death in 1936 of Governor Elmer A. Benson, it controlled the state government. Its radical program attracted much liberal attention throughout the Middle West. In 1935 Olson was talking of the necessity of a third party to "preach the gospel of government and collective ownership of the means of production." Whether a third party would be established on a national level, Olson said, "depends mainly on Mr. Roosevelt." [3] No such party materialized, and in 1936 Olson's followers supported F.D.R. in return for the withdrawal of the Democratic party's state ticket.

In Wisconsin, the traditional stronghold of agrarian liberalism, a Progressive party was organized in 1934 and was successful in electing several congressmen. The La Follette family continued to be powerful: Robert M. La Follette, Jr., was elected to his father's seat in the United States Senate, where he represented the state as a Republican from 1925 until

[3] Quoted in Schlesinger, *op. cit.*, p. 104.

64   THE ERA OF F.D.R., 1933–1945

1934, when he became an independent, and his brother Philip served three times as governor. In 1934 the La Follettes organized the Wisconsin Progressive party, but though they proclaimed it "a new national party," it did not become such until 1938, when dissatisfaction with the slowing down of the New Deal's reforms after the Supreme Court fight, apprehension about Roosevelt's growing interest in international affairs, and the La Follettes' own political ambitions caused them to launch the National Progressives of America. The new party never won much support, and in the Wisconsin gubernatorial election that year, Philip La Follette was defeated for reelection by a conservative Republican. Nonetheless, like the Minnesota Farmer Labor party, the Wisconsin movement caused the New Deal concern as to its ability to hold on to the liberal voters attracted by these two groups.[4]

Similar progressive and farmer-labor parties were also attracting much attention and winning considerable strength in various other states in the Mississippi valley and in the Far West, especially in Washington and California. In 1934 Upton Sinclair, the prolific socialist novelist, captured the Democratic party's nomination for governor of California and ran on a radical program, the EPIC (End Poverty in California) plan, which called for the state's acquisition of idle lands and factories so that they could be turned over to the unemployed, who would operate them for their needs. Sinclair was narrowly defeated by the conservative Republican Frank Merriam, but in 1938, when the Democrats won control of the state, the influence of the EPIC movement was readily evident. Not only were the Democrats in California considerably to the left of Roosevelt and the New Deal, but their candidates had the support of a number of Communists.

In the East, the most significant third party movement was in New York. In 1934 New York City conducted one of its periodic political housecleanings. Tammany Hall, which had controlled the city since 1917, was discredited by revelations of corruption made by a legislative investigation with Samuel Seabury as counsel. Fiorello H. La Guardia, officially a Republican but actually a progressive, was elected mayor. He gave the city a New Deal administration whose energy, efficiency, and liberality won wide applause. His strongest support came from the trade unions of the city, who organized in 1936 the American Labor party, the leadership of which came chiefly from the clothing unions. In 1936 nearly 250,000

[4] Donald R. McCoy, "The National Progressives of America, 1938," *Mississippi Valley Historical Review*, XLIV (June 1957), 75–93.

persons voted for Roosevelt on the Labor party ticket; and in 1937, when La Guardia was reelected mayor as candidate of both the Republican and Labor parties, the latter's vote reached nearly 500,000. The Labor party itself was not strong enough to elect candidates of its own to important offices, but it was in a position to hold the balance of power in New York State between the two major parties.

During the mid-1930's there was considerable talk of a national farmer-labor coalition which would bring under a single banner these various state and local parties, but as long as the Democratic party adopted liberal policies and supported progressive candidates, such a development was unlikely. The importance of these various third party movements was that they alerted Roosevelt and the administration's political leaders to the growing pressure for more liberal reform. If the Democratic party lost their support, it was quite likely that it might be defeated in 1936. The independent progressive vote represented in these third parties was strong enough to help convince the Democrats of the necessity for an advanced liberal program.

Roosevelt and the New Dealers were also concerned by the number of people attracted to the various "crackpot" groups that were peddling their panaceas across the country in the 1930's. Three depression-born demagogues—Senator Huey P. Long of Louisiana, Dr. Francis E. Townsend of Long Beach, California, and Father Charles E. Coughlin of Royal Oak, Michigan—were especially important. Although the movements which these men headed were at first purely American in their inspiration and ideals, to many observers they soon began to present alarming analogies to the fascist parties of Europe.

Huey P. Long, born on a Louisiana farm in 1893, studied law at Tulane University and then entered politics through service on the state's railroad commission and state attorney's office. In 1928 he was elected governor; three years later he resigned to become United States senator. As governor of Louisiana, he established a totalitarian regime over the state of a kind unprecedented in the annals of American government. He used his power not only for the benefit of himself and his friends but also to increase corporation taxes and to give the tenant farmers of Louisiana better schools and an excellent system of roads. During the depression he became a vitriolic enemy of high finance, and he began to build a broad popular organization for the redistribution of property, using the slogans "Share Our Wealth" and "Every Man a King." With his flamboyant personality, his inordinate ambition, his great ability for politics and mob oratory, and his oft-proclaimed egalitarian ideals, he combined the characteristics of an old-fashioned Populist leader and a Caribbean dictator. By 1935 Long's presidential ambitions posed a serious threat to the Democratic party in Louisiana and the South. However, he was assassinated in the Louisiana State capitol at Baton Rouge on September 8, 1935, by one of his opponents who, in turn, was immediately shot down by Long's henchmen. After Huey Long's death, the leadership of the "Share Our Wealth" movement was assumed by Gerald L. K. Smith, who had attached himself to Long's bandwagon. In 1936 Smith and the Long forces joined with those of Coughlin and Townsend in support of William Lemke's Union party candidacy for the presidency. Long's Louisiana political machine remained in power until 1940, when a reform Democrat became governor, but its influence and legacy continued to live on in various guises.

Dr. Francis E. Townsend, a leader of a very different type from Long, was born in a log cabin on an Illinois farm in 1867. He studied medicine, and after graduating from Omaha Medical College practiced in several middle-western states. During World War I he served in the Army Medical Corps, and in 1919 he settled in Long Beach, California, where he became one of the community's health officers. The incident which is said to have stimulated him, then a retired and impoverished physician, to become a political crusader was the spectacle during the depression of three elderly women searching a garbage can for food. In 1933 Townsend evolved an old age pension plan which would pay all retired persons past the age of sixty a monthly stipend of $200. The money to pay for the pensions was to come from a federal "transaction tax" of 2 per cent. In order to increase purchasing power and to stimulate industry, the pensioners were to be required to spend their pensions within a month of receiving their checks. Dr. Townsend saw in this plan a means whereby aged workers would retire so that their jobs would be made available to the young. The "national economic pattern" which would result from his proposal would create "a broad-scale safeguard to the aged and young alike."

Economists looked upon the Townsend plan as impracticable, and poked fun at it; but its simplicity, coupled with the sincerity and apostolic zeal of Dr. Townsend himself as well as the political cleverness of some of his associates, won for it wide popular support. During 1934 and 1935 probably as many as 5,000 Townsend clubs were organized all over the United States, and according to some estimates, as many as 25 million persons

THE NEW DEAL, II (1935-1936) 67

signed petitions in support of the plan. By organizing themselves as a pressure group and voting for congressmen who were willing to promise them assistance by introducing bills in Congress supporting the plan, the Townsendites developed into a formidable political force which Roosevelt could not long ignore.

In 1936, not satisfied with the New Deal's social security law, which he called "unfair and inequitable," Townsend joined Smith and Coughlin in supporting Lemke's candidacy for President. This move proved unpopular among his supporters, and many of them deserted him. After the election Townsend carried on with his National Recovery Plan, modifying it somewhat but keeping its essential features intact. As late as 1957, the Townsendites claimed 5 million members in 2,000 clubs. On September 1, 1960, Dr. Townsend died at the age of ninety-three. His son assumed the program's national leadership, but its political significance was now negligible.

Father Charles E. Coughlin, the third of the popular leaders to attract much attention and support in the 1930's, was a Canadian-born Irish Roman Catholic priest. He came to the United States in 1926 and was attached to the Shrine of the Little Flower at Royal Oak, Michigan, a Detroit suburb. His radio career started when he began to deliver radio addresses on religious subjects in the late 1920's. During the depression he turned his considerable histrionic talents to politics, denouncing Hoover and in 1933 and 1934 supporting F.D.R. by declaring that "The New Deal Is Christ's Deal." His highly emotional radio oratory won him a large audience of Protestants as well as Catholics. According to some estimates, Coughlin's political ideas in 1934 reached as many as 35 or 40 million listeners by radio and thousands of readers through his magazine, *Social Justice*. The reforms he advocated were derived partly from the papal encyclicals and partly from the traditions of American populism. By the spring of 1935, Coughlin, whose ideas were becoming increasingly radical, broke with F.D.R. and started to attack the President with the same bitterness that he expressed toward all "godless capitalists . . . Jews, Communists, international bankers, and plutocrats." In denouncing the Wall Street financiers, he demanded extensive government controls over banking and called for inflation by means of the coinage of silver. As time went on, he gradually abandoned the liberal elements in his program and developed red-baiting and anti-Semitism with marked Nazi sympathies. The extent of his influence was difficult to estimate, but certainly his maneuvers to create a third party, embracing the Long-Smith and Townsend

68 THE ERA OF F.D.R., 1933-1945

following, constituted an important political threat to Roosevelt and the Democratic party's chances for victory in 1936.

The demagogic appeals of Long, Townsend, and Coughlin drew strength from the hopes of the destitute and the aspirations of the aged, while the more advanced liberal programs of the farmer and labor parties attracted the support of those who believed the country required more serious economic reform than the Roosevelt administration was willing to initiate. The proposals of these various spokesmen of the left weakened the appeal which previously had attracted many people to the Socialist party. For a time in 1934 it still appeared as if the Socialists might be "going to go places," in the words of Norman Thomas, but the Roosevelt program of 1935–36 caused the Socialist party to fall upon evil days. By attacking the early New Deal measures as state capitalism and as not sufficiently radical, the party alienated almost all of its right wing supporters, who turned to F.D.R. or, after 1936, to the American Labor party. When the "second" New Deal enacted the Wagner Act, the Socialists also lost considerable labor support. In the election of 1936 the Socialist party polled fewer votes than it had in any presidential election since 1900, indicating the extent to which the liberal posture which F.D.R. assumed after June, 1935, had affected the fortunes of American socialism. To Norman Thomas, it was the President who "cut the ground pretty completely from under us . . . . You don't need anything more [to explain the near demise of the Socialist Party]." [5]

Meanwhile the Communists, numerically even weaker than the Socialists (the party had about 25,000 members in 1935), exercised an influence upon the American scene during the 1930's which was broader than their membership would suggest. They developed techniques for penetrating non-Communist organizations, which they often succeeded in controlling as a result partly of their secretiveness and partly of the energy and enthusiasm with which they undertook onerous and dangerous duties.

In the early days of the New Deal the Communists denounced Roosevelt as a Fascist, declaring that in political essence and direction his program was identical with that of Adolf Hitler. In 1935, however, the Communist International instructed its various subsidiary parties throughout the world to join other progressive organizations in a so-called Popular Front and to demand that the aggressive policies of the fascist states be checked by a program of collective security. The chief reason for this

[5] Quoted in David A. Shannon, *The Socialist Party of America: A History* (New York, 1955), p. 235.

change of policy appears to have been the fear of the Soviet government that it would be attacked by Nazi Germany. The Communist party of the United States thereupon abandoned its program of dual unionism, dissolved the Trade Union Unity League, and set about winning influence in the established labor unions by "boring from within." It formed numerous "transmission belt" organizations for middle-class liberals, most of whom were quite unaware that these organizations were under Communist control. And it began to support Roosevelt, approving particularly of his desire that the United States help the European democracies check Nazi Germany. In 1936, although the Communist party ran Earl Browder as its own candidate, many Communist sympathizers voted for Roosevelt in order to defeat Landon, who was being depicted by the party as a Fascist. The Communist cause was advocated by numerous writers, artists, and intellectuals—the so-called fellow travelers—and won a number of supporters in government agencies and among trade union officials.

Yet the extent of Communist influence was much exaggerated by both the friends and the enemies of the party. Perhaps the chief importance of its activity, in fact, was that it played into the hands of conservatives by enabling them to denounce as communistic many liberal movements that were temporarily receiving Communist support. Most of the individauls who joined the party were naïve idealists who had temporarily lost faith in American institutions and believed communism offered a better method of achieving universal liberty and equality; many of them quickly became disillusioned by close contact with Communist methods, and resigned their membership within a few years or even a few months. Most of the party's more intellectual supporters turned against it as a result of either the Moscow trials of the late 1930's or the Nazi-Soviet Nonaggression Pact of August, 1939, though it temporarily won new adherents, mostly on lower intellectual levels, during the war years when the Soviet Union and the United States were allies against Hitler. During the security hysteria of the early 1950's, this spread of Communist influence was to have tragic consequences for many individuals who had been—however briefly—involved in it.

During the winter of 1934–35 criticism of Roosevelt and the New Deal mounted steadily. From the Communists on the extreme radical left to the American Liberty League on the far conservative right, the administration was being continuously attacked, either for not doing enough for the "forgotten man" or for its bureaucratic meddling with free private enterprise. The various farmer-labor coalitions, the followers of Coughlin,

70   THE ERA OF F.D.R., 1933-1945

Long, Smith, and Townsend, and the more radical parties all insisted upon federal government action to guarantee security and eliminate privilege. The business community, at least those segments of it represented by the American Liberty League and the United States Chamber of Commerce, demanded more individual (including corporate) freedom and opportunity through a minimum of government intervention. All of these pressures bore down heavily upon the administration, especially after the midterm elections of 1934.

FROM THE "FIRST" TO
THE "SECOND" NEW DEAL

Because of the Twentieth Amendment, which advanced the date when Congress was to meet from December to January, the Seventy-fourth Congress did not assemble until January 3, 1935. Two months earlier the voters had sent huge Democratic majorities to both houses so that the President whould have, as *The New York Times*'s Arthur Krock expressed it, "a clear mandate to proceed with his policies in his own way." On January 4, while delivering his State of the Union message, F.D.R. indicated the general course he proposed to follow for the next two years. "The attempt to make a distinction between recovery and reform," he declared, "is a narrowly conceived effort to substitute the appearance of reality for reality itself. When a man is convalescing from illness, wisdom dictates not only cure of the symptoms, but also removal of their cause . . . . We find our population suffering from old inequalities, little changed by past sporadic remedies. In spite of our efforts and in spite of our talk, we have not weeded out the overprivileged and we have not effectively lifted up the underprivileged. Both of these manifestations of injustice have retarded happiness." What the President proposed was a comprehensive program that would assure every American "a proper security, a reasonable leisure, and a decent living throughout life." The task before the Congress in 1935, and the one F.D.R. hoped it would make central to all of its deliberations, was threefold: to establish "security of . . . livelihood through the better use of the natural resources of the land . . . ; security against the major hazards and vicissitudes of life; [and] security of decent homes." These recommendations were intended to consolidate and complete the moderate programs inaugurated during the last session rather than extend them or inaugurate radically different ones. Roosevelt was convinced that the key to recovery and "purposeful

THE NEW DEAL, II (1935–1936)

progress" was a middle-of-the-road approach. The "security" legislation he proposed, as he termed it, was aimed to satisfy the most insistent demands of the left without jeopardizing the confidence and the goodwill of the right.

This approach to the nation's problems, however, proved a hazardous one. Congress, without consistently firm leadership from the White House, took its obligation to enact the President's recommendations in a leisurely manner. During the first three months it accomplished substantially nothing. Commenting upon this barren legislative record, *Time* stated, "If a drowsy member of the 74th Congress had on Jan. 3 lain down to nap on a cloakroom sofa, and if by some miracle he had slept until last week [March 31], he would, on awakening, have had no reason to believe that he had taken more than three winks." [6] Congressional lethargy reflected the indecision which prevailed in the White House during the early months of 1935. Attacked by the right, criticized by the left, and unsure himself of the means to realize his long-term though still ill-defined objectives, Roosevelt during these months followed what James MacGregor Burns has characterized as "a wobbling way . . . [which] threatened . . . to mire his program in a legislative swamp." [7] And not even after Congress reorganized the system of unemployment relief (creating the Works Progress Administration on April 8), passed the Soil Conservation Act (April 27), set up the Resettlement Administration (May 1), and established the Rural Electrification Administration (May 11) was there any reason to believe that the first session of the Seventy-fourth Congress would distinguish itself. Then, on May 27, the Supreme Court declared the NRA unconstitutional. This decision, by destroying the principle of "national planning" as the means to achieve recovery, ended the "first" New Deal. Along with the mounting pressure from the left, the growing dissatisfaction of the right, the coolness with which the Seventy-fourth Congress—a more liberal body than its predecessor—received the administration's middle of the road proposals, and the necessity to devise a new program, the NRA case forced Roosevelt into a rush of activity.

Beginning early in June, when the President once again assumed the vigor characteristic of his first days in the White House, he drove the Congress into legislating an impressive program of far-reaching social and economic reform. Between June 26, when Congress established the National Youth Administration under the WPA, and August 26, when the

---

[6] *Time*, XXV (April 1, 1935), 11.
[7] James MacGregor Burns, *Roosevelt: The Lion and the Fox* (New York [1956]), p. 220.

THE ERA OF F.D.R., 1933–1945

first session of the Seventy-fourth Congress came to a close, it passed the Wagner Labor Relations Act, enacted social security legislation—probably its most distinguished achievement—adopted a revenue act which was denounced by the Republicans as a "soak the rich" measure, and passed a new banking statute, the Public Utilities Holding Company Act, and other laws. These were the major legislative achievements of 1935, constituting what the historian Basil Rauch later termed the "second" New Deal. The legislation of these two months was aimed at assisting those groups—principally the small farmer, the small businessman, the aged, and the unemployed—which had benefited least from the legislation of 1933 and 1934. The effect of these laws upon the social and economic fabric of American society as well as upon the body politic was to be far-reaching.

What caused the New Deal to shift direction in the summer of 1935? Opinions vary as to whether it was primarily the pressure from the left and the demands of the liberals in Congress, the growing hostility of the conservatives and the business community, or the disappointment with the Supreme Court's decision in the NRA case, necessitating new statutes to continue the programs initiated during the first two years. On the other hand, others have suggested, the "second" New Deal was due primarily to Roosevelt's own progressivism and humanitarianism which were now becoming more explicit and more clearly defined. Probably no single one of these explanations is adequate, for the transition from the first to the second New Deal was neither carefully planned nor executed according to a prearranged schedule. Most likely it was, as James MacGregor Burns has suggested, "the convergence of a number of trends and episodes at a crucial point—June 1935—that left Roosevelt in the posture of a radical." [8] Whatever the explanation, the second New Deal certainly proved popular with the great majority of the American people.

THE LEGISLATION OF THE SEVENTY-FOURTH CONGRESS

Unemployment Relief

Since the spring of 1933, when the administration extended the federal relief program, the New Dealers had hoped that the unemployment prob-

[8] *Ibid.,* p. 224.

THE NEW DEAL, II (1935-1936)

lem would prove to be a temporary one and that a quick economic recovery would solve it. By the beginning of 1935, however, it had become apparent that unemployment would have to be regarded as more or less permanent. At that time 5.5 million persons were receiving relief for themselves and their dependents. The total number of persons living on relief amounted to more than 20.5 million, 17 per cent of the entire population, more than 7 million of them being children under sixteen. This did not include those who were unemployed but receiving no relief and those who were working under government projects like workers with the CCC. In his January, 1935, message to the Congress, Roosevelt proposed that the federal government assume control of work relief and that direct relief be left to the local governments. "The Federal Government," he said, "must and shall quit this business of relief. I am not willing that the vitality of our people be further sapped by the giving of cash, market baskets, of a few hours of weekly work cutting grass, raking leaves or picking up papers in the public parks. We must preserve not only the bodies of the unemployed from destitution but also their self-respect, their self-reliance and courage and determination." The federal government, the President asserted, should assume only the burden of work relief for the 3.5 million citizens who were on relief because they could find no work. "This group," he said, was the victim of a nation-wide depression caused by conditions which were not local but national. The Federal Government is the only governmental agency with sufficient power and credit to meet this situation. We have assumed this task and we shall not shrink from it in the future. It is a duty dictated by every intelligent consideration of national policy to ask you to make it possible for the United States to give employment to all of these three and one half million employable people now on relief, pending their absorption in a rising tide of private employment."

In accordance with these proposals, on April 3, 1935, Congress passed the Emergency Relief Appropriation Act, which established the Works Progress Administration (in 1939 its name was changed to Works Projects Administration). Under the supervision of Harry Hopkins, this agency, with an initial $4.8 billion appropriation, was to furnish the unemployed with work of a kind which would be useful and which as far as possible would eventually return money to the government. Wage rates varied from $19 a month in the South to $55 a month in the northern cities, with higher schedules for professional workers; minimum hours were at first 140 a month.

74 THE ERA OF F.D.R., 1933-1945

The number of persons employed by the WPA varied between 1.4 and 3.4 million. It was handicapped by the difficulty of finding projects which would not compete with private business, as well as by the fact that a large majority of its employees were unskilled or too old to find jobs in private industry. Since the program was generally regarded as primarily for relief rather than for work, as F.D.R. had intended it, morale and discipline among the employees were often low. Also, local administrators were not always efficient or nonpartisan. The result was that the WPA quickly became one of the most hotly criticized of the many New Deal agencies. Nonetheless, the WPA built or repaired 651,087 miles of streets and roads, constructed 23,000 new schools and other public buildings and improved more than 100,000 others, and completed numerous other useful projects by the time it was terminated in 1943. It conducted a large number of enterprises in the field of adult education, reducing the rate of illiteracy among persons above the age of ten from 4.3 per cent to less than 1 per cent, and it established a number of projects for professional workers in literature, art, music, and the theater. Particularly notable was the Federal Theater, supervised by Hallie Flanagan, a drama professor at Vassar College, which in 1937 gave employment to 12,700 persons and put on performances seen by 22 million persons. Sixty per cent of these performances were in communities where the legitimate theater had hitherto been unknown. The work of the Federal Theater was remarkable both for the high quality of its productions and for its remarkable freedom from government censorship. The art projects, most of which consisted of painting murals for public buildings, were equally laudable examples of public patronage exercised with a due regard for freedom of aesthetic expression.

Another federal relief agency, established as part of the WPA, was the National Youth Administration, created in June, 1935, and supervised by Aubrey Williams, an efficient, capable, and idealistic social worker from Alabama. The National Youth Administration provided part-time work for high school and college students in laboratories and libraries at a maximum rate of $6 a month for the former and $15 a month for the latter. Its chief purpose was to permit students to stay in school and finish their course work, but it also established a number of classes for vocational training. The greatest number of persons employed at any one time by the NYA was about 750,000.

The relief rolls decreased throughout 1936 and the early part of 1937. By September, 1937, when the lowest point was reached, 4.4 million families were living on relief. After this date, however, there was a rapid in-

THE NEW DEAL, II (1935–1936) 75

crease in unemployment and in the number of persons on relief. In 1939 the number of workers unable to find employment in private industry was probably about 11 million, although some authorities regarded this figure as a considerable overestimate. In 1938, at Roosevelt's request, Congress increased the appropriations for the WPA and for various forms of public works. In 1939, on the other hand, Congress favored economy: the WPA appropriation was reduced, and consequently a number of its employees were transferred to the local relief agencies, and the Federal Theater and some of the other professional projects were abolished. There was also a reduction in the WPA wage schedules, except in the South.

Down to June, 1940, the Roosevelt administration spent on relief agencies (chiefly the FERA and the WPA) a total sum of $16.23 billion and on public works (including various housing and power projects not covered by the WPA) a total sum of $7.03 billion. The smallest appropriations were for the year ending June, 1938, when $1.96 billion was spent on relief and $880 million on public works; the largest appropriations were for the year ending June, 1939, when relief cost $2.74 billion and public works cost $1.23 billion.

The relief agencies of the New Deal, particularly the WPA, were vigorously attacked by conservatives. It was argued that the government could not afford to spend such large sums, that those employed by the WPA did little work and were being pampered and demoralized, and that the WPA and the other public works and relief agencies constituted a vast pork barrel designed to secure votes for the Democratic party. Many Republicans declared that the federal government should abandon relief and that it should be given back to the local governments—a change which would probably have been followed by large reductions in the scale of payments. It was true that in some states, notably in Pennsylvania, Kentucky, Maryland, and Tennessee, there was a tendency to use the WPA as an election agency for the benefit of Democratic candidates, although Hopkins and his associates in Washington appear to have been sincerely anxious to maintain its nonpartisan character. In order to prevent this, Congress passed in August, 1939, the Hatch Act against "pernicious political activity," which forbade employees of the federal government (with the exception of policy-making officials) from taking part in politics. There was also a growing tendency among persons who were not unemployed to treat WPA workers as a kind of inferior caste, to be viewed with contempt by respectable citizens. Conservatives, however, often refused to recognize the real sufferings caused by unemployment and the genuine desire of most of those employed by the WPA to find permanent jobs. Men who lived in daily fear of receiving the pink slips indicating dismissal from the WPA were far from being pampered; and if they were demoralized, it was more from poverty and uncertainty than because they were receiving temporary support from the federal government. The WPA necessarily had some of the elements of an election agency for the Democratic party as long as the size of the relief appropriations was determined by the President and Congress, rather than by economic needs, and as long as the right of unemployed persons to receive either work or relief was not generally recognized and established.

The real weaknesses of the relief program were not administrative ones, no matter how serious some of these may have been. Of far greater importance was the reluctance with which the administration first accepted and then applied Keynesian principles. In other words, the fundamental error, as one observer phrased it, "was not that it spent too much, but rather that it spent too little." [9] Reluctant to accept and employ deficit financing boldly as a weapon to combat the depression, the American people were finally forced to adopt it in order to pay the defense bills necessitated by the growing threat of Axis aggression, and when they did so, the prosperity which had eluded them previously returned as fast as the government increased its armaments program.

Labor under the New Deal

During the depression the trade unions had declined both in members and in importance. The official membership of the AFL decreased from 2,769,700 in 1929 to 2,317,500 in 1933, and the real decrease in dues-paying members was considerably larger. The membership of unions outside the AFL amounted in 1933 to 655,500. The growth of unemployment reduced the financial resources of the unions and made successful strikes impossible. Moreover, William Green and many of the other AFL leaders, conservatives who had voted for Hoover in 1928, were incapable of making the militant demands for reform which many workers believed that the situation required, and were fully as helpless and bewildered when confronted by the depression as were the leaders of organized capital.

The coming of the New Deal brought an immediate and decisive change. The administration was known to be sympathetic with organized labor; and the inclusion of Section 7a in the National Industrial Recovery Act

[9] Randolph E. Paul, *Taxation in the United States* (Boston, 1954), p. 243.

meant that workers now had a legal right to join unions of their own choosing. The economic recovery, moreover, meant that labor was in a stronger position to win concessions. In its struggle to do so, labor was stimulated by all the antagonisms which had accumulated during the years of wage cuts and dismissals. While employers hastily tried to protect themselves from Section 7a by forming company unions or supporting independent ones, tens of thousands of workers who had been hitherto wholly unorganized began to flock into the AFL, declaring that the government wished them to join unions and that it was their patriotic duty to obey. During 1934, a total of 1,466,695 workers participated in strikes —a figure which had been exceeded only in 1916, 1917, and 1919. Particularly notable were the ten-day San Francisco general strike of July, which was precipitated by the grievances of the longshoremen and marine workers, and the textile workers' strike of September.

Three unions in particular were able to take advantage of this situation in order to make large permanent additions to their membership—the United Mine Workers under the leadership of John L. Lewis, the International Ladies Garment Workers under David Dubinsky, and the Amalgamated Clothing Workers under Sidney Hillman. The growth of the United Mine Workers was especially rapid. In 1932 its membership had not exceeded 150,000 and may have been as low as 50,000; by 1935 it had increased to 500,000 and had established itself in areas where the "yellow dog" contract had prevailed hitherto and where union organizers had been excluded by terroristic methods. John L. Lewis had formerly been regarded as one of the most conservative of union leaders: he had fought a long battle to prevent progressive and radical leaders from capturing the union, he had been accused by his opponents of retaining control by fraud and intimidation, and in 1928 he had been a supporter of Herbert Hoover. After 1933, however, Lewis joined forces with his former enemies in the United Mine Workers, who were headed by John Brophy, and displayed great energy, aggressiveness, and political skill in rebuilding the union.

Meanwhile other AFL leaders failed to capitalize on the new prounion sentiment of American workers. While the workers were militant and enthusiastic, the old-fashioned labor leaders were slow-moving, conservative, and wedded to a policy of collaboration with the employers. Faithful to the traditions of the AFL, they endeavored to distribute the new union members among the different craft unions; and workers who wanted vigorous action to consolidate their right to collective bargaining found that the chief activity of the union officials was the settlement of jurisdictional boundaries and disputes. The inapplicability of craft union methods to the new situation was particularly marked in the steel, automobile, and rubber industries. It became apparent that such industries could most effectively be organized by the methods of industrial unionism, already used in the United Mine Workers, under which all the workers in an industry, whatever specialized task they might perform, belonged to the same organization.

THE WAGNER-CONNERY NATIONAL LABOR RELATIONS ACT

Early in 1935, while the trade unions were in the throes of their organizational struggle, the nation's labor leaders were pressing for a federal statute to guarantee the workers the rights they had been granted under the NRA's Section 7a. In February, 1935, in the face of a mounting "chorus of discontent" among the country's industrial workers, Senator Robert F. Wagner of New York introduced a bill aimed "to strengthen and clarify" Section 7a and to satisfy a number of labor's demands, such as outlawing company unions, which by 1935 were becoming a serious threat to the AFL's leadership of the trade union movement. Though the Wagner bill was enthusiastically supported by most of the country's labor leaders and workers, it did not receive the administration's endorsement. Roosevelt showed little interest in it and for a time was even opposed to it. The Wagner bill, Roosevelt felt, was special legislation, and he disapproved of any federal law which promoted only the interests of one group rather than those of the country as a whole. But when the New York senator succeeded in getting Senate approval for his bill with only four Democrats and eight Republicans voting against it, and when it appeared that the House would support it too, Roosevelt endorsed it and made it a part of his second New Deal program. Less than two weeks after the President announced his support of the Wagner bill, the Supreme Court declared the NRA unconstitutional. The administration was now compelled to take action, and on July 5, 1935, Congress passed the Wagner-Connery National Labor Relations Act, commonly known as the Wagner Act.

Workers were guaranteed the right of collective bargaining through unions of their own choice, and employers were forbidden to discriminate against union members or to support company unions. A National Labor Relations Board (NLRB), composed of three members and modeled on the principles of the Federal Trade Commission, was to supervise enforcement of the act. The board was to hold elections, when necessary,

THE NEW DEAL, II (1935–1936)

in order that workers might choose which union should represent them, and workers whose rights were violated might complain to the board, which could summon employers for hearings and could issue cease-and-desist orders enforceable by the courts. J. Warren Madden, a law professor from the University of Pittsburgh, was appointed chairman of the board.

Many employers expected that the Wagner Act would be declared unconstitutional, and for eighteen months the NLRB was paralyzed by injunction suits. In 1937, however, through its decisions on *NLRB v. Jones and Laughlin Steel Corporation* and *NLRB v. Friedman–Harry Marks Clothing Company*, two cases which marked an epoch in American labor history, the Supreme Court upheld the Wagner Act, declaring that workers had a "fundamental right" to organize and that unions were "essential to give laborers opportunity to deal on an equality with their employer." The NLRB could then proceed with the duties assigned to it. During its first five years the board and its subsidiary agencies finished 26,724 cases, of which 48 per cent were settled by agreement, 27 per cent withdrawn by the unions, 17 per cent dismissed, and only 8 per cent ended by decisions of the board. It also prevented 869 strikes, settled 2,161 strikes which had already been called, and ordered the reinstatement of 21,163 workers who had been dismissed for union activities.

The NLRB nevertheless probably provoked more violent controversy than any other New Deal agency. In two respects the board could exercise considerable discretion in the performance of its duties. In the first place, it was difficult to say what constituted discrimination against union members: whereas an employer could maintain that he had dismissed or refused employment to a worker on the ground of incompetence or refusal to obey orders, the board might argue that the real reason was membership in a union. In the second place, when there were two or more competing unions so that it was necessary to hold an election to determine which of them represented a majority of the workers, the board could decide whether the bargaining unit should be the craft or the industry; in other words, it had to choose between the claims of craft unionism (represented by the AFL) and, after November, 1935, those of industrial unionism (represented by the CIO). Conservatives violently attacked the NLRB, declaring that in the exercise of its discretionary authority it displayed bias against employers and against the AFL, that it was acting both as prosecutor and as judge, and that many of the young lawyers whom it employed were radical and incompetent. The defenders of the NLRB pointed out in reply that a number of its decisions had been hostile to the

80   THE ERA OF F.D.R., 1933-1945

CIO. They argued that the real objection was not to any bias on the part of the board but to the principle of collective bargaining.

The Wagner Act marked a major milestone in the history of labor-management relations, and it did much to bring about the rise of "big labor." Neither F.D.R. nor the administration's leaders understood clearly the effect this law would have upon the structure of American trade unionism or the augmented influence which organized labor would have in national politics. On the day Roosevelt signed the bill into law, he announced that the Wagner Act "should serve as an important step toward the achievement of just and peaceful labor relations in industry." Events quickly proved how sanguine this hope was—not only was the law challenged continuously by employers, but organized labor itself continued its bitter intraorganizational fight.

THE RISE OF THE CIO

At the AFL convention of 1934, which met at San Francisco, the advocates of industrial unionism secured passage of a compromise resolution admitting the need for industrial unions in certain industries. The leaders of the craft unions disliked this program, which would tend to diminish their own jurisdictions, and the AFL took no action to implement it. In the 1935 convention, meeting at Atlantic City, the industrial unionists demanded action and were defeated by a vote of 10,933 to 18,024. The industrial unionists then decided to ignore the AFL, and on November 9, 1935, their leaders formed the Committee for Industrial Organization. Lewis was elected chairman and John Brophy director. The CIO began its career with nearly 1 million members, a large majority of whom belonged to the United Mine Workers, the International Ladies Garment Workers, and the Amalgamated Clothing Workers. In August, 1936, when the AFL suspended the CIO unions, the split became definitive, and in November, 1938, the CIO was reorganized on a permanent basis. It changed its name to the Congress of Industrial Organizations and adopted a constitution. Lewis was elected president, Sidney Hillman and Philip Murray vice presidents, and James Carey of the Electrical, Radio, and Machine Workers secretary.

The most spectacular successes of the CIO were in steel and automobiles —two industries in which trade unionism had hitherto been negligible. In the steel industry the labor movement had suffered three crushing defeats, in 1892, in 1902, and in 1919. In 1933 only 4,800 steel workers were unionized, and the AFL Amalgamated Association of Iron, Steel, and Tin Workers had been dormant for more than a decade. In June, 1936, the CIO formed the Steel Workers Organizing Committee, headed by Philip Murray of the United Mine Workers. The SWOC rapidly gathered members, and was assisted by the sympathetic attitude of Governor George H. Earle of Pennsylvania. On March 1, 1937, Myron C. Taylor, chairman of the board of United States Steel Corporation, which had traditionally been regarded as the chief stronghold of antiunionism in the country, agreed to establish collective bargaining with the SWOC. The workers gained a forty-hour week and a 10 per cent increase in wages. By the end of the year a large number of other steel corporations had accepted collective bargaining, and the membership of the SWOC had risen to more than 400,000.

A group of powerful corporations in Pennsylvania, Ohio, and Illinois, generally known as Little Steel, refused, however, to abandon their traditional hostility to unions. In May and June the SWOC called strikes against Republic Steel, Youngstown Sheet and Tube, Inland Steel, and Bethlehem Steel. The chief spokesmen of the employers were Tom Girdler of Republic and Eugene Grace of Bethelehem. Girdler's vituperative denunciations of the Roosevelt administration and of the CIO and his adherence to the ideals of the era of President McKinley made him, for a period, a figure of national prominence. Some 90,000 steel workers went on strike, but the employers made extensive use of propaganda and of strikebreakers and were aided by the local police authorities. In July the SWOC had to accept defeat. The most important episode of the strike was the Memorial Day, 1937, massacre in South Chicago. A group of strikers who were engaged in peaceful picketing outside a plant belonging to Republic Steel were attacked by the police. Ten of the workers were killed, seven of them being shot in the back, fifty were wounded by gunfire, and twenty-five were injured by clubbing. Of the policemen, who declared that they had acted in self-defense, three were slightly injured. The defeat of the SWOC by Little Steel was not permanent, however, since the National Labor Relations Board, in a decision upheld by the Supreme Court, subsequently ordered Republic Steel to reinstate several thousand of the strikers and to accept collective bargaining with the SWOC.

Workers in the automobile industry began to join unions in 1933 but soon became disillusioned with the leaders given them by the AFL. In April, 1936, a convention of the United Automobile Workers repudiated AFL control and elected Homer Martin, a former clergyman, as their president. Soon afterward they joined the CIO. In December a series of strikes began in the plants of General Motors which eventually included 140,000 workers. These strikes were notable for the extended use of a new technique, the sit down, which had been first adopted by the rubber workers at Akron, Ohio, in January. Governor Frank Murphy of Michigan refused to use force to expel the strikers from the plants and endeavored to bring about a settlement by arbitration. On February 11 General Motors agreed to bargain with the union, although without accepting the closed shop, and the subsequent negotiations brought about an increase in wages. In March, 1937, the UAW called a sit-down strike in the Chrysler plant, and a month later Chrysler agreed to a settlement similar to that made by General Motors. The Ford Motor Company continued to be an uncompromising enemy of unionism, but by the end of 1937 the UAW had made contracts with every other important automobile corporation and claimed a membership of 400,000. Subsequently the union was split by factional quarrels, provoked chiefly by the personality and tactics of Homer Martin. In 1939 Martin was expelled from leadership and replaced by R. J. Thomas. Martin and his followers formed a small rival union, which was admitted into the AFL.

The CIO also established unions in a number of other industries. Among the more important were the Textile Workers; the Electrical, Radio, and Machine Workers; the Rubber Workers; the Transport Workers; the Oil Workers; the Shoe Workers; and a number of different sailors' and longshoremen's organizations. Through its Cannery, Agricultural, Packing and Allied Workers it endeavored to extend unionism to agriculture; and it included also several unions of white-collar and professional workers, the most successful of which was the American Newspaper Guild, which had been started at Cleveland, Ohio, in the summer of 1933 and had joined the CIO in 1937. At the time of the 1938 convention the CIO included 42 national unions and organizing committees. It claimed an enrollment of 3,787,877, although the actual number of dues-paying members was probably considerably smaller.

THE CIO VERSUS THE AFL

Meanwhile the AFL had also been making large gains. It profited by the growth of union sentiment among the American working class, and it was assisted by a number of employers who hastened to sign contracts with AFL unions in order to protect themselves from the militant CIO. By 1940 each organization was claiming a membership of about 4 million.

THE NEW DEAL, II (1935–1936)

The conflict between them had become exceedingly acrimonious, and efforts on the part of President Roosevelt and members of his cabinet to bring about a reunion of the labor movement were unsuccessful. It was difficult to arrange a satisfactory compromise between the claims of craft unionism and those of industrial unionism. Both organizations, moreover, had internal weaknesses.

In 1939 and 1940 officials of certain union locals affiliated with the AFL were indicted as criminals and racketeers, and the AFL leaders were denounced for having allowed such men to occupy responsible positions. The CIO, on the other hand, was open to attack because the Communist party, which had decided to support it in 1937, had captured control of some of the CIO unions. There was considerable discontent within the CIO because of this growth of Communist influence and also because of the increasingly erratic policies and egotistical attitudes of John L. Lewis. One powerful organization, the International Ladies Garment Workers, left the CIO in 1938 and two years later joined the AFL. In 1940 some students of the labor movement believed that the CIO, in spite of its claims to increased membership, was showing signs of considerable weakness.

Meanwhile the conflict between the two organizations was weakening the labor movement. By accusing the New Deal and the Labor Relations Board of being sympathetic to the CIO and by opposing New Deal candidates who had CIO support in the elections of 1938, the AFL strengthened the forces of conservatism. Struggles between AFL and CIO unions, moreover, resulted in strikes, picketing, and other labor disturbances, which tended to discredit the whole union movement with the general public.

OPPOSITION TO UNIONISM

In spite of the growth of collective bargaining, many employers continued to fight unionism by the traditional methods. A Senate Committee on Civil Liberties, headed by Robert M. La Follette, Jr., discovered in 1936 and 1937 that almost every big corporation in the country employed professional detective agencies to break up labor organizations. Between January, 1934, and July, 1936, General Motors alone spent nearly $1 million on espionage: 304 Pinkerton detectives had joined unions as spies and *agents provocateurs*, and 100 of these had become union officials, one of them becoming the national vice president of a union and fourteen others being elected presidents of union locals. The Ford Motor Company created

A scene from the seamen's strike in New York City (1936). Striking workers engaged in picketing often had cause to complain of police brutality. (Brown Brothers)

an organization known as the Ford Service Men whose function was to spy on labor organizations and to intimidate them by physical attacks on union leaders. According to a report published in December, 1937, by the National Labor Relations Board, the Ford Service Men had "been vested with the responsibility of maintaining surveillance over Ford employees, not only during their work but even when they are outside the plant, and of crushing at its inception, by force if necessary, any signs of union activity. . . . The River Rouge plant has taken on many aspects of a community in which martial law has been declared and in which a huge military organization . . . has been superimposed upon the regular civil authorities." Employers also carried on extensive propaganda campaigns in order to create the impression that all labor leaders were self-interested agitators with communistic tendencies. When a strike occurred, they frequently obtained help from the local police to crush picketing, and they created and financed organizations of vigilantes and "citizens' committees."

The technique of strikebreaking was explained by James H. Rand of

THE NEW DEAL, II (1935–1936)

Remington Rand Corporation in a bulletin published by the National Association of Manufacturers. This technique, known as the "Mohawk Valley Formula," was applied in a strike at the Remington Rand plant at Ilion, New York. The employer, said Mr. Rand, should represent the labor leaders as agitators and declare that they represent only a minority of the workers. He should create a citizens' committee to defend law and order, and he should win the support of storekeepers and other middle-class citizens by pointing out that they lose money through the strike. He should threaten that if the strike were not defeated, the plant might close down permanently and thus ruin the town. He should organize a back-to-work movement to demoralize the strikers, and he should call on the police to protect those workers who return to work.

That workers had a right to bargain collectively through unions of their own choosing had been stated by Congress in the Wagner Act and had been subsequently affirmed by the Supreme Court. The Roosevelt administration, through its Labor Relations Board, had considerable success in making this right a reality. In consequence, organized labor under the New Deal had made its greatest advances in American history, and by 1940 about one-quarter of the American working class had been unionized. But whether labor would hold the ground it had won was uncertain. Some of the new unions used their powers irresponsibly, calling strikes unnecessarily and abusing the sit-down technique (which was finally declared illegal by the Supreme Court in 1939, in the Fansteel Metallurgical Corporation case). After the Republican victories in the elections of 1938, a number of states passed laws limiting the right to strike and restricting picketing and other forms of labor struggle, and in the spring of 1940 the national need for a rapid increase in the construction of armaments provided an additional argument for limiting the powers of unions.

Social Security

The Wagner Act earned for Roosevelt and the New Deal the overwhelming support of most of the country's organized workers, just as the social security law was to win for him the support of the aged and the unemployed. Conservatives and influential spokesmen of the business community opposed it unconditionally and branded it "un-American and socialistic." Moreover, they prophesied that it would bankrupt the country. "Never in the history of the world," cried New York Congressman John Taber, "has any measure been brought in here [the House of Rep-

86 THE ERA OF F.D.R., 1933–1945

resentatives] so insidiously designed to prevent business recovery, to enslave workers, and to prevent any possibility of the employer providing work for the people." Many liberals, on the other hand, criticized it for not providing enough security. Despite its critics and opponents, the Social Security Act passed both houses of Congress with strong majorities and was signed by the President on August 14, 1935.

This law was the only attempt by the New Deal to provide a permanent unemployment policy. Roosevelt placed responsibility for drafting the law with the Committee on Economic Security, headed by the University of Wisconsin economist Edwin Witte. The principle of state insurance for unemployment and old age had already been accepted by all other important nations, and the United States could therefore profit by their experience. The American social security system differed, however, from those of most other nations in that it provided for a smaller scale of payments and made no provision for health insurance.

It was decided that unemployment insurance should be administered by the states, which were to be allowed considerable liberty to experiment with different methods. The money was to be raised by a tax on payrolls. The federal government would make no direct contribution, but would hold the reserve funds, which would be drawn on by the states as needed. Prior to 1935, Wisconsin was the only state that had established unemployment insurance; by the summer of 1938, however, all the state governments had adopted satisfactory plans. The amount of the payroll tax averaged 2.7 per cent a year. About 27 million persons were covered—agricultural laborers, domestic servants, casual laborers, various categories of salaried employees; in many states, employees of small businesses were excluded. In 1938 the largest payment was $15 a week, the average payment $10.93 a week, and the longest period during which an unemployed person might continue to receive payments sixteen weeks. Persons unemployed for more than this period were expected to apply for regular relief.

Generous old age pensions were demanded by the followers of Dr. Townsend, and pressure from this group was partly responsible for the passage of the Social Security Act. "We have to have it," F.D.R. told his advisers. "The Congress can't stand the pressure of the Townsend Plan unless we have a real old-age insurance system, nor can I face the country without having devised at this time, when we are studying social security, a solid plan which will give some assurance to old people of systematic

THE NEW DEAL, II (1935-1936) 87

assistance upon retirement." [10] The act provided both for federal assistance to state pension plans and for the establishment of a separate federal annuity system. The states were to pay half the cost of their pension plans and were to receive the other half from the federal treasury, but the federal contribution was not to exceed $15 per person. By the summer of 1938 it was estimated that 22 per cent of the population past the age of sixty-five was receiving pensions. Payments varied between $32.33 a month in California and $4.79 a month in Mississippi, the average being $19.48 a month. The Townsendites continued to agitate for larger pensions; but schemes of this kind, put forward in California and Ohio in the elections of 1939, were defeated. In 1939 the Social Security Act was amended to provide for greater federal control over state pension systems in order to prevent their abuse for political purposes.

The federal annuity system, as drafted in 1935 and amended in 1939, was to be financed by equal contributions from employers and employees, which would amount at first to 1 per cent of wages but which was to be increased later. About 46 million persons were covered by the act, each of whom would have a right to a pension when he reached the age of sixty-five, regardless of need. Payments were to begin in 1940 and would be proportionate to contributions. The maximum payment would be $85 a month. In order to receive this an individual would be required to have worked for forty-three years at a salary of more than $3,000 a year. The act of 1935 also provided for the creation of an enormous reserve fund, which would have amounted to $50 billion by 1970. This feature of the plan was sharply criticized and was virtually abandoned in 1939. The act was also attacked because its scheme of payroll taxation diminished purchasing power and had a deflationary effect; this caused the scheme of payments provided for in 1935 to be revised downward in 1939.

Plans for health insurance were not discussed in Congress until 1939, though the Economic Security Committee recommended that provision be made for it when it was studying social security. Opposition from the medical profession to "socialized medicine" and F.D.R.'s fear that the Congress would never approve such a radical proposal made any immediate action on it impossible in 1935. Roosevelt looked upon the Social Security Act as "a cornerstone" in the new social and economic structure which his administration was trying to erect. "The law will flatten out the peaks and valleys of deflation and inflation . . . . [and it] will take

[10] Quoted in Frances Perkins, *The Roosevelt I Knew* (New York, 1946), p. 294.

88 THE ERA OF F.D.R., 1933–1945

care of human needs and at the same time provide for the United States an economic structure of vastly greater soundness."

Banking and Utility Legislation

The process of building a new and strong economic system went on quickly during August, 1935, as Roosevelt pressed the Congress into finishing his legislative program. Nine days after the social security law went into effect, the President signed the Banking Act of August 23, 1935, which increased government control over bank credit and centralized it in a reorganized Federal Reserve Board (FRB), thenceforth to be known as the Board of Governors of the Federal Reserve System. All its members were to be appointed by the President, with fourteen-year terms. An Open Market Committee, consisting of the Board of Governors and five representatives of the federal reserve banks, was to control bank credit by buying and selling government securities and by raising and lowering the reserve requirements of the member banks. The act placed responsibility for maintaining economic stability in the Board of Governors, which, with its augmented authority, was now able to exercise central bank control. Its decision to increase or curb the flow of money gave it a decisive voice in determining the performance of the whole economy. From this time on, Washington rather than Wall Street was to be the dominant voice in the nation's financial and economic affairs. Roosevelt appointed Marriner S. Eccles of Utah, who had been instrumental in drawing up the law, as the board's chairman.

By the summer of 1936 the easy-money policy adopted by the FRB seemed to have overshot the mark; excess reserves were accumulating in the banks, and there seemed to be danger of a speculative boom. The Open Market Committee then began to raise the reserve requirements of the banks, while the Treasury sterilized part of its gold reserve by refusing to issue gold certificates for it. A year later the economic system was again entering a depression, so these policies were reversed. Whether central monetary management as allowed under this act is a sufficiently effective weapon to check inflation and deflation remains in doubt, and economists continue to debate the question. The experience of the last twenty-five years provides no conclusive answers.

To promote financial stability in the utility industry and to correct the corporate abuses exposed by the depression, Congress enacted the Wheeler-Rayburn Public Utility Holding Company Act on August 28, 1935. The

THE NEW DEAL, II (1935–1936)   89

Federal Power Commission was given extended powers and was to regulate all companies which transmitted power across state lines. The SEC was to supervise the acquisition of new properties by utility companies, and "as soon as practicable after January 1, 1938," it was to limit the operations of the holding companies so that each of them would control only "a single integrated public utility system." This "death sentence" for holding companies aroused the wrath of the power corporations, who tried to influence Congress against it by sending thousands of telegrams of protest, but to no avail. In 1938 the Supreme Court upheld it, and the utility companies were forced to divest themselves of all holding company affiliates which were beyond one degree removed from their operating companies or which were not part of their operational or administrative system. The kind of holding company pyramiding which was so typical of the utility empires of the 1920's was now forbidden. Despite the anguished outcries of a large segment of the industry, the law's long-term effects caused few losses to the investors, strengthened the financial condition of the industry, increased the profits of the operating companies, attracted new investment, and helped reduce utility prices to the consumer.

Meanwhile the Public Works Administration gave funds to a number of municipalities for building publicly owned power plants, and the Rural Electrification Administration, established May 11, 1935, and headed by Morris L. Cooke, a long-time student of public utilities and the requirements of rural power, began to build generating plants and power lines in rural areas. The purpose of the REA was to bring electric power to farm regions which, because of the poor prospects for profitable operations, the private utility companies had been unwilling to serve. By September, 1939, the REA had built 135,000 miles of line supplying 300,000 homes, and had made plans for 240,000 more miles of line which would supply an additional 700,000 homes. Less spectacular than the hydroelectric projects, like Boulder Dam or TVA, the REA nonetheless did much to bring cheap electricity to marginal farm families, thus improving the living standards of a long-neglected segment of the population.

Tax Revision

Among the last measures sent to the White House before Congress adjourned was the Revenue Act of 1935, more commonly known as the Wealth Tax Act—or, as it was termed by its critics, the "soak the rich"

90 THE ERA OF F.D.R., 1933-1945

law. The New Deal had made few important alterations in the tax system in 1933 and 1934, the only significant changes being the imposition of liquor taxes and tightening of the income tax regulations to block loopholes. On June 19, 1935, Roosevelt recommended tax revision in a message to the Congress. "Our revenue laws," he stated, "have operated in many ways to the unfair advantage of the few, and they have done little to prevent an unjust concentration of wealth and economic power." To correct this, F.D.R. asked Congress for higher taxes on large incomes and inheritances and on big corporations. The purposes of this proposal were social and political rather than financial. What Roosevelt hoped to do was to strike at the "concentration of wealth," check the growth of big business, and, in the process, probably also steal some of the thunder from Huey Long, whose "Share Our Wealth" movement was reaching dangerous proportions. While Congress did not accept all of Roosevelt's recommendations in the Revenue Act of 1935, it did impose higher taxes on gifts and estates; raise income taxes on incomes above $50,000, the maximum being 75 per cent on those above $5 million; raise the corporation income tax, setting the maximum at 15 per cent; and impose an excess profits duty, with a top of 12 per cent on profits exceeding 15 per cent.

The next year, the Revenue Act of June, 1936, provoked even more controversy, especially from corporation directors. The chief features were a tax of from 7 to 27 per cent on undistributed corporation profits and a heavy levy on profits realized through transfer of capital assets. In the opinion of the New Dealers, the failure of corporations to distribute their profits was often a device resorted to by wealthy stockholders to evade income tax payments; such undistributed profits, moreover, were often spent uneconomically on unwise expansion. Businessmen, on the other hand, vigorously opposed these two new taxes. They declared that corporations accumulated surpluses for use in depression periods, that taxing these surpluses would weaken business, and that the tax on capital gains would discourage new investments. In 1938 Congress made drastic reductions in both these taxes, and Roosevelt expressed his disapproval by allowing the Revenue Act to become law without his signature. In 1939 the undistributed profits tax was abolished, while the corporation income tax was raised to a maximum of 18 per cent. Another feature of the 1939 Revenue Act was that for the first time federal taxes were imposed on the employees of state and municipal governments, a measure which had been made possible by a recent Supreme Court decision.

The best that can be said for the New Deal's tax laws is that they introduced some long-needed reforms. The income tax bite was distributed more equitably and a number of loopholes were filled; but at the same time, because some of these reforms alarmed business, they worked against recovery by slowing down new investments. Even more important, however, was the failure of the administration to employ fiscal policy to promote economic recovery. Until 1938, at least, Roosevelt and Congress, partly because of business criticism and partly because of their own fear of incurring large deficits, adopted a high tax policy, thus depriving the country of the full benefits of the money that government was spending for relief and recovery. Since the Keynesian principle of lowering taxes and increasing government expenditures in order to combat depressions was not widely recognized in the United States during the 1930's, this consideration cannot be ignored in assessing the New Deal tax policy.[11]

Completing the "Second" New Deal

The first session of the Seventy-fourth Congress, which had started out slowly, ended in a frenzy of activity. During the last four months, from the beginning of June to the end of August, Congress had enacted an impressive amount of significant legislation, fully warranting Roosevelt's claim that "When a calm and fair review of . . . [its] work . . . is made, it will be called a historic session." To be sure, not all of the laws passed in this session were equally significant. Some, like the Guffey-Snyder Bituminous Coal Stabilization Act (August 30, 1935), which F.D.R. insisted was absolutely necessary to stabilize the soft coal industry, were aimed to fill the void created by the Supreme Court's decision against the NRA. This law provided for the establishment of a National Bituminous Coal Commission authorized to draw up a regulatory code similar to the one under the NRA, whereby production quotas, minimum prices, maximum hours, and minimum wages were all clearly defined. In 1936, the Supreme Court reviewed "the little NRA," as this law was commonly called, and declared it unconstitutional. The next year it was replaced by the Guffey-Vinson Act, which was upheld in *Sunshine Anthracite Coal Company v. Adkins* (1940).

Other legislation was aimed at satisfying certain long-felt needs; such were the Motor Carrier Act (August 9, 1935), which, with certain exceptions, brought the interstate passenger bus and trucking industries under ICC regulation, and the Wagner-Crosser Railroad Retirement Act

[11] Paul, *op. cit.*, pp. 243–44.

(August 29, 1935), which replaced the Railroad Pension Act of 1934, declared unconstitutional by the Supreme Court on May 6, 1935 (*Railroad Retirement Board v. Alton Railroad Company*). Demand for motor carrier legislation, for example, was at least ten years old. The Motor Carrier Act tried to establish a regulatory code for the interstate motor transport industry comparable to the one which had been evolved for the railroads. The law prohibited rate discrimination; provided for review of certain financial practices, such as mergers and consolidations; and established maximum hours of labor.

In order to provide aged railroad workers with pensions, which were neither universal nor uniform at this time, the administration, after its first effort in 1934 to establish a uniform and legally enforceable pension system upon the railroads was invalidated by the Supreme Court, sponsored a second measure in 1935 which was strongly opposed and quickly contested by the carriers. In 1936, after F.D.R. intervened and brought the representatives of the railroads and the workers together in a series of conferences, a mutually satisfactory pension plan was hammered out. The next year Congress enacted a new railroad retirement act which amended the bill passed in 1935 and incorporated the essential proposals negotiated earlier by the employers and the employees.

Except for the bitter controversy which accompanied the debate on the Revenue Act of 1936, the second session of the Seventy-fourth Congress, which met from January 3 through June 18, 1936, was rather dull and phlegmatic. Roosevelt's annual message, apart from its attack on "resplendent economic autocracy," "entrenched greed," and all those who would "steal the livery of great national constitutional ideals to serve discredited special interests," proved to be more of a political campaign piece than a report to the Congress on the state of the union. Partly because of this, partly because he indicated no specific "must" legislation for the Congress to consider, and partly because the members themselves were as aware of the forthcoming elections as F.D.R., the Congress, without strong direction from the White House, prepared to wait out the months until it could adjourn for the party conventions. The political spirit was apparent from the start.

In May, 1935, Congress had passed the Patman bonus bill, which called for the payment to World War I veterans of their "adjusted compensation certificates" immediately instead of in 1945, when they fell due. Roosevelt, unwilling to increase the federal deficit by some $2 billion for this purpose, went before Congress at that time in person to read his veto

THE NEW DEAL, II (1935–1936)

message. The House overrode it but the Senate sustained it. On January 24, 1936, the Congress enacted a similar measure; F.D.R. vetoed it again and for the same reason. But this time, realizing the political exigencies of an election year, he showed no indication that he would fight as he had done before to make his veto stick. The result was that the Congress quickly overrode it.

As soon as the Congress had disposed of the bonus bill, it was forced to devise a substitute farm measure as a result of the Supreme Court's action of January 6, 1936, which declared the AAA unconstitutional. On February 29, the Congress passed the Soil Conservation and Domestic Allotment Act. Under its provisions, the federal government was to pay subsidies to the producers of staple crops (wheat, corn, cotton, oats, and tobacco) who would agree to withdraw part of their land from commercial production and use it for soil conservation crops. By this method, the administration was able to avoid the objections of the Court's majority to the processing tax and the contract agreement provisions.

During the last week of June, 1936, the Congress, wanting to devote itself entirely to the business of election year politics, rushed through two other bills. On June 20 it passed the Robinson-Patman Federal Anti-Price Discrimination Act, also known as the anti–chain store law, which authorized the Federal Trade Commission to protect the independent retailers from the price-cutting practices of the large interstate chains. And on June 26 it passed a new merchant marine law.

Like the railroads and the housing industry, shipping had required and received attention from the federal government after World War I. But despite the subsidy programs of 1920 and 1928, American shippers found it impossible to compete successfully with those of other nations. Relatively few ships were built after 1918, and by 1933 the bulk of the American merchant fleet was rapidly becoming obsolete. According to the liberals this situation was due to mismanagement by the shipping companies, while the conservatives attributed it to high labor costs. The New Deal's Merchant Marine Act, under which a Maritime Commission was set up, aimed to rebuild the merchant marine not only to carry the goods of the United States in time of peace but to provide a carrier fleet "capable of serving as a naval and military auxiliary in time of war." The commission was given wide powers to plan trade routes and to work out a long-range building program, including both subsidies to private builders and, if necessary, direct building by the government. The old formula of providing subsidies through mail contracts was ended. In 1938 the act was

94   THE ERA OF F.D.R., 1933–1945

amended to give the commission power to prescribe wages and working conditions, while a Maritime Labor Board was to arbitrate labor disputes. This latter provision was repealed in 1941. In the opinion of Joseph P. Kennedy, the first head of the commission, at least $2.5 billion was required for new shipping. Since private capital seemed unlikely to enter the industry to this extent, the commission adopted a program of building by the government which would provide fifty new ships a year for ten years. When completed, the ships were to be operated by the private shipping companies. Through new construction, acquisitions, and other measures the commission succeeded in increasing both the tonnage and the quality of the American merchant fleet, and with the coming of World War II, the government inaugurated an emergency building program of huge proportions.

THE ELECTION OF 1936

During the first six months of 1936, the political excitement of a presidential election year increasingly distracted the nation's attention from the course of the administration's legislative program. On June 9 the Republicans met in Cleveland, and despite the magnitude of their defeat in the midterm elections of 1934, they entertained some hope that they could win. The "second" New Deal had alienated many conservative Democrats, who looked upon F.D.R. as a traitor to the party's Jeffersonian heritage. Moreover, the administration had failed, as the unemployment statistics clearly indicated, to bring about real recovery. This, along with the fact that Townsend, Coughlin, and Gerald L. K. Smith were demanding Roosevelt's defeat and the evidence that F.D.R.'s control over the Seventy-fourth Congress had shown several signs of weakness, heartened the GOP. The most important decision facing the Republicans was to find an attractive candidate with a national reputation. In 1936, this was no easy task.

Theoretically, at least, Hoover was the titular leader of the party and still highly popular with much of the rank and file, but as everyone realized, his political liabilities were such that they made him unacceptable. Two weeks before the convention he declared himself out of the running. The congressional elections of 1934 had left so few Republicans in office from whom the party could choose a candidate that by convention time only two senators (Michigan's Arthur H. Vandenberg and Idaho's Wil-

THE NEW DEAL, II (1935–1936)

liam E. Borah) and a governor (Alfred M. Landon of Kansas) had attracted sufficient public attention to be considered serious contenders. But Vandenberg, who enjoyed only limited national appeal at this time, did not seek the nomination very actively; and Borah, who wanted it, was disqualified by his liberal progressivism and by his public attacks on the conservative, big business wing of the party, which he blamed for the GOP's low repute and disastrous defeat in 1934. With virtually no opposition to contest his claim, Landon became the Republican standard-bearer on the first ballot. Frank Knox, the proprietor-publisher of the Chicago *Daily News*, also unopposed, received the party's unanimous nomination for Vice President.

Both Landon and Knox were admirers of Theodore Roosevelt, had supported the Bull Moose ticket in 1912, and were regarded as liberal Republicans. Landon, a University of Kansas Law School graduate, started his career in banking, but quickly followed his father into the oil business, where he accumulated a comfortable fortune. In 1932 he was elected governor of Kansas, and, even more significant politically, he was re-elected two years later. Knox, a Rough Rider in the Spanish-American War and a veteran of World War I, had been an independent newspaper publisher most of his adult life except for a three-year stint with the Hearst press.

There was much in Landon's record which made him appear an impressive candidate in 1936. Since he had been in no way connected with Hoover, he was removed from any association with the depression. The fact that he had supported Theodore Roosevelt in 1912 and the elder Robert M. La Follette in 1924 made him appear sufficiently independent to please the GOP's liberals, while his fiscal conservativism in administering Kansas appealed to the more orthodox in the Republican party. At a time when most state governors were struggling to keep state deficits at a minimum, Landon regularly balanced the Kansas budget. For this he was widely acclaimed; his partisans started to call him "the Great Budget Balancer" and "the Kansas Coolidge." Landon himself, however, knowing that his ability to achieve this fiscal respectability was not due entirely to his own efforts, never claimed exclusive credit for having done what other state executives had failed to accomplish. But apart from extolling the necessities of fiscal soundness—an objective which F.D.R. had never abandoned in principle and one which he hoped soon to regain—Landon's record indicated a considerably liberal bent. There was nothing in it which indicated he believed in returning to negative government or to

96 THE ERA OF F.D.R., 1933–1945

one which placed the interests of "the great industrial plutocracy" before those of the people. It was to the means rather than to the ends of the New Deal that he was opposed. "We have had," he said, "too much of the slap-dash, jazzy method." What the country required was "clear-cut, definite and vigorous administrative leadership." [12]

Partly because of Landon's own moderate views and partly because of the necessity to placate Borah and his followers, the Republican platform did not promise to repudiate the New Deal, though it did demand changes in detail. The unemployed, for example, were still to receive some relief from the federal government, but it was to be administered by the states; the farmers were to be given federal subsidies, but they were to be assisted in finding foreign markets for their surpluses; the antitrust laws were to be enforced, a provision which the antimonopolist Borah had insisted be included in the platform; labor was to be guaranteed the right to collective bargaining; and, according to Landon, the Constitution should, if necessary, be amended to allow regulation of wages and hours. The platform's foreign policy plank was completely isolationist, reflecting Borah's extreme opposition to the League of Nations and to American participation on the World Court. All these party proposals were strung together with bitter denunciations of the New Deal's "tyranny," "socialistic experiments," and "unconstitutional dictatorship." Roosevelt was accused of having established a "monstrous, reckless propaganda machine" which threatened the safety of the republic and undermined the age-old traditions of opportunity for self-improvement. The Republicans, joined by the Liberty Leaguers, declared that the college professors whom Roosevelt had called to Washington and the labor leaders who supported him were Communists and propagandists for alien ideologies. "America is in peril," the GOP warned. "The welfare of American men and women and the future of our youth are at stake."

When the Democrats met at Philadelphia two weeks later, it was a foregone conclusion that they would renominate Roosevelt and Garner and endorse the administration's record. Apart from replacing the two-thirds rule for nomination (which Andrew Jackson had forced upon the party in 1836) with one requiring only a majority vote, the Democrats spent five days endlessly singing the praises of their leader. The platform, written under the President's supervision, reaffirmed the government's responsibility for the welfare of its citizens, promised further domestic reforms, and declared that if the Supreme Court continued to prohibit

[12] Quoted in Schlesinger, *op. cit.*, pp. 534–35.

THE NEW DEAL, II (1935–1936)

federal regulation of economic conditions, the Democratic party would seek a "clarifying amendment." This clause of the platform was phrased so as to imply that the barrier to federal regulation was not the Constitution but the manner in which the Supreme Court had interpreted it.

On the night of June 27, more than 100,000 people assembled in Franklin Field to listen to F.D.R. deliver his acceptance speech. He asserted in this address that the political independence which the generation of 1776 had won at Philadelphia on July 4 needed to be reinforced by a similar declaration against the "economic royalists," who had "created a new despotism and wrapped it in the robes of legal sanction." Continuing his attack upon those who "conceded that political freedom was the business of the Government, but . . . economic slavery was nobody's business," Roosevelt declared "that Government in a modern civilization has certain inescapable obligations to its citizens, among which are protection of the family and the home, the establishment of a democracy of opportunity, and aid to those overtaken by disaster. . . . In the place of the palace of privilege we seek to build a temple out of faith and hope and charity . . . . There is a mysterious cycle in human events. To some generations much is given. Of others much is expected. This generation of Americans has a rendezvous with destiny."

There were the usual number of minor party candidates, among them Norman Thomas for the Socialists; John W. Aiken, the candidate of the Socialist-Labor party; Earl Browder, the Communist party's standard bearer; and Dr. D. Leigh Colvin, who ran on the Prohibitionist ticket. But a new party of discontents also entered the race. The Union party, composed largely of the followers of Coughlin, Townsend, and the late Huey Long, nominated the insurgent Republican farm politico and Non Partisan Leaguer Representative William Lemke of North Dakota for President. As his running mate, the party chose a Massachusetts Democrat and labor lawyer, Charles O. Brien, who was an attorney for the Brotherhood of Railway Trainmen. The party's platform, a mélange aimed to satisfy the programs of its three principal followers and to appeal to laborers and farmers as La Follette had tried to do in 1924, called for more inflation, "reasonable and decent security for the aged," and jobs for everybody.

The campaign was exceptionally heated, with the voters divided more along socioeconomic class lines than at any time since the Bryan-McKinley race in 1896. Few concrete issues were presented to the electorate. Roosevelt ran on his record and promised the country more of the same kind of thing, but he made few definite commitments, preferring to answer Re-

98 THE ERA OF F.D.R., 1933–1945

publican charges against him by asking the voter to compare his condition in 1936 with what it was in 1933. Roosevelt defended himself against the charge that he enjoyed Communist support by repudiating it and all other foreign ideologies, and he answered the charge that he was a radical by saying that "the true conservative is the man who has a real concern for injustices and takes thought against the day of reckoning. The true conservative seeks to protect the system of private property and free enterprise by correcting such injustices and inequalities as arise from it. The most serious threat to our institutions comes from those who refuse to face the need for change. Liberalism becomes the protection of the far-sighted conservative."

Landon began his campaign with considerable moderation, criticizing the administrative inefficiency and wastefulness which characterized many of the New Deal's programs, but neither rejecting their objectives nor questioning their need or usefulness. There was much in the New Deal of which he approved. "I cannot criticize everything that has been done in the past three years and do it sincerely," he informed Borah early in the campaign. "Neither do I believe that such an attack is good politics." [13] Landon's views on the issues of the campaign were diametrically opposed to those of the Old Guard, but in the end it was the voice of the latter which prevailed. As the campaign progressed, Landon's liberalism grew less and less evident and his denunciations of the New Deal more and more inconsistent with what he believed and had expressed previously. Meanwhile, the influence of Hoover and the GOP stalwarts grew more and more pronounced. The liberal-conservative split in the Republican party leadership produced glaring inconsistencies, precluded the development of an effective campaign strategy, and, worst of all, made Landon appear insincere and a puppet of the discredited Old Guard. Landon himself, moreover, was no match for the President as a personality, as a campaigner, or as a radio speaker. On the stump or from the back of a train or on the radio, F.D.R. was always poised, friendly, and charming. Landon, on the other hand, was tense, serious, and colorless, and his talks were usually uninspiring.

Nearly three-fourths of the major metropolitan press was against the New Deal in 1936, and many of the influential newspapers which had supported Roosevelt four years before were now far less enthusiastic in their endorsement of his administration. On the other hand, F.D.R. had the support of most of the trade unions, whose leaders had formed Labor's

[13] Quoted in *ibid.*, p. 603.

THE NEW DEAL, II (1935-1936)

Nonpartisan League in April, 1936, to campaign for his reelection, and particularly of the United Mine Workers, who gave him a campaign contribution of $469,870. Roosevelt could also rely on most of the farm organizations as well as on the unemployed. Liberals, progressives, independents, and most of the middle class, many of them under the banner of the Progressive National Committee and the Good Neighbor League, joined together to reelect Roosevelt. Also, for the first time, the Democrats received the votes of most of the northern Negro population—a change of party allegiance which had and would continue to have considerable importance.

Except for *The Literary Digest,* which predicted that Landon would win thirty-two states with 370 electoral votes, most of the other pollsters conceded a Roosevelt victory, but no one with the prophetic accuracy of Jim Farley. "In my humble judgment," he said a day before the election, "President Roosevelt will carry every State in the nation except Maine and Vermont." And he was right. The next day, Roosevelt was reelected in the most sweeping political victory since James Monroe's reelection in 1820. Roosevelt, with 60.2 per cent of the popular vote (27,478,945), won an electoral college vote of 523. Landon polled 16,674,665 popular votes, but carried only Maine and Vermont, which gave him eight electoral votes. Not since William Howard Taft's defeat in 1912, when he carried only Vermont and Utah, had a Republican can-

James A. Farley of New York, Roosevelt's able campaign manager in 1932 and 1936, broke with F.D.R. over the latter's decision to seek a third term. (Brown Brothers)

100   THE ERA OF F.D.R., 1933–1945

didate been beaten so decisively. Among the minor contenders, the Union party's William Lemke polled 882,479; Norman Thomas, the Socialist candidate, 187,752; Earl Browder, the Communist party's choice, 80,159; and the Socialist Labor and Prohibitionist candidates 12,779 and 37,847 respectively. The congressional vote was also a Democratic landslide. Of the 435 House seats, 333 went to the Democrats, the Republicans holding on to only 88. In the new Senate, the Democratic membership was increased to 75, the number of Republicans reduced to 16. The gubernatorial races indicated a similar GOP rout: the Democrats won 26 of the 33 that were contested, and the Republicans won only 5, losing even Landon's home state to the Democrats.

The election verdict, according to *The New York Times*'s Arthur Krock, was "the most overwhelming testimonial of approval ever received by a national candidate in the history of the nation." But it was more than that. The presidential vote indicated also that the American people, in reelecting Roosevelt so decisively, had repudiated both the radical left and the extreme right. The people voted for F.D.R. because, as *The New York Times* editorialized the morning after the election, his administration "helped greatly to restore hope, to equalize opportunity, to prevent the excesses of the recent past and to conserve American institutions by adapting them to changing times." The people clearly endorsed the "broad principles" of the New Deal, and their "vote of confidence" in the Roosevelt administration "carried with it," according to the same newspaper, "the hope that . . . [F.D.R.] may prove to be a master builder for a still damaged and troubled America." Roosevelt's second term, however, was to fall far short of realizing the goals he and many of his supporters expected of it.

Suggested Readings

Almost all of the general accounts cited in Chapter 1 contain pertinent information on developments during the years 1935 and 1936. The third volume of Arthur M. Schlesinger, Jr., *The Age of Roosevelt*, subtitled, *The Politics of Upheaval*, already cited, is devoted entirely to these years.

On the New Deal attack from the right, George Wolfskill, *The Revolt of the Conservatives: A History of the American Liberty League, 1934–1940* (Boston, 1962) and C. Frederick Rudolph, "The American Liberty League, 1934–1940," *American Historical Review*, LVI (October 1950), 19–33, cover the organization's activities in detail. Other manifestations of the rightist oppo-

THE NEW DEAL, II (1935–1936)

sition to the New Deal are described in Raymond G. Swing, *Forerunners of American Fascism* (New York [1935]) and G. Brett, *The Fifth Column Is Here* (New York [1940]). Two accounts of F.D.R. by a strong critic of the New Deal, who voted for the President nonetheless, are James P. Warburg, *Hell Bent for Election* (Garden City, N.Y., 1935) and the same author's *Still Hell Bent for Election* (Garden City, N.Y., 1936).

The attack from the left is discussed in Murray Kempton, *Part of Our Time: Some Ruins and Monuments of the Thirties* (New York, 1956), which is especially good on the Communists; James Oneal and Gustave A. Werner, *American Communism: A Critical Analysis of Its Origins, Development, and Programs* (new rev. ed., New York, 1947); and Eugene Lyons, *The Red Decade, The Stalinist Penetration of America* (Indianapolis [1941]), "an informal history of Bolshevism" in the United States between 1930 and 1940. See also Earl R. Browder, *The People's Front* (New York [1938]) and the "tortured" autobiographical tale of Whittaker Chambers, *Witness* (New York, 1952), a one-time Communist who repented.

The opposition of the left to the New Deal is discussed generally in Alfred M. Bingham, *Insurgent America* (New York, 1945) and by The Unofficial Observer [J. Franklin Carter], *American Messiahs* (New York, 1935). Father Coughlin's appeal is analyzed in Alfred M. and Elizabeth B. Lee, eds., *The Fine Art of Propaganda: A Study of Father Coughlin's Speeches* (New York, 1939). One of the best accounts of Huey Long is Allan P. Sindler, *Huey Long's Louisiana* (Baltimore, 1956), but see also Harnett T. Kane, *Louisiana Hayride: The American Rehearsal for Dictatorship* (New York, 1941), a good analysis; Carleton Beals, *The Story of Huey P. Long* (Philadelphia, 1935); Stan Opotowsky, *The Longs of Louisiana* (New York, 1960), an interestingly written but somewhat thin history of the careers of Earl and Huey Long; Thomas Martin, *Dynasty: The Longs of Louisiana* (New York [1960]); and Abbott J. Liebling, *The Earl of Louisiana* (New York, 1961).

Upton Sinclair tells the EPIC story himself in *I: Candidate for Governor and How I Got Licked* (Pasadena, Calif. [1935]). Not specifically on Sinclair, but related to the movement he represented and the protest he exemplified, are Clarke A. Chambers, *California Farm Organizations, 1929–1941* (Berkeley, Calif., 1952) and Robert E. Burke, *Olson's New Deal for California* (Berkeley, Calif., 1953).

The Floyd Olson story is discussed in George H. Mayer, *The Political Career of Floyd B. Olson* (Minneapolis [1951]).

On labor in the New Deal, see the excellent collection of essays on labor problems and issues during the 1930's by Milton Derber and Edwin Young, eds., *Labor and the New Deal* (Madison, Wis., 1958). The essay by Selig Perlman, "Labor and the New Deal in Historical Perspective," in this volume is an especially useful general appraisal. The advances of the labor movement from the Wagner Act to the attack on Pearl Harbor are expertly detailed in Walter Galenson, *The C.I.O. Challenge to the A.F. of L.: A History of the American Labor Movement, 1935–1941* (Cambridge, Mass., 1960). See also Harry A. Millis and Emily C. Brown, *From the Wagner Act to Taft-Hartley:*

102 THE ERA OF F.D.R., 1933–1945

A Study of National Labor Policy and Labor Relations (Chicago [1950]). Older works on this subject include Emanuel Stein and Jerome Davis, eds., *Labor Problems in America* (New York [1940]); Kenneth White, *Labour and Democracy in the United States* (Liverpool, England, 1939); and Gordon S. Watkins and Paul A. Dodd, *Labor Problems* (New York, 1940). More specialized, but first-rate on its subject, is Irving Bernstein, *The New Deal Collective Bargaining Policy* (Berkeley, Calif., 1953). See also Robert R. Brooks, *Unions of Their Own Choosing: An Account of the Labor Relations Board and Its Work* (New Haven, Conn., 1937), an account of union efforts to secure collective bargaining rights and of their experience in exercising those rights. The other works on this subject, including Joseph Rosenfarb, *The National Labor Policy and How It Works* (New York, 1940); Louis G. Silverberg, ed., *The Wagner Act after Ten Years* (Washington, D.C., 1945); and the Twentieth Century Fund study by Samuel T. Williamson and Herbert Harris, *Trends in Collective Bargaining: A Summary of Recent Experience* (New York, 1945), all bring the story to more recent times.

The CIO break with the AFL is told in Herbert Harris, *Labor's Civil War* (New York, 1940). On the CIO, see the account by Benjamin Stollberg, *The Story of the C.I.O.* (New York, 1938); other works on this subject include John R. Walsh, *C.I.O.: Industrial Unionism in Action* (New York, 1937); Robert R. Brooks, *When Labor Organizes* (New Haven, Conn., 1937); Walter Galenson, *Rival Unionism in the United States* (New York, 1940); and Edward Levinson, *Labor on the March* (New York, 1938).

Among the many specialized studies of labor and government policy, see John B. Andrews, *Labor Laws in Action* (New York, 1938); Herbert O. Eby, *The Labor Relations Act in the Courts* (New York, 1943); and Howard S. Kaltenborn, *Government Adjustment of Labor Disputes* (Chicago, 1943). The unionization of one important industry is told in Robert R. Brooks, *As Steel Goes . . .* (New Haven, Conn., 1940).

Opposition to the labor movement is told in Bruce Minton and John Stuart, *Men Who Lead Labor* (New York, 1937) and Harold Seidman, *Labor Czars: A History of Labor Racketeering* (New York, 1938). Some of the findings of Senator La Follette's investigation between 1936 and 1940 and employers' efforts to curb labor's newly gained rights are summarized in Leo Huberman, *The Labor Spy Racket* (New York [1937]).

Useful biographies of labor leaders include Matthew Josephson, *Sidney Hillman: Statesman of American Labor* (Garden City, N.Y., 1952); Saul D. Alinsky, *John L. Lewis: An Unauthorized Biography* (New York, 1949); and James A. Wechsler, *Labor Baron: A Portrait of John L. Lewis* (New York, 1944).

On social security, see Eveline M. Burns, *Toward Social Security: An Explanation of the Social Security Act and a Survey of the Larger Issues* (New York, 1936), an early view of the law before it went into effect. Domenico Gagliardo, *American Social Insurance* (New York, 1955) surveys the whole development of the social security program, with primary emphasis upon old age, unemployment, health, and disability benefits. Paul H. Douglas, *Social*

THE NEW DEAL, II (1935-1936)   103

Security in the United States: An Analysis and Appraisal . . . (New York, 1939) is a penetrating discussion. Abraham Epstein, *Insecurity: Challenge to America, A Study of Social Insurance in the United States and Abroad* (2d rev. ed., New York, 1938) is more general. Isaac M. Rubinow, *The Quest for Security* (New York [1934]) is useful on the background to the passage of the 1935 law, but consult also Marietta Stevenson and Ralph E. Spear, *The Social Security Program* (Chicago, 1936); Maxwell J. Stewart, *Social Security* (New York, 1937); and Lewis Meriam, *Relief and Social Security* (Washington, D.C., 1946).

Besides the studies cited in Chapter 1 on relief, unemployment, and welfare, see Betty and Ernest K. Lindley, *A New Deal for Youth* (New York, 1938), the story of the NYA. Other useful works on later developments are U. S. National Resources Planning Board, *Security, Work and Relief Projects* (Washington, D.C., 1942); E. Wight Bakke, *The Unemployed Worker* (New Haven, Conn., 1940); and Arthur W. McMahon, *et al.*, *The Administration of Federal Work Relief* (Chicago, 1941).

On the banking and securities legislation of the "second" New Deal, see the references in Chapter 1. On regulation of the public utilities, consult Marion L. Ramsay, *Pyramids of Power: The Story of Roosevelt, Insull and the Utility Wars* (Indianapolis [1937]).

On federal-state relations under the New Deal, see Jane C. Carey, *The Rise of a New Federalism* (New York, 1938).

Randolph E. Paul, *Taxation in the United States* (Boston, 1954) is a comprehensive survey by a knowledgeable tax lawyer, and is mostly devoted to post-World War I developments. The chapters on the New Deal laws are especially good and quite readable. See also the pertinent parts of Sidney Ratner, *American Taxation: Its History as a Social Force in Democracy* (New York, 1942). The book's chief interest is on "the endeavor of the American people . . . to forge taxes which should be not only sources of revenue but also instruments of economic justice and social welfare."

On the statistics of the 1936 election, see Edgar E. Robinson, *The Presidential Vote, 1936* (Stanford, Calif. [1940]). There is no first-rate biography of Landon. Frederick Palmer, *This Man Landon* (New York, 1936) was issued as a campaign portrait. Of similar calibre are Millis Thornton, *The Life of Alfred M. Landon* (New York, 1936) and Richard B. Fowler, *Deeds Not Deficits: The Story of Alfred M. Landon* (Kansas City [1936]).

3

The New Deal, III

1937-1939

BECAUSE OF the Twentieth Amendment, Roosevelt's second inaugural occurred on January 20, 1937. The President took this occasion to address the country on the still unfulfilled tasks of reform and rehabilitation which he believed required immediate attention. "In this nation," he declared, "I see tens of millions of its citizens—a substantial part of its whole population—who at this very moment are denied the greater part of what the very lowest standards of today call the necessities of life. I see millions of families trying to live on incomes so meagre that the pall of family disaster hangs over them day by day. I see millions whose daily lives in city and on farm continue under conditions labeled indecent by so-called polite society half a century ago. I see millions denied education, recreation, and the opportunity to better their lot and the lot of their children. I see millions lacking the means to buy the products of farm and factory and by their poverty denying work and productiveness to many other millions. I see one-third of a nation ill-housed, ill-clad, ill-nourished." These conditions, Roosevelt declared, should be reasons not for despair but rather for determination, a clear indication for democratic government to prove its ability to meet the needs of the people. "The test of our progress," he said, "is not whether we add more to the abundance of those who have much; it is whether we provide enough for those who have too little."

This address, along with some of the promises he had made during the closing weeks of the 1936 campaign, suggested that he intended to extend the New Deal's social and economic justice programs still further. The landslide victory in the election proved that the majority of the people enthusiastically supported the New Deal. Opposition to it, however, was strongly entrenched in the Supreme Court, and whatever legislative plans F.D.R. may have had for his second term, they were shattered within a month by his proposal to "rejuvenate" and reorganize the Court.

THE SUPREME COURT FIGHT

The Supreme Court which Roosevelt inherited in 1933 was an essentially conservative body. All its members, with the exception of two Wilson appointments (James C. McReynolds and Louis Brandeis), had been selected by Republican Presidents. The nine justices, with the dates of their appointments, were as follows: four were conservatives—Willis Van Devanter (1911), James C. McReynolds (1914), George Sutherland (1922), and Pierce Butler (1922); three were liberals—Louis Brandeis (1916), Harlan F. Stone (1925), and Benjamin Cardozo (1932); and two occupied the middle of the road—Chief Justice Charles Evans Hughes (1930) and Owen J. Roberts (1930)—sometimes called "the roving conservatives." Throughout the depression the Court had maintained a conservative trend and had frowned upon attempts by state legislatures to regulate economic conditions. In 1934, on the other hand, it showed liberal tendencies; in particular, in a five to four decision in the *Nebbia v. New York* case, in which the majority decision was written by Justice Roberts, it upheld a New York State law fixing the minimum price of milk.

The year 1935 brought a return to conservatism. The Court voided several minor New Deal measures, and on May 27, in the Schechter case, it declared the NRA unconstitutional by a unanimous vote. The reasons for the decision were, first, that Congress had unconstitutionally transferred legislative power to the Executive, and second, that the scope of the NRA had been unconstitutionally extended beyond the sphere of interstate commerce. January, 1936, brought a veto of the other main pillar of the New Deal recovery program, the AAA. By six to three, the majority opinion being written by Justice Roberts, the Court declared in *United States v. Butler* that the AAA was an unconstitutional interference with the rights of the states and that Congress had made an unconstitutional use of its power to levy taxes. The decision was notable because of an eloquent dissenting opinion by Justice Stone, in which he warned his colleagues against the assumption that the courts were "the only agency of government that must be assumed to have capacity to govern." Later in the year several other New Deal measures were invalidated, making a total of eight decisions against it and only two in its favor. In June a New York State minimum wage law for women was declared unconstitutional by five to four—a decision which appeared to conflict with the ruling in a previous case. The voiding of this state wage law, coupled with the earlier voiding of the NRA, meant that according to the Court no government body in the country had authority to regulate wages. In the opinion of the Court the Constitution of the United States still enforced the rules of laissez-faire economics.

Roosevelt expressed bitterness over the decisions of the Court, declaring that the justices had interpreted the Constitution according to the practices of "horse and buggy days" and pointing out that they defined interstate commerce very broadly when it was a question of issuing injunctions against strikers and very strictly when Congress attempted to raise wages and reduce hours. He did not, however, commit himself as to what policy he proposed to adopt until after the election.

Then, on February 5, 1937, he startled the country by proposing a general reorganization of the federal judiciary. Declaring that its "personnel . . . [was] insufficient to meet the business before them" and that many of the judges were too old to perform their duties efficiently, Roosevelt recommended that whenever a federal judge passed the age of seventy without retiring, the President should have the power to appoint an additional judge to assist him. In 1937, six of the justices were over seventy, and of these three were archconservatives. Under this plan the membership of the Supreme Court might, if necessary, be increased to fifteen. Provision was also made to increase the number of lower federal judges, so that with those on the Supreme Court the President could appoint altogether as many as fifty new ones. These and the other changes which the bill proposed were designed, as Roosevelt said, "to eliminate congestion of calendars and to make the judiciary as a whole less static by the constant and systematic addition of new blood to its personnel . . . to make the judiciary more elastic by providing for temporary transfers of circuit and district judges to those places where federal courts are most in arrears . . . to furnish the Supreme Court practical assistance in supervising the conduct of business in the lower courts . . . [and] to eliminate inequality, uncertainty and delay now existing in the determination of constitutional questions involving federal statutes." But whatever merits some of these proposals may have had, they were lost in the widespread and bitter opposition which arose over enlarging the number of Supreme Court justices.

Roosevelt expected protests from the conservatives, but he did not anticipate them from his strongest liberal supporters in and out of Congress or from so many of the people who had voted for him only a few months before. The Court plan was the most serious political mistake of his career. It alienated public opinion from his programs, it destroyed the Democratic party coalition which had made possible the landslides of 1934 and 1936, and it weakened Roosevelt's leadership and undermined his influence in guiding legislation through Congress. Moreover, it did much to help revive the Republican party and to indicate to GOP conservatives that by joining with the anti-New Deal Democrats in the Congress, together they could form a powerful bipartisan coalition capable of thwarting, if not halting, any liberal legislation which the administration might propose.

Why did Roosevelt's Court plan end in what Merlo J. Pusey has called the "most humiliating defeat of his career"? [1] In part it was the result of the secrecy with which the President, Attorney General Homer Cummings, and one or two other White House intimates prepared the bill. This was attributed by Roosevelt to the need for guarding against premature leaks to the press. Roosevelt neither consulted the Democratic leaders in Congress nor sought the advice of his cabinet. They learned of the bill only an hour before it was presented to the Congress and just before F.D.R. released it to the press. Except for Cummings and Secretary Ickes, who approved of it, the members of the cabinet, like the congressional leaders who would have to fight for the bill on Capitol Hill, were astounded by it. As James MacGregor Burns has suggested, Roosevelt's handling of the Court bill satisfied "two Rooseveltian traits—his instinct for the dramatic and his instinct for the adroit and circuitous stratagem rather than the frontal attack." [2] But whatever his motives,

---

[1] Merlo J. Pusey, "F.D.R. *vs.* the Supreme Court," *American Heritage,* IX (April 1958), 24.
[2] James MacGregor Burns, *Roosevelt: The Lion and the Fox* (New York [1956]), p. 297.

the way he moved against the Court was immediately criticized by his friends and enemies alike. Many agreed with *The New York Times* when it declared that "cleverness and adroitness in dealing with the Supreme Court are not qualities which sober-minded citizens will approve."

Many persons who disagreed with the Court's decisions against the New Deal would have preferred some other method of dealing with the problem—a constitutional amendment, for example, or a law restricting the Court's power of review; but Roosevelt rejected both these alternatives. The former, he claimed, could be easily thwarted or delayed by conservative minorities; the latter violated cherished legal precedents and could be invalidated by the Supreme Court itself. His proposal, which the ultraconservative Justice James C. McReynolds had once suggested himself when he was Wilson's Attorney General, was, he insisted, the only practicable one. But a large number of people, including many progressives, disagreed with the President. They opposed his proposal because they believed that it would seriously impair the dignity and independence of the judiciary. Moreover, they were aware that the arguments with which Roosevelt supported his plan were very disingenuous; and many also believed that his failure to publish his proposal until after the election, although he had been asked about his plans for the Court before November and had been thinking of ways to reform it for some time, made him appear indifferent, if not disrespectful, toward the democratic process. But Roosevelt refused to be deterred by the outcries of the conservatives or the protests of his friends.

Almost at once a strong opposition to the "Court-packing" bill developed throughout the country, and in the Congress, Democratic Senator Burton K. Wheeler, a long-time progressive and friend of the New Deal reform program, assumed leadership in defending the Court and safeguarding the Constitution against executive usurpation. Wheeler, like other liberal Democrats, sympathized with F.D.R.'s desire to liberalize the Court, but he was shocked by the means the President proposed to achieve his ends. With the Democrats fighting among themselves and at odds with the White House, the Republicans allowed the President's own party to carry the burden of defeating the bill, thus giving the battle the appearance of being one of fundamental principle and entirely removed from petty partisan politics.

As the storm in Congress gained momentum, Roosevelt tried to muster support for his proposal. On March 4, while addressing a Democratic

THE NEW DEAL, III (1937–1939)

victory dinner, he warned the party that unless it remained "a natural rallying point . . . of all those who truly believe in political and economic democracy," the voters in the future would not reward it with public office. Then he proceeded to point out the immediate need to prevent the "personal economic predilections" of the majority of the Supreme Court from paralyzing the efforts of Congress and the Chief Executive to fulfill the mandate of the country.

On March 9, F.D.R. took his case to the people in a fireside chat, and struck back at his critics by reviewing the administration's defeats and narrow victories at the hands of a conservative judiciary. "The Courts . . . have cast doubts on the ability of the elected Congress to protect us against catastrophe by meeting squarely our modern social and economic conditions," he declared. He criticized the Supreme Court's failure to give a law of Congress "the benefit of all reasonable doubt" before declaring it unconstitutional, and he accused it of "acting not as a judicial body, but as a policy-making body." Quoting from the Court's minority opinions, F.D.R. used the words of the dissenting justices to show that the Supreme Court had "improperly set itself up as a third House of the Congress—a super legislature . . . reading into the Constitution words and implications which are not there, and which were never intended to be there. We have . . . reached the point as a Nation where we must take action to save the Constitution from the Court and the Court from itself. . . . We want a Supreme Court which will do justice under the Constitution . . . not over it. In our Courts we want a government of laws and not of men." He denied that he was trying to pack the Court with "spineless puppets" who would do his bidding. "This plan of mine is no attack on the Court; it seeks to restore the Court to its rightful and historic place in our system of Constitutional Government and to have it resume its high task of building anew on the Constitution 'a system of living law.' "

While F.D.R. appealed to the country and the Democratic party for support, the Senate Judiciary Committee was holding hearings on his proposal. Wheeler and several other members of the committee suggested to the Chief Justice that he appear before them to inform the committee whether the Court actually was behind schedule in its work. Hughes was willing to appear, but did not want to go alone. "It seemed to me," he said, "that at least one other member of the Court should accompany me—preferably Judge Brandeis—because of his standing as a Democrat and his reputation as a liberal judge."[3] After discussing the matter with Brandeis, who refused to go and disapproved of any justice's attending the committee's hearing, Hughes agreed to write Wheeler a letter, if called upon to do so, describing the work schedule of the Court. Wheeler immediately asked for such a statement and Hughes prepared one for him. After it had been submitted to Brandeis and Van Devanter for their approval, Hughes's letter was read to the committee on March 21. "An increase in the number of Justices of the Supreme Court," Hughes asserted, "apart from any question of policy, which I do not discuss, would not promote the efficiency of the Court. . . . There would be more judges to confer, more judges to discuss, more judges to be convinced and to decide. The present number of Justices is thought to be large enough as far as the prompt, adequate, and efficient conduct of the work of the Court is concerned." Between 1930 and 1935, the number of cases which had come before each session of the Court for adjudication ranged from 1,023 to 1,132. Of these, not more than 139 or fewer than 102 per term failed to be considered. By showing that the Court was "fully abreast of its work," Hughes's letter demolished the President's claim that additional judges were needed "because the personnel of the Federal Judiciary is insufficient to meet the business before them."

Meanwhile the Court proceeded to take the wind out of its opponents' sails by spectacularly reversing itself. On March 29, by another five to four decision, the Court in *West Coast Hotel Company v. Parrish* upheld a minimum wage law enacted by the State of Washington, a statute very similar to both the New York minimum wage law declared unconstitutional in 1936 and the District of Columbia minimum wage statute for women declared unconstitutional in 1923. The West Coast Hotel Company decision had been reached before Roosevelt presented his Court bill to Congress, but because Hughes had not wanted to sustain this law by a tie vote when a similar one had been overruled only a year before, announcement of the decision had been delayed until Justice Harlan Stone, ill since October, returned to the Court on February 1. Justice Owen J. Roberts, whose switch in the West Coast Hotel Company case meant that wage-fixing legislation was no longer unconstitutional, had voted against the New York law only because at that time the Court appeared to be unwilling to overrule the 1923 decision. It is

[3] Quoted in Dexter Perkins, *Charles Evans Hughes and American Democratic Statesmanship* (Boston [1956]), p. 178.

probable that Hughes, who was aware of the liberal temper of the times, may have influenced Roberts' decision to uphold the Washington law. Thus, while it is impossible to explain Roberts' change of mind with any surety, it is certain that it preceded the President's attempt to pack the Court and was therefore not a response to the threat of political pressure.

This liberal decision was followed by others. On April 12, 1937, the Supreme Court, adopting a broader definition of interstate commerce than the one it had employed in the Schechter case, upheld the Wagner National Labor Relations Act in five separate decisions, the first of which, by a five to four vote, was in *NLRB v. Jones and Laughlin Steel Corporation*. And in May the Court, abandoning the narrow interpretation of the taxing power which had caused it to invalidate the AAA, accepted the Social Security Act. The result of these decisions and of the one upholding the Frazier-Lemke Farm Mortgage Moratorium Act of 1935 was that another of the chief arguments in favor of the President's plan had been removed.

Roosevelt's case against the Court was weakened further when Justice Willias Van Devanter, a conservative and a determined foe of the New Deal, announced on May 18 that he would step down at the end of the Court's session in June. Roosevelt thus had his first opportunity to appoint a justice to the high bench. Then, on July 14, Senator Joseph T. Robinson, who had legislative charge of the President's plan in the Senate, died suddenly. With his death, Roosevelt quietly accepted defeat. His bill died in the Senate Judiciary Committee; Congress passed, and on August 26, 1937, F.D.R. signed, a Judicial Reform Act, limiting certain minor abuses of judicial power; and the proposal to enlarge the Supreme Court was, thus, abandoned.

The fact that the Court upheld the New Deal after 1936 cannot be interpreted to mean, as F.D.R. claimed later, that the Court fight was "a lost battle which won a war." There is no evidence to suggest that F.D.R. frightened the "nine old men" out of their conservatism. On the contrary, the main explanation for the Court's approval of New Deal measures during and after the Court fight is to be found, as Merlo Pusey suggests, in the "greater care" with which the Congress framed legislation and in its increasing reliance upon the commerce clause rather than upon the tax power to support its regulatory legislation.[4]

For his first appointment to the Supreme Court, to succeed Van De-

[4] Pusey, *op. cit.*, p. 106.

vanter, Roosevelt chose Senator Hugo L. Black of Alabama. A controversy was immediately provoked by the discovery that Black had once been a member of the Ku Klux Klan. But the appointment was confirmed and the new justice soon showed himself a vigorous champion of civil liberties, and the able dissenting opinions in which he maintained that the Fourteenth Amendment should not apply to corporations were of remarkable interest. Between 1938 and the time of his death in April, 1945, Roosevelt appointed seven other members to the high Court. In 1938 Justice Sutherland resigned and was succeeded by Stanley Reed, former Solicitor General. In 1939 F.D.R. made two appointments. The first one, to succeed to Benjamin Cardozo's seat after his death in December, 1938, went to a personal adviser of the President, Felix Frankfurter of the Harvard University Law School. The second one that year went to William O. Douglas, formerly of the Yale University Law School and for the two previous years chairman of the Securities and Exchange Commission. Douglas succeeded to Louis Brandeis' chair. In 1940 Justice Pierce Butler, who had died in November, 1939, was succeeded by Frank Murphy, former Philippine High Commissioner, governor of Michigan, and Attorney General of the United States. In February, 1941, when James C. McReynolds, the last of the conservative "Old Guard," retired, he was replaced by Attorney General Robert H. Jackson, a strong and long-time foe of monopolistic big business. When the Court adjourned in June, 1941, Chief Justice Hughes retired, and Roosevelt elevated the distinguished "liberal nationalist" Harlan Stone to the top place. Stone's vacancy was filled by Senator James F. Byrnes of South Carolina, who resigned in October of the next year to become director of economic stabilization. In February, 1943, Roosevelt made his last appointment to the Supreme Court, when he replaced Byrnes with Wiley Rutledge, a former professor and dean of the State University of Iowa and Washington University law schools and, at the time of his appointment, a judge of the United States Court of Appeals.

Thus, from 1937 on, for the first time since before the Civil War, the Supreme Court had a liberal majority. The dissenting opinions which had been delivered in earlier years by Holmes, Brandeis, Stone, and Cardozo now became the official interpretations of the Constitution. The Court allowed much more latitude than formerly to the legislative power, particularly in the series of decisions in which it upheld the Wagner Act; and in a number of cases it defended, more fully and vigorously than had been its custom, the civil liberties guaranteed by the first article of

THE NEW DEAL, III (1937–1939)   113

the Bill of Rights. This revolution on the Supreme Court was probably as important a development in American constitutional history as had been its swing toward conservatism in the 1880's and 1890's.

THE MEAGER LEGISLATIVE RECORD
OF 1937

During 1937 the first session of the Seventy-fifth Congress was chiefly occupied with the President's Court bill, and Roosevelt, with a large part of his own party in open revolt against him, did not quickly regain sufficient prestige to exercise the kind of authoritative leadership which had characterized so much of his administration before the Court fight. The consequences of his battle with the high tribunal, especially the ill effects it had upon Roosevelt's influence over the Congress, became apparent when the record of this congressional session was measured against the goals the President had set for it in his second inaugural address.

The only major piece of new domestic legislation passed during this session was the Wagner-Steagall National Housing Act (September 1, 1937). The purpose of this law was to satisfy the great need for low-cost apartment buildings for working-class families. The needs of wealthier families had been adequately met before 1929, but private enterprise seemed to be incapable of providing new apartments at rentals the working class could afford to pay. A large proportion of the urban population continued, therefore, to live in slum tenements. The high cost of housing was due to a number of different factors, among them heavy real estate taxes, excessive real estate speculation, the high cost of material caused by monopolistic price fixing by business corporations, and the high cost of labor caused by monopolistic wage fixing by the AFL building unions. From the outset of the New Deal, it was frequently suggested that housing was one of the industries which might carry America out of the depression, but the problems involved were so complex that these hopes were not fulfilled.

The FHA, which insured construction loans and limited rates of interest, gave some stimulus to the building of houses for middle-income families. By 1940 it had underwritten loans for new houses totaling about $2 billion, and half of the 460,000 houses being built each year were covered by the FHA. The only attempt to solve the problems of low-cost housing in the early stages of the New Deal was through the PWA.

In three years, however, the Housing Division of the PWA was responsible for building only 30,000 family units.

The Wagner-Steagall Act set up the United States Housing Authority with Nathan Straus, a former New York State legislator, becoming administrator. The USHA was empowered to loan $800 million to local governments for low-cost housing. Ten per cent of the cost was to be raised locally, and the loans were to be repaid in sixty years, with 3 per cent interest. The USHA could also grant annual subsidies of $28 million for the reduction of rents on the condition that costs and rentals be kept below a certain figure and that only families earning less than a certain income be accepted as tenants. By the spring of 1940 it had loaned $600 million for 134,000 family units in 179 different projects in 24 states. The average rental to be charged was $14 a month per unit, and only those families were to be admitted whose incomes did not exceed five times the rent. However, although the USHA had given a considerable stimulus to housing, it seemed likely that the industry could never become really healthy until some method for reducing costs had been discovered. In 1939 and 1940 the federal government began to take action against the building unions under the antitrust laws, but the more complicated problems presented by local real estate taxes and by the high cost of material remained unsolved.

Dissatisfied with the way in which the first session of the Seventy-fifth Congress had dismissed his other legislative recommendations, Roosevelt decided to call it back into special session. On October 12, he issued a proclamation asking Congress to convene on November 15, and that evening he addressed the nation in a fireside chat explaining the reasons for his action. What the President told the country was essentially a recapitulation of the programs he had called for in January, 1937—"a new and permanent national farm act," wages and hours legislation, reorganization of the Executive branch of the government to bring about "the improvement of administrative management," and a comprehensive planning program for the "conservation and development of our natural resources." Roosevelt suggested "that the country be divided into the seven great regions into which Nature divided those resources—that in such regions local authorities be set up to arrange projects into some kind of comprehensive and continuing plan for the entire region—and that only after such consideration should regional projects be submitted to the Executive and to the Congress for inclusion in a national development program of such size as the budget of the year will permit." Not one of these proposals, however, was enacted by the special or second session of the Seventy-fifth Congress. Conservative Southern Democrats joined with stalwart Republicans from the North, as they had first done during the Court fight, to force the New Deal to a standstill.

THE BUSINESS RECESSION
OF 1937–1938

To detract further from Roosevelt's popularity and to add to the administration's mounting difficulties in the late summer of 1937, the mild boom which had been accompanying the country's recovery from the depths of the 1933 depression collapsed even more quickly than it had developed. By March, 1938, the stock market registered a major decline, unemployment increased, and industry found itself back almost where it had been when Roosevelt first entered the White House. For several months the administration hesitated. Roosevelt himself was undecided on what course to follow. He wanted a balanced budget. He had accepted deficit spending only because of the economic emergency. The idea of adopting Keynesian principles of deficit spending and low taxes as fundamental economic policy was too doctrinaire for him. Moreover, his advisers were divided on which was the right economic policy to apply. As a result, while Roosevelt was groping for a solution, the administration denounced big business one week and tried to promote business confidence the next. The more influential of the New Deal economists attributed the recession to monopolistic price raising and called for immediate government spending. Roosevelt finally accepted their point of view and decided to act. On April 14, 1938, abandoning his commitment to a balanced budget, he called upon the third session of the Seventy-fifth Congress to attack the recession by a $3 billion relief and works program. "Let us unanimously recognize the fact," he told the Congress, "that the Federal debt, whether it be twenty-five billions or fifty billions, can only be paid off if the Nation obtains a vastly increased citizen income." The purpose of the expenditures he recommended, along with the other proposals he suggested to this session of Congress, such as reducing bank reserves and increasing the Treasury's expenditures, were all aimed to increase the national income and thereby bring closer the day when the country would be "out of the red." That evening, in another fireside chat to the people, he reviewed for them

116   THE ERA OF F.D.R., 1933-1945

the message he had sent to the Congress. In June, Roosevelt's relief and works program was enacted by the Congress.

On April 29, in a second message to the Congress, Roosevelt analyzed the American economic system in detail and denounced the growth of monopoly and inequality. On June 16, Congress appointed a Temporary National Economic Committee. This body conducted an elaborate study of the workings of American corporate enterprise and made a number of very illuminating discoveries about the structure and performance of the economy. Its recommendations, which appeared in its final report on March 31, 1941, suggested numerous ways in which the government should act to curb monopoly and prevent the further concentration of business. Meanwhile the immediate policy of the administration was to enforce the antitrust laws. Thurman Arnold, a former law professor and prominent government attorney, was appointed to take charge of the antitrust division of the Department of Justice, and he instituted a campaign against both business corporations and trade unions with the purpose of forcing down prices which were being kept high by monopolistic practices. But with the outbreak of war, the work of Arnold's division was virtually suspended.

THE SECOND AGRICULTURAL ADJUSTMENT ACT

One of the first measures which the third session of the Seventy-fifth Congress considered was Roosevelt's recommendation for a comprehensive farm law, which he had recommended to it in July, 1937, and which had been set aside along with his other legislative proposals during the previous session. Meanwhile the farm problem was growing worse. The harvests of 1937 and 1938 were the largest since World War I, and farm prices, partly because of the recession and partly because of the growing surpluses, began to fall sharply. In his annual message of January 3, Roosevelt asked that the Congress prepare "an all-weather farm program" which would guarantee the farmers of the country "relatively constant purchasing power." The Congress responded quickly to the President's demand and on February 16, 1938, F.D.R. signed the second Agricultural Adjustment Act into law.

This measure, an extraordinarily complicated one, was the means by which Secretary Wallace hoped to achieve his ideal of an "ever-normal granary." The government was to allot acreage quotas among the producers of staple crops, allowing for the normal domestic and foreign demand and for a surplus which would be stored as a reserve in case of crop failures in future years. Farmers were not compelled to keep to these quotas, but those who did so would receive subsidies, "parity payments," which would be planned with a view to raising farm incomes to the 1909–14 level. If there was overproduction in spite of the quota system, the government would store surplus crops and make loans to the producers; and if two-thirds of the producers agreed, the government might restrict sales by means of marketing quotas and impose taxes on those who sold above their quotas. The act also established a Federal Crop Insurance Corporation to insure farmers against the uncertainties of the weather. By 1939 nearly 6 million farmers were included in the AAA program, and about 30 million acres had been taken out of production; subsidies totaled $482 million in 1938 and $675 million in 1939. As a result of overproduction in 1937, farm prices and farm incomes in 1938 and 1939 did not fully recover the ground which had been lost. How far the second AAA was "an effective instrument to serve the welfare of agriculture and all . . . [the] people" is impossible to say, since soon after it had gone into effect, World War II intervened and raised a host of new farm problems.

In order to reduce certain farm surpluses, Congress adopted the Food Stamp Plan in May, 1939, whereby the Federal Surplus Commodities Corporation, which had been purchasing surplus foodstuffs for distribution among the unemployed, now would distribute them through regular commercial channels. Persons on relief were entitled to receive 50 cents of surplus foods simply by presenting their grocer with the free stamps they received whenever they purchased $1 worth of food. This device, which was first tried in Rochester, New York, stretched relief payments and increased the business of retail stores. When it proved highly popular, it was quickly adopted in a large number of cities, and it remained in effect until the war.

THE FAIR LABOR STANDARDS ACT

Like the new agricultural program of 1938, the Fair Labor Standards Act, or as it was more commonly known, the Wages and Hours Law, was a measure Roosevelt had recommended to the Congress in May,

1937. The need to guarantee every worker, especially those in certain sweated industries, "a fair day's pay for a fair day's work" and to safeguard children against exploitation was obvious. "A self-supporting and self-respecting democracy," Roosevelt declared, "can plead no justification for the existence of child labor, no economic reason for chiseling workers' wages or stretching workers' hours." But like most of Roosevelt's other proposals that spring, serious consideration of a comprehensive wages and hours law was delayed first by the Court fight and then by the opposition of influential labor leaders, who were afraid that once a minimum wage was established there would be little likelihood of ever going beyond it. The improvement of hours and wages by federal law was complicated further by several other considerations.

Social legislation of this kind had formerly been left to the state governments. The states, however, were unable to regulate labor conditions effectively since industries were able to move from areas where labor was protected to other areas where low wages and long hours still prevailed. The New Dealers favored labor legislation not only as a step toward a more genuine democracy but also in the belief that reduced hours would bring about greater employment and that higher wages would mean increased purchasing power and hence greater production

Wages and hours legislation, moreover, involved also the question of prices, about which the New Deal did not adopt a consistent policy. If industrialists were required to pay higher wages, they would compensate themselves by charging higher prices, as a result of which the increase in purchasing power would be canceled. A number of New Deal economists, moreover, believed that the high prices exacted by semimonopolistic industries constituted the basic weakness of the economic system. But in 1933 the New Deal's chief spokesmen declared that a generally higher price level was desirable in order that debt obligations might become less burdensome. In 1938, on the other hand, government economists apparently believed that a number of prices ought to be reduced, but they were unable to devise any effective method by which this might be accomplished.

Political considerations, especially the influence exercised by conservative Southerners in the Democratic party, also raised difficulties. Many of the more backward industries likely to be affected by a minimum wage and maximum hours law were in the South, and some Southern spokesmen regarded low wages and long hours as a method by which their section could deprive the North of the economic supremacy it had enjoyed since the Civil War. The improvement of wages and

THE NEW DEAL, III (1937–1939)   119

hours, however, a long-time objective of the New Deal, had first been incorporated into the NRA. When the Supreme Court invalidated that law, other alternatives were sought. On June 30, 1936, Congress passed the Walsh-Healy Public Contracts Act, requiring businessmen making contracts with the federal government to pay "prevailing minimum wages" as set by the Secretary of Labor, to limit workers' hours to eight a day and forty a week, and to employ no one under the age of sixteen.

The Walsh-Healy law was an important beginning; but the President wanted a more comprehensive statute, and asked for it in May, 1937, and again in his November 15 message to the special session of the Congress. During November and December, 1937, the administration's minimum wage bill, which was still opposed by the AFL, was bitterly fought in the House of Representatives by a conservative bloc of Northern Republicans and Southern Democrats. When AFL President William Green denounced it, enough other congressmen, who were tired of the crusading zeal of the New Dealers and opposed to further reform, joined the conservatives from the North and the South to defeat it. A major defeat for the administration, this showed the extent to which Roosevelt's control and leadership over the Democratic majority in the House had deteriorated. After the bill was redrafted to incorporate various concessions, the Fair Labor Standards Act finally passed both houses of Congress on June 14. In a fireside chat ten days later, Roosevelt called it "the most far-reaching, far-sighted program for the benefit of workers ever adopted here or in any other country."

The law fixed minimum wages and maximum hours for all industries engaged in interstate commerce. Minimum wages were to begin at 25 cents an hour and were to rise to 40 cents an hour within seven years; maximum hours were to begin at forty-four a week and were to be reduced to forty a week within two years. Wage committees were to determine minimum wages for different industries, making allowances for differences in cost of production and transportation. Industries in which work had to be completed quickly were exempt from the maximum hour regulations. An administrator was to enforce the decisions of the committees, employers having the right of appeal to the courts. Employers who violated the regulations were liable to a fine of $10,000 or imprisonment for six months. Shipment of goods made by child labor (except in agriculture) was forbidden. It was calculated that the act meant an increase in wages for 650,000 workers, and a decrease in hours for 2,380,000 workers.

Before adjourning, Congress also passed the Wheeler-Lea Food, Drug,

120   THE ERA OF F.D.R., 1933–1945

and Cosmetic Act, on June 24, 1938, which broadened and revised the provisions of the Pure Food Act of 1906 by giving the Department of Agriculture stronger power to prohibit the sale of adulterated foods and harmful drugs. This law closed the legislative record of the Seventy-fifth Congress, but it was the Fair Labor Standards Act which marked the end of the New Deal's domestic reform legislation. From 1938 on, public attention became increasingly concentrated on the rapidly developing international crisis, and at home the voters showed a growing tendency toward conservatism.

THE DECLINE OF THE NEW DEAL

During the summer of 1938 Roosevelt, though still very popular as an individual, had not yet regained the national prestige and the political authority he had lost as a result of the Court fight and the business recession. Moreover, as the struggle over the Fair Labor Standards Act had shown, a considerable segment of the Democratic party was strongly opposed to more New Deal reform and increasingly disposed to defy the President's wishes. Congress had accepted Roosevelt's $3 billion spending program to fight the recession and, with less enthusiasm, had passed the new farm program and the minimum wage law. On the other hand, it refused to do anything about his proposal for river valley projects or to grant him the authority, which he had requested in January, 1937, to reorganize the Executive branch of the government.

For many years, political scientists and other students of the federal Executive had agreed that the rapid growth of administrative boards, bureaus, and agencies in the presidential office had created a "headless fourth branch" of the government. If the President was to perform his constitutional duties effectively, reform and a reorganization of these various offices were imperative. Virtually all the experts also agreed that only the President could bring about the required changes efficiently. But the fears of conservatives in both parties, aroused during the Court fight, that Roosevelt was aiming at a dictatorship and the pressure from various bureaucratic groups who were afraid that any changes would bring about a diminution of their influence caused Congress to reject Roosevelt's proposal twice, in 1937 and in 1938. It was finally passed in a modified form, however, in April, 1939. The Administrative Reorganization Act brought about a number of changes, the most important of which was the assembling of most of the New Deal bureaus into three major agencies: the Federal Security Agency, the Federal Works Agency, and the Federal Loan Agency. The first administrators of these three agencies were, respectively, Paul V. McNutt, a former governor of Indiana and High Commissioner to the Philippines; John Carmody, an industrial engineer and a former administrator of the Rural Electrification Administrator; and Jesse Jones, the Texas millionaire and Hoover-appointed chairman of the Reconstruction Finance Corporation. The law also provided for six administrative assistants to the President and for the establishment of eight new divisions in the Executive Office of the President. The Committee on Administrative Management, known as the Brownlow Committee, had also suggested the reorganization of some fifteen or more other agencies, among them the Interstate Commerce Commission, the Federal Trade Commission, and the Federal Communications Commission, and had recommended changes in the structure and operations of various cabinet departments, but the Congress refused to approve them. Other changes were brought about in 1940, and in 1947 Congress established the Hoover Commission to study the problems of the Executive offices and to propose further reorganization.

THE CONGRESSIONAL ELECTIONS
OF 1938

Several months before the midterm elections of 1938, a small group of ardent New Dealers close to the President, the most important of whom were Harry Hopkins, Thomas Corcoran, and Interior Secretary Harold Ickes, had convinced themselves that Roosevelt should abandon his long-time policy of not interfering in congressional elections and strike back openly at those conservative Democrats who had refused to support the social and economic reform program he had proposed in his second inaugural address. By ridding the Democratic party of its "Old Guard," most of whom were southern "Bourbons," these men hoped to transform the party into a consistently progressive organization. At any other time, Roosevelt would have been appalled at the idea of directing an out-and-out intraparty fight publicly, especially one involving the stamping of individuals with conservative or liberal labels. Such a scheme not only violated Roosevelt's practical and intuitive political sense but, as James MacGregor Burns has stated, it limited his maneuver-

THE ERA OF F.D.R., 1933–1945

ability and forced him to make an "almost complete commitment to a specific method and a definite conception of party." [5]

Roosevelt inaugurated the party "purge" on the evening of June 24, 1938, with a fireside chat, the ostensible purpose of which was "to report on the progress of national affairs to the real rulers of this country—the voting public." After reviewing the accomplishments and shortcomings of the Seventy-fifth Congress, he proceeded "to say a few words about the coming political primaries," and while he disclaimed any intention of intervening in any of them, he pointed out that he intended to speak out "in those few instances where there may be a clear issue between candidates for a Democratic nomination involving . . . [liberal versus conservative] principles, or involving a clear misuse of my name."

The "few instances" in the Democratic primaries in which Roosevelt chose to intervene involved one congressman, Representative John J. O'Connor of New York City, and three senators: Walter F. George of Georgia, Millard F. Tydings of Maryland, and Ellison D. ("Cotton Ed") Smith of South Carolina. Representative O'Connor, as chairman of the House Rules Committee, had kept the hours and wages bill in his committee, thereby preventing its passage in 1937. Senator George, whom Roosevelt personally accused of not "belonging to the liberal school of thought," had been a foe of many of the second New Deal's reform measures, outspokenly critical of the President's Court bill, and responsible, along with other Southern senators, for killing the Wagner-Van Nuys Antilynching bill. Senator Tydings was also a long-time critic of F.D.R. and the New Deal leadership of the Democratic party. He had opposed such New Deal measures as the NRA, TVA, AAA, FHA, and the Wagner Labor Relations Act, to name but a few. On one occasion, he accused F.D.R. and his advisers of trying "to run the government on hot air." The last of the President's major targets was Senator Smith, a "white supremacist" who had little sympathy for the "window-sill agriculturists" who were trying to save the farmers. The party "purge" was unsuccessful in every instance save one—the defeat of Congressman O'Connor.

In the November elections the liberal New Deal wing of the Democratic party suffered still another defeat. The results showed not only a strengthening of conservative influences in the Democratic party but also a revival of Republican strength. The GOP elected governors in Pennsylvania, Michigan, Minnesota, Wisconsin, and Oregon, all states which had previously been governed by Democrats or progressives; and they won 81 seats in the House of Representatives, raising their number

[5] Burns, *op. cit.*, p. 359.

THE NEW DEAL, III (1937–1939)   123

there from 88 to 169. In the Senate races the GOP captured seven seats, increasing its total in that body from 16 to 23. To be sure, the Democrats still had large majorities in both chambers: 69 to 23 in the Senate and 261 to 169 in the House, but the trend was unmistakably against the New Deal's liberalism.

The conservative influence was apparent as soon as the Seventy-sixth Congress convened on January 3, 1939. The Republicans, in cooperation with a group of sixty southern Democrats in the House, were able to prevent any significant extensions of the New Deal. The Congress, moreover, showed a marked inclination to amend a number of New Deal laws, particularly the Wagner Act, and it cut the relief and public works appropriations recommended by the President by some $200 million and forced him to accept other curtailments in relief activities. This victory for economy in relief expenditures, however, was counteracted by an increase in the benefit payments paid to the farmers. Congress also liberalized the Social Security Act by adopting on August 10, 1939, several important amendments recommended by the Social Security Board and the President. Among the more important were provisions which authorized benefit payments to the dependents of deceased workers; advanced the date of the first monthly old age insurance payments from January, 1942, to January, 1940; increased the number of workers covered (so that by 1940 some 35 million out of nearly 65 million were protected); raised monthly payments to the aged; and increased the amount the federal government paid to the states for unemployment compensation, maternity and infant care, and assistance to dependent or delinquent children. After World War II social security coverage was extended further. In spite of the outcries of Southern conservatives and the Republican denunciations of government extravagance, the Congress was not prepared to undo the New Deal. Congress was still, by preference, a spending agency; and in the end the total appropriations it voted were actually larger than those which Roosevelt had requested.

THE NEW DEAL AND
THE FEDERAL BUDGET

What had the New Deal accomplished, and what were its major weaknesses and limitations? Opinions varied considerably. Like Roosevelt, it was called everything from communism to fascism. Rightists denounced it for doing too much, leftists attacked it for not doing enough,

124   THE ERA OF F.D.R., 1933–1945

and a large number of people condemned it as a selfish political plot to satisfy the thirst for power of "that man" in the White House.

The feature of the New Deal which provoked most vigorous and widespread criticism, especially among conservatives, was its failure to balance the budget. Businessmen and orthodox economists believed that the continuance of deficit financing would result in steadily increasing taxes and might end in uncontrolled inflation. They further believed that the government was absorbing capital which would otherwise have financed business expansion, that these funds were being used wastefully and unproductively, and that a balanced budget was essential in order to create business confidence and thereby make an economic recovery possible.

Roosevelt himself originally favored a balanced budget; during his campaign for the Presidency he had criticized Hoover for his failure to prevent deficits, and one of the earliest measures of the Roosevelt administration was the Economy Act of March 20, 1933, which reduced government salaries and veterans' benefits. However, the promise to balance the budget was incompatible with other promises of the Democratic platform—with its support of adequate relief for the unemployed, reduction of agricultural production, and federal expenditures for public works. In March, 1933, moreover, any sudden contraction of government expenses would have diminished purchasing power and have had a deflationary effect that might have done more harm than good to the economic system.

Roosevelt therefore accepted an unbalanced budget as temporarily inevitable; the federal government spent large sums on public works and unemployment relief, and, with the expansion of government services under the New Deal, its normal expenditures also began to rise. Roosevelt continued to regard a balanced budget as a desirable goal, one to which he always aspired, but he continued to postpone achieving it because of the economic necessities of the times. And although the GOP leaders denounced the New Deal financial policies, few of them were willing to commit themselves as to where specifically economies should be made. Congressmen had always found that they were more likely to be reelected if they voted for the spending of money, and many Republican senators and representatives who denounced New Deal extravagance were, when confronted by concrete issues, willing to appropriate even larger sums than was the administration. This was conspicuously the case with the veterans' bonus, which Congress voted over Roosevelt's veto in 1935, and with subsidies for the farmers.

THE NEW DEAL, III (1937–1939)

Meanwhile some of the New Deal economists, influenced by the ideas elaborated by John Maynard Keynes in his major work, *The General Theory of Employment, Interest and Money* (1936), were putting forward a new point of view. They argued that large-scale government spending was essential during periods of depression in order to maintain purchasing power and compensate for the lack of spending by private capital. Eventually the growth of the national income would enable the budget to be balanced by increasing government revenues. The budget should be planned over long periods, with deficits in times of depression and surpluses in times of prosperity. It was suggested also that much of the government debt should be considered as an investment; insofar as government borrowings were used to finance public works, conservation, and improvements of health and education, they served, directly or indirectly, to increase the national wealth. When a private business corporation borrowed capital in order to enlarge its plant and equipment, it was regarded as a sign of prosperity; government borrowing, it was suggested, should be judged in the same manner.

The New Dealers argued further that much of the alarm provoked by the growth of the national debt reflected an inability to distinguish between a public debt and a private debt. A private debt was a burden upon the debtor, but a public debt was a debt owned by the nation to itself. Payment of a public debt meant merely the transference of wealth from one group of citizens to another; it did not diminish the wealth of the nation as a whole. The only question to be asked about an increase in the public debt was whether the government was making the best possible use of the capital and labor which it was putting into motion. Would the capital have been employed more advantageously if it had been left in private hands?

During the depression there was a decrease in government revenue, particularly in the income tax. A larger proportion of the revenue than formerly was represented by indirect taxes, which were paid by the whole population, not merely by those persons in the upper income brackets. The most important of the indirect taxes were those levied on liquor and tobacco, which accounted for nearly a quarter of all government revenues under the New Deal. During the ten years 1931–40 total revenues were $41.03 billion; income tax payments amounted to $15.79 billion, more than half of which was supplied by the corporation income tax, while internal indirect taxes brought in $16.03 billion.

Government expenditure increased during the Hoover administration

126 THE ERA OF F.D.R., 1933–1945

as a result of public works and the RFC. In 1933 normal government expenses were temporarily reduced, but they quickly began to rise as a result of the growth of the civil service, which contained 568,345 members in 1932 and 813,302 in 1937. Abnormal expenditure reached its peak in 1936 and 1937 as a result of payment of the veterans' bonus. During the fiscal year 1937–38, after a business recovery, relief spendings were reduced and the budget was almost balanced; during a part of the year, in fact, the government was taking in more money than it paid out. This was followed by a sharp business recession, and in the spring of 1938 the government embarked on another large-scale spending program. When the economic crisis showed no signs of improving, Roosevelt, once again temporarily, accepted the viewpoint of those New Deal economists who believed that an unbalanced budget was necessary in a depression period. In 1939 the conservatives in Congress insisted on a reduction of government spending, and the demand for a balanced budget began to win considerable support. In the spring of 1940, however, the United States was compelled to adopt a large-scale defense and armament program. This made a continuance of Treasury deficits inevitable.

In the spring of 1940 the gross national debt amounted to $44.45 billion, having increased by $21.92 billion since the beginning of the New Deal. In 1919, at the conclusion of World War I, the debt had amounted to $25.48 billion. However, since there was nearly $2.25 billion in the Treasury and another $2 billion in the Stabilization Fund, the net debt amounted to about $40.25 billion. The administration calculated, moreover, that it had spent $16.43 billion on public works and other durable improvements and on recoverable loans, and that of this sum $3.23 billion would eventually be paid back to the Treasury. Government borrowings had come almost wholly from the banks, and the interest rate had been abnormally low. Until 1940, interest payments on the national debt amounted to a smaller figure than in 1919.

THE NEW DEAL AND
THE ECONOMIC SYSTEM

The effects of the New Deal on the economic system remained a subject of violent controversy. Throughout 1933 and 1934 business conditions fluctuated. In the spring of 1935 there began a steady improvement which continued until August, 1937. The national income produced, which had amounted to nearly $83 billion in 1929 and $40 billion in 1932, reached $71.85 billion in 1937. The number of wage earners in employment increased from almost 26 million in 1933 to 32.5 million in 1937, 2.3 million less than in 1929. Corporate business, which had reported a deficit of about $5.64 billion in 1932, made a net profit in 1937 of about $4 billion, while payments of dividends for 1937 stood at 90 per cent of the 1929 figure. Industrial production was 77 per cent greater than in 1932, though it was still 7.5 per cent less than it had been in 1929. However, there were relatively few new investments, about 7.5 million persons were unemployed, and nearly 4.5 million families were still living on relief. The recovery was not maintained, and from September, 1937, until June, 1938, there was a sharp recession, during which unemployment increased by about 4 million. The autumn of 1938 brought an improvement which, however, was not fully maintained through 1939.

The working class—that part of it, at least, that was fortunate enough to retain employment in private industry—made definite gains under the New Deal. The average weekly wage for factory workers rose from $17.57 in 1933 to $25.14 in 1937. Prices remained somewhat lower than before the depression, so that by 1937 the real earnings of the average employed worker were nearly 10 per cent greater than they had been in 1929. Hours of labor in manufacturing decreased from an average of 37.9 a week in 1933 to 34.5 in 1934, chiefly as a result of the NRA; after the invalidation of the NRA they rose to 38.6 in 1937, but they remained considerably lower than before the depression. These figures seemed to support the claim of business leaders that recovery was impeded by high labor costs. Defenders of the New Deal pointed out, however, that there had been a considerable increase in the productivity of labor, chiefly as a result of new mechanical devices; fewer hours of labor were needed to produce the same quantity of goods. In 1939 industrial production was 12 per cent less than in 1929, but the total wages paid to factory workers were 17 per cent less.

Between 1932 and 1937 farm prices rose by 86 per cent, and the cash income of farmers increased from $4.6 billion to nearly $9 billion. Their real income in 1937, in terms of price levels, was about the same as in 1929. This was a result partly of the AAA and partly of the droughts of 1934 and 1936. After 1937, farm prices and incomes decreased as a result of overproduction after the voiding of the first AAA. In 1939 farm prices were 23 per cent lower than in 1937, and the cash income of farmers was $8.5 billion. Some progress had been made in reducing farm indebtedness: the total mortgage debt decreased from $9.2 billion in 1930 to $7 billion in 1937. In spite of a number of foreclosures, the number of owner farmers increased from 3.56 million in 1930 to 3.89 million in 1935, and the percentage whose farms were mortgaged decreased from 42.3 to 39.6 per cent. The growth of the ratio of tenancy was at least temporarily checked; while owner farmers increased by 9.3 per cent, the number of tenant farmers increased from 2.66 million to 2.86 million—a rise of only 7.5 per cent. But the problems presented by the tenant farmers and sharecroppers had been scarcely touched.

The most conspicuous feature of economic development in the 1930's was, however, the lack of business expansion and the consequent stagnation of the capital goods industries. New issues of stocks and bonds for productive investment, which had averaged about $5 billion a year throughout the 1920's, amounted to only $1.23 billion in 1937, $872 million in 1938, and $371 million in 1939. The function of borrowing capital and putting it back into circulation by investment, which had been performed by private business before 1929, was now being performed by the federal government. The American people still had many needs which could not be satisfied by means of the existing industrial equipment; in the fields of power production, housing, shipping, and railroad facilities, for example, there was room for great expansion. But private capital did not enter these fields in sufficient quantities.

The growth of mechanization, moreover, was increasing the maladjustments of the economic system. Industry needed a decreasing number of workers to produce the same amount of wealth and to pay the same quantity of dividends. Production in the 1930's was always lower than it had been in 1929; but even a return to the 1929 level of production would not have meant a return to the 1929 level of employment, except insofar as the growth of productivity was compensated by the decrease in hours of labor. Moreover, it would have left unemployed the millions of new workers who had been added to the adult population since that date.

A significant example of the decrease in the labor needs of industry was afforded by the record of American Telephone and Telegraph. Between 1929 and 1935 this corporation, by reducing the number of its employees from 454,000 to 269,000, cut its wage bill by $139 million. This reduction was chiefly due to an increased use of the dial system and to an increase in the work required of each operator from 134.6 units an

THE NEW DEAL, III (1937–1939)

hour to 173 units an hour. Use of the telephone by the general public decreased during the depression but rose after 1933, and by 1937 it had exceeded 1929 levels. During the same period the corporation continued to pay $9 dividends on its stock, and because of an expansion in its capital equipment, total dividend payments rose from $116 million in 1929 to $168 million in 1935. The gross revenues of the corporation decreased, but not to the same degree as the decrease in its wage bill. AT&T was a well-managed corporation, and in improving its equipment and putting the interests of its stockholders above all other considerations the managers of the corporation were only doing their duty.

In a healthy economic system the corporation's decreased need for labor would have been regarded as a sign of economic progress; in an expanding capitalism its dismissed workers would have found other jobs where they were more needed, and the increase in its dividends would have provided additional capital for new investments. In a period of economic contraction, however, such policies had a different effect. By performing honestly their functions as custodians of the stockholders' money, the managers of AT&T were extending unemployment, diminishing mass purchasing power, and increasing that proportion of the total national income which went to the rentier class. Nor were the policies of AT&T unique; they were to a greater or less degree the policies generally pursued by American corporate business.

Enemies of the New Deal declared that recovery had really begun in the summer of 1932, that the New Deal had impeded rather than assisted it, and that the lack of new investments and the recession of 1937–38 were caused by New Deal legislation which interfered with business, gave too many privileges to labor, and destroyed confidence. The New Dealers, on the other hand, argued that the continuance of the depression was due chiefly to the high prices charged by the big corporations and to the lack of sufficient purchasing power among the mass of the people. They maintained that the government was responsible for such recovery as had occurred and that the remedy for the nation's economic maladjustments was not to decrease the economic activities of the government but to extend them and make them more effective. The actual economic consequences of the various New Deal experiments cannot be calculated with any accuracy. The only fact which seems to be indisputable is that recovery was dependent upon large-scale government spending, and that when—as in 1937—the government began to economize there was an

130   THE ERA OF F.D.R., 1933–1945

immediate slump. Few people, including Roosevelt himself, however, maintained that heavy government borrowing and spending should become a permanent policy.

American participation in World War II ended these unresolved problems, at least for the time being. Large-scale armament manufacturing led to an industrial boom, and with the growth of America's armed forces and the expansion of munitions and aviation factories unemployment virtually disappeared. Faced with a struggle for national survival, the government forgot its inhibitions about increasing the national debt, and spent money in whatever amounts were needed to finance the war program. The results seemed to justify the Keynesian argument for deficit spending. The increase in the national debt, which had risen by 1945 to the astronomical figure of $247 billion, seemed to present no serious economic difficulties, and during the war years production expanded so enormously that in spite of the vast quantities of goods devoted to destructive purposes, average civilian living standards actually grew higher. Perhaps the New Deal had failed to restore full prosperity not because its methods had been wrong but because they had been applied too timidly.

Suggested Readings

The literature on F.D.R.'s fight with the Supreme Court is large. A popularly written general survey of the Court by a Yale University law professor whose thesis is to show that the judges have been "powerful, irresponsibe and human" is Fred Rodell, *Nine Men: A Political History of the Supreme Court from 1790 to 1955* (New York, 1955). Covering a shorter period of time and emphasizing the issues involved in the twin questions of "judicial review" and "judicial self-interest" is the study by Alpheus Thomas Mason, *The Supreme Court from Taft to Warren* (Baton Rouge, La., 1958). The same author and William M. Beaney discuss various constitutional law issues historically in *The Supreme Court in a Free Society* (Englewood Cliffs, N.J., 1959). Two other useful interpretative accounts of various aspects of the Supreme Court's role in American life are Dean Alfange, *The Supreme Court and the National Will* (Garden City, N.Y., 1937) and Beryl H. Levy, *Our Constitution: Tool or Testament?* (New York, 1941); the latter tries to appraise the effect of the personal conviction of the judges upon their legal opinions. The history of the Court since F.D.R.'s "war" upon it is well told in Bernard Schwartz, *The Supreme Court: Constitutional Revolution in Retrospect* (New York, 1957), but see also C. Herman Pritchett, *The Roosevelt Court: A Study in Judicial*

THE NEW DEAL, III (1937–1939)

Politics and Values, 1937–1947 (New York, 1948) and Wesley McCune, *Nine Young Men* (New York, 1947).

A convenient place to begin for older works on F.D.R.'s fight with the Court is Florence S. Hellman, comp., *The Supreme Court Issue* (Washington, D.C., 1938). The events leading to the Court struggle are detailed by a later justice of the high tribunal in Robert H. Jackson, *The Struggle for Judicial Supremacy* (New York, 1941). Louis B. Boudin, *Government by Judiciary* (2 vols., New York, 1932) is of interest because many of its criticisms of the Supreme Court were later adopted by those who defended Roosevelt's proposal to reform it. Robert K. Carr, *The Supreme Court and Judicial Review* (New York, 1942) is excellent on this subject.

The details of the "battle" itself are expertly analyzed in three books by Edward S. Corwin, *The Twilight of the Supreme Court* (New Haven, Conn., 1937); *Court over Constitution* (Princeton, N.J., 1938); and *Constitutional Revolution Ltd.* (Claremont, Calif., 1941), but see also the more popular account by Joseph Alsop and Turner Catledge, *The 168 Days* (Garden City, N.Y., 1938). The case against the Court is presented forcefully by Isidor F. Stone, *The Court Disposes* (New York, 1937), while Merlo J. Pusey, *The Supreme Court Crisis* (New York, 1937) is an equally strong indictment of F.D.R.'s plan. The following are also opposed to the President's scheme: Douglas W. Johnson, *The Assault on the Supreme Court* (New York [1937]); Walter Lippmann, *The Supreme Court: Independent or Controlled?* (New York, 1937); and David Lawrence, *Supreme Court or Political Puppets?* (New York, 1936). See also such other contemporary works as Irving Brant, *Storm over the Constitution* (New York, 1937); Morris L. Ernst, *The Ultimate Power* (Garden City, N.Y., 1937); and the convenient compilation of pieces on the various issues involved in William R. Barnes and Arthur W. Littlefield, eds., *The Supreme Court Issue and the Constitution* (New York, 1937). Osmond K. Fraenkel, *The Supreme Court and Civil Liberties* (rev. ed., New York [1960]) contains some useful information. A brief survey of the entire issue is presented by Merlo J. Pusey, "F.D.R. *vs.* the Supreme Court," *American Heritage*, IX (April 1958), 24–27 and 105–7.

Associate Justice Owen J. Roberts' memorandum, explaining his position on the minimum wage decision which played an important role in the Court fight, was published posthumously in Felix Frankfurter's article, "Mr. Justice Roberts," *University of Pennsylvania Law Review*, CIV (December 1955), 311–17. See also Owen J. Roberts, *The Court and the Constitution* (Cambridge, Mass., 1951).

For biographical data on the justices, consult Cortez Ewing, *The Judges of the Supreme Court, 1789–1937: A Study of Their Qualifications* (Minneapolis, 1937), which is largely a statistical compilation of facts on the lives of the men who have sat on the high bench. On the men whom Roosevelt "attacked," see Drew Pearson and Robert S. Allen, *The Nine Old Men* (Garden City, N.Y., 1936). Other important biographies include the very fine one by Alpheus Thomas Mason, *Brandeis: A Free Man's Life* (New York, 1946) and the same author's *Harlan Fiske Stone: Pillar of the Law* (New York, 1956), which is

132 THE ERA OF F.D.R., 1933–1945

scholarly and especially detailed on the years when Stone was on the Court. Samuel J. Konefsky, *Chief Justice Stone and the Supreme Court* (New York, 1945) is primarily concerned with analyzing Stone's constitutional ideas and his opinions on the bench. Joseph P. Pollard's *Mr. Justice Cardozo: A Liberal Mind in Action* (New York, 1935) is more an analysis of Cardozo's legal thought than a formal biography. On two other members of the Court, consult Joel F. Paschel, *Mr. Justice Sutherland* (Princeton, N.J., 1951) and John P. Frank, *Mr. Justice Black: The Man and His Opinion* (New York, 1949). The authorized biography of Roosevelt's Chief Justice during the crisis is the comprehensive and highly competent one by Merlo J. Pusey, *Charles Evans Hughes* (2 vols., New York, 1951), but see also the brief sketch by Dexter Perkins, *Charles Evans Hughes and American Democratic Statesmanship* (Boston [1956]), and Samuel Hendel, *Charles Evans Hughes and the Supreme Court* (New York, 1951). In no way directly concerned with the Court fight, but useful in revealing some of Hughes's thinking, is his own *The Supreme Court* (Garden City, N.Y., 1927). On Justice Frankfurter, consult his own *Of Law and Men* (New York, 1956) and his revealing comments upon his pre-Supreme Court career in Felix Frankfurter and Harlan B. Phillips, *Felix Frankfurter Reminisces* (New York [1960]).

On the public debt, see the general work by H. L. Lutz, *Public Finance* (4th ed., New York [1947]); Arthur E. Burns and Donald S. Watson, *Government Spending and Economic Expansion* (Washington, D.C., 1940); Jasper V. Garland, *Government Spending and Economic Recovery* (New York, 1938), which is good as an example of contemporary thinking; and Harold G. Moulton, *The New Philosophy of the Public Debt* (Washington, D.C., 1943), which is critical of Keynesian deficit spending.

4

American Foreign Policy and the Coming of World War II, 1933-1941

PRESIDENT ROOSEVELT and his advisers were as actively interested in the maintenance of peace abroad as they were in the restoration of prosperity at home. But since Roosevelt's belief in the need for a vigorous foreign policy was not reciprocated by Congress or by American public opinion, the New Deal administration was compelled to adopt a much more passive attitude toward world problems than its leaders would have preferred.

The international order established by the Treaty of Versailles had begun to break up in 1931 when Japan seized Manchuria and the League of Nations failed to give protection to China. In 1933 the Nazis set up a dictatorship in Germany and began to build armaments in order to avenge the defeat of their country in World War I and ultimately to achieve world domination. International peace and security during the 1930's were threatened by three aggressive and militaristic powers—Germany, Italy, and Japan—which were intent upon altering the world balance of power to their advantage and were contemptuous of treaty obligations and of the rights of weaker nations. In response to this challenge the governments of the two leading European democracies, Great Britain and France, both of which possessed large colonial empires coveted by the aggressor powers, failed to maintain their initial superiority in armaments or to cooperate effectively in implementing policies designed to curb the ambitions of the three militaristic states. Also, Britain and France refused, until too late, to rally the small nations in an effective program of collective security, and for a long time tolerated aggression as long as it was not directed against their own possessions. The weakness of the democracies was due partly to pacifistic sentiment, similar to that which prevailed in the United States, partly to concentration on domestic programs aimed to bring about recovery from the depression and to provide needed internal reforms, and partly to sympathy for fascism among the wealthier and more conservative classes, who looked upon Germany and Italy as lesser threats to their social and economic order than Communist Russia.

ISOLATION OR INTERVENTION?

In the decade before Pearl Harbor, opinion in the United States was sharply divided between isolationism and interventionism. The isolationists included many industrialists and farmers whose markets were at home; members of various ethnic minority groups, such as the Irish, Germans, and Italians, all of whom, for one reason or another, were anti-British; and those liberals who believed chiefly in avoidance of war. The interventionists or internationalists included, among others, certain economic groups, such as the cotton planters of the South and the bankers and exporters of New York, who were interested in foreign trade, and those liberals who believed that fascism was a menace to democracy everywhere.

The isolationists argued that since the United States was safely separated from the militarism of Europe and Asia by two great oceans, it had no reason to fear attack. This geographical contention was strengthened by the isolationists' appeals to tradition, especially their claim that America's peace and prosperity in the past were the result of its refusal to meddle in the sordid affairs of the Old World. Disillusionment with the results of American participation in World War I provided the isolationists with another important argument. Since, as the Treaty of Versailles had proved, the United States could not end the perpetual cycle of wars and rivalries in Europe, it would be foolish for the United States to become entangled in them for a second time. Moreover, many businessmen argued that it was World War I, with its economic losses and dislocations, which had caused the great depression.[1] American intervention in Europe meant, in practice, American support for British and French imperialism, which differed from German and Italian imperialism only in being satiated and hence passive but which was not intrinsically nobler. The chief responsibility of Americans was to build democracy and preserve freedom at home, saving the rest of the world by their example rather than by meddling in Europe. Many of the isolationists believed that democracy and freedom would be destroyed in the United States if America became involved in war. Businessmen, for example, were afraid of the economic "regimentation" which would accompany war. The isolationists concluded that the correct American foreign policy was to maintain the Monroe Doctrine and to exclude European political influences from any part of the Western Hemisphere, northern or southern. The weakness of the isolationist argument was that it overlooked the dangers to American security and democracy which would be presented by a Nazi victory over Great Britain and France. The United States navy was not strong enough to control both the Atlantic and the Pacific at the same time; and since the Washington Conference, by a tacit agreement with Great Britain, the American navy had been concentrated in the Pacific while the British policed the Atlantic. Destruction of the British fleet might be followed by a combined Japanese-Nazi attack on the Western Hemisphere, and the United States would then be compelled in self-defense to become a militaristic power. The major but unconscious premise of the isolationists was that British sea power would never be crushed by Nazi Germany.

The interventionists, on the other hand, maintained that Great Britain and France were the first line of defense of the American hemisphere against fascism and the United States should therefore support them. Fascism was necessarily hostile to all democracy everywhere, and if it were triumphant in Europe, it would immediately proceed—partly by open attack and partly by subsidizing American fascistic movements—to undermine democracy in the United States. Thus, since the United States could not divorce itself politically, economically, or ideologically from the remainder of the world, it should in its own interests act to

[1] Roland N. Stromberg, "American Business and the Approach of War, 1935–1941," *The Journal of Economic History*, XIII (Winter 1953), 58–78.

136 THE ERA OF F.D.R., 1933-1945

promote international peace, security, the rule of law, and adherence to treaty obligations. The weakness of the interventionist position was that prior to 1939 the two European powers with whom the interventionists proposed to cooperate—Great Britain and France—displayed no particular wish to check fascist aggression and, because of their own domestic and imperial problems, had little interest in supporting the security of small nations or the enforcement of treaties. The result was, as we have already seen, that American isolationists and British conservatives continued to play into each others' hands. While the isolationists pointed to the misdeeds of the British as an argument against American intervention, the British declared that they could not adopt a policy of collective security as long as America remained isolated.

The preferences of the Roosevelt administration were definitely for intervention. Roosevelt's personal attitude underwent some variations, but his general belief was that fascist aggression represented a danger which Americans could not safely overlook and that the United States, as the strongest and richest country in the world, had international responsibilities and obligations to fulfill. The viewpoint of Secretary of State Cordell Hull was even more strongly internationalist. Hull believed that the United States should use its influence on behalf of international law and the fulfillment of treaties. His strongest conviction was that trade barriers and economic nationalism constituted the chief cause both of economic depression and of war, and that the United States could most usefully promote world peace and prosperity by lowering tariffs and increasing world trade. In the pursuit of these objectives Hull showed a sincerity and a persistence which won the admiration even of those who disagreed with him.

Prior to 1940, however, American public opinion did not allow Roosevelt and Hull to take any very vigorous action in support of their policies. The arguments of the isolationists were strengthened by the general distaste of the American people for foreign adventures and entanglements and by their conviction that they could, if they chose, remain aloof from the next European war. Roosevelt and Hull were therefore unable to do much more than make speeches denouncing aggressors. American foreign policy consisted of little except a series of moral gestures which did not strengthen the hand of the democracies in their negotiations with the totalitarian powers but which caused some of the people of Britain and France to put too great a trust in American assistance in the event of war. Since these gestures neither reflected American strength nor were implemented by actions, they had no visible effect in checking the fascist nations.

THE HULL TRADE TREATIES

At the outset of his administration, Roosevelt appeared to be in favor of a program of economic nationalism, as his action during the debates of the London Economic Conference of June and July, 1933, indicated. F.D.R.'s "bombshell" message, which for all practical purposes scuttled the meeting, was loudly applauded by the isolationists and sincerely deplored by the interventionists. Three years later, however, the United States joined Great Britain and France in the stabilization of their respective currencies.

Cordell Hull refused to accept defeat, and he subsequently succeeded in winning Roosevelt's support for his ideals and in checking those individuals in the administration who opposed them. On June 12, 1934, Congress passed the Trade Agreements Act. The power to make tariff agreements was delegated to the Executive for three years. The act was renewed for another three years in 1937 and every three years thereafter until it was revised in 1951. Tariffs might be lowered as much as 50 per cent, although no changes might be made in the free list. Under this plan tariff schedules were worked out by government committees which heard any complaints that might come from business interests and then made recommendations to the Secretary of State. Tariff making was thus removed from Congress, which, because of the influence of pressure groups and the practice of logrolling, had always found it easier to raise schedules than to lower them. Henceforth, tariff rates were to be entrusted to experts.

By 1940 Hull had made treaties with twenty different countries, covering 55 per cent of America's export trade and 15 per cent of its import trade. The precise effect of the treaties was difficult to estimate. American exports to treaty countries increased by 61 per cent, while exports to nontreaty countries increased by only 37 per cent. On the other hand, imports from treaty countries rose by 35 per cent, and imports from nontreaty countries rose by 37 per cent. The most important effects of the treaties were probably psychological rather than economic; they removed much of the resentment which had been caused by the Smoot-Hawley Tariff and promoted friendly relations, especially with the

138 THE ERA OF F.D.R., 1933-1945

Latin American countries. The trend toward economic nationalism throughout the world was too strong for one country to stop it, however, and foreign trade in the 1930's remained much smaller than in the 1920's. In 1937, the year of greatest activity, American exports had a value of $3.34 billion, as contrasted with $5.24 billion in 1929, and imports had a value of $3.08 billion as contrasted with $4.39 billion in 1929. Moreover, there were few new foreign investments by Americans, and after 1935 capital tended to flow into the United States from abroad. European investors felt that the United States was the safest place for their money. By 1938 America's credit balance on investments was only $3.8 billion.

LATIN AMERICA

Probably the most successful achievement of the Roosevelt-Hull foreign policy was to bring about more friendly relations with Latin America. All groups in the United States were united in regarding this as desirable, whatever opinion they might hold with reference to the problems of Europe.

The Hoover administration had disclaimed any right on the part of the United States to intervene in the internal affairs of the Latin American countries. This attitude was reiterated by Roosevelt in his first inaugural address, when he declared, "In the field of world policy I would dedicate this Nation to the policy of the good neighbor—the neighbor who resolutely respects himself, and because he does so, respects the rights of others—the neighbor who respects his obligations and respects the sanctity of his agreements in and with a world of neighbors." In a speech delivered on December 28, 1933, Roosevelt declared that "the definite policy of the United States from now on is one opposed to armed intervention. The maintenance of constitutional government in other Nations is not a sacred obligation devolving upon the United States. The maintenance of law and the orderly processes of government in this hemisphere is the concern of each individual Nation within its own borders first of all. It is only if and when the failure of orderly processes of government affects the other Nations of the continent that it becomes their concern; and the point to stress is that in such event it becomes the joint concern of a whole continent in which we are all neighbors." In other words, the defense of the Monroe Doctrine was no longer to be

THE COMING OF WORLD WAR II 139

the responsibility of the United States alone; the doctrine was to become the joint policy of all the nations of the hemisphere, all of whom were to be regarded as equals in a common opposition to European encroachments.

In accordance with this policy American marines were withdrawn from Haiti in August, 1934; and in May of the same year the Platt Amendment, under which the United States enjoyed the right to intervene in Cuba, was repealed. In August, 1933, there had been a revolution in Cuba, due chiefly to bad economic conditions caused by American tariff policy, a fall in the price of sugar, and the necessity to pay interest on the loans made by American bankers. President Gerardo Machado was overthrown and was succeeded first by Grau San Martín and subsequently by a regime in which the dominant influence was exercised by an army leader, Fulgencio Batista. United States pressure was regarded as responsible for the rapid fall of Grau San Martín, who was somewhat radical, and for the consolidation of the more conservative Batista regime. On the other hand, the United States used its influence to try to persuade Batista to conform to democratic processes and to inaugurate social reforms; and Cuban economic conditions were improved by a trade treaty which reduced the American duty on sugar and by the Jones-Costigan Sugar Control Act which sought to stabilize the island's production by U. S. sugar purchases. Latin America was favorably impressed, moreover, by the fact that no American troops were landed in Cuba during the revolution. The Roosevelt administration also worked to improve relations with Panama, which were sorely strained by the limitations imposed on Panamanian sovereignty in the Hay–Bunau Varilla Treaty of 1903. In October, 1933, Panama's president, Harmodio Arías, visited Washington for discussions with Roosevelt, after which the two men issued a statement that paved the way for negotiating a new and more liberal treaty. The treaty was signed in 1936, and went into effect in 1939 when the United States Senate ratified it. One of the reasons the Senate delayed ratification was the insistence of American military and naval officials upon adequate safeguards that Panama would not interfere with United States defense policies in times of emergency or war.

The Good Neighbor Policy encountered its greatest difficulties in Mexico. The Mexican revolutionary movement, which had been checked since 1929, resumed its progress in 1934, when Lázaro Cárdenas was elected president. Cárdenas distributed land on a large scale to the peasants and reduced the estates of the big landowners, among whom were some Americans. He also supported the trade unions in their demand for a higher standard of living. In March, 1938, the foreign oil companies, both American and British, were expropriated after they had declared themselves unable to obey a government order to pay higher wages. While the Mexican government insisted that the companies deserved expropriation because they had refused to obey Mexican law, the oil interests replied that the wage increases would have ruined them and that the dispute about wages was merely an excuse, not a reason, for the expropriation.

The Mexican government stated that it was willing to pay the companies for their properties but that such payment should cover only what the companies had invested in equipment; the companies, on the other hand, claimed payment also for the oil, valuing their properties at $400 million. Moreover, the companies prevented Mexico from marketing its oil in Great Britain and the United States so that the Mexican government, although strongly opposed to fascism, was compelled to make contracts for the sale of oil with Germany, Italy, and Japan. Secretary Hull supported the claims of the companies to full compensation but did not condemn the expropriation itself. And in spite of considerable pressure from the oil interests and from American newspapers, he made no attempt to coerce the Mexican government. In 1940 the Sinclair Oil Company came to terms with Mexico and was paid the first installment of its compensation; and in 1941 and 1942, as the tide of Axis militarism swept across Europe and Asia, reemphasizing the need for hemispheric cooperation, the controversy was finally settled. In April, 1942, Mexico agreed to pay the oil companies $23,995,991,000 in addition to the earlier settlements it had reached with individual firms, as with Sinclair.

Roosevelt and Hull made their principal attempts to promote unity in the Western Hemisphere by continuing the Pan-American conferences, the first of which had been held in Washington, D.C., in October, 1889. At the seventh of these conferences, held at Montevideo in December, 1933, Secretary of State Hull, whom Roosevelt had asked to be chairman of the American delegation, warmly agreed to the conference's proposal that "No state has the right to intervene in the internal or external affairs of another." Official United States acceptance of the principle of nonintervention did much to bring about the "increasing understanding and accord" which was to be the touchstone of the Good Neighbor Policy. A special conference to discuss methods of preserving peace was held at Buenos Aires in December, 1936. Roosevelt visited the Buenos Aires

THE COMING OF WORLD WAR II 141

conference in person and declared that any non-American state seeking "to commit acts of aggression against us will find a Hemisphere wholly prepared to consult together for our mutual safety and our mutual good." But the attempts of the United States at Buenos Aires and at the Eighth Pan-American Conference held at Lima in December, 1938, to create a kind of American League of Nations, in which each state would have definite obligations to maintain collective security, were unsuccessful. At the Lima conference, however, a pact was signed for mutual consultation in case of danger; and in September, 1939, after the outbreak of the European war, a conference was held at Panama (October, 1939) at which plans were devised for keeping the war out of the Western Hemisphere.

The traditional hostility of Latin America to the United States and its traditional suspicion of Yankee imperialism were considerably reduced, but they by no means disappeared. The German and Italian governments engaged in vigorous campaigns to increase their trade with Latin America and to win sympathy and support. They were aided by the presence of considerable German and Italian populations in Brazil, Argentina, and elsewhere and by the fascist sympathies of many of the wealthier Latin Americans. In its official utterances the United States government found it wise to maintain the fiction that the Western Hemisphere was wholly dedicated to democracy, but in reality most of the Latin American governments were dictatorships. The Nazi government pushed its exports to Latin America by underselling its competitors and by using barter methods which compelled countries which sold to Germany to take German goods in exchange. Between 1933 and 1939 German trade with Latin America increased rapidly, chiefly at the expense of Great Britain. By 1940, it was obvious to many Americans that a Nazi victory in Europe would be followed by an even more vigorous German campaign to win political and economic control of South America.

The Roosevelt-Hull policies had, however, considerable success in counteracting this fascist penetration. In 1938 the United States government began to promote trade not only through the trade treaties but also through a government-owned Export-Import Bank, which made loans to Brazil and other Latin American countries. Between 1933 and 1938 the share of the United States in the import trade of Latin America increased from 29.2 per cent to 35.8 per cent. In 1937 Latin America bought 34.3 per cent of its imports from the United States, in contrast to 15.3 per cent from Germany, and sold 31.3 per cent of its exports to

142   THE ERA OF F.D.R., 1933–1945

the United States, in contrast to 8.7 per cent to Germany. The modesty and friendliness of Cordell Hull had made a most favorable impression upon Latin American diplomats, with the result that by 1940 the United States was certainly better liked by the Latin Americans than at any previous period.

THE FAR EAST, 1933–1940

In the Far East Japan continued its career of conquest in China, and talk of an eventual war between Japan and the United States grew more frequent. The most important American interest in the Far East was in the Dutch and British East Indies, from which the United States imported most of its rubber and its tin, and Japanese imperialists were now beginning to claim these islands as within the Japanese sphere of influence.

It was possibly on account of the aggressive policies of Japan that the Roosevelt administration decided to initiate diplomatic relations with Soviet Russia. This step was taken also in the hope of stimulating trade between the two countries. Maxim Litvinov, Soviet commissar for foreign affairs, came to Washington in November, 1933; and notes were exchanged in which the Soviet government pledged itself not to spread propaganda in the United States. No settlement was made about the debts which had been incurred by previous Russian governments and repudiated by the Bolsheviks, or about the claims to compensation of Americans who had owned properties in Russia which the Bolsheviks had confiscated.

The Philippines continued to be the Achilles heel of the American defense system. In the Jones Act of 1916, the United States had agreed to give the Filipinos independence as soon as they were capable of governing themselves. American opinion about withdrawal from the islands was divided, but by the early 1930's the depression strengthened the hand of those favoring immediate withdrawal—the traditional antiimperialists, the domestic sugar and cordage interests, and organized labor, which wanted to close the door to cheap Filipino labor. The combined pressure of these groups resulted in the passage, over President Hoover's veto, of the Hawes-Cutting Act in January, 1933. The Filipinos, resenting the motives which inspired the act, refused to accept it. Congress then passed, in March, 1934, the Tydings-McDuffie Act, which modified the provisions of the Hawes-Cutting bill referring to military and naval bases

THE COMING OF WORLD WAR II

and declared July 4, 1946, as the day of Filipino independence. During this transitional period the Philippines were to have a commonwealth government with a native chief executive, but the United States was to retain certain rights and obligations in the islands, and duties were gradually to be imposed on imports from the Philippines into the United States. Washington also agreed to relinquish its military bases in 1946 and to negotiate the question of its naval bases. Under this arrangement Manuel Quezon was elected the first president of the Philippines. Subsequently many of the Filipinos, alarmed by the power of Japan and by the prospect of exclusion from American markets, began to reconsider their desire for independence. Many Americans, on the other hand, realizing the difficulty of defending the Philippines in case of Japanese attack, felt that the United States should withdraw even sooner than 1946. Their fears proved justified, for on May 6, 1942, five months after the Japanese had attacked Pearl Harbor, the last American forces in the Philippines, those on Corregidor Island in Manila Bay, were forced to surrender to the Japanese.

With reference to the Japanese seizure of Manchuria, Roosevelt and Hull continued Stimson's nonrecognition policy. On the other hand, they stopped sending protests to Japan, and they endeavored to induce Great Britain, whose economic interests in China were far larger than those of the United States, to adopt a more vigorous policy. On July 7, 1937, after five years of relative peace, war again broke out between China and Japan. The Japanese undertook the conquest of large areas of central China, and the loss of life among both soldiers and the Chinese civilian population was enormous. Japan apparently proposed both to dominate the whole of China, thereby destroying whatever remained of the Open Door, and to deprive the Western nations of their economic privileges in the Far East. The American government took "parallel" action with Great Britain and with the League of Nations in protesting to Japan. Mere protests, however, were futile, and none of the Western Powers was able to take action. In November, 1937, representatives of nineteen nations, including the United States, met at Brussels to discuss the Far Eastern situation, but the conference adjourned without accomplishing anything. American citizens in China, of whom there were about 10,000, were urged by the State Department to leave, and warships were sent to protect them. On December 12 one of these warships, the gunboat *Panay*, and three American oil tankers were sunk by Japanese airplanes. The Japanese, however, quickly apologized and paid reparation. As the

144 THE ERA OF F.D.R., 1933-1945

war proceeded, American sympathies for China grew stronger. Under the neutrality legislation of 1937 the President was required to prohibit the export of munitions to countries which were at war, but Roosevelt did not apply the law to the war in China on the excuse that the war had never been officially declared. His real reason, however, appears to have been that an embargo on munitions would hurt China more than it would hurt Japan. Also, after 1937 the United States started sending Chiang Kai-shek small amounts of material assistance. At the same time, American protests to the Japanese government against its economic policies and its methods of waging war became increasingly stern. These diplomatic protests were soon followed by more direct indications of American displeasure at what the Japanese were doing in China. On July 1, 1938, the State Department informed 148 American firms manufacturing airplane parts that it "would with great regret issue any licenses authorizing exportation, direct or indirect, of any aircraft, aircraft armament, aircraft engines, aircraft parts, aircraft accessories, aerial bombs or torpedoes to countries the armed forces of which are making use of airplanes for attack upon civilian populations." Eighteen months later, on January 26, 1940, the United States government followed this "moral embargo" by refusing to renew the trade treaty of 1911 with Japan. American exporters, however, continued to ship to Japan large quantities of scrap iron and other materials for making munitions.

EUROPE, 1933-1940

At the outset of his administration Roosevelt made it plain that he was alarmed at the growth of aggressive policies and eager for the United States to use its influence on behalf of peace. In May, 1933, he sent a message in which he denounced aggression to the government of every nation in the world.

Meanwhile the general disarmament conference which had been convened at Geneva early in February, 1933, was still meeting; and Norman Davis, the financier and diplomat who represented the United States, promised that if a substantial degree of disarmament were achieved, the United States would pledge itself to do nothing which might interfere with the imposition of sanctions by the League of Nations to restrain an aggressor power. But because of the establishment of the Nazi dictatorship and Hitler's removal of Germany from membership in the League, it was now too late for any kind of disarmament, and the conference disbanded early in 1934 without having accomplished anything. In 1935 a naval conference met at London, as had been provided for in the naval treaty of 1930. Japan demanded naval equality with the United States, which the United States could not accept; and although in March, 1936, the United States, Great Britain, and France signed another naval treaty with one another, the conference could do nothing to prevent a new armaments race.

The isolationists were now becoming alarmed by the threat of another world war, and whereas Roosevelt believed that the United States should endeavor to prevent war, the primary concern of the isolationists was to ensure that when war came, the United States should stay out of it. In April, 1934, a Senate committee under Gerald P. Nye of North Dakota investigated the munitions industry, and paid special attention to its activities prior to April, 1917. Finding that bankers and munitions manufacturers had made large profits by supplying the Allies and that they had been generally in favor of American participation, the Nye Committee concluded, though without proving it, that this economic tie between the United States and the Allies had been one of the chief causes for the American entry into the war. The findings of the Nye Committee were strengthened by numbers of books and articles trying to show how America had been tricked or fooled into war in 1917, and denouncing the international bankers and the "merchants of death." Novels and moving pictures appeared which depicted the horrors of war and conveyed the impression that all wars were evil and that a country could avoid war by merely choosing not to fight.[2] Pacifistic sentiment grew rapidly, especially among the younger generation and in the colleges.

The Nye Committee and the isolationists argued that if the United States were to remain neutral in the next war, it should immediately adopt legislation that would prevent economic involvement. One such measure had already been taken in April, 1934, when Congress passed the Johnson Debt Default Act prohibiting the governments in default on their war debts from floating fresh loans in the United States. In August, 1935, Congress passed the first of a series of neutrality acts, according to which, when a war started, the President was to prohibit the export of munitions

---

[2] Examples of the more popular revisionist writings of the 1930's include Walter Millis, *The Road to War: America, 1914–1917* (Boston [1935]); Helmuth C. Engelbrecht and F. C. Hanighen, *Merchants of Death: A Study of the International Armaments Industry* (New York, 1934); and "Arms and Men," *Fortune*, IX (March 1934), 53 ff.

to belligerent countries, and he might also withhold protection from American citizens who traveled on ships belonging to the belligerents. This measure meant that the United States would have to abandon its long-held ideas on the economic and commercial rights of neutrals in wartime, principles which America had allegedly fought to guarantee in 1812 and 1917. The act was disliked by the administration, which would have preferred a measure allowing it to discriminate against an aggressor nation. F.D.R signed it with grave reservations, declaring that "the inflexible provisions [of this law] might drag us into war instead of keeping us out."

In October, 1936, when war started between Italy and Ethiopia, Roosevelt declared the Neutrality Act in force. Meanwhile the League of Nations, for the first and last time, attempted to maintain peace by the adoption of economic sanctions. The British conservative government was unwilling to use force to prevent Italy from conquering Ethiopia; but in the summer of 1935 British public opinion became aroused, and, in deference to the popular demand for action, the British government took the lead in condemning Italy. The sanctions voted by the League were mild, however, and did not cover any commodities which Italy bought from the United States. In particular, they did not include oil, the most vital of all the materials needed for modern warfare. Roosevelt and Hull gave a clear invitation to the League of Nations to adopt more rigorous sanctions by declaring, in their Neutrality Proclamation, that the United States government would give no protection to American citizens who traded with Italy. In other words, if the League powers chose to blockade Italy, the United States would not interfere. The State Department tried by moral pressure to prevent Americans from selling Italy oil and other raw materials needed for war. But since these materials were not covered by the League sanctions, American exporters saw no reason why they should obey this moral embargo, and Italian purchases of oil and metals from the United States increased by between 200 and 300 per cent.

It soon appeared that the British government was not in earnest in its support of sanctions. In November there was a general election in Great Britain, and the government, appealing for support on the basis of its foreign policy, was returned to power. This was followed in December by the announcement of the Hoare-Laval Pact, which revealed that the British and French were willing to allow Italy to absorb a large part of Ethiopia. The following spring, after Italy had completed its conquest, the sanctions were abandoned. The British declared that they would have asked the League to adopt more effective sanctions if they had been assured of American cooperation. Most Americans, on the other hand, believed that the British government had never been genuinely desirous of the defeat of Italy.

In July, 1936, civil war began in Spain. The Spanish democratic government, which was composed of a Popular Front coalition of liberals, Socialists, and Communists, was attacked by conservative elements under the leadership of General Francisco Franco, who planned to establish a dictatorship with the assistance of the Italian and German governments. The British and French governments then adopted a "nonintervention" program, which was supposed to prevent either of the two factions from receiving foreign assistance. Actually, however, "nonintervention" helped the rebels, who continued to receive troops and munitions from Italy and Germany, while the government could obtain only some very meager assistance from the Soviet Union.

In February, 1936, the United States Neutrality Act had been extended to May 1, 1937, and amended to prohibit the granting of loans and credits to belligerents. And in January, 1937, at the request of the administration, which wished to cooperate in the "nonintervention" program, Congress passed a joint resolution extending its neutrality legislation to cover civil as well as international war. Shipments of munitions to Spain were then embargoed. This measure was vigorously condemned by liberals, who pointed out that the Spanish government, both by international law and by a treaty signed in 1902, had a legal right to buy munitions from the United States. They also held that by participating in the Anglo-French "nonintervention" policy, the United States was, in practice, helping fascism. Isolationists argued that this was a fresh proof of the duplicity of the British and of the dangers of Anglo-American cooperation.

After two years of debate about the neutrality laws of 1935 and 1936, Congress passed another one on May 1, 1937, which provided that upon the outbreak of a war the President was to prohibit the sale of munitions to belligerents, the sale of securities in the United States by belligerents, and travel by Americans on belligerent-owned ships. The President might also, at his discretion, enforce "cash and carry" rules, by which belligerents purchasing other commodities from the United States would be required to pay cash for them and to transport them in their own ships. This act was a compromise which pleased neither the interventionists nor the isolationists. The administration wanted more power to use American

148 THE ERA OF F.D.R., 1933-1945

influence to restrain aggression. The isolationists, on the other hand, distrusted Roosevelt and felt that more stringent measures were required to keep America neutral.

One such proposal, which attracted much attention and was very popular in the mid-1930's, was the so-called "peace amendment" sponsored by a Democratic representative from Indiana, Louis Ludlow. First introduced into the House in 1935 and again in February, 1937, the Ludlow resolution called for a constitutional amendment limiting the power of Congress to declare war by requiring that a majority of the voters express themselves in "a nation-wide referendum" before the United States could go to war. Only "in the event of the invasion of the United States or its territorial possessions" could the Congress declare war without first going to the electorate for its approval. The idea of letting those "who would have to go to a foreign land to do the fighting and the dying . . . decide whether the cause is worth the sacrifice," as one of the commentators supporting the Ludlow resolution phrased it, gained considerable support, and the popularity of the proposal among large segments of the population caused serious concern to the administration.[3] In October, 1937, for example, 73 per cent of the people polled answered affirmatively the question, "In order to declare war, should Congress be required to obtain the approval of the people by means of a national vote?"[4] In January, 1938, a few days before the House of Representatives was to vote on the Ludlow proposal, Roosevelt wrote a letter to Speaker William B. Bankhead urging the resolution's defeat. "Such an amendment to the Constitution," F.D.R. declared, "would cripple any President in his conduct of our foreign relations, and it would encourage other nations to believe that they could violate American rights with impunity." Two days later, Secretary Hull, in a letter to the chairman of the House Committee on Foreign Affairs, stated that the Ludlow proposal "would most seriously handicap the Government in the conduct of our foreign affairs generally, and would thus impair disastrously its ability to safeguard the peace of the American people." The administration succeeded in defeating the "peace amendment," but only by a narrow margin, the vote in the House of Representatives being 209 to 188.

Meanwhile international conditions were steadily degenerating, and a

[3] William F. Bigelow, "The Fight Goes On," *Good Housekeeping*, CVI (March 1938), 4.
[4] "American Institute of Public Opinion—Surveys, 1938-1939," *Public Opinion Quarterly*, III (October 1939), 581-607.

THE COMING OF WORLD WAR II 149

second world war seemed to be rapidly approaching. On October 5, 1937, in a speech at Chicago, Roosevelt declared that 90 per cent of the peoples of the world wanted peace and that only 10 per cent were warmongers, and he called for concerted action by the peace-loving powers to quarantine the aggressors. The immediate occasion for this declaration was the outbreak of the war in China. The general reaction to the President's speech was hostile, and when it became obvious that the American people were unwilling to support Roosevelt in taking action to prevent aggression, the European democracies ignored Roosevelt's proposal. After the failure of the Chicago speech, Roosevelt drew the conclusion that since any hope of maintaining security by collective action must be abandoned, the United States must arm in self-defense. In January, 1938, therefore, he asked Congress to pass a billion-dollar naval expansion program to provide the United States with a "two-ocean" navy, and later in the year he recommended an enlargement of the air force to 6,000 planes. There was considerable opposition to these proposals, most of the opponents being—somewhat paradoxically—isolationists who had refused to support collective security; and Congress did not pass the Naval Expansion bill until May.

In August, 1938, in a speech at Queen's University in Kingston, Ontario, Roosevelt declared that the obligations of the United States under the Monroe Doctrine included the defense of Canada against foreign aggression. "I give to you assurance," he said, "that the people of the United States will not stand idly by if domination of Canadian soil is threatened by any other Empire." The next month, on September 27, during the Czechoslovakian crisis, Roosevelt sent notes to Germany and Italy urging a settlement by negotiation. The crisis ended with the Munich conference, at which Great Britain and France agreed to German annexation of a large part of Czechoslovakia. In November came violent anti-Semitic persecutions in Germany. Roosevelt protested to the Nazi government and recalled the American ambassador. In January, 1939, it became known that Roosevelt had approved of the sale of American-built airplanes to Great Britain and France. When the isolationists denounced this action, Roosevelt held a secret conference with a number of congressmen at which he apparently explained that Great Britain and France were America's first line of defense. When, however, the press announced this explanation, such widespread hostility was aroused that Roosevelt denied having made the statement. In March, Germany annexed what was left of Czechoslovakia, and in April Italy absorbed Albania. Roosevelt once again sent messages to the German and Italian governments denouncing aggression.

It cannot be said that American diplomacy was of any avail in postponing the advent of war. The sympathies of a large proportion of the American people were against fascism, but as long as they were unwilling to take any effective action against aggressors, the European dictators knew that they could safely ignore Roosevelt's messages and speeches. Nor were relations between the people of the United States and those of the European democracies particularly friendly. While the British and French felt that the United States ought to promise them assistance in case of war, the Americans deplored the Anglo-French policy of surrender which had culminated at Munich. If—in the words of the title of a book by an American author—many Englishmen expected every American to do his duty, many Americans would have been willing to defend the independence of Czechoslovakia to the last drop of English and French blood.

On March 31, 1939, the British and French governments, abandoning the policy of surrender, promised to defend Poland against Nazi attack. Believing that war was imminent, Roosevelt and Hull asked Congress to alter the neutrality legislation to make greater American assistance to the Allies possible, hoping that such a measure would serve as a warning to Germany. The isolationist leaders in the Senate declared, however, that war was improbable; and despite the combined efforts of Roosevelt and Hull to convince them that all the facts indicated otherwise, Congress refused to change the neutrality laws before adjourning on August 5.

Less than three weeks later, on August 23, the Nazis concluded a nonaggression pact with the Soviet Union, thus safeguarding Germany's eastern frontier. On August 24, Roosevelt cabled the heads of the German, Italian, and Polish governments with more appeals for peace. A week later, on September 1, 1939, the German army invaded Poland, and on September 3 Great Britain and France declared war on Germany. In a radio address that evening, Roosevelt asked the American people to realize "a simple but unalterable fact" of international affairs: "When peace has been broken anywhere [the] peace of all countries everywhere is in danger." At the same time he reassured the people by saying, "I hope the United States will keep out of this war. I believe that it will. And I give you assurances that every effort of your Government will be directed toward that end." Two days later the United States declared its neutrality, and on September 21 Roosevelt called the Congress into special session and asked it to make the amendments in the neutrality laws which it had been unwilling to make in the spring. Congress debated the question for six weeks, but finally agreed, in the Neutrality Act of November 4, 1939, to repeal the embargo on munitions and thus make it possible for the Allies to purchase airplanes and guns in the United States. They were to be sold under cash and carry rules, the Allies paying for them immediately and transporting them in their own ships. As an additional safeguard against American involvement, no American ships were to be allowed to enter the European combat zone.

The Nazis completed their conquest of Poland in seventeen days, after which there was a lull in the war until the following spring. Most Americans hoped that Germany would be defeated, but since the Allies did not appear to be in any need of immediate assistance, scarcely anybody in the United States advocated American participation. The British, moreover, had once again declared a blockade of Germany, and as in the previous war, the British blockade regulations caused some irritation in the United States. Meanwhile American exporters were shipping considerable quantities of metal to Italy and the Soviet Union, some of which was probably resold to Germany.

The American feeling of security abruptly ended in the spring of 1940. On March 29, 1940, Roosevelt announced that information he had just received from Under Secretary of State Sumner Welles, who had recently returned from a six-week fact-finding trip to Europe, indicated that the outlook for an early peace was "scant." Eleven days later, on April 9, the Nazis suddenly invaded Denmark and Norway; and on May 10 the German army, violating neutral rights even more brutally than in 1914, smashed through Holland and Belgium and inflicted crushing defeats upon the Allied armies in Flanders. A complete Nazi victory within a few months now appeared to be not at all impossible. The change in American sentiment was immediate and cataclysmic.

The American people suddenly became aware that their own interests were much more deeply involved in the European conflict than they had realized, and that if Germany seized the British fleet the United States itself would be confronted by the gravest peril in the whole of its history. Although even at this time relatively few persons demanded any immediate entry into the war, only a small minority of the population continued to advocate the kind of isolationism that had prevailed since the repudiation of the League of Nations. Earlier, on January 3, 1940, in his annual message, Roosevelt had asked the Congress to spend $1.8 billion for national defense, and now, on May 16, he appeared before Congress in person to ask for an additional $1.18 billion for the armed services and to recommend expansion of the American aviation industry to the point where it could construct 50,000 planes a year. With scarcely a dissenting voice, Congress voted billions of dollars for the army, the navy, and the air force, and the United States set about the task of arming itself with as much speed as possible. Whatever achievements or catastrophies the future might hold, the events of May, 1940, certainly marked a decisive turning point in both the internal and the external history of the American people.

THE ELECTION OF 1940

After the German victories in the spring of 1940 the people of the United States realized that they must now concentrate their energies on the tasks of national defense, and a substantial majority of them believed that they should also give support to the nations which were fighting aggression in Europe and Asia. The first steps toward mobilizing the nation's resources, creating effective armed forces, and sending aid to Great Britain were taken during the summer of 1940. A National Defense Research Committee headed by Dr. Vannevar Bush, the president of the Carnegie Institution, was created on June 15 under the White House Office for Emergency Management. The chief function of this committee was to correlate the scientific research of the nation and to promote further study "on the instrumentalities, methods and materials of modern warfare." To safeguard the country against subversion and to equip the federal government to control the aliens within its borders, Roosevelt signed the Smith Alien Registration Act on June 29, requiring all noncitizens to register their addresses with the federal authorities. The full adoption of defense policies, however, had to be postponed until after the presidential election in November.

The result of the Republican convention, which met at Philadelphia on June 24, was an encouraging proof of the vitality of American democratic processes. The leading contenders for the GOP presidential nomination were District Attorney Thomas E. Dewey of New York City,

Senator Robert A. Taft of Ohio, Senator Charles L. McNary of Oregon, and Senator Arthur H. Vandenberg of Michigan. All of these men were inclined toward isolationism; none of them had shown any understanding of the revolutionary forces which were destroying democracy in Europe and carrying mankind into the greatest conflict in history; and not one of them commanded much popular enthusiasm or support.

Fortunately these were not the only available candidates. Many of the rank and file of the Republican party, demanding a more inspiring leader, had found one in Wendell Willkie, a native of Indiana and a former Democrat who had distinguished himself as an able corporation lawyer, first in Ohio and, after 1929, in New York City. In 1933 Willkie became president of the Commonwealth and Southern Corporation, a large public utility holding company. Though interested in public affairs and at one time active in Democratic party politics, Willkie had never held any political office. In spite of his Wall Street associations, he was a man of genuinely liberal convictions who was opposed to Roosevelt not because he failed to appreciate the need for reform but because he believed that the New Deal had been applied inefficiently and extravagantly and with too much bureaucratic regimentation; and in spite of his German descent and Indiana background, he was an outspoken advocate of aid to Great Britain. Moreover, he was refreshingly free from the timidity and insincerity which characterized so many of the nation's professional politicians. It became obvious early in the convention that whatever the Republican party bosses might want, the rank and file, as the cheering galleries in the convention hall indicated, wanted Willkie.

The GOP leaders were already in a turmoil from the fact that three days before the delegates assembled in Philadelphia, Roosevelt had appointed two of the party's most eminent figures, Henry L. Stimson and Frank Knox, to his cabinet as Secretary of War and Secretary of the Navy, respectively; and they were determined to prevent, if at all possible, the nomination from going to a recent convert whose allegiance to Republican principles was suspect. Their efforts to "stop Willkie," however, quickly came to naught. Popular pressure, journalistic support, and the fact that there was little public interest in the other contenders resulted in Willkie's receiving the nomination on the sixth ballot. To strengthen and balance the ticket, the Republicans persuaded Charles L. McNary to run for the Vice Presidency. A western liberal who had opposed Willkie's nomination from the start, McNary's views on public power, foreign policy, and the tariff were opposed to those of his running mate.[5]

The Republican platform accepted most of the New Deal's domestic legislation, in principle at least, but it castigated the administration for its inefficiency and incompetence and for having created a vast federal bureaucracy. It reassured the aged with its promise to improve the administration of the social security system and to extend its benefits to others still unprotected by it. Relief for the needy was to be continued, but through the states rather than the federal government. Farmers were guaranteed their benefit payments, and industrial workers were told that the Wagner Act would be amended to assure them "true freedom for, and orderliness in, self-organization and collective bargaining." During the campaign Willkie appealed to labor by promising to "appoint a Secretary of Labor directly from the ranks of organized labor." Just as in domestic affairs, the foreign policy plank of the GOP platform endorsed the principal measures of the Roosevelt administration. The party declared itself for "Americanism, preparedness and peace" and "the extension to all peoples fighting for liberty, or whose liberty is threatened. of such aid as shall not be in violation of international law or inconsistent with the requirements of our own national defense." It censured the President, however, for his "explosive utterances," claiming that he was undermining America's neutrality and the sincere desire of the American people to stay out of the war. Moreover, the GOP held the President and the New Dealers entirely responsible for America's "unpreparedness and for the consequent danger of involvement in war. . . ."

Meanwhile it had become apparent that the Democratic party was going to challenge tradition by nominating President Roosevelt for a third term. Roosevelt himself, as he afterward explained, had originally planned to retire, but had changed his mind and decided to accept renomination on account of the unprecedented world crisis. He made no public pronouncement of his intentions, but his silence prevented any alternative candidate from gathering support. A number of the Democratic leaders, among them James Farley and Vice President John Garner, disliked this violation of the no-third-term tradition, but they were unwilling to disrupt the party by openly opposing its leader; and when the Democratic convention met at Chicago on July 15, Roosevelt was re-

[5] Joseph W. Martin, Jr., as told to Robert J. Donovan, *My First Fifty Years in Politics* (New York [1960]), p. 160; Donald Bruce Johnson, *The Republican Party and Wendell Willkie* (Urbana, Ill., 1960), pp. 101-2.

nominated on the first ballot with 946 votes. The other ballots, less than 150, went to four candidates, Farley, Garner, Hull, and Senator Millard Tydings, all of whom quickly withdrew and, at Farley's suggestion, made Roosevelt's third nomination unanimous. At Roosevelt's insistence and contrary to the wishes of a number of the delegates, Henry A. Wallace, the Secretary of Agriculture, was nominated for the Vice Presidency.

As was to be expected, the Democratic platform extolled the administration's achievements during the past seven years, promised to extend and strengthen the liberal programs of the New Deal, such as social security coverage, and pledged continued aid to the farmer, the worker, and the unemployed. To placate the isolationists and those who favored aiding Britain but were afraid that it might lead to American participation in foreign wars, the platform adopted an ambiguously worded plank calling for "all the material aid at our command consistent with law and not inconsistent with the interests of our own national defense." At the same time, the Democrats went on record against American participation in "foreign wars" or the use of the country's armed forces "in foreign lands outside of the Americas, except in case of attack."

The campaign showed that the American people did not regard the third-term question as a matter of vital importance. The essential issue was whether Roosevelt or Willkie would provide more effective leadership in the task of defending the American way of life. The two candidates were substantially in agreement on domestic affairs. Willkie declared in his August 17 acceptance speech, delivered in his home town, Elwood, Indiana, that he was "a liberal Democrat who [had] changed his party affiliation because he found democracy in the Republican party and not in the New Deal party." Much to the discomfiture of the stalwart Old Guard, Willkie went on to assert "that the forces of free enterprise must be regulated," that he was "opposed to business monopolies," and that he endorsed wholeheartedly the principle of "collective bargaining, by representatives of labor's own free choice, without any interference and in full protection of those obvious rights." By the time he had finished this address, Willkie had accepted all of the New Deal's reform programs of the past seven years, including the minimum wage and social security laws, and the federal banking, securities, and public utilities statutes to boot. He supported rural electrification and agreed "that the Federal government has a responsibility to equalize the lot of the farmer with that of the manufacturer. If this cannot be done by parity of prices, other means must be found—with the least possible regimentation of the farmer's affairs." In his approach to domestic policies, Willkie differed from Roosevelt only in details, though he did point to a number of weaknesses in the President's administration of the New Deal. The most serious charges Willkie made against Roosevelt and the New Deal were the administration's failure to bring about full recovery and its adherence to "the philosophy of distributed scarcity."

Willkie and Roosevelt were also in fundamental agreement on the general aims of American foreign policy and in their appraisal of the international crisis. "No man," Willkie said, "can guarantee to maintain peace. Peace is not something that a nation can achieve by itself. It also depends on what some other country does. It is neither practical nor desirable to adopt a foreign program committing the United States to future action under unknown circumstances." Like Roosevelt, he advocated stronger defense measures and agreed "that some form of selective service is the only democratic way in which to secure the trained and competent manpower we need for national defense." Willkie realized too that aid to Britain was essential, and he supported enthusiastically Roosevelt's statement: "We will extend to the opponents of force the material resources of this nation, and at the same time we will harness the use of those resources in order that we ourselves, in the Americas, may have equipment and training equal to the task of any emergency and every defense." Willkie's chief criticisms were directed, once again, at Roosevelt's methods of handling foreign affairs. He indicted the President for his "inflammatory statements and manufactured panics" and for his failure to explain his policies clearly or "to take the American people into his confidence." Willkie's criticisms of Rooseveltian diplomacy, however, were far less plausible or justified than those he directed against the President's conduct of domestic affairs. He accused F.D.R., for example, of seeking "a war for which the country is hopelessly unprepared—and which it emphatically does not want." Moreover, he declared that Roosevelt "has secretly meddled in the affairs of Europe, and he has even unscrupulously encouraged countries to hope for more help than we are able to give."

As the campaign progressed, Willkie showed an increasingly dangerous propensity for rash and reckless utterances which alienated a number of voters. In September, for example, he declared that at the time of the Munich conference Roosevelt had "telephoned to Hitler and Mussolini and urged them to sell Czechoslovakia down the river." [6] Afterward,

[6] Quoted in Johnson, *op. cit.*, p. 136.

THE COMING OF WORLD WAR II   157

however, he admitted that he had been wrong about this. In October, he questioned the sincerity of Roosevelt's desire to keep the United States out of the war. "I ask you," he cried out, "whether . . . [Roosevelt's] pledge for peace is going to last any longer than his [1932] pledge for sound money. On the basis of his past performance with pledges to the people, you may expect we will be at war by April, 1941, if he is elected." [7] After the election, Willkie admitted that this statement had been just "a bit of campaign oratory."

The attention Willkie attracted by his blasts against Roosevelt's foreign policy, unwarranted and erroneous as some of them were, and the fact that he was a highly attractive personality, doubtlessly the strongest opponent F.D.R. had yet faced, frightened Democratic politicos sufficiently to cause them to insist that the President engage actively in the campaign. At the time Roosevelt accepted the nomination, he stated, "I shall not have the time or the inclination to engage in a purely political debate. But I shall never be loath to call the attention of the nation to deliberate or unwitting falsification of fact." Except for a series of "inspection trips" to defense plants and visits to military and naval installations, Roosevelt did not plan to campaign vigorously across the country, though he did not fail to take whatever political advantage accrued to him from his visits to defense plants and bases.

On October 18, however, the White House announced that because of the "misrepresentations" of the Republicans, the President would deliver five major campaign addresses before election day, the first of which he made in Philadelphia on October 23. This speech, and the four others which followed, were generally conceded to be among the most effective of his political career. Roosevelt limited himself to answering what he called the "more fantastic" charges which Willkie and the Republicans were leveling against him. He denied over and over again that he was plotting war, and accused the Republicans of spreading panic among the people by their careless and false talk; he pointed to the record of domestic reform and the achievements in economic progress and asked his audience to compare the facts of the day with the GOP's charge that the country was on its way to bankruptcy; and he accused the Republican leaders in Congress of having voted against the administration's defense bills because they believed that the country's armed forces were adequate, and suggested that their concern with the strength of the army, the navy,

[7] Quoted in Basil Rauch, *Roosevelt: From Munich to Pearl Harbor* (New York, 1950), p. 266.

and the air force now was purely political. "The simple truth is that the Republican Party, through its leadership, played politics with defense, the defense of the United States, in 1938 and 1939. And they are playing politics with the national security of America today." Citing the Republican votes in Congress on defense and on the repeal of the arms embargo—which permitted aid to Britain—Roosevelt declared that "if the decisions had been left to [GOP] Congressmen Martin, Barton and Fish," neither Britain nor "a lot of other nations would . . . have received one ounce of help from us. . . ."

Despite the President's devastating rebuttals to Willkie's charges, Democratic party leaders insisted that F.D.R. reassure the people that peace and defense were the sole aims of his policies. On October 30, while speaking in Boston, he repeated his pledge against war: "I have said this before, but I shall say it again and again and again: Your boys are not going to be sent into any foreign wars. . . . The purpose of our defense is defense." This was the most extreme no-war statement F.D.R. ever made. Heretofore he had always qualified his declarations against war with the phrase "except in case of attack." Roosevelt explained its omission on this occasion to Sam Rosenman by saying it was "not necessary," for "If we're attacked it's no longer a foreign war." [8]

In the end a majority of the electorate decided that they did not want to entrust their destinies to a new and untried Chief Executive. A number of voters disapproved of Willkie's more irresponsible charges, while others were alarmed by the quality of some of his supporters, a fact which Roosevelt was quick to point out. "There is something very ominous," he told a Brooklyn audience on November 1, "in this combination that has been forming within the Republican Party between the extreme reactionary and the extreme radical elements of this country." The reactionaries who wished to return to the Coolidge era and the isolationists who hated Great Britain or sympathized with Nazism were all trying to defeat Roosevelt, and in spite of Willkie's liberalism and internationalism they would inevitably have regarded his election as a victory for themselves. As in the campaign of 1936, many Americans voted for Roosevelt because of the enemies he had made.

The result was the reelection of the President, but with a reduced majority. The middle-western farm states reverted to their traditional Republicanism, but the Democratic party retained its hold over the cities

---

[8] Quoted in James MacGregor Burns, *Roosevelt: The Lion and the Fox* (New York [1956]), p. 449.

and also over organized labor, despite the support given to Willkie when John L. Lewis turned against Roosevelt late in October. With a popular vote of 27,243,466 (54.7 per cent), Roosevelt carried thirty-eight states with 449 electoral votes. Willkie received a popular vote of 22,304,755 (44.7 per cent), nearly 6 million more than any previous Republican candidate, but he carried only ten states with 82 electoral votes. The only two states he won outside the Middle West were Maine and Vermont. All the minor parties running presidential candidates (Socialist, Communist, Prohibitionist, and Socialist-Labor) won less than 50 per cent of the votes they had polled in 1936. The Democrats made a small gain in their number of House seats (from 261 to 268), but their loss of 3 in the Senate reduced their majority in that body from 69 to 66. Of the 34 gubernatorial chairs at stake in 1940, the Republicans won 17. The war in Europe, improved economic conditions at home, and the conviction of the "little fellow" that F.D.R. was his "friend and protector," as the political analyst Samuel Lubell pointed out after the election, did much to ensure the President's reelection. But it is also an undeniable fact, which Roosevelt proved once again—and perhaps more strikingly in 1940 than he had ever done before—that he had mastered the political arts and knew how to employ them with effective timeliness.

THE ROAD TO WAR, 1940–1941

While the United States had been engaged in political campaigning, the nations across the Atlantic had been passing through one of the most terrible and momentous summers in their entire history. The German offensive in the West, after overrunning Holland and Belgium, broke through the French lines near Sedan and within four weeks virtually destroyed the French army, which military experts only a month before had believed to be the best in the world. On June 10 Mussolini, convinced that German victory was now certain and eager for a share in the plunder, entered the war; and on June 17 a new French government, headed by the semifascist hero of Verdun, Marshall Henri Philippe Pétain, ended democracy in France and sued for an armistice, which was signed on June 22. After one of the shortest and most brilliant military campaigns on record, Hitler had become master of most of Western Europe.

To many observers, both in Europe and in the United States, it seemed certain that the Nazis would now complete their victory by subduing

160   THE ERA OF F.D.R., 1933-1945

Great Britain. The British army had been rescued from capitulation by the evacuation at Dunkirk at the end of May, but it had abandoned the whole of its equipment. Great Britain had barely begun to organize its energies for war, and until May it had been governed by men who had shown a tragic inability to understand the enemy they were facing. But the British people now displayed a courage and a capacity in meeting the crisis which showed that free institutions had not lost their virtue and which earned the admiration of all democratic nations throughout the world. They had already found a leader equal to the occasion in Winston Churchill, gifted both in knowledge of war and in command of eloquence, who succeeded Neville Chamberlain as prime minister on May 11; and after Dunkirk they prepared to deal with the threatened invasion. Hitler never ventured to send troops across the Channel; he attempted first to secure mastery of the skies and to knock out Great Britain from the air. In a series of battles over British cities (August 6 to October 31, 1940), the Royal Air Force won a decisive victory over the German Luftwaffe. On one day alone, September 15, the Germans lost 56 planes. Between July 10 and October 31, 1940, the Battle of Britain cost Hilter 1,733 planes by German count, while the greatly outnumbered Royal Air Force lost 915.[9] Despite the heavy losses in lives and property which Hilter inflicted upon the British, their determination to continue fighting never weakened. By the end of October, the losses which the Royal Air Force had inflicted upon the Luftwaffe forced Hitler to abandon daylight raiding and to postpone his invasion plans until the following spring, and then, after June 22, 1941, when he attacked Russia, indefinitely. The German air force, however, continued its heavy night bombings and incendiary attacks of English cities. But despite all the terror of these night raids, the Battle of Britain—one of the most important battles of all times—had been won, and the ultimate victory of the democracies, even though they were to suffer still greater losses, had at least become possible.

Meanwhile, in the Far East Japan was preparing to take advantage of the European war in order to satisfy its imperialist ambitions. The Japanese war lords had been engaged in war with China for three years, but although their armies had occupied a large part of that country, they had never been able to end the resistance of the Chinese people under the leadership of Chiang Kai-shek. The German victories now opened easier and more profitable areas for conquest. For a generation or more,

[9] Churchill claimed that 2,698 enemy planes were destroyed.

Japanese militarists had been looking forward to the conquest of the French, Dutch, British, and American possessions in the Far East with their vast resources in rubber, oil, tin, and other raw materials; and the prospect of a German victory in Europe was too good an opportunity to be overlooked. The European powers could no longer defend their Asiatic possessions, and the United States, it was believed in Japanese circles, could be intimidated by a show of force.

The Berlin Pact

On September 27, 1940, a Tripartite Alliance among Germany, Italy, and Japan was signed at Berlin. Tokyo now became officially attached to the Rome-Berlin Axis. The Nazis and the Japanese war lords agreed to support each other in their plans for a "new order" in Europe and Asia respectively, and promised to come to each other's assistance "with all political, economic and military means" if any one of the three powers was "attacked by a Power at present not involved in the European War or in the Chinese-Japanese conflict." Since Article 5 of the Berlin Pact excluded Russia from its "terms," it was obvious that the statement could refer only to the United States. The reason Hitler entered into the pact with the Japanese at this time was clear. He hoped that if the United States was faced with the prospect of having to fight Japan, Germany, and Italy simultaneously, the American government would be forced to reenforce its Pacific defenses; and in order to accomplish this, it would have to reduce its aid to Great Britain. The advantages to Japan from an alliance with Hitler and Mussolini appeared equally attractive to Tokyo. For one thing, once the Japanese government recovered from the initial shock of the Nazi-Soviet Nonaggression Pact of 1939, which forced Nippon to abandon its expansionist ambitions at the expense of Russia in the north, Japan decided to satisfy its imperialist drive by moving against the French and British interests in South Asia.[10] The Japanese now saw in the Axis alliance the means to obtain German sanction for their absorption of French Indochina. Japanese troops had already begun to occupy bases in that region, and on September 22 the Pétain government at Vichy approved Tokyo's *fait accompli* and agreed to other concessions as well. Japan also sought to use its alliance with Berlin to deter the United States from aiding China and supporting

[10] Jules Davids, *America and the World of Our Time: United States Diplomacy in the Twentieth Century* (New York [1960]), pp. 180–81.

162 THE ERA OF F.D.R., 1933–1945

Britain in the Far East, which would greatly facilitate the realization of Nippon's greater coprosperity sphere. Finally, Tokyo also believed that the pact would prove useful in improving Russo-Japanese relations, which had been strained since the Japanese attack on Manchuria in 1931.

The purposes of this alliance—to keep the United States out of the European war and to force it to recognize Japan's primacy in greater East Asia—were never realized; and because of the disastrous consequences the pact had upon American opinion of Japanese intentions, it seriously undermined the possibility of negotiating the differences which divided the two countries.[11] When the text of the tripartite pact was made public in the United States, many Americans interpreted it as indisputable proof that the Axis was out to remake the map of the world to suit its own interests and in total disregard of the security and legitimate needs of the United States. "Hitler," Secretary Hull told the French ambassador, "was out to become the ruthless and destructive conqueror of Europe, and . . . the Japanese military clique was bent on the same course in the Pacific area from Hawaii to Siam."[12]

Because of the tripartite pact, Americans felt, the United States was in danger of finding itself confronted by aggressive militaristic powers across both oceans. Hitler had failed to conquer Great Britain by direct attack, but he might starve it into submission by submarine warfare; and the British, as their prime minister admitted, could not hope to defeat him without American assistance. Japan could occupy the East Indies whenever it felt that the time was ripe, and only the armed forces of the United States could prevent Nippon from acquiring permanent control of the whole of the western Pacific. The summer crisis of 1940 precipitated one of the most important debates in American history. Should the United States take action to prevent hostile powers from controlling the European and African coasts of the Atlantic and the Asiatic coast of the Pacific, or should America assume that it could do business with a victorious Germany and Japan and could successfully defend itself if either or both of these powers chose to attack the United States?

Of the numerous organizations which endeavored to mobilize public

[11] Paul W. Schroeder, *The Axis Alliance and Japanese-American Relations, 1941* (Ithaca, N.Y. [1958]), pp. 20–22.
[12] Cordell Hull to Gaston Henry-Haye, September 11, 1940, in U. S. Department of State, *Peace and War: United States Foreign Policy, 1931–1941* (Washington, D.C., 1943), p. 568.

The America First Committee was the most powerful isolationist organization to oppose President Franklin Roosevelt's anti-Axis policies. One of its most popular spokesmen was the beloved American hero of 1927, Charles A. Lindbergh, who is shown here addressing a committee rally at Fort Wayne, Indiana, two months before the Japanese attacked Pearl Harbor. (Wide World Photos)

opinion, the most influential were the interventionist Committee to Defend America by Aiding the Allies and the isolationist America First Committee. The Committee to Defend America, headed by the Kansas Republican William Allen White, was established in September, 1939, and was supported from the outset by a majority of the most respected leaders of American opinion. As the war proceeded a large number of former pacifists and isolationists began to reconsider their opinions. The United States, they declared, could not hope to preserve its free institutions and its traditional ideals if all Europe and Asia passed under the rule of aggressive and cynical military dictatorships; and it was improbable that the United States could defend the Western Hemisphere from German and Japanese attack if it had no allies in other parts of the world. British seapower had always been America's first line of defense; if the British empire were overthrown, not even the United States, in spite of

164   THE ERA OF F.D.R., 1933-1945

its vast resources, could hope to outbuild the Nazis in a race for naval and air superiority. Both the ideals and the security of America required that adequate aid be given to the British and the Chinese. These arguments were supported by a growing majority of the American people, particularly in the Northeast and in the South.

The isolationists, on the other hand, though vociferous and influential, especially in the Middle West, were handicapped in their appeals to public opinion by the quality of their supporters. They included many sincere and patriotic citizens who genuinely believed that the United States had no interest in the preservation of British seapower and that neither Germany nor Japan would ever venture to attack America; but they included also men whose motives were much more dubious. Nazi sympathizers who believed that democracy had failed and that fascism represented the "wave of the future," businessmen who wanted to end the New Deal and preferred Hitler to Roosevelt, Irish Americans whose hatred of Great Britain outweighed their loyalty to the United States, anti-semitic agitators who propagated the Nazi doctrines of racial hatred, office seekers who believed that the American electorate wanted primarily to stay out of war and would be pleased by assurances that they were not in danger, and politicians who had based their careers on the theory that all wars were provoked by bankers and munitions manufacturers and were now unwilling to admit that they had been wrong—men of this kind supported the America First Committee, which was formed in September, 1940, and headed by Robert E. Wood of Sears, Roebuck and Company. This group fought William Allen White's committee by preaching isolationist doctrines in Congress and circulating their opinions widely through the mails, often using the franking privileges of friendly congressmen and senators who belonged to it or sympathized with its ideas. The committee also used the press to propagate its views, and both the Hearst and McCormick newspapers gave it liberal coverage. The America Firsters, despite the majority of honest men and women who had joined the organization, made it increasingly obvious that a victory for isolationism would mean a victory also for all the most sinister forces in American public life.

The Swing to Interventionism

Supported by a majority of the electorate, the Roosevelt administration began slowly to give help to the British and the Chinese. When

Italy entered the war, on June 10, 1940, Roosevelt vigorously denounced the Italian dictator in a speech at Charlottesville, Virginia, in which he declared that the American government would "extend to the opponents of force the material resources of this nation." Surplus guns, ammunition, and planes were released by the War Department for sale to Great Britain; and on September 3, an agreement was concluded with the British government by which the United States leased a number of bases situated on British territory in Newfoundland, the West Indies, and Guiana which were necessary for the security of the Western Hemisphere. The British, in return, received fifty over-age destroyers, which they particularly needed for defense against the submarine campaign. When France capitulated, American influence was exerted to prevent the French navy and North African colonies from falling into German hands, but the Pétain government refused to send the navy to American ports for safekeeping. On July 3, 1940, units of the British Mediterranean fleet entered the Algerian port of Oran, where some of France's largest warships were anchored. When the French commander refused to entrust his ships to Britain or to sail them to the French West Indies, where they could pose no threat to the Royal Navy, British naval guns sank or crippled most of them. A few fled to Toulon, only to be sunk two years later, on November 27, 1942, when their crews, reacting against Hitler's occupation of all of France, scuttled them.

In the Far East, the United States answered the concessions which Japan had forced upon France in Indochina by giving loans to China and extending the embargo against Japan, which already contained numerous commodities, to include sales of iron and steel scrap. The State Department also ordered American citizens in Japanese-controlled territory to return home. The United States began to cooperate with the Chinese, the British, and the Dutch in defense of their common interests, and it was made obvious to Japan that the democratic powers would not submit to intimidation.

Meanwhile progress was made in unifying the nations of the Western Hemisphere against Nazi penetration. The United States began to buy up the surplus commodities of the Latin American nations to compensate them for the loss of their European markets and to outbid the German offer of profitable contracts to be fulfilled at the end of the war. On June 16, 1940, Congress passed the Pittman Resolution to reenforce the defenses of the Latin American countries. Under its provisions the states of the Western Hemisphere were permitted to acquire arms and mu-

166 THE ERA OF F.D.R., 1933–1945

nitions from the United States. And at the Inter-American Conference which met at Havana in July, 1940, it was agreed that the American nations should exercise a collective trusteeship over any European possessions, such as the French West Indies, which might be in danger of transference to Nazi control. The Declaration of Havana also warned the Axis that "any attempt on the part of a non-American State against the integrity or inviolability of the territory, the sovereignty or the political independence of an American State shall be considered as an act of aggression against the States which sign this declaration." The North American defenses of the United States were strengthened further when Roosevelt and Prime Minister W. L. Mackenzie King of Canada, meeting at Ogdensburg, New York, announced on August 18 that the two countries had agreed to establish a Permanent Joint Board on Defense.

Through the summer of 1940 the chances of continued British resistance seemed uncertain; and since the American economic system was not yet geared for war production, it was difficult to decide whether the United States should gamble on British strength by sending all its available resources abroad or concentrate on building its own defenses. By the end of the year, however, it had become evident that Great Britain was capable of defending itself provided it had the planes, ships, and other urgent matériel of war to do so. After the presidential election in November, public opinion in the United States strongly favored a bolder program of aid to assure Britain's survival.

At the end of the year, American policy, not neutral since the fall of France, assumed an even more definite form. Roosevelt declared to the American people in a radio address on December 29 that "The Axis powers are not going to win this war," that there could be no negotiated peace, and that nothing but a democratic victory could ensure the kind of world in which nations could live in security. Roosevelt had pledged himself during the presidential campaign that the United States would not enter into any foreign war, but he had promised that it would give the democracies sufficient material aid to enable them to defeat the aggressor powers. "We must be the great arsenal of democracy," the President declared in December, 1940. "There will be no 'bottlenecks' in our determination to aid Great Britain. No dictator, no combination of dictators, will weaken that determination by threats. . . ." To assure that America would become "the great arsenal of democracy" and that an increased and uninterrupted flow of war matériel reached Britain, on

December 20 Roosevelt established the Office of Production Management under the direction of William S. Knudsen, the president of General Motors. This agency was charged with the responsibility of coordinating all defense production, purchases, and priorities.

In addition to strengthening American defenses and increasing the amount of war matériel shipped to Great Britain, the United States also endeavored to check Hitlerism in other directions. Admiral William D. Leahy was sent as American ambassador to the Vichy government of Pétain in December, 1940, with the task of encouraging the Vichy officials to resist their Nazi overlords, and every effort was made to improve political and economic relations with the Soviet Union. During the Russo-Finnish War (October, 1940, through March, 1941) public opinion in the United States was strongly pro-Finn, but despite the desire of certain individuals in the State Department to condemn the Russian aggression, Roosevelt and Hull urged prudence.[13] American diplomats believed that a rupture between Moscow and Berlin was likely, if not inevitable, and that American patience and proof of friendship and good intentions might encourage Stalin to "come over to the side of the Allies." "We had to be careful," Hull argued, "not to push her in the other direction." [14] Improved relations between Moscow and Washington did not materialize quickly nor without first undergoing some serious setbacks. American policy, however, remained constant—to cultivate Russian friendship. As early as January, 1941, acting on secret information acquired by an American diplomat in Germany, the State Department warned the Soviet Union to expect a Nazi attack before summer.

Meanwhile, in the Far East, American policy was to remain firm but passive; the United States would not surrender to Japanese demands, but at the same time it would not provoke Japan into aggressive action. The defeat of Hitler was to have priority, and an over-all strategic plan to this effect was worked out by American and British staff officers in a series of secret meetings held in Washington between January and March, 1941. Though it was made clear that the military and naval arrangements agreed upon at this time would go into effect only "should the United States be compelled to resort to war" against "Germany and the powers allied with her," the substance of these secret talks was incorporated in

---

[13] Donald F. Drummond, *The Passing of American Neutrality, 1937–1941* (Ann Arbor, Mich., 1955), p. 122; William L. Langer and S. Everett Gleason, *The Challenge to Isolation, 1937–1940* (New York, 1952), p. 332.
[14] Cordell Hull, *The Memoirs of Cordell Hull* (2 vols., New York, 1948), I, 707.

subsequent American planning. In spite of these arrangements and of American sympathy for China, the United States continued to ship oil to Japan because Washington believed that if oil were embargoed, the result would be a Japanese attack on the East Indies.

Hitherto, in accordance with the Neutrality Act of 1939, the British had been required to pay in cash for all American war materials and to transport them in their own ships. It was now becoming obvious that Great Britain would need more direct help. By the end of 1940, Britain's cash reserves were almost exhausted, and although London still had large foreign investments, these could not be liquidated quickly or without heavy sacrifices. Moreover, German submarines were inflicting severe losses upon British shipping. Operating alone or in groups known as wolf packs, German U-boats threatened to defeat Britain in the North Atlantic, while surface raiders like the *Altmark* and fast, powerful warships like the pocket battleship *Graf Spee* attacked merchantmen wherever they found them. By the middle of March, 1941, the shipping losses of the Allies exceeded 3 million tons. It was absurd for the United States to export war materials which would only go to the bottom of the Atlantic.

On December 17, during a press conference, Roosevelt proposed a method for dealing with the first of these problems. Credits to Great Britain were prohibited by both the Johnson Act and the Neutrality Act; the history of the war loans made during World War I, moreover, did not encourage the repetition of such a policy. Roosevelt suggested instead that goods should be lent to Great Britain to be repaid after the war not in money but in kind. Out of this proposal, which F.D.R. justified to the nation as a means of assuring "the defense of the United States" by providing "all-out" aid to the nations fighting Hitler, grew the Lend-Lease Act, which Congress passed with an original appropriation of $7 billion on March 11, 1941. Goods now might be shipped to any country "whose defense the President deems vital to the defense of the United States," and the return to the United States might be "payment or repayment in kind or property, or any other direct or indirect benefit." In a series of agreements with nations which received lend-lease aid, it was stipulated that they should promote freer international trade after the war. Between March 11, 1941, and August 21, 1945, when President Harry S. Truman stopped lend-lease, the total value of goods sent to the Allies under this program amounted to nearly $50.3 billion.

The problem of ensuring that American goods actually reached the British could be solved only by sending American merchant ships into the

THE COMING OF WORLD WAR II   169

combat zone and by giving them adequate defenses against submarines. The first of these measures was prohibited by the Neutrality Act, while the second would mean that America would become a belligerent. In April, 1941, Roosevelt declared that the Red Sea and Indian Ocean were not a combat zone, and this enabled American ships to supply the British army in Egypt; and the air force was instructed to patrol the Atlantic as far as Iceland in order to warn British merchant ships of the locality of submarines.

On April 9, the Danish minister in Washington agreed to allow the United States to fortify Greenland to assure its safety and to facilitate the defense of the Western Hemisphere. In June, American troops and construction crews began to occupy the Danish colony. On July 7, Roosevelt informed Congress that by arrangement with the Icelandic government American forces had arrived at Reykjavik "to insure the adequate defense of that country," a responsibility which Britain had assumed in May, 1940, but could no longer fulfill. The American occupation of Iceland, which was to be terminated at the end of the war, was also undertaken, as in the case of Greenland, Roosevelt declared, to deprive Germany "of strategic outposts in the Atlantic to be used as air or naval bases for eventual attack against the Western Hemisphere."

On September 4, the American destroyer *Greer*, while proceeding to Iceland, was attacked by a submarine, the presence of which it had been broadcasting to British naval and air units. A week later in a fireside chat, Roosevelt announced that henceforth the American navy would defend the freedom of the seas "in any waters which America deems vital to its defense" by attacking these "rattlesnakes of the Atlantic" whenever encountered. And he went on to say, "Let this warning be clear. From now on, if German or Italian vessels of war enter the waters, the protection of which is necessary for American defense, they do so at their own peril." Shortly thereafter, the United States navy was assigned to protect convoys to Iceland. On October 9, Roosevelt asked Congress to repeal Section 6 of the Neutrality Act of 1939 which prohibited "American vessels engaged in commerce with any foreign state to be armed." While Congress was considering the President's request, two other American destroyers, the *Kearny* and the *Reuben James*, were attacked in the North Atlantic. The former was damaged, the latter sunk. On November 13, Congress approved the arming of American merchantmen and allowed them to deliver their goods "into belligerent ports." The undeclared war in the Atlantic had begun.

Meanwhile the growing partnership of the United States and the

British Commonwealth had become even more intimate. Roosevelt and Churchill met and conferred with each other secretly for several days on the H.M.S. *Prince of Wales* and the U.S.S. *Augusta*, anchored in Placentia Bay near the coast of Newfoundland. The two statesmen discussed the progress of the war and set forth their ideas on postwar reconstruction in an eight-point program which became known as the Atlantic Charter. In his message to Congress on January 6, Roosevelt had already formulated the Four Freedoms which he believed should be guaranteed everywhere: freedom of religion, freedom of speech, freedom from want, and freedom from fear. The Atlantic Charter, which was announced on August 14, declared further that the peace settlement should be based on the following principles: no nation should seek territorial aggrandizement; no territorial changes should be made except by the wish of the population concerned; all nations should be allowed to choose their own form of government; all nations should have equal access to markets and to raw materials; nations should collaborate with each other in the raising of standards of living; there should be security against war; the seas should be free to all in time of peace; and the aggressor nations should be deprived of their weapons, and efforts should be made to lighten the burden of armaments for all nations. The eight points of this Atlantic Charter were in some respects reminiscent of the Fourteen Points of President Wilson, but the differences were perhaps more significant than the similarities. Unlike the Fourteen Points, the Atlantic Charter was not merely an American program; it was formulated jointly by the Americans and the British. It confined itself to general statements of policy and did not attempt to forecast specific territorial changes. It laid considerable emphasis on economic cooperation. And it did not propose that the victorious nations should themselves disarm, or that they should commit themselves to freedom of the seas in wartime. The American government, it appeared, had taken warning from some of the errors which had been made in 1918 and 1919.

The Expansion of Axis Power

By the time of the Placentia Bay meeting the European war had spread eastward, and another group of unoffending neutrals had become the victims of Nazi imperialism. The winter of 1940–41 had been relatively quiet except for the night raids of the Luftwaffe over British cities and the continuous pressure of the submarine campaign. The British had made use of the lull in Nazi activity to deliver a crippling blow to the Italian fleet in its harbor at Taranto (November 11–12, 1940), to complete the liquidation of Mussolini's East African empire, and to destroy the Italian armies in Libya. By the spring of 1941, Hitler was forced to intervene to save the Italians. Meanwhile, that spring and summer saw more demonstrations of the Nazi blitzkrieg. Hungary, Romania, and Bulgaria had already been absorbed into the Nazi "New Order" during the previous autumn and winter without resistance, but the Yugoslavs and the Greeks proved less compliant. Hitler's drive into the Balkans began on April 6, and within less than three weeks the Yugoslav and Greek armies were crushed. By the end of April the Nazis were on the Aegean. The seizure of Crete, accomplished by troops transported entirely by air and in spite of British control of the sea, followed in May; and it seemed inevitable that the next move would be the conquest of the entire Middle East. German troops led by General Erwin Rommel took over the Libyan campaign from the Italians on April 3. In a ten-day offensive, Rommel drove the British back into Egypt. Except for the Australian force at Tobruk, which fought on desperately until it was relieved on November 27, Rommel's Afrika Korps appeared to be ready to march on to Cairo.

Hitler, however, had other plans. The Soviet government had shown a disconcerting unwillingness to abide by the terms agreed upon with Germany in 1939. Russia had viewed the Nazi conquest of the Balkans with obvious displeasure, and Stalin had informed Hitler that the USSR would collaborate with the Axis in bringing about a "New Order" in the world only if Germany removed all its troops from Finland, guaranteed Russia a naval base on the Dardanelles, recognized the USSR's "aspirations" in the Persian Gulf, and forced Japan to renounce its "rights and concessions for coal and oil in Northern Sakhalin." [15] This was more than Hitler was willing to pay. Moreover, he felt that it was unsafe for him to engage in an all-out struggle with Great Britain so long as he had a potentially hostile army on his eastern border. Too, Hitler had based his whole career on the thesis that communism meant disorder and degeneracy, and he was incapable of a realistic appraisal of Soviet military power. On December 18, he had issued a secret order calling for preparations *"to crush Soviet Russia in a quick campaign";* six months later, on June 22, 1941, the German army began its invasion of the Soviet Union,

---

[15] U. S. Department of State, *Nazi-Soviet Relations, 1939–1941: Documents from the Archives of the German Foreign Office* (Washington, D.C., 1948), pp. 258–59.

hoping to defeat the Red armies in a single campaign. During the next five months, the Wehrmacht occupied half a million square miles of Russian territory. The Soviet armies were nevertheless able to conduct an orderly retreat; and by the end of November the German advance was definitely halted, and the Russians were able in some sections to take the offensive. For the second time Hitler had failed to achieve his objective. The Nazis may have hoped that their attack on the Soviet Union would create divisions among the democracies, but the British and American governments, in spite of their hostility to communism, believed in cooperation with any power opposed to Germany, and immediately extended aid to the Soviets. The vigorous resistance made by the Russian army and people in defending their homeland won the sincere admiration of the people of the United States.

The conflict in Europe had the front place in the minds of most Americans, and by the autumn of 1941 the United States had come as close to belligerency as it was possible to go without ceasing to be officially at peace. Nevertheless, as many students of foreign affairs had always predicted, it was the course of events in the Far East which finally precipitated the entry of the American people into open war.

The German invasion of Russia created a major crisis in Japanese government circles. Tokyo was neither informed of it in advance nor diplomatically prepared for it. Despite the Tripartite Alliance, neither the Germans nor the Japanese ever wholly trusted each other. From the very beginning, Hitler had shown little respect for the ambitions of his Far Eastern ally and little sense of obligation to keep Japan informed of his plans. Tokyo, for example, had been seriously offended by the Nazi-Soviet Pact of August, 1939, which had forced a basic alteration in Japanese policy. Berlin was similarly displeased with Tokyo when on April 13, 1941, only a month before the originally scheduled German attack against Russia, the Japanese signed a five-year nonaggression pact with the Soviet Union. The Japanese had allied themselves with Germany and Italy against the democracies in the hope of achieving their ambition for a "greater East Asia" by frightening the United States into a Far Eastern agreement favorable to Tokyo while the Nazis were defeating Britain in Europe. The invasion of Russia changed everything, and in Japanese eyes for the worse. "To be frank," Yosuke Matsuoka, the Japanese foreign minister, confided to the Russian ambassador in Tokyo on July 2, 1941, "Japan finds herself in the most awkward position faced with the war between Germany and Italy, her allies, on one hand, and the USSR on the other, with whom she has but recently begun to improve relations." [16]

The last week of June and the first days of July, 1941, were a time of difficult decision making for the Japanese government. In view of the German-Russian war, what policy should Japan now follow to further its ambitions? There were several alternatives from which the Japanese could choose, and each had its official champion. Matsuoka insisted upon war against Russia, delay in fulfilling Japan's southern ambitions at the expense of Britain, France, and the Netherlands, and, if at all possible, peace with the United States. Matsuoka's program, however, was unacceptable to the prime minister, Prince Fumimaro Konoye, and certain other high government officials. Konoye, disturbed by Germany's attack on Russia, a move he interpreted as a "betrayal," and by Matsuoka's efforts to influence the government to support war against the USSR, had his own plan to propose.[17] He advocated war against neither Russia nor the democracies. He believed Japan's best interests could be achieved through diplomacy, and he proposed that renewed efforts be made toward reaching a satisfactory understanding with Washington and London. Konoye's plan would require concessions, mostly at the expense of China and Indochina, but he believed that the Western democracies would pay this price to get Japan to renounce its alliance with Hitler and to guarantee its neutrality. The third possibility, the one sponsored by General Hideki Tojo, the aggressive minister of war, called for a drive to the south. Japan, he argued, needed the food and resources of Southeast Asia; in addition, the area was necessary also for bases from which to plan further advances or to defend the territories which would be gained. Tojo and the military caste he represented had been gaining steadily in influence over the Japanese government and people; and in July, 1941, they were prepared to go to war with the United States to satisfy their imperialist ambitions, though they doubted it would come to such since they were reasonably certain that America would not fight.

At the imperial conference of July 2, these various alternatives were carefully considered, and it was decided to reject Matsuoka's plan for war against Russia and to adopt the proposals of Tojo and Konoye. Japan would move south, but at the same time real efforts would be made to avoid war with America. Should this dual policy prove impossible of attainment, then Japan would prepare for war "against the

[16] Quoted in Schroeder, *op. cit.*, p. 48.   [17] Davids, *op. cit.*, pp. 221–23.

174 THE ERA OF F.D.R., 1933–1945

United States, Great Britain, and the Netherlands, in addition to China, and, if necessary, or appropriate, the Soviet Union." [18] Defeated, Matsuoka left the cabinet two weeks later. He was succeeded as foreign minister by Admiral Teijuro Toyoda. As soon as Japan notified its embassies of the July 2 decision, the United States, which had broken the Japanese Foreign Office code early in the spring of 1941, learned of it also.

Japanese-American Relations, 1941

Even before the Foreign Office crisis of June and July, 1941, Tokyo had already initiated negotiations with Washington. In March, 1941, the Japanese ambassador to the United States, Kichisaburo Nomura, a retired admiral of limited diplomatic experience and skill who spoke and understood little English, inaugurated a series of talks with Secretary Hull which lasted until December 7 and which numbered no less than sixty meetings. Originally involved in sponsoring these conversations were two Roman Catholic missionaries who had recently returned from Japan and who, as a result of their own conversations with high diplomatic and military officials in Tokyo, were convinced that the Japanese government was sincere in its desire to improve relations with the United States and was prepared to make concessions to realize this goal. Through the good offices of Roosevelt's Catholic Postmaster General, Frank C. Walker, the two clerics presented their views to the President and Secretary Hull at a White House meeting. Roosevelt and Hull, though somewhat skeptical, suggested that the two missionaries "continue their contacts with the Japanese Embassy on a purely private basis," and that when they learned "*what the Japanese had in mind*," they should inform Walker, who in turn would bring the matter to the attention of the State Department.[19] The result of all this was a series of conversations between Hull and Nomura in April. In the opinion of the State Department, the Hull-Nomura talks were not sufficiently encouraging to warrant the opening of more formal negotiations. Nomura, however, misunderstood much of the essence of these conservations, and his reports of them allowed the Japanese leaders in Tokyo to reach "unwarrantable con-

[18] Quoted in *ibid.*, p. 223.
[19] Quoted in Robert J. C. Butow, "The Hull-Nomura Conversations: A Fundamental Misconception," *American Historical Review*, LXV (July 1960), 823.

THE COMING OF WORLD WAR II 175

clusions," which became painfully evident in the official Japanese government proposal of May 12, 1941.[20]

The purpose of this proposal was to establish the terms by which the difficulties which had long embittered Japanese-American relations could be resolved and a general Far Eastern settlement worked out. The Japanese Foreign Office considered this statement as its "answer" to a supposedly earlier official American communication. It was, of course, no such thing. What Tokyo had replied to was a "Draft Understanding" which had been drawn up by a Japanese army officer in the Japanese embassy in Washington and which Nomura had used in his informal discussions with Hull. Neither Hull nor anyone else in the United States government ever looked upon this document as expressing the official position of the United States. Indeed, it included none of the "basic principles" which Washington regarded as indispensable for a real settlement. Hull was greatly disturbed by the Japanese proposal of May 12 because, as he said, "it offered little basis for an agreement, unless we were willing to sacrifice some of our most basic principles, which we were not." But at the same time Hull, believing that this was the beginning of Tokyo's "official propositions" rather than its "answer" to an official American statement, decided "to begin conversations." "To have rejected it outright," he believed, "would have meant throwing away the only real chance we had had in many months to enter . . . into a fundamental discussion of all the questions outstanding between us. . . ."[21]

In replying to Tokyo's proposal of May 12, the State Department informed Nomura that before cordial relations could be resumed, Japan must agree to four conditions: it must "(1) respect . . . the territorial integrity and the sovereignty of each and all nations; (2) support . . . the principle of non-interference in the internal affairs of all countries; (3) support the principle of equality, including equality of commercial opportunity; (4) [and endorse the principle of] non-disturbance of the *status quo* in the Pacific except as the *status quo* may be altered by peaceful means." The Japanese were neither prepared nor willing to accept these conditions. In their May 12 proposal they had asked for a cessation of American support to China and American intervention in the Sino-Japanese conflict to bring about a settlement favorable to Tokyo as well as other political and economic concessions, such as repealing all

[20] *Ibid.*, p. 832.   [21] Quoted in *ibid.*, p. 834.

restrictions upon Japanese trade. It was obvious, therefore, that no fundamental agreement between the two powers was likely so long as each held to its declared positions. Negotiations were not terminated, however, though by mid-June it was quite clear that the Chinese question and Japan's continued adherence to the Axis alliance created a grave diplomatic impasse insofar as potentially fruitful conversations were concerned. The situation was aggravated further by the misconceptions arising out of the Hull-Nomura conversations. Inadequately informed by its ambassador in Washington of what the American government regarded as a suitable basis for a real settlement, Tokyo came to believe that the United States government had become less friendly disposed toward Japan than it had been in April.

This was the state of American-Japanese relations when the Imperial Council decided to realize Nippon's coprosperity sphere by pushing south. With Russia retreating in Europe, Tokyo initiated its first move on July 24 when it ordered Japanese troops to complete the occupation of French Indochina. Two days later, after Japan had refused to withdraw from southern Indochina, President Roosevelt signed an Executive order freezing all Japanese assets in the United States and placing an embargo upon oil, Japan's most vital need. The result of this order was to halt "all financial and import and export trade transactions" between the two countries. Britain and the Netherlands adopted similar policies. The American action of July 26 came as a terrible shock to the Japanese, and it caused a marked change in Tokyo's diplomatic negotiations with Washington. The economic restrictions against Japanese trade which the United States had applied in 1940 had made for hardships; the embargo on oil, unless it was quickly repealed, would prove disastrous. An early and acceptable settlement with the United States was now imperative.

The first Japanese move in this direction came on August 6, when Nomura presented Hull with a proposal whereby Japan would withdraw from Indochina as soon as the "China incident" had been settled, "guarantee the neutrality of the [Philippine] islands," and cease from making any other military moves southward, implying it would leave the East Indies alone. In return, the United States would have to "suspend its military measures in the Southwestern Pacific" and "advise" Britain and the Netherlands to do likewise; recognize Japan's "special status" in French Indochina, "even after the withdrawal of Japanese troops from that area"; refrain from any embargoes or restrictions upon Japanese trade; and help Japan negotiate "a speedy settlement of the

China Incident." Nomura's proposal was utterly unacceptable to the United States, and two days later, when Hull replied to it, he reiterated the traditional policies of the United States.

Meanwhile in Tokyo Prince Konoye, adopting a proposal made several months earlier, sought to resolve the diplomatic impasse by personal diplomacy. On August 17 Nomura asked Roosevelt whether he would be willing to meet with Konoye in order to reach a settlement of the differences which divided the two countries. Roosevelt avoided a direct reply. Whether such a meeting or further conversations on the ambassadorial level were in order depended, the President said, upon Japan's willingness "to suspend its expansionist activities" in the Pacific. For the next six weeks Tokyo and Washington exchanged more notes, but no agreement could be reached between the two capitals which promised fruitful negotiations or warranted a personal meeting between Konoye and Roosevelt. Except for the United States ambassador in Tokyo, Joseph C. Grew, neither Hull nor other American diplomats held much hope that a real settlement would result from a meeting of the two leaders. In view of Japan's recent record in the Far East and its declared future ambitions in that area, Hull distrusted Nomura's repeated pledges of peace and friendship. Moreover, Hull also doubted whether Konoye was strong enough to win the support of the militarists in his own cabinet for policies acceptable to the United States.

While neither Konoye nor the militarists paid the slightest attention to Japan's obligations under its alliance with the Axis or to Germany's insistence that Tokyo use the tripartite pact to curb American naval interference with the Nazi U-boat campaign against Britain in the Atlantic, this obvious rift between Tokyo and Berlin had little effect upon United States policy. The fundamental issue which precluded a Japanese-American understanding was and remained the China question. As long as Washington insisted upon Japan's withdrawal from China, no number of high-level meetings would amount to anything. The Japanese government knew this, and at a second imperial conference, held on September 6, it agreed that if diplomacy failed to produce results "by the end of October, the Japanese Government and the High Command should make up their minds to undertake a war against the United States, Great Britain, and the Netherlands, while making a special effort to prevent America and the Soviet Union from joining in united action against Japan."

On October 2, Secretary Hull informed Nomura that there should be "an agreement in principle upon fundamental questions" before a meeting between Roosevelt and Konoye could take place. Since such agreement was impossible as long as Japan refused to withdraw its troops from China and Indochina, the meeting between the two never occurred, and the Konoye government was forced to resign. On October 17 General Hideki Tojo, the leader of the militarist faction, became prime minister. In November Nomura was joined in Washington by the able and experienced diplomat Saburu Kurusu for a final attempt at negotiation. The Japanese government, already determined to go to war should negotiations fail, was pressing its envoys for a solution before Tojo's deadline of November 25, which was later extended to November 29. The United States, on the other hand, wanted to prolong talks, since Allied preparations for the defense of American, British, and Dutch possessions in the Pacific were still incomplete. Throughout these last fevered efforts to avoid war, Washington neither was deceived by nor was ignorant of Japanese intentions, though it was not aware of the specifics of Japan's war plans. Even before the final series of talks between the Japanese envoys and Hull were undertaken, Ambassador Grew warned the State Department on November 17 "to guard against sudden Japanese naval or military actions in such areas as are not now involved in the Chinese theater of operations."

On November 20, Nomura informed Hull of Japan's final proposal. Since the United States was intercepting Tokyo's secret instructions to its Washington embassy, the State Department knew the contents of the Japanese proposal before Nomura and Kurusu presented it officially. There was little in this proposal which differed substantially from the one of August 6. And even though Hull found it unacceptable, he was unwilling to reject it outright. His first move was to take up Roosevelt's idea, discussed at a cabinet meeting earlier that month, of offering the Japanese a temporary *modus vivendi* while renewed efforts at working out a general settlement were underway. This plan, however, was bitterly opposed by the Chinese, who were frightened that any concessions Japan might receive would be at their expense. And when Australia and Britain showed little enthusiasm for the proposal, the idea was dropped. In its place Hull offered the Japanese, on November 26, a ten-point program which reiterated all of the American principles.

Nomura and Kurusu were so distressed upon learning the unyielding nature of these terms that they were reluctant to submit them to their own government. The reason for their distress was real. Like Hull, who had access to the information which the United States government was getting from the decoded Japanese Foreign Office messages, they knew that further discussion was pointless. Moreover, they had been informed by Tokyo a few days earlier that if the United States rejected the Japanese proposal of November 20, then "things are automatically going to happen." These "things" were the Japanese preparations for a surprise strike at Pearl Harbor.

Hull, Roosevelt, and other high officials in Washington realized now that war with Japan was unavoidable. Hull admitted as much. "I have washed my hands of it," he told War Secretary Stimson on November 27, "and it is now in the hands of you and Knox—the Army and the Navy." On the same day the United States government cautioned London about the possibility of a Japanese attack on its Asiatic possessions, and it sent warnings to American military and naval commanders that war was imminent. George C. Marshall, the Chief of Staff, alerted Douglas MacArthur, the Commander in Chief of the Far Eastern forces of the United States in Manila; and Admiral Harold R. Stark, the Chief of Naval Operations, sent a "war message" to Admiral Husband E. Kimmel, the Commander in Chief of the Pacific Fleet at Pearl Harbor.

The American proposal of November 26 was never intended as an ultimatum, but that it left the Japanese with little hope of resolving their difficulties with the United States through further negotiations is undeniable. To Japan it was now a question of submitting to America's proposals, which would mean a humiliating withdrawal from China and abandonment of long-held plans for a "new order" in Asia, or going to war to try to realize them. For America to accept Japan's terms, even with the concessions the Japanese were willing to make on Indochina, meant yielding or compromising historic and cherished principles. Moreover, public opinion in the United States by this time had associated Japanese ambitions in Asia with Hitlerism in Europe, and it was unlikely that it would have tolerated any concessions at China's expense or anything that appeared to appease Japanese militarism.

The majority of the American people, on the other hand, did not appreciate the gravity of the situation. Underestimating the military and economic power of Japan, they never suspected that the Japanese would have the audacity to launch an attack upon the United States. Nor did the highest officials in Washington anticipate such an action. As late as November 25, at a special meeting of the cabinet, Roosevelt, Hull, Stimson, Knox, Marshall, and Stark reviewed the developing Far Eastern crisis

180   THE ERA OF F.D.R., 1933-1945

and concluded that Japan would attack the British and Dutch possessions and bypass Guam, the Philippines, and other American territories. What "troubled us very much" at this meeting, Stimson recalled later, was how the administration could win the full support of the American people in a war against Japan if Tokyo limited its attack to the British and Dutch territories.[22] Like the majority of the American people, Stimson and the administration believed "that the Japanese, however wicked their intentions, would have the good sense not to get involved in war with the United States." Moreover, the American government, as Stimson remarked, "paid the Japanese the compliment of assuming that they would take the course best calculated to embarrass their potential enemies. It seemed obvious that by limiting their overt attack to such areas as Thailand or the Dutch East Indies or even Singapore they would insure a serious division of opinion among Americans." [23]

The Japanese, however, had already determined that the success of their plans in the South Pacific depended upon their wiping out the United States Pacific fleet at Pearl Harbor. Preparations for the Hawaiian attack, which had been going on for nearly a year, moved quickly after the end of October. On November 7, Admiral Chuichi Nagumo was made commander of the task force which was to hit Pearl Harbor, and ten days later the first of the twenty-five warships which were assigned to him for the operation left Japan for Tankan Bay in the Kurile Islands to await further orders. On November 25 Tokyo instructed Nagumo to proceed toward Hawaii the next day. Since Japan had not yet irrevocably decided to go to war against the United States (this decision was reached on December 1) and since total secrecy and surprise were of the utmost importance, Nagumo was instructed to return to Japan if his task force was discovered before December 6 by American naval or air patrols. He was never detected, and with complete surprise, while negotiations in Washington were still continuing and no declaration of war had been made, the first of Nagumo's carrier-based planes appeared over Pearl Harbor at 7:55 A.M., Sunday, December 7, 1941. With this paralyzingly successful blow, the United States, like so many nations in Europe, Asia, and Africa during the previous decade, had become the victim of aggression.

On the following day Congress, with but the single dissenting vote

[22] Richard N. Current, "How Stimson Meant to 'Maneuver' the Japanese," *Mississippi Valley Historical Review*, XL (June 1953), 67–74.
[23] Henry L. Stimson and McGeorge Bundy, *On Active Service in Peace and War* (New York, 1948), pp. 385, 390.

THE COMING OF WORLD WAR II   181

of Montana's Congresswoman Jeannette Rankin, declared that a "state of war" existed with Japan. Three days later Germany and Italy, removing any doubts as to the ultimate purposes of the aggressor nations and in accordance with their pledge to support Japan against the United States, declared war upon America. Meanwhile, on December 8, Great Britain had declared war on Japan. The European and Asiatic conflicts were thus merged into a single global war.

Suggested Readings

General accounts of American foreign policy since 1933 include the brief survey volume in the *Chronicles of America* by Allan Nevins, *The New Deal and World Affairs* (New Haven, Conn., 1950); Walter Lippmann and William O. Scroogs, *et al.*, eds., *The United States in World Affairs, 1933 . . . 1939* (New York, 1934–40), a series of annual volumes published by the Council on Foreign Relations, containing much useful documentary material; and Wilfred Funk, ed., *Roosevelt's Foreign Policy, 1933–1941* (New York, 1942).

All of the general diplomatic texts, such as Thomas A. Bailey, *A Diplomatic History of the American People* (6th ed., New York [1958]), and Samuel F. Bemis, *A Diplomatic History of the United States* (4th ed., New York [1955]), and the more recent one by Nelson M. Blake and Oscar J. Barck, Jr., *The United States in Its World Relations* (New York, 1960) contain useful chapters with suggestions for further reading.

An especially useful work, Jules Davids, *America and the World of Our Time* (New York, 1960), has excellent bibliographies and is particularly detailed on events of the 1930's and 1940's.

Roosevelt's ideas and thinking on foreign policy questions are analyzed in Willard Range, *Franklin D. Roosevelt's World Order* (Athens, Ga. [1959]). The effect of the European war on the Chief Executive's authority is ably told in Louis W. Koenig, *The Presidency and the Crisis: Powers of the Office from the Invasion of Poland to Pearl Harbor* (New York, 1944).

There are numerous diaries and memoirs which are useful and revealing. Besides those of Cordell Hull, already cited, see William C. Bullitt, *Report to the American People* (Boston, 1940), the story of the American ambassador to France; Joseph E. Davies, *Mission to Moscow* (New York, 1941), the account of the American ambassador to the Kremlin; William E. and Martha Dodd, eds., *Ambassador Dodd's Diary, 1933–1938* (New York, 1941), containing the analysis of the American ambassador to Berlin on the rise of Hitler; and Joseph C. Grew, *Ten Years in Japan . . .* (New York, 1944), which covers the years Grew was ambassador (1933–42), but should be supplemented with his lengthier study edited by Walter Johnson, ed., *Turbulent Era: A Diplomatic Record of Forty Years, 1904–1945* (2 vols., Boston [1952]). Other personal records of value include volume III of Harold L. Ickes, *The Secret Diary of Harold L. Ickes*, already cited, which covers the years 1939–41;

Raymond Moley, *After Seven Years* (New York, 1939); Elliott Roosevelt, *As He Saw It* (New York, 1946), which covers some of the events of the years 1941 to 1945; Elliott Roosevelt, ed., *F.D.R.: His Personal Letters, 1928–1945* (4 vols., New York, 1947–50); Samuel I. Rosenman, *Working with Roosevelt* (New York, 1952); John Morton Blum, ed., *From the Morgenthau Diaries*, cited previously; Edward R. Stettinius, *Lend-Lease: Weapon for Victory* (New York, 1944); Henry L. Stimson, *The Far Eastern Crisis . . .* (New York, 1936) and the same author with McGeorge Bundy, *On Active Service . . .* (New York, 1948); William L. Shirer, *Berlin Diary, 1939–1941* (New York, 1941), the perceptive observations of an informed reporter; and Sumner Welles, *The Time for Decision* (9th ed., New York, 1944) as well as the same author's two other works, *Seven Decisions That Shaped History* (New York, 1950) and *Where Are We Heading?* (New York, 1946).

Among the foreign personal records, the most comprehensive and beautifully written are those of Winston S. Churchill, *The Second World War* (6 vols., Boston, 1948–53); but see also Galeazzo Ciano, *The Ciano Diaries, 1939–1943* (Garden City, N.Y., 1946), the views of Italy's foreign minister; the brief statement by Kichisaburo Nomura, "Stepping Stones to War," *Proceedings of the United States Naval Institute*, LXXVII (September 1951), 927–31; and Adolf Hitler, *Mein Kampf* (New York, 1939), a work which should not be minimized.

Nearly all of the Roosevelt biographies that cover the presidential years have something to say about F.D.R.'s conduct of foreign affairs. Robert E. Sherwood, *Roosevelt and Hopkins*, cited previously, is especially valuable. See also Harold B. Hinton, *Cordell Hull*, also cited before.

On New Deal tariff and trade policies, see Raymond L. Buell, *The Hull Trade Program* (New York, 1938); Grace L. Beckett, *The Reciprocal Trade Agreements Program* (New York, 1941); Francis B. Sayre, *The Way Forward: The American Trade Agreements Program* (New York, 1939); John M. Letiche, *Reciprocal Trade Agreements in the World Economy* (New York, 1948); Herbert Feis, *The Changing Pattern of International Economic Affairs* (New York, 1940); and Carl J. Kreider, *The Anglo-American Trade Agreement: A Study of British and American Commercial Policies, 1934–1939* (Princeton, N.J. [1943]).

Among the many works on the New Deal's Latin American policy, see Bryce Wood, *The Making of the Good Neighbor Policy* (New York, 1961) and the short but very good account by Edward O. Guerrant, *Roosevelt's Good Neighbor Policy* (Albuqerque, N.M., 1950). A highly competent review of the past thirty years is Donald M. Dozer, *Are We Good Neighbors?: Three Decades of Inter-American Relations, 1930–1960* (Gainesville, Fla., 1959). More specialized accounts include Henry F. Guggenheim, *The United States and Cuba* (New York, 1934); Rexford G. Tugwell, *The Stricken Land* (Garden City, N.Y., 1947), on Puerto Rico; Nathaniel and Sylvia Weyl, *The Reconquest of Mexico: The Years of Lázaro Cárdenas* (London, 1939); and E. David Cronon, *Josephus Daniels in Mexico* (Madison, Wis., 1960), for the details of Daniels' eight-year term as F.D.R.'s ambassador to Mexico.

The "great debate" between the isolationists and the interventionists can be studied in several works. Wayne S. Cole, *America First: The Battle against Isolation* (Madison, Wis., 1953) is a detailed and carefully documented monograph on the America First Committee. The internationalist cause is equally well treated by Walter Johnson, *The Battle against Isolation* (Chicago, 1944). An excellent work on the isolationism of the 1930's is Selig Adler, *The Isolationist Impulse: Its Twentieth Century Reaction* (London, 1957). Contemporary works reflecting the mood of the times include Charles A. Beard, *The Open Door at Home: A Trial Philosophy of National Interest* (New York, 1934); the same author's *A Foreign Policy for America* (New York, 1940); and Edwin M. Borchard and William P. Lage, *Neutrality for the United States* (New Haven, Conn., 1937). Other useful works on this subject are Allen W. Dulles and Hamilton F. Armstrong, *Can America Stay Neutral?* (New York, 1939); Jerome Frank, *Save America First: How to Make Democracy Work* (New York, 1938); Harold Lavine and James Wechsler, *War Propaganda and the United States* (New Haven, Conn., 1940); Raymond L. Buell, *Isolated America* (New York, 1940); and Charles G. Fenwick, *American Neutrality: Trial and Failure* (New York, 1940). For a more specialized account, see F. Jay Taylor, *The United States and the Spanish Civil War* (New York, 1956).

Convenient references for public opinion are Hadley Cantril, ed., *Public Opinion, 1935-1946* (Princeton, N.J., 1951) and the same author's more specific article, "America Faces the War: A Study in Public Opinion," *Public Opinion Quarterly*, IV (September 1940), 387-407. But see also William A. Lydgate, *What America Thinks* (New York, 1944); Archibald McLeish, *American Opinion and the War* (New York, 1942); and the pertinent sections of Thomas A. Bailey, *The Man in the Street: The Impact of American Public Opinion on Foreign Policy* (New York, 1948). For an article which sheds considerable light on the changes in American opinion, consult Philip E. Jacob, "Influences of World Events on United States 'Neutrality' Opinion," *Public Opinion Quarterly*, IV (March 1940), 48-65.

The most convenient place to begin to sift through the large amount of literature on the events leading to American participation in World War II is Wayne S. Cole, "American Entry into World War II: A Historiographical Appraisal," *Mississippi Valley Historical Review*, XLIII (March 1957), 595-617.

One of the most balanced and carefully researched analyses of the events leading to American participation is the two volume work by William L. Langer and S. Everett Gleason, *The Challenge to Isolation, 1937-1940* (New York, 1952) and *The Undeclared War, 1940-1941* (New York, 1953). Also internationalist in point of view is the able work of Basil Rauch, *Roosevelt: From Munich to Pearl Harbor* (New York, 1950). Donald F. Drummond, *The Passing of American Neutrality, 1937-1941* (Ann Arbor, Mich., 1955) is careful and judicious.

Emphasizing the Far Eastern origins of American involvement is the first of an excellent series of volumes by Herbert Feis, *The Road to Pearl Harbor: The Coming of the War between the United States and Japan* (Princeton, N.J., 1950). See also the careful study of Robert J. C. Butow, *Tojo and the*

184   THE ERA OF F.D.R., 1933-1945

Coming of the War (Princeton, N.J., 1961); Paul W. Schroeder, *The Axis Alliance and Japanese-American Relations, 1941* (Ithaca, N.Y. [1958]), a persuasive statement of the influence of the Tripartite Treaty in bringing about the failure of Japanese-American diplomacy; Richard N. Current, *Secretary Stimson: A Study in Statecraft* (New Brunswick, N.J., 1954), which is critical of its subject's role in the War Department; and Samuel Eliot Morison, *The Rising Sun in the Pacific, 1931–April 1942* (Boston, 1948), the well-written third volume in the author's fourteen-volume *History of United States Naval Operations in World War II.*

The isolationist interpretation is revealed in the two studies by Charles A. Beard, *American Foreign Policy in the Making, 1932–1940* (New Haven, Conn., 1946) and *President Roosevelt and the Coming of War, 1941* (New Haven, Conn., 1948). Another strongly revisionist indictment of F.D.R.'s diplomacy is Charles C. Tansill, *Back Door to War—Roosevelt's Foreign Policy, 1933–1941* (Chicago, 1952). Revisionism and extreme anti-Rooseveltian bias are shown in William H. Chamberlain, *America's Second Crusade* (Chicago, 1950); John T. Flynn, *The Roosevelt Myth*, already cited; George E. Morgenstern, *Pearl Harbor: The Story of the Secret War* (New York, 1947); Frederic R. Sanborn, *Design for War: A Study of Secret Power Politics, 1937–1941* (New York, 1951); Harry Elmer Barnes, ed., *Perpetual War for Perpetual Peace: A Critical Examination of the Foreign Policy of Franklin Delano Roosevelt and Its Aftermath* (Caldwell, Idaho, 1953); and Robert A. Theobald, *Final Secret of Pearl Harbor: The Washington Contribution to the Japanese Attack* (New York, 1954).

Several articles have appeared which analyze the work of the revisionists. See especially Herbert Feis, "War Came at Pearl Harbor: Suspicions Considered," *Yale Review*, XLV (March 1956), 378–90; Robert H. Ferrell, "Pearl Harbor and the Revisionists," *The Historian*, XVII (Spring 1955), 215–33; Samuel Eliot Morison, "Did Roosevelt Start the War—History through a Beard," *The Atlantic Monthly*, CLXXXII (August 1948), 91–97; and Arthur M. Schlesinger, Jr., "Roosevelt and His Detractors," *Harper's Magazine*, CC (June 1950), 62–68.

The United States' relations with Germany are carefully appraised in Hans L. Trefousse, *Germany and American Neutrality, 1933–1941* (New York, 1951), but see also the more general account by Samuel Eliot Morison, *The Battle of the Atlantic, 1939–1943* (Boston, 1947), volume I in the author's *History of United States Naval Operations in World War II.* On the destroyer deal, see the article by Edwin Borchard, "The Attorney General's Opinion on the Exchange of Destroyers for Naval Bases," *American Journal of International Law*, XXXIV (October 1940), 690–99, and Herbert W. Briggs, "Neglected Aspects of the Destroyer Deal," *American Journal of International Law*, XXXIV (October 1940), 560–87. For the Atlantic Charter, see Harold L. Hoskins, *The Atlantic Pact* (Washington, D.C., 1949).

Russian-American relations are surveyed from the beginning in Thomas A. Bailey, *America Faces Russia* . . . (Stanford, Calif., 1951); Foster Rhea Dulles, *The Road to Teheran: The Story of Russia and America, 1781–1943*

THE COMING OF WORLD WAR II   185

(Princeton, N.J., 1944); and William A. Williams, *American-Russian Relations, 1781–1947* (New York, 1952). See also Meno Lovenstein, *American Opinion of Soviet Russia* (Washington, D.C. [1941]).

J. Fred Rippy, *South America and Hemisphere Defense* (Baton Rouge, La., 1941) and the same author's *Caribbean Danger Zone* (New York, 1940) are useful on hemispheric problems. Consult also the pertinent sections of Maurice Matloff and Edwin M. Snell, *Strategic Planning for Coalition Warfare, 1941–1942* (Washington, D.C., 1953), a volume in the *United States Army in World War II* series.

The reasons for Japan's successful attack on Pearl Harbor have been investigated in great detail. A convenient place to begin is Louis Morton, "Pearl Harbor in Perspective: A Bibliographical Survey," *Proceedings of the United States Naval Institute*, LXXXI (April 1955), 461–68. The largest official collection is U. S. Congress, House of Representatives, Joint Committee on Investigation of Pearl Harbor Attack, *Hearings . . . Authorizing Investigation of Attack on Pearl Harbor . . . and Events and Circumstances Relating Thereto*, 79th Cong., 1st and 2d sess. (39 parts, Washington, D.C., 1946). A useful documentary selection has been collected by Hans L. Trefousse, ed., *What Happened at Pearl Harbor?* (New York, 1958), but consult also Tracy B. Kittredge, "The Muddle before Pearl Harbor," *U. S. News & World Report*, XXVII (December 3, 1954), 52–63. Largely on the basis of the evidence disclosed at the congressional hearing, Walter Millis wrote *This Is Pearl! The United States and Japan, 1941* (New York, 1947), an able summary of the events of that year. Equally dramatic in its presentation is Walter Lord, *Day of Infamy* (New York, 1957). One of the best short accounts is the article by Robert E. Ward, "The Inside Story of the Pearl Harbor Attack," *Proceedings of the United States Naval Institute*, LXXVII (December 1951), 1271–83. Walter Karig and Wilbourn Kelley, *Battle Report: Pearl Harbor to Coral Sea* (New York, 1944) is based on official navy records.

Among the personal recollections of varying merit, see Kazuo Sakamaki, *I Attacked Pearl Harbor* (New York, 1949), the somewhat vague story of one of the Japanese midget-submarine officers; William A. Maguire, *The Captain Wears a Cross* (New York, 1943), the eye-witness account of a Pearl Harbor chaplain; and by far the best of these accounts, Mitsuo Fuchida, "I Led the Air Attack on Pearl Harbor," *Proceedings of the United States Naval Institute*, LXXVIII (September 1952), 939–52. Husband E. Kimmel, *Admiral Kimmel's Story* (Chicago, 1955) is the apologia of the American naval officer in charge.

On Wendell Willkie and the election of 1940, consult James A. Farley, *Jim Farley's Story*, already cited, which deals with the third term question. Mary E. Dillon, *Wendell Willkie, 1892–1944* (Philadelphia [1952]) is a full-length portrait, but see also Joseph Barnes, *Willkie: The Events He Was Part of, The Ideas He Fought for* (New York, 1952) and Donald Bruce Johnson, *The Republican Party and Wendell Willkie* (Urbana, Ill., 1960). Willkie's foreign policy ideas are summarized in his own book, *One World* (New York, 1943).

5

The United States in

World War II, 1941-1945

ENTRY INTO the war as a belligerent made the United States a member of a worldwide combination of nations engaged in defending themselves against aggression. On January 1, 1942, a pact was signed at Washington, D.C., by the representatives of twenty-six governments, in which they accepted the Atlantic Charter, pledged themselves "to employ . . . [their] full resources, military or economic" to defeat the Tripartite Powers and not "to make a separate armistice or peace with the enemies," and—at Roosevelt's suggestion—assumed the title of the United Nations. Immediate steps were taken to coordinate the activities of the United States with those of its allies.

THE ALLIED NATIONS ON
THE DEFENSIVE, 1941–1943

The Anglo-American war program, which had been decided upon in the secret staff talks held in Washington during the early part of 1941, called for taking the offensive first against Germany, if possible in 1943. This plan, named ABC-1, also stipulated that Britain and the United States would not undertake any large-scale operations against

Japan until Germany had been defeated. Hitler, it was agreed, posed a far greater immediate threat than Tojo. But during most of 1942 neither the United States nor its allies could expect to be strong enough for offensive action anywhere. The initiative, therefore, would necessarily remain with the Axis. This was particularly true in the Pacific.

The War against Japan: From Pearl Harbor to Guadalcanal

The forces which the Americans, the British, and the Dutch could immediately muster for the defense of the East Indies were very weak, and the Japanese enjoyed initially an overwhelming superiority. Japanese military and naval operations, moreover, had been planned with great skill and care. As a result, during the winter and spring following Pearl Harbor the American people tasted a series of bitter and humiliating defeats.

The results of the December 7 raid on the United States' army, navy, and air force installations in the Hawaiian Islands were not made public for a year so that the American people were not at once aware of the extent of Toyko's victory over their fighting forces in the Pacific. In this bold opening strike of the Pacific war, the Japanese had employed a total of 353 aircraft, including high-altitude and dive bombers, torpedo planes, and fighters. The raid lasted one hour and fifty minutes, during which time the Japanese lost 29 planes. The damage they inflicted upon the United States was staggering. Total deaths numbered 2,403, of which 2,335 were servicemen and 68 civilians. Another 1,178 Americans were wounded, of whom 1,143 were members of the armed forces and 35 were noncombatants. The army and the navy lost 188 of their 476 planes. Hangars, repair shops, supply and oil depots, and all the islands' airfields were bombed and strafed. But it was the navy, America's chief deterrent against Japan's aggressive ambitions, which suffered the heaviest losses. The Japanese hit nineteen American warships, including every one of the eight battleships of the Pacific fleet. Although only one of these, the U.S.S. *Arizona*, was considered a total loss, four others were damaged so severely that they could not be put back into service for many months. Japanese ship losses amounted to five midget submarines. Tokyo had intended to use these small craft to guard the entrance to Pearl Harbor and to sink any American ships attempting to escape. This aspect of Japan's plans came to naught, but by the time the Japanese fliers had

188   THE ERA OF F.D.R., 1933–1945

completed their raids (9:45 A.M.), they had succeeded in inflicting upon the United States one of the worst naval disasters suffered by any power in modern times. With one strike, Japan had made it impossible for the American fleet to interfere with the invasion of the East Indies or with any of Tokyo's other immediate objectives in the Far East.

Japan's success, as later investigations concluded, was due to several factors. The Pacific commanders at Hawaii (Admiral Husband E. Kimmel and Lieutenant General Walter Short) were found to be at fault for failing to take adequate precautions against a surprise attack, in spite of the warnings they had received from Washington. Their "errors in judgment" stemmed partly from overconfidence—like their Washington chiefs, they did not believe Japan would attack Pearl Harbor—and partly from lack of cooperation and understanding among themselves and with their superiors in the Pentagon. Responsibility for the Pearl Harbor disaster, however, did not rest solely with the Hawaiian commanders. Washington officialdom, including the President, secretaries Knox and Stimson, General Marshall, and others, was also seriously at fault. In 1946 the government published the findings of a lengthy joint congressional investigating committee appointed to study the Pearl Harbor attack and the events leading to it.[1] The findings of this committee, which included six Democrats and four Republicans, were released in two reports. The *Majority Report*, signed by eight of the committee's members, blamed Kimmel and Short for their failure to heed Washington's warnings and to take every precaution to safeguard their forces; and it censured the administration in Washington for the inadequate measures it had taken to defend the country's armed forces against such an attack. "I think that the facts . . . clearly demonstrate," added one of the eight signers of the *Majority Report*, "that Hawaii was always the No. 1 point of danger and that both Washington and Hawaii should have known it at all times and acted accordingly." The two senators who signed the *Minority Report* asserted that the administration mishandled its intelligence in Washington and that its warnings to Kimmel and Short allowed for misinterpretation and failed to convey clearly the danger of an imminent surprise attack. Neither the facts disclosed by this committee nor the evidence discovered since then has succeeded in fixing the blame more specifically or in quelling the debate.

The Japanese success at Pearl Harbor was quickly followed by a series

[1] U. S. Congress, Joint Committee on the Investigation of the Pearl Harbor Attack. *Hearings*, 79th Cong., 1st sess. (39 pts., Washington, D.C., 1946).

THE UNITED STATES IN WORLD WAR II   189

of other major gains. On December 8 Japan moved against Malaya and Thailand. Two days later when the British Far Eastern fleet appeared off the Malayan coast to shell the invaders, Japanese torpedo planes and bombers sank two British capital ships, the 35,000-ton battleship H.M.S. *Prince of Wales* and the H.M.S. *Repulse*, a 32,000 ton battle cruiser. This terrible blow, which cost 840 seamen their lives and underscored the vulnerability of capital ships operating with inadequate air defenses and support, was as grievous to Britain's sea power in the Pacific as the attack upon Pearl Harbor had been to the United States. Not only did it further increase Japan's naval superiority, but it left Singapore and the whole of Southeast Asia virtually defenseless. On December 13, the Japanese captured Guam; ten days later, after encountering a gallant resistance, they took Wake; and on Christmas Day, the British forces on Hong Kong surrendered. Meanwhile the Japanese invasion troops, putting into effect plans which had been carefully prepared months before, proceeded to conquer other Allied possessions in the Western Pacific. Armies operating from Indochina invaded the British colony of Malaya and forced its defenders back to the island fortress of Singapore, which had long been regarded as the key to the defense of the whole East Indian Archipelago. Allied hopes for a long siege were quickly disappointed when the fortress, along with 70,000 British troops, fell into Japanese hands on February 15, 1942. Thailand had already been occupied without resistance, and Japanese troops were advancing into Burma, planning to cut the road by which supplies from the Western powers were being shipped to China. Neither the combined British and imperial forces nor two Chinese armies under the command of Lieutenant General Joseph W. Stilwell, whom Chiang Kai-shek had recently made his chief of staff, could stem the Japanese advance. By the end of May, 1942, all of Burma had been occupied, the supply road to China closed, and Japanese planes were bombing Indian cities. In Stilwell's words, the Japanese had given the Allies "a hell of a beating. We got run out of Burma and it is humiliating as hell." [2]

On the same day as the attack on Pearl Harbor Japanese planes, by means of another successful surprise attack, crippled the American air force in the Philippines. On December 10 Japan started to invade Luzon, the largest island in the archipelago. Other small landings followed quickly, and on December 22 the major Japanese invasion force, Lieutenant General Masaharu Homma's Fourteenth Army, landed at Lingayen

[2] Joseph W. Stilwell, *The Stilwell Papers* (New York [1948]), p. 106.

190 THE ERA OF F.D.R., 1933–1945

Gulf. Deprived of effective air or naval assistance and with his supply routes to Australia and Hawaii severed, General Douglas MacArthur realized that his inadequately trained and poorly equipped defending army of Filipino troops, aided by fewer than 25,000 American soldiers, was incapable of holding back the Japanese advance. On December 23, MacArthur decided to abandon most of the territory of the islands, to declare Manila an open city, which he did on December 26, and to take up defensive positions on the rock peninsula of Bataan. He made his headquarters at Corregidor, the fortified island guarding the entrance to Manila Bay. General Homma's conquering army occupied Manila on January 2, 1942, and on the same day the United States naval base at Cavite also fell to the enemy. The prolonged and heroic defense first of Bataan, which lasted until April 9, and afterward of Corregidor, which was not finally captured until May 6, provided the American people with the only note of encouragement among the events of this gloomy winter. To the Japanese, Bataan and Corregidor were embarrassing irritants. For four months these two battered outposts prevented General Homma from enjoying completely the results of his December victories and from engaging in other conquests.[3]

Elsewhere the Allies were unable even to delay the Japanese advance. Borneo, Celebes, and New Britain were occupied during January. During the last week of January, Allied warships succeeded in smashing a convoy of Japanese transports in their first naval engagement of the Pacific war, the Battle of the Macassar Straits. Three weeks later another Japanese convoy was destroyed off Bali, but Tokyo was prepared for heavy losses, and continued to enjoy an overwhelming superiority in manpower and equipment. Macassar and Sumatra were taken during February, and Java, the richest and most densely populated of all the East Indian islands, could now be attacked from three sides. Dutch, British, and American warships in the region tried to delay the island's capture, but in a three-day naval engagement beginning on February 27, the Japanese annihilated the Allied striking force of five cruisers, six destroyers, and a sloop. By March 10 all resistance in Java had ended. Meanwhile the Japanese had landed on the northern coast of New Guinea, and Australia was now in danger of being invaded.

By the end of the first five months of war Japan had almost completed its conquest of the East Indies. Whether the Allied nations would

[3] Louis Morton, "The Decision to Withdraw to Bataan," in Kent Roberts Greenfield, ed., *Command Decisions* (Washington, D.C., 1960), pp. 151–72.

succeed in retaining any strongholds in the western Pacific seemed more than doubtful. Only Major General James H. Doolittle's successful raid on Tokyo (April 18) provided any relief from the seemingly endless reports of retreat, disaster, and defeat which came from the Pacific during the early months of 1942. Doolittle's sixteen B-25 army bombers, which took off from the aircraft carrier *Hornet,* inflicted far less damage on the enemy than the Japanese had upon Pearl Harbor. Still, it was a daring exploit which brought momentary panic to Japan and aroused jubilation in the United States, and it served as a small example of what the Japanese might expect in the future.

Early in May, 1942, the tide of Japanese victory was halted. The Allied nations were able to hold India and Australia, the two essential bases for future offensives against the Japanese positions in the southern Pacific. India was primarily a British responsibility, although the inability of London's officials to secure cooperation in the defense of the country from the Indian nationalist leaders caused much concern in Washington and among the American people. Sir Archibald Wavell, the British general who had defeated the Italians in Africa early in 1941, was appointed to command the Allied forces in India. Despite numerous difficulties, he succeeded in keeping India in the fight against Japan.

Australia, on the other hand, although a British dominion, turned to Washington rather than to London for assistance. American troops were sent to this island continent, and on March 17 General MacArthur, who had earned both the applause of military experts and the admiration of the public by his skillful defense of Bataan, arrived in Darwin, Australia, to take command of the Allied forces in the Southwest Pacific. "The President of the United States ordered me to break through the Japanese lines and proceed from Corregidor to Australia," he declared upon arriving, "for the purpose, as I understand it, of organizing the American offensive against Japan, a primary purpose of which is the relief of the Philippines. I came through and I shall return." [4] Early in May, a Japanese armada on its way to attack Port Moresby in southern New Guinea appeared in the Coral Sea, off the northern coast of Australia. In the naval battle which followed (May 7–8), the first in the history of sea warfare to be fought exclusively with planes operating from the aircraft carriers of the two opposing fleets, American flyers inflicted serious damage upon the Japanese. More important, it forced Tokyo to abandon

[4] Quoted in Louis L. Snyder, *The War: A Concise History, 1939–1945* (New York [1960]), pp. 218–19.

192   THE ERA OF F.D.R., 1933–1945

its effort to take Port Moresby. The Americans, however, also suffered serious losses, the most important of which was the carrier *Lexington*.

Thwarted in their plans for an attack on Australia, the Japanese then turned eastward for a direct assault upon American bases. On June 3 they bombed the Alaskan base at Dutch Harbor, but their plans to capture this northern outpost were frustrated when American planes, operating from two recently constructed air bases unknown to Tokyo, attacked the Japanese warships. Caught by surprise and unwilling to risk the possibility of superior American forces, they abandoned their projected invasion of Dutch Harbor. They succeeded, however, in occupying Attu and Kiska in the Aleutians.

Meanwhile a huge Japanese naval force of some 200 ships of all kinds was moving across the Pacific to capture Midway Island, Hawaii's strategic western outpost. The advance against Midway, planned and executed by Admiral Isoroku Yamamoto, the Commander in Chief of the combined Japanese fleet, was timed to coincide with the strike at Dutch Harbor in the hope that the American fleet would be diverted to the north, thus permitting the Japanese carriers to attack Midway's airfields, destroy the island's defenses, and prepare the way for the transports to unload the invading army. Admiral Yamamoto's plans also called for the liquidation of the American fleet, and for this job he had assembled his fastest and most powerful capital ships. This grandiose project, intended to eliminate the United States as a Pacific power, not only failed but was turned into the first and probably the most decisive American victory of the Pacific war. "At one stroke," Churchill wrote later, "the dominant position of Japan in the Pacific was reversed." [5] Though greatly outnumbered (three American carriers against the Japanese's eight and not a single United States battleship to oppose Yamamoto's eleven), the American fleet nonetheless enjoyed certain other advantages. Admiral Chester W. Nimitz, who had succeeded Kimmel as Commander in Chief of the United States Pacific fleet, was prepared for the Japanese attack, having been apprised of it from intelligence gained from the enemy's secret code, and he deployed his three carriers in such a way as to "inflict maximum damage" upon the Japanese armada. In addition, Nimitz could count upon land-based bombers and fighters from Midway itself. The battle began on June 4, with the first round going to the Japanese. Midway's installations and air strips were bombed, but the raid, though damaging, failed to destroy the airfields. The initial American attack, a

[5] Winston S. Churchill, *The Second World War* (6 vols., Boston, 1948–53), IV, 253.

General Douglas MacArthur and Admiral Chester Nimitz, shown here conferring with F.D.R., were the leading American commanders in the war against Japan. (Navy Department)

squadron of twenty-six Midway-based planes, scored some hits against the invading task force but was badly beaten. Only nine of the twenty-six survived this sortie. But the battle was not over. While the enemy carriers were busily arming and fueling their planes for a second hit on Midway, American fliers from the carriers *Hornet, Enterprise,* and *Yorktown,* which were poised for just such a strike, fell upon the surprised Japanese flotilla with torpedoes and bombs and rained destruction upon three of Tokyo's carriers, one of which, the *Akagi,* was the flagship of Admiral Chuichi Nagumo. The Japanese, in the words of one of their flight commanders, "had been caught flat-footed in the most vulnerable condition possible—decks loaded with planes armed and fueled for an attack." [6] That afternoon dive bombers from the *Enterprise* attacked the fourth Japanese carrier. She sank the next day. Besides these four carriers, the Japanese lost a cruiser, some 300 planes, and 5,000 men. They also suffered considerable damage to other ships. The United States lost the carrier *Yorktown* and close to 150 aircraft. The victory at Midway was won by planes operating from carriers and from land bases on the island itself, reinforced by others from Hawaii. The two opposing fleets never even sighted each other.

The importance of the Battle of Midway in determining the course of the war in the Pacific cannot be overestimated. It ended the possibilities of further Nipponese conquests; it eliminated at once all danger to the security of Hawaii and the Pacific coast of the United States; and it deprived Toyko of the ability it had enjoyed for the past six months of fighting on its own terms. The Japanese would win other victories and the United States would suffer some serious reverses, but the ultimate victory of the Allied nations in the Pacific was now almost certain.

Two months after stopping the Japanese at Midway, the United States launched its first offensive in the Pacific. On August 7, American marines landed on Guadalcanal and Tulagi in the Solomon Islands, where the Japanese were constructing an airfield to attack Australia and to bomb the Allied convoys going there with vital supplies from the United States. Control of the Solomon bases, only 1,500 miles north of Sydney, was essential to both sides. The Japanese needed them to strike at Australia, and the Allies, aside from the necessity to secure that continent against attack, were dependent upon them to destroy the heavily fortified stronghold Japan held at Rabaul on the island of New Britain. The fighting which followed was long, desperate, and costly, but by the first week

[6] Quoted in Desmond Flower and James Reeves, eds., *The Taste of Courage: The War, 1939–1945* (New York [1960]), p. 503.

of February, 1943, despite the persistent attempts of Japanese land, air, and sea forces to regain the jungles and malarial swamps of Guadalcanal, the Americans succeeded in taking over the entire island. During this six-month campaign the United States navy, which had supported the initial landings and then defended the supply and troop ships bringing reinforcements, engaged the Japanese fleet in a series of naval battles, the most decisive of which was the one fought between November 12 and 15, in which a large Japanese task force was repulsed with even heavier losses than in the battles of Midway and the Coral Sea. The naval Battle of Guadalcanal, as this engagement has come to be called, more than avenged the naval defeat the Japanese had inflicted upon the United States in the Battle of Savo Island two days after the marines had landed on Guadalcanal.

As the struggle for Guadalcanal raged on, MacArthur, commanding Australian and United States troops, undertook a painful and difficult offensive against the Japanese in the jungles and mountains of New Guinea. At stake was Port Moresby on the island's southeastern coast. The Japanese had attempted to take Port Moresby earlier by sea, but their defeat in the Battle of the Coral Sea forced them to abandon the effort, at least temporarily. In mid-July they tried again, but this time decided to make an overland attack from their beachhead on the island's northeastern coast, and for two months fought on relentlessly, their prize nearly within grasp. On September 15 MacArthur launched a successful counteroffensive, and within less than two months the Japanese, back where they had been in July, were fighting stubbornly to stay on the beaches.

By the end of December, 1942, the Allies were beginning to inflict some serious defeats upon the Japanese war machine. And even though Guadalcanal and New Guinea were of minor importance, this operation served a useful purpose, as did the preparations which Stilwell and Wavell were making to reconquer Burma and to strengthen the Chinese armies by building a new road from Ledo in India to Myitkyina in Burma, where it would connect with the old Burma Road. These moves engaged the Japanese and deprived them of the full benefits of their conquests, they provided the Allied soldiers with invaluable combat experience in jungle fighting and amphibious operations, and they underscored the importance of cooperation among the commanders of the various armed services. Taken together, the Allied military and naval exploits of 1942 were essential preliminaries to that general Pacific offensive which would be undertaken whenever the United States could spare enough troops and resources from the European war fronts. Prior to such an attack, the American and Allied commands in the Pacific set themselves the task of weakening Japan by capturing the strategic islands Tokyo had recently occupied to defend the perimeters of its new and far-flung empire. It was this empire which the Allies were determined to take in preparing for future operations against the Japanese home islands. No effort was made to dislodge the Japanese from all the islands they occupied since, as Allied strategists indicated, it was only the key enemy bastions which guarded the empire that were vital. Once one of these was taken, the Japanese forces on the other islands, dependent upon supplies and support from the fallen base, were left defenseless, isolated, and quite often at the mercy of American naval guns. During 1942 the United States navy also weakened Japan's ability to fight by a process of attrition, sinking ships and destroying planes faster than the Japanese could replace them. In this endeavor, American and Allied submarines were especially successful. Japanese losses of merchant ships from United States submarine attacks were particularly heavy, as American undersea raiders increasingly penetrated the coastal waters of the home islands themselves.

The War against Germany

During 1942, while the United States was waging a limited though increasingly effective war against the Japanese in the Pacific, most of its energy and resources were being marshaled to defeat Germany. And while the country's military leaders generally believed that the campaigns of 1942 against Hitler would be of crucial importance, they also admitted that, as was the case in World War I, it would be at least a year before American troops could reach Europe in any large numbers. Meanwhile Hitler's war machine, taking advantage of America's inability to challenge the German armies in Europe, would doubtlessly employ all its resources in an effort to achieve victory before the United States could prevent it. As a result, the Allied leadership was prepared to accept some serious reverses. The all-important question which they had to face was how to prevent these German successes from being decisive.

THE ANGLO-AMERICAN FRONT: FROM DEFEAT
TO VICTORY IN AFRICA

Africa was the only theater of war where the British and the Americans met the Germans in land fighting, except for the commando raids against

THE UNITED STATES IN WORLD WAR II 197

the French ports of Saint-Nazaire and Dieppe in March and August, 1942. Although the Anglo-American forces engaged in the North African campaigns were relatively small, the strategic importance of the area was considerable. On January 7, 1942, the German Afrika Korps, commanded by the bold and highly capable Field Marshal Erwin Rommel, stopped the British Eighth Army's drive into Libya at El Agheila, some 500 miles west of Egypt. Two weeks later Rommel counterattacked, forcing the British to retreat. For the next four months Rommel's armored divisions pushed on relentlessly, inflicting crushing defeats on the British forces and driving them deep into Egypt. The Axis offensive was finally stopped on June 29, 1942, at El Alamein, some sixty miles from Alexandria. The British, secure behind defenses the enemy could neither penetrate nor outflank, now prepared for a new offensive. In August General Bernard Montgomery was given command of the British Eighth Army, and its forces were strengthened with tanks, planes, artillery, and other supplies from the United States. On October 23, with air and artillery superiority on its side, Montgomery's army took the offensive. The battle of El Alamein, concluded on November 4, was the first occasion in the war when any German army was decisively defeated. The remnants of Rommel's forces were driven back to Libya, beyond El Agheila, and into Tripolitania, leaving behind them thousands of prisoners and hundreds of tons of equipment; Montgomery had forced Rommel to retreat 1,200 miles. There would be other battles with the Afrika Korps before the Axis was entirely evicted from North Africa, but after the Battle of El Alamein Rommel's battered army no longer posed a serious threat. "The Battle of El Alamein," as Churchill noted, "was the turning point in British military fortunes during the World War. Up to Alamein we survived. After Alamein we conquered."

El Alamein was quickly followed by the first important American action in the European theater of the war. The convoying of American troops to the British Isles had started in January, and by the summer a considerable army, commanded by General Dwight D. Eisenhower, had been formed, but they had not yet been engaged in battle. On November 8, as Montgomery's Eighth Army was pushing west into Libya, an amphibious force of more than 800 ships from Britain and the United States landed American and Allied troops in the French colonies of Morocco and Algeria. Operation Torch, as this project was called, was one of the fruits of the long and much criticized maintenance of American diplomatic relations with the government of Vichy France. Apart from the two immediate objectives of American diplomacy, to establish friendly relations with the French officials in North Africa and to prevent the Nazis from taking over that region, both Roosevelt and Churchill hoped that Operation Torch would also placate Stalin, who was insisting upon a second front; strengthen the Allied naval and military situation in the Mediterranean, provide a steppingstone for an attack on Germany through southern Europe, assure Spain's continued neutrality, and guarantee Rommel's defeat. The whole operation was carefully planned and beautifully coordinated. At the end of five days all French resistance had ceased. The Vichy officials in the area, under the leadership of Admiral Jean François Darlan, who had earlier cooperated with the Nazis but had now rejected them, agreed to support the Allied nations. When Darlan was assassinated in December, 1942, he was succeeded by Henri Giraud, a French general who had fled to England from Nazi imprisonment and had joined the Anglo-American invasion forces to Africa. Meanwhile the reluctance of the French officials to adopt democratic policies, the hatred which French liberals felt toward men who had served the Vichy government, and the contest for power between Giraud and Charles de Gaulle, the leader of the Free French in London, all combined to cause the Allies a number of disheartening disputes.

The Allies had hoped that Operation Torch and the cooperation of the French in North Africa would be followed immediately by the expulsion of the remaining Axis forces in the region. Unfortunately German troops, ferried across from Sicily and from airfields and ports in Italy and France, reached Tunisia ahead of the Allies and were able to establish a number of strong positions there. They were soon joined by the retreating army of Marshal Rommel. And while few doubted that the Germans would eventually be expelled from Tunisia, it became quickly apparent that fighting would be prolonged and costly. Finally on May 13, 1943, after repulsing several strong German offensives, one of which, in mid-February, drove the Americans back more than a hundred miles, the Allies succeeded in defeating all the Axis forces. Two years and nine months after the first Italian offensive, the African phase of the European war had ended, and the Allies could now use the northern shores of that continent as a base for the invasion of Europe.

THE EASTERN FRONT

During the winter and spring of 1941 and 1942, the Russians had succeeded in pushing back the German invaders, although they had failed to capture any important strongholds. In June, 1942, the German armies, resuming the initiative, ended Russian resistance in the Crimea, and at the end of the month they launched a general offensive across the plains of southern Russia, hoping to drive through to the Caspian Sea and cut off the Soviet armies from the oil of the Caucasus. Continuing through the summer, by September the German advance had reached the Volga. Here, at the city of Stalingrad, the Soviet forces made a final stand, knowing that the fate of Russia depended on the outcome. For two months the Germans assaulted the city, but the Soviet defenses held. German losses were so heavy that by the third week in November they started to lose the initiative. The Battle of Stalingrad, like those of El Alamein and Midway, was one of the real turning points of the war. If the Battle of Britain, two years earlier, meant that Hitler had failed to win the war, the defense of Stalingrad marked the point when he began to lose it.

Hitler's failure to capture Stalingrad made possible a Soviet winter offensive, which was launched on November 19. During the next four months the Russians encircled and destroyed considerable sections of the German army, regained most of the territory lost during the summer of 1942, and threatened to drive through into the plains of the Ukraine and cut off even larger bodies of German troops from their sources of supply. These victories, like those of the Anglo-American Allies in the African desert, were convincing proof that military superiority had passed to the Allies.

The titanic struggle on the Russian front, in which larger armies and greater material resources were employed than in any previous war in history, dwarfed all other military operations. It was hoped that the British and Americans would be able to relieve the strain on the Russians by invading the continent of Europe and thereby initiating a second front, but during 1942 the Western Allies lacked men, supplies, and particularly ships for such an enterprise. The experimental raid on the French port of Dieppe had indicated the strength of the German defenses: more than half the invading force of about 6,000 men failed to return. In spite of repeated Soviet appeals for help, the Western Allies were forced to limit themselves to shipping supplies to Russia and to crippling German production by bombing raids.

The thousand-plane British bomber raids of the spring of 1942, like those of the Americans that summer, were far heavier than the biggest efforts of the Luftwaffe in the Battle of Britain, and considerable areas of Germany's industrial cities and railroad centers, among them Cologne, Essen, and Bremen, as well as those in Nazi-occupied countries, were destroyed. The military results of the Allied air war over Germany were controversial. Some authorities at the time, all of whom were outside the highest and most knowledgeable government circles, maintained that Hitler could be defeated by such air raids alone, and at considerably less expense than by an invasion of the continent. But as subsequent events were to prove, neither Germany's productive capacity nor its ability to wage war effectively was destroyed or seriously reduced. After the war, the *United States Strategic Bombing Survey*, appraising the results of the 1942 raids, declared that they "had no appreciable effect either on German munitions production or on the national output in general," and that it was the concentrated bombing of the German transportation system after September, 1944, which "was the most important single cause of Germany's ultimate collapse." [7]

THE ROAD TO VICTORY, 1943–1945

The European War

By the summer of 1943 the Allied nations had wrested the initiative from the Axis in both Europe and the Pacific, but while it was becoming increasingly certain that sooner or later Germany and Japan would be compelled to accept defeat, no one could predict whether the Russians would be able to continue their offensive or how soon the Western Allies could come to their aid by invading the continent. The Germans continued to show a remarkable capacity for defending themselves, despite their losses in Africa and Russia. Moreover, Allied operations were greatly hampered by the success of the Nazi submarine campaign. In one month alone—November, 1942—U-boat losses exceeded 700,000 tons. By December 31 of that year German submarines operating in the most vital sea lanes of the Allies, from the Arctic and the North Atlantic to the Caribbean, off the coastal waters of the United States, in the Gulf of Mexico, and along the strategic convoy routes to Europe, had destroyed more Allied tonnage than the British and the Americans had been able to build. Furthermore, the Germans were reported to be building submarines twice as fast as they were being sunk, and during the first months of 1943 more than 200 of them were in action. The U-boats took a heavy toll of British and American ships in March (514,744 tons), but by May,

[7] Quoted in Snyder, *op. cit.*, p. 399.

with improved radar and sonar detection, extended air patrols, and the addition of small aircraft carriers armed with antisubmarine planes to accompany the convoys across the Atlantic, the Allies succeeded in defeating what Churchill called the "worst evil" of World War II. So long as Hitler's U-boats were able to prevent the full strength of the United States from reaching Europe, the German military machine could not be decisively crushed, despite the blows it had received in Africa, at Stalingrad, and from the growing Allied air offensive of 1942. "The Battle of the Atlantic," as Churchill noted later, "was the dominating factor all through the war. Never for one moment could we forget that everything happening elsewhere, on land, at sea, or in the air, depended ultimately on its outcome. . . ." [8]

SICILY AND ITALY

By the summer of 1943, with effective control of the Atlantic sea lanes once again in Anglo-American hands, Britain and the United States prepared for their first major assault against the Axis in Europe. The invasion of Sicily (Operation Husky) had been agreed upon in January, 1943, when Roosevelt and Churchill met at Casablanca in French Morocco to plan future Anglo-American strategy in Europe. At that meeting Eisenhower, who was to command the Sicilian campaign, proposed that "if the real purpose of the Allies was to invade Italy for major operations to defeat that country completely," they should avoid Sicily and strike against Sardinia and Corsica. The only advantage in taking Sicily, argued Eisenhower, was "in opening up the Mediterranean sea routes." But the capture of Sardinia and Corsica "on the flank of the long Italian boot . . . would force a very much greater dispersion of enemy strength in Italy than would the mere occupation of Sicily. . . ." [9]

The defeat of the Axis was as vital to the British as it was to the Americans, but whereas Eisenhower and General Marshall insisted upon pursuing this objective with undeviating constancy, Churchill and his advisers pressed for greater flexibility. Opportunity for political advantage, whether immediate or after the war, should never be overlooked, for as Churchill commented, "political forces play their part" in achieving a substantial and meaningful victory. The Americans never subscribed to Churchill's position, and the divergent views of the two sides on this question were never satisfactorily reconciled. The issue arose over and

[8] Churchill, *op. cit.*, V, 6.
[9] Dwight D. Eisenhower, *Crusade in Europe* (New York, 1948), p. 185.

over again as new decisions had to be made, and after the war it was heatedly debated by writers on both sides of the Atlantic. At Casablanca the British succeeded in winning American approval for the Sicilian campaign, but only after the United States's military leaders made it clear "that everything done in the Mediterranean would continue to be subsidiary to and in support of the main purpose of attacking across the Channel in early 1944." [10]

On the morning of July 10, after more than two weeks of heavy bombardment, Anglo-American troops commanded by General Sir Harold Alexander landed on Sicily. Because the place of the landings was unexpected and because the weather had been bad the previous day, the defenders were taken partially by surprise. The initial assault was therefore speedily executed. Welcomed by the Sicilians and finding few Italian soldiers intent upon resisting the invaders, the Allied force advanced inland quickly. The United States Seventh Army, under the command of General George S. Patton, Jr., pushing west and then north, captured Palermo on July 22 and Marsala the next day. Along Sicily's east coast, General Montgomery's Eighth Army was driving north into Catania toward the port city of Messina, just two miles from the Italian mainland. The Allies had hoped to take this city quickly in order to isolate and capture the Axis forces on the island, but the Germans, aware of this, concentrated most of their troops in Catania, where, aided by the region's natural defenses, they staged a stubborn resistance. This, together with poor roads and malaria, slowed down Montgomery's advance. Catania fell to the Eighth Army on August 5, and twelve days later, with the surrender of Messina to the Americans, Operation Husky was completed. The success of the thirty-eight-day Sicilian campaign was marred by the fact, as Montgomery pointed out later, "that most of the German troops [about 60,000] got away across the Straits of Messina to Italy, and this when *we* had complete air and naval superiority." [11] For this the Allied command was strongly censured.

The invasion of Sicily precipitated a crisis in the Italian government which had been in the making for months. The defeat in Africa followed by the invasion of Sicily brought the Italian people face to face with the grim consequences of Mussolini's "shameful leadership." Tired of sacrifices and hardships for promises which never materialized, the Italian

---

[10] *Ibid.*, p. 186.
[11] Bernard Law, Viscount Montgomery of Alamein, *The Memoirs of Field-Marshal Montogomery* (Cleveland [1958]), p. 167.

Generals Omar N. Bradley (left) and George S. Patton (right), shown here conferring with Dwight Eisenhower, were the outstanding American field commanders during the liberation of Western Europe. (Culver Pictures, Inc.)

people were quite ready to rid themselves of their "Sawdust Caesar." The king, Victor Emmanuel III, and many of his ministers and other high government officials felt likewise, but in Churchill's words, "Who would 'bell the cat'?" A week after the Allies had landed in Sicily, on July 17, British and American fliers showered Italy's principal cities with a message from Churchill and Roosevelt appealing to the Italian people to repudiate the German alliance and their "own false and corrupt leaders. . . . The time has come for you to decide whether Italians shall die for Mussolini and Hitler—or live for Italy, and civilization." Two days later, while 500 American bombers were dropping more than 1,000 tons of high explosives on airfields, rail networks, and other military targets in and around Rome, Mussolini was at Rimini appealing to Hitler for help. But the only thing the Fuehrer could offer was to urge the Duce to continue to fight "so that Sicily may become for the enemy what Stalingrad was for us." Less than a week later, on July 25, Mussolini was forced to resign, and the king asked the elderly Marshal Pietro Badoglio to form a new government. For more than a month Badoglio tried to bargain with the Allied high command, hoping to avoid the unconditional surrender provisions Roosevelt and Churchill had announced at Casablanca. The Allies, surprised by Mussolini's sudden downfall, still had to decide among themselves upon what terms they would accept Italy's surrender. Should Badoglio be recognized? What should be expected of Italy? While these questions were being resolved and Eisenhower's headquarters was negotiating with Badoglio and his emissaries, the Germans entrenched themselves in northern and central Italy, occupying Rome on September 10. Two days later the Badoglio government accepted the unconditional surrender terms it had been trying so hard to avoid.

By this time the Allies had already invaded Italy. On September 3 Montgomery crossed the Straits of Messina and the Eighth Army proceeded to occupy the Calabrian peninsula; and on September 9, while a British naval squadron with 6,000 men steamed into Taranto and occupied that Italian base, General Mark Clark, commanding the United States Fifth Army, landed at Salerno. For six days the Germans, despite heavy Allied air attacks and naval gunfire, kept the Americans close to the beaches. Their resistance in the end proved futile, and on September 15 they withdrew. In the next two weeks Clark's army pushed steadily on to Naples, entering the city on October 1, just as Montgomery's forces on the Adriatic side of the peninsula were occupying Foggia. Southern Italy was now securely in Allied hands.

On October 13, the Badoglio government declared war on Germany, and Italy joined the fight against Hitler as a "cobelligerent." Much long and difficult fighting still remained, however, before Rome and central Italy were wrested from the Nazis. To expedite the liberation of Italy and to destroy the German army which was holding up the Allied march on Rome, on January 22, 1944, the British and the Americans landed a large amphibious force at Anzio and Nettuno, two villages some thirty miles south of Rome and approximately sixty miles behind the German lines.

Taken by surprise, the Germans offered "practically no opposition," according to Major General John P. Lucas, who commanded the invasion force. But instead of using this initial advantage to press ahead, Lucas chose to strengthen his beachhead and protect the port. As a result, Field Marshal Albert Kesselring, Rommel's successor in Italy, succeeded in establishing a strong defense, from which he launched a powerful counter-attack which nearly forced Lucas' men back to their ships.[12] Only after four months of the most dogged fighting did the Allies succeed in breaking through the German defenses. As is to be expected, Lucas' decision to delay has provoked considerable debate, especially since Kesselring's chief of staff declared that "The road to Rome was open, and an audacious flying column could have penetrated to the city." [13]

To relieve the pressure on Anzio, the Allies in February and March launched offensives against the town of Cassino, some fifty miles to the south of Anzio and a strong point in the German defenses along the Gustav Line. Little was accomplished, and the fight for Cassino, like the one at Anzio, proved prolonged and bitter. On May 11 the Allies opened another offensive. This time they were successful: a week later German resistance at Cassino was finally smashed, and along with it the town's famed sixth-century Benedictine abbey. While the Allies were piercing the Gustav Line at Cassino, the British and the Americans at Anzio were preparing to break the deadlock there, which they succeeded in doing before the end of the month. At last the two great obstacles to the occupation of Rome had been removed, and on June 4, 1944, General Mark Clark's Fifth Army entered the Eternal City. Two days later, the Allies invaded France; the war in Italy now became secondary to the events taking place in Western Europe. The liberation of the rest of Italy, however, was to occupy the Anglo-American armies for another year. By the time the Germans in Italy finally did surrender—the same day the Russians reached Berlin, May 2, 1945—the British and American armies were advancing into the Po valley.

FROM NORMANDY TO THE ELBE

The decision to destroy Hitler's *"Festung Europa"* by invading Germany through France grew out of the Anglo-American war plans agreed upon at Washington between Roosevelt and Churchill during the last week of December, 1941. At this meeting, the so-called Arcadia Conference, the two war leaders decided upon the defeat of Germany as their primary objective, and within the next several months initial plans calling for an invasion of the European continent early in the spring of 1943 were drafted by the American military chiefs and approved by the British "in principle." The need to aid the Russians, who were crying for a

[12] Martin Blumenson, "General Lucas at Anzio," in Greenfield, *op. cit.*, pp. 336, 340.
[13] Quoted in *ibid.*, p. 350.

second front, was great, and while the Western Allies realized the need of keeping the Soviet Union in the war, they were faced with difficult problems of their own which forced them to delay the invasion of Western Europe for a year. Production problems, especially the huge demand for landing craft and shipping, the U-boat menace, and Rommel's victories in North Africa, made it obvious to the British that a cross-Channel invasion had little chance of success in 1943. As an alternative, Churchill insisted upon a combined Anglo-American operation in North Africa or elsewhere in the Mediterranean, and Roosevelt, who was more sympathetic with the British in this case than with his military advisers, agreed and approved the North African project.

By the end of July, 1942, all hopes for an assault on Western Europe in 1943 had evaporated, and at a conference in Moscow in August Churchill and W. Averell Harriman, the lend-lease administrator at the time and F.D.R.'s personal representative, informed Stalin of the necessity to delay the opening of a second front for another year. Nine months later, in May, 1943, Roosevelt and Churchill met in Washington, this time with the combined chiefs of staff and their advisers, and fixed May 1, 1944, and the coast of Normandy as the date and place of Operation Overlord, the now much discussed second front. In August, at their Quebec meeting, the two Western leaders reasserted their intention to invade Western Europe in May, 1944, and agreed to support the operations in Normandy by attacking the Germans in southern France. Stalin was informed of these plans late in November when Roosevelt and Churchill conferred with the generalissimo at Teheran. A few days later, while meeting in Cairo, Roosevelt and Churchill agreed upon Dwight D. Eisenhower to command Overlord.

Intensive preparations were begun in mid-January, 1944, when Eisenhower arrived in London and assumed full responsibility of Supreme Headquarters, Allied Expeditionary Force (SHAEF). At his insistence, SHAEF was to have ultimate authority over all of the forces involved in Overlord—air, ground, and sea. To command the entire assault force, which was to be made up of a British and an American army, Eisenhower chose Montgomery. The battlefield commander of the American army was to be General Omar N. Bradley; later, when another American army was organized, Patton was selected to command it. During January, final plans for Overlord were completed, and D-Day was set for early June, the additional month's delay being necessitated by a shortage of landing craft.

To provide the huge invasion force with adequate supplies, southern England was turned into "one vast military camp, crowded with soldiers . . . and piled high with supplies and equipment. . . ." [14] To prepare for the initial assault and to sustain the beachheads, the Allies "assembled 150,000 men, 1500 tanks, 5300 ships and craft, and 12,000 planes." [15] One division alone, according to Eisenhower, "consumed about 600 to 700 tons of supplies per day," and the plan for Overlord called for putting five divisions on the beaches at once. As D-Day approached, "this mighty host," as Eisenhower described it, "was as tense as a coiled spring . . . a great human spring, coiled for the moment when its energy should be relieved and it would vault the English Channel in the greatest amphibious assault ever attempted." [16]

In the meantime British and American bombers pounded the industrial and military targets of Germany and occupied Europe day and night. In January the Allies began their strategic air offensive, and from then on a concerted effort was made to destroy the German air force, the aviation industry, oil refineries, transportation networks, and communication facilities. With increasing strength, sometimes as many as 800 bombers and 700 fighters in a single raid, the Allies dropped thousands of tons of high explosives upon Hitler's war plants. In April Anglo-American air fleets dropped 80,000 tons on Germany, twice the amount which Goering's Luftwaffe fleets had loosed on England in 1940 during the Battle of Britain. During the spring of 1944, while the Reich's productive capacity was being methodically blasted by British heavy bombers and American flying fortresses, the tactical air force attacked the German defenses all along the French coast, including the roads, bridges, and rail lines upon which they depended for supplies.

To deceive the Germans on the exact time and place of the invasion, the Allies delayed their heavy bombing of the Normandy coast until the early morning hours of D-Day. On that day, June 6, 1944, while the strategic and tactical air forces were striking at Normandy's defenses and hitting other vital inland targets, three paratroop divisions were dropped behind the enemy's lines. At dawn British and American naval units started bombarding the coast, and at 6:30 A.M. the first assault troops landed on the beaches of the Cotentin peninsula. Except on Omaha Beach, where the Americans encountered heavy opposition the first day, the landings were accomplished more easily than had been expected. Hitler,

[14] Eisenhower, *op. cit.*, p. 282. [15] Snyder, *op. cit.*, p. 364.
[16] Eisenhower, *op. cit.*, p. 364.

hoping to delay Nazism's doom, retaliated by terrorizing London with his "secret weapon," the V-1 robot bomb, but despite the heavy damage which these flying bombs inflicted upon life and property, Englishmen bore their ordeal with fortitude. The V-1 attacks on London had no effect upon Overlord, and by the end of the month the Allied invasion had advanced in some places as much as twenty miles beyond the beaches. For seven weeks the British and the Americans were locked in the Battle of the Beachheads. The fighting was difficult, and progress was slow. Cherbourg fell on June 27, but its harbor facilities, which the Allies needed badly, were completely shattered. The British, after failing once, took Caen on July 9, but only because Allied bombers pounded the city for two days before Montgomery's troops made their attack. On July 18, Saint-Lò fell to the Americans, and a week later Bradley, with a strong assist from the air force's bombers, launched a major offensive which demolished the German defenses and opened the way to the liberation of France. After the Saint-Lò breakout the Allied advance toward Germany moved quickly, sometimes as much as seventy-five miles a day. Hitler's troops, besides being assaulted on the ground by four Allied armies, were subjected continuously to heavy aerial attack and increasingly harassed by the bold strikes of the French underground and of other patriots who joined together to form the French Forces of the Interior.

August and September, 1944, were disastrous months for Hitler's Wehrmacht outside Germany. On August 15, while the Allied armies in northern France were pushing the Germans back on all fronts, French and American troops, commanded by General Jean de Lattre de Tassigny and Alexander M. Patch, landed on France's Mediterranean coast. Resistance to Dragoon, the code name for this operation, was slight; and by August 28, Nice, Marseilles, and Toulon—France's three principal southern ports—were all in Allied hands. Dragoon's next objective, to drive to the north and join with the Allied armies there, was also speedily accomplished. French and American troops took Lyons on September 3, and eight days later, west of Dijon, they met Patton's forces from the north. During the twenty-seven days that it took the Franco-American armies to reach Dijon, the Allied forces in northern France had liberated Paris (August 25) and, by the end of the month, nearly all of France, as well as Antwerp and Brussels (September 4). The Germans now proved as incapable of stopping Eisenhower's advance as the French and the British had been in halting the Nazi blitzkrieg in 1940. Once again,

Hitler tried to delay the Allied onslaught against Germany by resorting to terror. Early in September the first V-2 rockets struck London. Defense against these high-speed (approximately 3,400 miles per hour) missiles was practically impossible, and Britain was forced to withstand Hitler's vengeance until the Allies captured the launching sites. Like the V-1, however, Hitler's newest "wonder weapon" had no effect upon military operations, except to press the Allies to drive against Germany with even greater speed and determination.

By mid-September, six Allied armies were pressing against Germany's borders, anxious to pursue Hitler's forces across the Rhine and deprive him of the industrial Ruhr. But the very success of Eisenhower's armies, especially the unexpected speed with which they crossed France after the Saint-Lô breakout, complicated his logistics. Allied supply lines, still largely dependent upon recently captured French ports, many of which were not fully operational, were heavily burdened and becoming dangerously long. British and Canadian troops had already taken Antwerp, but as long as the Germans held on to the Schelde Estuary, this fine harbor was of no use to the Allies. "Our port position today [September 13]," Eisenhower informed Montgomery, "is such that any stretch of a week or ten days of bad Channel weather . . . would paralyze our activities and make the maintenance of our troops even in defensive roles exceedingly difficult." [17] Partly to relieve this logistical crisis, but primarily to get his armies across the Rhine and into the Ruhr without incurring the costly consequences of a direct frontal attack against the Siegfried Line, Eisenhower attempted to outflank the heavy fortifications of Germany's "West Wall" by a combined ground and airborne assault in the eastern Netherlands. Operation Market Garden, as this bold plan was designated, went into effect on the morning of September 17. Some 20,000 troops were landed at three strategic points in Holland—Eindhoven, Nijmegen, and Arnhem. The objective of this force was to capture the bridges which spanned the Meuse and the Rhine and to provide, in Montgomery's words, "a 'carpet' of airborne forces" for the British Second Army's northward push to Arnhem, the Dutch port city on the Lower Rhine. Once here, beyond the defenses of the Siegfried Line, Montgomery intended to turn south and enter the Ruhr. Two of the landings, those at Eindhoven and Nijmegen, succeeded, but heavy German resistance, bad weather, and poor coordination prevented the British from achieving

[17] Quoted in Charles B. MacDonald, "The Decision to Launch Operation Market-Garden," in Greenfield, *op. cit.*, pp. 432–33.

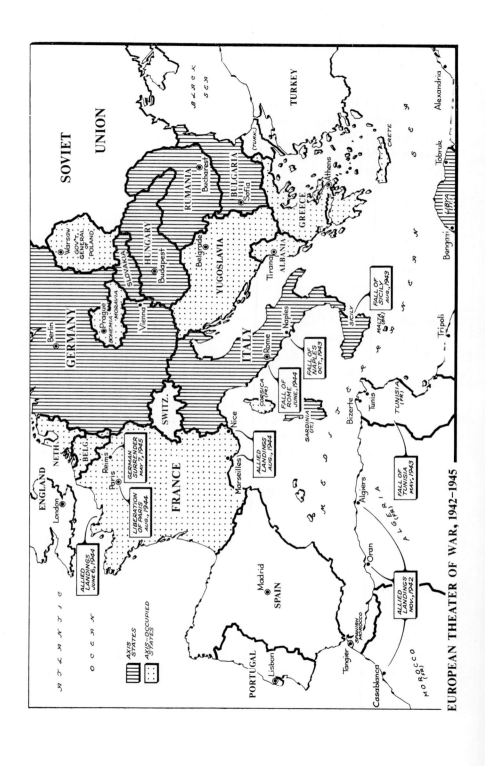

their main objective, the capture of Arnhem. By the end of September all Allied hopes of an easy jump across the Rhine were dashed.

The defeat at Arnhem and stiff German resistance along the Siegfried Line slowed the Allied war machine to a near halt during October and November. The battle to pierce Germany's West Wall was proving slow and costly. Aachen fell to General Courtney H. Hodges' American First Army on October 21 after nineteen days of difficult combat, and a month later General Patton took Metz and Strasbourg. These autumn offensives had weakened the American line in the Belgian Ardennes. And here, on December 16, Hitler struck with all his remaining fury. Three panzer armies commanded by Field Marshal Karl von Rundstedt launched a heavy counterattack aimed against General Troy H. Middleton's Eighth Corps. Taking Middleton by surprise, the Germans quickly destroyed his meager defenses, and with Allied air power immobilized by bad weather, they swiftly pushed ahead, creating a huge, fifty-mile-deep "bulge" in the American lines. Eisenhower responded quickly to Von Rundstedt's challenge by ordering Montgomery and Bradley to drive against the enemy's northern and southern flanks respectively, while Patton was assigned the task of relieving the isolated troops defending Bastogne. As soon as the weather permitted, Eisenhower brought his air power into action, and on December 23 and 24 Von Rundstedt's armies and supplies were subjected to aerial attacks by thousands of planes. Finally, on December 26, Hitler's last great offensive in the west was stopped. Except for the heavy American casualties, the Battle of the Bulge did not damage the Allied positions grievously, though it took the British and the Americans nearly a month to recover the territory Von Rundstedt had seized from them in ten days. For Germany, however, the consequences of Hitler's gamble in the Ardennes were disastrous. German casualties exceeded 100,000, and these, like the planes, tanks, and all the matériel the Allies had destroyed, could never be replaced. Hitler's defeat here also made it impossible for the German army to withstand the next Russian and Anglo-American offensives.

By January 21, 1945, the Western Allies were back where they had been before the Battle of the Bulge. By February 1 seven Allied armies (four American, one British, one Canadian, and one French) from Nijmegen in Holland to Colmar in Alsace were poised for the final assault upon Germany's western defenses. The Allied offensive started in the north on February 8 with Montgomery's British and Canadian armies pushing across Holland to the Lower Rhine, which they reached on February 21, just before the other Allied armies were to make their strike. During the next two days British and American planes from England, Italy, and France pounded the enemy's transportation and communication systems, destroying them almost completely. Meanwhile, on February 23, the American armies under General Bradley moved into the Saar-Palatinate and the Ruhr. On March 7, as the U. S. First Army's Twelfth Corps reached the Rhine at Cologne and was occupying that battered city, its Ninth Armored Division entered Remagen. Finding the Ludendorff railroad bridge across the Rhine partly damaged but still usable, General Bradley quickly ordered four divisions to cross it. Thus was established the first Allied bridgehead across the Rhine. After ten days of almost ceaseless effort, German planes and artillery finally succeeded in destroying the Ludendorff Bridge. But by then the initial bridgehead had been greatly strengthened and the other temporary structures which the Allies had built across the Rhine were already in use. By the end of the month, all seven Allied armies were across the Rhine and speeding eastward to the Elbe, the predetermined point where the Western Allies were to meet the Soviet forces.

On the Russian front, German resistance was crumbling as fast as it was in the west. Since the summer of 1943, when Hitler's third great effort to destroy the Soviet Union had failed, Russian troops had continuously been forcing the Nazis to yield more and more territory. By January, 1944, one Russian army had already entered Poland. During the next four months Soviet troops chased the remaining Germans out of Russia, including the Crimea, and advanced deep into Poland and penetrated the Nazi defenses of Rumania. Less than three weeks after the Western Allies had invaded Normandy, Stalin, with some 5 million men in his armies, launched a huge offensive which by the end of the year had brought the Russians into the Baltic, East Prussia, Rumania, Bulgaria, and Hungary. Early in 1945, while the Western Allies were occupied with the Ardennes bulge, the Soviet forces repulsed a German attack with an offensive of their own which destroyed or encircled Hitler's eastern armies and established the Russians in Warsaw, Budapest, Memel, and Vienna. On April 25 the advanced patrols of the Ukrainian First Army met those of the U. S. First Army at Torgau on the Elbe. Five days later Adolf Hitler, after marrying his mistress and naming Grand Admiral Karl Doenitz as his successor, committed suicide in his fortified bunker under the Reich chancellery in Berlin. On May 2 the Russians occupied the city, and shortly before 3:00 A.M. on May 7, Field Marshal

Alfred Jodl and two high German officers sat down in Eisenhower's headquarters at Reims to sign the official document specifying the details of Germany's unconditional surrender.

The War in the Pacific

While the Allies were defeating the Axis in Europe, the United States bore the principal burden of fighting Japan. Neither the United States nor its allies believed it possible to wage two large-scale wars simultaneously. Anglo-American plans, therefore, were originally aimed at preventing new Nipponese conquests, attacking enemy shipping and supply lines, and staging limited offensives against Tokyo's distant outposts. But the unprecedented productiveness of American war industry and the success of the United States at Midway and Guadalcanal made it feasible for the Allies to undertake larger and bolder offensives in the Pacific long before the landings in Normandy sealed the fate of Nazism.

Early in 1943, while the Japanese were being driven from Guadalcanal and Papua in New Guinea, the U. S. Joint Chiefs of Staff, who directed over-all strategy in the Pacific, were planning Japan's ultimate defeat. Executing decisions agreed upon at Casablanca and at subsequent meetings, the Joint Chiefs planned a series of coordinated offensives in the southern and central Pacific designed to destroy or isolate the enemy's key bases in those two areas and in the process to secure for themselves naval supremacy in the western Pacific. Once this was done, the way would be prepared for an all-out naval and air assault upon the Japanese home islands.

NEW GUINEA AND THE SOLOMONS

Japan's most vital air and naval bastion in the South Pacific was Rabaul, a small town on the northeastern coast of New Britain Island in the Bismarck archipelago. The invasion of Guadalcanal and MacArthur's campaign on New Guinea in 1942 had been launched partly to check Rabaul's threat to Australia, but also as a preliminary move against the base itself. The Japanese, determined to hold on to Rabaul at any cost, decided to strengthen their garrisons against MacArthur's forces on New Guinea. On February 28, 1943, eight troopships escorted by four destroyers left Rabaul for Lae on New Guinea's northern coast. The next day Australian and American bombers caught the enemy convoy in the Bismarck Sea and, in the four-day air battle which followed, sank all twelve ships,

214 THE ERA OF F.D.R., 1933–1945

killing 3,664 of the 6,912 soldiers on board and destroying more than 100 Japanese planes. The price the Allies paid for this victory was 25 casualties and four planes.[18]

Early in the summer the Allies launched the first of a series of offensives aimed at encircling and isolating Rabaul, thereby making it unnecessary to wage a costly campaign to capture it. On June 30, General MacArthur and Admiral William F. Halsey, in command of the South Pacific area, attacked the Japanese simultaneously. While MacArthur landed troops at Nassau Bay in New Guinea, Halsey, operating under MacArthur's "general directives," invaded Rendova and New Georgia, two islands northwest of Guadalcanal, in the central Solomons. The Japanese fought stubbornly, but by the middle of September MacArthur had driven them out of Lae and Salamaua on Huon Gulf and was preparing to move farther west along New Guinea's northern coast. Less than three weeks later Halsey secured New Georgia, but only after a bitter campaign in which nearly 1,100 Americans lost their lives and another 3,800 or more were wounded. Halsey's next target was Bougainville in the northern Solomons, the largest island in the entire chain. On November 1, against stiff enemy resistance, the Marines established a beachhead at Empress Augusta Bay. It took more than four months of hard fighting before the Japanese admitted defeat and evacuated the island. By mid-December, however, Bougainville's air fields were in operation and Allied bombers started using them to pound Rabaul and clear the Solomon Sea of Japanese shipping. With the Allies firmly established on Guadalcanal, New Georgia, Bougainville, and several lesser islands, the Japanese hold on the Solomons was ended, the remaining enemy garrisons were isolated and impotent, and Rabaul's western flank was exposed.

On December 15, MacArthur started to move against Rabaul from the east by invading Arawe in New Britain. Eleven days later Allied troops landed at Cape Gloucester. In March the Admiralty Islands were occupied, and in April, with the invasion of Hollandia in Dutch New Guinea, MacArthur completed Rabaul's encirclement.

THE NORTH AND CENTRAL PACIFIC

In the meantime, Admiral Chester W. Nimitz, Commander in Chief of the Pacific Ocean area, was advancing against Japan in the North and

[18] John Miller, Jr., *United States Army in World War II: The War in the Pacific, Cartwheel, The Reduction of Rabaul* (Washington, D.C., 1959), p. 41.

THE UNITED STATES IN WORLD WAR II 215

Central Pacific. On May 11, 1943, American troops invaded Attu in the western Aleutians, and after nearly a month of hard fighting, made worse by intense cold and almost continuous fog, they defeated the Japanese garrison. Kiska, the chief enemy stronghold in the Aleutians, was occupied on August 15 without opposition, the Japanese having evacuated the island before the American and Canadian forces arrived.

In November, Nimitz began his "kangaroo leaps" across the Central Pacific. His strategy, like that of MacArthur and Halsey in the South Pacific, was designed to pierce Japan's peripheral defenses, neutralize major enemy strongholds—in this case Truk in the eastern Carolines—and secure bases from which Allied planes and warships could strike at Japan and cut the enemy's access to raw materials. Nimitz began his campaign by invading Tarawa and Makin in the Gilbert Islands. After four days of fanatical resistance, which cost the marines nearly 3,000 casualties, "bloody Tarawa" was won. From here Allied planes attacked Eniwetok and Kwajalein in the Marshall Islands, which were invaded early in February, 1944. To reduce casualties, the preinvasion naval and air bombardment was greatly increased; and though the pattern of the enemy's resistance was similar to the one encountered on Tarawa, the marines lost fewer men than before. The occupation of Kwajalein provided Allied fliers with a base from which to strike at Truk, and once it was immobilized the American fleet, growing stronger almost daily, penetrated Japan's inner defenses. On June 15 the marines landed on Saipan, the largest island in the Marianas, less than 700 miles from Truk and 1,500 from the Philippines. Loss of this island, which Japan had acquired in 1914, forced the imperial navy to challenge the American task force in the area. On June 19 and 20, in the Battle of the Philippine Sea, Admiral Raymond A. Spruance's fliers destroyed more than 400 Japanese planes in a day-long air battle and then proceeded to strike at the enemy's powerful surface force, sinking two carriers, two destroyers, and a tanker. By the end of the second day, in what came to be known as the "Great Marianas Turkey Shoot," American fliers damaged three other cruisers, a battleship, two destroyers, and three tankers. American losses amounted to 106 planes. This decisive battle, like the ones off Midway and in the Coral Sea, was fought exclusively by planes from carriers; the surface ships never fired at each other. With Japanese naval and air strength seriously impaired by their disastrous losses in this two-day battle, the United States continued to strike closer and closer to the Japanese islands.

In July, just before the invasion of Guam and Tinian completed the occupation of the Marianas, Premier Tojo's government resigned, and in the hope of turning defeats into victories a new one, led by General Kuniaki Koiso, took over. Koiso's intentions, however, had little effect upon Nimitz's plans, and in September the marines landed on Palau. Two months of fighting and the Japanese were deprived of another naval and air base, this time only 500 miles from the Philippines.

By October, 1944, Nimitz and MacArthur had achieved the basic purposes of the Joint Chiefs' strategic plans for the Pacific. Now the next major phase of the drive against Japan could be executed—the reconquest of the Philippines. On October 20, supported by the U. S. Seventh Fleet and strong air cover, MacArthur landed with four divisions of the U. S. Sixth Army on Leyte in the center of the Philippine archipelago. The Japanese, determined to stop the invasion before MacArthur could establish a firm foothold, sent their combined fleet to destroy the invasion troops and the naval task force which protected them. But Vice Admiral Thomas C. Kinkaid's Seventh Fleet and Admiral William F. Halsey's Third Fleet engaged the Japanese, discovered by American submarines, in a three-day naval and air action. The Battle of Leyte Gulf, "the greatest sea engagement in all history," began auspiciously for the United States with an overwhelming victory in Surigao Strait, between Leyte and Mindanao. And though the Americans also inflicted considerable damage on the enemy in the two actions which followed, those off Samar and Cape Engaño, the wisdom of Halsey's decision to take his powerful fleet north in order to engage the Japanese off Cape Engaño has been seriously questioned. In any case, the Japanese were decisively defeated, losing altogether three battleships, four carriers, ten cruisers, and nine destroyers. The Americans lost the light carrier *Princeton,* two escort carriers, two destroyers, and a destroyer escort. With the Japanese fleet no longer a threat, other Philippine landings followed. On December 15, the island of Mindoro was invaded as a preliminary to the drive against Luzon, which occurred at Lingayen Gulf on January 9, 1945. The battle for Manila lasted nearly a month, but by the last week in February the Japanese were evicted from the city. Mindanao was invaded in March, and in April and July two other landings were made. Though the whole Philippine archipelago was now securely in American control, fighting continued until the end of the war.

While MacArthur was clearing Manila Bay, the American fleet and

THE UNITED STATES IN WORLD WAR II   217

air force were blasting tiny Iwo Jima in the western Pacific, only 750 miles from Japan. On February 19 two marine divisions landed on this eight-mile-square island. Despite three days of heavy naval and aerial bombardment, the Japanese force continued to defend the island desperately. Against this suicidal resistance, the marines advanced slowly and at heavy cost. It took the United States five weeks to reduce the island, and by the time the last pockets of enemy resistance were eliminated, marine casualties, including dead, wounded, and missing, exceeded 20,000, about one-third the total force engaged in the action. The capture of Iwo Jima exacted a high price in American lives, but it also yielded great strategic rewards. Japan's four home islands could now be bombed and blockaded effectively. The next Allied jump, to Okinawa, the largest island in the Ryukyu chain, would bring Allied power within 360 miles of Japan.

"The enemy now stands at our front gate," Premier Koiso declared after Iwo Jima. On April 1 the army and the marines tore down that gate by invading Okinawa, the last and by far the costliest operation of the war. On the first day the defending troops offered small resistance, preferring to force the invaders to assault them in their fortified island strongholds. The greatest damage was inflicted by the kamikazes. These bomb-laden and piloted suicide planes, which the Japanese had first used to attack the American fleet during the Philippine invasion, were now employed far more extensively, and they exacted a heavy toll of Allied ships. Meanwhile, in a desperate attempt to save Okinawa, Admiral Kantaro Suzuki's government, which had succeeded the Koiso ministry on April 5, decided to send the surviving units of Japan's home fleet to attack the invasion force. Vice Admiral Marc A. Mitscher's fast carrier task force intercepted the Japanese fleet, and on April 7, in the Battle of the East China Sea, destroyed it, sinking the huge 72,000-ton battleship *Yamato*, Japan's only remaining capital ship, along with a light cruiser and four destroyers. The fight to capture Okinawa raged on until June 22, and when it was all over 49,151 Americans had been killed or wounded or were missing. Largely because of the kamikaze attacks, the Allies lost 36 ships and suffered damages to 368 others.

By the end of June, 1945, less than two months after V-E Day, the United States had destroyed or isolated Japan's defense armaments, shattered its overseas empire, and crushed its naval power. Despite this overwhelming series of defeats and the fact that the more responsible Japa-

218   THE ERA OF F.D.R., 1933–1945

nese statesmen were aware the war had been lost, the militarists in power insisted upon continuing the struggle. In China, moreover, Japan was still strong and, except for minor skirmishes, undefeated militarily.

Since May, 1942, when the Japanese had completed their occupation of Burma and deprived the Allies of their last overland route to China, neither the United States nor Britain had been able to provide Chiang Kai-shek with the supplies he needed to prosecute the war against Japan effectively. War goods from India were flown to Chungking over the Himalayan hump, but the amount that could be airlifted in this way was limited by the weather, the height of the mountains over which the planes had to fly, and the size and number of transports available. By the summer of 1943, the Himalaya airlift was delivering about 3,000 tons of supplies a month, a mere trifle in terms of China's immense needs. The supply problem remained acute until the end of January, 1945, when the Ledo or Stilwell Road was finally finished and in operation. The war in China was complicated further by Chiang's hostility toward the Chinese Communists, whom he "hated" as much as he did the Japanese. The result, as General Stilwell observed, was that the Nationalists and the Communists in China were so busy keeping an eye on each other that "neither gives a damn" about fighting the Japanese.[19] But neither Roosevelt nor Churchill was prepared to allow Japan to hold on to its gains in Burma and China. At the Quebec conference in August, 1943, Admiral Lord Louis Mountbatten was named Supreme Commander for Southeast Asia, and on December 21 Stilwell started his campaign to reconquer Burma, which was finally liberated in June, 1945. In the meantime Roosevelt, at the insistence of Chiang Kai-shek, had recalled Stilwell and on October 28, 1944 assigned Major General Albert C. Wedemeyer to act as Chiang's Chief of Staff. The war in China, however, remained secondary to developments elsewhere in the Pacific.

FROM OKINAWA TO TOKYO BAY

Originally the United States had intended to use bases in China for its B-29 superfortress attacks against Japan, and the first such raid, on the island of Kyushu on June 15, 1944, took off from there. But after the United States had driven the Japanese from their strategic western Pacific islands, the B-29's increasingly used the captured airfields on the Marianas. The first of the bombing attacks from these bases occurred on

[19] Stilwell, *op. cit.*, pp. 321–22.

PACIFIC
THEATER
OF WAR
1941-1945

November 24, 1944, when 111 superfortresses pounded Tokyo's industrial section. With the end of the European war and the seizure of Okinawa, the air offensive against Japan's four home islands opened in earnest. Heavy day and night bombing attacks started in June, 1945. These strikes were aimed primarily at softening Japan for a projected November 1,

1945, invasion. During June and July industrial plants, oil refineries, air fields, and the islands' transportation system were hit hard. Meanwhile carrier planes and American and British capital ships struck at Japan's coastal cities and defenses. Since opposition to this combined air and sea offensive was slight, by the middle of June it was quite apparent that Japan had lost the war.

The crucial question facing Allied strategists was to decide upon the quickest way to force Tokyo to surrender. On this, military and naval authorities in the United States were divided. Admiral William D. Leahy, along with others, argued for heavier aerial bombardment and a complete naval blockade. "I was unable to see any justification for an invasion of an already thoroughly defeated Japan," Leahy declared. "I feared the cost would be enormous in both lives and treasure." MacArthur and Marshall, on the other hand, were as equally convinced of the need to invade Japan proper, and ultimately their views prevailed. By the middle of June plans to this effect were already in progress.

Meanwhile the "peace group" in Japan, realizing they had lost the war, earnestly sought to end it, but only if a way could be found which did not call for unconditional surrender. The militarists in the government, however, still insisted upon fighting to the bitter end. The United States was aware of the acrimonious debate going on within the Japanese cabinet and of Tokyo's earlier efforts to get Sweden and Switzerland to act as mediators in trying to bring an end to the war, just as it knew of Foreign Minister Shigenori Togo's current attempt "to use the Soviet Union to terminate the war." On July 26, during the Potsdam meetings, the United States, Britain, and China warned the Japanese government that the alternative to unconditional surrender was "prompt and utter destruction."

The development of an American atomic bomb went back to August 2, 1939, when Albert Einstein, the distinguished German scientist and Nazi refugee, wrote to President Roosevelt, saying that research in uranium fission had reached the stage where it could be employed militarily, and that it was "conceivable, though much less certain—that extremely powerful bombs of a new type may be . . . produced." One month after Roosevelt received Einstein's letter, Europe was at war. Now the need to beat Hitler's scientists in developing an atomic bomb became urgent. To expedite research, construct and finance the huge plants and installations required, and carry on this vital work beyond the range of Goering's Luftwaffe, Roosevelt and Churchill arranged to transfer

Britain's research scientists and laboratories to the United States and to make the atomic bomb project a combined Anglo-American and Canadian enterprise. On August 31, 1942, the Manhattan Engineer District was established under the command of Major General Leslie R. Groves and charged with the responsibility of coordinating all uranium research and of developing an atomic bomb. In May, 1943, the research activities formerly carried on by Dr. Vannevar Bush and his staff under the Office of Scientific Research and Development were included in the Manhattan District. The atomic bomb project was now given top priority, and the activities of its three great plants—Oak Ridge, Tennessee, Hanford, Washington, and Los Alamos, New Mexico—were kept highly secret.

Research on splitting the uranium atom had been going on at various American universities since 1939. Many of the atomic physicists engaged in these studies were native Americans, among them Ernest O. Lawrence and J. Robert Oppenheimer at the University of California, Arthur H. Compton at the University of Chicago, and Harold C. Urey at Columbia University. But many others were European exiles who had come to the United States during the 1930's to escape from Hitler and Mussolini. It was one of these refugees, Enrico Fermi, a renowned Italian physicist at the University of Chicago, who succeeded in establishing "the first self-maintaining nuclear chain reaction on record." [20] On that day, December 2, 1942—the "birthday of the atomic age"—Fermi and his colleagues "lighted the first atomic fire on earth." This "pile," as Fermi called it, was the world's first nuclear reactor, the predecessor of the ones the Manhattan District built at Hanford, Washington. But another two and a half years of concentrated scientific teamwork and the expenditure of nearly $2.5 billion were to follow before "Fat Man," the first atomic bomb, was ready. And then, not until one was tested on July 16, 1945, at Alamogordo Air Force Base in New Mexico, was anyone certain the bomb would do what its designers claimed. Admiral Leahy, for example, believed the entire project was "the biggest fool thing we have ever done." He was convinced that "the bomb will never go off." Others were less skeptical. "I knew that if it worked out right," Dr. Vannevar Bush recalled later, "the war was over." [21]

The decision to use the bomb against Japan was reached after careful deliberation by the highest civilian officials in the government. It was

---

[20] James Phinney Baxter, III, *Scientists against Time* (Boston, 1946), p. 432.
[21] Quoted in John W. Finney, "The Men around 'Fat Man,'" *The New York Times Magazine*, July 10, 1960.

222   THE ERA OF F.D.R., 1933–1945

based upon the belief, in the words of Secretary of War Stimson, one of the important officials in the discussions, that in order "to extract a genuine surrender from the Emperor and his military advisers, they must be administered a tremendous shock which would carry convincing proof of our power to destroy the empire. Such an effective shock would save many times the number of lives, both American and Japanese, than it would cost." [22] The proposal of giving the Japanese a preview of the bomb's destructivity so that they could surrender before it was used against them, as one group of scientists suggested, was rejected on several grounds. For one thing, the fact that no more than two bombs could be assembled for use in August dictated against it. Another reason was fear of the consequences which would follow should the demonstration bomb fail to work. The best-informed opinion in the United States recommended using the bomb for military purposes, but it also appears quite probable that some Washington officials, already disturbed by Russia's territorial and political ambitions in Eastern Europe, hoped that if the bomb were used Japan would surrender before Russia entered the war, thereby preventing the Kremlin from complicating the Far Eastern settlement. By the summer of 1945, however, this was too much to expect, for as W. Averell Harriman, the American ambassador to Russia, informed Leahy in May, "Russia would come into the war regardless of what we might do." [23] For military reasons, and probably for political ones as well, the United States decided to use the bomb to bring about Japan's surrender as quickly as possible, and to do so without giving Tokyo any advanced warning other than the one contained in the Potsdam declaration.

On July 29, Premier Suzuki, who had been trying to get Japan out of the war since taking office in April, issued a statement to the Tokyo newspapers in which he declared that "the Government . . . does not find any important value in . . . [the Potsdam declaration] and there is no other recourse but to ignore it entirely and resolutely fight for the successful conclusion of this war." [24] A week later, on the morning of August 6, a single B-29 dropped "Lean Boy," a uranium-235 bomb, on the city of Hiroshima. Its destructive force exceeded 20,000 tons of high

---

[22] Quoted in Louis Morton, "The Decision to Use the Atomic Bomb," in Greenfield, *op. cit.,* p. 498.

[23] Quoted in *ibid.,* p. 504.

[24] Quoted in Herbert Feis, *Japan Subdued: The Atomic Bomb and the End of the War in the Pacific* (Princeton, N.J., 1961), p. 97.

THE UNITED STATES IN WORLD WAR II 223

explosives, and its impact, according to Radio Tokyo, was "so terrific that practically all living things, human and animal, literally were seared to death by the tremendous heat and pressure engendered by the blast. All the dead and injured were burned beyond recognition. . . . Those outdoors burned to death, while those indoors were killed by the indescribable pressure and heat." [25] More than one-third of the city's 344,000 people were killed, missing, or injured. On August 8, two days later, Stalin, fulfilling his agreement with the Western Allies to declare war on Japan, sent Soviet troops into Manchuria and southern Sakhalin and started to invade Korea. On August 9 a second atomic bomb—the last one the United States then possessed—was dropped on Nagasaki, killing nearly 74,000 of the city's 220,000 inhabitants. The Nagasaki bomb was so far superior to the Hiroshima one that no other "Lean Boys" were ever built or used.

Hiroshima, Russia's hurried intervention, and the atomic disaster at Nagasaki created a grave crisis in the Japanese government. The military clique still refused to surrender, and nearly another full day of angry debate followed before the emperor himself intervened and forced his ministers to inform the Allies that Japan was "ready to accept" the Potsdam declaration, provided it did "not compromise . . . the prerogatives of His Majesty as a sovereign ruler." [26] Hostilities ceased on August 14, and on September 2, 1945, General MacArthur, as Supreme Commander for the Allied Powers, accepted Japan's official surrender aboard the U.S.S. *Missouri* in Tokyo Bay.

After six years—almost to the day—World War II came to an end with the total defeat of the powers responsible for having started it. As in World War I, the United States was the last of the major world powers to become an active belligerent. For the American people World War II began with the attack on Pearl Harbor, nearly three years and eight months before the Japanese surrendered. The price of America's victory was high. Some 12,466,000 Americans served in the armed forces, of whom 322,188 were killed and 700,000 wounded. Had it not been for the new "wonder drugs"—antibiotics like penicillin and the various sulfa compounds—and the extensive use of blood plasma on the battlefields, the number of deaths would have been far greater. Considerable progress was also made in rehabilitating the injured, and wartime developments in physical medicine—many of them pioneered by the St. Louis internist, Dr. Howard A. Rusk, at the Convalescent Training and Re-

---

[25] Quoted in Snyder, *op. cit.*, p. 493.   [26] Morton, *op. cit.*, pp. 515–17.

224 THE ERA OF F.D.R., 1933–1945

habilitation Center of the Air Surgeon's Hospital—were later adopted at more than 200 other institutions. Every effort was made to return amputees and other seriously disabled veterans to useful lives.

Besides the human resources destroyed or crippled, the American people spent $281 billion to fight the war, and if property losses are included the total would jump another $70 billion. In both human and natural resources, World War II was the costliest conflict in the history of the United States, but the death, suffering, and destruction it inflicted upon the peoples of Europe and Asia—victor and vanquished alike—were far, far greater. After Hiroshima and Nagasaki, a great many people seriously questioned mankind's ability to survive another total war.

Suggested Readings

The literature on the military and naval aspects of World War II is already immense and continues to grow. The most comprehensive studies are the multivolume service histories, of which there are four major ones for the United States. The series, Office of the Chief of Military History, Department of the Army, *United States Army in World War II* (50 vols., Washington, D.C., 1947–) is divided into the following nine groups: *European Theater of Operations; The War in the Pacific; The Middle East Theater; The China-Burma-India Theater; The Army Ground Forces; The War Department; The Technical Services; Special Study;* and *Pictorial.* When completed, the army's story will total eighty volumes. Kent Robert Greenfield, the general editor of this massive history, tells some of the problems encountered in preparing these volumes in a fascinating little book of less than one hundred pages, *The Historian and the Army* (New Brunswick, N.J., 1954). Greenfield has also edited *Command Decisions* (Washington, D.C., 1960), an especially useful collection of essays covering twenty-three great wartime decisions. Samuel Eliot Morison, *History of United States Naval Operations in World War II* (14 vols., Boston, 1947–60) is the official account of the navy; Wesley F. Craven and James L. Cate, eds., *The Army Air Forces in World War II* (7 vols., Chicago, 1948–58) and U. S. Marine Corps, *Monographs* (14 vols., 1947–) are the official accounts of these two services.

Among the one-volume surveys, Louis L. Snyder, *The War: A Concise History, 1939–1945* (New York [1960]) is recent and well written, but see also such older works as Fletcher Pratt, *War for the World* (New Haven, Conn., 1951) in the *Chronicles of America;* Walter P. Hall, *Iron Out of Calvary: An Interpretative History of the Second World War* (New York, 1946); Francis T. Miller, *History of World War II* (Philadelphia, 1945); Roger W. Shugg and Harvey A. DeWeerd, *World War II: A Concise History*

THE UNITED STATES IN WORLD WAR II 225

(Washington, D.C., 1946); and Herbert C. O'Neill, *A Short History of the Second World War* (New York, 1950). A useful aid in following the shifting battle lines is Francis Brown, ed., *The War in Maps: An Atlas of The New York Times Maps* (3d ed., New York, 1944). The pictorial story is reproduced in *Life's Picture History of World War II* (New York, 1950).

Chester Wilmot, *The Struggle for Europe* (New York, 1952) is the interpretative account of an Australian newspaperman which combines military and diplomatic aspects. Readable, scholarly, and somewhat argumentative, this work criticizes Allied strategy, especially the American military's decision to stop at the Elbe. Wilmot's interpretation is challenged by Arthur M. Schlesinger, Jr., "Wilmot's War or Churchill Was Right," *The Reporter*, VI (July 29, 1952), 36. Also critical of Allied strategy and wartime diplomacy is the well-written account by Hanson W. Baldwin, *Great Mistakes of the War* (New York, 1950). Another indictment of American strategy in Europe is Reginald W. Thompson, *The Price of Victory* (London [1960]). Trumbull Higgins, *Winston Churchill and the Second Front, 1940–1943* (New York, 1957) censures Churchill for delaying the second front and accuses him of following an "opportunist strategy." See also Samuel Eliot Morison, *American Contributions to the Strategy of World War II* (New York, 1958).

John Toland, *But Not in Shame: The Six Months after Pearl Harbor* (New York, 1961) ably describes the extent of the Allied losses during these grim six months.

Among the many specialized works on various aspects, battles, and issues of World War II, consult the following: Richard Collier, *The Sands of Dunkirk* (New York, 1961), which describes the evacuation in detail; Alexander McKee, *Strike from the Sky: The Story of the Battle of Britain* (Boston, 1961), a first-rate treatment; Walter Ansel, *Hitler Confronts England* (Durham, N.C., 1961), an excellent account of the projected Nazi invasion; Bernard Ash, *Someone Had Blundered: The Story of the "Repulse" and the "Prince of Wales"* (Garden City, N.Y., 1961); Correlli Barnett, *The Desert Generals* (New York, 1961), which is less than complimentary toward Montgomery; Desmond Young, *Rommel: The Desert Fox* (New York, 1950); James A. Field, *The Japanese at Leyte Gulf* (Princeton, N.J., 1947), which presents the Japanese strategy of this greatest of all sea battles; Erich Kern, *Dance of Death* (New York, 1951), a German's explanation of why Hitler failed in Russia; Albert R. Buchanan, ed., *The Navy's Air War: A Mission Completed* (New York, 1946), which discusses various aspects of its subject; Duncan S. Ballantine, *U. S. Naval Logistics in the Second World War* (Princeton, N.J., 1947); Wynford Vaughan-Thomas, *Anzio* (New York [1961]), a discussion of this controversial campaign; John Toland, *Battle: The Story of the Bulge* (New York, 1959), a complete story; Holland M. Smith and Percy Finch, *Coral and Brass* (New York, 1949), a marine's battles in the Pacific against the Japanese and the "brass"; Richard F. Newcomb, *Savo: The Incredible Naval Debacle off Guadalcanal* (New York, 1961); Robert L. Sherrod, *History of Marine Corps Aviation in World War II* (Washington, D.C. [1952]); C. D. Becker [Hans D. Berenbrok], *Defeat at Sea: The Struggle and Eventual De-*

226 THE ERA OF F.D.R., 1933–1945

struction of the German Navy, 1939–1945 (New York [1955]); Harold Busch, *U-Boats at War* (New York, 1955); Anthony K. Martienssen, *Hitler and His Admirals* (New York, 1949); William D. Puleston, *The Influence of Sea Power in World War II* (New Haven, Conn., 1947); Walter D. Edmonds, *They Fought with What They Had: The Story of the Army Air Forces in the Southwest Pacific, 1941–1942* (Boston, 1951); Walter Karig and Wilbourn Kelley, *Battle Report, I: Pearl Harbor to Coral Sea* (New York, 1944); Jeter A. Isely and Philip A. Crowl, *The U. S. Marines and Amphibious War: Its Theory and Its Practice in the Pacific* (Princeton, N.J., 1951); Milton Shulman, *Defeat in the West* (London, 1947), the revealing story of Germany's disintegration; Hugh R. Trevor-Roper, *The Last Days of Hitler* (New York, 1947); Desmond Flower and James Reeves, eds., *The Taste of Courage: The War, 1939–1945* (New York [1960]), "a documentary conspectus"; Basil H. Liddell Hart, ed., *The Soviet Army* (London, 1956), a collection of useful miscellaneous pieces; Nicholas Monsarrat, *The Cruel Sea* (New York, 1951), which is excellent on the war in the Atlantic, as is Donald McIntire, *The Battle of the Atlantic* (New York [1961]); Peter Fleming, *Operation Sea Lion* (New York, 1957), which describes Britain's plight during the terrible year, 1940; David Hawarth, *D-Day* (New York, 1959), Cornelius Ryan, *The Longest Day: June 6, 1944* (New York, 1959), and S. L. A. Marshall, *Night Drop: The American Airborne Invasion of Normandy* (Boston [1962]), all dealing with the Normandy invasion; and Robert Payne, *The Marshall Story* (New York, 1952), a good and informative biography which suffers from the fact that the author did not have access to his subject's personal and official papers.

Among the countless memoirs, reminiscences, and personal records of the war, consult Winston Churchill, *The Second World War*, already cited, which is by far the best of the lot; Dwight D. Eisenhower, *Crusade in Europe* (Garden City, N.Y. [1948]), which is indispensable for the war against Germany, but see also his *Report by the Supreme Commander to the Combined Chiefs of Staff on Operations in Europe . . . 6 June 1944 to 8 May 1945* (Washington, D.C., 1946); Henry C. Butcher, *My Three Years with Eisenhower* (New York, 1946), the story of a staff officer; Kathleen Summersby, *Eisenhower Was My Boss* (New York [1948]), which reveals the informal side of Ike at SHAEF; Omar Bradley, *A Soldier's Story* (New York, 1951); Henry H. Arnold, *Global Mission* (New York, 1949), which is good on air strategy, but see also his *The War Reports* (Philadelphia, 1947); Mark W. Clark, *Calculated Risk: A Personal Story of the Campaign in North Africa and Italy* (New York, 1950); Bernard Law, Viscount Montgomery of El Alamein, *The Memoirs of Field-Marshal Montgomery* (Cleveland, Ohio [1958]), the strong statement of a highly qualified, colorful, and opinionated field commander, but see also his briefer, *Normandy to the Baltic* (Boston, 1946), in which he argues for a drive to Berlin; Sir Arthur Bryant, *The Turn of the Tide* (Garden City, N.Y., 1957), which was written from the diaries of Field Marshal Lord Alanbrooke; Albert B. Cunningham, Viscount of Hyndhope, *A Soldier's Odyssey* (London, 1951), which is good on the submarine and Allied shipping; Ernest J. King and Walter M. Whitehill, *Fleet Admiral King: A Naval Record* (New York, 1952), which

THE UNITED STATES IN WORLD WAR II

is good on strategy and wartime high-level diplomacy, but see also Ernest J. King, *U. S. Navy at War, 1941–1945: Official Reports to the Secretary of the Navy* (Washington, D.C., 1946); William D. Leahy, *I Was There: The Personal Story of the Chief of Staff to Presidents Roosevelt and Truman* (New York, 1952), useful primarily on diplomacy and high-level strategy; Saul K. Padover, *Experiment in Germany: The Story of an American Intelligence Officer* (New York [1946]), which contains useful information on Germany's last days; Theodore H. White, ed., *The Stillwell Papers* (New York, 1948); Charles de Gaulle, *War Memoirs* (2 vols., New York, 1955–59), covering the years 1940–44; Walter Bedell Smith, *Eisenhower's Six Great Decisions* (New York, 1956); George C. Marshall, *Report: The Winning of the War in Europe and the Pacific* (New York, 1945), which describes the last phases of the war; Lewis H. Brereton, *The Brereton Diaries: The War in the Air in the Pacific, Middle East, and Europe, 3 October 1941-8 May 1945* (New York, 1946); Lucius D. Clay, *Decision in Germany* (Garden City, N.Y., 1950); Albert C. Wedemeyer, *Wedemeyer Reports!* (New York [1958]); Jonathan M. Wainwright, *General Wainwright's Story* (Garden City, N.Y., 1946); and Henry L. Stimson and McGeorge Bundy, *On Active Service in Peace and War*, already cited, which contains useful information on the war.

Since General MacArthur has neither written his own memoirs nor made his papers available, the only account of his labors in the Pacific is the account written by his aide, Charles A. Willoughby, assisted by John Chamberlain, *MacArthur, 1941–1951* (New York, 1954).

For recollections of defeated soldiers, see Erwin Rommel, *War without Hate* (Heidenheim, Germany [1950]) and Basil H. Liddell Hart, ed., *The Rommel Papers* (New York, 1953); Desmond Young, *Rommel: The Desert Fox*, already cited, a good biography of this much publicized soldier; Heinz Guderian, *Panzer Leader* (London [1952]), the story of the 1940 blitzkrieg; Karl Doenitz, *Memoirs: Ten Years and Twenty Days* (Cleveland, Ohio [1950]); Louis P. Lochner, ed., *The Goebbels Diaries, 1942–1943* (Garden City, N.Y., 1948); and Mitsuo Fuchida and Masatake Okumiya, *Midway: The Battle That Doomed Japan* (Annapolis, Md., 1955).

On the scientific developments during the war, see James Phinney Baxter, III, *Scientists against Time* (Boston, 1946), which covers all phases, including the atomic bomb project. On the latter, see especially Henry L. Stimson, "The Decision to Use the Atomic Bomb," *Harper's Magazine*, CXCIV (February 1947), 97–107. There are several good nontechnical accounts on the development of the atomic bomb, of which Ronald W. Clark, *The Birth of the Bomb* (New York [1961]) and Michael Amrine, *The Great Decision: The Secret History of the Atomic Bomb* (New York, 1959) are the most recent. See also the very able older work by John W. Campbell, *The Atomic Story* (New York, 1947) and the one by *The New York Times* correspondent, William L. Laurence, *Dawn over Zero: The Story of the Atomic Bomb* (New York, 1946). One of the important scientists on the project, Arthur H. Compton, tells his story in *Atomic Quest: A Personal Narrative* (New York, 1956).

228   THE ERA OF F.D.R., 1933–1945

The history of the "atomic capital" is told by George O. Robinson, Jr., *The Oak Ridge Story* (Kingsport, Tenn., 1950).

On the decision to use the bomb, see the above as well as the superb article by Louis Morton, "The Decision to Use the Atomic Bomb," in Kent Roberts Greenfield, ed., *Command Decisions* (Washington, D.C., 1960), pp. 493–518. Herbert Feis's excellent analysis of the bomb, diplomacy, and military policy is well told in his *Japan Subdued: The Atomic Bomb and the End of the War in the Pacific* (Princeton, N.J., 1961).

6

Mobilizing the Home Front and Allied Diplomacy, 1941-1945

"WITHOUT AMERICAN PRODUCTION the United Nations could never have won the war." This statement was made by Premier Stalin at Teheran in 1943, in the presence of the assembled Allied leaders, as a toast to President Roosevelt. Whether the Soviet leader was sincere or not in proposing it no one will ever know, but that the productivity of the United States was decisive in determining the war's outcome is beyond dispute. So great were the amounts and varieties of finished war goods which flowed out of America's factories that within two years after Pearl Harbor it became possible for the United States to fight the European war, supply many of the needs of its Allies in that theater, and prosecute the war against Japan with greater vigor than had been anticipated when Churchill first came to the United States in December, 1941, to plan the strategy of the two Western Allies.

THE HOME FRONT, 1941–1945

The immediate task of preparing the United States for total war began in the summer of 1940. The three major necessities of the war program were to build a large army and navy, transform industry to war pro-

230 THE ERA OF F.D.R., 1933–1945

duction, and establish controls over the economic system which would assure an equitable distribution of the available commodities and prevent inflation. For these three purposes it was necessary for the government to assume far-reaching powers over the lives and activities of all Americans. This necessity was generally recognized; and in spite of much distrust of the New Deal among conservative Democrats and Republicans, it was agreed that the government must have the requisite authority.

Recruiting the Armed Forces

The United States adopted peacetime conscription for the first time in its history with the Burke-Wadsworth Selective Training and Service Act of September 16, 1940. All men between the ages of twenty and thirty-six were required to register and were subsequently classified by local draft boards into four groups according to their relative ability for service. Those not given deferments on account of occupation, support of dependents, or physical disability were to be called for a year's military training, the order being determined, as in 1917, by lottery, and the total number of drafted men at any one time was not to exceed 900,000. On August 18, 1941, the Congress, by a very narrow vote (203 to 202 in the House and 45 to 30 in the Senate), extended the term of service to eighteen months. It was hoped that the Selective Service System would provide a body of trained soldiers who could be called back for duty if there were an emergency or if the United States entered the war.

After Pearl Harbor, by a new draft law passed on December 19, 1941, all men between the ages of eighteen and sixty-five were required to register, and all those between the ages of twenty and forty-five were made liable to service. In the autumn of 1942, it was decided that a larger number of younger men were required; consequently, in November the age of eligibility for service was lowered to eighteen, and men past the age of thirty-eight were deferred. By October, 1942, there were 4.25 million men in the army and 1.3 million in the navy, with plans for an expansion of the army to 8.2 million and of the navy to 2.6 million by the end of 1943. It was apparent that if these totals were to be reached, it would be necessary for many men with dependents to be called into service. Before the end of 1942, draft boards were beginning to call up married men without children, and in February, 1943, the government announced that men of draft age who had dependent children would be drafted if they were not working in an essential occupation. By May 31, 1945, when the coun-

THE HOME FRONT & ALLIED DIPLOMACY   231

try's armed forces were at their peak strength, there were nearly 8.3 million men in the army, of which some 66 per cent were serving overseas, and more than 3.88 million in the navy.

In order to free as many servicemen as possible from noncombatant duties, the armed forces accepted women into the services on a voluntary basis, and in May, 1942, Congress established the Women's Auxiliary Army Corps (WAAC) for the army and the Women Appointed for Voluntary Emergency Service (WAVES) for the navy. Before the end of the year Congress authorized the establishment of a Women's Reserve for the coast guard, *Semper Paratus* Always Ready Service (SPARS), and in 1943 the Marine Corps Women's Reserve was activated. All together more than 210,000 women joined these various services, performing hundreds of useful jobs at home and overseas.

The Civilian Labor Force

The calling of men for military service and the movement of workers into those war industries which paid high wages resulted in a shortage of labor in many occupations which were equally important to the prosecution of the war. Agriculture, for example, was particularly hard hit, despite improved farm wages. In order to meet the great wartime demand for agricultural products, more and more farmers mechanized their operations so that by 1945 fewer farmers were producing more agricultural commodities than ever before, a fact which was to have serious repercussions after the war. To some extent the scarcity of labor was met by the employment of older and younger workers, the handicapped, and individuals formerly regarded as unemployable. Women, however, proved to be the single most important addition to the wartime labor force; many of them became factory, shipyard, and aircraft plant workers in large numbers. Between 1941 and 1944 the number of women in the labor force increased by 4.73 million; by the end of the war it had swelled to nearly 6 million.

Soon after Pearl Harbor it became apparent that if the manpower needs of the armed services and the war industries were to be met, the government would have to assume much greater authority over the disposition and utilization of the labor force, and it might be necessary also to conscript men and women for work in industry and agriculture. Such a proposal, in the form of a national service law, was recommended by the War Department, and a bill to that effect was introduced in Congress on

February 8, 1943. But the combined opposition of organized labor, business, and other groups was strong enough to block it in committee. Meanwhile, in April, 1942, Roosevelt had already established the War Manpower Commission (WMC), headed by Paul V. McNutt, the Federal Security administrator. The WMC was entrusted with all questions concerning the country's manpower needs. It classified jobs, recruited workers on a voluntary basis to fill jobs wherever there existed critical shortages, organized training within industry programs, and fulfilled various other functions aimed to mobilize the labor force effectively. The commission's authority was strengthened further in February, 1943, when the President increased the work week in defense industries to forty-eight hours, with time and a half pay for all additional hours beyond forty. To prevent workers performing essential jobs from leaving them to accept higher-paying ones, Roosevelt issued a "hold the line" order on April 8, 1943, which authorized the WMC to freeze some 27 million essential war workers to their jobs. These policies, along with the decision of the Selective Service System—which was included under the WMC's authority on December 5, 1942—to grant deferments on the basis of essentiality of employment, solved many of the country's manpower difficulties. There were enough serious labor shortages, however, to keep alive the possibility of having to use compulsion to meet the labor needs of war factories and farms until the defeat of Hitler.

Once the government sought to provide the war machine with its manpower requirements, its next step was to prevent labor-management disputes from interfering with production. The first step in this direction was taken on March 19, 1941, when the administration established the National Defense Mediation Board (NDMB), headed by the New York City attorney William H. Davis. The NDMB included on its panel representatives of labor, management, and the public, and its function was to prevent work stoppages by mediating employer-employee disputes. Since its decisions were not legally enforceable, the board's success in preventing strikes depended entirely upon the willingness of labor and management to accept its recommendations. When the NDMB failed to prevent several major strikes, the most important of which was the one following John L. Lewis' refusal to accept its decision against the union shop in the "captive coal mines" (those owned by and producing coal for the steel companies), the board's authority was seriously undermined. And then when the CIO's representatives on the NDMB resigned from it because of the adverse decision it had rendered in this case, the NDMB's effectiveness was all but ended.

Roosevelt's response to this threat to industrial peace was to call the representatives of management and labor into conference and force them to agree upon a program which would guarantee the uninterrupted production of goods so long as the country was at war. Before the conference adjourned, late in December, 1941, Roosevelt secured from both labor and management a pledge that henceforth there would be "no strikes or lockouts and all disputes shall be settled by peaceful means." In return, he promised to establish a National War Labor Board (NWLB) to help arbitrate and mediate serious disputes which labor and management could not resolve themselves and, after October, 1942, to supervise wages. The NWLB was established on January 16, 1942; like its predecessor, it was headed by Davis, and its membership included representatives from labor, management, and the public. The board resolved the union or closed shop controversy, which had defeated the NDMB, in April, 1942, by adopting the "maintenance of membership" principle, whereby a union's rights to organize were protected.

The NWLB's wage policy, based upon the President's recommendations to the Congress to prevent inflation (April, 1942) and announced in connection with a 15 per cent increase to the workers in "Little Steel," was to allow raises which would compensate for increases in the cost of living since January 1, 1941. The effectiveness of the Little Steel Formula, as the NWLB's basis for wage increases came to be known, was increased considerably when Congress passed the Economic Stabilization or Anti-inflation Act of October 2, 1942. Among other things, this law fixed wages and froze the salaries of many workers earning less than $5,000 a year. These restrictions irked labor sufficiently to bring about a considerable increase in the number of strikes, from 2,968 in 1942 to 3,752 in 1943. Most of them, however, were brief, inconsequential, and had little effect upon the war industries. The most serious one involved, once again, John L. Lewis' United Mine Workers, who insisted upon a $2.00 a day wage increase and other benefits. When the operators refused to grant the UMW's demands, the miners failed to report to work. The next day— May 1, 1943—Roosevelt seized the mines and turned them over to Interior Secretary Ickes, who operated them until an agreement was reached in October. The miners received an additional $1.50 a day with the approval of the NWLB, but the other benefits they won, such as paid vacations, went beyond the Little Steel Formula.

The coal strike and labor's growing restlessness in 1943 were denounced by antiunion spokesmen and critics of the administration, all of whom disapproved of the NWLB's willingness to allow wage increases. The

234 THE ERA OF F.D.R., 1933-1945

demands of these groups resulted in the Smith-Connally War Labor Disputes Act of June 25, 1943, which aimed to prevent strikes by imposing a thirty-day cooling off period before a strike call went into effect, and required the National Labor Relations Board to conduct a secret election to determine whether the workers wanted to go on strike. No strike could be called until the results of the election were known. The law also enlarged the authority of the federal government to seize strike-threatened companies, prohibited workers from leaving their jobs in government-operated plants, and forbade unions from contributing money toward the election of federal officials. Roosevelt opposed the measure as unduly harsh and "discriminatory," but the Congress passed it over his veto. Despite the many strikes and government seizures which followed the Smith-Connally Act (one of the most notable of which was the army's bodily removal of Montgomery Ward president Sewell Avery from his Chicago offices), labor's wartime record was an outstanding one. Its contribution to victory was indispensable.

Mobilizing Industry

The process of shifting industry to war production also started in June, 1940, with the appointment of an advisory commission of seven members to supervise the armament program. There was a lack of centralized and responsible authority, however, and the various members of the commission lacked adequate powers. As in World War I, it was gradually recognized that efficient production could best be obtained by giving full authority to a single individual. A move in this direction was taken on December 20, 1940, when the Office of Production Management (OPM) was established with William S. Knudsen, formerly president of General Motors, as director and Sidney Hillman, formerly president of the Amalgamated Clothing Workers, as assistant director. This dual control, under which authority was divided between an industrialist and a trade union leader, impeded efficiency; and the OPM also lacked adequate power. Finally, on January 13, 1942, the OPM was replaced by the War Production Board (WPB), and Donald Nelson, formerly of Sears, Roebuck, was placed at its head with full responsibility over the country's production. Other agencies were established to perform special duties, such as the Rubber Administration, which spent $14 billion to develop and produce synthetic rubber, and the Office of Economic Warfare, which was charged with providing the war industries with "critical strategic materials" and was authorized to buy any that appeared on the world market, thereby preventing the enemy from acquiring them.

In spite of many unnecessary delays and much waste and inefficiency, American industry responded to the challenge presented by the national crisis even more remarkably than in World War I. The building of new factories and the transfer of labor and equipment to war production necessarily required much time, although some observers believed that it might have been accomplished more quickly. But once the WPB stopped all nonessential construction (April 8, 1942) and the new war industries were in operation, they began to produce war materials in quantities which justified the most optimistic prophecies and with which the Axis powers could not hope to compete. The total sums spent by the United States for war purposes increased by leaps and bounds, from $6.3 billion for the year 1941 to $26 billion for fiscal 1942, $72.1 billion for 1943, and $87 billion for 1944. The federal government's total expenditures for the year 1944 reached the staggering sum of $100.4 billion—an amount larger than the total income of all the American people in any year of peace.

The war production statistics were equally staggering. In September, 1939, the total ship tonnage of the United States was 11.4 million gross tons; by the end of 1945 it was 45.8 million gross tons. During these six years American shipyards produced 38.25 million gross tons, more than ten times the amount lost during the war. The production of other war material was similarly impressive: 297,000 planes of all kinds, nearly 86,400 tanks, 315,000 artillery guns of various sizes, 4.2 million tons of artillery shells, and 4.4 billion rounds of ammunition for rifles, machine guns, and other light arms. For this and all the other matériel of war, the United States spent nearly $187 billion. With the industrial complex engaged in producing these vast quantities of war goods, many cherished and long-accepted features of American life were perforce altered. Whenever the manufacture of civilian goods—from automobiles to women's nylon stockings—interfered with the production of an article of war, the output of the consumer item was either halted entirely or severely curtailed.

Efforts to Control Inflation

The most complicated of the problems which confronted the government was that of trying to prevent a price inflation which would vastly increase the cost of the war and cause acute suffering and dislocations among the civilian population. The quantities of goods and services avail-

236 THE ERA OF F.D.R., 1933–1945

able for civilian use were being drastically reduced, while at the same time payments of wages and salaries were being raised through government purchases of war materials to the highest totals in American experience. Between 1939 and 1945 wages and salaries increased from $44.2 billion to $111.4 billion, and net farm incomes from $4.3 to $12.5 billion. The disposable income of individuals, or the amount left to them after they had paid all taxes, rose from $67.7 billion in 1939 to $124.6, $137.4, and $139.5 billion respectively for 1943, 1944, and 1945. Consumer expenditures for these years were as follows: 1939, $61.7 billion; 1943, $91.3 billion; 1944, $98.5 billion; and 1945, $106.4 billion. If inflation was to be avoided, the excess of purchasing power over goods and services available had to be recaptured by the government through taxes and loans, and wage and price levels had to be stabilized. Adequate controls over the economic system were rendered difficult by the influence of different pressure groups, each of which was afraid of incurring more than its due share of the necessary sacrifices. To reconcile the divergent interests of business, labor, and agriculture and apportion equitably the costs of winning the war was an exceptionally difficult task; and while some observers maintained that economic controls could have been exercised more effectively, the federal government's record in World War II surpassed that of any other wartime period in the history of the United States.

FINANCING THE WAR

Taxes on all incomes were steadily increased, and the total number of persons liable to the income tax was enlarged from less than 4 million in 1939 to nearly 40 million in 1943. Never before had so many Americans been required to file income tax returns. Because of the cut in personal exemptions enacted in the Revenue Act of October 21, 1942 ($500 for single individuals and $1,200 for married persons), the income tax, for the first time, became a "mass tax," affecting, in the words of two economists, men and women "from the country club group district down to the railroad tracks and then over to the other side of the tracks." [1] Besides recruiting new taxpayers from the low-income groups, the law greatly increased the tax burden of everyone else, especially the wealthy, by raising the "normal tax" from 4 to 5 per cent and the surtax from 77 to 82 per cent. In addition, individuals with a net income of more than $624 a year were required to pay a 5 per cent victory tax, which was deducted from their paychecks. As originally enacted, the Revenue Act of 1942

[1] Quoted in Randolph E. Paul, *Taxation in the United States* (Boston, 1954), p. 318.

THE HOME FRONT & ALLIED DIPLOMACY 237

stipulated that the government would refund a certain percentage of the victory tax after the peace had been won, but two years later Congress invalidated this provision. The Revenue Act of 1942 also raised corporate tax rates from 31 to 40 per cent and the excess profits tax was boosted to an all-time high of 90 per cent. These increases, together with those imposed on gifts and estates and the numerous other new levies that were written into the law, made the Revenue Act of 1942, in the words of F.D.R., "the greatest tax bill in American history." Government revenues rose from $7.6 billion in 1941 to $12.8 billion in 1942, $22.3 billion in 1943, $44.1 billion in 1944, and $46.5 billion in 1945. In 1942–43, between one-fourth and one-third of the total government expenditures were being met by taxes.

To expedite collections, reduce losses, and avoid evasions, the government introduced, in the Current Tax Payment Act of June 9, 1943, the pay as you go or payroll deduction system, whereby all employers were required to withhold the federal taxes of all individuals in their employ each payday and to forward the taxes collected to the Collector of Internal Revenue every three months. The self-employed and those whose wage or salary deductions were not large enough to meet their tax bill were required to file an estimate and to pay the additional tax in quarterly installments. The government met the difference between its receipts and expenditures by borrowing from individuals and banks. As a result the total debt of the United States rose from $57.9 billion in 1941 to $278.1 billion in 1945. These figures meant that in spite of greatly increased tax collections and in spite of the general public's purchase of approximately $43.3 billion of war bonds out of a total $185.7 subscribed, there was still a large surplus of purchasing power, which some economists believed should have been reduced still further by increasing the tax levies. This, of course, would have been the most effective way to limit inflation, for when the government borrows by selling war bonds to individuals it only reduces the public's purchasing power temporarily.

Besides taxing and borrowing from individuals, the government also borrowed heavily from banks, and the money it received from them, unlike that raised by taxes or by selling bonds to individuals, was based on credit. In other words, it was not money that was already in existence; it was a new addition to the total money supply. Between 1939 and 1944, the Federal Reserve System and the nation's commercial banks increased their holdings of government securities by about $78.1 billion. During these same years the total money supply increased by about $77.6 billion.

238 THE ERA OF F.D.R., 1933–1945

The expansion of the money supply at a time when civilian goods and services were being reduced forced prices up just when the government was endeavoring to keep them down.

PRICE CONTROLS AND RATIONING

On January 30, 1942, the Congress passed the Emergency Price Control Act, which entrusted the task of preventing price increases to the Office of Price Administration (OPA). The OPA was established on April 11, 1941, and headed by Leon Henderson, a former economic adviser to the President and a member of the Securities and Exchange Commission. But because the OPA at first lacked adequate powers, by April, 1942, the cost of living was 15 per cent higher than in September, 1939, while the increases in most wholesale prices were considerably larger. Congress passed a price control act in February, 1942, authorizing the OPA to fix price ceilings, but pressure from the farmers caused it to include a clause authorizing an increase in farm prices to 110 per cent of parity and giving the Secretary of Agriculture the right to veto price ceilings on agricultural products.

By the spring of 1942 there seemed to be a real danger of a disastrous inflation. In April, Roosevelt sent a message to Congress laying down a five-point antiinflation program, and in September he asked for full authority over prices and wages, declaring that if the Congress failed to act he would assume the necessary power himself. The result was the enactment on October 2 of the Stabilization of the Cost of Living Act. Salaries, wages, and prices were in general to be frozen at the levels they had reached two weeks earlier, on September 15, 1942. Proposals to allow further increases in farm prices were defeated, although it was stated that such prices should allow for increased costs of farm labor. On the day after the passage of this law, Roosevelt appointed Supreme Court Justice James F. Byrnes to the post of director of the Office of Economic Stabilization (OES), whose chief job was to work with the OPA and the NWLB in a concerted effort to keep prices and wages down. The over-all record of the government in preventing inflation might have been better, as some critics of the administration were quick to point out, but despite its faults, it was a marked improvement over the performance of World War I. Between 1940 and 1945 consumer prices rose 31 per cent, whereas the increase in the production of consumer goods and services rose only 15 per cent. What the public could not spend, it saved, so that by the

THE HOME FRONT & ALLIED DIPLOMACY   239

end of the war individuals were saving about 20 per cent more of their disposable incomes than they had been setting aside in 1939.

Early in the war as certain acute shortages in articles for civilian consumption developed, the OPA began to put into effect a gradual program of rationing, beginning on December 27, 1941, with automobile and truck tires. Sugar, gasoline, and coffee were rationed before the end of 1942, and in 1943 meat, canned foods, oil, butter, fats, and cheese were added. Each individual was issued ration books for meat, fats, and canned goods containing stamps of various denominations with which he purchased his rationed items. The number of points each person was allotted for these commodities in any specified period depended, of course, upon available supplies. Many housewives, for example, learned to make their meat points last longer by buying low-point cuts or substituting one variety for another. For a time in 1943 it appeared that many other articles of food and clothing would also be limited, but in the end only shoes and a few other items were added, and all told only thirteen items were rationed. Except for sugar, which remained under OPA controls until June, 1947, rationing ended by the close of 1945. As was to be expected, a few people tried to hoard scarce items and petty cheats found ways to circumvent the rationing rules, but the number of these offenders was small. At first there was a considerable amount of grumbling against the OPA, but it was difficult to decide how much of it indicated an inability among some sections of the population to realize that winning the war required sacrifice and how much of it was due to the blunders and officiousness of the volunteers who staffed the local rationing boards, or the lack of political tact among OPA officials. Leon Henderson, against whom most of the complaints were directed, resigned in December, 1942, and was succeeded first by Prentiss Brown, a former United States senator from Michigan, and after October, 1943, by Chester Bowles, a Connecticut journalist and advertising executive.

Civil Liberties and Internal Security

One of the most satisfying features of the war at home was that civil liberties were much more generally respected than in 1917 and 1918. Enemy agents were taken into custody by the Federal Bureau of Investigation; subversive literature and some obviously fascist newspapers were removed from circulation; and a few thousand of the most outspoken

240   THE ERA OF F.D.R., 1933–1945

German and Italian enemy aliens were interned. But the general public showed little of that intolerance toward alleged pro-Germans that had so disfigured the American record in World War I. Critics of the war program continued to express their opinions with great freedom, and in one case, where twenty-eight alleged seditionists were accused of having advocated Nazism, thereby violating the Smith Alien Registration Act of June, 1940, the Circuit Court of Appeals of the District of Columbia, after a lengthy and somewhat amusing trial, finally dismissed the case.

The ugliest violation of civil liberties was directed against the 112,000 Japanese on the Pacific Coast, nearly 70,000 of whom were nisei, American-born children of native Japanese parents. The latter, called issei, were ineligible for citizenship, but the nisei and their children, the sansei, were citizens of the United States. As the tide of Japanese victories neared its crest during January, 1942, the American people, especially those living in California, Oregon, and Washington, grew increasingly frightened, suspicious, and intolerant. There was much talk, though no evidence, of Japanese plans to sabotage army and navy bases and to interfere with civilian defense programs. The presence of the Japanese in California, warned the state's attorney general, Earl Warren, "may well be the Achilles' Heel of the entire civilian defense effort." Government officials and responsible private citizens joined the popular outcry against the Japanese, insisting that citizens and aliens alike, regardless of their legal rights, should be removed from the West Coast. "A Jap's a Jap," declared Lieutenant General John DeWitt, the officer in charge of the Western Defense Command at San Francisco's Presidio. "It makes no difference whether he's an American citizen or not. I don't want any of them here." On February 19, 1942, Roosevelt, by Executive order, authorized DeWitt to begin the "evacuation," and by the end of March, 1942, most of the Japanese had been "relocated" in nine centers, two of which were in California's interior and the rest east of the Sierra Nevada Mountains.

The relocation centers to which the Japanese were sent were much like concentration camps, with families broken or crowded together into quickly and poorly built camp sites. Many of them were forced to abandon homes, businesses, valuable farm lands, and other properties or to sell them at great loss. Not only did the Japanese accept the government's decision with equanimity, but the 33,000 nisei who fought for the United States in combat units of their own proved themselves to be among the most courageous and decorated troops in the service.

In contrast to the experience of their countrymen in California, the

121,500 or more Japanese in the Hawaiian Islands were carefully watched but allowed to go about their affairs. But as with all residents of the islands, their life was made difficult by having to live under martial law for nearly four years.

In December, 1944, in the case of *Korematsu v. United States*, the Supreme Court, in a six to three vote, upheld the government's authority on the grounds of "military necessity." Three dissenting justices—Owen J. Roberts, Frank Murphy, and Robert Jackson—wrote strong minority opinions, declaring that the exclusion order "falls into the ugly abyss of racism" (Murphy), and that it was "a clear violation of Constitutional rights" (Roberts). After the war, when most of the Japanese had returned to the West Coast, the government made an effort to reimburse them for part of their losses, but the most alarming legacy of the Japanese relocation episode was the fact that the Supreme Court upheld the government's exclusion order, thereby establishing the dangerous precedent that "military necessity" can nullify the individual's protection under the Bill of Rights.

The federal government's wartime efforts toward ending racial discrimination against the Negro, especially for the 1 million or more who moved to the cities between 1940 and 1944 in search of jobs in industry, provide a gratifying contrast to its deplorable treatment of the Japanese. On June 25, 1941, by Executive order, Roosevelt established the Fair Employment Practices Committee (FEPC), first under the WPB and, after July 30, 1942, under the WMC. The FEPC's chief function was to investigate discriminatory employment practices and to eliminate them wherever they were found to exist in government offices and in the defense and war industry. The authority of the committee was strengthened on May 27, 1943, when the President, again by Executive order, placed it in the Executive Office of the President and required that henceforth all government contracts include a clause "obligating the contractor not to discriminate against any employee or applicant for employment because of race, creed, color, or national origin and requiring him to include a similar provision in all subcontracts." A similar provision was made to apply to all government agencies. Although the FEPC was entrusted with protecting the rights of all minority groups, nearly 80 per cent of the complaints it investigated concerned discrimination against the Negro, almost all of which were quickly and amicably settled.

Partly because of the FEPC and partly because of employers' needs for workers, discrimination in industry was greatly reduced, and the number of Negroes working in war plants increased rapidly. In 1940 they constituted less than 3 per cent of the nation's war workers; by the end of 1944 they made up about 8.3 per cent, and a great many of them had succeeded in securing and holding skilled and responsible jobs, including supervisory positions. The social and economic advance of the Negro during World War II did not occur without some ugly instances of race prejudice, the worst one being the June, 1943, race riots in Detroit. Order was restored quickly, but only after Roosevelt sent federal troops into the city to help the local and state law enforcement authorities. Considerable progress was made also in eliminating discrimination in the armed forces, but while the navy started to commission Negro officers during the war, segregation in the services was reduced only very slowly, even after President Harry S. Truman issued an Executive order in 1948 in which he stated his intention to promote "equality of treatment and opportunity of all persons in the armed services."

During the war the government also undertook to publicize its aims and activities both at home and in foreign countries. For this purpose the Office of Facts and Figures (OFF) was established in February, 1942, and headed by Archibald MacLeish, the Pulitzer Prize-winning poet and Librarian of Congress. In June, the OFF was expanded into the Office of War Information (OWI), and Elmer Davis, a former newspaper and radio commentator, was given general charge of government publicity. For the most part the OWI and its subsidiary agencies restricted themselves to the function of giving out information, and except for the opening of bond drives there was little attempt to stir up popular excitement. The chief danger on the home front was not fanaticism but rather apathy, especially after the Allied nations took the offensive and victory became increasingly certain. But the conduct of the men in the armed forces and the merchant marine proved that American civilization had not weakened in any degree the capacity for heroism in facing danger, and by the end of the war those observers who had doubted whether the civilian population of the United States would be prepared to surrender the comforts of a high standard of living with the same patrictism which characterized the men in the service were proved wrong.

The Election of 1944

Ten months before victory, when Allied arms in Europe were pressing against Germany's West Wall and MacArthur's troops were advancing in the Philippines, the people of the United States were preparing to hold a presidential election, the first one in wartime since Abraham Lincoln defeated George B. McClellan in 1864. The Republicans had made a strong comeback in the congressional elections of 1942, winning 46 additional seats in the House of Representatives and increasing their numbers in the Senate from 28 to 38. The Congress elected in 1942 remained Democratic, but by greatly reduced majorities: 222 Democrats to 208 Republicans in the House, while the division in the Senate was 57 to 38 in favor of the Democrats.

These majorities did not mean that the President could have his way, for there were enough conservative or anti-Roosevelt southern Democrats who voted with the Republicans to thwart the wishes of the White House. Except on essential war measures, the President was forced to accept several legislative defeats. His request to simplify the tax laws was ignored, and the Revenue Act of 1943, which provided the government with $2.2 billion in additional taxes instead of the $10.5 billion the administration had requested, was passed over his veto. In exceptionally strong language, Roosevelt called the law "not a tax bill but a tax relief bill providing relief not for the needy but for the greedy." He accused the Congress of being responsible for the fact "that the income taxpayers are flooded with forms to fill out which are so complex that even Certified Public Accountants cannot interpret them." He ended his denunciation of the revenue bill by saying that Congress had used language in drawing up this measure "which not even a dictionary or a thesaurus can make clear." When the President's veto message was read in Congress, Senate Majority Leader Alben Barkley resigned his post, and though he was reinstated, as the President had hoped and so telegraphed Barkley, the conservative anti-New Deal temper of the federal legislature which manifested itself on this measure became more obvious as the session continued.

By convention time, the obvious displeasure with which the southern Democrats viewed Roosevelt and the congressional gains which the Republicans had registered in 1942 caused the GOP to look to 1944 with considerable confidence. Willkie, the Republican standard-bearer in 1940, was so badly defeated in the Wisconsin primaries that he withdrew shortly thereafter, leaving the nomination to the other contenders, the strongest of whom was New York's Governor Thomas E. Dewey. There was some talk of running General MacArthur, but late in April he declared that he was not a candidate. Minnesota's Governor Harold E. Stassen, at the time serving in the navy, and Governor John W. Bricker of Ohio enjoyed

244   THE ERA OF F.D.R., 1933-1945

moderate support, but neither proved a serious threat to Dewey, with the result that when the Republican convention met in Chicago on June 26 Dewey won the nomination on the first ballot. Only one Wisconsinite, who insisted upon casting his vote for MacArthur, prevented Dewey from winning the nomination unanimously. For Vice President, the delegates chose Bricker.

The Republican platform that year, like the one four years earlier, endorsed almost all the New Deal's domestic reforms, including the Wagner Act, social security, and the Wages and Hours Law; and it promised the farmers "an American market price . . . and the protection of such price by means of support prices, commodity loans or a combination thereof." Having "accepted the purpose" of the social and economic reform legislation of the New Deal, the platform limited itself largely to criticizing the incompetence with which the Democrats had administered the laws. In foreign policy, the GOP platform, much to the chagrin of the isolationists, advocated "responsible participation by the United States in a postwar cooperative organization . . . to prevent military aggression and to attain permanent peace . . . ." It supported the United Nations declaration and, of course, it agreed with the administration on prosecuting the war until total victory had been won.

Three weeks later, on July 19, the Democrats moved into Chicago to nominate Roosevelt for the fourth time. "All that is within me cries out to go back to my home on the Hudson River," he wrote to the Democratic party's national chairman, Robert E. Hannegan, on July 11, but he went on to say that if the American people, "the Commander in Chief of us all," asked him to serve another term, he would be willing to do so. A group of southerners cast 89 votes for Senator Harry Byrd of Virginia and one vote was cast for James Farley, but Roosevelt won the convention's remaining 1,086 on the first ballot. The problem of finding a running mate proved more difficult. Vice President Henry Wallace, who had the President's "personal" approval, had won the confidence of the country's liberals and enjoyed considerable popular support, especially from organized labor, but he was unacceptable to the South because of his ardent New Dealism and his strong stand on civil rights. To avoid a convention fight which might impair his and the Democratic party's chances for victory in November, F.D.R. "sacrificed" Wallace by informing the convention chairman that he did not "wish to appear in any way as dictating to the convention." A few days later he wrote Hannegan saying that he would be "very glad to run with either" Senator Harry S. Truman of Missouri or Supreme Court Justice William O. Douglas. As a result, by the time the delegates were ready to cast their votes, twelve candidates had been nominated, but the real contest was between Truman, who had now become the official choice of the White House, and Wallace. On the second ballot, a combination of southern and northern city votes secured Truman's nomination.

The Democratic platform, as was to be expected, stood on the party's record in both domestic and foreign affairs. It took credit for the triumph of Allied arms and the way in which the country had been mobilized to win the "battle of production." In foreign policy it promised American participation in an effective international body strong enough to enforce the peace, while in domestic affairs it endorsed an extension of the kind of legislation that had brought so many benefits to every group in American society and had provided security to nearly every American. Addressing the convention by radio from the San Diego, California, naval base, F.D.R. told the delegates, as he had in 1940, that "in these tragic days of sorrow . . . [and] of global warfare," he would "not campaign in the usual sense," but he promised to "report to the people the facts about matters of concern to them and especially to correct misrepresentations."

To compensate for the Republican advantage in money and newspaper support, the Democrats enjoyed the vigorous and effective aid of labor's Political Action Committee, which the CIO's leaders had organized the previous year. The PAC labored indefatigably to alert the country's workers to get to the polls and vote for Roosevelt, just as the National Citizens Political Action Committee did in appealing to the liberal and independent voters. Many of Willkie's supporters in 1940 turned to Roosevelt this year, and when Willkie died early in October without having endorsed the GOP ticket, a number of people interpreted his silence to mean that he had intended to support the President. It was an open secret that the two men had been communicating with each other for some months, since both of them were sympathetic to the idea of remaking the Republican and Democratic parties into "two real parties —one liberal and the other conservative." This was an old pet project of the President's. He had tried this maneuver before, notably in 1938, and failed; and now, because he could not agree with Willkie on the proper time to inaugurate the change, he failed again. With Willkie's death and Roosevelt's preoccupation with the war and the peace, the President dropped his efforts at party realignment.

246 THE ERA OF F.D.R., 1933–1945

Since the two parties were in such fundamental agreement on most basic issues, the campaign turned to the question of who was most qualified to execute the proposed programs. Dewey campaigned vigorously, accusing the "tired and quarrelsome old men" in the administration of incompetence and inefficiency in planning and operating the war effort and declaring that it was "time for a change.' Roosevelt, except for the usual "nonpartisan" trips to inspect military bases and war plants, limited himself at first to fulfilling his duties as Commander in Chief. By September, however, Dewey's efficiently run campaign was gaining momentum and attracting sufficient attention to worry the Democrats. Dewey proved himself a capable campaigner whose fighting speeches made Roosevelt "pretty mad." Late in September, F.D.R. decided to reply to "that little man," and in a series of six major addresses he once again proved himself to be what Willkie had dubbed him, "the old champ." Roosevelt's first scheduled speech attracted much attention from friends and enemies alike since there were indications that his health was failing. The fact that six weeks earlier, on returning from a month's trip to Hawaii and Alaska, he had considerable difficulty in delivering a speech at the Puget Sound navy yard in Bremerton, Washington, seemed to confirm the reports of the President's poor health. But on September 23, while speaking before the Teamsters' Union, Roosevelt allayed many of these stories, if only temporarily, and reasserted beyond doubt his supremacy as one of the greatest political speakers of all times He deprecated the Republican party's endorsement of the social and economic reform legislation of his administrations and accused it of trying to "pass itself off as the New Deal." In reply to the GOP's and Dewey's assertion that the Republicans were better qualified than the Democrats to win the war and the peace, he reminded his listeners of the pre-Pearl Harbor isolationists who had fought lend-lease and the other defense measures he had proposed. And finally, he concluded by cataloguing the inconsistencies between the Republican party's current statements on a world organization and its past voting record by questioning whether the GOP Old Guard could achieve collective security without losing "a single isolationist vote or a single campaign contribution." To Dewey's reference to the "Roosevelt recession," F.D.R. replied, "If I were a Republican leader speaking to a mixed audience, the last word in the whole dictionary that I think I would use is that word 'depression.'" But the President's most shattering blow was still to come, and he delivered it when he answered a widely circulated rumor that he had sent a destroyer to the Aleutians to pick up his dog,

THE HOME FRONT & ALLIED DIPLOMACY 247

Fala, at great cost to the taxpayers. "I am accustomed to hearing malicious falsehoods about myself—such as that old, worm-eaten chestnut that I have represented myself as indispensable. But I think I have a right to resent, to object to libelous statements about my dog." After this speech, according to one Democratic wag, "the race was between 'Roosevelt's dog and Dewey's goat.' "[2] But talk about Roosevelt's declining health continued, and when the President decided to ride through four of New York City's five boroughs in an open car during a cold October rain, the press reaction was that he was trying to end rumors that he was a sick man.

Whatever may have been the state of Roosevelt's health in the autumn of 1944—and there is considerable difference of opinion among those who saw him daily during these months—the voters decided that they wanted him to carry on for another four years.[3] On November 7, some 48 million Americans went to the polls and reelected Roosevelt by a plurality of nearly 3.6 million votes. Roosevelt carried thirty-six states with 432 electoral and 25,602,505 popular votes; Dewey won twelve states, seven of them in the Middle West, with 99 electoral and 22,006,278 popular votes. The Democrats increased their strength in the House from 222 to 242, and the Republicans lost 18 seats, reducing their numbers there to 190. The Democratic majority in the Senate was reduced by one, so that the line-up in that body was 56 Democrats, 38 Republicans, and the Wisconsin Progressive, Robert M. La Follette, Jr.

As usual, the minor parties ran presidential candidates—Norman Thomas (Socialist), Claude A. Watson (Prohibitionist), and Edward A. Teichert (Socialist-Labor)—but all three together polled only a little over 200,000 votes; and Norman Thomas received the smallest endorsement of his long career—80,518 votes. The election of 1944 demonstrated more than Roosevelt's continued popularity and his ability to hold a seriously divided Democratic party together, if only to win an election. Much more important was the fact that a large bipartisan majority of Americans had rejected the old isolationism, at least temporarily. Both parties had endorsed internationalist planks, but the electorate appeared to go even beyond them by depriving a number of long-time Republican isolationists of their seats in the United States Senate, among the more important of whom were Gerald P. Nye of North Dakota, John A. Danaher of Con-

---

[2] Quoted in James MacGregor Burns, *Roosevelt: The Lion and the Fox* (New York [1956]), p. 468.
[3] Herman E. Bateman, "Observations on President Roosevelt's Health during World War II," *Mississippi Valley Historical Review*, XLIII (June 1956), 93–97.

necticut, and James J. Davis of Pennsylvania. One of the most outspoken isolationists in the House, Representative Hamilton Fish of New York, was also rejected by his constituents.

WARTIME DIPLOMACY

The Western Hemisphere

The Japanese attack on Pearl Harbor brought into the common struggle not only the resources of the United States but also those of nearly all of Latin America. The sagacious and patient labors Cordell Hull and Sumner Welles had devoted to implementing the spirit of the Good Neighbor Policy met with a most gratifying response. A conference of the foreign ministers of the American nations was held at Rio de Janeiro during the last two weeks of January, 1942, and the sentiments of most of the participants were voiced by Ezequiel Padilla, the Mexican secretary of foreign relations, who declared, "The attack by Japan was not on the United States but on America. In the Philippines that small force of men are dying not for the United States but for America. . . . We are going to defend America." As a result of opposition from Argentina, which had its own brand of isolationism, the conference could go no further than to "recommend" that all the American states break diplomatic relations with the Axis. All the Latin American states except Argentina and Chile followed the recommendation immediately, and Chile did so within a year. Between December, 1941, and August, 1942, eleven of the twenty Latin American countries, including Mexico and Brazil, entered the war as belligerents. Mexico and the United States had already agreed to cooperate with each other in defending themselves against the Axis. On January 28, 1943, President Roosevelt flew from the Casablanca meeting to Natal, Brazil, where he and President Getulio Vargas, along with their military staffs, devised plans to improve antisubmarine warfare against the German U-boats, then near the peak of their strength in the Atlantic.

By this date, the only American state which remained entirely neutral was Argentina, and even in this country the sentiment of large segments of public opinion, if not of the government, was strongly in favor of the Allied nations. In June, 1943, however, Argentina came under the rule of a profascist military clique. In October, when Roosevelt learned of Argentina's suspension of several Jewish newspapers, he condemned the action as a violation of the Lima Declaration of 1938, which asserted that "any persecution on account of racial or religious motives which makes it impossible for a group of human beings to live decently is contrary to the political and juridical system of America." Nearly a year later, in September, 1944, Roosevelt described the situation in Argentina by saying that it "presents the extraordinary paradox of the growth of Nazi-Fascist influence and the increasing application of Nazi-Fascist methods in a country of this hemisphere, at the very time that those forces of oppression and aggression are drawing ever closer to the hour of final defeat and judgment. . . ."

If Argentina was failing to comply with what F.D.R. called "its solemn inter-American obligations," the other nations of the Western Hemisphere, meeting at Mexico City's Chapultepec Castle in February and March, 1945, agreed to strengthen the hemisphere's war effort against Germany and Japan; to promote greater postwar cooperation and solidarity, for which the delegates adopted the Economic Charter of the Americas; and to participate in the work of the United Nations Conference, which was scheduled to meet in San Francisco in April. Among the numerous proposals adopted at this meeting, officially known as the Inter-American Conference on Problems of War and Peace, the most important, in terms of the relations of the United States with the other American states, was the Declaration of Reciprocal Assistance and American Solidarity. The Act of Chapultepec, as it was called, provided that an attack against any one of the nations of the Western Hemisphere was to be "considered as an act of aggression against the other States which sign this Act," and it authorized, among other things, the use of "armed force to prevent or repel aggression." Argentina, because of its badly strained relations with the United States, was not invited to attend the Chapultepec meeting. But before the conference adjourned, the delegates registered their desire to have "the Argentine nation" subscribe to the principles agreed upon at the meeting. Less than three weeks later, on March 27, 1945, Argentina went through the motions of declaring war on Germany and Japan, though without any fundamental change of policy.

Except for a Brazilian division in Italy and the training of Mexican and other American air cadets at Corpus Christi naval base in Texas, some of whom saw action in the liberation of the Philippines, the overseas military contribution of Latin America was insignificant. But its assistance in thwarting Axis espionage, in providing sites for the construction of American naval and air bases to combat German U-boats in the South

250 THE ERA OF F.D.R., 1933–1945

Atlantic, and in supplying the United States with vital raw materials was considerable and important. By the end of World War II, the Western Hemisphere was more nearly united than ever before. Much of the suspicion and hostility which Latin America had formerly felt for the United States had disappeared, and the New World's regional security system, enunciated at Chapultepec, was stronger and more firmly established than at any other time. Whether this wartime solidarity and cooperation would continue in the postwar era and lead to the realization of those social and economic goals proclaimed at Chapultepec was the great challenge facing Pan-Americanism at the close of World War II.

Allied Diplomacy

GREAT BRITAIN AND THE UNITED STATES

Anglo-American relations, which had been growing steadily closer since June, 1940, when Britain stood alone against the Rome-Berlin Axis, became even more intimate after Pearl Harbor. Roosevelt and Churchill differed on many questions, notably on the timing of a second front in France and on the future of colonial empires, but these were made easier to reconcile by the fact that the fundamental, long-term interests of the two powers were not inimical to each other and also that the two men respected, admired, and understood each other. Partly because of this, partly because of their unusual degree of trust for each other, and partly because of the urgent need of the time, neither Churchill nor Roosevelt ever allowed their differences to obscure their common goal. Since their first wartime meeting, off the coast of Newfoundland in August, 1941, their relationship, like that of the two countries which they represented, grew in depth and strength.

Two weeks after Pearl Harbor Churchill arrived in the United States to confer with Roosevelt. Shortly thereafter joint boards were established in Washington for common planning of war operations and of the production and allocation of munitions, shipping, raw materials, and food. In June, 1942, Churchill returned to Washington to discuss the critical shipping losses in the Atlantic and to plan further strategy against Hitler. Since it was obvious that the Anglo-American Allies were too weak militarily to gratify Stalin's demands for a second front, Roosevelt and Churchill agreed to the joint invasion of North Africa, and the Russian delegates at the conference were so informed. Early in August, Churchill flew to

THE HOME FRONT & ALLIED DIPLOMACY 251

Moscow, and with W. Averell Harriman appraised Stalin of the Anglo-American decisions reached in Washington.

Two months after the invasion of North Africa, Churchill and Roosevelt met again, at Casablanca in mid-January, 1943, to decide upon over-all strategy for that year. They had invited Stalin to join them, but the generalissimo declined because of the Russian offensive then in progress, though his continued suspicions of Anglo-American intentions about opening a second front and his distrust of what the Western Allies were planning in Southern Europe and the Mediterranean appear also to have played a part in keeping him from going to Casablanca. Besides the more routine matters of supplies, shipping, and field command, Roosevelt and Churchill were forced to tackle three major questions: (1) where to strike next, (2) what to do about France, and (3) how to win Stalin's confidence.

The first one was decided in favor of Sicily, but since there was considerable difference of opinion between the British and the Americans on where to launch subsequent offensives that year, it was agreed to delay a final decision until after the end of the war in Africa.

The second question, that of trying to establish a united provisional government for France, involved bringing together the two rival and quarreling French generals, Charles de Gaulle, the leader of the Free French in London, and Henri Giraud, Darlan's successor in North Africa. Angry and insulted that he had not been informed of the North Africa landing, De Gaulle at first refused to go to Casablanca, but the combined pressure and threats of Roosevelt and Churchill finally prevailed, and De Gaulle flew to the meeting and agreed to meet Giraud, where the two disputatious Frenchmen, in Churchill's words, were "forced . . . to shake hands in public before . . . reporters and photographers." After several more months of difficulties, a French Committee of National Liberation, headed jointly by De Gaulle and Giraud, was established in Algiers. Nearly a year later, in June, 1944, the committee became the French provisional government in exile. By this time, however, Giraud was out and De Gaulle was in full command.

To reassure the Russians, who suspected that Britain and the United States were purposely delaying a second front and might even be contemplating a separate peace with Hitler, Roosevelt, with Churchill's approval, announced at a joint press conference that they were determined upon securing the unconditional surrender of Germany, Japan, and Italy. In the future the wisdom of this announcement would be questioned, first on military grounds and later because it had become apparent that the total destruction of German and Japanese power would leave the Soviet Union dominant in Europe and Asia. At the time, however, Roosevelt hoped that this forthright declaration would dispel whatever fears or suspicions Stalin might entertain about British and American intentions to fight until total victory had been won. Roosevelt also wanted to make certain that the Germans would be made to realize their defeat. "Practically all Germans deny that they surrendered in the last war," he stated later, "but this time they are going to know it."

Four months after Casablanca, Churchill and his staff came to Washington to review plans for the Sicilian campaign and, more important, to settle upon the next theater of action. At this conference, code-named Trident, the divergent British and American views on whether to launch an attack against "the soft underbelly of Europe" or to strike at Germany through northern France were finally compromised. Sicily was to be followed by a campaign against Italy, thus satisfying Churchill, whom General Marshall and others in the Pentagon suspected of being motivated by political considerations; and the cross-Channel invasion which the American military chiefs had been advocating was set for May 1, 1944. This date was reconfirmed in August, 1943, when Roosevelt and Churchill met in Quebec to plan further military operations, and at their meeting in Cairo, early in December, 1943, Eisenhower was chosen to command the operation.

Besides these personal meetings, Roosevelt and Churchill were in constant communication with each other, and the military and production chiefs of their two countries crossed the Atlantic Ocean frequently for consultations. But although there was much greater coordination between the two Western Allies than had been achieved in World War I, there could be no real unity of command in a war which covered so vast an area and included so many diverse peoples. Great Britain and the United States nonetheless succeeded in establishing a very close partnership in which the policy was adopted of appointing single commanders, sometimes British and sometimes American, with full powers in different theaters of war.

THE SOVIET UNION

Anglo-American cooperation with the Soviet Union, much more distant and difficult, was complicated by mutual suspicions, distrust, and recriminations. In part this resulted from the long legacy of ill will,

On June 24, 1941, two days after Germany invaded Russia, President Roosevelt assured the Soviet Union of America's material assistance. This promise was subsequently formalized when, as shown here, Soviet Ambassador Maxim Litvinov (left) and Secretary of State Cordell Hull signed the lend-lease agreement. (Brown Brothers)

strained political relations, and the near diplomatic isolation of the Soviets since the close of World War I. Even more fundamental, however, was the unfortunate fact—too often overlooked or minimized during the war years—that Stalin's postwar aims in Europe were essentially identical to those which had motivated him to sign a nonaggression pact with Hitler in 1939.[4] The only thing that had changed was that the German attack had forced the Soviet Union to fight alongside Britain and the United States if it hoped to hold on to the spoils it had gained in 1939 and to realize the other objectives Hitler had denied it in 1940. The enemy—Nazi Germany —was the only common ground between Russia and the West during the war years. Under such circumstances, there was little room for much mutual confidence. Each side suspected the other's motives and even its loyalty to the common military cause. The possibility that Russia might

[4] George F. Kennan, *Russia and the West Under Lenin and Stalin* (Boston [1960]), ch. 23.

254   THE ERA OF F.D.R., 1933–1945

be forced or might choose to sign a separate peace with Germany frightened the West to the point where, as George F. Kennan has suggested, neither Roosevelt nor Churchill dared to refuse Stalin's demands categorically. Similarly, as pointed out above, the possibility of a Western *rapprochement* with Hitler alarmed the Russians too. That Stalin would not share his military intelligence with Britain and the United States, permit them to assist his armies in the Caucasus with air power, or allow them to use Soviet airfields freely made effective cooperation, much less coordinated strategy, extremely difficult.

Both Washington and London, but especially President Roosevelt, sought earnestly to dispel the suspicions and fears of the Russians and to earn their goodwill and support, first in winning the war and then in establishing an equitable and durable peace structure. Roosevelt's idea that it was possible to reform Stalin and win his cooperation by tokens of sincerity was, of course, a highly dangerous policy, but in 1941 and 1942 the Anglo-American military chiefs were convinced that the Soviet armies were indispensable to an Allied victory. The Soviet Union needed help, and London and Washington decided to provide it with lend-lease supplies of all kinds and in increasing quantities, sometimes even at the risk of shortages for the American and British forces. But regardless of the amount of matériel the United States shipped to the Soviet Union, the Kremlin remained aloof and suspicious, and when the war was over it never acknowledged the $11 billion of lend-lease it had received. Major General John R. Deane, who went to Moscow in November, 1943, at the head of a reorganized American military mission, reported to General Marshall his reaction after a year's association with the Kremlin: "The truth is that they want to have as little to do with foreigners, Americans included, as possible. We never make a request or proposal to the Soviets that is not viewed with suspicion. They simply cannot understand giving without taking, and as a result even our giving is viewed with suspicion. Gratitude cannot be banked in the Soviet Union. Each transaction is complete in itself without regards to past favors. The party of the second part is either a shrewd trader to be admired or a sucker to be despised." [5] Only two things were important in Stalin's military calculations with the West: "more lend-lease and a second front." [6] These he pressed for from

[5] John R. Deane, *The Strange Alliance: The Story of Our Efforts at Wartime Cooperation with Russia* (New York, 1947), pp. 84–85.
[6] Maurice Matloff, *United States Army in World War II: The War Department, Strategic Planning for Coalition Warfare, 1943–1944* (Washington, DC., 1959), p. 16.

the very beginning, when Soviet Foreign Minister Vyacheslav M. Molotov first came to Washington, in May, 1944, to confer with Roosevelt and other American war officials. When it became apparent that no second front was to be launched in 1942, Churchill and Ambassador Harriman, representing the President, met in Moscow (August, 1942) to confer with Stalin. The generalissimo was quick to show his intense displeasure, and, among other insults, he accused the West of having violated its pledges. The antagonism which marked this meeting continued into the early months of 1943, with Stalin reminding Roosevelt and Churchill regularly "to fulfill their obligations fully and on time" and complaining that it was the Soviet Union "alone" which "was bearing the whole weight of the war." Neither lend-lease nor the invasions of Africa, Sicily, or Italy dissipated Russian suspicions entirely, but by late spring signs appeared which were interpreted to indicate the approach of more cordial relations with the Kremlin.

Moscow's announcement in May of the dissolution of the Third International (Comintern) was greeted by London and Washington as a happy omen. In August Churchill informed his monarch that he had "heard from the Great Bear and that . . . [they were] on speaking, or at least growling, terms again." The idea that it was possible to secure Russian cooperation was strengthened further in October at the Moscow meeting of the "big three" foreign ministers—Cordell Hull, Anthony Eden, and V. M. Molotov. Reassured of a second front in France in 1944, Stalin promised Hull that after Hitler had been defeated Russia would join the United States and Britain against Japan. General agreements were also reached on several other questions. A European Advisory Commission was established in London to investigate all "questions arising out of the war" and to recommend policy to the "big three," thereby supposedly assuring unified action. Several declarations were published, one of which was signed by the Chinese ambassador to Moscow. It called for "establishing at the earliest practicable date a general international organization, based on the principle of sovereign equality of all peace-loving states, and open to membership by all such states, large and small, for the maintenance of international peace and security." The three governments at war with Hitler, through their foreign secretaries, also guaranteed "the right of the Italian people ultimately to choose their own form of government," declared their intention "to see re-established a free and independent Austria," and vowed to bring to trial those responsible for German atrocities. The lack of conflict with which these agreements were reached was greeted with jubilation in the West as a sign of the beginning of a new era in which international amity and goodwill would guarantee peace and security in the future. Roosevelt hailed the meeting as "a tremendous success"; Hull, in reporting to the Congress, declared that henceforth there would be no "need for spheres of influence, for alliances, for balance of power, or any other of the special arrangements through which, in the unhappy past, the nations strove to safeguard their security or to promote their interest." [7] Even Churchill, who was never overly optimistic about Russia's intentions in the postwar world, conceded that the West "had every reason to be content with these results."

One of the agreements reached at Moscow involved a meeting of the "big three" themselves, which was to be held at the Iranian capital, Teheran, between November 28 and December 1, 1943. Roosevelt and Churchill had been seeking such a conference for months, but for one reason or another Stalin was never able to leave Russia, and his decision to meet at Teheran, and nowhere else outside the Soviet Union, imposed great hardship upon the President. But Roosevelt, convinced that a personal meeting with Stalin would remove many of the generalissimo's suspicions and most of the obstacles which had made for inter-Allied difficulties in the past as well as prevent others from arising in the future, was prepared to assume whatever burdens and inconveniences were necessary. Right or wrong, Roosevelt was certain that Soviet intransigence originated from fear, apprehension, and memories of past struggles and defeats against powerful European coalitions. But if, as Roosevelt believed, these deep-rooted fears could be allayed, Russia's security and legitimate interests guaranteed, and proof of Anglo-American goodwill rendered, the bases for postwar peace and cooperation could be firmly established. "As I have said to you before," Roosevelt wrote Stalin before Teheran, "I regard the meeting . . . as of the greatest possible importance, not only to our peoples as of today, but also to our peoples in relation to a peaceful world for generations to come."

On their way to Teheran, Roosevelt and Churchill stopped at Cairo for a five-day meeting with Chiang Kai-shek. The President had invited Molotov to attend, but Stalin vetoed the idea since Russia was not at war with Japan. The Cairo meeting, for which Churchill had little enthusiasm and saw little need, failed to accomplish much since the promises which were made to Chiang—increased aid and a stepped-up offensive in Burma

[7] Cordell Hull, *The Memoirs of Cordell Hull* (2 vols., New York, 1948), II, 1314-15.

—later had to be broken because all available supplies were needed for the cross-Channel invasion. Before adjourning, the three Pacific war leaders issued a joint communiqué declaring that the Allies had "no thought of territorial expansion," that "the enslavement of the people of Korea" would be ended and that "Korea shall become free and independent," and finally that the war would be continued until Japan's unconditional surrender had been secured.

Two days later, Roosevelt and Churchill were at Teheran for their long-sought first "big three" conference. Roosevelt's belief that it was possible for the West to win Russia's friendship and cooperation through personal diplomacy with Stalin himself was strengthened as a result of his first confrontation with the Soviet leader. And Churchill, though with far greater restraint, was also pleased with the results. His plans for a Balkan or an eastern Mediterranean campaign in conjunction with the projected 1944 invasion of France, however, were shattered. Opposed by both Roosevelt and Stalin, the two strongest members of the Grand Alliance, Churchill was forced to accept defeat. The chief results of this conference were military. The May date for the second front was fixed, and it was agreed also that as soon as possible after the cross-Channel invasion, the Western Allies would invade southern France as well. Stalin promised to launch a Russian attack "at about the same time" and reaffirmed his earlier pledge to declare war on Japan soon after Germany's collapse. Apart from coordinating their military operations for 1944 as best they could, the "big three" also agreed to support the Yugoslav "partisans" headed by Marshal Tito, to try to secure Turkish intervention against Germany, and to guarantee "the independence, sovereignty, and territorial integrity of Iran." The issues raised at this meeting dealing with postwar affairs were left for future study and discussion. It was these, of course, especially the problem of what to do with Germany, which were to occupy more and more of Roosevelt's time. The possibility that conflicts among the "big three" might arise over the resolution of these issues occurred to Roosevelt, but he minimized them and continued to believe that patience, goodwill, and friendly negotiation would reduce their significance and allow for workable compromises.

On the day he returned to the United States, Roosevelt held a press conference, and when a reporter asked him to describe Stalin, F.D.R. replied: "I would call him something like me—he is a realist." A week later, in his Christmas Eve fireside chat to the nation, Roosevelt reviewed the results of his meeting with Stalin and assured the American people that

258 THE ERA OF F.D.R., 1933-1945

he did "not think any insoluble differences will arise among Russia, Great Britain, and the United States. . . . I may say that 'I got along fine' with Marshal Stalin. . . . I believe that we are going to get along very well with him and the Russian people—very well indeed."

Planning the Peace

The war aims of the United States were first stated in the Atlantic Charter and were later formally accepted by all the United Nations. During the war they were elaborated in speeches by Roosevelt, Vice President Wallace, and Under Secretary of State Sumner Welles, as well as by other high government officials. What the United States government looked forward to was a world in which all peoples would enjoy security against war, in which prosperity would be assured through freer international trade, in which government would be based on the free consent of the governed, and in which—much to Churchill's displeasure—the imperialist control of subject races would be ended. Roosevelt never once believed that these propositions were utopian visions plainly impossible of fulfillment. To him they were sober necessities—essential to the preservation of civilization and the prevention of another and even more catastrophic war. All these goals, moreover, were in harmony with the historic ideals which had always animated the American republic and with the hopes of the oppressed nations of Europe and Asia. What remained in doubt at the beginning of 1944 was whether the United States, Great Britain, and Russia would strengthen their wartime efforts at cooperation and try to reconcile their long-term interests and objectives equitably, and then proceed to conduct their foreign policies in accordance with these objectives.

As the tide of battle began to turn and the day of victory grew closer, Roosevelt and men of goodwill throughout the world recalled how, after World War I, the United States had attempted to withdraw from Europe and adopt a policy of shortsighted and complacent isolationism, disclaiming all responsibility for defending the victory its armed forces and industries had helped win. They remembered too how the United States had subsequently adopted a tariff and a war debt policy which showed a total ignorance of the economic interdependence of all nations. The fruit of this evasion of responsibility and of the errors which the other victors had committed during the interwar years was a decade of disaster, followed by a great global war which all of them were now in

THE HOME FRONT & ALLIED DIPLOMACY 259

the costly process of trying to win and which unfortunately, as too few people in the West realized, would inevitably leave in its wake as many vital and complex problems as it would resolve. For foe and friend alike, World War II was killing thousands of young men, consuming hundreds of billions of dollars and huge quantities of natural resources, and lowering the standard of living of millions of people. As the economic crisis of the 1930's and the outbreak of war in 1939 had shown, the world had become a unity. Whatever happened in any part of it would affect, for good or ill, the lives of all peoples everywhere. No nation—and particularly not the richest and the most powerful of all nations—could hope to escape its obligations to defend the peace of the world and promote the common welfare. "The well-intentioned but ill fated experiments of former years did not work," Roosevelt told the American people on his return from the Teheran conference. "It is my hope that we will not try them again. No—that is putting it too weakly—it is my intention to do all that I humanly can as President and Commander in Chief to see to it that these tragic mistakes shall not be made again."

Throughout the war neither Roosevelt nor his top advisers ever lost sight of these long-range objectives, though there is considerable room for argument whether the administration devoted enough attention to devising realistic means to implement them. A beginning was made in discarding the old isolationism when the United States adopted the Atlantic Charter and the United Nations declaration, but even more important was the action taken by the House of Representatives on September 21, 1943, when it strongly approved Democratic Congressman J. William Fulbright's resolution "favoring the creation of appropriate international machinery with power adequate to establish and to maintain a just and lasting peace." Meanwhile, in the Senate, a bipartisan group had been at work on a similar proposal since March, which it adopted on November 5, four days after the Moscow Conference of Foreign Ministers announced its declaration on general security. The Senate's resolution, introduced by the Texas Democrat Tom Connally and endorsed by the overwhelming majority of the membership (85 to 5), incorporated word for word the statement of the Moscow announcement on an international organization to guarantee the peace. Senate approval for America's participation in any such organization, of course, would have to be secured, but it was generally admitted that Roosevelt would not have to experience what Wilson had suffered with the League of Nations. The adoption of these two resolutions, the many public statements in their support made by Republican and Democratic leaders throughout 1943 and 1944, the widespread appeal of Wendell Willkie's book *One World* (New York, 1943), and the foreign policy statements in the party platforms of 1944 as well as many other indications of the public's support for international cooperation provided considerable assurance that not partisan politics, war weariness, unwillingness to make sacrifices, or suspicion of foreign entanglements would deter the American people from trying to fulfill their international responsibilities.

The American and Allied peace plans which were announced after the Moscow, Cairo, and Teheran conferences were general statements of postwar objectives whose execution, according to the United States, should wait upon the defeat of the Axis. In the meantime, however, the United States took the lead in promoting international cooperation on other levels. In May, 1943, American officials conferred for two weeks with the representatives of forty-three other nations at Hot Springs, Virginia, on ways to improve dietary habits in certain parts of the world and to improve the agricultural standard of living. The Food and Agriculture Organization (FAO) which grew out of this meeting was later brought under the United Nations. To help the starving and destitute victims of Axis aggression in the countries which the Allies had liberated, the United Nations Relief and Rehabilitation Administration (UNRRA) was established in November, 1943, with Herbert H. Lehman, the former New York governor, as its first director. The United States, along with the other participating countries whose territories had not been invaded by the Germans or the Japanese, contributed 1 per cent, later increased to 2 per cent, of their national income to raise the money required to buy and distribute the food, clothing, medicine, and other commodities and services the agency dispensed. By the end of September, 1946, when other United Nations organizations started to assume some of UNRRA's responsibilities, the agency had spent some $3.8 billion, of which nearly 75 per cent had been contributed by the United States. In July, 1944, the representatives of forty-four nations met at Bretton Woods in New Hampshire's White Mountains and established the International Bank for Reconstruction and Development; the bank would begin operations with a capital of $9 billion, of which the United States would contribute about 35 per cent. The purpose of this bank was to provide loans to its members and to protect private investors engaged in rebuilding devastated industries or in developing new ones which promised long-term growth. The conference also established an International Monetary Fund of $8.8 billion, for which the United States was assessed some \$2.2 billion. The fund was to help its members to evaluate and stabilize their currencies and, in time, to fix rates of exchange, thereby facilitating foreign trade.

The real accomplishments in international cooperation represented by the establishment of these social and economic organizations were overshadowed, however, by the conference which took place between August and October, 1944. Meeting at Dumbarton Oaks, a Georgetown estate in suburban Washington, D.C., Britain, Russia, and the United States agreed upon the general structural outlines for the new international peace organization. Since Russia was not at war with Japan, the two Western Allies consulted China separately on these questions. Though several important issues were left unresolved, the most significant being the use of the veto by the members of the Security Council, where the four Allies were to occupy permanent seats, the over-all character of the Dumbarton Oaks plan squared well with Roosevelt's ideas that all nations would in time be admitted into the world body but that the responsibility for safeguarding the peace would rest with "the four policemen"—the chief wartime Allies. It was they who would have to intervene, with force if necessary, to enforce the law and to prevent or stop aggression. That "the four policemen" might disagree sufficiently to go to war with one another was a possibility which Roosevelt hoped would never occur and for which he made no provision. Unfortunately, the tie which bound the "big three" together—fear of being defeated—became weaker each time they inflicted a decisive defeat upon the enemy, so that as the day of ultimate victory approached, what emerged was the substantial differences which existed among them rather than their common interests or objectives. And these differences, which involved vital political questions of national security, interest, and territorial readjustments and settlement, could not be decided satisfactorily on the basis of those broad, idealistic objectives announced at the beginning of the war or by the plans which came out of the conference at Dumbarton Oaks.

This became especially evident during 1944, as the Russian armies occupied Poland and the Balkans. The future of these countries had to be settled, but even more important was the necessity to learn the Soviet's intentions in these areas. Early in December, 1941, Stalin had tried to get Britain to accept the Russian frontiers of the 1939 Nazi-Soviet pact as its postwar boundaries, but neither Britain nor the United States was willing to do so, and at the time, in the words of Under Secretary of State Sumner Welles, London and Washington "reached a firm agreement that

262   THE ERA OF F.D.R., 1933–1945

no commitments upon post-war political and territorial settlements should be made until the peace conference." [8] At the same time, the military's fears of losing the help of the Soviet armies prevented the West from refusing flatly to consider sacrificing Poland or any other Eastern European state simply to satisfy the Russians. The result was that the Soviet proposition was neither denied nor approved. The reason for this evasiveness was primarily military, but it was also motivated by the fact that neither Britain nor the United States was then prepared to discuss territorial settlements, especially these which involved obvious violations of the Atlantic Charter. Moreover Hull was strongly opposed to any kind of spheres-of-influence diplomacy, and Roosevelt continued to believe that most of these questions could be settled later through personal negotiations. For much the same reasons, nothing was decided in September, 1944, when Roosevelt and Churchill met for a second time in Quebec. Roosevelt's refusal at this later date was understandable, since any decision taken on the Polish or the Balkan question could be used against him in his campaign for reelection, which was then just about to get under way.

Churchill, however, was becoming increasingly concerned with Central and Eastern Europe, and a month later, early in October, realizing the future significance of the Soviet occupation of these countries, he determined that a meeting with Stalin to discuss these matters could be delayed no longer. At least a temporary agreement had to be reached. Since it was impossible for F.D.R. to leave the country a month before the presidential elections, Churchill and Eden left for Moscow themselves to "reach an understanding" with Stalin on the Balkans and Poland.

"Let us settle about our affairs in the Balkans," Churchill suggested to Stalin on the evening of his arrival in Moscow. "Your armies are in Rumania and Bulgaria. We have interests, missions, and agents there. Don't let us get at cross-purposes in small ways. So far as Britain and Russia are concerned, how would it do for you to have ninety per cent predominance in Rumania, for us to have ninety per cent of the say in Greece, and go fifty-fifty about Yugoslavia." [9] With this, and a similar fifty-fifty arrangement for Hungary and a seventy-five–twenty-five division of interests in favor of Russia for Bulgaria, the Balkans were quickly divided into Soviet and British spheres of influence. The Polish question proved more difficult. Churchill had several stormy sessions with Stanislaw Mikolajczyk, the prime minister of the Polish government in exile, who had been sum-

[8] Sumner Welles, *Seven Decisions That Shaped History* (New York, 1951).
[9] Winston S. Churchill, *The Second World War* (6 vols., Boston, 1948–53), VI, 227.

The "big three" (Roosevelt, Churchill, and Stalin) with their principal aides at the Yalta Conference, February, 1945. (U.S. Army Photograph)

moned to Moscow to arrange Poland's eastern frontier. But when Churchill failed to get him to accept the Curzon Line as the Polish-Soviet border, the issue was left for settlement by the "big three" at their next meeting. The United States was represented at this nine-day conference by Ambassador Harriman, who attended the meetings only as "an observer." The President had emphasized this fact in a cable to Harriman in which he said that it was "important that I retain complete freedom of action after this conference is over." At the same time, F.D.R. also notified Stalin that it was his "firm conviction that the solution to still unsolved questions can be found only by the three of us together" and that he viewed the "talks with . . . Churchill merely as a preliminary to a conference of the three of us which can take place, so far as I am concerned, any time after our national election." [10]

THE YALTA CONFERENCE

The meeting that was to solve these and the other outstanding difficulties among the "big three" took place between February 4 and 11, 1945, at Yalta, the Crimean resort city on the Black Sea, where at one time the tsarist nobility found refuge from the rigors of Moscow's cold winters. At this, the second of the "big three" meetings, Churchill, Stalin, and

[10] Quoted in Robert E. Sherwood, *Roosevelt and Hopkins: An Intimate History* (New York [1948]), p. 834.

264 THE ERA OF F.D.R., 1933–1945

Roosevelt reached a series of agreements which have since aroused more vigorous criticism and more embittered dispute than any other decisions of World War II. The five major questions with which the conference occupied itself were (1) the proposed world organization, (2) Poland, (3) the liberated European countries, (4) Germany, and (5) Russian participataion in the Far Eastern war.

Like Wilson in 1918 and 1919, Roosevelt believed that world peace depended upon the continued cooperation of the "big three" through an effective world organization, and he was prepared to go to great lengths to assure its success. If this meant making concessions to Stalin to dispel his suspicions about the West or to satisfy his fears about the need to safeguard security of his country's frontiers, he was prepared to do so. Thus, Britain and the United States acceded to Stalin's request that the Ukrainian and Byelorussian republics be admitted to the world body's General Assembly with the same status and rights enjoyed by the other sovereign members. It was also agreed that the members of the Security Council would each have one vote and that, except "on procedural matters," all decisions "should be made by an affirmative vote of seven members including the concurring vote of the permanent members." By this provision the "big three," along with China and France, both of which were later admitted to permanent seats, assured themselves the right to veto all substantive decisions they might oppose. Britain favored the veto as a safeguard against interference in its imperial affairs, and the United States approved of it because, as Secretary of State Edward R. Stettinius, Jr., Cordell Hull's successor, declared, the American military chiefs and the Congress insisted that "the United States should not join any world organizataion in which its forces could be used without its consent." [11] The Soviet Union for its part wanted to make certain that the new world organization could not be used against Russian interests, as had been the case during the Finnish war, when Britain and France succeeded in "isolating and expelling the Soviet Union from the League." Stalin reminded Churchill of this at Yalta and demanded "some guarantees that this sort of thing will not happen again." Thus, each of the "big three" had his own reason to support the veto, and in the end it was accepted almost precisely as the American delegation proposed it.

Poland presented a far more difficult problem. With the Soviet armies occupying Warsaw and the Anglo-American forces not yet across the

[11] Edward R. Stettinius, Jr., *Roosevelt and the Russians: The Yalta Conference* (New York, 1949), p. 296.

Rhine, the advantage in negotiating Poland's future rested clearly with the Russians. The two questions which precipitated the controversies pertained to the establishment of a Polish provisional government and the determination of Poland's eastern frontier. Britain and the United States supported the Polish government in exile, the so-called London Poles. The Soviet Union recognized the Polish Committee of National Liberation, which had been set up in Moscow but which later moved to Lublin. Neither government was entirely satisfactory to the West, but the British could not betray the London Poles, whom they had recognized as the legitimate government of Poland since 1939, and Stalin refused to consider any Polish government which was not "friendly" to the Soviet Union. After considerable debate, it was agreed to reorganize the Lublin government "on a broader democratic basis with the inclusion of democratic leaders from Poland itself and from Poles abroad." The Western powers accepted this solution, which admittedly was much less satisfactory than they had hoped, because the new government was to be only an interim one and because the Soviet Union agreed that the provisional government was "pledged to the holding of free and unfettered elections as soon as possible on the basis of universal suffrage and secret ballot." Churchill's and Roosevelt's chief interest in Poland was to see it reestablished as a free and independent state in which the Poles would determine for themselves the government they wanted. The compromise solution they accepted appeared to guarantee this, even though neither Britain nor the United States had any way of assuring itself that the elections would be "free and unfettered." Stalin, claiming the Poles would be insulted by outside "supervision" of their elections, refused to consider Roosevelt's suggestion to this effect, and Churchill and the President were forced to settle on the "reports" of their ambassadors after the event.

The question of Poland's boundaries proved easier to resolve, since all three powers were basically agreed upon the Curzon Line in the east, and this, with slight "digressions from it . . . in favour of Poland," was announced in the joint communiqué. For the territorial losses which Poland suffered in the east, it would "receive substantial accessions of territory in the North and the West," but the specifics of these "accessions and the final delimitation of the Western frontier" were to be settled later at a peace conference.

As subsequent events were to prove, the agreements on Poland were entirely to Stalin's advantage, and the Poland which the Western Allies had hoped to see emerge from the war was never established. What arose in its stead was a totally different state, one in which frontiers were defined to allow Russia to hold on to the territories it had acquired from Hitler, and the government of which was a virtual puppet of the Kremlin. The unfortunate fate which befell the Poles did not stem from any Anglo-America sellout or surrender at Yalta. As Charles E. Bohlen, Roosevelt's interpreter and Stettinius' adviser at Yalta, declared later before the Senate Foreign Relations Committee, it was the result of "the progress of the war." By February, 1945, with the Soviet armies occupying most of Poland, there was very little the West could do to alter the situation.

Similar problems arose and similar solutions were adopted for the other Eastern European countries which the Russians had "liberated" and which their armies were now occupying. Bowing to the principles of the Atlantic Charter, Stalin, Roosevelt, and Churchill issued the Declaration on Liberated Europe, which asserted "the right of all peoples to choose the form of government under which they will live—the restoration of sovereign rights and self-government to those people who have been forcibly deprived of them by the aggressor nations." Once again, the fulfillment of these optimistic promises rested upon the Soviet Union, and unpleasant as it was to have to admit it, there was little the West could do in 1945. "We felt," Bohlen stated, that "it was the best we could do. The alternative of doing nothing was worse. That was the judgment."

Insofar as Germany was concerned, Churchill, Roosevelt, and Stalin had already agreed earlier that it was to be dismembered. At their second meeting in Quebec in September, 1944, Churchill and Roosevelt had given their tentative approval to Treasury Secretary Henry Morgenthau's proposal to turn over parts of Germany to its neighbors—Poland, Russia, Denmark, and France—and to create an International Zone out of the industrial Ruhr to be governed by the postwar world organization. What was left of Germany was to be divided into two sovereign states, permanently separated from each other. In addition, the Morgenthau plan called for the imposition of extremely harsh economic terms, "looking forward to converting Germany into a country primarily agricultural and pastoral in character." The State Department, War Secretary Stimson, and Harry Hopkins opposed these proposals vigorously. Hull called Morgenthau's proposal "a plan of blind vengeance" which would not only destroy Germany but "partly wreck" the entire European economy, including Britain's. A month later, Roosevelt rejected it. When Stalin introduced the subject of dismembering Germany at Yalta, Roosevelt and Churchill informed him that while they were agreed "on the principle" of dismemberment, they were "not yet ready to specify boundaries." At Roosevelt's suggestion, the question was referred to the foreign secretaries for further study. Meanwhile, Germany was to be divided temporarily into four zones of occupation, one for each of the "big three" and, at Churchill's recommendation, one for France. The French zone was to be created out of the Anglo-American ones. Stalin strongly opposed allowing France, a country which had "opened the gates to the enemy," a zone of its own, but Churchill was insistent. Roosevelt had declared that while he could "get [the American] people and Congress to co-operate fully for peace," he was not at all certain he could get either to agree "to keep an army in Europe for a long time. Two years would be the limit." This statement made it imperative that Britain secure help in the occupation, and in the end Stalin yielded.

Berlin's fate was decided when Roosevelt, Churchill, and Stalin approved the protocol which had been drawn up in London in September, 1944, by the European Advisory Commission. This agreement, originally signed by the "big three" but later amended to include France, provided for "an Inter-Allied Governing Authority . . . [to] direct jointly the administration of the 'Greater Berlin' area." Each of the four powers was to have a voice in the city's government, and each was designated a section in which to station its troops.

Everyone agreed that Germany should be forced to pay for the losses it had inflicted upon the Allies. To avoid a repetition of the painful experience which resulted from the reparation policy following World War I, the three powers agreed to impose payments "in kind" rather than in money and to establish a sum within Germany's ability to pay. Roosevelt and Churchill were disposed to be lenient, but Stalin thought differently. He proposed an indemnity of $20 billion, one-half of which was to be paid to the Soviet Union. Since payments were to be "in kind," he argued that they should be collected in three ways: reducing Germany's "national wealth" by about 80 per cent, establishing a ten-year schedule of "annual deliveries of goods from current production," and using German workers to rebuild the ruined cities, industries, and farms of the Allies. Since Churchill violently opposed this scheme, it was decided to establish a Reparations Commission to study the question further.

The last important issue to be discussed at Yalta pertained to Russia's participation in the Pacific war. That Stalin intended to do so had been known since October, 1943. What remained to be decided at Yalta was the timing of Russia's declaration of war and settling the price for its assistance. Roosevelt and Stalin began their Far Eastern discussions on February 8, just at the time when MacArthur was entering Manila and when the military chiefs were calculating Japan's defeat in terms of eighteen months after the surrender of Germany. The atomic bomb, of course, was to prove the military's timetable entirely wrong, but at Yalta no one knew whether such a bomb would work. Because the Joint Chiefs of Staff could not count upon it, they placed great importance upon Russian assistance. Just before Roosevelt sailed for Yalta, they informed him and the State Department that "We desire Russian entry at the earliest possible date consistent with her ability to engage in offensive operations . . . ." Since then, with the benefit of hindsight, a considerable controversy has arisen on the need for Soviet help, with MacArthur disputing the recollections of those who, like Navy Secretary James V. Forrestal, asserted that he had strongly favored an "active and vigorous . . . [Russian] campaign against the Japanese in Manchukuo . . . to pin down a very large part of the Japanese army." [12]

At Yalta, Roosevelt, Stalin, and Churchill signed a secret agreement whereby the Soviet Union promised to go to war against Japan "two or three months after Germany has surrendered and the war in Europe has terminated." In return, Roosevelt and Churchill agreed that the territories and rights which Russia had held before "the treacherous attack of Japan in 1904"—the southern half of Sakhalin and the lease on Port Arthur —would be restored. The Soviet Union's "preeminent interests" at Dairen, the ice-free port on the Liaotung Peninsula, were acknowledged, but the port itself was to be internationalized; and provision was made for the establishment of a joint Chinese-Russian company to operate the two railroads leading into Dairen from Manchuria. These concessions would make the Soviet Union the dominant power in Manchuria, even though the three signatories acknowledged the "full sovereignty" of China over the region. It was agreed further that the "status quo in Outer Mongolia (the Mongolian People's Republic) shall be preserved," and finally that Russia was to receive also the Kurile Islands. Stalin's demands did not strike Roosevelt as unreasonable, and Churchill declared that he was "in favour of Russia's losses in the Russo-Japanese War being made good."

To grant Stalin these railway and port concessions, it was necessary to secure Chiang Kai-shek's assent. Stalin left this up to Roosevelt, but he assured himself that his demands would be met by a provision in the protocol whereby the "big three" agreed "that these claims shall be un-

[12] Walter Millis, ed., *The Forrestal Diaries* (New York, 1951), p. 31.

THE HOME FRONT & ALLIED DIPLOMACY   269

questionably fulfilled after Japan has been defeated." Chiang Kai-shek accepted these decisions, and even saw advantages in a pact of "friendship and alliance" with the Soviet Union. On August 14, 1945, a Sino-Soviet treaty was signed in Moscow embodying the concessions which had been granted to Stalin and formalizing the two nations' postwar relations. The accord was hailed by both sides, as well as by the United States, "as an augury of peace on the continent of Asia and healing unity in China." [13]

No other decision at Yalta was to arouse such intense controversy as the ones on the Far East. Roosevelt's willingness to accede to Stalin's claims against China was, of course, a clear violation of the Atlantic Charter's provision against territorial changes "that do not accord with the freely expressed wishes of the people concerned." While his action in this instance cannot be justified on moral grounds, it is understandable in terms of the great importance the Joint Chiefs of Staff placed upon Russia's aid in defeating Japan. In view of this and also of Russia's interests and ambitions in the Far East, it is difficult to see what else the United States might have done in February, 1945, to restrain the Soviets. Roosevelt's concern with the necessity of securing Stalin's cooperation in the postwar era, his belief that Soviet policy could be made to serve world peace, and his hope that the wartime alliance would be continued and strengthened after the defeat of the enemy caused him to make, in Bohlen's words, "an honest attempt . . . to see if any form of arrangement with the Soviet Union could be arrived at that would have any value for the future of the world." The unfortunate fact was that by February, 1945, the shape of the postwar world had already been determined. By then it was too late to undo the consequences of the military events and the political decisions of the earlier years.

Few people realized this at the time, for the news of the Yalta meeting was welcomed as the dawn of a new era in international amity and accord. On February 12, when the results of the meetings were announced, the American people and most of the country's newspapers greeted them enthusiastically. Winston Churchill declared to the House of Commons that the Yalta meeting "leaves the Allies more closely united than before, both in the military and the political sphere . . . . The impression I brought back from the Crimea, and from all my contacts, is that Marshal Stalin and the Soviet leaders wish to live in honourable friendship and

[13] Herbert Feis, *Japan Subdued: The Atomic Bomb and the End of the War in the Pacific* (Princeton, N.J., 1961), p. 132.

270   THE ERA OF F.D.R., 1933-1945

equality with the western democracies. I feel also that their word is their bond. I know of no Government which stands to its obligations, even in its own despite, more solidly than the Russian Soviet Government . . . . Sombre indeed would be the fortunes of mankind if some awful schism arose between the Western democracies and the Russian Soviet Union." [14] And President Roosevelt asserted in his report to the Congress, "I came from the Crimea Conference with a firm belief that we have made a good start on the road to world peace."

THE DEATH OF
FRANKLIN D. ROOSEVELT

This was Roosevelt's last appearance before Congress. The President's health, a topic of rumor since his campaign for reelection, had become by inauguration day a subject of serious concern to several of his associates. He appeared to be weary, to tire easily, and to lack his customary vigor and joviality. When he returned from Yalta he gave the impression of being exhausted, but almost everyone expected him to recover his strength as soon as he could take a rest. On March 29, he left Washington for a month's vacation at Warm Springs, Georgia, and there, on the afternoon of April 12, he died of a "massive intra-cerebral hemorrhage." [15]

The President died knowing that victory over Germany and Japan was certain. And although, like Wilson before him, F.D.R. did not live to see the United States become a member of the international organization for which he had labored so hard and in which he had placed so much hope, he died knowing also, as *The New York Times*'s James Reston reported, that "the chances for the success of his league seemed . . . better than President Wilson's." Roosevelt's death struck the American people like a thunderbolt. For twelve years, through unprecedented domestic and international crises, Roosevelt had provided them with courage and leadership. His policies were not always clearly defined and many of them fell short of their objectives, but the great majority of the American people overlooked these shortcomings because of "the fresh and spontaneous interest which this man took, as naturally as he breathed air, in the troubles and the hardships and the disappointments and the hopes of little men and humble people." [16] Roosevelt, in the words of Anne O'Hare Mc-

[14] Churchill, *op. cit.*, VI, 400-401.   [15] Bateman, *op. cit.*, p. 101.
[16] Editorial, *The New York Times*, April 13, 1945.

THE HOME FRONT & ALLIED DIPLOMACY   271

Cormick, "so fused" the Presidency "with his own personality" that to millions of Americans it seemed almost inconceivable that anyone else could occupy the office. No one realized this fact more than his successor, Harry S. Truman.

Suggested Readings

The story of the war at home has been told less fully than the military aspects of the conflict, but a useful, brief survey of the highlights is the *Chronicles of America* volume by Eliot Janeway, *The Struggle for Survival* (New Haven, Conn., 1951). Francis Walton, *Miracle of World War II* (New York [1956]) tells the industrial story of the war, emphasizing the burgeoning role of government in business. John Dos Passos, *State of the Nation* (Boston, 1943) is a good contemporary account, as are Seymour E. Harris, *Economics of America at War* (New York, 1943) and Selden Menefee, *Assignment: U.S.A.* (New York, 1943). See also the relevant chapters in Allan Nevins and Louis M. Hacker, eds., *The United States and Its Place in World Affairs, 1918–1943* (Boston [1943]). Essays of varying quality on many aspects of American society during the war are collected in Jack Goodman, ed., *While You Were Gone: A Report on Wartime Life in the United States* (New York, 1946). Some of the "spirit" of wartime America can be savored in Mercedes Rosebery, *This Day's Madness: A Story of the American People against the Background of the War Effort* (New York, 1944).

Among the specialized studies, see Walter W. Wilcox, *The Farmer in the Second World War* (Ames, Iowa, 1947) and U. S. Bureau of Agricultural Economics, *The Impact of the War on the Financial Structure of American Agriculture* (Washington, D.C., 1944); and Joel Seidman, *American Labor from Defense to Reconversion* (Chicago, 1953), a good treatment on its subject. Joseph R. Ross, *American Wartime Transportation* (New York, 1953) treats all phases of World War II developments, but see also Frederic C. Lane, et al., *Ships for Victory: A History of Shipbuilding under the United States Maritime Commission in World War II* (Baltimore, 1951). Lester V. Chandler, *Inflation in the United States, 1940–1948* (New York, 1951); William J. Fellner, *A Treatise on War Inflation* (Berkeley, Calif., 1942); and Seymour E. Harris, *Inflation and the American Economy* (New York, 1945) are analyses by professional economists. Consult also Julius A. Furer, *Administration of the Navy Department in World War II* (Washington, D.C., 1959); Harold M. Groves, *Production, Jobs, and Taxes* (New York, 1944); and Robert H. Connery, *The Navy and Industrial Mobilization in World War II* (Princeton, N.J., 1950), which emphasizes the administrative problems. See also the pertinent volumes in the series *United States Army in World War II*, already cited, especially Byron Fairchild and Jonathan Grossman, *The Army and Industrial Manpower* (Washington, D.C., 1959); Kent Robert Greenfield, et al., *The Organization*

272   THE ERA OF F.D.R., 1933–1945

of Ground Combat Troops (Washington, D.C., 1947); and Richard M. Leighton and Robert W. Coakley, *Global Logistics and Strategy, 1940–1943* (Washington, D.C., 1955).

Important memoirs include Donald M. Nelson, *Arsenal of Democracy: The Story of American War Production* (New York, 1946), the well-told account by the head man. Edward R. Stettinius, Jr., *Lend-Lease: Weapon for Victory*, already cited, is an inside view, as is Jesse H. Jones and Edward Angly, *Fifty Billion Dollars*, also cited previously. Many of the memoirs cited before, such as Henry L. Stimson and McGeorge Bundy, *On Active Service;* Frances Perkins, *The Roosevelt I Knew;* Eleanor Roosevelt, *This I Remember;* and William D. Leahy, *I Was There*, are also useful on certain aspects of the home front.

On the violation of Japanese-American civil rights, see Carey McWilliams, *Prejudice; Japanese-Americans: Symbol of Racial Intolerance* (Boston, 1944). The story of the internment and resettlement episode is told in much detail in Dorothy S. Thomas, *et al., The Spoilage, the Salvage: Japanese-American Evacuation and Resettlement* (2 vols., Berkeley, Calif., 1946–52); and Morton Grodzins, *Americans Betrayed* (Chicago [1949]). The Hawaii experience in race relations is detailed in Andrew W. Lind, *Hawaii's Japanese* (Princeton, N.J., 1946); Stanley D. Porteus, *And Blow Not the Trumpet: A Prelude to Peril* (Palo Alto, Calif., 1947); and Gwenfread Allen, *Hawaii's War Years, 1941–1945* (Honolulu [1950]). William S. Tsuchida, *Wear It Proudly* (Berkeley, Calif., 1947) tells the experiences of a Japanese-American soldier.

Nearly all of F.D.R.'s associates have commented on the President's health in their memoirs, and many of their opinions, along with those of others, are summarized in the article by Herman E. Bateman, "Observations on President Roosevelt's Health during World War II," *Mississippi Valley Historical Review*, XLIII (June 1956), 82–102, and in the last chapter of Rudolph Marx, *The Health of the Presidents* (New York [1960]). The impact of F.D.R.'s death on the country is described in Bernard Ashbel, *When F.D.R. Died* (New York, 1961).

A great many of the memoirs, diaries, and personal accounts cited in Chapter 5 are of great value in revealing certain phases of wartime diplomacy; see, for example, those of Churchill, Leahy, Hull, Welles, Wedemeyer, and Stimson. In addition, consult also James F. Byrnes, *Speaking Frankly* (New York, 1947) and the same author's *All in a Lifetime* (New York [1958]); John R. Deane, *The Strange Alliance: The Story of Our Effort at Wartime Cooperation with Russia* (New York, 1947); Elliott Roosevelt, *As He Saw It: The Story of the World Conferences of F.D.R.* (New York [1946]), strongly anti-Churchill; Carlton J. H. Hayes, *Wartime Mission in Spain, 1942–1945* (New York, 1945); Walter Millis, ed., *The Forrestal Diaries* (New York, 1951); Arthur H. Vandenberg, Jr. and Alex Morris, eds., *The Private Papers of Senator Vandenberg* (Boston, 1952); Edward R. Stettinius, Jr., *Roosevelt and the Russians: The Yalta Conference* (Garden City, N.Y., 1949); and Charles de Gaulle, *The Call to Honor, 1940–1942* (New York, 1955), the abbreviated statement of this influential Frenchman. His more detailed

THE HOME FRONT & ALLIED DIPLOMACY

views and reflections on the events of 1940–44 are in his *Memoirs,* already cited.

Revealing wartime accounts of peace plans include Herbert Hoover and Hugh Gibson, *The Problems of Lasting Peace* (New York, 1942); Henry A. Wallace, *The Century of the Common Man* (New York, 1943); Wendell Willkie, *One World* (New York, 1943); and Emery Reeves, *The Anatomy of Peace* (New York, 1945).

On planning the peace and the background of the United Nations, see Vera M. Dean, *The Four Cornerstones of Peace* (New York [1946]), an excellent account of the UN's origins, and Leland M. Goodrich and Edward I. Hambro, *Charter of the United Nations: Commentary and Documents* (2d rev. ed., Boston, 1949), which contains detailed historical background and analysis. Eugene P. Chase, *The United Nations in Action* (New York, 1950) also has useful historical material. Louis W. Holborn, ed., *War and Peace Aims of the United Nations* (2 vols., Boston, 1943–48) is a valuable documentary collection. On the later history and development of the UN, see the very able study by John MacLaurin, *The United Nations and Power Politics* (New York, 1951). Consult also the brief account by Clark M. Eichelberger, *U.N.: The First Fifteen Years* (New York [1960]) and the more interpretative study by Lincoln P. Bloomfield, *The United Nations and United States Foreign Policy: A New Look at the National Interest* (Boston [1960]).

The diplomacy within the Grand Alliance between 1941 and 1945 is expertly told by Herbert Feis, *Churchill-Roosevelt-Stalin: The War They Waged and the Peace They Sought* (Princeton, N.J., 1957) and to 1946 in the equally competent study by William H. McNeill, *America, Britain, and Russia: Their Cooperation and Conflict, 1941–1946* (New York, 1953). Consult also David J. Dallin, *The Big Three* (New Haven, Conn., 1945) and William L. Neumann, *Making the Peace, 1941–1945* (Washington, D.C., 1950). An excellent interpretative essay is the chapter "Russia and the West as Allies," in George F. Kennan, *Russia and the West under Lenin and Stalin* (Boston [1960]), but see also the chapter in the same author's *American Diplomacy, 1900–1950* (Chicago, 1951).

Some of the basic documents on wartime diplomacy are conveniently collected in U. S. Department of State, *A Decade of American Foreign Policy, 1941–1949* (Washington, D.C., 1950) and in Francis O. Wilcox and Thorsten V. Kalijarvi, eds., *Recent American Foreign Policy* (New York, 1952).

There is valuable material on the influence of the military upon diplomacy and vice versa in several of the volumes in the series *United States Army in World War II.* See especially Maurice Matloff and Edward Snell, *Strategic Planning for Coalition Warfare, 1941–1942* (Washington, D.C., 1953) and its sequel, Maurice Matloff, *Strategic Planning for Coalition Warfare, 1943–1944* (Washington, D.C., 1959); Roy S. Cline, *Washington Command Post: The Operations Division* (Washington, D.C., 1951); and Forrest C. Pogue, *The Supreme Command* (Washington, D.C., 1954). The fifth volume in the official British history of World War II, John Ehrman, *Grand Strategy* (London, 1956) should be consulted as well.

274   THE ERA OF F.D.R., 1933–1945

Certain aspects of the Latin American diplomacy of the United States in wartime are covered in the volume in the *U.S. Army in World War II* series by Stetson Conn and Byron Fairchild, *The Framework of Hemisphere Defense* (Washington, D.C., 1959). The basic diplomatic history of the decade 1938–48 is told in Edward O. Guerrant, *Roosevelt's Good Neighbor Policy*, already cited, and more interpretatively in Laurence Duggan, *The Americas: The Search for Hemispheric Security* (New York, 1949). Arthur P. Whitaker, *The Western Hemisphere Idea: Its Rise and Decline* (Ithaca, N.Y. [1954]) is an historical appraisal since the eighteenth century.

On the Yalta Conference the best analysis and interpretation is to be found in the essays in John L. Snell, *The Meaning of Yalta: Big Three Diplomacy and the New Balance of Power* (Baton Rouge, La., 1956). The official account is told in U. S. Department of State, *The Conferences at Malta and Yalta, 1945* (Washington, D.C., 1955). Other relevant documentary evidence is collected in U.S. Senate, Committee on Foreign Relations, *A Decade of American Foreign Policy: Basic Documents, 1941–1949* . . . (Washington, D.C., 1950). Raymond J. Sontag analyzes these papers in his article, "Reflections on the Yalta Papers," *Foreign Affairs*, XXXIII (July 1955), 615–23. Critical accounts of American diplomacy at Yalta include William H. Chamberlain, *America's Second Crusade* (Chicago, 1950), the pertinent sections of Chester Wilmot, *The Struggle for Europe*, already cited, and Hanson W. Baldwin, *Great Mistakes of the War*, also cited before. The labors of Roosevelt and Churchill at Yalta are defended by McGeorge Bundy, "The Test of Yalta," *Foreign Affairs*, XXVII (July 1949), 618–29, and by Rudolph A. Winnacker, "Yalta, Another Munich?" *Virginia Quarterly Review*, XXIV (October 1948), 521–37.

There is a considerable specialized literature that can be consulted on the background and the events leading to the various decisions taken at Yalta. On Poland, for example, see Arthur Bliss Lane, *I Saw Poland Betrayed* (Indianapolis [1948]); Stanislaw Mikolajczyk, *The Rape of Poland* (New York, 1948); and the appraisal in Edward J. Rozek, *Allied Wartime Diplomacy: A Pattern in Poland* (New York, 1958). The future of Germany is discussed by Henry Morgenthau, Jr., *Germany Is Our Problem* (New York, 1945) and by Otto Butz, *Germany: Dilemma for American Foreign Policy* (Garden City, N.Y., 1954), an able presentation. See also Redvers Opie, *et al.*, *The Search for Peace Settlements* (Washington, D.C., 1951), which is more general but contains many useful insights into the problems of peacemaking.

On China and the Far East in Allied wartime diplomacy, consult the comprehensive and balanced study by Herbert Feis, *The China Tangle: The American Effort in China from Pearl Harbor to the Marshall Mission* (Princeton, N.J., 1953). Also good are Kenneth S. Latourette, *The American Record in the Far East, 1945–1951* (New York, 1952) and Harold M. Vinacke, *The United States and the Far East, 1945–1951* (Stanford, Calif., 1952). Two strong indictments of the administration's China policy are John T. Flynn, *While You Slept: Our Tragedy in Asia and Who Made It* (New York, 1951) and Freda Utley, *The China Story* (Chicago, 1951). The official documents on the Far East are collected in U. S. Department of State, *United States Relations*

THE HOME FRONT & ALLIED DIPLOMACY 275

with China, with Special Reference to the Period, 1944–1949 (Washington, D.C., 1949). On the final events leading to Japan's defeat and surrender, from May to August, 1945, see the excellent account in Herbert Feis, *Japan Subdued*, already cited, and the brief article by Samuel Eliot Morison, "Why Japan Surrendered," *The Atlantic*, CCVI (October 1960), 41–47.

PART II THE UNITED STATES AND THE POSTWAR WORLD

1945–1961

7

The Beginning of the Truman Era, 1945-1947

OF THE SEVEN Vice Presidents who have succeeded to the Presidency, none has entered upon his new duties under more difficult circumstances than Harry S. Truman. With no executive training or experience, with only a minimum knowledge of his predecessor's policies and commitments, and with no intimate friends or advisers in any of the major Executive departments, Truman was forced to assume at once all of the responsibilities involved in concluding successfully the nation's worst war, establishing a new international order, and guiding the country's transition to peace. The resolution of any one of these problems would have required all of Roosevelt's knowledge, ability, and prestige. On April 12, 1945, a great many Americans, including some of the highest government officials, questioned Truman's capacity to fulfill the difficult responsibilities fate had thrust upon him. What seemed even worse was the fact that there was nothing in his public record to dispel the fears, doubts, and concern brought about by Roosevelt's death at this critical juncture in history. Only a very few people knew anything about Harry S. Truman.

Unlike his predecessor, whose family had belonged to the American equivalent of Britain's landed aristocracy, Truman was the oldest child of a moderately successful Missouri farmer and livestock merchant. Born in Lamar, a small town in the southwestern part of the state, on May 8,

280 THE U.S. & THE POSTWAR WORLD, 1945-1961

1884, Truman moved with his family to the Jackson County seat at Independence before he was seven years old. There he attended the public schools and, after graduating from high school in 1901, held several minor jobs in Independence and in neighboring Kansas City. By 1906 he was back operating his father's farm, where he remained until 1917, when he was commissioned a first lieutenant in the National Guard. On March 20, 1918, he sailed for France, and in September he was a captain of artillery on the Alsatian front, seeing action at Saint-Mihiel, Somme-Dieu, and in the Meuse-Argonne. Discharged as a major in May, 1919, he returned to Independence, married his boyhood sweetheart, and, in partnership with one of his former army friends, opened a men's apparel store in Kansas City. Forced to close in 1922 because of the postwar depression which hit the farm states, Truman refused to declare himself bankrupt and in time paid all his creditors. Meanwhile, his long-time interest in local politics and his acquaintance with Boss Tom Pendergast's brother helped him secure his first elective office, an "administrative judgeship" on the Jackson County Court, a position equivalent to a county commissioner or supervisor in other states. For the next two years, while holding this job, Truman studied law in Kansas City. Defeated for reelection in 1924, he spent the next eighteen months working for the Kansas City Automobile Club, and in 1926 he was elected presiding judge of the Jackson County Court, a position he held until 1934 when he entered the United States Senate.

Truman brought with him to Washington an intimate knowledge of precinct politics and a great reverence for the high office to which he had been elected. "Even before I had left Kansas City," Truman wrote later, "I had read the biographies of every member of the Senate and had studied every piece of information I could find on our chief lawmaking body." [1] As a senator Truman worked diligently on his assignments, and with but few exceptions he voted to support Roosevelt's New Deal. Not until his second term, when he was appointed chairman of the Senate Special Committee to Investigate the National Defense Program, did he attract national attention, but even then few expected him to achieve any great distinction. When he was nominated and elected Vice President in 1944, almost everyone admitted that it was his political availability rather than his accomplishments in the Senate or his friendship with Roosevelt and the administration's policy-makers that brought him the prize. Five months after his election he was in the White House.

[1] Harry S. Truman, *Memoirs* (2 vols., Garden City, N.Y., 1955-56), I, 142.

As President, Truman displayed many of the qualities and characteristics of the typical small-town, middle-class citizen of the Middle West. His optimistic and uncomplicated philosophy of life and his undeviating faith in the righteousness of his principles and ideals appealed to millions of Americans. They admired the pride he took in his heritage, the devotion he showed for his family, and the loyalty with which he stood by his friends. Truman's sincere, unaffected, and forthright manner sometimes caused him to appear tactless and impulsive, and when he failed to control his easily strained temper, he could be petty, willful, and obstinate. For this, along with the mistakes he made, he was loudly and strongly denounced by his critics, many of whom deplored his humble origins, his simple faith, and his lack of sophistication as much as his policies and his partisanship. But like his most ardent admirers, they were agreed that whatever his faults, Truman was a strong and forceful President who, once he had the facts, never lacked the courage or the self-confidence to make a decision.

"All my life," Truman once said, "whenever it comes time to make a decision, I make it and forget about it." He sought and listened to the advice of government experts to a far greater extent than Roosevelt ever had, but he made it quite clear from the very first days that he was the President that he intended to be the nation's unquestioned leader, and that he alone would make and was accountable for "all final policy decisions." Truman, as the little sign on his White House desk declared, subscribed to and understood fully the meaning of the dictum, "The buck stops here." And though he was humble enough to realize that there was much that he had to learn, he never doubted his ability to master any of the tasks or responsibilities with which he might be faced. Hard work and determination had always provided him with the answers in the past; he was certain that they would do so again. "The Presidency," he said after leaving the office, "is the toughest job in the world, and it's getting tougher as time goes on. But if you work at it all the time, every day, and don't let the hard decisions pile up on you, it won't get you down. At least, it never got me down." For nearly eight years, Truman was forced to make one momentous decision after another. When he retired to Independence in 1953, few could deny his contribution to the growth of presidential leadership in foreign affairs, regardless of their opinion of the wisdom of some of his policies. Because of his many courageous actions, Truman was, in the words of one student of his administrations, "the first President to give the presidency an enduring 'peacetime' global

282   THE U.S. & THE POSTWAR WORLD, 1945–1961

orientation."[2] Recalling those days, Truman said, "As President . . . you never have time to stop. You've got to keep going because there is always a decision ahead of you that you've got to make, and you don't want to look back. If you make a mistake in one of those decisions, correct it by another decision and go ahead. That's all you can do." The first of the many significant decisions he was forced to make during his years in the White House was the one which resulted in the United Nations Conference at San Francisco.

EFFORTS TO ESTABLISH THE PEACE

Building the United Nations

On April 25, 1945, the representatives of fifty nations assembled in San Francisco's War Memorial Opera House to discuss the plans which the British, American, Russian, and Chinese delegates had agreed upon at the Dumbarton Oaks meeting the previous August and September. After considerable debate, negotiation, and compromise a United Nations Charter acceptable to both the large and the small powers was finally agreed upon, and it was signed on June 26. Its main provisions, following closely the recommendations put forth by the sponsoring governments, called for an international body composed of a General Assembly, in which all member nations were to have equal representation, and a Security Council of eleven members, five of whom (Britain, France, the United States, Soviet Russia, and China) were to hold permanent seats. The other six, the so-called nonpermanent members, were to be chosen by the General Assembly for a term of two years. The chief function of the General Assembly, which was to meet annually and in special session when necessary, was to consider questions which threatened the peace or which might lead to international rivalry. The "primary responsibility for the maintenance of international peace and security" was vested in the Security Council, which could employ any policy it chose to safeguard or restore the peace, including the armed forces of the members of the General Assembly. The authority of the Security Council in enforcing the peace greatly exceeded the power that had been conferred upon the League of Nations, but the council's ability to exercise it was seriously curtailed by Article 27 of the

[2] Louis W. Koenig, "Truman's Global Leadership," *Current History*, XXXIX (October 1960), 228.

Charter, which required that all "substantive" decisions "shall be made by an affirmative vote of seven members including the concurring votes of the permanent members." This meant, of course, that the Security Council could act only when the "big five" permitted it to do so. The negative vote (or veto) of any one of them was sufficient to prevent it from taking any consequential action, and had Truman not asked Harry Hopkins, who was then in Moscow, to get Stalin to endorse the right of the Security Council to discuss any dispute brought before it, the Soviet delegation at San Francisco would have insisted upon the approval of all the permanent members to allow such questions to be introduced for discussion.

The Charter also provided for an eighteen-member Social and Economic Council to "make or initiate studies . . . with respect to international economic, social, cultural, educational, health, and related matters" and "to obtain regular reports from the specialized agencies" which were affiliated with the United Nations—the International Labor Organization (ILO), United Nations Educational, Scientific, and Cultural Organization (UNESCO), the Food and Agriculture Organization (FAO), and half a dozen others. To administer territories placed under the UN's jurisdiction and "to promote the political, economic, social, and educational advancement of the inhabitants of the trust territories," the Charter established a Trusteeship Council, whose membership was to be "equally divided between those Members of the United Nations which administer trust territories and those which do not." The United Nations was to be administered by a Secretariat, headed by a secretary general appointed by the General Assembly and recommended by the Security Council. An International Court of Justice, modeled upon the World Court, was established as the United Nation's "principal judicial organ."

On July 2, immediately upon returning from addressing the San Francisco Conference, Truman appeared before the United States Senate to recommend the Charter's ratification, which was achieved on July 28 by the overwhelming vote of 89 to 2. Senators William Langer, the North Dakota Republican, and Henrik Shipstead, the former Minnesota Farmer-Laborite who had joined the Republicans in 1940, cast the two negative votes. Truman was informed of the Senate's action in Potsdam, the German city made famous by Prussia's Frederick II, where he was conferring with Stalin and Churchill. On July 28 Clement Attlee, who had just become Britain's prime minister as a result of his party's victory in the general elections, took Churchill's seat at the conference table.

284 THE U.S. & THE POSTWAR WORLD, 1945-196:

The Potsdam Conference

Even before Truman left for Potsdam, the Soviet Union had already shown its unwillingness to allow the Yalta agreements to interfere with its political and expansionist ambitions in Central and Eastern Europe, and as James F. Byrnes, who succeeded Stettinius as Secretary of State on July 3, was to record later, the "high hopes" which followed the Yalta Conference quickly gave way to "great concern." [3] The Soviet's direct intervention in the reorganization of the Rumanian government in March, 1945, violated the Yalta Declaration on Liberated Europe, just as its obstinacy in demanding that the United States and Britain recognize the Lublin Poles as the "kernel" of a "new" Polish provisional government was an obvious distortion of the compromise solution agreed upon by the "big three" at the Crimea conference. A month before Roosevelt died, Stalin accused him of allowing American and British officers to conduct secret peace negotiations with the Germans, an accusation which was entirely false and sufficiently insulting to cause F.D.R. to inform Stalin that unless such "vile misrepresentations" were curbed, the solidarity of the Grand Alliance, and with it the future peace of the world, would be jeopardized even before victory had been won. Molotov's intransigence during the San Francisco debates on the proposed United Nations Charter provided further grounds for questioning the Soviet Union's professed desires to cooperate with the West. As was to be expected, Washington's and London's concern with Russian violations of the Yalta agreements, which were then less than six months old, was received in Moscow with suspicion. The Kremlin, for example, mistrusted the motives of the West with respect to Poland's future. Truman's "brutal" (in Stalin's word) cessation of lend-lease assistance to Russia early in May and the West's insistence upon French representation on the Reparations Commission did not help to allay Soviet suspicions. In the hope of resolving some of these difficulties and in an effort to reestablish good relations, Truman had sent Harry Hopkins to Moscow in late May to confer with Stalin. The results of Hopkins' mission to the Kremlin were sufficiently encouraging to warrant Truman's optimism as he sailed for his first meeting with the Soviet chief.

The four principal items of business to be discussed at Potsdam were (1) settling the administration for occupying Germany, (2) deciding

[3] James F. Byrnes, *Speaking Frankly* (New York [1947]), p. 49.

upon the "machinery and procedures" for writing the peace treaties, (3) agreeing upon methods to be employed in guaranteeing the people of Central and Eastern Europe that the Yalta Declaration on Liberated Europe would be honored both in principle and practice, and (4) devising a new policy toward German reparations. For nearly two weeks, from July 17 through August 2, the "big three" debated these and related subjects, but without much success at reconciling the fundamental differences which divided them. The conference accepted Truman's proposal to establish a Council of Foreign Ministers, composed of the foreign secretaries of the "big three," France, and China. Its first task would be to prepare preliminary drafts of the Italian, Rumanian, Finnish, and Hungarian peace treaties and "to propose settlements of territorial questions outstanding on the termination of the war in Europe." By assigning this work to the council, the United States hoped to avoid the strife and confusion which

Clement Attlee, who succeeded Winston Churchill as Britain's Prime Minister (left), President Truman, and Josef Stalin are shown here with their four principal aides at the Potsdam Conference of July, 1945. This was the last meeting to achieve any substantial agreement between the Western powers and the Soviet Union. (Navy Department)

286   THE U.S. & THE POSTWAR WORLD, 1945–1961

had occurred at Versailles in 1919. To allow the small powers a role in the peacemaking, provision was made for the United Nations to review the treaties once the council had concluded its work and secured the approval of the principal victors.

On the far more complex subject of drawing up a German peace treaty, the "big three" instructed the council to begin working on the problem, but agreed that no settlement was to be made with Germany until "a government adequate for the purpose is established." Meanwhile, Hitler's former Reich was to be divided into four zones, each occupied by one of the principal allies, including France, as had been decided at Yalta. While each occupying power was allowed considerable flexibility and authority in its zone, the Potsdam Declaration asserted that "uniformity of treatment" should prevail whenever "practicable." The purpose of the occupation, the "big three" declared, was not "to destroy or enslave the German people," but to make certain "that Germany never again will threaten her neighbors or the peace of the world."

In order to secure these ends and to "prepare for the eventual reconstruction of German political life on a democratic basis," Germany was to be completely disarmed, its capacity to make war destroyed, and every institution, law, or organization formerly associated with the army or the Nazi party eliminated. Every effort was to be made to decentralize German political and economic life. The thorny issue of how Germany was to be made to pay for the damages Hitler's war machine had inflicted upon the United Nations had aroused considerable controversy at Yalta. Since then, however, the views of the United States on this subject and on the related issue of Germany's future role in Europe had undergone considerable change. Neither the State Department nor the administration was at all convinced that it was in the best interest of the United States to impose reparations aimed at crushing Germany. Aware of its recent difficulties in negotiating with the Kremlin and realizing the menace presented by further Soviet penetration into Central Europe, the American delegation at Potsdam was unwilling to see Germany saddled with a reparations bill which would prevent or excessively delay it from becoming a unified, sovereign, democratic state capable of resuming its place in the European balance of power. Since the Russians, on the other hand, were determined to avoid the rebirth of a new Germany as long as possible, they were prepared to employ reparations as one possible way to achieve this end. As a result, only after considerable difficulty was it possible to get Stalin to drop the $20-billion figure which had been discussed at Yalta. Stalin viewed this amount, of which one-half was to go to the Soviet Union, as already agreed upon, whereas Byrnes looked upon it as Roosevelt had—only as a "basis for discussion" by the Reparations Commission. The question of German payments was complicated further by the fact that the Soviet armies in Germany were taking all kinds of "property and equipment that could in no sense be classified as war booty," except by Russian definition, which, according to Byrnes, included "furniture, bath fixtures, silverware, coal, and other nonmilitary supplies." In the end, it was agreed that no total reparations figure should be fixed and that the four occupying powers were to collect their claims from their own zones and "from appropriate German external assets." It was agreed also that the Soviet Union was to receive from the Western zones "15 per cent of such usable and complete industrial equipment . . . as is unnecessary for the Germany peace economy . . . in exchange for an equivalent value of food, coal, potash, zinc, timber . . . and such other commodities as may be agreed upon." Moreover, the Soviet Union was to receive an additional 10 per cent of Germany's "industrial capital equipment" located in the Western zones "without payment or exchange of any kind in return." It was hoped that the compromises which went into the solution of the reparations problem would end the controversy, but as events were soon to prove, the arrangements reached at this time only served to provide bases for further disputes.

The question of Poland's western frontier still remained to be settled, and since it was apparent that no mutually satisfactory solution could be found, it was decided "that the final delimitation of the western frontier of Poland should await the peace settlement." On the surface this appeared to be no more than the postponement of a currently difficult impasse among the "big three." In actuality, however, it meant that while the search for a solution was being investigated, Soviet arms and influence, the latter exercised through the pro-Communist Polish government, were to entrench themselves as far west as the Oder-Neisse, the boundary the Soviet Union insisted upon and the West refused to concede. Among the other territorial questions discussed at Potsdam was the one involving the Baltic port and former East Prussian capital city of Königsberg. The conference "agreed in principle" that this historic city "and the area adjacent to it" should be transferred to the Soviet Union.

Except for the decision to bring the Nazi war criminals "to swift and sure justice," the agreements reached at Potsdam were more apparent than real. At the conclusion of the conference, "the American delegation

288   THE U.S. & THE POSTWAR WORLD, 1945–1961

that headed for home," in Byrnes's words, "was less sanguine than the one that had departed from Yalta." Still, neither he nor Truman looked upon the meeting as a failure. "We thought," Byrnes said, "that we had established a basis for maintaining our war-born unity." This idea, enriched with even greater optimism about the future, was shared by almost every American. Only a very few of them realized at the time that final victory in World War II, which came only one week after the end of the Potsdam meeting, meant no more than the end of the German and Japanese military threat to the security of the United States. Unfortunately, in August, 1945, too many Americans interpreted victory as meaning that they had won the "war to end wars." The facts, however, were otherwise, as Acting Secretary of State Joseph C. Grew stated a week after Germany's surrender. The triumph of American arms, he told Ambassador Harriman and Soviet expert Charles E. Bohlen, meant only "the transfer of totalitarian dictatorship and power from Germany and Japan to Soviet Russia which will constitute in the future as grave a danger to us as did the Axis." [4]

At the time, however, all that appeared to interest the American people, as they celebrated their victory, was the speed with which the government would permit them to resume their peacetime pursuits. In August, 1945, the United States was the most powerful military nation on earth. No state or coalition of powers approached its armed strength or doubted its ability, should it so desire, to impose its will on friend and foe alike. What was equally obvious was that rarely, if ever, in the annals of human history had a nation with such power been so uninterested in conquest or so unwilling to employ its forces for its own selfish ends. Neither the United States government nor the American people desired anything more than peace and security. No greater proof of this can be found than the determination and speed with which both turned their attention to domestic affairs in the autumn of 1945.

DEMOBILIZATION

As soon as Germany surrendered, the public started to demand that the government begin demobilizing; and when Japan sued for peace the pressure from servicemen's families upon Washington officialdom to "bring the boys home" as fast as possible grew relentless. Since 1943, when the military first began to consider demobilization, it had planned a two-stage program: the first, following the end of the war in Europe, would involve discharging some men and redeploying others to the Pacific; the

[4] Joseph C. Grew, *Turbulent Era* (2 vols., Boston [1952]), II, 1445.

second was to occur after Japan's defeat, which the service chiefs assumed would take place twelve to eighteen months after V-E Day. On May 12, 1945, four days after Germany's surrender, the army began to move its forces to the Pacific and to discharge servicemen according to their Adjusted Service Rating or, as the program was more commonly called, the point system. Discharges were to be determined on the basis of length of service, time overseas, combat record, awards, decorations, and number of dependents. Japan's surrender, three months after V-E Day, resulted in widespread public demand to expedite the demobilization program, and in September the services reduced the required "points" for discharge. Within one month after V-J Day the army stepped up its daily discharge rate by 11,000 men, from 4,200 to 15,200, and President Truman announced that the rate would be increased still further "to more than 25,000 per day by January 1946." Every available ship was used to return soldiers to their families, and even though the public continued to criticize the government and to accuse it of unwarranted delay, the strength of the army was reduced so rapidly that, as Truman declared, it "was no longer demobilization . . . it was disintegration." By June 30, 1946, nine months after V-J Day, the United States army had discharged more than 6.1 million men, thereby reducing its size from 8 to 1.8 million men.

Meanwhile the need for occupation troops forced Congress to extend the Selective Service Act, but its reluctance to do so in the face of public hostility was obvious. The first extension, which Congress passed on May 14, 1946, lengthened the life of the original law to July 1, 1946, with amendments excluding fathers and men below the age of twenty. When the number of June volunteers proved inadequate to meet the services' requirements, on June 29 Congress extended selective service through March 31, 1947, and by further amendments made all men between the ages of nineteen and forty-four, with the exception of fathers and draftees who had already served six months or more overseas, liable to induction for eighteen months.[5] On June 16, at the request of the military, Truman

---

[5] On June 24, 1948, Congress enacted a new Selective Service Act, requiring all men between the ages of eighteen and forty-five to register, but only those nineteen to twenty-five were made liable to twenty-one months of service. With the outbreak of the Korean War (June 25, 1950), Congress on June 30 extended the law for another year and allowed the President to call into service for twenty-one months the National Guard and the "organized reserves." The next year, on June 19, 1951, the draft law was extended to July 1, 1955, and to meet the manpower needs of the armed services the age to which men were made liable to service was lowered to eighteen and a half.

changed the age limits of those liable for service to men between nineteen and twenty-nine years old. During July and August and from October through December no men were drafted. As a result of these "draft holidays," the limitations written into the extensions of the selective service law, and the various provisions which were made in 1946 to defer certain essential workers and students, the size of the country's armed forces was reduced to a dangerously low level. By January, 1947, the total strength of the army, navy, and marine corps was only 1.1 million men, a fact which heartened the great majority of Americans but the significance of which to the political and diplomatic role of the United States in the world was not lost upon the Kremlin or upon observant and knowledgeable men everywhere. Navy Secretary Forrestal voiced his alarm at the speed and abandon with which the United States was reducing its military and naval strength. On September 19, 1945, while testifying before the House Naval Affairs Committee, he reminded the congressmen that "the outstanding lesson of the past quarter-century is that the means to wage war must be in the hands of those who hate war." [6] But most of his listeners, like their constituents, were neither so realistic nor so skeptical about the future. The war had been won; it was now time for the government to release and reward its fighting men.

Veteran Benefits

The federal government prepared to assist the returning veteran through two wartime statutes. On March 23, 1943, Congress provided for disabled veterans who, through education and special training, could be restored to useful and self-sufficient lives; and the next year, on June 22, 1944, President Roosevelt signed the Servicemen's Readjustment Act, more widely known as the GI Bill of Rights.[7] Under the latter's provisions, any nondisabled veteran who had served in the armed forces for ninety or more days and who had been honorably discharged was qualified to apply for assistance to begin or continue his secondary or college education; to borrow funds through loans secured by the Veterans' Administration to buy or improve a house, farm, or business; and to receive the help of the Veterans' Placement Service to find a job. If he was

---

[6] Walter Millis, ed., *The Forrestal Diaries* (New York, 1951), p. 97.
[7] The letters *GI* refer to *government issue*, a term widely employed during the war to everything provided by the federal government. Servicemen soon came to apply it to themselves.

unable to secure employment or accepted a position which paid less than $1,200 a year, he was entitled to a weekly "readjustment allowance" of $20, which could last as long as a year. By July, 1949, when this provision generally ceased to apply, close to 9 million veterans had been benefited by "readjustment allowances," though only a small percentage of these had made use of it for longer than several weeks. The availability of jobs and the law's educational benefits proved far more attractive than the government's weekly compensation checks. By July, 1956, when the schooling provisions of the GI Bill were about to expire, more than 7.8 million veterans had received government-subsidized educations. Of these, the largest number, 3.5 million, had enrolled in various specialized and secondary schools, 2.2 million had attended colleges and universities of their choice, 1.4 million had received on-the-job training, and 700,000 had entered upon agricultural programs which combined schooling with actual farm experience. These benefits could last as long as four years, depending upon length of service. Educating the veterans of World War II, many of whom used all their benefits, cost the government $14.5 billion, of which 80 per cent went to the former GIs as "subsistence allowances." Originally these were fixed at $50 and $75 a month for single and married veterans respectively, but subsequent increases raised the amounts to $75 and $105. In addition each veteran received an annual grant of $500 to meet the costs of his tuition, books, and whatever other supplies were required. The government also provided generously for the less fortunate veterans who required long medical or psychiatric care, hospitalization, and physical rehabilitation.

RECONVERSION

Although the legislative efforts of the government to ease the servicemen's transition from war to peace were effected harmoniously and without partisanship, the reconversion of the economy was accomplished by prolonged political controversy between the President and Congress and by even greater strife between labor and management. The return to a peacetime economy began in August, 1944, two months after D-Day, when the War Production Board (WPB) allowed a number of industrialists whose supplies and labor force exceeded the requirements of the war program to resume the manufacture of civilian goods. On October 3, 1944, Congress established the Office of War Mobilization and Reconversion (OWMR), which succeeded and undertook the functions of the Office of War Mobilization (OWM). The OWMR's principal task was to study the problems of reconversion and to recommend policies designed to facilitate the economy's return to peacetime production as quickly and smoothly as possible. Headed first by former Supreme Court Justice James F. Byrnes, the OWMR worked closely with other government agencies and with representatives of industry and labor in settling and terminating war contracts and disposing of war surpluses. After V-E Day the amount of resources allocated for civilian production was increased, and when Japan surrendered three months later the public's demand for goods and business' insistence upon a speedy end to wartime controls brought a stepped-up reconversion program. In September, 1945, the WPB removed many of the controls it had exercised during the war and liberalized its priority system. A month later, on October 4, 1945, President Truman announced that the WPB would be dissolved within the next thirty days and a Civilian Production Administration (CPA) established in its place under the OWMR. The declared purpose of the CPA was "to further a swift and orderly transition from wartime production to a maximum peacetime production in industry free from wartime government controls, with due regard for the stability of prices and costs."

Strikes and Inflation

The CPA's plans for an "orderly transition" to peace, like the administration's hopes to avoid the difficulties which had accompanied the "great demobilization" of 1919, were shattered by labor's bitter disputes with management, which, along with soaring prices, soon came to dominate the country's attention. The workers, determined to maintain their take-home pay at wartime levels, insisted upon wage increases which would compensate them for their loss of overtime. When employers resisted their demands for wage boosts, the workers became belligerent. Their dissatisfaction was increased further by fear of a major postwar depression. The reduction in war production following V-E Day had doubled the number of unemployed, and after V-J Day it trebled, reaching nearly 3 million. In the meantime, business was also apprehensive about the effects of government cutbacks on profits and concerned with the costs and difficulties of reconversion. Under these circumstances the business community was convinced that it could not afford to increase wages.

Early in November, as threats and talk of strikes multiplied, Truman called a National Labor-Management Conference and asked it to agree upon an equitable and mutually satisfactory method whereby employers and employees could reconcile their differences amicably without resort to strikes. The conferees met for three weeks, but without significant results. The next month Truman asked Congress for legislation which would empower him to set up fact-finding boards to investigate industrial disputes and recommend settlements, but the Congress, intent upon drawing up its own labor law, refused to enact the President's recommendation.

In the meantime labor-management relations continued to deteriorate, and beginning with the General Motors strike, which lasted from November 21, 1945, to March 13, 1946, the country was faced with a series of work stoppages which tied up a number of major industries, prolonged reconversion, and, before they were settled, resulted in a runaway "wage-price spiral" which appeared incapable of being stopped. On January 15, 1946, the electrical equipment workers went on strike and did not return to their jobs for nearly two months; on January 16, the meatpackers struck for ten days; and on January 21, the steel industry was forced to close down for nearly four weeks. The country had just recovered from this wave of labor troubles when John L. Lewis ordered his United Mine Workers to strike, and between April 1 and May 29, the soft coal mines ceased to operate, threatening to force all industries dependent upon soft coal to shut down also. Meanwhile, an even greater threat to the nation's economy occurred when two railway brotherhoods—the Locomotive Engineers and the Railway Trainmen—refused to join the other unions and the carriers in accepting the government's wage compromise solution. Despite the fact that Truman had seized the railroads on May 22 and placed them under the control of the Office of Defense Transportation, the engineers and the trainmen ordered a strike on May 23 which stopped all rail transportation in the United States. Truman moved at once to end the strike. He addressed the country by radio on May 24, declaring that unless the strikers returned to their jobs at once he would order them drafted and charge the army with running the trains. The next day, while he was before Congress asking for "strong emergency legislation" to prevent strikes against government-operated industries, the two striking unions announced that they would accept the government's proposal and order their men to return to work.

In all these labor-management disputes, as in others which were settled without work stoppages, union leaders argued that industrial profits were high enough to permit hourly wage increases without increasing prices. Indeed, it was to industry's advantage to do so, declared the United Auto Workers' Walter Reuther during the General Motors strike. Without additional purchasing power, how could the workers afford to buy the growing number of products which were beginning to roll off the assembly lines in ever-increasing quantities? Management, as was to be expected, vigorously denied the validity of labor's arguments, claiming that it was unrealistic if not unjust to expect business to pay its present labor costs out of past profits. Spokesmen for General Motors declared that they would refuse to do so. Others said the same. Moreover, most businessmen asserted, it was not up to labor to determine whether management could or could not afford to increase wages. The administration tried to resolve the impasse by appointing fact-finding boards to investigate the conflicting arguments but to no avail, since it had been unable to get a law to compel management to open its financial records to these boards. Unwilling to allow these crippling strikes to disrupt reconversion further or to precipitate a grave national economic crisis, the administration was forced to make concessions, and beginning with the steel strike, in February, 1946, it allowed industries which granted wage increases to raise prices. This concession, which in 1946 amounted usually to 17 or 18 per cent boosts, is significant, for it established a pattern adopted by many industries and laid the basis for subsequent wage-price increases, with the result that the two soon chased each other to higher and higher levels.

Like many other people, the workers had welcomed Truman's speedy end to most rationing and were now opposed to the remaining wartime controls which prevented or delayed them from using their savings to buy what they wanted. Many people who would never have considered patronizing a black market during the war years now showed themselves increasingly disposed to pay dealers and merchants a considerable bonus to get a new automobile or other hard-to-find items. Only a few Americans were sympathetic with the ideas voiced by OPA Director Chester Bowles or for that matter with those of most economists, who called for strong government controls over wages and prices and a return to rationing of scarce items in order to hold down prices. The public complained about soaring prices and shortages, but with employment at a high level and with plenty of money available for spending, it was opposed to any controls which interfered with its freedom. As a result, many Americans, like the spokesmen for the business and industrial community, a large and influential segment of which supported the National Association of Manufacturers' campaign for a quick return to a "free" economy, believed that as soon as business was liberated from government controls and interference, production would increase so rapidly that it would provide them with all the goods they required or desired. Once business prospered, so the NAM's argument went, irksome scarcities and greedy black marketeers would disappear and prices would return to their proper levels.

Partly because of these business claims, partly because of the public's impatience with regulations and controls, and partly because of its own conservative sympathies and reluctance to continue in peacetime the President's enlarged wartime powers, the Congress agreed to support Truman's request to extend the Office of Price Administration for only one more year, and only after amending the original law to such an extent as to make it virtually useless as an effective antiinflation weapon. On June 29, Truman vetoed this bill on the grounds that it "was not a choice between continued price stability and inflation, but a choice between inflation with a statute and inflation without one." Two days later, with all OPA controls and ceilings no longer in force, prices began to move up, and by July 25, when Truman "reluctantly" accepted a bill only slightly more effective, the Bureau of Labor Statistics reported that its index of consumer prices had climbed 25 per cent. The ineffectiveness of the revised OPA law, as Truman asserted at the time he signed it, failed to prevent inflation, and as more and more commodities were decontrolled and the ceiling prices on others increased, the cost of living index rose higher and higher. And when on August 20 the government tried to use its limited authority to stop the soaring price of meat by reimposing ceilings, livestock growers refused to market their animals. As consumers found it increasingly difficult to buy meat of any kind, they complained loudly, and together with the cattle growers and the packers they exerted sufficient pressure to force the administration to abandon its effort to stabilize meat prices, which it did on October 14. Less than a month later, on November 9, Truman declared that the government was ending all controls, except those regulating rents, sugar, and rice. By the end of the year, the advocates of decontrolling the economy swiftly had won their fight, but at the cost of considerably higher prices. The price index of consumer goods, which had risen less than 30 per cent during the war years, shot up 31.7 per cent during 1945 and 1946.

As prices continued to soar to new heights in 1947, with no indication that they were about to level off, Truman called Congress into special session and on November 7 asked it to legislate an effective antiinflation program which would provide the government with the power to fix wages and prices and to ration scarce commodities. But the Congress, under Republican leadership since the midterm elections of 1946, was opposed to reviving wartime controls. Senator Robert A. Taft, who spoke for the conservative majority, strongly opposed Truman's recommendation, calling it a "step toward a complete totalitarian nation." Congress replied to the President's request by drawing up its own bill, which Taft claimed would provide the administration with sufficient authority to curb the inflation, if Truman "really wanted to do so." The bill which came out of Congress did not incorporate any of the President's major recommendations, and when Truman signed it on December 28, 1947, he warned the country that this "pitifully inadequate" measure would not provide price stability or prevent further inflation. Events quickly proved him right: the consumer price index jumped from 159.2 in 1946 to 171.2 by June, 1948. Since both the Democratic and Republican party conventions had just gone on record in favor of legislation to curb further price rises, Truman called Congress into special session on July 26, 1948, and urged it "to take strong, positive action to control inflation." The comprehensive program he proposed called for reenacting the excess profits tax law, providing controls on consumer credit, enlarging the powers of the Federal Reserve to regulate bank credit, reestablishing priorities and price controls where required, and granting the administration "standby authority . . . to ration those few products in short supply which vitally affect the health and welfare of our people." Three weeks later, on August 16, Truman signed the Antiinflation Act into law, but it was hardly what he had asked for. While the law increased the government's control over consumer and bank credit, which the board of governors of the Federal Reserve exercised the next day, it did not provide for any of the other principal antiinflation curbs he had demanded. Not until September, 1952, when the Korean crisis precipitated another major price rise did Truman succeed in getting a strong antiinflation bill through Congress.

LAUNCHING THE "FAIR DEAL"

During Truman's first eighteen months in the White House, the Congress, like the nation, was so preoccupied with the price-control fight, the struggle between labor and management, and the difficulties and inconveniences accompanying reconversion that it overlooked almost all of his domestic recommendations, which he outlined first in his "twenty-one points" address of September 6, 1945. "This message," Truman wrote later, "marked the beginning of the 'Fair Deal,' and . . . symbolizes for me my assumption of the office of President in my own right." [8] And though he did not officially term his policies as such until his State of the Union address of January 5, 1949, the guiding principles of his domestic program were set forth clearly in this earlier message, and in his words they "set the tone and direction for the rest of my administration and the goals toward which I would try to lead the nation." The policies he proposed in September, 1945, and elaborated almost continuously thereafter were drafted with the assistance of Roosevelt's trusted adviser, Judge Samuel I. Rosenman; and they aimed, as Truman explained, to extend "the progressive and humane principles of the New Deal." Up to this time many observers had questioned his loyalty and commitment to the liberal policies of his predecessor, but in this message he dispelled all doubts as to his political philosophy and, like Roosevelt before him, asserted his faith in progressive reform and his coviction that the federal "government exists not for the benefit of a privileged few, but for the welfare of all the people." But while he continuously urged the Congress to enact his program, Truman's success as a legislative leader capable of getting his domestic policies translated into law was mixed at best.

Regardless of the party that controlled Congress during his Presidency, the conservative coalition composed of southern Democrats and conservative Republicans either shelved his recommendations (as they did in 1946, when they refused to establish a permanent Fair Employment Practices Committee or extend and enlarge the social security program) or postponed acting upon them from one session to another. And when the Congress did consider his Fair Deal proposals, it amended or revised them so extensively that by the time they were ready for his signature he was almost always forced to accept less than he had originally requested. The public, concerned with getting back to peacetime pursuits or worried about the deteriorating international scene, showed little interest in the President's struggle to get Congress to accept his domestic reforms, unless it was a question of expediting reconversion, decontrolling the economy, or disciplining the strikers, whom a great many people accused of being responsible for the shortages and inconveniences they had to suffer.

[8] Truman, *op. cit.*, I, 481.

Truman himself, however, was also partly responsible for failing to get more of his program through Congress. Unlike Roosevelt, who submitted his recommendations in bill-like drafts, Truman rarely employed this technique of legislative control, thereby providing Congress with the opportunity to satisfy its desire to assert a greater role in shaping policy than it had been able to exercise during the war years. But even though little of the Fair Deal became law, its influence upon subsequent administrations and the fact "that it kept the flame of reform alive in an era that was unfavorable for reform" cannot be minimized.[9]

The Employment Act

Among the twenty-one legislative requests which Truman presented before the second session of the Seventy-ninth Congress in September, 1945, the full employment proposal was one of the major domestic statutes which that body wrote into law. Afraid that it would be faced with large-scale unemployment and a severe depression similar to the one following World War I, Congress adopted the Employment Act on February 20, 1946, in the hope that the law would ease any economic crisis which might arise. The economic principles upon which this statute was based were those of John Maynard Keynes, who claimed that it was the responsibility of government to maintain full employment and, when necessary, to spend public funds to prevent or lessen the social and economic costs cf a depression. These ideas, which had already won the support of many economists, had been accepted and elaborated by Roosevelt into an "economic Bill of Rights," in which he declared that it was the task of postwar America to establish "a new basis of security and prosperity." Support for a full employment law arose also as a result of the government's impressive wartime record. By planning and cooperating with business and labor leaders, Washington had succeeded in mobilizing the nation's human, natural, and industrial resources to an unprecedented degree. Was it not possible, if a similar policy were adopted, to maintain a high level of employment and productivity in peacetime as well? The results would guarantee every citizen the opportunity to contribute to the growth and to participate in the benefits of a prosperous, stable, and abundant economy.

Since almost no one questioned the need or the desirability of securing these objectives, the debate on the full employment bill centered on

[9] Koenig, *op. cit.*, p. 227.

whether the federal government or private enterprise should be made primarily responsible for achieving the law's purposes. Most liberals and progressives insisted that it was the responsibility of the former; most conservatives were equally emphatic in their conviction that it should be left to the latter. The exponents of free enterprise discovered in *The Road to Serfdom* (Chicago, 1944) by Friedrich A. von Hayek, a Viennese economist who had studied and taught at the London School of Economics before joining the faculty of the University of Chicago, a book they felt proved their arguments and refuted those of Keynes, which New Deal liberals were hoping to have accepted in the administration's full employment bill. In far more restrained and academic phrases than the New Deal's critics had ever employed to castigate the Roosevelt policies, Von Hayek expressed all the antipathy which conservatives had long felt toward F.D.R.'s programs. Von Hayek's conclusions, which were in essence that any form of government planning or interference with the free working of the economy meant the end of individual liberty and democratic government, were precisely those which sober-minded critics of the administration's bill had been voicing and which they had been urging the electorate in the past to express at the polls.

The fears of these conservatives, all of whom were opposed to the government's "meddling" in economic affairs, together with the conservative temper of the times were not strong enough to kill the administration's bill, but they were sufficient to cause Congress to dilute Truman's original recommendation considerably and to substitute "maximum" for "full" employment as the law's objective. Great as were the concessions the administration was forced to accept, the Employment Act which was finally passed retained at least one significant and novel feature, incorporated in its declaration of purpose: that "it is the continuing policy and responsibility of the Federal Government to use all practicable means . . . to promote maximum employment, production, and purchasing power." To achieve these goals and at the same time "to foster and promote free competitive enterprise," paradoxical as these aims appeared to many, the Employment Act provided the President with a Council of Economic Advisers composed of three members, all of whom were to be "exceptionally qualified to analyze and interpret economic developments . . . and to formulate and recommend national economic policy." The council was "to assist and advise" the President in preparing a detailed annual economic report to the Congress in which he would review the nation's employment, production, and purchasing power, summarize and appraise the economic activities of the federal government, indicate any "foreseeable" changes in the performance of the economy, and recommend policies to fulfill the law's basic objectives. In addition, the act also called for the creation of a bipartisan congressional joint committee on the economic report to review and study the President's recommendations and to advise the Congress "on broad economic policy." [10] It was hoped that the Employment Act would provide the federal government with all the information it required to enable it to employ its resources swiftly and effectively whenever changes occurred in the economy's performance which increased unemployment or posed other cyclical threats to the nation's well-being.

The Atomic Energy Act

With the passage of the Employment Act, Congress devoted itself to the even more difficult and controversial task of framing a policy for the domestic "control, use, and development" of atomic energy, which Truman first requested at the time he announced the dropping of the bomb on Hiroshima. Two months later, he again urged Congress to decide upon a policy and to establish a federal agency to implement it. The nation's wartime atomic investment, he recommended, should be employed and directed toward "the promotion of the national welfare, securing the national defense, safeguarding the peace, and the acquisition of further knowledge concerning atomic energy." The necessity to protect technical secrets and the huge expense involved in atomic research made it mandatory for the government to exercise control over future developments. The power of the atom, Truman decided, was "too important to be made the subject of profit seeking." And while industry, universities, and other private research institutes were to share in its development and benefit from its exploitation, the government would determine the means and the extent of both. What remained for Congress to decide was whether to allow the military, which had exercised authority over atomic research during the war, to continue to do so in peacetime. Army and navy leaders hoped that this would be the case, and they opposed, as Admiral Leahy expressed it at a White House conference, turning "over the making of one of the most effective weapons of war to a civil commission

[10] E. Ray Canterberry, *The President's Council of Economic Advisers: A Study of Its Functions and Influence on the Chief Executive's Decisions* (New York [1961]), p. 21.

THE TRUMAN ERA, 1945-1947

which would dole out its product, if it decided to make any, as it saw fit." [11]

Early in October, 1946, with the approval of the War Department, Colorado's Democratic Senator Edwin C. Johnson and the chairman of the House Military Affairs Committee, the Kentucky Representative Andrew J. May, introduced a bill which would have left the control of atomic energy in the hands of the military. The May-Johnson bill, which at first appeared to have Truman's approval, immediately brought forth a storm of protest from most of the nation's atomic scientists, many of whom had been intimately associated with developing the atomic bomb. They were soon joined by others: educators, religious leaders, newspaper editors, and liberals who distrusted the military generally and were strongly and vociferously opposed to allowing it to determine or influence national atomic policy. The spokesmen of these groups insisted that the government should concentrate its effort upon developing atomic energy for peaceful, productive, and humanitarian purposes. Their views found expression in the recommendations of the Senate's Special Committee on Atomic Energy headed by the Connecticut Democrat Brien McMahon, who introduced a bill on December 20, 1945, calling for an independent government commission whose members were all to be civilians.

On February 9, 1946, Truman wrote McMahon expressing his agreement with the latter's bill, but the inflamed controversy over military versus civilian control raged on for another five months. In the hope of striking a compromise which would end this legislative impasse, Michigan's Republican Senator Arthur Vandenberg proposed an amendment to the McMahon bill on March 12 which required the President to appoint a "military liaison board" which would "advise and consult" with the civilian commission "on all atomic energy matters which the board deems to relate to the common defense and security." This was to be the board's only function, and Vandenberg assured the Senate that it was neither intended to nor could it "challenge civilian control." After further revision, months of debate and controversy elapsed before the opposition of the House Military Affairs Committee and the fears of the House Un-American Activities Committee were allayed sufficiently to allow the amended bill to come to a vote. Finally, on August 1, 1946, Truman signed it into law.

The Atomic Energy Act of 1946, the statute's official title, established, in Vandenberg's words, a "government monopoly . . . of fissionable

[11] Quoted in Millis, *op. cit.*, p. 133.

material." He admitted that it called for "a degree of centralized control which is out of step with all our essential principles in respect to free enterprise," but he justified this unprecedented departure from tradition to one of his constituents by saying that he knew of "no other answer for the time being which will protect the national security." [12] The law established an Atomic Energy Commission (AEC) of four civilian members, headed first by David E. Lilienthal, the former TVA director, and entrusted to it complete control over all fissionable material. The commission's declared policy, "subject at all times to the paramount objective of assuring the common defense and security," was to be "directed toward improving the public welfare, increasing the standard of living, strengthening free competition in private industry, and promoting world peace." To foster these goals, the AEC created several programs and divisions and charged them with the responsibility of working with private business and educational institions in studying and developing the medical and industrial uses of atomic science. Shortly thereafter, the commission began to provide medical schools and hospitals with radioactive materials for cancer research and treatment, and within a few more years started to approve contracts with private power companies to build nuclear reactors for the production and sale of electricity.

The Legislative Reorganization Act

The day after Truman signed the Atomic Energy Act into law, he affixed his signature to the Legislative Reorganization Act, which Congress had been discussing since March, when the Joint Committee on the Organization of Congress, headed by Senator Robert M. La Follette, Jr., and Representative Mike Monroney, had reported the results of its year-long study and hearings. That reforms in congressional procedures, organization, and practices were necessary had long been acknowledged and advocated by most of the country's political scientists and many of the federal lawmakers themselves. Earlier efforts to improve and expedite the legislative process had resulted in eliminating some of the inefficiencies, but as the La Follette committee's report indicated, there were still many congressional practices which needed to be improved or discarded. Some of these the committee ignored entirely, most notably the difficult problems presented by the filibuster, seniority, and the Rules Committee, and

[12] Arthur H. Vandenberg, Jr., ed., *The Private Papers of Senator Vandenberg* (Boston [1952]), p. 252.

for this it was strongly criticized. The Congress, moreover, did not accept all the joint committee's recommendations, and some of those it refused to act upon, such as the one calling for a legislative-Executive council to improve congressional relations with the President, appeared to some students of American government to be more important than those it adopted.

Still, the law did effect some important changes which facilitated congressional procedures. Among these, some of the most significant were those aimed to "modernize and strengthen" Congress by reorganizing and reducing the number of committees in each house and stipulating their responsibilities, requiring each committee chairman to "report . . . any measure approved by his committee and to take . . . necessary steps to bring the matter to a vote," prohibiting the introduction of certain kinds of private bills, establishing the Legislative Reference Service as a permanently operating body with enlarged duties in assisting committees with their assignments, and requiring lobbyists to register with each house of Congress and to divulge the funds spent to sway legislators. In addition, the act increased the salaries of senators and representatives and provided for their retirement. Like previous efforts to improve congressional practices, not all the reforms instituted by the Legislative Reorganization Act proved to be as effective as their advocates had anticipated, and because of tradition, expediency, or self-interest, the law left many problems untouched. The experts who had proclaimed the need for Congress to "streamline" itself were only moderately satisfied with what it had achieved in 1946, and the same might be said of its entire domestic legislative record.

DEMOCRATIC PARTY DISCORD
AND DISUNITY

Truman's efforts to push the Fair Deal alienated conservatives, many of whom had hoped that he would bring them a respite from the reform crusade of the prewar years, while his inability to get an effective extension of price controls disappointed all those who had expected him to protect them against soaring prices. Organized labor, too, was unhappy with the President, accusing him of failing to protect the gains which the worker had won during the war and decrying his action in the railroad dispute, especially his threat to draft the strikers. In addition to incurring the dis-

304 THE U.S. & THE POSTWAR WORLD, 1945–1961

pleasure of these and other politically influential groups, Truman's disagreements and open conflict with several of his cabinet members seemed to provide further evidence of the administration's inability to govern effectively and its lack of purpose or direction. Attorney General Francis Biddle, dissatisfied with Truman, resigned on June 15, 1945, and his post was filled by the Texan Thomas C. Clark. In the case of Treasury Secretary Morgenthau, Truman's obvious distaste for the already rejected Treasury plan to reduce Germany to a "pastoral" economy and his refusal to accede to Morgenthau's request to accompany the White House party to Potsdam brought forth the latter's speedy resignation. On July 6, 1945, Truman appointed Fred M. Vinson, the director of the OWMR, to Morgenthau's place, but Vinson served only a year in this capacity. On June 21, 1946, Truman appointed him Chief Justice of the Supreme Court and selected the conservative Missouri banker and former government official John W. Snyder to head the Treasury Department. As soon as Secretary of State Stettinius returned from the United Nations Conference at San Francisco, he resigned his post. It was rumored that Stettinius quit the cabinet because he disagreed with Truman, and Vandenberg, condemning the President's acceptance of his resignation as "grossly unfair," privately asserted that Stettinius "deserved better treatment after his rare performance at Frisco." On July 2, 1945, Byrnes was named Secretary of State.[13]

None of these disputes, however, caused anything like the controversy or the political repercussions which accompanied the resignations of Ickes and Wallace in 1946. Early in January, Truman proposed the California businessman and Democratic party benefactor Edwin W. Pauley as Under Secretary of the Navy. The Senate Naval Affairs Committee called upon Ickes to testify on Pauley's abilities, and the Secretary told them that during one of his talks with the Californian concerning the federal government's title to the state's tideland oil, he had received from Pauley the "rawest proposition ever made to me." When Truman suggested in a press conference that Ickes "might be mistaken," the "old curmudgeon" resigned and explained his action over the radio by saying that he was unwilling to continue as Secretary of the Interior if he was "expected to

[13] The following cabinet changes also occurred in 1945: Robert E. Hannegan of Missouri replaced Frank C. Walker as Postmaster General (May 8), Lewis B. Schwellenbach of Washington took Frances Perkins' place in the Labor Department (June 1), Clinton P. Anderson of New Mexico followed Claude R. Wickard in the Department of Agriculture (June 2), and Robert P. Patterson of New York succeeded to Henry L. Stimson's job in the War Department (September 27).

commit perjury for the sake of party." Less than a month later, Truman appointed Julius W. Krug, the Wisconsin engineer and chairman of the War Production Board, to Ickes' place.

The last and the most serious cabinet fight of 1946 involved Commerce Secretary Wallace. Occurring only two weeks before election day, it precipitated a serious controversy which indicated, among other things, the extent to which the prewar fissures in the Democratic party had widened since Roosevelt's death. Wallace looked upon himself as the "true heir" of the New Deal and the person most qualified to explain and elaborate its domestic and foreign policies, both of which he and a good many other people believed were being rejected or perverted by the Truman administration. On September 12, while speaking in New York City, he deplored the growing rivalry between the United States and Russia and blamed the advocates of a "tough" American policy for the postwar deterioration in Soviet-American relations. "The real peace treaty we now need," Wallace asserted, "is between the United States and Russia." His criticisms of postwar American diplomacy, especially of what he considered to be its departures from Roosevelt's efforts to cooperate with and reassure the Kremlin of Washington's goodwill and friendliness, amounted to a serious indictment of the State Department and, in Truman's opinion, "an all-out attack on our foreign policy." What made this speech even more world-shocking was Wallace's statement that "when President Truman read these words, he said that they represented the policy of his Administration." From Paris, where he was at work on one of the peace treaties, Byrnes cabled Truman, "If it is not possible for you, for any reason, to keep Mr. Wallace, as a member of your Cabinet, from speaking on foreign affairs, it would be a grave mistake from every point of view for me to continue in office, even temporarily." And Vandenberg, who was in the American delegation with Byrnes, replied to Wallace's broadside against the Republican party as "the party of economic nationalism and political isolation" by saying that the "authority of American foreign policy is dependent upon the degree of American unity behind it," and that a successful bipartisan foreign policy "requires unity within the Administration." The GOP, Vandenberg concluded, "can only cooperate with one Secretary of State at a time."

Truman, faced by this storm of protest, called the White House reporters together and denied he had read or approved the speech. A week later, on September 20, he dismissed Wallace and appointed W. Averell Harriman, then ambassador to Great Britain, to head the Commerce De-

306 THE U.S. & THE POSTWAR WORLD, 1945–1961

partment. Wallace's departure from the cabinet may have reaffirmed the "confidence" of the world's diplomats in the administration's policies, as Byrnes asserted, but it did not allay the doubts the incident had aroused in the minds of many Americans. Nor was the controversy which it provoked or the larger ones of which it became a part quickly silenced.

The Congressional Elections of 1946

The timing of the Wallace affair, like the seven-week meat shortage with which it coincided, could hardly have been more politically inopportune for the Democratic party. It provided the Republicans with still another issue to add to their lengthy catalogue of charges against the administration, all of which the GOP orators summed up for the voters conveniently in one phrase: "Had Enough?" On election day some 36 million Americans went to the polls and emphatically registered their dissatisfaction with the administration's domestic policies by giving the Republicans majorities in both houses of Congress for the first time since 1931. The GOP won 13 Senate races, increasing its total there to 51; the Democrats lost 12 and thus found their number in the upper house reduced to 47. In the House of Representatives the two-party line-up was 246 to 188 in favor of the Republicans. The GOP victory was not limited to Congress: sweeping across the nation, it elected 25 governors and a host of lesser state officials. The administration's defeat was so decisive that Arkansas' Democratic Senator J. William Fulbright suggested that Truman appoint a Republican Secretary of State and then resign, thereby allowing the GOP to take over the White House as well. Truman, whom the Democratic party chiefs believed to be a liability to them this year and thus had not called upon to participate in the campaign, declined to comment upon Fulbright's suggestion. In the meantime, the Republican leadership, jubilant over its election triumph, proposed to assume the added legislative responsibilities the voters had just conferred upon them.

The Eightieth Congress

The two most influential Republican leaders of the newly elected Congress, which convened for its first session on January 3, 1947, were Michigan's Arthur H. Vandenberg, whose enlightened and untiring efforts in effecting and implementing a bipartisan foreign policy were to distinguish the Truman administration, and Ohio's Robert A. Taft, the undisputed

Senator Robert A. Taft of Ohio, here shown talking to newspapermen, was the ablest and most effective spokesman of conservative Republicanism from his election to the United States Senate in 1938 until his death in 1953. (Brown Brothers)

spokesman and the legislative whip of his party's domestic policies. The oldest son of the former President and chief justice, Robert A. Taft came from a wealthy, distinguished, and public-spirited Cincinnati family. A top honors student and graduate of Yale University and of Harvard Law School, Taft combined law and politics in a brilliantly successful career which began in the Ohio legislature in 1920 and which brought him to the United States Senate in 1938. A pre-Pearl Harbor isolationist and a bitter foe of the New Deal, Taft's conservatism, which he labeled a middle of the road position, endeared him to all who wanted to return to the

308   THE U.S. & THE POSTWAR WORLD, 1945–1961

"good old days" of pre-Rooseveltian America, while his great intelligence. dedication to work and principles, ability, honesty, and strength of character commanded widespread respect and "made him a natural leader." [14] On May 1, 1957, less than four years after his death, a bipartisan Senate committee named him, along with Henry Clay, Daniel Webster, John C. Calhoun, and the elder Robert M. La Follette, as one of the five outstanding senators of the past.

Taft believed that the federal government's chief responsibility was to guarantee liberty and opportunity rather than security. "We have got to break with the corrupting idea that we can legislate prosperity, legislate equality, legislate opportunity. All of these good things came in the past from free Americans working out their destiny . . . . That is the only way they can continue to come in any genuine sense." [15] This was the American tradition as Taft, or as he soon came to be called, "Mr. Republican," understood it. This was the spirit which dominated much of the Eightieth Congress and which the GOP leadership earnestly sought to reestablish in the place of the "false ideologies" which had been introduced by the New Dealers. Taft and the conservative Republicans started to prepare America's return to what they believed were its historic principles the very first day the Eightieth Congress was organized.

TAXES

Relief from high wartime taxes was a GOP campaign promise the party intended to redeem at once. On January 3, Harold Knutson, a Republican congressman from Minnesota, introduced a revenue bill calling for a 20 per cent cut in the federal income tax. The bill passed Congress by substantial majorities (220 to 99 in the House and 48 to 28 in the Senate) on June 16, only to be vetoed the next day by Truman, who declared that the tax cuts it allowed, ranging from 10.5 to 30 per cent, were aimed to benefit the rich, would promote inflation, and would bring about the "very recession we seek to avoid." When the House sustained the President's veto by two votes, the Republicans passed a second tax reduction bill in July, which Truman again vetoed. The House overrode this veto by 299 to 108, but the Senate sustained it by 5 votes. The tax fight between the White House and Capitol Hill continued on into the next session of Congress. On April 2, 1948, a third tax reduction bill was passed by Con-

[14] Herbert Agar, *The Price of Power: America Since 1945* (Chicago [1957]), p. 67.
[15] Quoted in Eric F. Goldman, *The Crucial Decade—And After: America, 1945–1960* (New York [1961]), p. 55.

THE TRUMAN ERA, 1945–1947

gress and vetoed by Truman, but this time the Republicans mustered sufficient Democratic strength to override the President's veto, and the $4.8 billion tax cut became law. The rates on all incomes were reduced, but as Truman indicated, "nearly forty per cent of the reductions would go to individuals with net incomes in excess of $5,000, who constitute less than 5 per cent of all taxpayers."

THE TAFT-HARTLEY ACT

An even more embittered controversy between Truman and the Eightieth Congress arose over a new labor-management relations law intended to curb the power of the nation's 15 million organized workers. Criticism of the Wagner Act, which many Americans felt was the source of labor's belligerence and irresponsibility, had gained considerable nationwide support even before Pearl Harbor, and partly because of this Congress had been able to override Roosevelt's veto of the Smith-Connally Act of 1943, which imposed a number of restrictions upon unions during the war. The long series of strikes which followed V-J Day and continued on into 1946 appeared to justify the arguments of all those who insisted upon the imperative need for a more stringent labor law. Reflecting the growing antilabor mood of the times and shocked by the two-day nationwide railway strike which had just come to an end, on May 29, 1946, Congress passed the Case bill by a large majority. This measure, in the tradition of the wartime Smith-Connally Act, required a union to notify management of its intention to strike and then to observe a sixty-day cooling-off period, during which time the workers were to remain on the job. Among its other provisions, it made unions liable to civil damage suits in cases involving contract violations, and it prohibited the secondary boycott. Truman, who believed that labor, like business, should be forced to respect the public interest and had already recommended to Congress corrective legislation of his own, vetoed the Case bill on June 11, saying it was a "punitive" measure which would give rise to more strikes than it would prevent. The House, by the narrow margin of 5 votes, upheld his veto. This pronounced antilabor trend in Congress was reinforced by the results of the off-year elections.

In the meantime, the public's indignation with the continuing deterioration in labor-management relations reached a climax on November 20, when John L. Lewis' UMW openly defied a federal restraining order prohibiting it from calling a strike in the government-operated mines. For seventeen days the mines remained closed, forcing factories to cease or reduce production, causing railroads to limit train schedules, and requiring many Eastern cities to revive the wartime brownout in an effort to save their dwindling coal supplies. On December 7, three days after Federal District Judge T. Alan Goldsborough imposed a $10,000 fine on Lewis and a $3.5 million one on his union for contempt of court, the UMW leader told the miners to return to work. Meanwhile union attorneys appealed Goldsborough's decision to the Supreme Court, claiming it violated the Norris–La Guardia Act. On March 6, 1947, the Supreme Court, by a 7 to 2 vote, upheld the contempt conviction, but reduced the union's fine to $700,000.

Lewis' tug of war with the government provided the Eightieth Congress with further evidence that labor was abusing its power and that its selfishness was a threat to the country's economic stability. During the spring of 1947, the House Committee on Education and Labor, headed by New Jersey's Fred L. Hartley, Jr., and the Senate Committee on Labor and Public Welfare, with Taft as chairman, held a number of hearings in which spokesmen for management pointed out what was wrong with the Wagner Act while labor representatives, conceding the possible need for some revision in the 1935 law, sought primarily, in Reuther's words, to prevent employers from taking "the guts" out of it. As the hearings progressed, it became increasingly apparent that the two committees, and Hartley's more so than Taft's, were determined to restrain the authority of organized labor and check the growing influence of its leaders. The chairman of the National Labor Relations Board, testifying on behalf of the public, declared that revising or repealing the Wagner Act "would not solve the primary problems that trouble our fellow citizens in 1947"; and he went on to add that the "need is to encourage industry and labor to sit down and reason together, and not to turn the clock back to the time when there was no precept that they do so." The Congress, however, was not persuaded by his judicious and moderate appraisal, and on June 16 passed the Taft-Hartley Labor-Management Relations Act of 1947 by a substantial vote, 320 to 79 in the House and 54 to 17 in the Senate. By incorporating many of the restrictions written into the original Hartley bill, the new law deprived the unions of some of the benefits and protection they enjoyed under the Wagner Act, though it was hardly the "slave labor act" union leaders labeled it. Edwin E. Witte, the distinguished University of Wisconsin labor economist and long-time government adviser, asserted that the most accurate description of the Taft-Hartley Act's intent had been made by *The New York Times* when it termed it a "labor-union control act."

THE TRUMAN ERA, 1945–1947

The most important changes introduced by this long and complex statute, and those which aroused labor to fight it with all the militancy at its command, were those which outlawed the closed shop, jurisdictional disputes, secondary boycotts, and the "check off," the requirement that the employer deduct union dues from the worker's pay envelope. Henceforth, this last practice was allowed only after each employee consented to it in writing. The law also prohibited the employees of the federal government from striking and forbade unions from making "a contribution or expenditure in connection with any election." Unions were made liable to damage suits and required to publish annual statements detailing their organization and finances, and their officials were obliged to submit affidavits declaring they were not Communists. In the case of a strike, the union was required to give "written notice" sixty days in advance; but if the threatened strike affected "an entire industry or a substantial part thereof" or if it might "imperil the national health or safety," then the sixty-day cooling-off period would be extended to eighty, and during the extra time the National Labor Relations Board would poll the employees by secret ballot and determine for itself whether the workers wanted to strike or to accept management's "final offer of settlement."

Truman opposed the Taft-Hartley bill, and in a vigorous veto message declared that it "would contribute neither to industrial peace nor to economic stability and progress." Moreover, he asserted, it violated the "national policy of economic freedom" to which the United States had always adhered; it "would encourage distrust, suspicion, and arbitrary attitudes"; it was biased against labor; its strike procedures were impractical; and it was a "clear threat to the successful working of our democratic society." On June 20, two days after he returned it to Congress without his approval, the House overrode the President's veto by 331 to 83. The bill became law three days later when the Senate supported the House by a vote of 68 to 25. The Republican leadership, with a strong assist from conservative Democrats, had succeeded in redeeming one of its major campaign promises, but in doing so it had earned the enmity of the country's labor leaders, who resolved to employ all their political power, financial resources, and influence to bring about the defeat of the legislators who had been responsible for the law's passage.

GOVERNMENTAL CHANGES IN
THE EXECUTIVE DEPARTMENT

Before Congress adjourned, it acted upon two of Truman's earlier recommendations. It adopted a new presidential succession law and it passed the National Security Act. During Grover Cleveland's first administration, when the memory of President James A. Garfield's death from wounds inflicted by an assassin's revolver was still fresh, Congress was forced by the death of Vice President Thomas A. Hendricks, only eight months after his inauguration, to provide for Cleveland's successor. On January 15, 1886, it adopted a law which established the succession in the cabinet according to the dates the various posts were created, beginning with the Secretary of State and going on down through the Secretary of the Interior, who then occupied the last Executive department formed.

Very soon after Truman became President, he began to consider seriously the problems posed by the death or incapacity of the Chief Executive, especially in cases like his and Cleveland's, when the Vice Presidency would remain vacant for nearly a full term. The succession established by the law of 1886 he found wanting, since it allowed the President to appoint his successor. "I do not believe," he told Congress on July 19, 1945. "that in a democracy this power should rest with the Chief Executive. In so far as possible, the office of the President should be filled by an elective officer." He proposed, therefore, that Congress draft a new law which would give the speaker of the House of Representatives and the president pro tempore of the Senate, in that order, precedence over members of the cabinet. By placing the speaker first in line of succession, it would keep the Presidency in the hands of an elected official who, next to the President and Vice President, was more directly responsible to the people than any other federal officeholder, since he owed his position to the voters of his district and to the other representatives of the people. But according to Truman's larger plan, the speaker was to serve as Chief Executive only temporarily. He hoped that Congress, by enacting also other appropriate legislation, would give the people an early opportunity to elect a new President and Vice President to serve the remaining term of the two who had died in office. In order to do this without upsetting the established quadrennial pattern of presidential elections, he suggested holding special elections or using the midterm congressional ones for this purpose, whichever could be held first.

The House approved Truman's plan on June 29, ten days after he had proposed it, but it failed to get through the Senate, as it did again in 1946. In February, 1947, Truman resubmitted his proposal, and Congress enacted the Presidential Succession Act on June 18, though without the provision for "a general or special election" as he had suggested. Some political scientists questioned the law's constitutionality and most of them criticized its failure to provide a way to determine presidential "disability" and to establish the procedure for running the Executive office when the President cannot do so himself. The latter problem had arisen twice before, in the cases of Garfield and Wilson; it was to present itself twice again in Eisenhower's administration.

With the memory of Roosevelt's successful violation of the two-term tradition and of the four political defeats he had inflicted upon the Republicans still gnawing at them, the GOP leadership, assisted by conservative and other anti-F.D.R. Democrats, determined to prevent another such performance by changing the Constitution's rules on presidential eligibility. During the last week of March, 1947, Congress adopted a proposal to limit the Presidency to two terms and, with the exception of Truman, to bar any individual's succeeding to that office and serving in it for more than two years from being reelected to it more than once. The proposal, which was ratified by the required thirty-six state legislatures on February 25, 1951, became the Twenty-second Amendment to the Constitution. The wisdom of a legally binding two-term limitation on the Presidency was immediately questioned by students of government, many of whom deplored the effect it would have upon the Chief Executive's ability to lead his party and to exercise his influence and authority effectively. "The Amendment," as one expert observed, "makes every second-term President a 'lame duck.'" Eisenhower's experience, as the first President to whom the new amendment applied, neither confirmed nor confuted this observation.

On July 26, one week after Congress had passed the presidential succession bill, Truman signed the National Security Act of 1947, one of the most significant achievements of his Presidency. Science and World War II had invalidated many of the traditional bases upon which the security of the United States had rested in the past, necessitating comprehensive reforms in the nation's total defense system. "One of the strongest convictions which I brought to the office of President," Truman wrote later, "was that the antiquated defense set up of the United States had to be reorganized quickly as a step toward increasing our future safety and preserving world peace." [16] Like other Presidents before him, Truman found strong opposition, especially among the navy's senior officers, to any reform schemes involving unification of the services which might threaten the Navy Department's independence, even though wartime experience and the urgent necessity to prevent wasteful and costly duplica-

[16] Truman, *op. cit.*, II, 46.

tion dictated otherwise. Army and navy officials acknowledged the need for reform too, but neither service had devised a mutually satisfactory scheme to achieve the desired results. Truman, however, refused to be deterred by past failures, and beginning in August, 1945, he called upon his military chiefs to study the defense of the country in terms of "the combined requirements of the armed forces." Seventeen months of extensive conference and committee work followed in which army and navy officers and legislators on Capitol Hill worked hard to reconcile the differences which kept the services apart. The successful results of these labors could hardly have been realized, however, without the intelligent and patient efforts of Navy Secretary Forrestal, who devoted all his energy and ability to bringing about unification. Throughout these difficult months of negotiations, Truman provided Forrestal with every means of support at his command. Whenever serious disputes threatened to undermine unification, the President intervened effectively. Finally, the army and the navy agreed upon "a compromise unification plan" which incorporated most of the provisions Truman and the military chiefs deemed essential. After further congressional revision, it passed as the National Security Act.

Achieving the law's declared purpose, "to provide for the security of the United States through the establishment of integrated policies and procedures," necessitated the effective coordination of the government's various military and civilian activities. The task was assigned to a newly created National Military Establishment,[17] headed by a Secretary of Defense with cabinet rank. Truman appointed Forrestal to the post, and on September 17, 1947, he became its first occupant. The Secretaries of War and the Navy were dropped from the cabinet and their departments, along with a newly created and independent one of the Air Force, were consolidated into the National Military Establishment. Each of the services was to have its own secretary, but the three were to "function under the direction, authority, and control of the Secretary of Defense." The Joint Chiefs of Staff, which Roosevelt had set up in February, 1942, were legally recognized and brought into the Establishment.[18]

The National Security Act also created a number of specialized agencies,

[17] On August 10, 1949, the National Security Act was amended. The authority of the Secretary of Defense was increased, and the National Military Establishment was reorganized and its name changed to the Department of Defense.
[18] By amendment in 1949, the Joint Chiefs of Staff were provided with a "nonvoting chairman." General Omar N. Bradley, appointed by Truman, was the first to hold the position.

THE TRUMAN ERA, 1945-1947

three of which—the National Security Resources Board (NSRB), the Central Intelligence Agency (CIA), and the National Security Council (NSC)—were assigned especially important tasks.[19] The NSRB's chief functions were to appraise all the nation's resources and provide for any strategic shortages which existed, to plan for the most effective use of these resources in time of war, and to develop comprehensive and integrated mobilization plans. The job of collecting, analyzing, coordinating, and interpreting the intelligence required to safeguard the national security was assigned to the CIA, which took over the functions previously carried on by various government departments. The tasks of the CIA and the NSRB were largely directed to one end: to supply the National Security Council with all the reliable evidence available, thus providing it with the information necessary to "advise and assist" the President in coordinating, developing, and executing national policy. Since its establishment, the five-man council, over which the President presides, has become, in the opinion of some observers, "the most powerful and most secret of all governmental agencies"; and its decisions, when approved by the President, determine the foreign and military policies of the United States and to a considerable degree the domestic ones as well. Not all of the reforms achieved under the National Security Act proved entirely effective or fulfilled all the expectations of its supporters; and as the changes brought about by the National Military Establishment went into effect, the need for further reforms became quickly evident. But despite the law's shortcomings, the long-overdue unification of the services and the coordination of the country's defenses which it made possible were in themselves major accomplishments.

THE DEVELOPMENT OF A
BIPARTISAN FOREIGN POLICY

The partisanship and controversies which embittered the relations between the President and the Eightieth Congress on domestic policy were far less evident on questions involving America's enlarged responsibilities in postwar international affairs. For this, a large measure of credit belongs to Senator Arthur H. Vandenberg, whose "inspired self-reversal and

[19] On June 12, 1953, after several previous changes, the NSRB was abolished and its functions assumed first by the Office of Defense Mobilization and then, after August, 1958, by the Office of Civil and Defense Mobilization.

316 THE U.S. & THE POSTWAR WORLD, 1945–1961

. . . brilliant, intelligent leadership" (in Truman's words) made possible some of the most significant and far-reaching decisions which have affected the peace and security of the United States since then. A long-time foe and critic of the New Deal's domestic and foreign policies, Vandenberg had been one of the Senate's most outspoken pre-Pearl Harbor isolationists and among its most effective leaders in fighting Roosevelt's efforts to repeal the arms embargo and to supply lend-lease assistance to Britain. The outbreak of war in the Pacific, however, led Vandenberg to reassess America's worldwide interests and its role in determining the course of international affairs. "In my own mind," he noted in his diary, "my convictions regarding international cooperation and collective security for peace took firm form on the afternoon of the Pearl Harbor attack. That day ended isolationism for any realist."

From then on he became increasingly convinced of the necessity to establish a bipartisan approach to winning the war and securing the kind of peace which would prevent another similar holocaust. As chairman of the Senate Foreign Relations Committee between 1947 and 1949 and as one of the most influential Republicans on Capitol Hill, Vandenberg was largely responsible for securing the congressional support and funds which made possible some of Truman's most significant diplomatic decisions. Never did the need for a strong, nationally endorsed bipartisan foreign policy appear more imperative than during the two years following the Potsdam Conference, when Vandenberg's wartime hopes for the future, like those of the American people, were shattered by the Kremlin's ideological and expansionist ambitions.

THE DISINTEGRATION OF THE GRAND ALLIANCE, 1945–1947

The worldwide Soviet-American power struggle which broke out almost immediately after Japan's surrender and has continued to dominate the international scene since then was the inevitable outcome of the conflicting objectives with which the United States and Russia entered and fought the war. Roosevelt's inability to reconcile these differences and to win the Soviet Union's friendship and assistance in building a new world order was becoming increasingly apparent even before victory had been won, but only a very few Americans realized this at the time or, even more important, understood the extent to which the military con-

THE TRUMAN ERA, 1945–1947 317

sequences of the war and the Kremlin's long-term goals were inimical to the interests and security of the United States.

Despite the growing evidence of Soviet hostility, the American people were slow to recognize that victory had not brought with it the peace and security for which they had hoped and sacrificed for nearly four years. And though the United States government had grown increasingly concerned with Soviet policy in Europe and Asia, especially since the Yalta Conference, Truman and Byrnes, like Roosevelt before them, believed that the difficulties which divided the two countries were negotiable. "I had assumed," Byrnes declared later, "that at the end of hostilities an era of peace would be so deeply desired by those nations that had fought the war in unity that the inevitable differences of opinion could be resolved without serious difficulty." All that was required to build a stable post-war structure which would satisfy the legitimate interests and safeguard the security of the United States and the Soviet Union, Byrnes believed, was mutual goodwill and cooperation. Unfortunately, the wartime pressures which had divided the Grand Alliance were strengthened by the victory it had achieved. As a result, the "deep anxiety" which Churchill had felt about Russia's intentions and which he had communicated to Truman in May, 1945, assumed a grim reality by September when the Council of Foreign Ministers, which the "big three" had established at Potsdam, met in London for the first time.

Taking advantage of its military occupation of Central and Eastern Europe, the Soviet Union proceeded to set up pro-Russian governments in the formerly Nazi-held areas which made a mockery of the free, independent, and democratic self-rule the "big three" had agreed to guarantee when they signed the Declaration on Liberated Europe at Yalta. And though Britain and the United States disapproved and protested the Soviet Union's violations of this and other wartime agreements, such as those concerning Poland and the occupation of Germany, neither London nor Washington was inclined or prepared to use force to prevent the Kremlin from turning Central and Eastern Europe into a Russian sphere of influence. Soviet troops occupied the area; the British, with their strength greatly diminished, could do little if anything without the assistance of the United States; and the American people, concerned only with expediting demobilization and reconversion and enjoying the benefits of the first flush of what was to become an unprecedented postwar boom, did not appreciate the significance of the fact that victory had turned their former ally into a potentially dangerous adversary. The realization

318   THE U.S. & THE POSTWAR WORLD, 1945–1961

of this disturbing reality was brought home to them during the next eighteen months, as the Truman administration sought without success to gain the Soviet Union's cooperation in establishing peace in Europe and Asia.

The Conflict over the Five
Minor Axis Peace Treaties

That the Soviet Union did not intend to compromise the victory its armies had won in Central and Eastern Europe simply to honor its wartime pledges or to satisfy the verbal protestations of the United States and Britain became immediately apparent when, on September 12, 1945, the Council of Foreign Ministers, representing Britain, France, China, the United States, and Russia, met to write the Italian, Hungarian, Rumanian, Bulgarian, and Finnish peace treaties. From the very beginning innumerable controversies and difficulties arose between the Soviet Union and the West, and negotiations stalled in a quagmire of procedural technicalities, accusations, and counteraccusations which occupied the better part of six different conferences, the last of which ended on December 12, 1946. Among the many questions which arose at these meetings to embitter East-West relations and to widen the rift which separated the Soviet Union from its wartime allies, one of the first involved Russia's opposition to permitting France and China to assist in writing the peace treaties. This dispute, which was largely responsible for wrecking the London meeting, was ultimately resolved in December, 1945, when the council met in Moscow for the second time. The "big three," by deciding to limit the writing of each treaty to the delegates of those powers which had participated in the defeated country's armistice arrangements, excluded China entirely from the council's deliberations on the minor European treaties and allowed France to take part only in drafting the Italian one. To placate the protests of the smaller and less powerful members of the Grand Alliance, whose representatives insisted upon being heard, Secretary Byrnes won Russia's and Britain's assent to holding a general peace conference in which all of the twenty-one wartime Allies would be represented.

The opening session of this conference, which was to be held in Paris and had originally been scheduled for May 1, 1946, did not occur until July 29, largely because of Molotov's delaying tactics and the wrangling which took place among the "big four" foreign ministers, who had been laboring in Paris negotiating the details to be incorporated in these preliminary drafts since April 25. On July 15, three days after the Council of Foreign Ministers had completed its work, Byrnes told the American people that while these five treaties were "not the best human wit could devise," they were "the best which human wit could get the four principal Allies to agree upon" and "as satisfactory an approach to the return of peace as we could hope for in this imperfect and war-weary world." The purpose of the twenty-one–nation Paris Peace Conference was to review the treaties drawn up by the foreign ministers and, according to the sentiments of the United States, to provide all the Allies, irrespective of size, an opportunity to offer suggestions or amendments, even though it was clearly understood that these proposals were not binding upon the ultimate decisions of the "big four." The Soviet Union, however, was opposed to allowing the small nations to express themselves freely or to influence the final texts of the treaties. As was to be expected, this issue gave rise to a new, prolonged, and bitter dispute between Byrnes and Molotov which carried over into other areas under consideration and continued for the duration of the conference, revealing once again the many conflicting interests which were driving the United States and Russia farther and farther apart.

By the time the conference adjourned on October 15, it had submitted to the Council of Foreign Ministers ninety-four recommendations for it to consider at its next meeting, in New York City on November 4. After considerable negotiation, much of it made difficult by Molotov's continued intransigence, the Russians finally agreed to accept a number of the Peace Conference's recommendations, thereby permitting the final texts of the treaties to be completed by December 12 when the fourth meeting of the "big four" foreign ministers came to an end.

The treaties, which the United States signed on January 20, 1947, and which the Senate ratified on June 4, were, in Byrnes's words, "not written as we would write them if we had a free hand." The Russians won nearly all the demands they had insisted upon in the Rumanian, Bulgarian, Hungarian, and Finnish treaties. The armaments of all four countries were carefully limited; heavy reparations, totaling $1.17 billion, were imposed upon them, of which the Soviet Union received $800 million; and their frontiers were redefined, with each ceding parts of its territory to Russia. The only concession Britain and the United States were able to get written into the Balkan treaties—free navigation of the Danube and equal trade opportunities—proved meaningless since the Kremlin subsequently refused to honor them.

The Italian treaty was the only one in which the West succeeded in winning any substantial concessions from the Soviets. Italy's reparation bill of $360 million, of which Russia received $100 million, was larger than the West believed necessary or desirable, but it was one of the few instances in which Britain and the United States deferred to the Soviet Union. Molotov's insistence upon Russian participation in administering Italy's former African colonies was rejected, and except for Ethiopia, which was reestablished as an independent state, Mussolini's former empire was turned over to Britain, which administered it temporarily. Subsequently most of these peoples gained independence. The other territorial changes imposed upon Italy involved transferring small bits of land to France along the Alpine border, ceding the Dodecanese Islands to Greece, and turning over to Communist Yugoslavia most of its eastern Adriatic possessions, which the Italians had taken over after World War I, including Fiume, the Istrian Peninsula, and a large part of Venezia Giulia. The future of the seaport city of Trieste and its adjacent area, which Italy had held since 1919, proved the most difficult problem to solve. The Russians supported the claims of Marshal Tito, who was then on good terms with Stalin, and the West was determined to prevent him from acquiring it. Ultimately a compromise solution was agreed upon. Trieste was declared a "free territory" under the control of the United Nations Security Council and divided into two zones, one occupied by British and American troops and the other by Yugoslav forces. After nearly seven years of wrangling and difficult negotiations, Italy and Yugoslavia agreed on October 5, 1954, to partition the territory, with Italy receiving the northern section, including the city of Trieste, and Yugoslavia the Istrian zone it had been occupying.

The East-West Impasse over
Austria and Germany

The patient, difficult, protracted efforts which finally produced the five minor Axis treaties failed to yield similar results in the case of Austria and Germany. In both instances the real stumbling block to an agreement was, of course, the inability of Russia and the West to reconcile their divergent views regarding the future map of Central Europe. The Soviet Union, by insisting upon its own liberal definition of what German assets in Austria it was entitled to receive as reparations and by demanding that the rich mineral and mining region of Carinthia, along with $150 million in reparations, be turned over to Yugoslavia, would have made Austria economically subservient to the Kremlin. When the West refused to accede to these conditions, the prospects of an Austrian peace treaty quickly disappeared, and the "big four" continued to occupy the country until May 15, 1955, when they finally agreed to a treaty "re-establishing Austria as a free, independent, and democratic State."

Negotiations on settling the far more complex German question resulted in some of the most bitter disputes of these years, poisoning East-West relations nearly to the point of war on several occasions. The Potsdam principle of a coordinated and uniform political and economic occupation policy for all of Germany was never effected, and as the Soviet Union proceeded to establish communistic programs and institutions in its zone, the United States, Britain, and France drew their zones closer and closer together. As a result, every effort to settle the German question broke down; and when the Soviet Union reintroduced its claim to $10 billion in reparations, the likelihood of a settlement in the near future became even more remote.

The difficulties facing Britain and the United States were complicated further by France, whose fears of a resurgent Germany led it to demand annexation of the Saar, control over the Rhineland, and internationalization of the Ruhr, only the first of which was acceptable to the United States. Without these concessions, France showed little interest in co-operating with Britain and the United States in reuniting Germany, and its resistance squared well with the Soviet Union's plans to keep Hitler's former Reich divided. The greater the economic and political difficulties the German people had to suffer, the greater the opportunities for Soviet communism to take a firm hold. That this rather than the requirements of Russian security dictated the Kremlin's tactics with respect to Germany became evident when Molotov rejected Byrnes's offer to negotiate a "big four" common security pact. Such a treaty, Byrnes told Molotov, would assure Europe against future aggression and help the American people "understand the exact aim of the Soviet Union—whether it is a search for security or merely expansion." The Russians, however, were not interested in any arrangements which would continue American participation in the affairs of Europe, and the proposal, which had the support of Truman, Senator Vandenberg, Britain, and France, was allowed to die of neglect.

The deadlock on Germany became even more evident in March, 1947, when George C. Marshall, who had succeeded to Byrnes's post on January 21, met with Molotov and Britain's Foreign Secretary Ernest Bevin in Moscow. Among the principal German issues argued at this meeting were those concerning the creation of a central authority to coordinate occupation policies, the structure of Germany's future government, and the still unresolved reparations issue. After nearly seven weeks of debate, the "big three" foreign ministers adjourned without reaching a single agreement, save the one to resume their talks at a subsequent conference, to be held in London on November 25. Marshall returned from the Moscow meeting depressed, and convinced, as Truman recalled later, that the Russians "were interested only in their own plans and were coldly determined to exploit the helpless condition of Europe to further Communism rather than cooperate with the rest of the world."

The Iranian Crisis

During the winter of 1945–46, while Byrnes and after him Marshall were trying to achieve a European settlement, American suspicions of Soviet expansionism were being confirmed in another and equally vital corner of the world. In January, 1946, the United Nations Security Council discussed, over Russia's protest, the charges of the Iranian government that the Kremlin was using its troops stationed in that country to interfere with Iran's domestic affairs. The presence of Soviet forces in this oil-rich and strategically located country, once known as Persia, dated from August, 1941, when Hitler's triumphant legions were threatening to deprive Britain of its Middle East petroleum resources and to sever Russia's vital supply line through Iran, over which Anglo-American aid reached the Soviet Union. Alarmed at the prospect of a Nazi invasion of the Middle East and disturbed by the pro-German sympathies of Iran's government, Britain and the Soviet Union occupied the country and compelled its ruler to abdicate in favor of his twenty-two-year-old son, Mohammed Reza Shah Pahlevi. Five months later, on January 29, 1942, Britain and the Soviet Union guaranteed Iran's "territorial integrity, sovereignty, and political independence" by a treaty which the "big three" reaffirmed at the Teheran Conference.

One of the treaty's provisions called for the withdrawal of all foreign troops by March 2, 1946, a condition Britain and the United States, which had also stationed forces in Iran, observed but which the Soviets did not. Indeed, during the autumn of 1945 there was every indication that the Kremlin was strengthening its forces and that, moreover, it had used them to foment a rebellion in Azerbaijan, Iran's northern province bordering on the Soviet Union. Russia's open violation of the tripartite agreement of 1942 and of the Teheran Declaration and its subversive activities within the country, which together had precipitated Iran's charges before the Security Council, not only revealed the Kremlin's indifference to its treaty obligations but posed, insofar as the United States was concerned, an alarming threat to American interests and security in the Middle East, which Truman was quick to reaffirm. After several efforts had failed to ease the crisis, he instructed Byrnes "to send a blunt message to Premier Stalin." This, combined with the Iranian protest, forced the Soviet Union to yield, and on March 24 the Kremlin declared that all its forces would be withdrawn by May 6. The fact that the Iranian crisis had been resolved, at least temporarily, and that, as Truman said, the "world was now able to look more hopefully toward the United Nations" in no way reduced Washington's increasing concern with the worldwide nature of the Soviet threat.

The Dispute over the Control of Atomic Energy

The political and diplomatic conflicts which divided and acerbated Russo-Western relations spilled over into United Nations debates on the international control of atomic energy. On November 15, 1945, Britain, Canada, and the United States, the three wartime atomic powers, issued a joint statement in which they declared their intention to make the benefits of atomic energy for peaceful development available to the members of the United Nations "just as soon as effective enforceable safeguards against its use for destructive purposes can be devised." The next month, at the Moscow meeting of the Council of Foreign Ministers, the "big four" endorsed this proposal, and Britain requested that the United Nations establish a commission to study the problem, which it did on January 24, 1946.

In the meantime Secretary Byrnes created a special five-man committee, headed by Under Secretary of State Dean G. Acheson, to pre-

324   THE U.S. & THE POSTWAR WORLD, 1945–1961

pare a plan the United States could present before the United Nations commission at its first meeting, which was scheduled for June 14. To assist Acheson's committee an advisory group was formed, and TVA's David E. Lilienthal was appointed its chairman. Among his advisers were some of the country's top scientists and industrialists, all of whom had previously been associated with the development of the bomb. The combined labors of these two groups resulted in the Acheson-Lilienthal report, which the State Department published on March 28. This carefully prepared and comprehensive document called for the international control of all fissionable materials through an autonomous international Atomic Development Authority under the United Nations. The proposed body would own and operate every process concerned with the manufacture of atomic energy throughout the world from the mines yielding the raw uranium and other fissionable materials to the plants which processed and distributed them. To safeguard the world against any possible military uses of these critical materials, provision was made for the authority to denature them, thereby making them useless for the manufacture of bombs and other weapons. Moreover, no nation was to possess all the facilities to produce atomic energy within its borders, and those which it was allowed were to be carefully supervised and inspected by the world authority.

Since the United States then possessed a monopoly on the atomic bomb and the most advanced nuclear plant facilities, Truman instructed Bernard Baruch, who was appointed to present the Acheson-Lilienthal report to the United Nations Atomic Energy Commission, that "We should not under any circumstances throw away our gain until we are sure that the rest of the world can't arm against us." To provide effective protection and immediate United Nations action against any possible aggressor, the United States proposal incorporated a provision, suggested by Baruch, which called upon the members of the Security Council to relinquish their veto right over all questions pertaining to atomic energy policies. "There must be no veto," Baruch told the United Nations, "to protect those who violate their solemn agreements not to develop or use atomic energy for destructive purposes. The bomb does not wait upon debate. To delay may be to die." Once the proposed international atomic commission was granted "control or ownership of all atomic energy activities potentially dangerous to world security" and its authority "to control, inspect, and license all other atomic activities" was assured, the United States would turn over to the world body all of its secrets, bombs, plants, and other manufacturing and research facilities. "Before a country is ready to relinquish any winning weapons it must have more than words to reassure it," Baruch declared. With the exception of conservative ultranationalists and radicals who called for universal disarmament, most Americans—78 per cent, according to one poll—approved of the plan.[20]

The Soviet Union immediately countered the American proposal with one of its own which Andrei A. Gromyko, the Russian delegate on the United Nations Atomic Energy Commission, presented on June 19. The Soviet plan called upon those nations possessing atomic weapons, which so far as anyone knew at the time meant the United States, Britain, and Canada, to destroy them and all other atomic devices for war within ninety days. The Gromyko plan's only provision to assure the world against a nuclear war was a clause calling for a multination treaty outlawing the manufacture of atomic weapons and imposing penalties upon those who violated it. The treaty was to follow the destruction of all nuclear weapons. It was at once obvious that fundamental differences existed between the two proposals; and these—involving the crucial questions of inspection, adequate safeguards, and abolishment of the Security Council veto in all nuclear matters—remained, despite the minor concessions each side indicated it was willing to make, the principal stumbling blocks which defeated every effort to arrive at an international agreement to prevent the use of atomic energy for war and to promote its development for constructive purposes. The impasse on the international control of atomic energy prevented the United Nations Commission on Conventional Armaments, also set up in 1946, from devising a scheme to lessen the world's nonnuclear arms burden.

On July 1 and 25, 1946, as a result of a Navy Department request issued shortly after Japan's surrender, the United States tested the effect of two atomic explosions on a surface fleet asembled for the purpose at Bikini, a coral atoll in the Marshall Islands. Besides navy, air force, and other official American observers, the government invited the press and representatives from the twelve nations on the United Nations Atomic Energy Commission. Whatever the reason for the government's decision to execute the tests at this time, other than to satisfy the Navy Department, its sole effect was to impress upon the world that civilization was, in the code word used to designate the operation, at its "crossroads."

[20] Margaret L. Coit, *Mr. Baruch* (Boston, 1957), p. 586.

The Trials of the Axis War Criminals

In one important area, the prosecution of the Axis war criminals, the United States and the Soviet Union cooperated harmoniously in implementing their wartime agreements. In January, 1942, the Allies agreed to "place among their principal war aims the punishment, through the channel of organized justice," of those responsible for precipitating the "war and for the crimes they perpetrated during it." The next year, on October 20, 1943, the United Nations War Crimes Commission, composed of the representatives of sixteen nations, was established to investigate and study all reports of inhuman enemy practices and to recommend action. Assisted by several committees created on the national level by each of the Allied governments, the commission accumulated a lengthy and shocking collection of instances of atrocity, large-scale murder, enslavement of war prisoners and conquered civilians, vice, and other similar examples of brutal inhumanity, looting, and plunder. The foul story of the Nazis' war crimes was revealed to an almost incredulous world in a lengthy trial conducted by the legal representatives of the "big four." The International Military Tribunal met in the old, historic city of Nuremberg from November 20, 1945, to October 1, 1946, with Associate Supreme Court Justice Robert H. Jackson acting as United States prosecutor. The court sentenced twelve surviving top Nazi officials to death. Reichsmarshal Hermann Goering poisoned himself and cheated the gallows by an hour, and Martin Bormann, whom Hitler referred to in his will as "my most faithful Party comrade," was never found. The other ten, however, among them Joachim von Ribbentrop, Field Marshal Wilhelm Keitel, and General Alfred Jodl, were hanged on October 16, 1946. Subsequent trials, conducted by each of the occupying powers in its own zone, resulted in numerous other convictions.

The legal principles upon which the European trials were held, like those conducted later in Tokyo by the International Military Tribunal for the Far East,[21] were questioned at once on various grounds. Some lawyers and jurists accused the tribunal of violating the long-held and universally honored principle that there can be no punishment of crime

[21] The Tokyo trials, lasting from June 3, 1946, to November 12, 1948, resulted in seven death sentences, including that of Premier Hideki Tojo. Sixteen high-ranking military and civilian officials were sentenced to life imprisonment. Lesser terms were given to numerous other officials. As in the case of Germany, a great many Japanese military leaders were tried also for violating the laws of war.

without a preexisting law; others were quick to observe that, considering its record between 1939 and Hitler's invasion, the Soviet Union was hardly qualified to pose as the champion of international morality and law; still others argued that officials of state are not accountable for the actions of their government; and there were those who cynically dismissed the trials as nothing more than evidence of the victor's wrath imposing sentence upon the vanquished. To all these criticisms, the tribunal's judges replied that the legal principle of *nullum crimen sine lege* was inapplicable, since Germany had signed the Kellogg-Briand Pact of 1928, which outlawed war. "In the opinion of the Tribunal," the judges declared, "the solemn renunciation of war . . . necessarily involves the proposition that such a war is illegal in international law; and that those who plan and wage such a war . . . are committing a crime in so doing." No less important a reason for holding the trials, in the opinion of Justice Jackson and many others, was the fact that it would force aggressors in the future to weigh carefully the consequences of their actions. The ten Nazi leaders who were executed at Nuremberg, asserted *The New York Times*, will provide "a grim warning to all who would emulate them in the future that mankind has entered a new world of international morality and that in the end the angered forces of humanity must triumph over those who would outrage it."

Soviet-American cooperation at Nuremberg did not dispel the serious concern which disturbed the Truman administration during 1946. The Kremlin's obvious efforts to impose its hegemony on Europe were bared by its obstructionist tactics in writing the minor Axis treaties, in preventing the drafting of an Austrian and German settlement, and in frustrating all hopes of concluding an international agreement to control nuclear energy. The East-West disputes which arose out of these issues, the threat posed by the Iranian crisis, and the growing evidence of Soviet subversion and infiltration in the Eastern Mediterranean confirmed Washington's growing suspicions that the differences which separated the two powers greatly outnumbered and were far more fundamental than those which bound them together.

The post-Potsdam assumptions of Russo-American cooperation and accord upon which Secretary Byrnes had hoped to build future American policy were already being scrutinized and revised by the end of 1945. The frustrating diplomatic experiences which followed that meeting brought forth a growing demand from congressional leaders of both parties that the United States reject any further efforts to placate the

328 THE U.S. & THE POSTWAR WORLD, 1945–1961

Soviet Union by compromising American principles or interests. Truman's comment that Byrnes had "lost his nerve" while negotiating with Molotov during the ten-day Moscow foreign ministers' conference in December, 1945, reflected Congress' stiffening attitude and his own disenchantment with the course of Soviet-American relations. By the time of the Paris Peace Conference (April–May, 1946), the new "firmness" in United States policy was already sufficiently apparent to lead one knowledgeable French diplomat to assert that Byrnes appeared to be primarily "interested in convincing the Russians that the sucker season has ended, and that henceforth, the Americans would be tough." [22] After Churchill's now widely hailed but at the time highly controversial speech of March 5, 1946, at Westminster College in Fulton, Missouri, in which he said that "an iron curtain has descended across the Continent," the American people were torn between Churchill's warnings of the new Soviet threat and Henry Wallace's attack on the administration's "get tough" policy. And even though at the time these two speeches were delivered Wallace's perhaps reflected the public attitude more accurately than Churchill's, the country's mood, like the administration's Russian policy, was changing. When Marshall succeeded Byrnes as Secretary of State in January, 1947, both public opinion and the administration had abandoned the effort of trying to salvage what was left of the Allied unity upon which Roosevelt had hoped to build and secure the world's peace. The new American approach toward the Soviet Union was to be a less idealistic one.

Suggested Readings

There is no entirely adequate biography of Harry S. Truman. The best place to begin is with Truman's own account of his life and presidency, *Memoirs* (2 vols., Garden City, N.Y., 1955–56). See also his *Mr. Citizen* (New York, 1960) for some of his other views on various subjects. Truman's public papers from April 12 through December 31, 1945, have been published under the title *Public Papers of the Presidents of the United States* (Washington, D.C., 1961). William Hillman, ed., *Mr. President* (New York, 1952) also contains a miscellaneous collection of Truman's statements. Excerpts from Truman's principal speeches, with brief editorial introductions, have been collected by Louis W. Koenig, ed., *The Truman Administration: Its Principles*

[22] Quoted in Richard D. Burns, "James F. Byrnes," in Norman A. Graebner, ed., *An Uncertain Tradition: American Secretaries of State in the Twentieth Century* (New York, 1961), p. 237.

THE TRUMAN ERA, 1945–1947

and Practice (New York, 1956). Morris B. Schnapper, ed., *The Truman Program* (Washington, D.C. [1949]) contains Truman's principal campaign speeches and the Democratic platform of 1948. Jonathan Daniels, *The Man of Independence* (Philadelphia [1950]) is a friendly biography.

On the men around Truman, see the popular books by Maurice M. Milligan, *Missouri Waltz* (New York, 1948) and Robert S. Allen and William V. Shannon, *The Truman Merry-Go-Round* (New York [1950]). Richard E. Neustadt, *Presidential Power: The Politics of Leadership* (New York [1960]) contains a brilliant section on Truman's conception and execution of his White House duties.

General accounts of the years since 1945 include Eric F. Goldman's well-written and perceptive, *The Crucial Decade and After: America, 1945–1960* (New York [1960]); Herbert Agar, *The Price of Power: America since 1945* (Chicago [1957]), a "lively and intelligent" summary; William F. Zornow, *America at Mid-Century: A Chronicle of Yesterday* (Cleveland [1959]), which covers the Truman and Eisenhower years briefly; and Hans W. Gatzke, *The Present in Perspective: A Look at the World since 1945* (2d ed., Chicago [1960]), which has a chapter (III) on American developments.

The American scene in its varied aspects is amusingly analyzed by a British newspaperman in Robert Waithman, *The Day before Tomorrow* (New York, 1951). Other books containing pertinent information include Thurman Arnold, *The Future of Democratic Capitalism* (Philadelphia, 1950), which treats the role of a "free" economy in world affairs; Adolph A. Berle, *The Twentieth Century Capitalist Revolution* (New York, 1954); John K. Galbraith, *American Capitalism* (Boston, 1952); Sumner H. Slichter, *What's Ahead for American Business* (Boston, 1951); David E. Lilienthal, *Big Business: A New Era* (New York, 1953); David Riesman, *The Lonely Crowd* (New Haven, Conn., 1950); Samuel Lubell, *The Future of American Politics* (New York, 1952); and Frederick L. Allen, *The Big Change* (New York, 1952), which traces some themes since 1900.

Many of the memoirs and other personal accounts cited in Chapter 6 are useful for developments covered in this chapter. Besides those, consult Walter Bedell Smith, *My Three Years in Moscow* (Philadelphia, 1950), the record of the American ambassador; Walter Millis, ed., *The Forrestal Diaries* (New York, 1951); William O. Douglas, *Strange Lands and Friendly People* (New York, 1951), the impressions of the justice's trip of 1949–50; and Herbert Hoover, *Addresses upon the American Record, 1949–1950* (Stanford, Calif., 1950), the views of the ex-President on some international questions.

An excellent account of the activities of the Eightieth Congress is William S. White, *The Taft Story* (New York, 1954).

On the problems of demobilization, see Ralph G. Martin, *The Best Is None Too Good* (New York, 1948).

Reconversion is treated in a number of works, among them Abraham D. H. Kaplan, *The Liquidation of War Production* (New York, 1944); Seymour E. Harris, ed., *Economic Reconstruction* (New York, 1945); and John M. Clark, *Demobilization of Wartime Economic Controls* (New York, 1944).

330 THE U.S. & THE POSTWAR WORLD, 1945-1961

Two official statements are Bernard M. Baruch and John H. Hancock, *War and Postwar Adjustment Policies* (Washington, D.C. [1944]) and U. S. Office of Contract Settlement, *A History of War Contract Terminations and Settlements* (Washington, D.C., 1947).

On specific legislation of the Truman era, 1945-47, E. Ray Canterberry, *The President's Council of Economic Advisers: A Study of Its Functions and Its Influence on the Chief Executive's Decisions* (New York [1961]) is good for one phase of the Employment Act, while Stephen K. Bailey, *Congress Makes a Law: The Story behind the Employment Act of 1946* (New York [1950]) is a detailed analysis of the act's legislative history. Many of the general ideas behind this law are discussed in George A. Steiner, *Government's Role in Economic Life* (New York, 1953).

Books on the Taft-Hartley Act include Harry A. Millis and Emily C. Brown, *From the Wagner Act to Taft-Hartley* (Chicago, 1950); Bert Cochran, "The Taft-Hartley Decade," in Bert Cochran, ed., *American Labor in Mid-Passage* (New York, 1959); and Edwin E. Witte, "An Appraisal of the Taft-Hartley Act," *American Economic Review*, XXXVIII (May 1948), 368-82, an exceptionally balanced analysis. The views of the law's framers are stated in Fred H. Hartley, Jr., *Our New National Labor Policy* (New York, 1948) and Robert A. Taft, "Toward Peace in Labor," *Collier's*, CXXI (March 6, 1948), 21, 38-42. Labor's opinion is expressed by George Meany, "The Taft-Hartley Law: A Slave-labor Measure," *Vital Speeches*, XIV (December 1, 1947), 119-23. A more general account of the organized worker after the war is Colston E. Warne, *et al.*, eds., "Labor in Postwar America," *Yearbook of American Labor*, II (1949). The leadership of labor is analyzed by sociologist C. Wright Mills in *The New Men of Power: America's Labor Leaders* (New York, 1945).

On the impact of atomic energy upon American life and society, see David V. Bradley, *No Place to Hide* (Boston, 1948); Daniel Long, *The Man in the Thick Lead Suit* (New York, 1954); and Vannevar Bush, *Modern Arms and Free Men* (New York, 1949). The official story of American efforts to control the atom internationally is in U. S. Department of State, *International Control of Atomic Energy* (3 vols., Washington, D.C., 1946-49). A highly competent survey is William T. R. Fox, *The Struggle for Atomic Control* (New York [1947]). See Chapter 8 for references on the military and strategic problems of the atomic era.

The story of America's occupation of Germany is told by Julian Bach, Jr., *America's Germany: An Account of the Occupation* (New York, 1946) and by Saul K. Padover, *Experiment in Germany: The Story of an American Intelligence Officer* (New York, 1946). The American view of the Nuremberg Trials is presented in two books by Justice Robert H. Jackson, *The Case against the Nazi War Criminals* (New York, 1946) and *The Nuremberg Case* (New York, 1947). The Russo-American split on Germany is treated by Drew Middleton, *The Struggle for Germany* (New York, 1949) and John P. Nettl, *The Eastern Zone and Soviet Policy in Germany, 1945-1950* (New York, 1951).

THE TRUMAN ERA, 1945-1947

The story of the Japanese occupation is briefly told in a Foreign Policy Association pamphlet by Richard Hart, *Eclipse of the Rising Sun* (New York, 1946) and in more detail by Russell Brines, *MacArthur's Japan* (Philadelphia, 1948) and, for the later period, by Robert A. Fearey, *The Occupation of Japan: Second Phase, 1948-1950* (New York, 1950).

A good sampling of the public documentation on American foreign policy is the Council on Foreign Relations, *The U.S. in World Affairs, 1945-1947* (New York, 1947), which appears annually. See also the pertinent State Department volumes, *Documents on American Foreign Relations*.

Among the many general interpretative accounts of American foreign policy since 1945, see Hans J. Morgenthau, *In Defense of the National Interest: A Critical Examination of American Foreign Policy* (Chicago, 1951), an excellent, though critical, analysis of the effects of "moralism" and "legalism" on American policy. In the same tradition is George F. Kennan, *Realities of American Foreign Policy* (Princeton, N.J., 1954) and the same author's last two essays in his *American Diplomacy, 1900-1950*, previously cited. H. Bradford Westerfield, *Foreign Policy and Party Politics* (New Haven, Conn., 1955) covers its subject well; Max Beloff, *Foreign Policy and the Democratic Process* (Baltimore, 1955) contains the views of one of England's Soviet experts on the problems of making and executing foreign policy in a democracy; William Y. Elliott, *et al.*, eds., *United States Foreign Policy* (New York, 1950) is a collection of essays aimed at appraising "the adequacy of our eighteenth-century Constitution and our structure of government to the demands of global crisis"; Norman A. Graebner, *The New Isolationism* (New York, 1956) analyzes the way in which the United States adjusted to its postwar problems; Walter Lippmann, *Isolation and Alliances: An American Speaks to the British* (Boston, 1952) consists of two lectures by the brilliant *New York Herald Tribune* columnist on the traditions of American foreign policy and their effect upon mid-century developments; Gabriel A. Almond, *The American People and Foreign Policy* (New York, 1950) relates the effect of the "American character" upon policy; Felix Morely, *The Foreign Policy of the United States* (New York, 1951) is a pamphlet attacking the post-1945 bipartisan approach to foreign policy and attributing to it "all our major blunders"; Robert A. Taft, *A Foreign Policy for Americans* (New York, 1951) presents the Ohio senator's views; James P. Warburg, *The United States in a Changing World: An Historical Analysis of American Policy* (New York, 1954) censures more than it analyzes post-1945 official policy; and Harold K. Jacobson, ed., *America's Foreign Policy* (New York [1960]) contains a collection of essays by various experts on different aspects of American foreign policy problems.

The basic events are presented in John W. Spanier, *American Foreign Policy since World War II* (New York [1960]) and by William Reitzel, *et al.*, *United States Foreign Policy, 1945-1955* (Washington, D.C., 1956). John Fischer, *Master Plan, U.S.A.* (New York, 1951) gives the basic "essentials." Foster R. Dulles, *America's Rise to World Power, 1898-1954* (New York [1955]) has four chapters (11-14) on post-1945 developments, but see also

332 THE U.S. & THE POSTWAR WORLD, 1945–1961

the excellent chapters (14–21) in Jules Davids, *America and the World of Our Time*, already cited. Brief, analytical biographical sketches of the secretaries of state for these years are in Norman Graebner, ed., *An Uncertain Tradition: American Secretaries of State in the Twentieth Century* (New York [1961]).

A large number of more specialized works have been published covering various problems of America's worldwide policies. On the Potsdam Conference, the most recent and comprehensive study is Herbert Feis, *Japan Subdued*, already cited.

On the United States and the United Nations, see the brief account by Vera M. Dean, *The Four Cornerstones of Peace*, cited before, and Ruth B. Russell and Jeanne E. Muther, *A History of the United Nations Charter: The Role of the United States, 1940–1950* (Washington, D.C., 1958), a detailed Brookings Institution study. On the background and the events leading to the UN, see also Daniel S. Cheever and H. Field Haviland, *Organizing for Peace* (Boston, 1954), and two works already cited, Clark M. Eichelberger, *UN: The First Ten Years* and Lincoln P. Bloomfield, *The United Nations and U.S. Foreign Policy*.

Lionel M. Gelber, *America in Britain's Place: The Leadership of the West and Anglo-American Unity* (New York [1961]) is a careful study of an important and neglected subject. John C. Campbell, *Defense of the Middle East* (New York, 1960) discusses ably American policy in this vital region, and Lewis V. Thomas and Richard Frye, *The United States and Turkey and Iran* (Cambridge, Mass., 1951) is equally competent.

The Russo-American conflict on writing the minor peace treaties is well treated in the Brookings Institution study by Redvers Opie, *et al.*, *The Search for Peace Settlements* (Washington, D.C., 1951).

8

The Truman Policies

1947-1952

THE FOREIGN POLICY OF "CONTAINMENT"

The Truman administration's reappraisal of American foreign policy during 1946 and the early months of 1947 was occasioned by several factors, the most immediate of which was, of course, the disillusioning diplomatic experience of trying to collaborate with the Soviet Union in establishing a stable postwar order. The fundamental difficulty which prevented these two nations from reaching any substantial agreement on the numerous problems confronting them arose out of the worldwide "power revolution" brought about by World War II and the opportunities it presented for Russia to satisfy its expansionist ambitions.

By eliminating the international authority previously exercised by four major nations—Germany, Japan, France, and Italy—and by seriously weakening that of a fifth—Great Britain—the war destroyed the old balance of power system, in which several nations, singly or in combination, had exercised a significant and sometimes decisive influence on the course of international affairs. Only the United States and the Soviet Union, despite the latter's heavy losses, came out of the war as undisputed world powers of the first rank. The greatly increased strength of these two nations and the marked decline of others brought about a

334 THE U.S. & THE POSTWAR WORLD, 1945–1961

radical redistribution of the world's power, now divided mainly between two giants with divergent objectives, clashing interests, and conflicting ideologies. The resulting postwar rivalry between these two "superpowers" compelled each to prevent the other from achieving any political, military, or strategic gains which would alter the world's power equilibrium to its own disadvantage.

The failure to resolve or indeed even to accommodate the issues dividing the United States and the Soviet Union and the realization that any further increase in the latter's power constituted a serious threat to America's security and interests forced the Truman administration, after more than eighteen months of frustrating and almost futile negotiations, finally to abandon the hope of friendly cooperation with the Kremlin. Early in March, 1947, as the challenge of Russian expansionism threatened the Eastern Mediterranean, the United States adopted a new policy vis-à-vis the Soviet Union. In the words of its principal formulator, George F. Kennan, then the chief of the newly created State Department Policy Planning Staff, the United States determined to follow in the future "a policy of firm containment, designed to confront the Russians with unalterable counter-force at every point where they show signs of encroaching upon the interests of a peaceful and stable world." What distinguished the containment policy from previous American efforts to deal with the Soviet Union was the fact that it rested upon a more realistic—some said less naïve—appraisal of the structure and operation of the postwar balance of power. Kennan asserted, in a brilliant article published anonymously in the July, 1947, issue of *Foreign Affairs*, "that the United States cannot expect in the foreseeable future to enjoy political intimacy with the Soviet regime. It must continue," he said, "to regard the Soviet Union as a rival, not a partner, in the political arena."

The Truman Doctrine

The first indication of an "adroit and vigilant application of counterforce," which Kennan had called for and which marked the beginning of America's effort to "contain" the Soviet Union, occurred on March 12, 1947, when President Truman appeared before a joint session of Congress to ask for $400 million in emergency assistance for Greece and Turkey, whose governments were being undermined by Communist subversion and threatened by Soviet force. "I believe," Truman told the Congress, "that it must be the policy of the United States to support free peoples who are resisting attempted subjugation by armed minorities or by outside pressures. I believe that we must assist free peoples to work out their own destinies in their own way. . . . It is necessary only to glance at a map to realize that the survival and integrity of the Greek nation are of grave importance. . . . If Greece should fall under the control of an armed minority, the effect upon its neighbor, Turkey, would be immediate and serious. Confusion and disorder might well spread throughout the entire Middle East."

The Greek and Turkish crises, both of which had been in the making since the end of the war, assumed critical proportions during the last week of February, 1947, when Britain informed the United States that it could no longer maintain its military mission in Greece or provide the economic assistance necessary to uphold the free world's interests in the Eastern Mediterranean. The decline of British power in this region, where it had once been dominant, revealed Britain's greatly weakened postwar status, which was aggravated at this time by the serious economic effects of the terrible winter of 1946–47. In the spring of 1947, the peoples of Western Europe and the British Isles were nearly destitute, and all that the London government possessed was required at home.

The effect of the British crisis upon the Greek situation was immediately obvious to the United States. Threatened by internal political divisions and defied by a strong Communist minority which the Soviets assisted through their Balkan satellites, the Greek government was not strong enough either to maintain internal order or to withstand the Kremlin's external pressure. The Communists, moreover, were greatly aided in their efforts to seize power by the economic distress and hardship which plagued the country and which the legitimate government was incapable of alleviating. In Turkey, the situation was much the same: economic and political strain internally and an external Soviet threat, in this instance against the strategic Dardanelles. Should either of these countries fall to the Communists, the interests and security of the United States in the Eastern Mediterranean and the Middle East would be seriously jeopardized. "The choice," Secretary Marshall told a White House conference of eight top congressional leaders, "is between acting with energy or losing by default." And though this group supported Truman's decision and the Congress responded enthusiastically to his message of March 12, nearly nine weeks of debate followed before the legislators provided the $400 million the President had requested.

The debates on the Truman Doctrine, as the program soon came to be called, concerned themselves with questions of precedent and expense, which disturbed many conservatives; fear of imperialism and disapproval of the Greek monarchy, which jarred liberal sensibilities; and the effects of a unilateral American action upon the influence and prestige of the United Nations. Senator Vandenberg, for example, disapproved of bypassing the world organization, even though he admitted that "Greece could collapse fifty times before the U.N. itself could ever hope to handle a situation of this nature." Nonetheless, he believed it was necessary for the United States to "proceed as far as possible within the United Nations," and in order to assure this end and to placate its supporters, Vandenberg introduced an amendment, which was accepted, asserting that the Truman program was "an emergency and temporary one" and that "the United Nations and its related agencies should assume the principal responsibility . . . for the long-range tasks of assistance required for the reconstruction of Greece. . . ." On April 22, the Senate voted 67 to 23 in favor of Truman's recommendation, and on May 9, the House did likewise by a 287 to 107 vote. Even before the law went into effect (May 22), Truman had already begun sending Greece and Turkey whatever assistance he could legally provide.

The Truman Doctrine inaugurated the beginning of a new era in the diplomatic policy of the United States. In the opinion of some observers, it was "the most significant development in American foreign relations since the Monroe Doctrine." It saved the Greek and Turkish governments from collapse; it effectively checked the Soviet Union's drive into the Mediterranean; and it strengthened the purposes of American policy in that part of the world. As such, it was entirely successful, but it was not, as Senator Taft declared at the time he voted for it, "a commitment to any similar policy in any other section of the world." As the British journalist Barbara Ward Jackson termed it, it was "a specific act to meet a specific danger." At the very time these words were being expressed, the State, War, and Navy Departments were already at work preparing a long-term plan for American economic assistance to Europe which, it was hoped, would prevent other emergencies similar to the Greek and Turkish ones.

The Marshall Plan

The idea of encouraging social and economic stability by helping the Europeans restore their war-torn economies was strongly supported by

George C. Marshall, a career soldier, served President Roosevelt as army Chief of Staff, and President Truman as ambassador to China (1945), Secretary of State (1947–49), and Secretary of Defense (1950–51). (Brown Brothers)

Secretary Marshall, who was convinced that the security and well-being of the United States rested upon a strong, free, and prosperous Europe. The first public indication of the administration's evolving European policy came on May 8 from Under Secretary of State Dean Acheson, who had been instrumental in sponsoring and working on the program. Speaking in Cleveland, Mississippi, a small cotton town in the northwestern part of the state, Acheson outlined many of the fundamental principles which, after further review by the President and other appropriate officers in the government, were formally announced by Marshall on June 5, 1947, while delivering the commencement address at Harvard University.

Speaking of the distress, suffering, and privation of the Europeans, Marshall asserted that apart "from the demoralizing effect on the world at large and the possibilities of disturbances arising as a result of the desperation of the people concerned, the consequences to the economy of the United States should be apparent to all. It is logical that the United States do whatever it is able to do to assist in the return of normal economic health in the world, without which there can be no political stabil-

338   THE U.S. & THE POSTWAR WORLD, 1945–1961

ity and no assured peace. Our policy is directed not against any country or doctrine but against hunger, poverty, desperation, and chaos." All that the United States asked of the Europeans was that they help themselves, agree upon their needs, and indicate how they proposed to employ American assistance to facilitate and expedite the Continent's recovery. "It would be neither fitting nor efficacious," Marshall continued, "for this Government to undertake to draw up unilaterally a program designed to place Europe on its feet economically. This is the business of the Europeans. . . . The role of this country should consist of friendly aid in the drafting of a European program and of later support of such a program so far as it may be practical to do so. The program should be a joint one, agreed to by a number, if not all European nations."

One of the principal purposes of the Marshall Plan, or the European Recovery Program (ERP), as it was also known, was to put an end to what Marshall called the "series of piecemeal relief measures" of the past, such as the special $3.75 billion loan to Britain made at the end of 1945 and the $350 million relief appropriation for Austria, Greece, Italy, Hungary, and Poland voted by Congress in May, 1947. In addition, during the two years following Germany's surrender, the United States had contributed $11 billion to UNRRA for European relief and reconstruction assistance. Since most of UNRRA's funds were spent to aid the liberated states of Eastern Europe, where the Communists, it was claimed, distributed the supplies they received among their "political supporters," considerable opposition arose against the agency in the United States. Many Americans agreed with former Secretary Byrnes when he stated that "foreign relief should be allocated by the United States and should go to those countries who would not denounce us for granting them the relief they asked for." But even more important than this consideration was the fact of Western Europe's desperate need. It was to ease its crisis rather than to provide it with relief that the Marshall Plan was proposed. "Its purpose," as Marshall stated, "should be the revival of a working economy in the world so as to permit the emergence of political and social conditions in which free institutions can exist."

Marshall's proposal was widely acclaimed in Western Europe, and on June 27, 1947, three weeks after it was first announced, the British, French, and Russian foreign ministers met in Paris to discuss the project and to plan for a twenty-two–nation conference which would appraise Europe's resources, determine its needs, and prepare a comprehensive report for America's consideration. The Russians, to whom the Marshall

THE TRUMAN POLICIES, 1947-1952 339

Plan also applied, rejected it, charging that it was a cunning scheme of the capitalist and imperialist interests of the United States aimed "to overwhelm Europe and bring it into subjection to themselves." On July 3, Molotov and the Soviet delegation left the Paris conference and later forbade Russia's Eastern European satellites from participating in the Marshall assistance program.

All the European states except Spain, which was not asked, accepted the American offer of assistance, and on July 12 the delegates of sixteen nations met in Paris and formed the Committee for European Economic Cooperation (CEEC).[1] For ten weeks the delegates, assisted by their technical staffs, studied the resources and needs of the European economy, and on September 22 they issued a detailed and comprehensive report indicating the extent of their assets, the ways they intended to employ them to help themselves, individually and collectively, and the amount of American assistance they required over the next four years, which they estimated at $16.4 to $22.4 billion. Truman referred the CEEC's report to three special committees and other government officials for study, and on the basis of their recommendations asked Congress on December 19, 1947, to approve a total of $17 billion in ERP assistance over the next four years.

While the administration was reviewing the CEEC's requests and appraising America's ability to meet them, economic conditions in Europe deteriorated steadily and the need for immediate assistance became urgent. During September and October, Truman called upon the American people to conserve food and to eat less meat and poultry so that there would be enough to send to the needy Europeans. When it became apparent that Europe required far more substantial help, Truman called Congress into special session; and when it met, on November 17, he asked it to provide Italy, France, and Austria with immediate "stop-gap aid" and to enact a workable and effective antiinflation bill which would permit the government to meet all its foreign relief and assistance programs while protecting the American people from the ravages of inflation. Congress ignored the President's request for price control legislation, but responded to his appeal for European relief on December 24 by passing the Foreign Aid Act of 1947, which provided $540 million of emergency assistance. Except for $18 million, which the Congress

[1] The sixteen nations were Austria, Belgium, Denmark, France, Greece, Iceland, Ireland, Italy, Luxembourg, the Netherlands, Norway, Poland (until it became Communist), Sweden, Switzerland (which later chose not to participate), Turkey, and the United Kingdom.

340   THE U.S. & THE POSTWAR WORLD, 1945–1961

chose to allocate to China, the remaining $532 million went to help France, Italy, and Austria, the three countries Truman and Secretary Marshall had singled out as being in the most serious economic danger.

Two weeks later, when the Eightieth Congress convened for its second session, the hearings on the Marshall Plan opened in earnest. The strong support of Vandenberg in the Senate and the able leadership of another Republican in the House, New Jersey's Charles A. Eaton, the chairman of the Committee on Foreign Affairs, greatly expedited proceedings, and their efforts to secure the bill's approval were further facilitated by the vehemence of the Kremlin's opposition to it. The Soviet leaders denounced it unsparingly and accused the plan's supporters of being warmongers. In October, 1947, together with Communist party chiefs in eight other European countries, they had formed the Communist Information Bureau, or Cominform, whose purpose, along with other related propaganda activities, was to frustrate the proposed American aid program. These activities, like the Russian offer to assist Europe through an enlarged trade program, the so-called Molotov Plan of November, 1947, did not go unnoticed on Capitol Hill.[2] But it was the suppression of Czechoslovakian independence on February 25, 1948, through a Soviet-supported *coup d'état*, against the background of the serious deterioration in East-West relations over Germany, that revealed the Kremlin's real intentions and impressed upon Congress and the American people the imperative need of strengthening Europe against Russian subversion and expansion. In March, the Congress accepted by substantial majorities the administration's $17 billion European assistance program and agreed to appropriate the required moneys annually for the next four years. On April 2, 1948, Truman signed the ERP bill into law under the official title of the Economic Cooperation Act, and two days later he appointed a Republican business executive, Paul G. Hoffman, the president of the Studebaker Corporation, to head the Economic Cooperation Administration (ECA) which was to direct the program.[3]

The great majority of the American people, like most of the nation's

[2] In January, 1949, the Russians announced the formation of the Council of Mutual Economic Assistance, a foreign aid program for the five iron curtain countries—Bulgaria, Czechoslovakia, Hungary, Poland, and Rumania.

[3] On December 10, 1951, when the ECA law expired, the foreign aid program was taken over by the Mutual Security Administration (MSA); when the latter organization was terminated (August 1, 1953), its functions were transferred to the Foreign Operations Administration (FOA); and finally, on May, 9, 1955, the entire economic and military assistance programs were reorganized and brought into the State and Defense Departments.

editorial opinion, strongly approved of the Marshall Plan. Some supported it for purely selfish reasons and others accepted it for more altruistic ones, but those who understood its purposes generally subscribed to the view *The New York Times* expressed in its April 4 editorial: "If we can make Western Europe happy, free, and prosperous, we erect a barrier which communism cannot peacefully pass, and which it will be less tempted to try to pass by force." The ECA's opponents, among them Henry A. Wallace and many of his supporters, criticized Truman because the program was established outside the United Nations and, in Wallace's words, because it was designed primarily "as an instrument of Cold War against Russia." The extreme radical left, as was to be anticipated, looked upon it in much the same way as did the Kremlin. To them the "Martial Plan" was what the American Labor party's New York Congressman Vito Marcantonio labeled it: a law aimed "to safeguard and protect the expansion of Wall Street monopoly capital all over the world" and a ruse to secure the votes of the American people to "support the bankers and generals who want to spend billions to make the world safe for the new imperialism."

The results of the Marshall Plan were impressive. Senator Taft, who was always skeptical about "handouts" in any form, joined the ECA's supporters when he realized the threat Soviet expansionism posed to America. "Our assistance," he wrote in 1951, four years after the ECA law had begun operations, "undoubtedly enabled . . . [the European countries aided by it] to recover in three or four years to a point which they might not have reached without our aid for perhaps ten years. Time was important in the fight against communism, and the assistance we gave enabled some of those countries to bring about a recovery wherein communism found a much less fertile soil." [4] All the economic indicators attested to the extent and speed of Europe's recovery. But the significance of the Marshall Plan was far more than economic. It greatly weakened the influence of the Communists upon the Italian and French governments, and it turned despair into hope and fear into courage. "Within two years," Barbara Ward Jackson noted, "it had created, if not a continent without problems, at least a community with a sense of promise and purpose. . . ." [5]

With respect to Soviet-American relations, the Marshall Plan, like the

[4] Robert A. Taft, *A Foreign Policy for Americans* (New York, 1952), p. 86.
[5] Quoted in Robin W. Wenks, ed., *The Marshall Plan and the American Economy* (New York [1960]), p. 51.

342 THE U.S. & THE POSTWAR WORLD, 1945–1961

Truman Doctrine before it, officially proclaimed the end of the era of optimistic wartime hopes, and it heralded the beginning of what that perceptive newspaper columnist Walter Lippmann called the "cold war," a state of international tension which was neither war nor peace. Less than three years after the end of the costliest war in human history, mankind's search for a real peace remained unfulfilled; and as the rift between East and West grew wider, the world divided itself into two hostile camps, as if determined to realize Alexis de Tocqueville's prophecy of more than a century earlier. "The Anglo-American," he wrote at the close of the first volume of his *Democracy in America* (1834), "relies upon personal interest to accomplish his ends and gives free scope to the unguided strength and common sense of the people; the Russian centers all the authority of society in a single arm. The principal instrument of the former is freedom; of the latter, servitude. Their starting point is different and their courses are not the same; yet each of them seems marked out by the will of Heaven to sway the destinies of half of the globe."

The Western Alliance System

On March 7, 1948, less than a month before Congress passed the Marshall Plan bill, Britain, France, and the Benelux nations (Belgium, the Netherlands, and Luxembourg) signed, with America's enthusiastic approval, the Brussels Pact. This fifty-year defensive military alliance, binding each of the signatory powers "to assist the others in the event of military aggression," was partly an outgrowth of the Anglo-French Treaty of Dunkirk, signed in March, 1947; but unlike the latter, which still reflected the old fear of a resurgent Germany, the Brussels Pact was a multilateral alliance aimed against Soviet militarism and requiring of its members an increasing degree of cooperation and coordination. Such an arrangement was highly satisfactory to the United States, which was sponsoring the Marshall Plan as a joint recovery measure and whose military chiefs were already thinking in terms of an integrated Western European defense system. In addressing a joint session of Congress ten days after the signing of the Brussels Pact, Truman declared that this treaty was "a notable step in the direction of unity in Europe for [the] protection and preservation of its civilization," that it merited "our full support," and that he was certain "the determination of the free countries of Europe to protect themselves will be matched by an equal determina-

THE TRUMAN POLICIES, 1947–1952

343

tion on our part to help them to protect themselves." Without American participation, the Brussels Pact nations were incapable of deterring Soviet power. What was required was a clear guarantee of United States support. But how was this to be achieved, in view of the long American tradition against entangling alliances?

The solution was found in the precedent established by the Treaty of Rio de Janeiro and in Congress' approval of the Vandenberg Resolution. The former, also known as the Inter-American Treaty of Reciprocal Assistance, was signed by nineteen Western Hemisphere nations on September 2, 1947. Designed to strengthen the Act of Chapultepec, the treaty established a regional alliance system in which the signatories agreed to help each other against an assault upon any of them and to do so "in the exercise of the inherent right of individual or collective self-defense recognized by Article 51 of the Charter of the United Nations." The next year, meeting at Bogotá for its ninth session, the International Conference of American States accepted the Pact of Bogotá (May 2), which established the Organization of American States (OAS) as the regional body designed to promote the welfare, security, and defense of the Americas.

Employing the principle of the Rio treaty and the provisions of Article 51 of the United Nations Charter, Senator Vandenberg and Marshall's able Under Secretary Robert A. Lovett devised a formula which made possible United States participation in regional security systems outside the Americas. On June 11, 1948, by the large majority of 64 to 4, the United States Senate approved the Vandenberg Resolution, officially known as Senate Resolution 239, which asserted that it was "the policy of the United States to achieve international peace and security through the United Nations" and which provided for the "Association of the United States by constitutional process, with such regional and other collective arrangements as are based on continuous self-help and mutual aid. . . ." With the passage of this highly significant resolution, the road was cleared for an even more precedent-shattering step, the Senate's ratification of the North Atlantic Treaty Organization (NATO) on July 21, 1949.[6]

Negotiations on the NATO treaty, also known as the North Atlantic

[6] The NATO treaty was signed in Washington, D.C., on April 4 by Belgium, Canada, Denmark, France, Great Britain, Ireland, Italy, Luxembourg, the Netherlands, Norway, Portugal, and the United States. It was signed in February, 1952, by Greece and Turkey, and in 1955 by West Germany.

344   THE U.S. & THE POSTWAR WORLD, 1945–1961

Pact, were begun immediately following the Senate's adoption of the Vandenberg Resolution and were pressed vigorously after the presidential election of 1948. Numerous questions arose among the European powers which delayed writing the treaty's final draft; furthermore, once these were resolved, the treaty met considerable opposition in the United States Senate. A number of legislators, one of the most notable being Taft, fought it on various grounds, principally because they believed it violated the "spirit" of the United Nations, ran counter to American tradition, and might interfere with Congress' exclusive right to declare war. "I voted against it," Taft declared, "because I felt it was contrary to the whole theory of the United Nations Charter, which had not then been shown to be ineffective, because I felt that it might develop aggressive features more likely to incite Russia to war than to deter it from war, and because I thought . . . it committed the United States to the policy of a land war in Europe, when we might find that a third world war could better be fought by other means." [7]

But despite the opposition of Taft and others, the Senate ratified NATO by a large vote (82 to 13), thereby committing the United States to what Truman called "an offensive-defensive alliance to maintain the peace in the North Atlantic area but without automatic provision for war." Article 5 of the treaty, its most important one, provided that "an armed attack against one or more of . . . [its members] in Europe or North America shall be considered an attack against them all; and . . . each of them, in exercise of the right of collective or self-defense recognized by Article 51 of the Charter of the United Nations, will assist the Party or Parties so attacked by taking forthwith, individually and in concert with the other Parties, such action as it deems necessary, including the use of armed force. . . ." The purpose of the North Atlantic Pact, Truman told the nation, was to deter aggression. "If we can make it sufficiently clear in advance that any armed attack affecting our national security would be met with overwhelming force, the armed attack might never occur."

To implement the treaty's purposes, Congress approved Truman's request for funds to provide the NATO countries, Turkey, Greece, Iran, Korea, China, and the Philippines with "military assistance in the form of equipment, materials, and services" by passing the $1.3 billion Mutual Defense Assistance Act in September, 1949. The next year, after Britain, France, and the United States agreed that Germany should be permitted

[7] Taft, *op. cit.*, p. 89.

THE TRUMAN POLICIES, 1947–1952 345

to "reenter progressively the community of free peoples of Europe," the Federal Republic and West Berlin were included under the protection of the North Atlantic Pact; and after the serious doubts and fears of France were sufficiently allayed, Germany was allowed to rearm, and in 1955 was invited to participate in NATO's defense system. On December 19, 1950, at the Brussels Conference of the NATO foreign ministers, General Dwight D. Eisenhower was appointed the Supreme Commander of the Allied Powers in Europe, with his military headquarters (known as SHAPE) in suburban Rocquencourt, just outside Paris; and finally, on May 27, 1952, after much difficulty, the United States, Britain, Italy, West Germany, and the Benelux countries established the European Defense Community (EDC) and agreed to integrate their armed forces and place them under NATO's command.[8] By 1952, the Truman administration's efforts to contain Soviet power had brought to an end a long era in American foreign policy and had inaugurated a new one in which the American people were obliged to recognize that the United States, as the most powerful nation in the free world, was compelled to assume the principal burden for its defense.

Germany and the Berlin Crisis

At the very time the United States Senate was about to vote on the Marshall Plan and the State Department was considering America's participation in a European defense system, the Soviet Union created a new crisis in Berlin which lasted 321 days and brought the world closer to war than at any time since V-J Day. The Berlin crisis of June, 1948, arose out of the West's efforts to prevent Russia from converting Germany into a Soviet satellite. Since the Yalta and Potsdam meetings, the question of Germany's postwar status had precipitated the bitterest disputes in the East-West power struggle for Europe. As it became increasingly obvious that the Soviet Union was bringing East Germany completely into its orbit and that it would permit the reunification of Germany only if the West accepted its terms, first Britain and the United States and then France agreed to expedite the rehabilitation of their respective zones. In May, 1946, the United States stopped stripping the industrial plants in its sector and using the confiscated capital equipment to pay Russian reparation claims; in September Secretary Byrnes de-

[8] France had also signed the treaty, but after two years of discussion and delay, the National Assembly declined to accept it in August, 1954.

clared, in a speech at Stuttgart, that the United States was opposed to "a prolonged alien dictatorship" over Germany; and in December Britain and the United States agreed to unite their two zones in a single administrative and economic unit. The failure of the London Conference of Foreign Ministers in November and December, 1947, to resolve the East-West impasse on a German treaty and the obvious need to use Germany's productive capacities to supplement Marshall Plan assistance in facilitating the recovery of Western Europe resulted in a meeting, held in London in February, 1948, in which France and the Benelux countries joined Britain and the United States in preparing for the creation of a single united German government to replace the three separate Western jurisdictions then existing.

In protest against these efforts at consolidating and rebuilding West Germany, the Soviets, beginning in the spring of 1948, started to harass and ultimately blockaded the West's rail, canal, and highway traffic from their zones across the Soviet sector into Berlin. According to the European Advisory Commission's wartime agreement of September 12, 1944, signed by the "big three" and subsequently amended to include France, each of the Western Allies was to occupy a section of Hitler's former capital. While this agreement did not include a written statement of the West's right of access to its garrisons in Berlin, it had been verbally agreed at a later meeting that each of the occupying powers in the city had the right to move troops and supplies in and out of its section along certain designated land and water routes. In the case of access to Berlin by air, a written agreement had been signed which specified the West's air corridors into the city.

The immediate event which precipitated the Berlin blockade was the decision of the Western Allies on June 18, 1948, to strengthen the economic stability of their occupation zones by introducing a new, uniform currency which would give the people of West Germany a sound mark. On June 23, Russia issued a new Soviet mark for East Germany, but unlike the Western powers, the Kremlin introduced it also into its sector of Berlin. The next day Britain, France, and the United States countered this unilateral Russian action by extending their recently issued *Deutsche Mark* throughout West Berlin. The Soviet Union, accusing the three Western Allies of having repudiated the Potsdam agreements on Germany to suit their militaristic interests, replied by blockading all of the greater Berlin area and ordering Red troops on June 25 to close all of the West's land and canal routes into the city.

The Kremlin's intentions were obvious. "What the Russians were trying to do," Truman wrote later, "was to get us out of Berlin. . . . What was at stake . . . was not a contest over legal rights . . . but a struggle over Germany and, in a larger sense, over Europe." This was precisely the view of General Lucius D. Clay, the United States military governor in Germany. In mid-April, when Soviet interference with the West's land and river routes was becoming increasingly intolerable, he had informed Washington that "if Berlin falls, Western Germany will be next. If we mean . . . to hold Europe against Communism, we must not budge . . . [for] if we withdraw, our position in Europe is threatened. If America does not understand this now, does not know the issue is cast, then it never will, and Communism will run rampant. I believe the future of democracy requires us to stay."

In order "to stay" and at the same time to minimize the possibilities of incidents and avoid taking any action which might incite the Kremlin to adopt measures which could lead to war, Truman decided upon two courses of action: he ordered General Clay to expand the emergency airlift that had been bringing in supplies into "a full-scale organized" operation; and in agreement with the other Western Allies, he countered the Soviet blockade with an Anglo-French-American one, thus severing all East-West trade. Beginning on June 26, hundreds of British and American planes flew in and out of Berlin, carrying all the food, coal, and other supplies required to feed and care for the city's 2.1 million blockaded inhabitants. The success of the airlift, which flew a total of 2.3 million tons of goods into the hard-pressed city before the blockade came to an end on May 12, 1949, was made possible by the superb efforts and efficiency of the Anglo-American air and ground transport services and by the determination and courage of the West Berliners, who joined their former Western enemies in order to avoid being ravaged by their Eastern one.

In the meantime, the West sought a solution by negotiating with the Soviets, including a meeting between Ambassador Walter Bedell Smith and Stalin; when these discussions solved nothing, the dispute was referred to the Security Council. But the compromise the neutral nations on the council proposed was not acceptable to the Soviet Union. Only after the Kremlin realized that the West intended to fulfill General Clay's earlier assertion that the Russians "can't drive us out by any action short of war" did Russia abandon its stubborn unwillingness to enter into reasonable negotiations. Early in May, 1949, the Kremlin pro-

348 THE U.S. & THE POSTWAR WORLD, 1945–1961

posed to open all the routes the Western Allies had previously used if they would end their own counterblockade and agree to a meeting of the Council of Foreign Ministers to discuss the Berlin and the German question, two conditions which the West was happy to accept. A week after Britain, France, and the United States assented to these terms, the blockade came to an end, and on May 23 the foreign ministers met in Paris. But after nearly a month of talks, they adjourned without reaching any solution to the German problem, though they did agree on a *modus vivendi* for Berlin which allowed the West access to the city.

The Berlin blockade proved to be a major blunder for the Kremlin. Not only did the Soviet Union suffer a significant diplomatic setback, but the eleven-month crisis strengthened the advocates of containment in the United States and, by expediting Western efforts to push Germany's economic recovery and reunification, brought about the very result the Russians were hoping to avoid—a united West Germany. By the time Stalin ordered the blockade lifted, the citizens of West Berlin, despite the threats of Soviet officials and the proximity of the Red army, had defeated the Communists by an overwhelming vote in the city elections of December, 1948, and the people of "Trizonia," as the three integrated Western zones came to be called, had adopted a democratic constitution establishing the Federal Republic of Germany. The new nation, composed of the eleven states in the British, French, and American sectors, established its capital at Bonn and on September 15, 1949, organized its own government with Christian Democrat Konrad Adenauer as its first chancellor. Three weeks later, the Soviet Union proclaimed the German Democratic Republic as the new government of its zone, thereby giving Europe two Germanies and two Berlins. On August 2, 1952, the United States signed a peace treaty with the Bonn government, and for all practical purposes West Germany was rid of most of the limitations defeat had imposed upon it, except certain military ones.

THE ELECTION OF 1948

The Berlin issue developed during the months of the presidential primaries. Almost as if the men in the Kremlin were intent upon depriving America's politicos of their quadrennial monopoly of the front pages of the country's newspapers, the crisis reached its climax three days after the opening of the Republican National Convention in Philadelphia on

June 21. Their hopes greatly buoyed by the GOP triumph in the mid-term elections of 1946 and by what they interpreted to be the party's successful performance in frustrating Truman's domestic program and in legislating part of their own, the Republicans convened for what they were certain amounted to electing the next President. To add to the general excitement of the occasion, the convention's proceedings were televised for the first time, and some million owners of sets witnessed the spectacle.

Of the party's seven principal contenders, its two military heroes had been eliminated by convention time: on January 23, 1948, General Eisenhower, who was then the president of Columbia University, declared flatly that he refused to run, and the next month General Mac-Arthur, the Supreme Commander of the occupation forces in Japan, who was not at all opposed to the nomination, was decisively defeated in the Wisconsin primary. The other candidates were Harold E. Stassen of Minnesota, who still enjoyed considerable public support but who suffered a serious setback in the Oregon primary when he was badly hurt in a national radio debate with New York's Thomas E. Dewey; the liberal and popular governor of California, Earl Warren, who was strongly supported on the Pacific Coast; Senator Vandenberg, who, despite his repeated declarations that he was not a candidate, continued to be "boomed" for top place; Senator Taft, a declared and campaigning candidate since October, 1947; and Governor Dewey of New York, the party's titular leader and Taft's most important and dangerous rival.

Before the delegates got down to the important business of nominating candidates, they adopted a platform which revealed the party's domestic conservatism, as reflected in Taft's leadership of the Eightieth Congress, and its recently acquired internationalism, as defined by Vandenberg, who wrote the GOP foreign policy plank. Despite the protests of the isolationists and the followers of the *Chicago Tribune*'s Colonel Robert McCormick, the Republican party declared its support for "collective security against aggression," the United Nations, and "regional arrangements as prescribed by the [UN] Charter," and it asserted its intention to build a "foreign policy on the basis of friendly firmness which welcomes cooperation but spurns appeasement." And while the GOP did not endorse the Marshall Plan by name, it did so indirectly by approving American assistance, "within the prudent limits of our own economic welfare," to friendly and peaceful nations.

The domestic planks supported the GOP's record in Congress, and

350 THE U.S. & THE POSTWAR WORLD, 1945-1961

though it censured the inefficiency and wasteful spending of the burgeoning federal bureaucracy and decried the corrupting influences of the New Deal and the Truman policies, it did not propose to repeal any of the social and economic legislation of the past fifteen years. Some of the programs the platform called for, such as the appropriation of federal funds to clear urban slums and to construct low-cost housing, appeared to be at variance with the position taken by the party's leaders in Congress, but the delegates endorsed the proposals nonetheless. The GOP took credit for reducing the people's tax burden and for the Taft-Hartley Act, which it called "a sensible reform of the labor law," asserted its determination to defend "both workers and employers against coercion and exploitation," and advocated a strong civil rights plank. Since the platform was not one with which conservatives could find offense, it was quickly adopted.

While the platform was being written and debated, the Taft and Dewey forces were busily engaged in gathering votes. For a time it appeared as if an anti-Dewey coalition might lead to the nomination of Taft, who was supported by the more conservative elements of the party and, because of his reluctant internationalism, by the isolationists as well. But the carefully organized and smoothly efficient Dewey forces could not be stopped. The New Yorker's "blitz," noted Vandenberg, "was a thing of beauty," and Dewey won 434 votes on the first ballot to Taft's 224. On the second roll call, Dewey increased his total to 515, only 32 short of nomination, while Taft added just another 50 to his; and before the third ballot was taken, the Ohioan withdrew, thereby opening the way for Dewey's unanimous nomination. For second place, the convention acclaimed Earl Warren of California, the choice of its standard-bearer and his close advisers.

Three weeks later, on July 12, the Democrats assembled in Philadelphia with very little enthusiasm and considerable pessimism about the party's chances of victory. After Eisenhower's refusal to run for the GOP, a group of Democratic leaders tried to get him to accept an offer from them, but he refused their proposal as emphatically as he had the Republicans' approach. These and other Democrats then sought to interest Supreme Court Justice William O. Douglas. But when he would hear none of it, the nomination went on the first ballot to Truman, who, knowing from the beginning that he had enough votes to secure his own nomination, was never greatly concerned by the efforts of those Democrats who wanted to bypass him. Many Southerners, opposed to the

President's strong civil rights stand, refused to vote for him, thereby depriving him of the honor of a unanimous endorsement. For Vice President, the delegates chose the Senate's minority leader, the seventy-one-year-old Alben W. Barkley of Kentucky, who was unopposed.

As was to be expected the Democrats endorsed the party's legislative record and blamed the Republicans for not having been able to redeem all their pledges. The platform's foreign policy plank was outspokenly internationalist, approving all of the administration's important decisions and asserting the party's readiness to assume the nation's leadership in its struggle to safeguard the free world. To protect America's economic strength, the Democrats promised to "curb the Republican inflation," for which they held the Eightieth Congress responsible; to enact slum-clearance and housing legislation; to reduce taxes "whenever it is possible to do so without unbalancing the nation's economy"; to promote "a permanent system of flexible price supports for agricultural products"; to increase the minimum wage from 40 to 75 cents an hour; to repeal the Taft-Hartley Act, which they branded a total failure; and to extend the social security system "to all workers not now covered," reduce the "eligibility age for women from 65 to 60 years," and raise the level of benefit payments. The platform also called for "a national health program" and "federal aid for education administered by and under the control of the states."

The adoption of none of these planks caused anything like the bitter fight which accompanied the writing of the party's civil rights platform. In opposition to the mild, states'-rights–oriented proposal of the Southerners, the party's New Deal liberals offered a vigorous and forthright declaration of their own written by Minneapolis Mayor Hubert H. Humphrey, Jr., which the convention ultimately accepted. The provision that the South found especially offensive and that caused the Mississippi and part of the Alabama delegations to storm out of the convention was the one asking the Congress "to support our President in guaranteeing these basic and fundamental American Principles: (1) the right of full and equal political participation; (2) the right to equal opportunity of employment; (3) the right of security of person; (4) and the right of equal treatment in the service and defense of our nation."

In addition to the usual collection of minor parties, two others—the States' Rights Democratic party (better known as the Dixiecrats) and a new Progressive party—nominated presidential and vice presidential candidates this year. The former, composed of disgruntled antiadministration Democrats and die-hard foes of civil rights, met in Birmingham, Alabama, three days after the Democratic convention had committed itself "to eradicate all racial, religious and economic discrimination," and nominated two southern governors, James Strom Thurmond of South Carolina and Fielding Lewis Wright of Mississippi, for President and Vice President respectively. Though the Dixiecrats appealed almost exclusively to the more reactionary and negative elements in the South, many of the party's leaders exercised considerable influence on the election machinery in their states and were in a position to deprive the regular Democratic party candidates of important electoral votes.

A week after the Dixiecrat convention, the Progressive party met in Philadelphia and nominated Henry A. Wallace, who had declared his intention to run for President on a third-party ticket, on December 29, 1947. For his running mate, the party chose Senator Glen H. Taylor of Idaho. Wallace explained that his decision to seek the Presidency was prompted by Truman's failure to continue the Roosevelt policies, both domestic and international, and by his belief that what the American people wanted was a "positive peace program of abundance and security, not [one of] scarcity and war." Wallace's ideas were translated into a party platform which blamed the administration for the cold war and denounced the new policy of containment as exemplified by the Truman Doctrine, the Marshall Plan, and increased armaments. Instead of these warlike policies, Wallace proposed strengthening the United Nations and developing a more friendly and cooperative approach to the Soviet Union, one which would assuage its fears and satisfy its needs for security. On the domestic side, the Progressives, like the Democrats, called for repealing the Taft-Hartley Act, enacting a strong antiinflation law, including a revival of many wartime controls, and effectively guaranteeing the civil liberties of all the people. As was to be expected, they favored also a strong program of social justice legislation. Many of Wallace's supporters and most of the party's leaders belonged to the Progressive Citizens of America, a group of ardent liberals and New Dealers who had joined together in 1946 when it appeared to them that a new conservatism was taking hold of the Democratic party. Along with these honest and sincere liberal-progressives, the Wallace movement attracted also a goodly number of Communists and fellow travelers whose influence on the party's programs and policies soon became painfully apparent. In August, when Wallace and Taylor received the official endorsement of the Communist party, a great many Americans began to suspect, with not a few of them convinced, that the Communists were actually running the party.

With the Progressives and the Dixiecrats threatening to deprive the Democrats of substantial blocs of votes, Truman's chances of winning the election appeared dim indeed. Almost everyone, including the major pollsters and political pundits, with the notable exception of the President himself, predicted Truman's defeat. The Republicans were certain of it, and Dewey conducted himself accordingly. He was aloof, reserved, and self-confident. His speeches possessed considerable stylistic elegance, and he delivered them with an easy informality. He promised peace with honor, "national unity," social progress, and continued prosperity. Rarely did he discuss specific issues, and when he did he was always careful to avoid offending either the conservatives or the liberals in his party. With ample funds, the support of nearly two-thirds of the press, and an energetic group of party workers on all levels, the GOP looked upon the Democratic campaign with a combination of indifference, contempt, and amusement. Just as the elation of certain victory possessed the Republicans, the gloom of inevitable defeat haunted the Democrats. Many of the party leaders, convinced that they had already lost the election, refused to exert themselves; campaign contributors, also of the same opinion, held on to their money, with the result that the party was continuously hard pressed to meet its radio and transportation expenses. The whole Democratic campaign, as one of *The New York Times*'s reporters summed it up later, "was patched together with scotch tape, rubber checks, and sheer bravado."

And it was Truman himself who contributed most of this last component, which he employed with keen political wisdom and seemingly inexhaustible energy. The President began his fight for election at the Democratic convention, when he declared that he was going to call the Republican Eightieth Congress into special session on July 26 and ask it to legislate a price control law; to appropriate money to aid education; to pass housing, civil rights, and health care bills; and to extend the social security program. The Republicans had endorsed every one of these proposals in their platform, and now Truman called upon them to redeem their promises. "Of course I knew," he wrote later, "that the special session would produce no results. . . . But I felt justified in calling the Congress back to Washington to prove to the people whether the Republican platform really meant anything or not." For nearly two weeks, the GOP's legislators were forced to sit and face a choice between two evils: refuse to enact the President's recommendations, thereby providing him with excellent campaign ammunition, or do his bidding, in which case they would alienate the conservative wing of their party. They decided on the former; and as was to be expected, Truman, ignoring entirely the fact that the conservative Democrats were as strongly opposed to much of his program as were their counterparts in the GOP, launched into a vigorous, fighting one-man crusade against the "party of privilege" and "Grand Old Platitudes" with its "old moss-backs in Congress."

He whistle-stopped across the country, traveling nearly 32,000 miles—twice as many as Dewey—and delivering, by his own count, a total of 356 speeches. And though Truman was not a sophisticated public speaker like Dewey, and not at his best before large audiences or the microphone, he proved to be exceptionally effective before small groups, where his extemporaneous, informal remarks revealed all the warmth, humanity, and friendliness of his personality. In forceful language, which was often earthily colorful, he castigated the Republicans for having renounced their own platform, and he lambasted the Eightieth Congress as a "do-nothing" one, "the worst" in American history.

President Harry S. Truman, here shown addressing a crowd in St. Louis, conducted a whistle-stop campaign which drew widespread attention during the election of 1948. (Brown Brothers)

THE TRUMAN POLICIES, 1947–1952   355

The result of his energetic fight for election, which the Republicans called a "one-man circus," combined with the strength of the Democratic party, many of whose candidates polled more votes than Truman, was the most surprising political victory in the country's history. Truman polled 24.1 million popular votes, representing 49.8 per cent of those cast, and he won 303 electoral votes, with California and traditionally Republican Iowa among the twenty-eight states in the Democratic column. Dewey received a total of 21.9 million popular votes, or about 45.1 per cent, and 189 electoral votes, including those of New York, where the Wallace Progressives polled 509,559 votes or nearly one-half of their national total of 1,157,172. The Dixiecrats, with 1,169,063 popular votes, won three states—Alabama, Louisiana, and Mississippi—with 38 electoral votes, to which Tennessee added another for a total of 39. The Democrats also recaptured both houses of Congress by comfortable majorities. The new party line-up on Capitol Hill was as follows: in the Senate, 54 Democrats and 42 Republicans; in the House, 263 to 171 respectively.

Since just about everyone had anticipated Truman's and the Democratic party's defeat, the size of their victory made it appear all the more unbelievable. "I just don't know what happened," admitted George Gallup, the oft-quoted and highly respected pollster. Senator Taft, reviewing the Republican party rout, dismissed the explanations. "It defies all common sense," he said, "for the country to send that roughneck ward politician back to the White House." [9] Despite the inability of Taft and many others to understand why the voters elected Truman, there were many reasons for the people's decision. The over-all campaign strategy Truman and his top advisers adopted was an exceptionally astute one. Essentially it was twofold: to hold Dewey responsible for the record of Taft and the conservatives in Congress, and to appeal to the various interest groups by warning them that a GOP victory would jeopardize all the benefits they had received from fifteen years of Democratic rule. Truman won the support of the foreign-born and the various nationality groups in key cities and states by his stand against further Soviet expansion in Europe, his foreign assistance program, and his determined efforts to get 400,000 displaced Europeans admitted into the United States. When the Congress, in the Displaced Persons Act of June 25, 1947, reduced the number to 205,000 and because of Republican pressure wrote into the law various discriminatory clauses against certain religious and

[9] Quoted in Eric F. Goldman, *The Crucial Decade—And After: America, 1945–1960* (New York [1961]), pp. 87, 90.

ethnic groups, Truman accused the GOP of denying the nation "the courage and skills" of these people because it did not "want homeless, suffering Europeans of certain religions to get in the United States." He reminded the middle- and fixed-income groups, both hard hit by rapidly accelerating prices, of his frustrated efforts to get the Republicans to pass an effective antiinflation law; he branded the GOP tax reduction bill "a rich man's" statute; in the Middle Western agricultural belt, he pointed out how the Eightieth Congress had already undermined various New Deal farm programs and warned the farmers that the Republicans would strike at price supports next; and he used, with equal effectiveness, the Taft-Hartley Act to frighten labor and the civil rights plank to appeal to the Negro vote. This strategy, combined with his fighting spirit and his claim that he was trying to protect and extend the reforms of the Roosevelt era which had brought so many benefits to the country's "common people," resulted in his victory.

THE FAIR DEAL, 1949–1952

The voters, responding to Truman's repeated campaign appeals for a Democratic Congress, gave him one in 1948 and, with reduced majorities, elected another in 1950.[10] The reaction of both these Congresses to the President's Fair Deal domestic program, which he first announced as such in his State of the Union message of January 5, 1949, was mixed. In some instances, the Democratic Eighty-first and Eighty-second Congresses treated his proposals with the same indifference, procrastination, and negativism with which they had been received by the previous "notorious" Republican one. The same southern bloc which had stopped the passage of a permanent Fair Employment Practices law in 1946 with a filibuster succeeded in preventing the enactment of a similar measure in 1950 and again in 1952. This same group also defeated the President's civil rights program. In October, 1947, the President's Committee on Civil Rights, which Truman had appointed the previous December to study "all areas of racial and religious discrimination," published its report, *To Secure These Rights;* and on the basis of its findings, Truman asked Congress (February 2, 1948) to guarantee all Americans "equal

[10] The congressional elections of 1950 increased the GOP's numbers in the Senate from 42 to 47 and in the House from 171 to 199. The Democratic count on Capitol Hill during the last two years of the Truman administration was 49 senators and 235 representatives.

opportunities for jobs, for homes, for education, for health . . . [and] for political expression, and equal protection under the law." He proposed a ten-point program designed to provide the country with a set of "modern, comprehensive civil rights laws, adequate to the needs of the day." When Congress continued to ignore his recommendations, Truman tried to do whatever he could by presidential action. He moved to end segregation in the armed forces and in the federal civil service, and he ordered the Justice Department to enforce the existing civil rights statutes vigorously.

If the Southerners frustrated his efforts in one direction, a conservative Democratic-Republican coalition stymied his attempts to repeal the Taft-Hartley Act, to establish a department of public welfare with cabinet rank, to pass the St. Lawrence–Great Lakes Seaway and hydroelectric power project, and to set up a Missouri Valley Authority which would, like the TVA, conserve and develop the region's natural resources. Truman's recommendations for similar projects along the Columbia and Colorado rivers were also blocked. But despite these failures, the President succeeded in expanding the flood control and irrigation programs and in extending the work of the Reclamation Bureau and the Rural Electrification Administration. When he left the White House, the conservationists looked upon him as a staunch friend.

Congressional conservatives, opposed to extending the authority of the federal government over the economy, which they looked upon as "regimentation" and "creeping socialism," joined with the spokesmen of large agricultural interests like the American Farm Bureau to defeat the administration's new farm program, the so-called Brannan Plan, named after Agriculture Secretary Charles F. Brannan, who succeeded to Clinton P. Anderson's post on June 2, 1948. The purpose of the Brannan Plan, the first comprehensive review of the country's agricultural policies in a decade, was to provide the farmer "a stable income" comparable to the one he received during the years 1939–48, to hold the price of food at a reasonable level, and insofar as possible to reduce the government's storage expenses. To achieve these ends Brannan devised a scheme whereby price supports would be employed to pay the farmer the difference between the established support price and the market one. "What was important about the Brannan Plan," Truman said, "was that it shifted the emphasis in price supports from commodity purchases to production payments," thereby giving "the consumer . . . the benefits of the lower price." The Brannan Plan was to apply to the producers of perishables;

358 THE U.S. & THE POSTWAR WORLD, 1945–1961

farmers growing other crops would continue to receive loans from the Commodity Credit Corporation or be provided with a government market for their surpluses. When the House refused to accept the administration's proposal, Truman settled for the Agricultural Act, which Congress passed in October, 1949. Under its provisions the "rigid" 90 per cent of parity base was to be continued for a year. Then, during the next twelve months, it was to be allowed to drop as much as 10 per cent, and after 1951 it was to become "flexible" at 75 to 90 per cent. The law was less than Truman had hoped for, but it was nonetheless consistent with the Democratic party's campaign pledge to seek "a permanent system of flexible price supports."

The antiadministration forces in Congress, ably assisted by powerful lobbying interests, also succeeded in defeating other liberal-progressive Fair Deal programs, two of the most notable being federal aid to education and a national health insurance program, which the President had repeatedly requested. In the case of the former, even though its need was widely recognized, prominent Roman Catholic leaders opposed any assistance law which excluded parochial school children from sharing in all of the government-subsidized benefits. And in the case of the latter, the American Medical Association's vigorous campaign against what it liked to call "socialized medicine" prevented the administration's health insurance bill from getting through the Congress.

The federal legislators did not cast aside all Truman's domestic recommendations, however. In 1950 and 1952 the social security system was broadened to cover some 10.5 million additional persons and the benefit payments were increased to meet the greatly changed economic conditions of the postwar era. The Social Security Act of 1950, the first major amendment to the law in eleven years, raised benefits 77 per cent; the one of 1952 boosted them another 12.5 per cent. To meet the additional expense, provision was made in the 1950 law to raise employer and employee contributions gradually over the next twenty years, from $1\frac{1}{4}$ per cent in 1950 to $3\frac{1}{4}$ per cent in 1970. Truman also succeeded in extending the federal rent control law through June, 1950, and in raising the minimum wage from 40 to 75 cents an hour. With the aid of Senator Taft and other Republican votes, he was also able to secure the passage of the National Housing Act of July 5, 1949, which reorganized the federal government's various housing agencies, provided loans and subsidies for slum clearance projects, and allocated sufficient funds for a six-year building program designed to add 810,000 units of low-cost public housing. In addition, in June, 1950, Truman secured a new Displaced Persons Act which increased the number of these suffering and persecuted individuals eligible for admission to 400,000. The new law, moreover, corrected some of the discriminatory clauses Truman had criticized in the 1948 statute.

Equally significant though far less publicized than the other domestic programs of his administration were Truman's efforts to simplify the structure and improve the efficiency of the Executive branch of the government. Early in 1949 the first Hoover Commission finished its exhaustive two-year study of the federal Executive and presented its findings to the Congress in the form of eighteen special task force reports. This distinguished bipartisan group found much that was wrong with the administrative practices and procedures of the Executive department. Almost all the inefficiencies, duplication, and lack of "responsibility and accountability" which the commission uncovered arose from the fact that there was no "clear line of authority from top to bottom." In many of the department's agencies, bureaus, and offices this was made even worse by inadequate staff services. To remedy these defects, which the Commission asserted prevented the Chief Executive from fulfilling the requirements of his office effectively, especially in times of crisis, Congress passed the Reorganization Act on June 20, 1949, authorizing the President to submit for its approval his plans for improving the performance of his department. Truman responded enthusiastically to the challenge, and in one year presented the Congress with more than thirty different reorganization plans, all of which the legislators accepted save the one calling for the creation of a department of public welfare. Most of the changes the President instituted involved reducing the number of agencies and bureaus, coordinating the activities of others, improving administrative and budgetary practices, and tightening Executive controls. By the time Truman left the White House, more than half the Commission's recommendations had been adopted, and while there still remained much to be done, he had achieved considerable success in making the government what he believed it should be—"an effective instrument of service to the people."

When compared to the many Fair Deal programs the President recommended to the Congress, the domestic reform legislation Truman was able to get accepted on Capitol Hill fell considerably short of his hopes and those of his liberal and progressive supporters, many of whom had at first doubted his allegiance to the principles of his predecessor. Truman soon proved, however, that he was as dedicated to reform, social justice, and public welfare legislation as Roosevelt had been; and in the case of his fight for civil rights, he was an even greater spokesman for equality of opportunity and freedom. Though the Truman administration did not provide the strikingly novel domestic reforms that distinguished the Roosevelt era, it was nonetheless a singularly constructive one, and its achievements were all the more remarkable because they were won in an era of grave international crises and unprecedented prosperity at home, when public attention was either frightened by the possibility of another global war or distracted by the thousands of new gadgets and fancy consumer goods rolling off the nation's assembly lines.

"Point Four"

While the Truman administration sought to satisfy the hopes of the American people for a secure and more abundant life and to help the Europeans rehabilitate their economies, it offered also to assist the discontented and less fortunate peoples of the world in raising their standards of living and bringing their aspirations closer to realization. On January 20, 1949, while delivering his inaugural address, Truman outlined a four-point program designed "to strengthen the free world," three items of which—supporting the United Nations, carrying out the Marshall Plan, and drafting a North Atlantic security pact—were already well known. It was the last, or "Point Four," which, because of its far-reaching implications, fired the imagination. "We must embark on a bold new program for making the benefits of our scientific advances and industrial progress available for the improvement and growth of under-developed areas," Truman said. "More than half the people of the world are living in conditions approaching misery. . . . Their poverty is a handicap and a threat both to them and to more prosperous areas. . . . The United States is preeminent among nations in the development of industrial and scientific techniques. The material resources which we can afford to use for the assistance of other peoples are limited. But our imponderable resources in technical knowledge are constantly growing and are inexhaustible." American know-how and show-how techniques and the investment of private capital in the world's underdeveloped regions could help the people of these countries "raise themselves from the level of colonialism to self-support and ultimate prosperity." To dispel any doubts about the purposes of American investments in these countries, Truman declared that these "new economic developments must be devised and controlled to benefit the peoples of the area in which they are established. Guarantees to the investor must be balanced by guarantees in the interest of the people whose resources and whose labor go into these developments." In other words, this was not a scheme to revive the old imperialism in a new garb.

More than a year later, on June 5, 1950, Congress passed the Act for International Development, and in September the Point Four program went into effect with a $35 million grant to meet the expenses of its first year. The State Department, which administered the program, had had some experience in managing technical assistance projects in Latin America, and it was hoped that it could employ its knowledge and administrative skills to launch the Point Four program effectively and secure the full cooperation of the recipient countries. Six months after the program had been inaugurated, Truman reported that "about 350 technicians were at work on more than a thousand technical co-operation projects in twenty-seven countries"; some thirty or more underdeveloped Asian, African, and Latin American states had applied for Point Four assistance; and 236 individuals representing 34 governments were being trained in the United States. Much of the Point Four aid was used to stimulate and develop basic industries, like agriculture and transportation, and to improve the people's health. The benefits of the program to the recipient countries as well as to the United States became quickly apparent, and Congress more than quadrupled its appropriations for 1952. Like the Marshall Plan and NATO, the Point Four program was intended also to promote the basic purposes of American foreign policy, and as Truman stated later, it was to be "a practical expression of our attitude toward the countries threatened by Communist domination." By 1949, this threat had assumed ominous proportions in the Far East.

Latin America

It was unfortunate that with so many new commitments in other parts of the world, the United States after World War II could spare little attention or economic aid for its Latin American neighbors. During the war years all but one of the American nations—Argentina—had been united against the Axis powers. The Latin Americans had made substantial contributions to the common cause, especially in the production of raw materials needed for the American war program, and the United

States had assured them that it would not forget their economic needs after the victory had been won. But because many Latin Americans felt this promise was not fulfilled, there was a marked deterioration in hemispheric relations. The process of building a Pan-American security system transforming the Monroe Doctrine into a hemispheric obligation, which had been initiated during the 1930's, continued with the Rio Treaty of 1947 and the formation of the Organization of American States (OAS) at the Bogotá Conference of 1948; but Latin Americans resented the priority given to Europe and the Far East by American policy-makers, particularly after they had been bluntly told by Secretary Marshall at the Bogotá Conference that they would have to rely mainly on the investment of private capital, not on government grants or loans. Their resentment against the United States was exploited by Communists, who made considerable progress in a number of countries, especially Brazil, Chile, and Cuba.

Latin Americans were still afraid of United States domination, despite the hands-off promises that had been made again and again at Pan-American conferences during the 1930's. They were alarmed by attempts to put pressure on Argentina during the later war years and by United States intervention in the Argentinian elections of February, 1946. Colonel Juan Domingo Perón had now emerged as the leading figure in the military clique that had governed the country since June, 1943, and his dynamic personality and promises of social and economic reform had won him wide popularity among the impoverished masses, despite his avowedly dictatorial and fascistic program. He now felt strong enough to offer himself as presidential candidate in an election. His chief opponent, José Tamborini, was a colorless figure who offered little to the Argentinian people except promises to defend democracy. Concerned about the threat of totalitarian dictatorship, the United States made it abundantly plain that it hoped to see Perón defeated, and shortly before the election the State Department published a "blue book" of documents showing the pro-Axis activities of Perón and his associates during the war years. Chiefly associated with this well-intentioned but unwise attempt to influence Argentinian politics was Spruille Braden, a career diplomat who served as minister to Argentina during the summer of 1945 and subsequently as Assistant Secretary in charge of Latin American affairs in the State Department. Declaring that his real opponent was Braden rather than Tamborini and appealing to the nationalistic senti-

THE TRUMAN POLICIES, 1947-1952   363

ments of the Argentinian electorate, Perón was elected president in what appears to have been, on the whole, a free election. The United States, left in the humiliating position of having backed a loser, was compelled to repudiate the Braden policies and make friends with Perón. Latin American democrats, in fact, were soon complaining that the United States was giving Perón even more support than was necessary. The middle road between giving too much aid and comfort to dictators and intervening in Latin American affairs too deeply in the hope of promoting democracy was, indeed, hard to find. Perón continued to govern Argentina until 1955, when, having virtually bankrupted the country, he was overthrown by revolution.

In its treatment of one Latin American country, however, the Truman administration gave a convincing demonstration of the falsity of Communist charges of Yankee imperialism. Puerto Rico, an American possession since 1898, was transformed into a self-governing commonwealth freely associated with but no longer controlled by the United States.

The American record in Puerto Rico had been disappointing. Although the islanders had been permitted to elect their own legislature and had been granted citizenship by the Jones Act of 1917, the ultimate authority belonged to the United States government in Washington, D.C., which was represented in Puerto Rico by an appointed governor. There was a growing demand among Puerto Ricans for political freedom, although most of them recognized that complete independence would intensify their economic problems, which were steadily becoming more acute as the result of a rapid population growth. The economy of the island was dominated by big landowning corporations, mostly controlled by American investors, which produced sugar and tropical fruits and paid meager wages to their Puerto Rican employees. During the 1940's and early 1950's hundreds of thousands of impoverished islanders migrated to the United States, mostly to New York, where they found homes in congested slum areas. Bad as such conditions were, however, Puerto Rican laborers fared better in the United States than in their homeland.

A new era in Puerto Rico began with the emergence of Luis Muñoz Marín as leader of a new political party, the *Partido Popular*, which controlled the legislature from 1940 on. Muñoz Marín's inspiring but realistic leadership, his complete dedication to democratic ideals, and his friendly attitude toward the United States did much to convince Americans that the Puerto Ricans were ready for self-government. In 1947

Puerto Rico was given the right to elect its own governor, and in the following year Muñoz Marín was so elected. Puerto Rico was then invited to decide by popular vote among statehood, commonwealth status, and complete independence. In 1951 the islanders made their choice for commonwealth status, and a new constitution was drafted and put into effect in 1952. Only a small group of fanatical nationalists headed by Albizu Campos continued to demand independence. Members of this group were responsible for an attempt to assassinate President Truman in 1950 and for the wounding of five congressmen in a shooting affray in the House of Representatives in 1954.

Under Muñoz Marín's leadership Puerto Rico also embarked on a long-range program of industrial development, known as Operation Bootstrap. Investment of American capital was invited on easy terms, but with adequate protection against exploitation of native labor. Living standards, though still abysmally low by contrast with the United States, were soon showing a remarkable improvement. The whole Muñoz Marín program was a significant illustration of how much could be achieved by a backward country working with rather than against the American government and American capital. Puerto Rico was beginning to perform a most useful function as intermediary between the United States and Latin America.

RUSSIA AND THE UNITED STATES IN THE FAR EAST, 1945–1952

When Truman succeeded to the Presidency in April, 1945, the United States was at war with Japan, the government of Chiang Kai-shek occupied the Chinese mainland, and the Soviet Union had already committed itself to joining them in destroying the last vestiges of Nipponese imperialism in the Far East. Less than eight years later, when Truman left the White House in January, 1953, Japan was allied to the United States, Russia was America's principal rival in the Far East, Chinese Communists had taken over all of China and forced Chiang Kai-shek to move his government to the island of Formosa, and a quarter of a million American soldiers and marines were fighting a war in Korea under the flag of the United Nations. Of all these events, none so disturbed the American people or had more important consequences upon their domestic affairs than the so-called fall of China.

Failure in China

Chiang Kai-shek's China came out of the war with its prestige greatly enhanced, and largely because of the United States, was accorded—officially, at least—recognition as a major world power with a permanent seat on the Security Council. To assist China's rehabilitation, the United States loaned Chiang money, provided him with substantial material aid, and intervened on his behalf in promoting the Sino-Soviet treaty of August, 1945. But not America's optimistic hopes nor diplomatic recognition as a world power nor economic assistance could make Chiang's regime what it was not—a unified, effective, representative, and responsible government—just as together these could not transform China into a great power. Chiang's internal policies soon caused him to lose the respect and allegiance of his people, who were suffering unbelievable hardships and experiencing profound social and economic changes. Instead of assisting them by effecting some of the desperately needed political, economic, and social reforms his American advisers had repeatedly urged upon him, Chiang and the corrupt and reactionary officials in the Nationalist (Kuomintang) government ignored both the advice of their American friends and the many great needs of their people.

China's numerous and complex economic troubles, which were reflected in widespread political disorder and in a severe inflation which ravaged the country, were complicated further by the bitter animosity that still existed between Chiang and the Chinese Communists. The latter had used the war against Japan to extend their authority, and by introducing some moderate reforms wherever they assumed power, they had won the confidence and support of the peasantry, the petty merchant class, and many of the intelligentsia. After the war, despite the Yalta agreements and the subsequent Sino-Soviet treaty of friendship, Russia delayed its evacuation of Manchuria, removed whatever capital equipment it could, claiming it as war booty, and permitted the Chinese Communists to entrench themselves in the region and take over whatever captured Japanese military equipment they found.

Aware of the increasing influence of the Chinese Communists and the weaknesses of Chiang's regime, American policy sought to strengthen the Kuomintang by encouraging it to accept reform and by urging Chiang to agree to the formation of a coalition government with Communist representation. What the United States feared most was a resumption of the civil war between the Nationalists and the Communists, which, according to the many reports of military clashes and local outbreaks, appeared to be imminent. To prevent these incidents from degenerating into an all-out test of strength, which the United States did not believe Chiang could win and which, even worse, might lead to Russian and American intervention, President Truman sent General George C. Marshall to China on December 15, 1945.

Marshall's instructions were "to persuade the Chinese Government to call a national conference of representatives of the major political elements to bring about the unification of China and, concurrently, to effect a cessation of hostilities. . . ." Marshall was also instructed to inform Chiang that as soon as "peace and unity" had been secured, the United States government was "prepared to assist the National [Chinese] Government in every reasonable way to rehabilitate the country, improve the agrarian and industrial economy and establish a military organization capable of discharging Chinese national and international responsibilities for the maintenance of peace and order." At first it appeared as if Marshall might succeed, and on January 10, 1946, a cease-fire agreement was signed, but the high hopes with which this news was received in Washington were quickly shattered. In mid-April the Communists violated the order, and the next month the Nationalists did likewise. With the exception of an occasional, short-lived, and reluctantly agreed upon truce, neither side showed any real interest in compromising differences, and early in January, 1947, Marshall was back in the United States, blaming the "dominant reactionary group" in the Kuomintang and the "irreconcilable Communists" for the failure of his mission.

Three weeks after Marshall's return to the United States, the Truman administration declared it was abandoning its attempt to mediate the Chinese civil war. And though the United States continued to supply the Nationalists with military assistance for nearly another three years, it was already recognized, as the State Department revealed later, that Chiang's forces and American arms alone could not defeat the Communists, and that "to underwrite permanently the success of the Chinese government's military operations," the United States would have to intervene directly with troops. Neither the American people nor the Truman administration was prepared to go this far. The American public was in no mood to mobilize for another war; the administration, faced by the growing Greco-Turkish crisis and the economic deterioration of Western Europe, was forced to choose between allowing the Soviet

Union to take over Europe and the Mediterranean or permitting the Chinese Communists to overwhelm Chiang. Since the United States lacked the strength to rescue both continents simultaneously, Truman, like Roosevelt in 1941, decided that the nation's interests and the greater likelihood of ultimate success for its efforts dictated that priority be given to the rehabilitation of Europe and the containment of Soviet power at the iron curtain. This decision, which later was to incite a bitter storm of controversy in the United States, sealed Chiang's fate.

During 1947 and 1948 the Communists made steady gains, and by February, 1949, they had secured control over all of Manchuria. From there, with the covert assistance of the Soviet Union, the large-scale capture of American arms and supplies, and the widespread desertion of Nationalist troops, the Communists moved south, inflicting one defeat after another upon Chiang's decimated forces, until they had taken over all of China. On August 6, 1949, the State Department stopped military shipments to the Nationalists, since, as Truman noted later, "many of . . . [Chiang's] generals took their armies, equipped through our aid, into the enemy camp." Six weeks later, on September 21, Mao Tse-tung, the leader of the Communist forces, proclaimed the founding of the People's Republic of China; the next month a Communist government was organized at Peiping, to which the Soviet Union accorded diplomatic recognition; and finally, on December 7, 1949, eight years to the day after the Pearl Harbor attack—for which the question of Nationalist China's independence and territorial integrity bore a considerable responsibility—Chiang Kai-shek fled to Formosa. The American people were now faced with the grim reality that 450 million Chinese, whom they had always held to be their friends, had become their potential enemies. Recognizing Chiang's defeat for what it was, the British quickly granted Communist China diplomatic recognition.

However, partly because many Americans looked upon the Nationalist government, despite all its faults, as representing the "good" China of former years and partly because Chiang became the symbol of anti-communism in Asia, the United States was unable to follow suit, even though the highly capable diplomatist Dean G. Acheson, who succeeded the ailing Marshall as Secretary of State on January 21, 1949, warned the nation of the danger of associating itself with a regime which had become repugnant to its own people. If America followed the misguided advice of Chiang's supporters, Acheson declared, it would "mobilize the whole of Asia's millions solidly against the United States and destroy the pos-

368 THE U.S. & THE POSTWAR WORLD, 1945–1961

sibility in our time of a friendly power, and friendly peoples, in Asia." Acheson expressed his realistic approach to the question of the diplomatic recognition of Red China in September, 1949: "We maintain diplomatic relations with other countries primarily because we are all on the same planet and must do business with each other. We do not establish an Embassy in a foreign country to show approval of its Government." Unfortunately, emotion rather than reason appeared to be determining the issue, and American recognition was withheld.

Chiang's defeat precipitated a long and unusually acrimonious controversy in the United States which affected every aspect of government policy and seriously divided the American people. On August 6, 1949, the State Department published its official explanation of the disaster in China in a white paper,[11] attributing Chiang's defeat to the internal economic and political weaknesses of China, the inefficiency and corruption of the Nationalist government, the superior strength and leadership of the Communists, and the despair and disillusionment of the people. The conclusion was that "the ominous result of the Civil War in China was beyond the control of the government of the United States." These views were confirmed by General Albert C. Wedemeyer, who had undertaken a special mission to China for Truman in July, 1947. On his return he had advised the President that the National government required "drastic, far-reaching political and economic reforms." Later testifying before a joint meeting of the Senate Foreign Relations and Armed Services committees, Wedemeyer declared, "The [Chinese] people were tired of war. All they wanted . . . was food, shelter, and peace. And the Communists exploited these basic, fundamental desires of the people; and they exploited the corruption and the maladministration that were present, to such a degree that Chiang Kai-shek . . . was repudiated as a leader. The troops were dispirited and they didn't fight." General Omar N. Bradley, at the time the chairman of the Joint Chiefs of Staff, defended the administration's decision to avoid committing itself further in China and to devote its energies to stemming the Soviet advance in Europe by saying that while the United States could effectively supply Europe with aid, it could not do so in the case of China.

A large number of Americans, however, refused to accept these official explanations, even though they were to prove entirely correct. Because the debacle was so great and because the bipartisan foreign policy did

[11] U. S. Department of State, *United States Relations with China with Special Reference to the Period 1944–1949* (Washington, D.C., 1949).

One of the principal architects of American foreign policy after World War II, Secretary of State Dean Acheson is shown here testifying before a congressional committee. (Brown Brothers)

not apply to China, Truman's opponents in and out of Congress attacked the administration without restraint. Many of the most influential Republican leaders, moreover, were "Asia Firsters" who, like California's Senator William F. Knowland and New Hampshire's Senator Henry Styles Bridges, believed in all-out aid to China, even if it required cutting down on or (as some of them would have wished) entirely eliminating America's commitments in Europe. Others, like former President Herbert Hoover, believed in turning the Western Hemisphere into a "fortress America" guarded by a powerful navy and air force. Never having rid themselves entirely of their prewar isolationism, many of the Asia Firsters, ultranationalists, and other self-proclaimed friends and supporters of the Kuomintang labeled the State Department's white paper a whitewash and blamed Chiang's defeat upon Truman, Dean Acheson, and the State Department's Far East experts, some of whom Senator Taft accused of entertaining a pro-Communist policy. These critics asserted that China could have been "saved" if the administration had given Chiang adequate assistance, minimizing the fact that the United States had already provided the Nationalists with some $2 billion in aid since 1945. They also censured Truman for adopting one policy for Europe and another for Asia.

370   THE U.S. & THE POSTWAR WORLD, 1945–196:

In the midst of this rapidly developing verbal battle and just two days after Mao Tse-tung announced the formation of the People's Republic, Truman declared (September 23, 1949) that the United States possessed "evidence that within recent weeks an atomic explosion occurred in the U.S.S.R." Two days later the Soviet Union confirmed Truman's statement, adding that it had possessed an atomic bomb since 1947. This frightening announcement, which stripped away the sense of security the United States had enjoyed from its monopoly of atomic weapons, along with the growing disclosures of Soviet espionage in the United States was immediately injected into the China debate, igniting it with a new intensity. Did China actually fall, or had it been intentionally betrayed? Were the administration's errors in China the result of misguided New Deal liberals and Russian sympathizers, or were they the consequences of Communist agents in the State Department and spies in other "high places"? Such possibilities were suggested with increasing frequency.

The Korean War, 1950–1953

While the American people were debating the responsibility for Chiang's defeat and while Washington was appraising the effect of Mac's victory upon the United States's position in the Far East and revising its over-all Asian policies, America and the United Nations were precipitated into a war to defend the Republic of Korea. This ill-fated country, which Japan had annexed in 1910, had been promised its freedom and independence in November, 1943, when Churchill, Roosevelt, and Chiang conferred at Cairo. Two years later, at Potsdam, the "big three" agreed that the Soviet Union and the United States were to occupy the country and that the thirty-eighth parallel was to be the dividing line, with Russia to the north of it and America to the south. As in the case of Germany, the victors failed to agree upon a mutually satisfactory government for a unified and independent Korea, and on September 17, 1947, the United Nations was asked to resolve the dispute. It recommended holding a general election and established a temporary commission to supervise the voting. The Soviet Union, however, refused to allow the commission into its zone, and the United Nations instructed the United States to prepare for an election in its sector, which was held under the commission's supervision on May 10, 1948. Two months later, the long-time nationalist and conservative leader Dr. Syngman Rhee was elected president; on August 15, 1948, the Republic of Korea was established at

Seoul; and the United States started to withdraw its occupation troops, the last of whom, except for a small token police force, left by the end of June, 1949.

In the meantime the Soviet Union was also sponsoring a government for Korea, and on September 9, 1948, the People's Democratic Republic was proclaimed at Pyongyang. Like the Americans, the Russians quickly evacuated their zone, and Korea was left with two hostile governments, each claiming sovereignty over all of this rugged, mountainous peninsula. From the beginning, the two regimes found it impossible to coexist peacefully. Border clashes along the thirty-eighth parallel became a common occurrence and threatened to spread into an all-out civil war. For nearly two years the Korean situation remained alarmingly tense. Then, on June 25, 1950, the Russian-trained troops of the People's Democratic Republic, equipped with Soviet-made armor, aircraft, and arms of all kinds, invaded South Korea.

Since December, 1948, the United States had been supplying the Seoul government with Marshall Plan aid through the Economic Cooperation Administration. But despite Washington's knowledge of the growing military power of the North Korean Communists and Rhee's repeated demands for armaments, the United States declined to build up South Korea's defenses or guarantee its security against an armed attack. South Korea, Secretary Acheson declared in January, 1950, did not fall within the defensive perimeter of the United States, which he asserted extended from the Aleutians to Japan and included the Ryukyus and the Philippine Republic, whose independence had been proclaimed on July 4, 1946. This significant policy statement was consistent with the administration's reappraisal of its Far Eastern interests and responsibilities as expressed in Truman's statement earlier in the month that the United States would not "pursue a course which will lead to involvement in the civil conflict in China" or "provide military aid or advice to Chinese forces on Formosa." The safety and freedom of South Korea, Formosa, and the other Asiatic countries outside America's defensive perimeter, Acheson stated, must rest "on the people attacked . . . and . . . upon the commitments of the entire civilized world under the Charter of the United Nations. . . ."

The North Korean invasion, Truman decided, called for quick United Nations action, and an emergency session of the Security Council was called at once. Since the Russians were then boycotting the United Nations because of its refusal to admit Red China, there was no veto to

372 THE U.S. & THE POSTWAR WORLD, 1945–1961

prevent the council's ordering the North Korean government to cease all hostilities and to withdraw its troops to the thirty-eighth parallel. In the meantime, Truman took a series of decisive steps of his own: he called General MacArthur in Tokyo and asked him to "evacuate the Americans from Korea" and to provide "ammunition and supplies to the Korean army by airdrop and otherwise"; and he ordered the United States Seventh Fleet from Cavite in the Philippines to the Formosa Strait, where it was to "repel any attack on Formosa and . . . [prevent] attacks from Formosa on the mainland." The latter decision, enlarging Acheson's earlier definition of America's defensive perimeter, was to have consequences far beyond those involved in the Korean conflict.

Truman never believed that the North Koreans would observe the United Nations resolution, and in order to be prepared to assist the Rhee government if asked to do so by the Security Council, he alerted all the services, ordered the defenses of the Philippines and French Indochina strengthened, and asked MacArthur to dispatch a survey party to look over the Korean situation. After returning from his inspection trip, MacArthur informed Washington "that a complete collapse is imminent" and that "only American ground units could stop the North Korean advance." On June 27, the Security Council voted 7 to 1 for a resolution asking "that the Members of the United Nations furnish such assistance to the Republic of Korea as may be necessary to repel the armed attack and to restore international peace and security in the area." [12] Within hours of the adoption of the resolution, Truman ordered American "air and sea forces to give the Korean government troops cover and support"; three days later United States ground forces were committed; and on July 8, at the request of the Security Council, Truman appointed General MacArthur to command the United Nations forces, to which forty-two nations ultimately contributed their support. As was to be expected, the United States assumed the largest burden, both militarily and financially. "The prompt action of the United Nations to put down lawless aggression and the prompt response to this action by free peoples all over the world," Truman told the American people, "will stand as a landmark in mankind's long search for a rule of law among nations." An equally significant "landmark," however, was the fact that the American people strongly supported Truman's decision. Senators Vandenberg and Taft,

[12] Yugoslavia cast the opposing vote; the other two members of the Security Council, India and Egypt, remained silent.

both critical of the administration's Far East policies, applauded the President's decision, the former calling it "courageous and indispensable."

The strength of the North Korean offensive forced Rhee's ill-equipped and poorly trained troops into a general retreat, which quickly belied Truman's first estimate that the conflict was a "police action" against a "bunch of bandits." For two and a half months, from June 25 to September 15, ten North Korean divisions, one of them armored, pushed steadily south, capturing Seoul three days after the initial attack. The first American reinforcements sent to Korea were neither trained nor equipped for combat, and though superior to the almost totally unprepared South Koreans, they proved incapable of stopping the invader's seasoned fighters. By August the North Koreans had occupied nearly all of the peninsula except for a 140-mile perimeter around Pusan, the chief port city in the south and MacArthur's principal supply base. Repeated North Korean attacks failed to break through the Pusan defenses of the U. S. Eighth Army under the field command of General Walton H. Walker. While the Americans fought stubbornly to hold on to the Pusan perimeter and British and American seapower brought in reinforcements and blockaded the Korean coast, General MacArthur, in a frighteningly daring and brilliantly executed amphibious operation, landed a division of Marines at Inchon, on the other side of the Korean peninsula, on September 15. Taken by complete surprise and hit by naval gunfire and air attack, the North Koreans offered almost no resistance and quickly withdrew. The next day General Walker's Eighth Army opened an offensive of its own. Two weeks later MacArthur and Rhee were back in Seoul, and by October 1 all of South Korea had been retaken, the surviving invaders having fled beyond the thirty-eighth parallel.

In the meantime, the Joint Chiefs of Staff had decided that MacArthur's next assignment should be the "destruction of the North Korean armed forces" beyond the thirty-eighth parallel. MacArthur was warned, however, that these instructions, which he received on September 27, applied only if the North Koreans were fighting alone. They did not apply if the North Koreans were being assisted by Soviet or Chinese Communist troops. On October 7 the General Assembly of the United Nations approved a resolution calling for the adoption of "all appropriate steps . . . to insure conditions of stability throughout Korea." The American decision and the United Nations resolution were criticized by many, both in the United States and abroad, as a dangerous move which

374   THE U.S. & THE POSTWAR WORLD, 1945–1961

might incite Red China to war. The fears of these people were strengthened a few days later when Chou En-lai, Peiping's foreign minister, announced that his countrymen would not "supinely tolerate seeing their neighbors being savagely invaded by imperialists." The success of the United Nations offensive in North Korea and MacArthur's firm conviction that there was little likelihood that the Red Chinese would intervene reassured the President, and he returned from his October 14 Wake Island conference with MacArthur persuaded "that the victory was won in Korea" and that "all resistance would end . . . by Thanksgiving." Less than two weeks later, on October 26, Chinese Communist troops from Manchuria crossed the Yalu River into North Korea. On November 25 they launched a powerful and relentless offensive which drove MacArthur's forces below the thirty-eighth parallel and resulted in the recapture of Seoul on January 4, 1951. From there the Eighth Army, now commanded by General Matthew B. Ridgway, regrouped its forces and prepared to recapture the ground it had lost below the thirty-eighth parallel and then to fight a war in which the major objective was not in pushing ahead but, as Ridgway defined it, "only in inflicting maximum casualties to the enemy with minimum casualties to ourselves."

THE TRUMAN-MAC ARTHUR CONTROVERSY

MacArthur attributed the success of the Chinese offensive and the failure of the one he had launched on November 24, which at the time he claimed would end the war by Christmas, to the "extraordinary inhibitions" Washington had placed on him. The administration's and the United Nations' refusal to permit him to bomb "the privileged sanctuary of Manchuria," blockade China, employ Nationalist Chinese troops in Korea, and allow Chiang to raid the China coast were the reasons for his setback. During the early months of 1950, the divergent opinions of MacArthur and his superiors in Washington on the strategy and objectives of the Korean War grew more and more pronounced. MacArthur, like many of his Republican supporters and "Asia First" friends, believed that the Korean conflict had become "an entirely new war" and that it was necessary to strike at Communist China, even though the latter had been an ally of the Soviet Union since the Sino-Soviet treaty of February, 1950. The administration, on the other hand, while as opposed to the expansion of Communist influence in Asia as MacArthur, was also concerned with containing Soviet power in Europe and elsewhere, supporting United Nations collective security policies, and preventing World

THE TRUMAN POLICIES, 1947–1952

War III, especially since the United States was now vulnerable to a Russian atomic attack. Truman and his military chiefs as well as America's allies rejected MacArthur's suggestions, and on January 13, 1951, the President sent MacArthur a personal message explaining carefully the position of the United States. "Our course of action at this time," Truman said, "should be such as to consolidate the great majority of the United Nations. This majority is not merely part of the organization but is also the nations whom we would desperately need to count on as allies in the event the Soviet Union moves against us."

MacArthur never accepted the administration's policy and on several occasions criticized it publicly, even after Truman had ordered all government officials, both civilian and military, "to exercise extreme caution in public statements, to clear all but routine statements with their departments, and to refrain from direct communication on military or foreign policy with newspapers, magazines, or other publicity media in the United States." MacArthur refused to be bound by this presidential order, and on March 20, 1951, replying to a letter from Joseph W. Martin, Jr., the Massachusetts representative and GOP minority leader, he set forth his views on "Red China's entry into the war against us in Korea." MacArthur declared that he believed in "meeting force with maximum counterforce" and agreed fully with Martin's expressed views on the desirability of using Chiang's troops on Formosa to open "a second Asiatic front to relieve the pressure on our forces in Korea," and he concluded his letter with a blast against the administration: "It seems strangely difficult for some to realize that here in Asia is where the Communist conspirators have elected to make their play for global conquest, and that we have joined the issue thus raised on the battlefield; that here we fight Europe's war with arms while the diplomats there still fight it with words; that if we lose the war to Communism in Asia the fall of Europe is inevitable, win it and Europe most probably would avoid war and yet preserve freedom. . . . There is no substitute for victory."

Three days later, even before Martin read the General's letter to the House, MacArthur, without conferring with Washington, issued another unauthorized statement, declaring that despite "the inhibitions which now restrict the activity of the United Nations forces . . . [Red China] has . . . shown its complete inability to accomplish by force of arms the conquest of Korea. The . . . enemy must by now be painfully aware that a decision of the United Nations to depart from its tolerant effort to contain the war to the area of Korea, through an expansion of our military operations to its coastal areas and interior bases, would doom Red China to the risk of imminent military collapse." He then went on to say that he stood "ready at any time to confer in the field with the commander-in-chief of the enemy forces in the earnest effort to find any military means whereby realization of the political objectives of the United Nations in Korea . . . might be accomplished without further bloodshed." In view of the administration's declared policies, this was a shocking statement, and it petrified America's allies. The State Department was deluged with anxious queries about America's intentions in Korea. Truman, of course, interpreted MacArthur's statement as "a challenge to the authority of the President under the Constitution," and as he wrote later, "MacArthur left me no choice—I could no longer tolerate his insubordination." The Joint Chiefs of Staff immediately cabled MacArthur, reminding him of the President's orders on policy statements and informing him "that in the event Communist military leaders request an armistice in the field," he was to confer at once with Washington. On April 5, Congressman Martin read MacArthur's letter to the House; six days later, after discussing the General's recent unauthorized declarations with his top advisers, Truman relieved MacArthur of his commands and replaced him with Ridgway. "If I allowed him to defy the civil authorities," Truman noted later, "I myself would be violating my oath to uphold and defend the Constitution."

The news of MacArthur's dismissal, which the White House had to release to the press before the General was informed because of a leak, caused a storm of controversy, and as was to be anticipated, Martin and other GOP leaders immediately arranged to have the famous soldier address the Congress. Returning to the United States for the first time in sixteen years, MacArthur was cheered and given a hero's welcome. On April 19 he appeared before a joint session of Congress and delivered a strongly emotional defense of his actions which some 60 million Americans viewed on television. The Truman-MacArthur controversy raged on into May and June as the Senate Armed Forces and Foreign Relations committees held combined hearings on MacArthur's recall and the administration's Korean and Far East policies. The nation's top military and civilian leaders were called to testify and, to the wonderment of America's friends and the gratification of its enemies, to divulge, as Truman stated, "every detail of our strategic planning."

The hearings revealed that while MacArthur and his supporters were willing to risk a global conflagration in order to defeat Red China decisively, even if it meant losing the support of America's allies, the administration believed the national interest could be served best through collective security, containment, and limitation of the fighting in Korea to the objectives defined by the United Nations. MacArthur's plan, General Bradley declared, "would involve us in the wrong war, at the wrong place, at the wrong time, and with the wrong enemy." Secretary Acheson, with his customary incisiveness and clarity of thought, asserted that MacArthur's proposal called for the United States "to undertake a large risk of general war with China, risk of war with the Soviet Union, and a demonstrable weakening of our collective-security system" in return "for measures whose effectiveness in bringing the conflict to an early conclusion are judged doubtful by our responsible military authorities." While the hearings produced no fundamental alterations either in over-all American policy or in Korean strategy, they documented fully the GOP's distrust and lack of confidence in the Truman-Acheson conduct of United States diplomacy in Asia. Moreover, as *The New York Times*'s military analyst Hanson W. Baldwin was to write later, the MacArthur affair underscored the administration's failure to define its objectives precisely, to adhere to them consistently, and, most important of all, to explain them fully to the American people.

By the time the MacArthur hearings came to an end on June 27 and the two Senate committees declared American policy had not changed, General Ridgway had finished evicting the Chinese Communists from South Korea. On July 10, 1951, both sides agreed to begin negotiating a truce; and for the next two years, as the fighting continued, the truce talks dragged on, the delegates arguing such questions as the location of the armistice line and the exchange of prisoners. Finally, on June 26, 1953, an armistice was agreed upon and the war came to an end. Korea was divided once again into two parts, with the Seoul government receiving some 1,500 square miles of additional territory; a two-and-a-half-mile demilitarized zone was created along the truce line separating the North and South Korean regimes; the opposing sides agreed to restrict their armaments; a Neutral Nations Supervisory Commission was established to safeguard the peace; and the difficult issue of repatriating prisoners, which had already defeated the negotiators once, was turned over to a Neutral Nations Reparations Commission.

The armistice was entirely unsatisfactory to Rhee, who hoped to see a united Korea emerge from the three-year struggle. At one point in the negotiations he endangered the armistice talks by proclaiming his

378 THE U.S. & THE POSTWAR WORLD, 1945-1961

intention to carry on the fight, alone if necessary. But the United States persuaded him to cooperate by promises of economic relief and rehabilitation assistance, which were met in August, 1953, when Congress appropriated $200 million for Korean aid. The administration also guaranteed South Korea's security, a promise the Senate made good on January 19, 1954, when it ratified the Korean Mutual Defense Treaty. As in the case of Germany, the armistice agreements were to be followed by a peace treaty, but Red China's charges that the United States had employed germ warfare, which Washington vehemently denied, the American countercharge that the Communists slaughtered some 35,000 United Nations prisoners and Korean civilians, for which the world organization condemned the Peiping government, and the numerous other accusations the two sides leveled at each other doomed every attempt to write a permanent peace pact.

KOREA AND THE HOME FRONT

Even though the administration looked upon the Korean War as a limited one, its effect upon the American economy was pronounced. Taxes were increased and the rearmament program was greatly accelerated. Airplane production between 1950 and 1953 jumped from 150 to 1,000 a month, and the government once again started ordering large numbers of tanks, forcing industry to resume their production at nearly 1,000 per month. Appropriations for the armed forces were greatly increased, from $14.8 billion in 1950 to $56.9 billion in 1952, of which some $22 billion went to finance the Korean War. To curb inflation and assure the defense industries the materials they required, on September 8, 1950, Congress passed the Defense Production Act, giving Truman extensive authority "to provide for effective price and wage stabilization . . . and to maintain uninterrupted production"; on December 15 the government's powers to meet the crisis were increased further by the President's proclamation of a national emergency; and in January, 1951, Truman appointed Charles E. Wilson, former president of the General Electric Corporation, to the post of Director of Defense Mobilization. Selective service calls were stepped up, and the armed forces increased from 1.5 to 3.6 million members, doubling the number of army divisions and increasing the strength of the marines from 74,000 to 232,000 men. By the time the armistice was signed, 250,000 Americans had fought in Korea, of whom some 23,000 lost their lives and 103,000 or more were wounded.

The impact of the Korean War defense program on the domestic economy brought a renewed fight over wage and price controls. As prices again started to soar, reaching a new high by July, 1953, labor demanded more effective controls and wage adjustments. Neither the people nor the Congress was disposed to reestablish effective wartime controls, and though some effort was made to tighten price and rent controls in the Defense Production Act of 1951, the results were far from satisfactory. As a result, labor continued to demand increases to compensate for the price rises. When these were not forthcoming, the workers struck. During all the years of the Korean War but especially in 1952, the country faced a rash of strikes. Most of these, however, were quickly settled and thus caused only slight production delays. The greatest threat to the defense program came in March, 1952, when the country's steel companies rejected the Wage Stabilization Board's recommendations for a 15-cent wage increase and recognition of the union shop. On April 3, 1952, Philip Murray, the president of the United Steel Workers of America, issued a strike call. Several hours before it was to go into effect, Truman seized the mills. That evening—April 8—the President explained the necessity for this drastic action to the country, blaming the companies for failing to accept the WSB's proposals, which he termed "fair to both parties and the public interest." Three weeks later, on April 29, Judge David A. Pine of the United States District Court declared the President's action illegal, denying the validity of the government's contention that the President acted on the basis of his inherent constitutional powers. On June 2, 1952, the Supreme Court, in *Youngstown Sheet and Tube Company v. Charles Sawyer*, upheld Judge Pine's decision by a 6 to 3 vote, though it "did not," as constitutional law expert C. Herman Pritchett wrote, "deny the constitutionality of the President's general power to meet emergencies by the exercise of inherent or residual powers." When the government ceased operating the mills, the workers struck; and after nearly two months of negotiations a new contract, granting most of the workers' original demands, was signed.

The Korean War alerted the American people to the need for continuous vigilance against Soviet and Communist threats, and it impressed upon them the price of their responsiblities as the principal guardians of the free world's security. As Adlai Stevenson, the Democratic party's presidential nominee in 1952 and 1956, asserted, "patience is the price of world power," and the American people "will have to learn to live with . . . [Korea] even as the British learned to live with the 'Northwest

380 THE U.S. & THE POSTWAR WORLD, 1945–1961

Frontier.'" One of the immediate effects of the Korean War upon American policy was to force Washington to strengthen its defenses, including those of NATO, and to reappraise its position and strategy in the Far East.

Japan

Like the collapse of Nationalist China, the Korean crisis greatly increased the importance of Japan in strengthening the American policy of containing the Soviet threat in Asia. The Moscow Foreign Ministers' Conference of December, 1945, had established an eleven-power Far Eastern Commission in Washington, representing the Pacific nations which had been at war with Japan, and a four-power Allied Control Council in Tokyo, in which the United States, France, the Soviet Union, and Britain (including the three commonwealths of Australia, New Zealand, and India) were represented. Neither of these international bodies, however, exercised much direct authority over the occupation, and the reforming and rehabilitation of Japan was left almost entirely to the discretion of Washington and MacArthur. Under American supervision, Japan was stripped of its ability to make war; its cartel-like industrial complex was considerably decentralized by introducing various American-style antitrust programs; trade unionism was promoted; large agricultural holdings were divided; the influence of the military over the country's political institutions was substantially reduced, if not entirely eliminated; the educational system was revamped; and a vigorous program was sponsored to promote democracy and to guarantee the Japanese people their civil liberties. In 1947, a new American-sponsored constitution, reflecting more the liberal heritage of the West than that of the people for whom it was written, went into effect. The emperor retained his position as head of state, but his functions were limited almost entirely to the ceremonial activities of his office. A parliamentary government similar to Britain's was established, though modified sufficiently to allow for a Supreme Court with the power of judicial review. The kind of government America intended for Japan was clearly stated in the constitution's preamble, which declared that "Government is a sacred trust of the people, the authority for which is derived from the people, the powers of which are exercised by the representatives of the people, and the benefits of which are enjoyed by the people."

The wisdom and effectiveness of the comprehensive reforms of the early postwar era were subjects of considerable debate, and while most observers agreed to their apparent success in liberating long-suppressed elements in Japan's society and in winning the goodwill of most of the Japanese people, their long-term effect was less clear. By 1947, however, as Soviet-American relations became increasingly strained, as international communism threatened to exploit the nationalistic ambitions and economic aspirations of the colonial and underdeveloped countries of Southeast Asia, and as the Kremlin sought to extend its power in the Far East, the United States became less concerned with reforming Japan and more determined to expedite its economic and political recovery. The Sino-Soviet Alliance of 1945 and Red China's intervention in Korea served to emphasize still further the need to reestablish Japan as a significant and friendly force in the Far East power equilibrium.

As early as March, 1947, MacArthur had called for a Japanese peace treaty, and in July the United States announced its intention to call an eleven-nation Far East conference to begin working on the document. Soviet intransigence on procedural questions, notably its insistence that the "big four" (Russia, Britain, China, and the United States) assume the principal role of peacemakers and that each have the right to veto all decisions, frustrated these and subsequent negotiations. In 1950, Truman authorized John Foster Dulles, an experienced international lawyer and a long-time foreign policy adviser to the Republican party, to begin negotiating a Japanese peace treaty with America's other Pacific allies. After a year of hard work and some 125,000 miles of travel, Dulles succeeded in securing the support of these nations for a treaty drafted by the State Department. At San Francisco on September 8, 1951, a "peace of reconciliation" was signed by Japan and forty-eight other nations. India, Burma, and Yugoslavia refused to attend the conference; neither the Nationalist nor the Communist Chinese were invited; and Russia, Poland, and Czechoslovakia, though present at the ceremonies, declined to sign the pact.

The terms of the treaty were unusually generous. Japan was deprived of Korea, the Pescadores, southern Sakhalin, the Kurils, and the other Pacific islands it held as mandates of the League of Nations. The Bonin, Ryukyu, and certain other island groups were to be designated as United Nations trusteeships, "with the United States as the sole administering authority." While the treaty "recognized that Japan should pay reparations," it left the problem for future negotiation. Japan's "resources," the treaty declared, were not "presently sufficient" to permit it "to make

382 THE U.S. & THE POSTWAR WORLD, 1945–1961

complete reparation for all such damage and suffering and at the same time meet its other obligations." The treaty also recognized Japan's right to "individual or collective self-defense," a fact which greatly disturbed Australia, New Zealand, and the Philippine Republic. Recalling the threat of Japanese militarism in the early 1940's, none of these states was disposed to grant Japan legal sanction to rearm. American defense policy in the Far East, however, required Japan's rehabilitation, including the ability to defend itself. To allay the fears of its wartime allies and to secure their approval of the treaty, which many of them regarded as "soft" and excessively liberal, the United States signed a mutual assistance treaty with the Philippines on August 30 and two days later, on September 1, a Tripartite Security Treaty with Australia and New Zealand. The former supplemented the Philippine Military Assistance Act of June 30, 1946; [13] the latter established ANZUS, the Pacific Council, to discuss mutual defense problems and to plan coordinated security measures.

A few hours after the close of the San Francisco Conference, the United States and Japan signed a bilateral security treaty in which the latter agreed to permit American bases and troops on its home islands so long as the two powers deemed them necessary to safeguard the peace and security of the Far East. The treaty also provided that the Japanese government could call upon the United States to assist it in restoring order in case of "large-scale internal riots and disturbances . . . caused through instigation or intervention by an outside power or powers." With this pact and the other Pacific treaties of 1952, the United States hoped to secure the peace in Asia, defend its interests in that part of the world, contain Soviet expansionism, and check the new threat posed by Red China.

Suggested Readings

Nearly all of the general works cited in the preceding chapter are useful for developments covered in this one. In addition to those, consult Walter Lippmann, *The Cold War* (New York, 1947) and Theodore H. White's perceptive and well-written account, *Fire in the Ashes: Europe in Mid-century*

---

[13] Economic assistance was provided by the Philippine Trade Act of April 30, 1946, which allowed the islands to ship their products to the United States tariff free until 1954, after which duties would be imposed "at the rate of 5 per cent progressively over a span of twenty years." A second measure, the Philippine Rehabilitation Act, also signed on April 30, 1946, provided for various other kinds of economic assistance.

THE TRUMAN POLICIES, 1947–1952   383

(New York, 1953). Blair Bolles, *The Big Change in Europe* (New York, 1958) carries White's story ahead five years, to 1957. John A. Lukacs, *A History of the Cold War* (Garden City, N.Y., 1961) is a brief and able account of the reasons for the development of the United States–Soviet conflict. Hugh Seton-Watson, *Neither War nor Peace: The Struggle for Power in the Postwar World* (New York [1960]) is a major effort to explain the world crisis of the years after 1945 in terms of "expansion of totalitarianism and the growth of anti-European nationalism."

General works on American foreign economic policy include Samuel Lubell, *The Revolution in World Trade and American Economic Policy* (New York [1955]); Clarence B. Randall, *A Foreign Economic Policy for the United States* (Chicago, 1954); and William Y. Elliott, *et al.*, *The Political Economy of American Foreign Policy* (New York, 1956).

Many of the memoirs and diaries cited in the last chapter apply to this one also. In addition, see the three excellent books by Dean Acheson, *A Democrat Looks at His Party* (New York, 1955); *Power and Diplomacy* (Cambridge, Mass., 1958); and *Sketches from Life of Men I Have Known* (New York, 1961). McGeorge Bundy, ed., *The Pattern of Responsibility: From the Record of Secretary of State Dean Acheson* (Boston, 1952) contains Acheson's most important public statements. Norman A. Graebner, "Dean G. Acheson," in Norman A. Graebner, ed., *An Uncertain Tradition*, already cited, is a capable analysis of Acheson as a diplomatist.

On the Truman policy and the Marshall Plan, see the excellent study by Joseph M. Jones, *The Fifteen Weeks (February 21–June 5, 1947)* (New York, 1955). Sidney S. Alexander, *The Marshall Plan* (Washington, D.C., 1948); Harry B. Price, *The Marshall Plan and Its Meaning* (Ithaca, N.Y. [1955]); and the brief collection of excerpts in Robin W. Winks, *The Marshall Plan and the American Economy* (New York [1960]) are all useful.

The NATO treaty and its role in American policy are detailed in Arthur C. Turner, *Bulwark of the West: Implications and Problems of NATO* (Toronto [1953]); but see also Klaus Knorr, ed., *NATO and American Security* (Princeton, N.J., 1959), an excellent analysis of the many problems facing the alliance; Ben T. Moore, *NATO and the Future of Europe* (New York, 1958); Royal Institute of International Affairs, *Atlantic Alliance* (London, 1952); Ronald S. Richie, *NATO, The Economics of an Alliance* (Toronto, 1956); Roy Sherwood, *NATO: A Critical Examination* (London, 1956); and the personal account of Lord Ismay, *NATO: The First Five Years, 1949–1954* (Paris, 1954).

Jonathan Bingham, *Shirt-sleeve Diplomacy* (New York, 1954) tells the story of "Point Four," and Merle Curti and Kendall Birr, *Prelude to Point Four: American Technical Missions Overseas, 1838–1938* (Madison, Wis., 1954) is what its title says.

Two books by Eugene W. Castle, *Billions, Blunders and Baloney* (New York, 1955) and *The Great Giveaway: The Realities of Foreign Aid* (New York, 1957) are strong attacks against the postwar relief and rehabilitation programs.

Germany and the Berlin crisis are covered in Lucius D. Clay, *Decision*

384 THE U.S. & THE POSTWAR WORLD, 1945–1961

in Germany (New York, 1950), the memoirs of the American commander. The personal story of the United States ambassador to the Kremlin at the time is in Walter Bedell Smith, *My Three Years in Moscow*, already cited. W. Phillips Davison, *The Berlin Blockade* (Princeton, N.J., 1958) is a comprehensive analysis. Consult also Russell Hill, *Struggle for Germany* (New York, 1948); Curt Reiss, *The Berlin Story* (New York, 1952); Hans Speier, *Divided Berlin: The Anatomy of Soviet Political Blackmail* (New York, 1961), on the later (1958) Berlin crisis; Drew Middleton, *The Struggle for Germany* (Indianapolis, 1949); John P. Nettl, *The Eastern Zone and Soviet Policy in Germany, 1949–1950* (New York, 1951); and U. S. Department of State, *Germany, 1947–1949: The Story in Documents* (Washington, D.C., 1950).

The Far Eastern policies of the United States are discussed generally in Kenneth S. Latourette, *The American Record in the Far East, 1945–1951*, already cited, and in most of the books on China and the Far East cited in Chapter 7. Francis C. Jones, *et al.*, *The Far East, 1942–1946* (London, 1955) appraises the impact of World War II on the Asian nations. Owen J. Lattimore, *The Situation in Asia* (Boston, 1944) presents the views of a controversial expert.

Besides Herbert Feis's excellent study, *The China Tangle*, already cited, see Tien Fong-cheng, *A History of Sino-Soviet Relations* (Washington, D.C., 1957), a survey covering seven centuries; Chiang Kai-shek, *Soviet Russia in China* (New York, 1957), the generalissimo's memoirs; David J. Dallin, *Soviet Russia and the Far East* (New Haven, Conn., 1948), which details Russia's penetration into Asia; Warner Levi, *Modern China's Foreign Policy* (Minneapolis, 1953), which surveys Chinese foreign policy from the beginning of the twentieth century to the Korean War; Robert C. North, *Moscow and the Chinese Communists* (Stanford, Calif., 1951), a detailed study; Henry Wei, *China and Soviet Russia* (New York, 1956), which analyzes Sino-Soviet diplomacy; and Aitchen K. Wu, *China and the Soviet Union* (New York, 1950).

On Japan, consult Robert J. C. Butow, *Japan's Decision to Surrender* (Stanford, Calif., 1954). Baron Evert J. Van Aduard, *Japan from Surrender to Peace* (New York, 1954) is an especially useful account, as are Russell Brines, *MacArthur's Japan* (Philadelphia, 1948); Robert A. Fearey, *The Occupation of Japan: Second Phase, 1948–1950* (New York, 1950); Frazier Hunt, *The Untold Story of Douglas MacArthur* (New York, 1954); and Edwin M. Martin, *The Allied Occupation of Japan* (Stanford, Calif., 1948).

The diplomacy of the Korean War is ably discussed in the Council of Foreign Relations volume by Leland M. Goodrich, *Korea: A Study of United States Policy in the United Nations* (New York, 1956). See also Robert T. Oliver, *Why War Came to Korea* (New York, 1950), a strong defense of Rhee's position; Rutherford M. Poats, *Decision in Korea* (New York, 1954); and Carl Berger, *The Korean Knot: A Military-Political History* (Philadelphia, 1957). More specialized studies include Robert E. Osgood, *Limited War: The Challenge to American Strategy* (Chicago, 1957). On the same subject, see the article by Hanson W. Baldwin, "Limited War," *The Atlantic Monthly*, CCIII (May 1959), 35–43, and Allen S. Whiting, *China Crosses the Yalu: The Decision to Enter the Korean War* (New York, 1960), a careful study of the reasons leading to Peking's intervention.

Personal records of the Korean War include Maxwell D. Taylor, *The Uncertain Trumpet* (New York [1960]); Matthew B. Ridgway, *Soldier: The Memoirs of Matthew B. Ridgway* (New York, 1956); and Mark Clark, *From the Danube to the Yalu* (New York, 1954). See the same author's article, "You Can't Win if Diplomats Interfere," *U. S. News & World Report*, XXXVII (August 20, 1954), 75–81. In the same vein is the article by Courtney Whitney, "The War MacArthur Was Not Allowed to Win," *Life*, XXXIX (September 5, 1955), 63–81.

The military aspects of the first six months of the Korean War are detailed in Roy E. Appleman, *South to Naktong; North to the Yalu: June–November, 1950* (Washington, D.C., 1961). Robert Frank Futrell, *The United States Air Forces in Korea, 1950–1953* (New York [1961]) is what the title states. David B. Duncan, *This Is War: A Photo Narrative* (New York, 1951) is an annotated picture book on the Korean War.

On Truman's dismissal of MacArthur, see John W. Spanier, *The Truman-MacArthur Controversy* (Cambridge, Mass., 1959) and Trumbull Higgins, *Korea and the Fall of MacArthur* (New York, 1960). Richard H. Rovere and Arthur M. Schlesinger, Jr., *The General and the President* (New York, 1951) defends Truman forcefully; Charles A. Willoughby and John Chamberlain, *MacArthur, 1941–1951* (New York, 1954) presents MacArthur's side with equal force. John Gunther, *The Riddle of MacArthur* (New York, 1951) contains some revealing insights. Courtney Whitney's *MacArthur: His Rendezvous with History* (New York, 1956) is extremely laudatory. John M. Pratt, ed., *Revitalizing a Nation: A Statement of Beliefs, Opinions, and Politics Embodied in the Public Pronouncements of General MacArthur* (Chicago, 1952) is a useful compilation. The official testimony and record of the MacArthur hearings are in U. S. Senate, Joint Senate Committee on Armed Services and Foreign Relations, *The Military Situation in the Far East and the Facts Surrounding the Relief of General MacArthur* (5 vols., Washington, D.C., 1951). The official record of the Truman-MacArthur conference at Wake Island is in U. S. Senate, Joint Senate Committee on Armed Services and Foreign Relations, *Substance of Statements Made at the Wake Island Conference* (Washington, D.C., 1951).

Two important works on the Korean truce negotiations are Charles T. Joy, *How Communists Negotiate* (New Haven, Conn., 1955) and William H. Vatcher, *Panmunjon* (New York, 1958).

On the election of 1948, Karl M. Schmidt, *Henry A. Wallace: Quixotic Crusade, 1948* (Syracuse, N.Y., 1960) covers one aspect. Jack Redding, *Inside the Democratic Party* (Indianapolis [1958]) is the well-told story of the Democratic Party's National Committee publicity director during the campaign. Jules Abels, *Out of the Jaws of Victory* (New York, 1959) is a general

386 THE U.S. & THE POSTWAR WORLD, 1945–1961

account of the famous political upset. The role of one labor group in the congressional election of 1950 is told in Fay Calkins, *The CIO and the Democratic Party* (Chicago, 1952).

In addition to the work cited in Chapter 7 on the Fair Deal, see also *To Secure These Truths: The Report of the President's Committee on Civil Rights* (Washington, D.C., 1947); *The Hoover Commission Report on Organization of the Executive Branch of the Government* (New York, 1949); and Alan F. Westin, *The Anatomy of a Constitutional Law Case* (New York [1958]), which includes summaries of the major documents on the steel seizure case.

9

The Fair Deal Yields to Modern Republicanism

THE TRUMAN ADMINISTRATION's diplomatic success in remaking Japan into an effective bulwark in the free world's security system was a notable and significant achievement. At the time, however, a great many Americans failed or refused to recognize this fact because of the continuing debate on the China policy, the controversy over the strategy of the Korean War, the issues arising out of the MacArthur dismissal, and related questions of Soviet espionage and subversion.

LOYALTY AND INTERNAL SECURITY, 1949–1953

The continuing crises of the postwar era and the growing realization of the serious threat Soviet communism posed to America's interests abroad and to the security of its institutions at home led Truman to order "a sweeping study of the government's loyalty procedures." On November 25, 1946, he established a Temporary Commission on Employee Loyalty, and after four months of careful study the commission issued its recommendations, which Truman embodied in an Executive order on March 22, 1947. Loyalty boards were established in all the Executive departments to hold preliminary investigations of cases involving sus-

388　THE U.S. & THE POSTWAR WORLD, 1945–1961

pected disloyalty. Individuals who disagreed with the findings of these departmental panels could appeal to one of the fourteen regional Civil Service Commission offices, which were authorized to review all such cases. Truman's order also established a special Loyalty Review Board, whose members were appointed by the President and whose decisions were final. With the assistance of the Federal Bureau of Investigation and the Civil Service Commission, the government ultimately checked the loyalty of all employees in the Executive branch of the government, and it searched into the past activities and associations of all new applicants. By May, 1953, the Civil Service Commission, according to its own report, had completed more than 4.7 million loyalty checks, including 26,000 full field investigations, which were carried out by the Federal Bureau of Investigation. As a result of these loyalty probes, the administration dismissed 384 government employees, representing, as Truman stated in a speech to the National Civil Service League, "nine one thousandths of one per cent of all those checked."

In the meantime, the House Un-American Activities Committee, set up permanently in January, 1945, to succeed the earlier committee headed by Martin Dies, was also investigating and collecting information on alleged Communist infiltration and espionage. It uncovered some evidence of Communist sympathizers and propagandists trying to influence unsuspecting Americans. But because of the committee's reckless charges and legally dubious tactics as well as the obvious interest of a few of its members in personal publicity, which often appeared to exceed their zeal for the truth, a large number of Americans expressed skepticism at many of its charges, such as those describing the federal Executive, the trade unions, the schools and colleges, and the entertainment world, particularly Hollywood's movie colony, as being crowded with subversives plotting to overthrow the Constitution and trying to impose a Communist tyranny upon America. The committee's rather low repute, however, was improved considerably, at least in the opinion of some people, by its role in the Hiss case, in which the young California Representative Richard M. Nixon played an active part that brought him national prominence.

The Hiss Case

On July 31, 1948, as a result of the testimony of the former Communist courier Elizabeth Bentley, the committee summoned the repentant one-

FROM FAIR DEAL TO MODERN REPUBLICANISM 389

time Communist Whittaker Chambers to testify. In a prepared statement, which he read to the committee on August 3, Chambers, then a senior editor of *Time* magazine, admitted he had joined the Communist party in 1924, and said he had repudiated it fourteen years later and confessed his error and his knowledge of its activities to the federal government in 1939. During his testimony, Chambers revealed the names of the "seven or so" of the highest officials of the "underground organization of the United States Communist Party" to which he had belonged. One of the names of the top-level cell leaders he divulged was that of Alger Hiss, a Johns Hopkins and Harvard Law School graduate who began his government career in 1929 as a secretary to Supreme Court Justice Oliver Wendell Holmes. After a three-year stint as a private practicing attorney, Hiss returned to Washington in 1933 as a staff lawyer for the Agricultural Adjustment Administration. In 1936 he entered the State Department, rising to the post of deputy director of the Office of Special Political Affairs, in which capacity he accompanied the American delegation to the Casablanca meeting. Subsequently, according to Secretary of State Stettinius, Hiss "performed brilliantly" at the Dumbarton Oaks, Yalta, and San Francisco conferences and at the first United Nations meeting in London. Stettinius' predecessor, Cordell Hull, had been equally impressed by Hiss's abilities, and Senator Vandenberg, James Byrnes, and Dean Acheson also spoke well of him.

Chambers' startling charge came as a great shock to most Americans, and at first many of them were reluctant to believe it, accusing Chambers and the committee of using the testimony of a confessed Communist to ruin the life of a capable and trusted public servant. Hiss, who was now the head of the Carnegie Endowment for International Peace, demanded a hearing, which the committee immediately granted him; and two days after Chambers' accusation Hiss declared under oath that he had "never been a member of the Communist Party or any of its front organizations nor . . . [had I] followed its line. . . . So far as I know, I have never laid eyes on . . . [Chambers]." Hiss's statement inaugurated one of the most sensational government hearings and court trials in American history. For nearly eighteen months, the nation occupied itself with arguing about the integrity of the two men.

During the course of its hearings, the committee brought Hiss and Chambers together for a personal confrontation, and after some hesitation, Hiss admitted having known Chambers earlier under a different name. But Hiss continued to deny that he had ever been a Communist, challenging Chambers with a libel suit if he repeated his charges outside the committee room. Chambers obliged on August 27: appearing on the radio program "Meet the Press," he said, "Alger Hiss was a Communist and may still be one." About a month later, Hiss sued for libel; and during the hearing which followed, Chambers introduced evidence indicating that Hiss had been engaged in espionage and had supplied Chambers with reproductions of secret government documents. These disclosures resulted in Hiss's indictment for perjury by a New York federal grand jury. The trial lasted six weeks; the jury, after deliberating for more than fourteen hours, failed to agree upon a verdict. On November 16, 1949, a second trial was held; and two months later, on January 21, 1950, the jury found Hiss guilty of perjury on two counts, for which he was sentenced to a five-year term in the federal penitentiary at Lewisburg, Pennsylvania. Denying Chambers' charges and protesting his innocence, Hiss entered prison on March 22, 1951. He petitioned for another trial, but his appeals were denied. After serving three years and eight months of his sentence, he was released on November 27, 1954.

The significance of the Hiss case went far beyond the confines of the hearings or the courtroom. For this, Truman himself was partly to blame. In his press conference of August 5, 1948, he dismissed the findings of the Un-American Activities Committee "as a red herring" designed to hide the dismal Republican record in Congress. After Hiss's conviction, while the emotionalism and the controversies aroused by the trial still disturbed millions of Americans, Truman's opponents latched on to his ill-advised words and employed them with telling effect, accusing him and the Democratic party of being "soft on communism." Meanwhile, to those people who had always held Roosevelt and Truman Democrats suspect, Hiss had become a symbol of everything that was wrong and evil in the United States and the world, "the personification of what worried them," as Herbert Agar stated it. Old Guard conservatives and anti–New Dealers of every shade of opinion saw in Hiss "all the upstart intellectuals," left-wingers, and peddlers of alien ideologies who had risen to power and prominence since 1933 and who were responsible for the downfall of "traditional America." [1] Richard Nixon confirmed the fears of these frightened and angry Americans when he cited the Hiss case as "the most treasonable conspiracy in American history." Liberals and progressives, on the other hand, interpreted this rightist attack on Hiss as an assault upon what he typified rather than upon his

[1] Herbert Agar, *The Price of Power: America Since 1945* (Chicago [1957]), p. 92.

FROM FAIR DEAL TO MODERN REPUBLICANISM 391

alleged treason. Fred Rodell, the Yale University professor of jurisprudence, summarized the outraged opinion of Hiss's defenders. Writing in *The Saturday Review*, he asserted that Hiss had been "framed" by a congressional committee "that was out, not for facts or truth or justice, but for New Deal–Fair Deal blood at any cost, in an election year," and that he had been convicted "largely on phony, fabricated evidence." One of the most important consequences of the Hiss case, aside from focusing increased public and government attention on the issues of Communist subversion and espionage, was that it provided unprincipled and publicity-seeking demagogues with an opportunity to exploit these serious questions for their own selfish ends, and to do so in the name of "loyalty" and "patriotism."

The reason the public debate on the loyalty issue aroused so many people to the point of hysteria can be found in the series of disturbing developments that struck the American people during the difficult, crisis-ridden years of Truman's second term. Chambers' accusations against Hiss came at a time when the Communists were driving Chiang out of China, when Truman was asking Congress to vote billions to stop Soviet expansionism in the Middle East and Europe, and when the Russians were acquiring their first atomic bombs. The impact of these events frightened and confused millions of Americans; and many of them were easily persuaded by the unsubstantiated charges of those irresponsible critics of United States policy who were attributing the diplomatic reverses of the administration in Asia and the growing strength of the Soviet challenge to spies and Communist sympathizers in the government. The issue was made to order for demagogic exploitation, and no one abused it more successfully than Joseph R. McCarthy, the junior Republican senator from Wisconsin.

McCarthyism

First elected to the Senate in the GOP upsurge of 1946, McCarthy's reputation as a lawyer and former circuit judge was debatable at best; and during his first four years on Capitol Hill he did little to improve it or to earn the respect of his fellow legislators. Not until February 8, 1950, did he begin to achieve the national recognition—notoriety might be the better word—to which he had always aspired. On that day, while addressing the Republican Women's Club of Wheeling, West Virginia, he asserted that the "reason we find ourselves in a position of impotency is not because our only powerful potential enemy has sent men to invade our shores, but rather because of the traitorous actions of those who have been treated so well by this nation." He then went on to declare that the State Department was "thoroughly infested with Communists," and he dramatized this claim in characteristic McCarthy fashion by waving a sheet of paper which bore, according to him, the names of the alleged Communists. Though the number of Communists or "bad security risks" he claimed to have discovered varied from speech to speech, and though neither he nor the Federal Bureau of Investigation ever substantiated even one of his charges, McCarthy was able to use what he called "the issue of Communism in government" to frighten, malign, and slander countless individuals, from lowly government clerks to the highest officials in the government, including some of his own colleagues in the Senate, as well as General Marshall and Dean Acheson. Neither Truman nor Eisenhower after him was spared from McCarthy's malevolence and abusive vulgarity. In the process of his four-year campaign of "rooting out the skunks" from public life (his own words), McCarthy trampled "with a heavy tread over large parts of the Constitution of the United States," as Richard H. Rovere, *The New Yorker* magazine's Washington correspondent, pointed out.

At the height of the new Red hysteria, which McCarthy's outrageous charges had done so much to create, some 50 per cent of the American people, according to one Gallup poll, held a "favorable opinion" of the senator. What is even more important is that a number of highly intelligent and honest men, among them Senator Taft, endorsed or gave tacit support to what McCarthy was doing, even though it remains highly uncertain whether he himself was convinced of his own charges and accusations. And though it may very well be that McCarthy was, as Rovere suggests, no more than "a poolroom politician grandly seized with an urge to glory," the fact that he was an exceptionally skillful demagogue who confused and embittered the public debate at home and did untold damage to the reputation of the United States abroad is indisputable. "If a major objective of Russian foreign policy is to undermine the faith of democratic peoples in their governments," *The New York Times* asserted, "then the Kremlin must rejoice every time that Joseph R. McCarthy opens his mouth in the Senate of the United States."

One of the immediate consequences of what came to be called McCarthyism was the strong popular reaction which set in against anyone

FROM FAIR DEAL TO MODERN REPUBLICANISM

who had been at any time remotely connected with left-wing groups or programs or who argued too strongly that the guarantees expressed in the Bill of Rights applied to all Americans. The loyalty of many citizens was questioned, and the charge of guilt by association was employed to ruin lives and reputations. And though the number of cases involving violations of civil liberties was never large, the efforts of various rightist groups to demand conformity was unmistakably apparent.

The Anti-Communist Crusade

Both the courts and the Congress now assumed a far more stringent attitude toward communism than ever before. In January, 1949, the government brought to trial the eleven top officials of the Communist party of the United States for violating the clause in the Smith Act of 1940 which made it illegal to "teach and advocate the overthrow and destruction of the Government . . . by force and violence. . . ." Nine months later a federal grand jury in New York City convicted them of the charge, and on October 21 Judge Harold R. Medina sentenced them to prison. When the Court of Appeals refused to reverse the lower court's verdict, the case was brought to the Supreme Court, where, on June 4, 1951, the high tribunal upheld Medina's action in a 6 to 2 decision. The significance of the Supreme Court's decision in this instance (*Eugene Dennis*, et al. *v. United States*) was underscored by Justice Douglas' dissent, in which he said that the conviction of these eleven Communist party leaders made "freedom of speech turn not on *what is said*, but on the *intent* with which it is said. Once we start down that road we enter territory dangerous to the liberties of every citizen." The decision in the Dennis case allowed the government to continue its proceedings against other lesser Communist party leaders.

THE SPY TRIALS

In the meantime, the government was also striking at Soviet espionage. In March, 1950, Judith Coplon, a young political analyst in the Department of Justice, and Valentine Gubitchev, a Soviet engineer and member of his country's delegation to the United Nations, were convicted of espionage. Each was given a fifteen-year prison term, which neither served. Gubitchev's sentence was suspended when he promised to leave the United States, and the Circuit Court of Appeals later reversed Miss Coplon's because of defective legal technicalities in the government's case. Shocking as it was, the Coplon story caused nothing like the public alarm which accompanied the atom spy trials.

On February 3, 1950, Dr. Klaus Fuchs, a prominent atomic scientist, was arrested for espionage in England. A native of Germany, Fuchs had emigrated to Britain in 1933 and joined that country's nuclear research program, and in 1943, along with a group of English and Canadian scientists, he arrived in the United States to work on the American atomic project at Los Alamos. At the time of his arrest he was in charge of theoretical physics at Harwell, a major center of British atomic research. Fuchs's confession revealed that since 1942 he had been supplying Soviet agents with much vital information on Anglo-American nuclear developments. Largely because of his espionage activities, the Soviet Union achieved a nuclear explosion long before the United States government had anticipated it would do so and at much less cost. "It is hardly an exaggeration to say," the Joint Congressional Committee on Atomic Energy reported later, "that Fuchs alone has influenced the safety of more people and accomplished greater damage than any other spy not only in the history of the United States but in the history of nations." For this, he was convicted on March 1, 1950, and given "the maximum sentence ordained," fourteen years in jail.

Fuchs's story led to the arrest of several key atom spies in the United States, the first of whom was his principal American confederate, Harry Gold, who was then the chief biological research chemist in one of the Philadelphia General Hospital's clinics. Like Fuchs, Gold quickly confessed. He was tried, convicted, and on December 9, 1950, given a thirty-year sentence. From Gold the trail led to David Greenglass, a wartime army sergeant and machinist at Los Alamos. Greenglass, it was learned, had supplied his sister, Ethel Rosenberg, and her husband, Julius, with detailed data on the world's first atomic bombs, which they in turn had passed to the Soviet vice consul in New York City. All three were arrested and convicted. Greenglass turned state witness and received fifteen years; the Rosenbergs, whom Federal Judge Irving R. Kaufman accused of having committed a "crime worse than murder," one which had "altered the course of history to the disadvantage of our country," were given the death penalty. After numerous appeals and reviews and several efforts to turn the case into an example of corrupt, anti-Semitic American justice, the Rosenbergs were executed at Sing Sing Prison in New York on June 19, 1953.

FROM FAIR DEAL TO MODERN REPUBLICANISM   395

The atom spy cases, along with the Hiss trial, led Congress to pass the McCarran Internal Security Act on September 23, 1950. This complex and highly restrictive statute required all Communists and organizations the Justice Department deemed to be Communist-inspired or -directed to register with the federal government and to supply it annually with information regarding their activities, finances, and membership. The act also barred Communists from being employed by the government or in defense plants, denied them the privilege of holding an American passport, forbade them or any other foreigner who had ever joined a "totalitarian organization" from migrating to the United States, and imposed various other penalties upon them, including the right of the government to confine them during wartime. Truman immediately vetoed the bill because the Justice, State, and Defense Departments, as well as the Central Intelligence Agency, were strongly opposed to it. The officials of these government departments and agencies declared that the McCarran bill "would seriously damage the security and intelligence operations for which they were responsible." Truman rejected it also because he was convinced that it was unworkable. The law's registration requirements, he declared, were "about as practical as requiring thieves to register with the sheriff." A far more important reason for the President's disapproval was the fact that the bill was "so broad and vague that it might well result in penalizing the legitimate activities [of individuals] who are not Communists at all, but loyal citizens." The Congress, however, was not persuaded by Truman's reasons. Reflecting the near hysteria of the times, it quickly overrode his veto.

The same fears and impulses that led Congress to pass the Internal Security Act produced the McCarran-Walter Immigration and Nationality Act of June 27, 1952, the first major revision of the immigration laws since 1924. When the Congress began its study of the accumulated rules, amendments, and Executive orders regulating the entry of foreigners into the United States, many Americans hoped its investigations would lead to a more liberal law, one which would reverse the national origins quota system of 1924. About a dozen civic and religious organizations, like the Americans for Democratic Action and the American Friends Service Committee, along with the spokesmen of various minority and nationality groups argued against the discriminatory and scientifically unsound features of the quota system, calling for either its outright elimination or its extensive liberalization. Their combined efforts, however, hardly equaled the pressure from advocates of continued restriction. Various patriotic and veteran organizations, among them the American Legion, strongly supported the quota system as an effective barrier against the admission of undesirable aliens with subversive ideas.

Largely because of the fear of Communist infiltration, the McCarran-Walter Act retained and in certain instances tightened the quota system. The bill's most outstanding liberal feature was the provision repealing the exclusion of Orientals, which gave them a quota and permitted them to become American citizens. Aside from this and certain minor increases and adjustments in other quotas, the law continued the national origins restrictions established earlier and tried to strike at communism by various exclusion and registration clauses. It authorized the Justice Department, for example, to deport immigrants accused of subversion even after they had become citizens, and it required all immigrants to register their addresses annually with the Commissioner of Immigration and Naturalization. Many of these restrictive provisions shocked liberals, and Truman vetoed it on the grounds that it was discriminatory and that it violated the principles of American decency and democratic government. Capitol Hill, however, was determined to have it, and Congress overrode the President's veto by substantial majorities. A year later, when the President's Commission on Immigration and Naturalization concluded its study, its report, *Whom We Shall Welcome*, declared that America's "growth as a nation has been achieved, in large measure, through the genius and industry of immigrants of every race and from every quarter of the world. The story of their pursuit of happiness is the saga of America." The provisions of the McCarran-Walter Act, however, as many observed, seemed intended to deny this fact.

THE END OF THE DEMOCRATIC ERA

During the last two years of Truman's administration the American people were seriously disturbed by the disclosures of the spy trials, the "treadmill" war in Korea, the President's fight with MacArthur, and the emotional turbulence created by McCarthy's demagoguery. Any one of these issues would have been sufficient to shake the people's confidence in its leaders. Coming as close together as they did, their combined impact reduced the prestige of the administration to an all-time low. And if this were not enough to worry the Democrats, the televised hearings of the Senate Subcommittee to Investigate Interstate Crime provided the country with considerable evidence of a profitable alliance between corrupt urban politicians, many of whom were in Democratic strongholds, and the principal leaders of organized crime. Under the chairmanship of the Tennessee Democrat Estes Kefauver, the committee exposed the wide extent and influence of the country's well-organized, effectively protected, and flourishing criminal industries, the most important branches of which were gambling, other kinds of rackets, prostitution, and the illegal sale and use of narcotics.

Corruption in Government

If the Kefauver investigation impugned the honesty of certain local public officials, similar examples of dishonesty and corruption also appeared on the federal level, much to the embarrassment of the President and other top administration leaders. And while none of the disclosures involved Truman himself or was in any way as extensive as the corruption among the members of Harding's "Ohio gang," there was enough of it for the opposition to use in discrediting the administration.

A number of the more publicized offenses involved the intervention of administration officials in the affairs of various government bureaus and offices. Major General Harry Vaughan, the President's military aide, was found to have used his White House position to win special consideration for several businessmen, one of whom rewarded him with a deep-freeze unit reputedly valued around $500. For services similar to those performed by Vaughan, other government bureaucrats, according to a Senate subcommittee, received a 5 per cent fee, and the opposition immediately dubbed them the "five percenters." But some of the most notable instances of skulduggery occurred in the Reconstruction Finance Corporation and in the Bureau of Internal Revenue. In the former, Democratic Senator William Fulbright's subcommittee discovered that when Democratic National Committee Chairman William J. Boyle, Jr., became the counsel for a firm whose loan application had previously been rejected by the RFC, the company's subsequent request was granted. In another case, a White House stenographer whose husband had once been employed by the RFC received a $9,540 mink coat from a law firm handling the affairs of a client who was applying for a loan. Like Harry Vaughan's freezer, mink coats became a political symbol of major import, much to the annoyance of the Mink Ranchers' Association, which tried to assure the country that these garments usually belonged to "highly respectable

398   THE U.S. & THE POSTWAR WORLD, 1945–1961

people of discriminating taste." [2] When Truman asserted there was "no evidence of illegal influence on the R.F.C.," Senator Fulbright replied by saying that in his opinion it was "setting a low level if our only goal for official conduct is that it be legal instead of illegal."

Disclosure of graft, corruption, and favoritism in the nation's tax offices led to the dismissal or forced resignation of the Commissioner of Internal Revenue, the collectors of the St. Louis, Boston, San Francisco, and Brooklyn offices, and some thirty other employees. T. Lamar Caudle, the Assistant Attorney General and head of the Tax Division in the Justice Department, and Charles Oliphant, the Treasury Department's Assistant General Counsel for the Revenue Bureau, also were forced to resign. Early in February, 1952, Truman assigned the wealthy New York City liberal Republican attorney Newbold Morris to clean out the corruptionists in the federal bureaucracy. A one-time member of the La Guardia reform group, Morris ran into difficulties with Attorney General J. Howard McGrath, who refused to cooperate. Disapproving of Morris' plans, McGrath summarily dismissed him. The next day Truman dismissed McGrath and appointed James P. McGranery as his Attorney General. A week later Truman asked Congress to approve his reorganization plan for the Bureau of Internal Revenue, which he declared was designed "to place under the civil service all the positions in the bureau, with the sole exception of the Commissioner. . . ." The Congress adopted Truman's proposal, but the reform came too late to help the Democrats in the following presidential elections, and the Republicans added corruption to the two other great issues of the day—communism and Korea.

THE ELECTION OF 1952

As in 1948, the leading Republican contender for the GOP nomination was Ohio's Robert A. Taft, who had declared himself a candidate as early as September, 1951, and had been campaigning for delegates ever since. Strongly supported by conservative and nationalist Republicans, Taft was acceptable neither to the liberal-internationalist wing of the party nor to its politically knowledgeable leaders, all of whom were afraid that the Ohioan's well-known views would guarantee the

[2] Quoted in Eric F. Goldman, *The Crucial Decade—And After: America, 1945–1960* (New York [1961]), p. 188.

The most popular military hero of World War II, Dwight D. Eisenhower was enthusiastically cheered wherever he appeared. This picture was taken in 1952, while he was campaigning for the Presidency in Chicago. (Brown Brothers)

party's defeat. Thomas E. Dewey, the twice-defeated titular head of the GOP, had declared himself out of the race, and neither California's Earl Warren nor Minnesota's Harold Stassen, both of whom were ideologically acceptable to the liberal Republicans, enjoyed a substantial national following. What the GOP needed was a popular leader who could attract enough independent and dissatisfied Democratic voters to ensure victory. Shortly after his 1948 defeat, Dewey started to push General Dwight D. Eisenhower's candidacy. Ably assisted by a group of influential Republicans, among them Governor Sherman Adams of New Hampshire and Senator Henry Cabot Lodge, Jr., of Massachusetts, Dewey and these men, along with other personal friends of the General's, placed Eisenhower's name on the ballot in several primaries. When the results of these races proved highly encouraging, his supporters finally persuaded Ike, as he was generally called by then, to resign his NATO post and return to the United States to campaign for the nomination, which he did on

400   THE U.S. & THE POSTWAR WORLD, 1945–1961

June 1, 1952. As was to be expected, everywhere Eisenhower appeared he was greeted as a hero. And though the Taft men accused him of being grossly uninformed of the great issues of the day and of mouthing "five star generalities," to quote the *Chicago Tribune*, it was obvious that the people admired Ike as an individual, even though they knew almost nothing about his ideas on government or economics.

When the Republican convention met in Chicago on July 7, the Taft men were in control of its machinery. Both the national chairman, Joseph W. Martin, Jr., of Massachusetts, and the keynote speaker, General MacArthur, were dedicated Taft men. It was only after Senator Lodge, Herbert Brownell, Jr.—a former Dewey campaign manager and now one of Ike's convention strategists—and a few others succeeded in changing the rules on the seating of a number of contested southern delegations that Eisenhower's nomination was made possible. Forty years earlier, in this same city, Taft's father had used these very rules to prevent the progressives in the GOP from nominating Theodore Roosevelt; this time the more liberal eastern wing of the party forced their amendment to defeat William Howard Taft's eldest son, "Mr. Republican," the symbol and the most articulate spokesman of GOP conservatism. The convention's vote on the disputed delegates previewed Eisenhower's successful nomination, which he won on the first ballot with 845 votes, as opposed to 280 for Taft, 77 for Warren, and 4 for MacArthur. Ohio's Senator John W. Bricker introduced a motion to make Ike's nomination unanimous, which the convention immediately adopted. In a detailed statement analyzing the reasons for his third failure to secure the Republican nomination, Taft attributed his defeat to "the power of the New York financial interest," the hostility of "four-fifths of the influential newspapers in the country," and the opposition of many Republican governors.

For Vice President, the convention nominated by acclamation Richard M. Nixon, the junior senator from California, who had already won the approval of Eisenhower's chief advisers. Young, energetic, and a loyal party supporter in Congress since 1947, Nixon had attracted considerable attention as the fledgling representative who had "helped break the Hiss case." Furthermore, his voting record in Congress was in no way offensive to the party's conservatives, and he came from a politically important state.

The Republican platform denounced the Democratic record unsparingly and promised to support farm prices at 90 per cent of parity, to extend social security, and to assist and cooperate with local government authorities in promoting slum clearance and urban renewal projects. It opposed federal aid to education and compulsory national health insurance, declaring that these were responsibilities which should be left to the states; and it came out in favor of keeping the Taft-Hartley Act, reducing federal expenditures and taxes, balancing the budget, and strengthening the nation's defenses by developing "a force in being . . . of such power as to deter sudden attack or . . . decisively defeat it." The foreign policy planks, once again largely written by John Foster Dulles, called for supporting the United Nations and promoting collective security. "We shall end neglect of the Far East," the platform asserted, and "we shall not sacrifice the East to gain time for the West." The "negative, futile and immoral policy of containment" was to be scrapped. In its stead, the GOP promised to inaugurate a program of "liberation" reflecting the "dynamic, moral, and spiritual force" of the American nation. Like most of the delegates, the American people soon indicated they were more interested in what Ike said than in the party platform, which, despite its apparent stand on so many issues, left considerable room for compromise and personal interpretation.

For the first time in twenty years, the Democrats were faced with the problem of finding a presidential candidate who was not already in the White House. Truman, who could have had the nomination—the Twenty-second Amendment did not apply to him—excluded himself on March 29, 1952, when he announced that he "would not be a candidate for reelection." His first choice was Chief Justice Fred M. Vinson, whom he had tried to persuade to go after the nomination as early as 1950. When Vinson "firmly declined," Truman turned to the governor of Illinois, Adlai E. Stevenson, the grandson and namesake of Grover Cleveland's Vice President during the latter's second term. A capable administrator with experience in the State Department and in various other government agencies, a former delegate to the United Nations General Assembly, and the popular and successful governor of Illinois since 1948, Stevenson had, in Truman's opinion, "the background and what it takes" to be a distinguished President. Stevenson, however, refused to commit himself or to help his supporters, declaring repeatedly that he was interested only in being reelected governor.

While Truman and other Democratic leaders were trying to convince Stevenson of his duty to run, Senator Estes Kefauver, whose televised investigations of organized crime made him a national celebrity, was busily engaged in recruiting delegates. The popularity he had earned in disclosing the activities and political influence of the nation's criminal syndicates made him unacceptable to certain big-city bosses, while his liberal voting record made him unpopular in the South. The fact that he had declared himself a candidate even before Truman had announced his own intentions earned him few friends among the administration's leaders. By convention time, neither his personal popularity—his trademark was a coonskin cap, reminiscent of Davy Crockett's—nor his victories in the primaries were sufficient to offset his other liabilities.

Among the other Democratic hopefuls, Senator Richard Russell cf Georgia represented the conservative South; Averell Harriman of New York, then the head of the Mutual Security Administration, enjoyed the support of labor and the liberals in the party; Senator Robert Kerr of Oklahoma, a friend of the oil interests in his state, was unacceptable to Truman and the liberals; and Vice President Alben Barkley, the "Veep," was rejected by the labor leaders on the first day of the convention because he was too old—seventy-four. "But for his age," Truman noted later, Barkley "would have been a most logical candidate." After labor's open refusal to endorse his candidacy, even though Truman had agreed to support him, shattered Barkley's hopes, he immediately announced he was no longer a candidate. With Barkley's withdrawal and Stevenson's repeated assertions that he was not available, the 1,230 Democratic delegates who followed the Republicans into Chicago on July 21 faced a situation which, according to one weekly news magazine, was "ready-made for a party regular."

The only issue that threatened to disrupt Democratic harmony was a proposal, sponsored by a coalition of northern liberals, requiring the delegates to pledge their support for whomever the party nominated. Coming on the first day of the convention, it had an obvious purpose—to prevent a repeat of the Dixiecrat bolt of 1948. When several influential Southerners refused to subscribe to it and after it became apparent that the anti-Kefauver delegates were also opposed to declaring their "loyalty" in this fashion, no effort was made to press the issue. Unlike 1948's, this year's Democratic platform produced no party crisis. The convention adopted a strong civil rights plank, endorsed the Truman policies, both foreign and domestic, guaranteed the farmer 90 per cent of parity, promised to assist the United Nations in preserving and promoting peace, reasserted its faith in the principle of collective security, claimed credit for introducing an effective and equitable loyalty program and for ex-

FROM FAIR DEAL TO MODERN REPUBLICANISM   403

posing and evicting corruptionists, and registered the party's continued opposition to the Taft-Hartley Act and to tax cuts which threatened the country's security.

While the convention was writing the platform, Stevenson changed his mind about running and on July 24 informed Truman he was prepared to make the race. Since in the President's opinion Stevenson was "the logical choice," Truman, despite his annoyance with the Illinoisan's tardy reversal, immediately moved to secure his nomination, which occurred the next day on the third ballot. For Vice President, the Democrats chose Alabama's Senator John J. Sparkman, a friend of the administration except on civil rights and a Southerner who had remained loyal in 1948.

The campaign quickly revealed that Stevenson, up to the time of his nomination scarcely known outside Illinois, was a man of great intelligence and high principles. He possessed an exceptional understanding of national and world affairs, which he discussed with great conviction and unusual knowledge. As a campaigner, Stevenson was at his best in formal talks and on television, where his carefully prepared and eloquently phrased speeches, delivered with an effectiveness reminiscent of Franklin Roosevelt's radio addresses, won him millions of loyal admirers, especially among the better educated, the so-called "eggheads," many of whom rallied to his banner with the same fervor and dedication with which they had moved to F.D.R.'s.

Eisenhower, on the other hand, was neither so conversant with all the issues nor anywhere near so articulate in expressing himself as Stevenson. Ike's most valuable assets, which he employed with great effectiveness, were his reputation and personality. A great war hero who was respected, admired, and honored all over the world, Eisenhower gave the impression of having been completely unspoiled by the many distinctions which had been bestowed upon him. The warmth, sincerity, and kindly friendliness of his personality appealed to millions, and neither the slim intellectual fare of his speeches nor the halting manner in which he delivered them (they improved in both content and style as the campaign progressed) lessened the people's enthusiasm or affection for him. Many Americans admired Eisenhower's simple, unaffected, and honest appeal all the more because they had come to distrust the very qualities which attracted the intellectuals to Stevenson. John Alsop, the one-time newspaper columnist, expressed the public reaction to the two candi-

404   THE U.S. & THE POSTWAR WORLD, 1945–1961

dates when he said that "while Stevenson was appealing and appealing strongly to the people's minds, Eisenhower, as a man and as a figure, was appealing far more strongly to far more peoples' emotions." [3]

Despite Eisenhower's personal popularity, the Republican party's leadership was seriously concerned with the unenthusiastic and grudging support he was accorded by the conservative Taft wing. Many of the party's stalwarts, moreover, resented the moderation with which Ike attacked the Truman policies, claiming that Eisenhower's internationalism and middle of the road views on domestic affairs were no different from those expressed by most Democrats. Influential Republican newspapers charged that he was "just another me-too candidate." For the sake of party unity, the disagreements and lingering animosities that separated the liberal and conservative wings of the GOP were reconciled, temporarily at least, on September 12 when Taft, after conferring with Eisenhower in New York City, announced that any differences remaining between them were only "differences of degree." The immediate effect of this statement was to bring the Taftites into the campaign, but because it appeared to be so obviously inconsistent with the previously declared opinions of the two men, it seriously disturbed many of Eisenhower's liberal friends, a number of whom seemed to find Stevenson's comment at the time—"It looks as if Taft lost the nomination but won the nominee"—embarrassingly true.

On a number of questions, however, such as fiscal responsibility and the need to reduce federal expenditures, balance the budget, and assure the people's "liberty against creeping socialism," Ike and Taft were in fundamental agreement; and after their New York City meeting, Ike gave these issues additional emphasis. But some of his later foreign policy statements, especially those in which he accused the administration of "bungling . . . into Korea" and of "appalling and disastrous mismanagement" of foreign affairs, raised more serious doubts as to his understanding of these complex diplomatic problems. Even more distressing was the increasing number of references to the three great issues Senator Karl Mundt, the conservative South Dakotan, declared would defeat the Democrats—Korea, communism, and corruption. The fact that Ike allowed himself or was forced because of political expediency to appear on the same platforms with such vicious critics of the Democrats as Senators William Jenner of Indiana and Joe McCarthy also disappointed many of his friends, especially among independents, because Ike thus appeared to

[3] Quoted in *ibid.*, p. 223.

FROM FAIR DEAL TO MODERN REPUBLICANISM 405

lend his prestige to these men and their false charges. Eisenhower's most effective campaign appeal came at Detroit on October 24 when after reviewing the "stalemate" in Korea he declared that if elected he would make "a personal trip to Korea." And though he made no specific promises to end what many Republicans referred to as "Truman's war," his assertion that he would "concentrate on the job of ending the Korean War . . . until that job is honorably done" was precisely what the American people desired most.

Stevenson, for all his high principles, intelligence, wit, and eloquence, simply could not match Eisenhower's reputation or the confidence the people had in his ability and integrity. Moreover, such issues as the Korean and cold wars, the threat of Communist subversion at home, and what the Republicans generally labeled "the mess in Washington" were so much part of the Democratic record that it was impossible for Stevenson to dissociate himself entirely from them without appearing to endorse the GOP's charges or repudiate the outgoing administration. In mid-September, when the *New York Post* disclosed that some seventy-five rich southern California business and professional men had collected $18,235 "to enable Dick [Nixon] to do a selling job for the American people in behalf of private enterprise," as one of the contributors declared, it appeared, momentarily at least, as if one of the Republican charges against the administration—corruption in government—might have to be dropped from the GOP's campaign arsenal. For a time there was even talk of Nixon's withdrawing from the ticket, but nothing came of it. In a brilliantly executed television performance, he defended his record of honesty and probity, asking his listeners to express themselves to the Republican National Committee, which would determine his political fate. The public response was overwhelmingly in his favor, and when the Republicans disclosed that Stevenson had used campaign money to reward a number of his assistants who were on the Illinois state payroll, the possibility of using the "Nixon fund" against the GOP effectively evaporated.

Despite Stevenson's impressive campaign, Truman's strenuous defense of his administration, and the efforts of Democratic campaign orators to impress upon the people that they "never had it so good," the results were an overwhelming Eisenhower victory. Out of a total popular vote of 61.5 million, Eisenhower won 33.8 million, or nearly 55 per cent, as opposed to Stevenson's 27.3 million, representing 44.3 per cent. Ike carried 39 states, including Virginia, Tennessee, Florida, Texas, Maryland,

406 THE U.S. & THE POSTWAR WORLD, 1945–1961

and Missouri, with 442 electoral votes. Stevenson won in West Virginia, Kentucky, and seven southern states with a total of 89 electoral votes. Except for Franklin Roosevelt's landslide sweep in 1936, no other presidential candidate had ever received such an enthusiastic endorsement from the electorate. Eisenhower's victory, however, was clearly his own and not the Republican party's. The GOP polled barely enough votes to give it control of the next Congress—48 to 47 in the Senate and 221 to 213 in the House. Eisenhower's "gigantic vote of confidence" was the result of many factors, among which the most important were his own personal popularity, his promise to safeguard the social and economic gains of the past twenty years of Democratic rule and to restore morality in government, and the people's disillusionment with the Truman administration's record. Ike attracted to his "crusade" millions of people representing every social and economic group in every section of the country, all of whom believed that his "personal and intellectual integrity," as *The New York Times* put it, would provide the United States with the kind of "effective and . . . forthright leadership" the times required.

THE BEGINNING OF THE EISENHOWER ERA, 1953–1956

Up to the time he was elected President, Eisenhower had never held any government office. Born on a farm in Denison, Texas, he moved with his family when he was less than a year old to Abilene, Kansas, where he spent all his youth and graduated from high school in 1909. Two years later he entered the Military Academy at West Point, graduating in 1915, sixty-first in a class of 164 cadets. During World War I he was assigned to command the tank training program at Camp Colt near Gettysburg, Pennsylvania. In 1922 he was transferred to the Canal Zone, where he served two years, returning to the United States to study at the General Staff School at Fort Leavenworth in Kansas and at the Army War College in Washington, D.C. Between 1929 and 1933 he was attached to the Assistant Secretary of War's office, and from there he went to the Philippines, serving as MacArthur's assistant until 1939. After Pearl Harbor, Eisenhower was assigned to various planning and operational positions in Washington, and on November 8, 1942, Franklin

FROM FAIR DEAL TO MODERN REPUBLICANISM 407

Roosevelt appointed him Commander in Chief of the Allied Forces in North Africa. Ike's success in evicting the Nazis from Africa, the first major American land victories in World War II, turned him from a relatively unknown lieutenant general into a prominent national figure. His subsequent leadership in directing the victorious Anglo-American assault on Sicily and Italy augmented his reputation still further, so that by the time he was appointed Supreme Commander of the Allied Expeditionary Force which invaded France, he was America's most famous soldier next to MacArthur and certainly its most popular one. In November, 1945, he returned to the United States to become Army Chief of Staff, a post he held until he retired from active duty (February, 1948) to become president of Columbia University. It was while he was in this position, his only civilian job up to this time, that President Truman, in December, 1950, asked him to command NATO, his last assignment before becoming the GOP's presidential candidate.

Because of his many years of experience in working with military staffs, and because of his limited knowledge of the machinery of government and the art of politics, Eisenhower sought to adopt in the Executive office the practices to which he had grown accustomed in the army. As a result, the roles of the cabinet and of his personal advisers assumed a far greater importance than had been the case with Truman, Franklin Roosevelt, or any of the other Presidents who believed in and exercised strong Executive leadership. The fact that as an army officer Ike had always been liberal in delegating authority and in relying upon his advisers for recommending, developing, and implementing policy strengthened the influence of the cabinet and his White House staff still further. Moreover, since he was not committed to any specific legislative program of his own, did not believe that it was the President's duty to initiate policy, and was not too interested in participating actively in the detailed work of the Executive departments, Eisenhower allowed his cabinet officers and staff to assume many responsibilities which previous Chief Executives had exercised themselves. The President's job, as Eisenhower understood it, was to study the carefully prepared proposals of his advisers, which he liked to have presented to him orally or in briefly written memoranda, preferably of a page or less, and to reach a decision after consulting with his aides. The policies which came out of the White House under Eisenhower were the results of close staff work in which the President participated only in the final stages. It was important to him, therefore, that he secure the assistance of a competent group of men who reflected his views and upon whom he could count to resolve the incessant torrent of problems which descended upon him.

The Cabinet

During the latter weeks of December, 1952, Eisenhower began recruiting his cabinet, and by the end of the month he had filled all nine posts. For Secretary of State he chose John Foster Dulles of New York. The grandson of Benjamin Harrison's Secretary of State and the nephew of Woodrow Wilson's wartime head of the State Department, Dulles had his first diplomatic experience in 1907 when, at nineteen years of age, he assisted his grandfather at the Second Hague Conference. Twelve years later he was at Versailles, working with the reparations commission. These and the other diplomatic assignments which he subsequently fulfilled, the wide experience he acquired as an international lawyer, and his long association with Senator Vandenberg seemed to make him exceptionally qualified to be Secretary of State. Eisenhower was convinced of it, and partly because of this and partly because of Dulles' own self-confidence, he was, in the words of *The New York Times,* "the strongest personality of the Eisenhower Cabinet" and one of the President's closest and most trusted advisers. Until April 15, 1959, when cancer forced him to resign (he died May 24), Secretary Dulles was the principal figure in American foreign policy, determining not only its conduct but much of its content as well.

Eisenhower's basically conservative views on domestic affairs were revealed in his choice of George M. Humphrey as Secretary of the Treasury. A prosperous and successful Ohio industrialist and financier, Humphrey believed that economy and fiscal probity were as desirable in government as they were in private enterprise. His opinions carried considerable weight with the President: "In cabinet meetings I always wait for George Humphrey to speak," Ike once said, because "I know . . . he will say just what I am thinking."

The third most influential member of the cabinet was Defense Secretary Charles E. Wilson, president of General Motors Corporation. Determined to introduce economy and efficiency into the nation's defense establishment, Wilson inaugurated his tenure by reducing the civilian personnel in his department by some 40,000 in a little over four months; and he diverted the government's defense purchases from the smaller to

FROM FAIR DEAL TO MODERN REPUBLICANISM 409

the larger and allegedly more efficient producers, thereby establishing what came to be known as the narrow base supply system. The Truman administration had followed a broad base program in which the government scattered its orders among many firms of various sizes, a practice Wilson regarded as wasteful, costly, and inefficient. Wilson's innovation was strongly criticized, but it caused nothing like the storm that arose after he decided to give the country's defenses a "New Look" by reducing the size of its conventional armaments and concentrating on developing atomic weapons capable of producing "a bigger bang for a buck" and of inflicting "massive nuclear retaliation." A strong and forceful individual, inclined to speak his mind freely, "Engine Charlie," as he was called, aroused the Senate's opposition even before it had confirmed his appointment. Reluctant to divest himself of General Motors stock valued at nearly $2.5 million, Wilson told the Senate committee which was to pass on his nomination that he saw no reason why he should be forced to incur a financial loss simply to satisfy the requirements of the conflict of interest law, especially since he was certain that "what was good for our country was good for General Motors and vice versa." As soon as this statement reached the headlines, Wilson was severely criticized for it, but when he announced that he would dispose of his General Motors holdings, the outcry subsided and the Senate approved his appointment.

All the remaining members of Eisenhower's cabinet save one also revealed the President's faith in "practical men of affairs" with a conservative bent. Sinclair Weeks, the Secretary of Commerce, was a respected Boston investment banker and businessman who believed in a minimum of government intervention in the economy; and Secretary of the Interior Douglas McKay, Oregon's former governor, was opposed to the federal government's assuming the leadership in developing regional projects along the Columbia and Missouri rivers. Ezra T. Benson of Utah, whom Taft promoted and Ike accepted as Secretary of Agriculture, believed that the farmer should be liberated from the controls, restraints, and subsidies the Democrats had imposed upon him; however, his efforts to reduce the cost of the government's agricultural programs aroused bitter criticism in the farm states, and Benson became the most disliked member of the President's cabinet. To the posts of Attorney General and Postmaster General, both traditionally filled by important political figures, Eisenhower assigned Herbert Brownell, Jr., of New York and Arthur E. Summerfield of Michigan, the latter being chairman of the Republican National Committee. When Congress, on April 1, 1953, estab-

410   THE U.S. & THE POSTWAR WORLD, 1945-1961

lished the Department of Health, Education, and Welfare, Eisenhower appointed Mrs. Oveta Culp Hobby to fill the new post. The World War II commander of the Women's Auxiliary Corps and the wife of a prominent Texas newspaper publisher, Mrs. Hobby was the only Southerner in the cabinet. Her appointment provided the required "geographical balance," and it was hoped that it would strengthen the GOP's prospects of keeping Texas in the Republican column and of breaking still further the Democratic hold on the solid South.

The only individual in Eisenhower's cabinet who was not wealthy, not a businessman, not a conservative, and not a Protestant was Secretary of Labor Martin P. Durkin of Maryland. The president of the AFL's International Union of Plumbers and Pipe Fitters and a Truman Democrat, Durkin's appointment shocked the sensibilities of many Republicans. Since he did not share the social, economic, or political ideas either of Eisenhower or of his colleagues, Durkin was often referred to as the "plumber in a group of millionaire businessmen" or the "square peg in a round hole." Whatever the reason for his appointment—whether because it provided occupational balance, because he was a Roman Catholic, or because Eisenhower hoped a union man could handle labor's problems—the results were unrewarding, and Durkin resigned after ten months. He was replaced by James P. Mitchell of New Jersey, a former New York City department store executive in charge of personnel and labor relations, who at the time of his appointment was Assistant Secretary of the Army.

SHERMAN ADAMS

Next to the President himself, and with the possible exception of Dulles, the single most influential individual in the Eisenhower administration was New Hampshire's former Governor Sherman Adams, "the assistant to the President." No presidential assistant—not even Wilson's Colonel House or Roosevelt's Harry Hopkins—ever exercised as much authority as Adams. As he reported himself, Eisenhower "never specifically defined my responsibilities or outlined their limits." The President, Adams went on to say, "simply expected me to manage a staff that would boil down, simplify and expedite the urgent business that had to be brought to his attention and to keep as much work of secondary importance as possible off his desk." [4] Because of the range of his responsibilities, the

[4] Sherman Adams, *Firsthand Report: The Story of the Eisenhower Administration* (New York [1961]), p. 50.

Assistant to the President, Sherman Adams was the chief of the White House staff and, until his resignation in 1958, the most influential member of the Eisenhower "team." (Wide World Photos)

determination with which he sought to lessen the President's burdens ("Don't bother the President" was an oft-repeated Adams rule), and the confidence Ike placed in his judgment and abilities, Adams was often referred to as "the second most powerful executive in the government" or "the ringmaster of the circus." The jobs Adams fulfilled were such that, in the opinion of one careful student of these years, they allowed Eisenhower to achieve "one of the most thoroughgoing withdrawals from the duties of the Presidency in the history of the office." [5] Adams did not usurp authority; nor did he ask for it. Eisenhower gave it to him even before he was inaugurated President.

Republican Policies and Domestic Affairs

When Eisenhower entered the White House, some of the more conservative members of his party would have had him undo most of the Roosevelt-Truman record which so many of them had been criticizing for the last twenty years; but neither the President nor the millions of Americans who had voted for him subscribed to the antediluvian views expressed by these extreme GOP right-wingers. In spite of all the campaign talk, Eisenhower's domestic program, which he labeled "moderate progressivism" on one occasion and "progressive moderation" on another, was not fundamentally different from the legislation of the previous Democratic administrations except perhaps in its emphasis, which was more conservative. While Eisenhower and his principal advisers were opposed to increasing federal expenditures, deficit financing, and enlarging the activities of the government in the economy, they were also aware that the international crises of the postwar era were largely responsible for the unbalanced budgets and the economic controls they had so strongly opposed. Similarly, while Eisenhower, Adams, and other administration spokesmen deplored the high costs of the government's various welfare programs, they accepted them, unlike some of their more conservative colleagues in the Republican party, just as they did the principle that it was Washington's responsibility to safeguard and promote human welfare.

At first Eisenhower had hoped that with Senator Taft's assistance he could overcome the conservative opposition to his program, and so long as Taft was alive (he died on July 31, 1953) a real attempt was made to reconcile the differences which divided the GOP in the hope of impressing upon the country the fact that the Republicans had not lost their ability to govern effectively or forgotten their preelection promises. But despite Ike's efforts, especially after California's William F. Knowland replaced Taft as the Senate GOP leader, the President often found the Republican Old Guard as frustrating as Truman had found the Democratic stalwarts. By joining together, the conservatives of both parties disappointed Eisenhower's efforts sufficiently for him to tell

[5] Louis W. Koenig, *The Invisible Presidency* (New York [1960]), p. 339.

FROM FAIR DEAL TO MODERN REPUBLICANISM 413

Adams early in his administration that the country needed a new political party, one Adams described as "accepting a role of leadership in world affairs, liberal in its policies affecting human welfare but taking a more conservative stand than the Democrats on domestic government control and spending. . . ." And though nothing ever came of Eisenhower's thoughts on this subject, the ideas he expressed on its domestic orientation reveal the broad principles which guided his administration and which came to be called the "Eisenhower equilibrium" or "modern Republicanism," terms employed to mean a central position on the political spectrum that would attract middle of the road citizens of both parties.

THE BUDGET AND TAXES

During the campaign the Republicans had declared that they intended to achieve the twin goals of prosperity and price stability by balancing the budget, cutting taxes, and freeing the economy from excessive government regulation. Once in office, they immediately set out to establish a free and fiscally sound economy. The Korean War controls over rents, wages, and prices were allowed to expire, and the responsibility for checking the still serious inflation was assigned to Treasury Secretary Humphrey who, with the assistance of the Federal Reserve System, instituted a tight money policy. The administration ordered the Executive departments to cut expenses and improve efficiency, but despite various efforts at economy, it soon learned that it was easier to talk about a balanced budget than to achieve one. Much to the discomfiture of the Republicans, Eisenhower's first budget, originally prepared by the outgoing Democrats but revised downward considerably by the incoming administration, still showed a deficit of $3.1 billion. When Eisenhower informed Taft of this unfortunate fact, the Senator's easily aroused ire got the best of him. "You're taking us down the same road that Truman traveled," he cried out at the President. "It's a repudiation of everything we promised in the campaign!" [6]

The principal items which prevented a balanced budget were, of course, the very same that had caused the Democratic deficits—the high defense and foreign aid costs, and these could be reduced significantly only by cutting or changing the bases of the country's military security program. Defense Secretary Wilson's economies and "New Look" approach were intended to reduce the defense bill without undermining

[6] Quoted in Adams, *op. cit.*, p. 21.

414 THE U.S. & THE POSTWAR WORLD, 1945–1961

the nation's security. In addition to the military requirements of the United States and its allies and the foreign assistance programs, the growing needs of the American people themselves, who increased in numbers by nearly 25 million (from 155 to 179.3 million) during the Eisenhower years, not only prevented the administration from reducing the size of the federal budget significantly but forced it to incur deficits in five out of its eight years. By the time Eisenhower left the White House in 1960, the public debt, which had stood at $271.3 billion in 1954, had risen to $280 billion.

The inability of the administration to balance its first two budgets did not prevent the conservative Republicans in Congress from pressing for a tax cut. Since this was a promise the GOP Old Guard intended to keep, it was with obvious displeasure that they were forced in July, 1953, to accept the administration's proposal to extend the corporate excess profits tax for another six months. The next year, frightened that the mild post–Korean War recession that had set in during the latter part of 1953 might degenerate into a real depression and concerned with the forthcoming midterm elections, the administration abandoned its antiinflationary tight money policy and moved to redeem the party's campaign pledge to cut taxes.

The Internal Revenue Act of August 16, 1954, the first major revision of the tax laws since 1939, cut certain excise taxes, such as those on toiletries, furs, jewelry, luggage, and theater tickets, by 50 per cent, and substantially reduced the federal taxes on telephone calls and travel. The principal levies that remained unchanged were those imposed on automobiles, tobacco, and alcoholic beverages. Income tax relief was provided by liberalizing deductions and by granting special consideration to various groups, among them widowers, working mothers, pensioners, retired persons, and heads of households. Businessmen and farmers were accorded additional benefits, and investors were allowed $50 of tax-free dividends and, under certain conditions, an extra 4 per cent tax credit. The opposition criticized the law, accusing the administration of refusing to increase personal exemptions so that it could provide tax relief to the groups which needed it least. The Republicans denied the charge and claimed that the law's new excise and income scales would save the taxpayers billions.

BENSON AND THE FARMERS

Just as the administration's fiscal and budgetary policies were to the right of those of the Fair Deal, its farm program revealed an even more conservative orientation. Since 1950, while the rest of the country had been enjoying prosperity, the farmer had watched his income decline steadily. To make matters worse, the drop in farm prices occurred at a time when nonagricultural ones were rising. These economic difficulties drove many thousands of farmers off the land, but even though the number of agricultural units declined by 11 per cent between 1950 and 1954, the output of those remaining so far exceeded the demand that the government's price and income stabilization programs cost the taxpayer $2.1 and $1.7 billion for 1953 and 1954 respectively, the first two fiscal years of the Eisenhower administration.

Secretary of Agriculture Benson was convinced that the rigid price support system was the single most important reason for the continually growing farm surplus. It induced the farmer to overproduce, thereby driving prices down and forcing the government to assume the heavy financial burden of subsidies. Early in 1953, when Eisenhower was struggling to reduce the deficit, Benson suggested cutting the 90 per cent payments established in the Agricultural Act of 1952 as a part of the administration's effort to trim expenses and as a beginning toward resolving the farm problem. The President rejected Benson's suggestion at this time because of his campaign statements, but soon thereafter, as he watched the huge farm surpluses in government storage grow larger and larger, he became more convinced of the wisdom of Benson's proposal. By lowering the high price supports under the crops in far greater supply than demand, the President and Benson hoped the farmers, threatened by glutted markets, would voluntarily reduce their output or cultivate something else which promised them a higher profit. The plan appeared reasonable, and it satisfied Benson's and Eisenhower's desire to limit government regulation and cut the cost of the administration's farm program as well.

Despite the powerful opposition of many farmers, who were alarmed at any change which threatened to lower their incomes, already considerably below the national average, Congress enacted the administration's flexible farm support system in the Agricultural Act of January 11, 1954. The law established supports for five crops—wheat, corn, rice, peanuts, and cotton—at 82.5 to 90 per cent of parity for 1955 and 75 to 90 per cent for subsequent years, the exact rate of support to be determined by the Secretary of Agriculture; and it revised the supports under other crops also. A few months later, on August 28, 1954, the administration also sought to dispose of surplus crops abroad by enacting the Agricultural Trade Development and Assistance Act, which allowed the government to exchange excess farm goods for strategic products required by the United States. The administration's high hopes that these policies would provide the answer to the nation's farm problem were quickly disappointed by the size of the 1955 surplus, the continuing decline in farm incomes, and the fact that instead of reducing the government's cost Benson's policies increased them by about $1.5 billion in one year. Even though the flexible support law "had failed so dismally," in Adams' words, neither the President nor Benson was disposed to scrap it; and Eisenhower, despite the bitter anti-Benson protests of many farmers and the political fears of a number of influential GOP congressmen and senators, refused to blame his Secretary of Agriculture by asking for his resignation, as so many worried Republicans suggested.

Early in January, 1956, Eisenhower tried to tackle the problem of the surplus by proposing a scheme whereby the government would pay the growers of certain basic staples to limit their production of these crops. The plan, which Congress legislated in the Agricultural Act of May 28, 1956, provided the farmer with various types of assistance, the two most significant of which were the establishment of an acreage reserve and a conservation reserve or soil bank. The former was designed as a temporary emergency measure to prevent further increases in the corn, wheat, rice, and cotton surpluses by paying the farmer not to cultivate these crops; the latter was intended as a permanent effort to end the overproduction of staples. Farmers who agreed to put part of their land in the soil bank for five years, which meant either planting nothing or growing soil-restorative grasses, received an annual payment from the government to compensate them for their loss of crop income. The principles behind the soil bank, for which Congress allocated $1.2 billion, were very similar to some of the New Deal's farm measures aimed to increase agricultural incomes by setting production limits. But like the policies of the 1930's, the Republican measures of the 1950's failed either to reduce the productivity of American agriculture or to cut the mounting costs of the government's various farm programs. Indeed, they had a reverse effect. In the Agricultural Act of August, 1957, the administration again tried to use the support and crop allotment systems to persuade the farmers to grow fewer staples, but the results of this law were no better than those of the 1954 act. By the time Eisenhower left the White House, the cost of the administration's farm laws had increased from about $3.5 billion a year for the period 1955 to 1958 to some $5.4 billion for fiscal 1959 and 1960. Despite these expenditures, which were becom-

FROM FAIR DEAL TO MODERN REPUBLICANISM   417

ing increasingly irksome to the country's urban citizens, and the substantial reduction in the number of acres cultivated, the crop yields during these years registered such impressive gains that by 1960, according to one expert, the Commodity Credit Corporation "had investments in price supports and inventories of more than $9 billion . . . and held enough wheat to feed the nation for the next two years if not another bushel were grown." [7]

CONSERVATION AND PUBLIC POWER

Just as Eisenhower's agriculture policies sought to place the responsibility for the economic welfare of rural America upon the farmers themselves, his attitude on conservation, as revealed in the tidelands oil bill and other measures, reflected a similarly conservative view. Unlike Truman, who had asserted that the tidelands or offshore oil and mineral deposits of the seaboard states—the undersea resources lying between the coastline and the three-mile limit (ten and a half for Florida and Texas)— belonged "to all the people of the country," Eisenhower believed that this wealth should be turned over to the states. The weight of legal opinion on this issue appeared to be clearly with Truman, since the Supreme Court had ruled on two earlier occasions that the federal government had "paramount rights" on these submerged lands. Attorney General Brownell was of this opinion, too, but Eisenhower was not; and with strong presidential endorsement and the effective assistance of the southern Democrats, especially those whose states would benefit by the law, Congress transferred title to these resources to the states. The federal government kept its rights to the deposits lying beyond the jurisdictional limits of the states. Despite the loud protests of the conservationists and the fact that shortly before Truman had left the White House he had ordered these lands set aside as a naval petroleum reserve, Eisenhower signed the bill on May 23.

In keeping with his desire to limit the regulatory powers of the federal government, Eisenhower was prepared to amend the pricing provisions of the Natural Gas Act of 1938, which authorized the Federal Power Commission (FPC) to determine "the rates, charges, and services" for natural gas piped across state lines. The President believed that relaxing or abolishing entirely the FPC's control over prices would stimulate the companies engaged in this business to expand gas production and enlarge

[7] Gilbert C. Fite, "Abundance: The Farmers' Problem," *Current History*, XXXIX (July 1960), 15.

their facilties for its transportation. The end result, he hoped, would be a lower price for the consumer. But just as Congress was about to pass a bill allowing these changes, which like the tidelands oil legislation was strongly supported by the southern Democrats as well as many GOP members of both houses, Senator Francis P. Case, a South Dakota Republican, declared he had just learned that an attorney representing one of the oil companies had contributed $2,500 toward his campaign expenses. Case, who had originally intended to vote for the amendment. now asserted that he refused to do so. Case's disclosure caused Eisenhower to change his mind too; and when the Congress passed the bill. he vetoed it because, as he told Adams, "he refused to leave his administration open to the charge that the oil industry could get a bill approved in Washington by throwing money around."

Eisenhower had expressed his strong preference for a free economy on numerous occasions, and his stand on offshore oil and the natural gas amendment seemed to confirm his intention to implement his views vigorously. During the summer of 1953, he reiterated his growing concern with "big government," declaring that in the past the federal authorities had assumed many responsibilities that properly belonged to the people and the states. One of his principal objectives, he said, was to reestablish the federal government in its rightful position, which, in his own words, meant "trying to make it smaller rather than bigger and finding things it can stop doing instead of seeking new things for it to do." The public power program presented the Eisenhower administration with a seemingly ideal opportunity to advance the cause of two of its most cherished objectives: trimming the powers of the federal government and strengthening the cause of private enterprise.

Whereas Roosevelt and Truman had been strong supporters of public power and proud of their accomplishments, such as those in the Tennessee and Columbia river valleys, Eisenhower and Interior Secretary McKay were generally opposed to such federally sponsored and operated projects. Their answer to the nation's growing electric power requirements was the "partnership idea," according to which the local population determined its own needs, decided upon the kind of project it wanted, whether privately or publicly owned, and assumed, insofar as possible, the responsibility for financing it. In August, 1957, for example, Eisenhower signed the Niagara Power Act authorizing the New York State Power Authority, a state agency, to spend some $720 million, not a cent of which came from the federal Treasury, to harness New York's share

FROM FAIR DEAL TO MODERN REPUBLICANISM 419

of the Niagara River's hydroelectric potential. But not every state, local community, or private utility company could afford the expenditures often required to develop new sources of reasonably priced electricity. In such instances, the Eisenhower administration agreed that federal assistance was in order. In April, 1956, it applied this principle when it approved the use of $760 million of government money to promote the upper Colorado's hydroelectric, irrigation, and other water supply resources.

The most notable partnership project was the completion of the 2,342-mile St. Lawrence Seaway which, besides opening the Middle West to ocean shipping, allowed Canada and the United States to exploit the river's hydroelectric potential. Since the beginning of the twentieth century, various private interests had been trying to tap the St. Lawrence River's water power for their own needs, but the right to develop the river involved Canada as well as the United States, and the Ottawa government refused to allow it to be used exclusively for the benefit of certain private firms. The growing need for power, amply demonstrated during World War I, finally led the two governments to take action, and in 1919 the International Joint Commission established earlier under the provisions of the Boundary Water Treaty of 1909 was authorized to study the power and navigation resources of the St. Lawrence and to recommend policies for their effective development.

Submitted in December, 1921, the commission's report, as well as subsequent engineering studies, recommended an integrated series of projects, including power plants and navigation canals, which both governments accepted in principle but neither was able to implement. Domestic politics in both the United States and Canada, disagreements between the federal government and New York over their respective rights on the St. Lawrence, and the strong opposition of private utility companies, Atlantic seaboard rail and shipping interests, and the coal miners and other groups all combined to defeat every effort to launch the project until after World War II, when Canada proposed to undertake the job itself. This and pressure from the steel companies of the Middle West, which were becoming increasingly dependent upon Canadian iron ore, finally persuaded Congress to pass the Wiley-Dondero Act on May 13, 1954, establishing the St. Lawrence Seaway Development Corporation to finance, construct, and operate the American portion of the waterway. Canada created a similar agency to build and operate its section of the seaway. The project's power developments were undertaken by the New

420   THE U.S. & THE POSTWAR WORLD, 1945-1961

York State Power Authority and the Hydro-Electric Power Commission of Ontario. Less than five years later, on June 26, 1959, President Eisenhower and Britain's Queen Elizabeth II dedicated the completed Great Lakes–St. Lawrence Seaway and Power Project.

Whatever satisfaction the proponents of public power received from Eisenhower's action in pushing the St. Lawrence and upper Colorado projects was dispelled by the position he adopted toward harnessing the Snake River in Idaho's Hell's Canyon near the Oregon border. They believed the federal government should develop this site by constructing a multipurpose high dam capable of providing the power, irrigation, and flood control facilities the region required. The friends of private enterprise opposed this scheme vehemently, claiming that all the benefits of the high dam could be realized at far less cost to the taxpayers by allowing the Idaho Power Company, a private utility corporation, to build three smaller and less expensive low dams. Since this project involved no federal funds and since the Eisenhower administration was not persuaded that the high dam would be of any more benefit to the area, it approved the Federal Power Commission's license to the Idaho Power Company to begin construction. Supporters of public power and conservationists, unwilling to accept defeat, continued to fight for the high dam, but all their efforts both in and out of Congress were unsuccessful.

The Dixon-Yates controversy. Eisenhower's policy to curb the government's participation in the power industry was not limited to new projects; it applied to the expansion of existing federal ones as well, and it was the future of one of these—the Tennessee Valley Authority— which embroiled his administration in a prolonged and embarrassing controversy. Unlike Truman, who had fought the TVA's congressional battles for funds to build new steam plants to augment its hydroelectric facilities, Eisenhower had little sympathy for what the TVA stood for, and he was especially opposed to its further expansion at the expense of the region's private utility companies, which he believed should not be forced to compete with a tax-exempt public enterprise.

Despite the TVA's remarkable growth, the economic development of the region it serviced (and for which the project itself had been largely responsible) was taxing the authority's capacities to the limit. The Atomic Energy Commission's installations alone used nearly one-half of the TVA's total output. If the needs of the area's people, agriculture, and industries were to be met satisfactorily, the TVA's generating capacity had to be increased considerably. Late in 1952 the authority's directors requested funds to build a steam plant at Fulton, Tennessee, which they claimed was needed to satisfy the electric power requirements of the Memphis area. Truman had approved the request and allocated money for it in his last budget; but the economy-minded Eisenhower staff, which reviewed the government's proposed expenditures for fiscal 1953, had canceled the application, asserting that the TVA's present facilities were adequate. Within months the administration was proved wrong, and it was faced with the problem of deciding how to supply Memphis and the government's atomic plants with enough power.

Determined to prevent the TVA from building another generating plant, the Eisenhower administration proposed a plan whereby the authority could supply Memphis with the electricity it required without adding to the TVA's facilities. Instead of the TVA's producing nearly all the power it sold to its customers as it had done in the past, the electricity it delivered to the Atomic Energy Commission's Paducah installations would be returned to the authority from a new privately built steam plant at West Memphis, Arkansas, a city of nearly 16,000 inhabitants just across the Mississippi River from Memphis, Tennessee. The cost of building this new generating plant, which was estimated at around $107 million, was to be borne by a utilities combination headed by Edgar H. Dixon of Middle South Utilities, Inc., an operating utility company, and Eugene A. Yates of the Southern Company, an electric power holding company. On October 5, 1954, the Atomic Energy Commission signed a $107,250,000 long-term power contract with this group, including a provision for an additional congressional appropriation of $6.5 million for building the transmission system over which the power from the West Memphis plant could be fed back to the TVA. The administration looked upon this partnership arrangement as an effective restraint upon the "creeping socialism" of the TVA's growing "power empire." The authority's friends and the country's public power advocates attacked the contract as false economy, pointing out that it would increase the government's annual power bill anywhere from $3.3 to $5.5 million. Moreover, they also charged it was a devious means of destroying the TVA's "yardstick" principle, which had kept down the price of electricity.

The Dixon-Yates contract became an issue in the midterm elections of 1954, and in February, 1955, Alabama's Democratic Senator Lister D. Hill added to the postelection furor by accusing the administration of having failed to disclose the fact that one of the government negotiators in preparing the agreement had been Adolphe H. Wenzell, an official of the First Boston Corporation, a security and investment house which was interested in underwriting the contract. When this apparently damaging information was revealed, the administration compounded the blunder by asking the Securities and Exchange Commission, which was then investigating the financing of the contract, to delay calling for Wenzell's testimony. This request gave the opposition an ideal opportunity to raise the conflict of interest issue, which it did, exploiting it fully, to the GOP's growing embarrassment. In the meantime, while official Washington was preoccupied with the possibility of uncovering a major scandal, Memphis officials announced that the city would construct its own power plant. This permitted Eisenhower to cancel the controversial contract, which he did on July 11, 1955. By this time, however, the Dixon-Yates group had already spent some $3.5 million on the West Memphis project, for which it expected to be repaid by the Atomic Energy Commission. When the AEC refused on the grounds that Wenzell had violated the conflict of interest laws, Dixon-Yates sued. For six years the case dragged through the courts until finally, in 1961, the Supreme Court ruled in favor of the commission.

In the end, Eisenhower's efforts to prevent the TVA from expanding failed completely. In November, 1960, the authority demonstrated that it possessed the "flexibility and initiative of a private enterprise" with which, at Roosevelt's suggestion, the Congress had endowed it by going directly to the people for new construction capital with a $50 million bond issue, the first of several others which followed. By the end of 1960, Eisenhower's last full year in office, the TVA had increased its generating capacity from the 1955 level of 7.8 billion kilowatts to 11.3 billion.

Nuclear power. The Eisenhower administration also applied the partnership idea to the development of nuclear power. Since the passage of the Atomic Energy Act of 1946, the federal government had exercised absolute control over this new source of energy. Eisenhower proposed to loosen this government monopoly by allowing private enterprise to enter the atomic power industry. After considerable debate, in which spokesmen for public power assured themselves that the private utility interests would not be allowed to turn the energy of the atom into a monopoly for their own profit and that the Atomic Energy Commission would reserve for itself the right to manufacture and sell electric power, Congress passed the Atomic Energy Act of August 30, 1954.

FROM FAIR DEAL TO MODERN REPUBLICANISM 423

Private utility companies could now acquire their own fissionable material and construct and operate their own nuclear reactors to produce electric power for commercial use. On December 18, 1957, the first of these civilian nuclear power plants, at Shippingport, Pennsylvania, began generating electricity for the city of Pittsburgh. By 1960 several others were in various stages of construction or operation.

The law also authorized the Atomic Energy Commission to provide friendly governments with information and assistance on the development and uses of atomic energy for peaceful purposes. The idea embodied in this provision had originated earlier in Eisenhower's "atoms for peace" speech, delivered before the United Nations on December 8, 1953. At that time he had suggested that the United States and the Soviet Union donate some of their fissionable material to a special United Nations agency which would use it "to serve the needs rather than the fears of mankind." The Russians refused; and when Congress passed the Atomic Energy Act, Eisenhower declared that the United States would assist in promoting a "new atomic technology for peace" itself. Congress' reluctance to appropriate adequate funds, however, delayed and limited the program's effectiveness. In the meantime, the Soviet Union reversed its earlier position and on April 18, 1956, agreed to join the United States and ten other nations in creating the International Atomic Energy Agency (IAEA), whose purpose was to promote the study and development of "atomic energy for peaceful uses throughout the world." On July 29, 1957, after the United States and seventy-nine other governments had signed the statute creating the IAEA, the agency took over the direction of the "atoms for peace" proposal. Meanwhile, on July 2, 1957, Congress had also passed the European Atomic Energy Community Act, allowing the United States to share some of its nuclear secrets and armaments with its allies and to participate with the six "Euratom" countries (France, the Netherlands, Belgium, Luxembourg, Italy, and West Germany) in pooling and developing their nuclear research.

WELFARE LEGISLATION

If the partnership idea indicated the middle course along which Eisenhower intended to steer his power policies, his attitude toward social welfare legislation was equally moderate. In the case of raising the minimum wage, for example, the administration recommended increasing it from 75 to 90 cents an hour, but on July 30, 1955, Congress boosted it to $1.00. During Eisenhower's term benefits under the Social Security Act were

424 THE U.S. & THE POSTWAR WORLD, 1945-1961

extended by a series of important amendments. In September, 1954, some 10 million previously unprotected workers, including farmers and household servants, were brought into the system, and the income from wages a retired worker could earn without forfeiting his benefits was raised from $900 to $1,200 a year. In August, 1956, the age at which women workers could begin receiving benefits was lowered from sixty-five to sixty-two; the coverage was again increased by allowing more self-employed into the system; and provision was made for totally disabled workers to begin collecting monthly payments when they reached fifty years of age. In August, 1956, and again in September, 1960, Eisenhower and a Democratic Congress liberalized the system still further by increasing payments, reducing the required retirement age for men from sixty-five to sixty-two, and relaxing some of the law's other requirements. Similarly, the benefits of railroad workers were increased in May, 1959, when Congress amended the Railroad Retirement and Railroad Unemployment Insurance laws.

In the field of public housing, Eisenhower was less liberal than many of the northern Democrats but more so than most of the Republicans on Capitol Hill. Instead of providing for the 140,000 units the President had recommended, the Housing Act of August 2, 1954, authorized the construction of only 35,000, a number nowhere near that required to meet the needs of a growing population or to replace the dwellings torn down through slum clearance and urban renewal projects. To stimulate the construction industry, the law liberalized the financing of FHA housing by lowering the required down payment and lengthening mortgages. A year later, on August 11, 1955, Eisenhower signed an amendment to the law authorizing another 45,000 units of public housing and providing funds for additional slum clearance and community construction work. Five subsequent housing laws, enacted between August, 1956, and September, 1960, eased mortgage and other financial requirements further, provided for more public housing, and allocated additional funds for slum clearance and other programs begun earlier. The passage of these laws was facilitated by the decline in business activity, both actual and threatened, and by the increasing Democratic strength in Congress. Yet despite all this legislation, the condition of the nation's housing was improved but slightly.

The Eisenhower administration proved more successful in rehabilitating the neglected and overcrowded highway system. Partly because it persuaded the GOP Old Guard that road building assisted the national defense effort in addition to satisfying the public demand, and partly because the program was strongly supported by the Democratic majority on Capitol Hill, on July 29, 1956, Congress passed the Federal-Aid Highway Act, which provided for the construction of 41,000 miles of interstate roads and highways over the next thirteen years at a cost of nearly $33.5 billion. In keeping with Eisenhower's partnership idea, the responsibility for completing the program was divided between the states and the federal government, the former undertaking the construction work and paying 10 per cent of the costs and the latter assuming the other expenses. To defray part of the program's costs, the government increased the tax on gasoline and "other highway user items." In April, 1958, when it appeared that the marked decline in business activity might become worse, Congress passed another highway act, allocating $1.8 billion to step up the government's road-building projects at once.

During Eisenhower's administration, two of the most important social problems of the 1950's—education and medical care—remained largely unresolved. Both issues aroused vehement public debate, which was intensified by the partisan attacks of both sides. Conservatives, for example, argued strongly against the national government's assisting the country's overcrowded and financially hard-pressed schools and colleges, and they fought with even greater vigor the use of federal funds to subsidize the high costs of hospital and medical care, two budget items which imposed especially heavy burdens on the retired elderly and on millions of middle- and low-income families. Liberals, on the other hand, asserted that since neither local nor state governments could afford to build and maintain the schools the population required, it was the duty of the federal government to provide assistance. Their attitude toward medical care was the same. Everyone, they claimed, was entitled to adequate medical and hospital services. The free enterprise system in medicine was prohibitively expensive for most people, and the various private health insurance plans either were too expensive or provided inadequate coverage. The administration was sympathetic toward some of these arguments, and Secretary Hobby of the Department of Health, Education, and Welfare proposed a plan calling for the establishment of a "federal reinsurance corporation" to assist the private health and hospitalization programs in existence and to promote other similar ones. Nothing ever came of it. The conservatives opposed it because of its cost and because it smacked too much of "socialized medicine"; the liberals attacked it as a poor substitute for a national health insurance law.

In the meantime, while her reinsurance plan was being debated, Mrs. Hobby and her department were being accused of negligence and gross mismanagement in distributing Dr. Jonas Salk's polio vaccine. This controversy limited Mrs. Hobby's usefulness still further, so that a few months after the vaccine storm blew over she resigned, ostensibly because of her husband's declining health. On August 1, 1955, the President appointed Marion B. Folsom of Georgia to succeed her. But even though he was far more favorably disposed than his predecessor toward a federally sponsored medical health program, the only measure Congress enacted was the "partnership" Medical Care Act of September 13, 1960. The law authorized the federal government to assist the states in meeting the expenses of the medically needy who were sixty-five years of age or more. The fact that the law was so limited and that it contained a needs test was denounced by many, and the question of an effective national health insurance program was made a campaign issue in 1960.

Eisenhower and Secretary Folsom were also strongly desirous of helping resolve the acute teacher and classroom shortage, but the administration's proposal for providing federal aid to the neediest states, modest as it was, failed to get through Congress. The Republicans themselves were seriously divided on the legality and the wisdom of federal assistance. Many of the GOP's more conservative members were opposed to government intervention in the school crisis in any form whatsoever, even if it involved no more than permitting the Treasury to purchase some school district bonds. The President and his advisers, moreover, showed little disposition to fight for the administration's program or to settle upon a satisfactory compromise with the liberal Democrats in Congress, who were demanding a more comprehensive assistance program than Eisenhower was willing to approve. The Republican opponents of school aid were greatly strengthened by the segregationist Democrats from the South, who were afraid that any school aid bill which was sponsored by a bipartisan coalition of liberals, many of whom were also supporters of civil rights, would be written to discriminate intentionally against their states. As a result, partisan politics, selfish interests, excessive concern with costs, and the fear of government interference defeated every administration plan for federal assistance to education.

The school aid controversy was intensified and complicated further by the Soviet Union. On October 4, 1957, the Russians launched Sputnik I, the world's first space satellite, and they followed this scientific achievement by firing a second one a month later. These Soviet successes and the

FROM FAIR DEAL TO MODERN REPUBLICANISM 427

fact that the United States was incapable of matching, much less surpassing, them alarmed many Americans, a large number of whom attributed the accomplishments of the Soviet Union to its superior education system. The public's concern with the teacher and classroom shortages now assumed a new urgency, while the increasing criticisms which certain renowned educators and other prominent national figures leveled against the content of the school curricula led to a widespread debate on the "crisis in education," as *Life* magazine labeled it. One of the results of this growing concern with the quality of American education, which many admitted was shockingly low, and the increasing apprehension over the Soviet Union's scientific progress was the National Defense Education Act, which Congress passed on September 2, 1958. To assist worthy students with rising college and education costs, the law allocated $295 million for low-interest loans of $1,000, payable in ten years. If the borrower agreed upon graduation to teach on the precollege level for five years, he was required to repay only 50 per cent of his loan. Provision was made as well for a fellowship program to help graduate students preparing for college teaching careers, and Congress also appropriated $280 million to improve science and foreign language instruction in state schools on a dollar-matching basis. Whatever its merits in correcting certain instructional deficiencies in the school system or in promoting the study of foreign languages, science, and mathematics, the National Defense Education Act did nothing to resolve the larger problems facing American education. Like the question of medical care, it was still being debated in 1960.

LOYALTY AND THE FALL OF MC CARTHY

Many Americans hoped that with a Republican in the White House Senator McCarthy would spare the United States government further embarrassment. Their hopes, however, were quickly disappointed. Despite the administration's efforts to cooperate with and placate the Wisconsin senator, McCarthy continued as he had in the past, and within two months of Eisenhower's inauguration the two clashed openly. At Secretary Dulles' suggestion, the President appointed Charles E. Bohlen, the distinguished career diplomat, as ambassador to Moscow. Because he had served Roosevelt and Truman capably, Bohlen was anathema to McCarthy and a few others like him, who were charging the Democrats with "twenty years of treason." When Bohlen's appointment went to the Senate for confirmation, McCarthy opposed it strongly, accusing the President of having se-

428 THE U.S. & THE POSTWAR WORLD, 1945–1961

lected "Acheson's architect of disaster" and a "security risk" to represent the United States at the Kremlin. The appointment precipitated an angry intraparty squabble, but with the assistance of Senator Taft, who assured his colleagues that he had personally investigated the appointee's record and found "no suggestion anywhere by anyone reflecting on the loyalty of Mr. Bohlen," the Senate confirmed the President's choice by a vote of 74 to 13.

Even before the struggle to secure Bohlen's appointment was over, McCarthy was attracting other headlines and embittering the public debate further by his "Red-hunting" activities into the staffs of "The Voice of America" radio broadcasts and the State Department's overseas libraries and information centers. He criticized the administration for failing to purge all the Communists from these and other government departments, and he claimed that two of his investigators had found subversive literature in the libraries the government maintained abroad. During the spring of 1953, the administration tried to cooperate with McCarthy by investigating his charges and tightening its security regulations. Such measures, however, did not satisfy McCarthy or deter the other two congressional investigating committees busily ferreting out the many Communists who had supposedly infiltrated the nation's schools and entertainment industry.[8]

Eisenhower deplored the publicity-seeking tactics of these committees, and he was especially disturbed by McCarthy's reckless attacks on the State Department, which interfered with its management of foreign affairs, and by his efforts to cleanse the government's information centers, which made a mockery of American freedom and democracy. On one occasion, at Dartmouth College, he expressed his dislike for "the book burners" and on another for those who would impose "thought control" over the country; and when he was asked about the issue of Communists in government, he expressed the hope that it would soon become a matter of history and memory. But partly because he wanted to avoid an open break with the more conservative and nationalist wing of his party, many of whom were sympathetic to McCarthy's anticommunism, partly because he was reluctant to exercise the authority of his office, and partly

[8] William F. Jenner of Indiana was the chairman of the Senate Internal Security Committee investigating communism in the schools, and Representative Harold R. Velde of Illinois headed the House Un-American Activities Committee's probe into the motion picture and theatrical world.

FROM FAIR DEAL TO MODERN REPUBLICANISM 429

because, to use his own words, he refused to "get in the gutter with that guy," Eisenhower never disciplined McCarthy openly. And since McCarthy was not the kind of person to be affected by the President's quiet displeasure, the senator continued to abuse the national interest with his grossly inaccurate accusations.

In December, 1953, having sown considerable fear and discord in the State Department and its agencies, McCarthy began searching for Communists in the army. In the course of his investigations he came across Dr. Irving Peress, a New York dentist, who had been drafted, commissioned an officer, and routinely promoted to major. When Peress refused under questioning to admit whether he was or had been a Communist by taking refuge under the Fifth Amendment, the army got rid of him as quickly as possible by discharging him honorably. The army agreed that this action, like Peress' previous promotions, was ill-advised, and it assured McCarthy that it was instituting reforms to prevent similar errors henceforth. But this was not enough for McCarthy, who summoned various officers from Peress' camp to testify before his committee. When one of them, Brigadier General Ralph Zwicker, following the instructions of his superiors, refused to answer certain questions pertaining to Peress' discharge, McCarthy accused Zwicker of being "ignorant," of "shielding Communist conspirators," and of being "a disgrace to the uniform."

Shocked by this unwarranted and humiliating assault upon a distinguished soldier and determined to protect his other officers from similar abuse, Secretary of the Army Robert T. Stevens, aided by a number of influential Republicans, met with the Wisconsin senator. But the "memorandum of understanding" which resulted from this conference was widely interpreted as the Secretary's surrender document, not the reassurances he had sought—that McCarthy would cease his attacks on the army. Stevens subsequently refuted parts of the memorandum with a statement of his own, but the impression remained that he had capitulated before McCarthy—that he had displayed "the white feather," as one newspaper put it. The Stevens fiasco, with its disastrous effect upon the military's morale, finally caused the administration to fight back, and on March 11 the army revealed that McCarthy and Roy M. Cohn, the chief counsel of the McCarthy subcommittee, had used various kinds of pressure to secure "preferential treatment" for one of their unsalaried assistants, G. David Schine, who had been drafted as a private. McCarthy struck back by accusing the army of trying to "smear" him and using Schine as "a hostage" to prevent him from continuing the investigation of subversion and Communist infiltration at Fort Monmouth, New Jersey, the Army Signal Corps center.

Beginning on April 22, 1954, the subcommittee of the Senate Permanent Investigating Committee listened to these charges and countercharges, and for five weeks the televised army-McCarthy hearings almost monopolized the nation's attention, much to the disgust of Eisenhower, who declared at one of his press conferences that he hoped "America may derive from this incident advantages that are at least comparable to what we have suffered in the loss of international prestige and . . . national self-respect." The results of the hearings did not vindicate either side, but they contributed materially to McCarthy's own self-destruction. The television cameras, recording accurately all his vulgarities, viciousness, and contempt for almost everything men hold sacred, exposed his falsity to millions of Americans. And though the subcommittee dismissed the Army's charges against him and his aides, neither McCarthy's influence

Senator Joseph R. McCarthy of Wisconsin sought national prominence; and he achieved it temporarily by exploiting the postwar fears of the American people. He is shown here during the army-McCarthy hearings (May, 1954). (Brown Brothers)

FROM FAIR DEAL TO MODERN REPUBLICANISM 431

nor his reputation survived the hearings. Several months later, on September 27, a Senate committee headed by the Utah Republican Arthur V. Watkins recommended McCarthy's censure for "conduct . . . unbecoming a member of the United States Senate . . . , contrary to senatorial traditions, and tend[ing] to bring the Senate in disrepute"; and on December 2, the Senate voted 67 to 22 to "condemn" McCarthy. Every one of the twenty-two senators who voted against condemning McCarthy was an ultra right-wing Republican, for example, Illinois' Everett Dirksen and Minority Leader William Knowland of California. The President, however, was well pleased with the results, and he so informed Senator Watkins of the fact publicly. This caused McCarthy to "apologize" to the American people for having asked them to vote for Eisenhower in 1952, thereby permitting him to add another year to the "twenty years of treason" under the Democrats. By this time, however, McCarthy's influence had fallen precipitously. Ignored by the administration, shunned by his colleagues and the press, he died in May, 1957, a disgruntled, lonely, and unlamented has-been.

While McCarthy was making headlines out of the loyalty issue, the administration was quietly strengthening the government's internal security system. Less than a month after Eisenhower took office he altered the loyalty regulations Truman had introduced, broadening them into a security risk program and enlarging the reasons for which government officials might be dismissed. At the same time he ordered the FBI to adopt fair but strict policies toward all cases involving matters that might affect the loyalty of federal employees. A short time thereafter he ordered the FBI to recheck the files of all persons against whom unfavorable information had been collected. By the end of his first year in the White House, Eisenhower announced that some 2,200 security risks had been separated from their government jobs. Unlike McCarthy, the administration refused to reveal the names of these individuals or the nature of their offenses. Nonetheless, the program was strongly criticized by a large segment of the press, which asserted that the inclusion of various unrelated offenses—from drunkenness to expressing Communist sympathies—under the heading *security risk* allowed for much misinterpretation and unfairly inflicted the disloyalty tag on all discharged government employees. Eisenhower, however, convinced that the new rules which had been adopted were both proper and just, was, in his own words, "perfectly indifferent to the shouting of some newspapers."

One of the first and most prominent individuals affected by Eisen-

432 THE U.S. & THE POSTWAR WORLD, 1945–1961

hower's new security order was J. Robert Oppenheimer, World War II chief of the Los Alamos atomic bomb project, former chairman of the General Advisory Board of the Atomic Energy Commission, and still a consultant with the AEC. On December 22, 1953, after a recheck of Oppenheimer's file, the President ordered Lewis L. Strauss, the AEC's chairman, to revoke the physicist's clearance and to accept his immediate resignation. When Oppenheimer chose to stand investigation rather than resign without learning the reason for having had his clearance withdrawn, a special five-man AEC commission was established to study his case. Beginning in April, 1954, the commission listened to the government charge that before 1942, the year Oppenheimer entered government service, he had associated with many Communists and had supported some of their causes. Oppenheimer admitted this was true, but he asserted that since that time he had had nothing to do with Communists and was no longer sympathetic with any of their ideas. The government also accused him of having opposed the development of the hydrogen bomb and of having failed to cooperate effectively in implementing President Truman's 1950 directive ordering full-scale work on its production. This appeared to be a more serious charge than the others, since it was strongly supported by the testimony of Edward Teller, a former colleague of Oppenheimer's at the University of California and one of the chief physicists in charge of the "superbomb" project. The commission weighed all the evidence and reported its findings to the Atomic Energy Commission, which issued its report on June 29, 1954. Upholding the recommendations of the special commission, the AEC, in a 4 to 1 vote, declared Oppenheimer to be "loyal" but refused to reinstate his clearance because of "fundamental defects in his character" and because his associations with Communists had "extended far beyond the tolerable limits of prudence and restraint."

The administration's efforts to combat Communist subversion continued uninterrupted as the new security system went into effect in the various federal departments. On August 24, 1954, Congress passed the Communist Control Act, legally outlawing the Communist party. By this time, however, with McCarthy in disrepute and the administration and the courts quietly enforcing the law, the loyalty issue fell increasingly into the background. And as the fear of Communist infiltration subsided, concern with safeguarding individual freedom reasserted itself. The Supreme Court, led by its new Chief Justice, Earl Warren of California, an Eisenhower appointee, showed an exceptionally strong respect for protecting the constitutional rights of the individual. In *Watkins v. United States* (1957), the Court admitted Congress' right to investigate, but declared that its "power of inquiry . . . is not unlimited" and that it did not possess the "general authority to expose the private affairs of individuals without justification in terms of the functions of Congress." During the same year, in at least three other equally significant decisions, the Court limited the government's right to prosecute under the Smith Act (*Yates v. United States*), forced state officials investigating subversives to respect the defendant's rights (*Sweezy v. New Hampshire*), and granted the accused the right to inspect the evidence against him, including information in the FBI files, if it was employed by the prosecution (*Jencks v. United States*). To abide by the Court's ruling and at the same time to protect the government's secret sources of information and safeguard its files, on August 30, 1957, Congress limited and regulated the use defendants could make of these materials. Except for a few superpatriots, some of whom wanted to impeach the Chief Justice, most Americans welcomed the Supreme Court's vigorous enforcement of the Bill of Rights.

Suggested Readings

The loyalty issue and the related questions of internal security and individual rights are discussed with considerable objectivity in Nathaniel Weyl, *Battle Against Disloyalty* (New York, 1951) and in Henry S. Commager, *Freedom, Loyalty and Dissent* (New York, 1954). Equally good is Robert K. Carr's study, *The House Committee on Un-American Activities, 1945–1950* (Ithaca, N.Y. [1952]). See also Telford Taylor, *Grand Inquest* (New York, 1956) on congressional investigations. Carey McWilliams, *Witch Hunt: The Revival of Heresy* (Boston, 1950); Bert Andrews, *Washington Witch Hunt* (New York, 1948); and the two books by Alan Barth, *The Loyalty of Free Men* (New York, 1951) and *Government By Investigation* (New York, 1955) are all useful. A judicious and perceptive collection of essays on the "cultural vigilantes" and the "ritualistic liberals" is Sidney Hook's *Heresy, Yes—Conspiracy, No* (New York, 1952). Reppy Alison, *Civil Rights in the United States* (New York, 1951) analyzes the Supreme Court's decisions involving these freedoms between 1948 and 1951. See also C. Herman Pritchett, *Civil Liberties and the Vinson Court* (Chicago, 1954).

Alistair Cooke, *A Generation on Trial: U.S.A. v. Alger Hiss* (2d enl. ed., New York, 1952) is a balanced account of this significant trial. Richard B. Morris, *Fair Trial: Fourteen Who Stood Accused from Anne Hutchinson to Alger Hiss* (New York, 1952) puts the Hiss case in perspective. Ralph de Toledano and Victor Lasky, *Seeds of Treason: The True Story of the Hiss-*

434 THE U.S. & THE POSTWAR WORLD, 1945–1961

Chambers Tragedy (New York, 1950) is as strongly anti-Hiss as Earl Jowitt's *The Strange Case of Alger Hiss* (New York, 1953) is in favor of him. Hiss and Chambers present their own views in Alger Hiss, *In the Court of Public Opinion* (New York, 1957) and Whittaker Chambers, *Witness* (New York, 1952).

David A. Shannon, *The Decline of American Communism: A History of the Communist Party of the United States since 1945* (New York, 1959) ably sets forth the party's postwar demise. Louis F. Budenz, *Men without Faces: The Communist Conspiracy in the U.S.A.* (New York, 1950) contains the confessions of a former Communist.

The atom spy story is interestingly told in two books: David J. Dallin, *Soviet Espionage* (New Haven, Conn., 1955) and Alan Morehead, *The Traitors* (New York, 1952).

Senator McCarthy's career is documented in Wisconsin Citizens Committee, *The McCarthy Record* (Madison, Wis., 1952). See also Richard H. Rovere, *Senator Joe McCarthy* (New York [1959]); Jack Anderson and Ronald W. May, *McCarthy: the Man, the Senator, the Ism* (Boston, 1952); and Richard Luthin, *American Demagogues: Twentieth Century* (Boston, 1954), which establishes McCarthy as "the foremost exponent of twentieth century demagoguery." Owen J. Lattimore, *Ordeal by Slander* (New York, 1950) is one man's reply to McCarthy's charges of disloyalty.

On the elections of 1952, 1954, and 1956 see, in addition to William S. White, *The Taft Story*, already cited, Paul T. David, *et al.*, *Presidential Nominating Politics in 1952* (Baltimore [1954]) and Angus Campbell, *The Voter Decides* (Evanston, Ill. [1954]). See also Charles A. H. Thompson and Frances M. Shattuck, *The 1956 Presidential Campaign* (Washington, D.C., 1960), a Brookings Institution analysis of that political contest. On the Truman-Eisenhower transition, Laurin L. Henry's *Presidential Transitions* (Washington, D.C., 1960), is first-rate.

On Eisenhower's administration see the references at the end of Chapter 10.

10

The Eisenhower Years

FOREIGN POLICY, 1953–1956

Among the many serious consequences and repercussions of the anti-Communist hysteria that gripped the country during the first years of Eisenhower's Presidency, probably none was more detrimental to the national interest than the inhibiting effect it had upon American foreign policy. Many of McCarthy's most ardent supporters on Capitol Hill were supernationalists and ultraconservatives who had stubbornly fought the domestic and foreign policies of Roosevelt and Truman. Able to defeat the Democrats in 1952 only by accepting a spokesman of the eastern, more liberal, and internationalist faction of the Republican party as presidential candidate, these congressional right-wingers were almost as suspicious of Eisenhower as they had been of his Democratic predecessors. Since the ideological orientation of the new administration was not entirely to their liking, they sought to determine its direction by strengthening their influence over the making of foreign policy, the one area in which their views had been most ignored during the past twenty years. There was little point in defending "the American way of life" by fighting communism and subversion at home if the President could undermine the national heritage by entering into all kinds of Executive agreements or secret understandings with foreign governments, as had occurred at Yalta. The most effective way Congress could assure itself that the President would respect its views in negotiating with foreign powers was to limit

436 THE U.S. & THE POSTWAR WORLD, 1945−1961

and carefully define his authority to enter into Executive agreements which, for all practical purposes, were as binding as duly ratified treaties. Moreover, since the United States was a member of the United Nations, an organization many of these supernationalists held to be suspect at best, there was always the possibility that it might require the United States to adhere to one of its resolutions which was contrary to American law. The apprehension these men felt about a postwar world they disliked and did not understand, their fears of the immense growth of presidential authority, and their desire to prevent further change were expressed in numerous ways, one of which was a concerted effort to trim the powers of the President by enlarging those of Congress, which they believed to be a better guardian of the country's interests and safety than was the White House.

The Bricker Amendment

On January 7, 1953, two weeks before Eisenhower was inaugurated President, Ohio's Republican Senator John W. Bricker introduced a resolution proposing a constitutional amendment which would render the provisions of treaties conflicting with the Constitution null and void, require that a "treaty shall become effective as internal law in the United States only through legislation which would be valid in the absence of a treaty," and empower Congress "to regulate all executive and other agreements with any foreign power or international organization." Bricker's proposal was strongly supported by such groups as the American Legion and the American Bar Association, but while neither Eisenhower nor Secretary Dulles was entirely opposed to limiting the President's role in foreign affairs in some respects, both of them disapproved strongly of the extensive restraints incorporated into Bricker's proposal. For nearly a year Eisenhower tried to devise a substitute that would satisfy Bricker's supporters without endangering the authority of the President to determine and execute the nation's foreign policy, but when no suitable compromise could be reached, he wrote Senate Majority Leader William Knowland that he was "unalterably opposed to the Bricker Amendment" and that if the Senate adopted it "in its present form . . . [it] would be notice to our friends as well as our enemies abroad that our country intends to withdraw from its leadership in world affairs." Dulles also submitted his protests. On February 26, 1954, the amendment failed to pass the Senate but received only a single vote less than the two-thirds required for amendments initiated in either house of Congress. Of the 31 votes that killed it, 17 were Democratic ones.

Eisenhower's struggle with the conservative-nationalist coalition over the Bricker amendment was duplicated in his efforts to lower the tariff and to prevent drastic cuts in the foreign aid and military assistance programs. In 1953, for example, Congress extended the Reciprocal Trade Act for a year, but only after the protectionists won concessions from the administration. The next year they forced Eisenhower to accept several other amendments reflecting their high tariff views. Subsequent extensions of this law, enacted in June of 1955 and in the Trade Agreements Extension Act of August 20, 1958, which was to remain in effect until June 30, 1962, also included protectionist clauses that nullified many of the President's proposals designed to enlarge American foreign trade with the non-Communist bloc and to make the tariff policy of the United States into an effective instrument to meet the Soviet Union's growing economic challenge in world markets. "We cannot find safety in economic isolation at a time when the world is shrinking," the President declared repeatedly, but his words went unheeded and Congress showed no interest in legislating the liberal trade policies he proposed year after year.

The same group of conservative and nationalist congressmen who opposed Eisenhower's foreign trade program also insisted upon cutting the overseas aid and assistance program. The President, Adams recalled, "argued himself hoarse" to prevent Congress from slashing the mutual security program, and though he succeeded in getting an annual appropriation, it was always considerably less than the amount he deemed necessary for peace and security. Congress was especially reluctant to help the underdeveloped or neutral countries, like India and the new African and Asian nations, even though it was abundantly obvious that the Soviet Union was trying to win them over to its side. Neither Eisenhower nor Secretary Dulles was able to persuade Congress of the necessity for these moneys. In 1957 the administration's request for mutual security funds was cut by a billion dollars; the next year, even after a special committee headed by the former president of the United States Steel Corporation, Benjamin Fairless, confirmed the vital importance of the foreign assistance program to the security of the United States and the President appealed for public support in a radio and television speech, Congress appropriated $1.6 billion less than he had requested.

438 THE U.S. & THE POSTWAR WORLD, 1945-1961

The Diplomacy of John Foster Dulles

Like the President, Dulles tried to assure himself of the support of right-wing Republicans by catering, at least verbally, to some of their prejudices. During the 1952 campaign the GOP had accused the Democrats of being responsible for the rise of Red China and the worldwide expansion of Soviet communism. The "tragic blunders" of Democratic diplomacy that had made these unfortunate events possible, the Republicans asserted, had undermined the vital interests and security of the United States, and the policy of containment, which Dulles repeatedly denounced as "negative, futile and immoral," was simply perpetuating the frustrations arising out of the Democratic party's errors and misconceptions. The "treadmill policies" of the Truman era, he declared, had to be replaced with dynamic and positive ones.

THE POLICY OF "LIBERATION"

Dulles believed that the nation's diplomacy must express the great "moral principles" upon which the United States was founded and had prospered. Instead of passively accepting the status quo as the Democrats had done, American policy must assume the psychological and political offensive necessary to change the world balance of power to the nation's advantage. The policy of containment must give way to what he called a policy of "liberation," designed to strengthen the cause of freedom among the oppressed and subjugated peoples behind the iron curtain. The United States, Dulles said, "should make it publicly known that it wants and expects liberation to occur. The mere statement of that wish and expectation would change, in an electrifying way, the mood of the captive peoples. It would probably put heavy new burdens on the jailers and create new opportunities for liberation." [1]

Statements like this one were soothing tonic to the nationalist-conservative faction of the GOP. Recalling the way these militant anti-Communists had harassed his predecessor, Secretary Acheson, Dulles was determined to prevent them from employing similar tactics against him by mollifying their fears with reassuring words. The policy of liberation, like his demand for the forceful execution of a new, stringent, and "positive loyalty" program in the State Department, was to avoid alienating the congressionally

---

[1] Quoted in John W. Spanier, *American Foreign Policy Since World War II* (New York [1960]), p. 100.

THE EISENHOWER YEARS 439

powerful right-wingers and, as he said, being "caught with another Alger Hiss on my hands." Because of the political necessity of satisfying and securing the support of the disparate elements within his own party and because of his own highly developed moralistic conscience, Dulles proclaimed a foreign policy that appeared to be considerably different from the one elaborated by his Democratic predecessor but that in practice turned out to be very much the same. In essence, the policy of liberation was containment under a different name.

The reason the content of Dulles' foreign policy was largely undistinguishable from Acheson's should have been immediately apparent to the American people, as it soon was to their friends and foes alike. To begin with, no responsible or knowledgeable member of the administration actually believed that America's insecurity stemmed from the secret Democratic sell-outs at Yalta or any other wartime conference, as some of the more neurotic members of the Republican Old Guard were asserting; and whatever the shortcomings of those agreements, both Dulles and Eisenhower understood clearly that it was not to the advantage of the United States to repudiate them. Moreover, the administration, America's allies, and the American people themselves were not disposed to inaugurate World War III in order to liberate the "captive peoples" or to reestablish Chiang Kai-shek on the Chinese mainland. Proof of this was amply apparent in the alarm Dulles created among large segments of the American and Allied peoples when, speaking before the Council on Foreign Relations on January 12, 1954, he declared that the top civilian and military leaders of the government had reached some new "basic policy decisions." Henceforth, he said, the United States would no longer meet the aggressor on his own terms, as the Truman administration had done in Korea, but would counter his moves by employing America's "great capacity to retaliate instantly by means and places of our own choosing." The doctrine of massive retaliation, as this policy soon came to be called, like the policy of liberation, had little effect upon the officials in Moscow and Peiping, for whom it was intended, because they realized that neither the United States nor its allies were willing to assume the risks it entailed. So long as the Communist powers did not threaten the West's vital interests, it was unlikely that the United States would precipitate a nuclear war to repel a Red thrust in a nonvital area of the world.

The loud protests that followed Dulles' speech, the fact that he subsequently limited the doctrine's applicability by saying that, like all disciplinary measures, this one too followed the well-known precept that "the punishment must always fit the crime," and the fact that neither the Soviet Union nor Red China was deterred from fomenting new crises appear to uphold the verdict of those who, like the columnist Walter Lippmann, called Dulles' efforts to elaborate a new policy "a case of excessive salesmanship." Five years later, at the time of Dulles' death, *The New York Times*, in reviewing his career as Secretary of State, affirmed Lippmann's earlier judgment when it concluded that "as things worked out," there was always "a wide margin between Mr. Dulles' bold words and the United States Government's actions." This disparity between what the administration announced as its policy and what it was prepared to do when confronted by an actual crisis revealed itself almost at once.

One week after Eisenhower's inauguration, on January 27, 1953, Dulles announced in a nationally televised speech that the captive peoples could count on the United States to help them regain their freedom and independence; and three weeks later the administration asked Congress to approve a resolution to this effect, but to which Eisenhower added an important qualification—that American assistance in "liberating" the subjugated peoples did not imply the use of force. Because the resolution limited the role of the United States to employing only peaceful means, it was strongly criticized by Senator Taft and other anti-Yalta Republicans for being too moderate and for not including a sweeping denuncia-

Secretary of State John Foster Dulles was one of the strongest figures in President Eisenhower's administration and largely responsible for the direction of American foreign policy from 1953 until the time of his death. (Brown Brothers)

tion of Democratic foreign policy. The news of Joseph Stalin's death on March 5, 1953, led the administration to ask the Republican leadership in Congress to withdraw the resolution, a move that suggested in many quarters that Eisenhower did not intend to enforce Dulles' policy of liberation. That this was the case was revealed to the whole world in June, 1953, when the workers of East Berlin, protesting against new Soviet-imposed work schedules, started a strike which led to widespread rioting throughout East Germany. The Soviet army moved in quickly to restore order, and while Eisenhower deplored the bloodshed that followed, he announced that the United States would send food but that it would not intervene on behalf of the rioting anti-Soviet East Germans. To have implemented the policy of liberation in this instance would have meant the possibility of precipitating a war with Russia.

The administration followed much the same policy when the Hungarian nationalists revolted against the Kremlin's domination in October, 1956. During this brief and bloody revolution, the Hungarians appealed to the West for help, but aside from offering them "sympathy, relief, and asylum," as Adams put it, there was little the United States could do to assist them. The State Department protested directly to Moscow, and Henry Cabot Lodge, Jr., the American ambassador to the United Nations, secured a resolution ordering the immediate withdrawal of Soviet troops from Hungary. Ignoring both Washington and the United Nations, Russian armored troops crushed the revolt and by November 4 had reestablished the Kremlin's firm hold over Hungary. To help the estimated 175,000 to 200,000 Hungarians who fled their Russian overlords during the uprising, Eisenhower announced that the United States would admit 5,000 of these refugees, a number subsequently increased to some 38,000. Once again, the unwillingness of the West to risk a war with the Soviet Union resulted in considerable sharp criticism of the United States for declaring itself forcefully and then acting meekly when the chips were down. Even though by this time the original policy of liberation had been considerably toned down by the President's and Dulles' own statements, the fact remains that it raised false hopes among the captive peoples and presented, on the surface at least, a highly distorted, confusing, and unrealistic picture of American policy and capabilities.

THE FAR EAST

Indochina. Just as the East German and Hungarian uprisings demonstrated that the policy of liberation was meaningless so long as the United States was unwilling to use force to implement it, the Indochina crisis of

1954 revealed that Eisenhower was no more inclined to apply Dulles' "deterrent of massive retaliatory power" than Truman had been to follow MacArthur's advice to end the Korean stalemate by risking total war. But unlike the way Truman and Acheson responded to the Communist challenge in Korea, Eisenhower and Dulles reacted to the Red threat in Indochina by what the London *Economist* described as "vociferous inaction."

The events that led to the defeat of America's objectives in Indochina and turned Dulles' threat of massive retaliation into a hollow boast were part of the twentieth-century worldwide revolt of colonial peoples against foreign rule. In the case of Indochina, the struggle for independence from France was accelerated by World War II, when nationalist and Communist groups fought against their new Japanese conquerors. After the war, when Japan had been ousted and the French sought to reestablish their dominion over their former colony, the same groups which had opposed Nippon's imperialism resisted the return of the French. One of these nationalist factions, led by Ho Chi-minh, the native Communist leader who headed the Independence League (Vietminh), carried on a protracted fight against the returning French forces. At first the United States government took little interest in Indochina's war against France, but as Ho Chi-minh's forces, strongly assisted by Red China, made steady headway against the Vietnamese regime of Emperor Boa Dai which the French had established in March, 1949, America became increasingly concerned, especially after the Communists had taken over China and had invaded South Korea.

Despite the United States government's dislike of associating itself with an imperial power which was trying to frustrate the desires of a colonial people for independence, the Truman administration, realizing that if the Communists were allowed to take over Indochina it would gravely damage the strategic interests of America and the free world in Southeast Asia, started to extend France increasing amounts of financial and military assistance. At the time Eisenhower became President, Truman told him the United States was "helping France to the extent of carrying between one-third and one-half of the financial burden of the Indo-Chinese war." Within less than a year the Eisenhower administration was paying for even more of France's war effort—between 75 and 80 per cent. Money and military equipment, however, were not enough to stem the Communist advance, and during Eisenhower's first year in the White House Ho Chi-minh's armed guerrillas advanced steadily, inflicting still heavier losses upon the French.

THE EISENHOWER YEARS 443

Early in 1954 the Indochinese crisis had become so acute that the Eisenhower administration was faced with the unpleasant choice between direct intervention, as Truman had done in Korea, and a Communist victory. In February Eisenhower declared he was "bitterly opposed" to committing American troops "in a hot war in that region," but at the same time he stressed the great importance of assisting the anti-Communist forces. On March 25 he said that Indochina was of "transcendent importance" to the security of the United States in Southeast Asia, and four days later Dulles elaborated upon the President's statement by saying that "the imposition on Southeast Asia of the political system of Communist Russia and its ally, by *whatever* means, would be a grave threat to the whole free community. The United States feels that that possibility should not be passively accepted, but should be met by united action. This might have serious risks, but these risks are far less than would face us a few years from now if we dare not be resolute today." These were strong words, but because the administration, America's allies, and the American people were not disposed to create another Korea by using force to give substance to Washington's warnings, Dulles' bold words proved meaningless.

By April, 1954, with its forces pinned down at Dienbienphu, France called upon the United States to send its carrier-based planes to bomb the Communist besiegers. In view of Eisenhower's and Dulles' recent statements on the necessity of defending Dienbienphu and Indochina, France's demand for assistance was an important test of the administration's determination to enforce its declared policies. When the President refused to help France because, as he said, he did not want to get the United States "involved alone in a power move against the Russians," whatever merit there was in the administration's policy of massive retaliation was nullified. Dulles had declared repeatedly that the purpose of American policy was to prevent further Communist expansion by warning the "potential aggressor . . . in advance that he can and will be made to suffer for his aggression more than he can possibly gain by it." The Communists gambled that Dulles was practicing Theodore Roosevelt's famous maxim —"Speak softly and carry a big stick"—in reverse. Events proved them right.

Except for Admiral Arthur W. Radford, the Joint Chiefs of Staff were opposed to using American planes to relieve Dienbienphu; the legislative leaders Dulles consulted refused to support his request for a congressional resolution authorizing the President "to use air and naval power" against

Ho Chi-minh's forces without the approval of America's allies; and the British, afraid of precipitating a general war, refused to move with the United States in a joint action to support France. These various considerations combined to assure the Communists of victory. Dienbienphu fell in May; and France, no longer able or willing to continue the Indochinese struggle alone, decided to end it. On July 21, 1954, at the Geneva Conference on Far Eastern Affairs, the French government agreed to an armistice which, as in the case of Korea, divided Indochina in two, with the seventeenth parallel separating the hostile forces. The northern section became the Communist state of Vietminh with Ho Chi-minh as its first president; the southern provinces organized themselves into the republic of Vietnam and in October, 1955, elected the aristocratic and anti-Communist nationalist Ngo Dinh Diem as president. The United States immediately began supplying him with various kinds of economic, military, and technical assistance, and by 1962 the Defense Department's Military Assistance Advisory Group (MAAG), through which President Truman had begun funneling aid to the French in 1951, had spent on Indochina a total of some $2 billion. The Geneva agreement of 1954 brought neither real peace nor security to Indochina: the seventeenth parallel remained an armed frontier, and a chronic guerrilla war, sporadically blazing into open conflict, remained a depressingly dangerous threat to world peace. After 1954 the United States became increasingly committed to the defense of Vietnam, and although American ground forces had not at that time been engaged in any battles with the Vietminh Communists, such a possibility could not be excluded.

The Indochinese crisis of April, 1954, which brought the United States so close to another war in the Far East was a serious defeat for American diplomacy, and Dulles moved quickly to prevent further Communist inroads into the free world's interests in Southeast Asia by seeking to establish a security system for the region similar to NATO. The idea of such a defensive alliance had preceded the collapse of Indochina, but the events of May, 1954, certainly accelerated its realization, and at Manila on September 8 the United States and seven other Pacific powers (Britain, France, Australia, New Zealand, Pakistan, the Philippines, and Thailand) signed the Manila Pact, which established the Southeast Asia Treaty Organization (SEATO). The SEATO treaty was essentially a "consultative pact," far less binding upon its members than NATO. Article IV of the treaty states that in case of an attack against any one of the signatories "or against any state or territory which . . . [they] may hereafter designate" will be construed by each of them as a threat to "its own peace

THE EISENHOWER YEARS 445

and safety and . . . [each of them] will . . . act to meet the common danger in accordance with its constitutional processes." The treaty was weakened further by the fact that Japan, India, Burma, Ceylon, and Indonesia chose not to become members. Moreover, because of the mixed reaction toward Nationalist China and South Korea on the part of SEATO's members, neither of these two states was included, and South Vietnam, Laos, and Cambodia (the latter two also formerly parts of French Indochina), while brought under the protection of Article IV, were not made official members of the Manila Pact. Finally, the responsibility of the United States under Article IV was limited by a special provision which stated that American involvement will "apply only to Communist aggression." Whether SEATO would prove effective was debatable, but that it indicated the Eisenhower administration's efforts to extend the Truman-Acheson policy of containment was clearly apparent.

Formosa. The question of American policy toward the Nationalist Chinese government on Formosa also revealed the differences between the administration and the "Asia First" Republicans in Congress, who were continuing to demand that the State Department adopt a new and more vigorous China policy. A number of these outspoken members of the GOP's Old Guard talked as if they were prepared to go to war against Red China in order to reestablish Chiang's government on the mainland, but Eisenhower was as opposed to becoming involved in a war in China as Truman had been. But whereas Truman and Acheson looked upon the fall of the Nationalist regime as an unfortunate and largely unalterable *fait accompli,* Dulles, partly to mollify the Asia Firsters and partly to persuade the Red Chinese to end their intervention in the Korean War, which was still going on when he became Secretary of State, spoke as if the United States was going to help Chiang regain the mainland. This impression was strengthened on February 20, 1953, when Eisenhower told Congress that he was revoking President Truman's order of June, 1950, by which the United States Seventh Fleet had been "instructed both to prevent attack upon Formosa and also to insure [that] Formosa should not be used as a base of operations against the Chinese mainland." Henceforth, Eisenhower continued, "the Seventh Fleet [would] no longer be employed to shield Communist China."

This statement, widely referred to as the "unleashing" of Chiang Kaishek, supposedly marked the beginning of a new China policy. In mid-August, 1954, when Red China's Foreign Minister Chou En-lai announced his long-held intention to take Formosa, Eisenhower declared that "any invasion of Formosa would have to run over the Seventh Fleet." Three

446   THE U.S. & THE POSTWAR WORLD, 1945–1961

weeks later Red Chinese artillery began shelling Quemoy, one of the several small islands just off the China coast which Chiang's troops were still holding. (The other principal islands were Matsu and the Tachens.) During the autumn of 1954, as the Red Chinese were firing upon these Nationalist-held islands, the Eisenhower administration debated whether to include them in its guarantee to defend Formosa. There were a few GOP spokesmen, among them Senator Knowland and other equally strong congressional friends of Chiang, who argued that the United States should use force to repel any attack against these islands even though General Matthew Ridgway, the Army Chief of Staff, indicated that their military and strategic value to Chiang and the United States was debatable at best. Like Truman, Eisenhower, in Adams' words, "had no desire to provoke a war with China unless Formosa itself was in jeopardy," and on December 2, 1954, this view was confirmed in a mutual defense treaty with Nationalist China. The United States agreed to assist Chiang in case of an attack upon Formosa or the Pescadores, a small group of islands in the Formosa Straits which sheltered some 83,000 Nationalist Chinese. No provision, however, was made for the offshore islands which had occupied so much of the recent news. The United States also received Chiang's pledge to refrain from any offensive action against Red China without first consulting Washington. The treaty's net effect was to "re-leash" Chiang, reestablish the Seventh Fleet's naval patrol around Formosa, and formally reassert the Truman-Acheson policies.

The treaty did not deter Communist China from continuing its bombardment of Quemoy and Matsu, and in January, 1955, when it appeared as if Premier Mao Tse-tung was prepared to take over the islands, Congress replied immediately to Eisenhower's request for additional authority to use the nation's armed forces to defend Chiang against attack. On January 28, 1955, by a large vote (409 to 3 in the House and 85 to 3 in the Senate), it authorized the President to use whatever means he thought "necessary for the specific purpose of securing and protecting Formosa and the Pescadores against armed attack, this authority to include the securing and protection of such related positions and territories . . . now in friendly hands as he judges to be required and appropriate . . . ." The resolution did not guarantee that America would go to the defense of Matsu and Quemoy,[2] but since, as Dulles subsequently stated, Mao Tse-

---

[2] In February, 1955, Chiang, with the assistance of the United States navy, evacuated the Nationalist forces and civilians from the Tachens Islands, the most northerly of the three coastal island groups under Red Chinese attack.

tung and Chou En-lai had repeatedly declared that the capture of these islands was a means to the conquest of Formosa, the two Red Chinese leaders had very clearly linked them to the defense of Formosa, to which the United States was firmly committed. Dulles' interpretation of the Formosa Resolution was far more "belligerent" than the President's. According to Adams, Eisenhower looked upon the Formosa Resolution as providing him with "a wait-and-see clause that gave him the privilege of deciding in the event of an attack on Quemoy and Matsu whether the safety of Formosa and the Pescadores was actually threatened before committing himself to a fight over the smaller islands." Dulles, on the other hand, used it—so he said to the author of a *Life* magazine article published on January 16, 1956—as a tool to force Red China to abandon its plans to destroy Chiang. Mao Tse-tung subsequently denied that Dulles' contention was true.

Dulles was also quoted in this article as saying that the Formosa Resolution was an example of the beneficial results achieved by his forcefully executed diplomacy. "Of course we were brought to the verge of war," he said. "The ability to get to the verge without getting into the war is the necessary art. If you cannot master it, you inevitably get into war . . . . We walked to the brink and we looked it in the face. We took strong action." Whether Dulles' "brinkmanship" diplomacy, as this policy was soon widely labeled, with its threat of massive retaliation actually brought an end to the immediate danger of a Red Chinese assault upon these islands is difficult to say. In any event, the danger passed, and for more than three years, while the representatives of the United States and Red China conferred on "relaxing tension" in the Formosa Straits, there were no new crises in the area.

Then, during the last week of August, 1958, Red China started to bombard the islands again and Chou En-lai spoke of an imminent invasion of Quemoy. Eisenhower ordered the Seventh Fleet to escort Nationalist supply ships bringing reinforcements to the islands but to stay out of Red China's three-mile limit, and Mao Tse-tung's Communist fighters were equally careful to avoid a direct clash with the American naval convoys. For forty-four days, while the Communists poured 475,000 pounds of artillery shells on the two islands, the United States sent Chiang arms, ammunition, and planes, including some light tactical atomic artillery. By the first week of October this second threat of an invasion also passed, and both sides reverted once again to guarding their ground. The presence of the United States Seventh Fleet and Chiang's determination to defend

448 THE U.S. & THE POSTWAR WORLD, 1945–1961

the offshore islands "to the last man" prevented the Chinese Communists from fulfilling their threat to invade the islands, if that was their real purpose in the first place. But whatever the explanation for the Formosa crisis of August and September, 1958, it served to remind Americans of the precarious peace in that region. Like the thirty-eighth parallel in Korea and the seventeenth parallel dividing Indochina, the Formosa Straits remained one of the real danger zones which could ignite World War III.

The Formosa crisis forced the Republicans, much to their discomfiture, to accept the same realities they had criticized Acheson for recognizing, to abandon the policy of liberation in Asia just as they had been obliged to do in Central and Eastern Europe, and to exercise the old policy of trying to contain Communist expansion. During the presidential campaign of 1960, the Democratic candidate, John F. Kennedy, declared in one of his television debates with Richard M. Nixon, the Republican standard-bearer, that the United States had not guaranteed the defense of the offshore islands. Moreover, he indicated that they were not militarily defensible, a position which Dulles' successor, Secretary of State Christian A. Herter, had asserted at the height of the September, 1958, crisis and which Eisenhower had also affirmed a few weeks later. Nixon, on the other hand, replied that Quemoy and Matsu were "bastions of freedom" which had to be protected. Realizing the sensitive and controversial ground upon which they were treading, neither candidate pressed the issue further, apparently satisfied to have made their points and, save to recognize America's commitment to Formosa, to drop the subject.

The Road to the Summit

On March 5, 1953, less than two months after Eisenhower became President, Stalin died, and the new government headed by Georgi M. Malenkov appeared, on the surface at least, to be less belligerent. The Kremlin replaced its uncompromising Stalinist line with talk of "peaceful coexistence" and reasserted the necessity to end the atomic arms race, which had now been made even more terrifying by the successful explosions of American and Soviet thermonuclear (hydrogen) bombs in August, 1952, and 1953, respectively. Moreover, Russia's words seemed to be confirmed by Chou En-lai's statements at the twenty-nine-nation Afro-Asian Conference which opened on April 18, 1955, at Bandung, Indonesia. Red China, Chou declared, was interested in easing tension in the Far East and in trying "to seek common ground and not create divergence." The next month Red China and the United States began their Geneva talks, and Peiping released fifteen captured American fliers. In the meantime, in Vienna on May 15, the Soviet Union and the "big three" Western Allies agreed to sign an Austrian peace treaty after eight years of negotiations. Despite these favorable indications that the Soviet Union was willing to permit a thaw in the cold war, neither Eisenhower nor Dulles was enthusiastic about a meeting "at the summit," as Churchill called it; but Britain's Conservative party, now led by Anthony Eden, was eager to have one in the hope that it would strengthen the party's appeal with the electorate. For these various reasons, as well as the President's real desire to end the arms race, Eisenhower agreed to confer with the British, French, and Soviet heads of state, and for the first time since the Potsdam Conference of 1945 the "big four" met at Geneva on July 18, 1955.

The two principal items which occupied most of the conferees' five-day meeting were the reunification of Germany and disarmament. Despite Soviet cordiality and expressions of friendship, the talks on Germany indicated that Marshal Nikolai Bulganin, who had succeeded Malenkov as premier on February 8, 1955, was as opposed to a reunified, independent Germany aligned with the West as Stalin had been. What kept Germany divided, Bulganin declared, was the "remilitarization of Western Germany and her integration into military groups of the Western powers." [3] In order to resolve the East-West impasse on Germany, Bulganin proposed a plan whereby each side agreed not to attack the other, to end using foreign territories for military bases, and to work toward dissolving the alliances aimed against each other, namely, NATO and the Warsaw Pact. Eisenhower tried to reassure Bulganin that the West had no aggressive designs upon the Soviet Union, but the President's words did not convince the Russian. Despite Prime Minister Anthony Eden's efforts to find a mutually satisfactory solution, the German question remained unresolved. The Soviet Union's real purpose was to get the American forces out of Germany and Europe; the United States was equally determined to keep them there so long as the Kremlin continued to threaten the freedom and security of the Continent.

For a time it looked as if the disarmament talks would prove as unrewarding as those on Germany. The Soviet proposal, with its provisions for each side to reduce the size of its armed forces and to ban the produc-

---

[3] Quoted in Jules Davids, *America and the World of Our Time: United States Diplomacy in the Twentieth Century* (New York [1960]), p. 503.

450   THE U.S. & THE POSTWAR WORLD, 1945–1961

tion and use of atomic bombs and weapons, contained little that was new, and it made no impression on the Western leaders. Eisenhower, on the other hand, had with him a plan prepared by the Quantico Panel, a special group of civilian and government disarmament experts under the direction of Nelson Rockefeller. Employing a principle very similar to the one proposed nearly a decade earlier by former Secretary Acheson, the panel had devised a scheme which would safeguard America's security and atomic defense system while satisfying world opinion that the United States's interest in promoting disarmament was real. As proof of America's peaceful intentions, Eisenhower reassured Bulganin that "the United States will never take part in an aggressive war," and on July 22 he announced the American plan for disarmament. With great sincerity and telling effect, the President proposed that the various nations provide each other with "a complete blueprint" of their military establishments and agree to allow each other's territory to be photographed from the air by "unarmed peaceful planes." The "open skies" plan, as Eisenhower's proposal came to be called, did not provide for disarmament—it was intended, as Eisenhower stated, to "convince the world that we [the United States and the Soviet Union] are providing . . . between ourselves against the possibility of great surprise attack"—but its impact upon world opinion was tremendous. Furthermore, it took the Soviet delegation completely by surprise. And even though Bulganin subsequently rejected it in its original form, the proposal opened new avenues of discourse. Throughout 1956 and 1957 several disarmament conferences were held to discuss the question further before the Russians finally discarded it, in August, 1957.

The summit conference did not resolve any of the important questions that divided the United States and the Soviet Union. Upon his return from Geneva, Eisenhower told the American people that he had gone to the meeting "to attempt to change the spirit in which . . . [East-West] negotiations and conferences were held." He believed that this had been accomplished, and that the "new spirit of conciliation and cooperation" which emerged from the sessions held great promise for the future of world peace. But the "spirit of Geneva" which appeared to mark the beginning of a new accommodation between the two rival power blocs did not survive the year. So long as it lasted, it provided the American people with a most welcome surcease from cold war tensions and allowed them to enjoy the unprecedented prosperity of that summer without the dampening effects of foreign crises.

THE ELECTION OF 1956

On August 14, 1955, Eisenhower left Washington for a vacation in Denver, Colorado; five weeks later, on September 24, 1955, he suffered a "moderate" heart attack. For the next several months, while the President was recuperating and the nation was following the accounts of Eisenhower's recovery, which Press Secretary James C. Hagerty released in great detail daily, the government of the United States was being run by an informal council composed of Sherman Adams, Vice President Nixon, secretaries Dulles and Humphrey, Attorney General Brownell, and Major General Wilton B. ("Jerry") Persons, a long-time friend of Eisenhower and one of his trusted White House aides. The most important job was entrusted to Adams, who, in his own words, was made "the sole official channel of information between Eisenhower and the outside world." In November, Eisenhower left Denver's Fitzsimons General Hospital for a brief visit to Washington on his way to his farm in Gettysburg, Pennsylvania.

One of the most frequently discussed questions during the months of Eisenhower's recovery was whether he would seek reelection, and while the official bulletins on the extent of the President's recovery and his growing ability to assume greater and greater responsiblity were increasingly optimistic, there remained considerable doubt as to his ability to perform all the presidential duties for another four years. Moreover, there was also the question of whether Eisenhower himself was interested in running. On February 14, 1956, Dr. Paul Dudley White, the eminent Boston cardiologist, answered part of the question when, after examining the President, he told the press, "Medically I think . . . that his present condition and the favorable chances in the future should enable him to be able to carry on his present active life satisfactorily . . . for five to ten years. . . ." The Republican party's leaders were elated by the medical verdict, of course, and they increased their pressure on Eisenhower to agree to run again. Two weeks later, on February 29, he told the American people that since his physicians had assured him that he was quite able to fulfill all the burdens of the Presidency effectively—a fact to which his own sense of well-being attested—he had agreed to serve for another four years if his party and the people so desired. At the same time, he wanted everyone to know that if chosen and elected, he would have to follow

452 THE U.S. & THE POSTWAR WORLD, 1945–1961

"a regime of ordered work activity, interspersed with regular amounts of exercise, recreation and rest." The nation and the GOP were frightened again on June 9 when the President had to undergo surgery for ileitis, but this too caused only momentary concern; and when Eisenhower left for Panama on July 21 to attend a meeting of the Organization of American States, whatever new doubts had arisen as to his earlier statement about a second term were quickly dispelled.[4]

With Eisenhower's renomination a certainty, the only discordant note among the Republicans before they met for their convention in San Francisco's Cow Palace on August 20 was struck by Harold E. Stassen, who was then serving as the President's disarmament adviser. On July 23, much to the chagrin of the GOP's leaders, Stassen declared that the Republican ticket would be strengthened by at least 6 per cent if the party replaced Nixon with Governor Christian A. Herter of Massachusetts as Ike's running mate. The Republican National Committee tried to offset the effect of Stassen's statement by declaring the next day that Governor Herter had already agreed to renominate the Vice President, but Eisenhower, who had not as yet endorsed Nixon officially, allowed Stassen to take a month's leave of absence "to pursue certain political activities without involving his official position at the White House." As was to be expected, Stassen's efforts were met with stern, outspoken disapproval by the party chiefs, and he ended his "dump Nixon" drive by seconding the Vice President's nomination.

The Republican convention unanimously endorsed the Eisenhower-Nixon team and adopted a platform extolling the peace, progress, and prosperity the GOP had provided the country during the past four years. In addition to endorsing already established policies, such as flexible farm price supports, the partnership principle in developing new power resources, and federal aid for new public school construction, the Republican platform called for effective enforcement of the Supreme Court's school desegregation decision with "all deliberate speed." The foreign policy plank was more outspokenly internationalist than it had been in 1952, calling for cooperation with United Nations peace efforts, aid to underdeveloped countries, and continuance of the security and alliance systems. With Eisenhower at the head of the ticket, neither the platform

[4] On November 25, 1957, Eisenhower suffered a "slight cerebral stroke" which impaired his speech for a few days. But he recovered quickly, and within two weeks he was again fulfilling his regular duties.

nor the issues which the party spokesmen elaborated received much attention.

The Democratic party's chances of winning the White House in 1956 were slight, even though they had regained control of Congress in the midterm elections of 1954 by a very small majority (one seat in the Senate and twenty-nine in the House). On November 15, 1955, Adlai Stevenson declared himself a candidate for renomination, and the next month Tennessee's Senator Estes Kefauver announced his candidacy. But despite his surprising victory over Stevenson in the Minnesota primary on March 20, Kefauver's strength deteriorated rapidly, and on July 31, two weeks before the Democratic convention met in Chicago, he withdrew from the race and endorsed Stevenson, whose only other serious challenger was New York's Governor Averell Harriman. Former President Truman supported Harriman and so declared himself, but the convention nominated Stevenson on the first ballot with 905½ votes, as opposed to 210 for the New York governor. The delegates then moved to make the nomination unanimous, and Truman promised to campaign vigorously for the nominee, which he did. Stevenson then startled the convention by appearing before the delegates to remind them that seven out of the thirty-four Presidents had died in office and that it was their "solemn obligation" to choose a Vice President who was "fully equipped" to assume the duties of the Presidency. Instead of allowing the choice to be made on the basis of "personal predilection or expediency," as was so often done, "I have decided," he said, "that the selection . . . should be made through the free processes of this Convention."

A number of the party's younger men immediately sought the prize, but despite the opposition of the South and most of the party leaders, Kefauver won the nomination on the second ballot with 755½ votes, 69 more than the required number. His closest competitor, with 589 votes, was the young junior senator from Massachusetts, John F. Kennedy, who won the votes of eighteen states, ten of which were from the South.

The Democratic platform, aside from accusing the Republicans of being "representatives of special privilege" and of having initiated "the wreckage of American world leadership," did not offer much that was new or significantly different from that of the GOP. It again called for repeal of the Taft-Hartley Act, rigid price supports at 90 per cent of parity, and public power development; it asserted the necessity to pro-

454 THE U.S. & THE POSTWAR WORLD, 1945–1961

mote world peace through the United Nations and to safeguard national security by promoting "the unity and strength of the free world"; and it stressed the need to develop "strong defenses so clearly superior in modern weapons" as to deter all possible aggressors. On the delicate subject of enforcing the Supreme Court's school desegregation decision, the Democratic platform declared its opposition to "illegal discriminations of all kinds," but it condemned "all proposals for the use of force to interfere with the orderly determination of those matters by the courts."

Neither the platforms nor the issues raised by the Democratic and Republican orators attracted much attention. As in 1952, the immense personal popularity of President Eisenhower dominated the presidential race of 1956. Stevenson, despite his extensive campaigning, simply could not match Eisenhower's appeal, and the fact that the country was enjoying peace and prosperity, for which the Republicans claimed credit, made it even more difficult for the Democrats to stir much voter interest. Labor Secretary Mitchell issued a report early in September, 1956, indicating that since Eisenhower entered the White House employment had risen by 5.5 million and that the average American factory worker was earning $13 a week more than he had four years earlier. "The level of the economy," the report concluded, "has never been higher in peace or war." When Stevenson proposed that the United States and the Soviet Union agree to stop testing hydrogen bombs, Eisenhower accused the Democrats of playing politics with national defense and of trying to cause "confusion at home and misunderstanding abroad." All Democratic charges proved similarly ineffective. Stevenson, for example, tried to equate Eisenhower and the Republicans with big business by pointing out that while corporate profits were rising to new heights, farm prices were declining appreciably; but this charge, too, was largely ignored. In October, as Eisenhower took a more active part in the campaign, the question of his health became less and less an issue; in like manner, the doubts and questions Stassen had raised about Nixon's past record and his fitness for the Presidency declined in importance. The fact that most citizens liked Eisenhower personally, trusted him, and credited him with ending the Korean War and keeping the peace, even though new crises in the Middle East and Hungary were threatening to disrupt it just as the American people were to go to the polls, earned him a huge vote of confidence.

On November 6, some 62.1 million people went to the polls and re-elected Eisenhower by a sweeping landslide vote—35.5 million as opposed

THE EISENHOWER YEARS 455

to 26 million for Stevenson. The electoral count was 457 to 74. Stevenson carried seven states, of which only Arkansas and Missouri were outside the deep South. No other candidate, save Franklin Roosevelt in 1936, ever polled such a huge majority. Like the election of 1952, Eisenhower's huge victory was again entirely a personal one: the Republicans lost both houses of Congress to the Democrats. The line-up in the new Eighty-fifth Congress was 49 to 47 in the Senate and 232 to 199 in the House, and the two parties divided the gubernatorial races evenly—15 apiece.

DOMESTIC DEVELOPMENTS, 1956–1961

The Integration Controversy

One of the most important and difficult domestic issues to occupy the attention of the American people during Eisenhower's second term arose out of the Supreme Court's ruling in *Brown v. Board of Education of Topeka* on May 17, 1954, which outlawed racial segregation in the public schools. Despite the great improvements during the past generation in the political, economic, and, to a lesser degree, social conditions of the northern Negro, no comparable progress had taken place for those living in the South, where rigid social barriers limited their opportunities and denied them the equality to which they were entitled by the Constitution and federal law. Nowhere was this more apparent than in the public school system, which adhered tenaciously to the "separate but equal" doctrine set down by the Supreme Court in 1896 in *Plessy v. Ferguson*. Since that time American society had undergone profound changes, and what the Court had ruled acceptable then was no longer consistent with the declared ideals of the American people. In contrast to the quiet legislative progress of the 1930's, which extended the Negro's political and economic equality, the Supreme Court's decision of May, 1954, striking down one of the major remaining social barriers, aroused much bitter controversy.

In this unanimous decision, the Court invalidated the "separate but equal" doctrine by asserting that "separate educational facilities are inherently unequal," that "segregation in public education" denied the Negro pupils "equal protection of the law," and that separating Negro children "from others of similar age and qualifications solely because of

456 THE U.S. & THE POSTWAR WORLD, 1945–1961

their race generates a feeling of inferiority as to their status in the community that may affect their hearts and minds in a way unlikely ever to be undone." The Court, recognizing the difficulties involved in implementing this decision, delayed issuing its plan for integrating the schools for a year. Then, on May 31, 1955, it ordered the federal district courts, from which the segregation cases had originated, to assume the responsibility for integrating the school system. "While giving weight to . . . public and private considerations," the high justices declared that "the [district] courts will require . . . a prompt and reasonable start toward full compliance with our May 17, 1954 ruling . . . [and] the district court . . . [will] enter such orders and decrees . . . as are necessary and proper to admit to public schools on a racially non-discriminatory basis with all deliberate speed the parties to these cases."

Southern segregationists denounced the Supreme Court for abusing its power and encroaching "upon the reserved rights of the states and the people," and they sought every legal refuge to frustrate and delay its order. While the number of Southerners who belonged to extreme racist groups—White America, Inc., the Christian American Segregation Association, or the various White Citizens' Councils established to fight integration by force and violence—was small, so was the number who favored desegregation. Most Southerners were opposed to integration, almost all of them hoped it could be postponed indefinitely, and many of them tried to delay it, but only a few of them refused to recognize its ultimate inevitability. The degree of success or failure to integrate was, in the words of a special *New York Times* report, determined largely by the "size and density of the Negro population." Since this fact more than any other motivated the South's response, the extent of segregation varied from state to state and from county to county within the same state. Opposition to it was strongest in the rural areas of the deep South, especially in the counties of the so-called black belt, which before the Civil War had been "the heartland of the slave South." In this region, where the concentration of Negro population was heaviest, very little progress was achieved. Resistance to integration was much less pronounced in the cities and in the border states, where the number of Negroes was smaller. Thus, the schools of the District of Columbia and most of those in the states of Delaware, Kentucky, Maryland, Missouri, Oklahoma, and West Virginia were desegrated quickly and with relatively little difficulty.

Elsewhere, however, obedience to the Supreme Court's ruling varied considerably. The strongest official efforts to resist and frustrate the

THE EISENHOWER YEARS   457

Court's purposes occurred in Alabama, Mississippi, Georgia, Louisiana, and South Carolina. In August, 1960, at the beginning of the sixth post-decision school year, not one of the school districts in these states, with the exception of a few in New Orleans, appeared disposed to abide by the law. In the six remaining southern states—Arkansas, Texas, Tennessee, Florida, North Carolina, and Virginia—a token beginning was made, but progress was often slow and on several occasions accompanied by outbursts of violence. In February, 1956, a Negro student was prevented from entering the University of Alabama because of the protests of white student rioters; in August, fighting accompanied the admission of twelve Negro students to a Clinton, Tennessee, school; and the same kind of disturbances occurred in Mansfield, Texas. None of these incidents, however, created anything like the crisis in Little Rock, Arkansas, in September, 1957.

This deplorable episode, which seriously strained federal-state relations and gravely injured the reputation of the United States abroad, especially among the emerging African and Asian nations, began on September 4, 1957, when nine Negro students attempted to enter the city's all-white Central High School in accordance with the federal district court's gradual desegregation order of the previous year. Some of the parents of the white students protested the integration order and tried to get it reversed on the grounds that integration would incite "mob violence and bloodshed." When the court refused to accept their petition, Governor Orval M. Faubus ordered units of the National Guard to the high school, explaining his action as an effort "to prevent racial violence." By preventing the Negro students from entering the school building, however, the guardsmen were violating the district court's order. Faubus tried to secure Eisenhower's support for his decision, but the President refused to promise anything except to uphold the Constitution "by every legal means at my command"; and even after the two men met at the Newport Naval Base on Narragansett Bay, where Eisenhower was vacationing, no mutually acceptable solution could be reached to resolve the impasse at Little Rock's Central High School. Faubus kept the guardsmen at the school for another week, removing them only after the federal court had ordered him to do so. On September 23, after the troops had been withdrawn, the Negro students appeared at the school but were prevented from entering the building by some 500 angry citizens, whose protests degenerated into a riot. The next day Eisenhower ordered 1,000 paratroopers to the scene. As the first contingent of the 101st Airborne Divi-

458   THE U.S. & THE POSTWAR WORLD, 1945–1961

sion was arriving at Little Rock, the President flew to Washington, and that night in a nationally televised address he told the American people that while he had hoped he would never have to use the army to enforce a federal court decision, the events at Little Rock left him no alternative. "The very basis of our individual rights and freedoms," Eisenhower declared, "rests upon the certainty that the President and the executive branch of the government will support and insure the carrying out of the decisions of the federal courts, when necessary, with all the means at the President's command. Unless the President did so, anarchy would result."

The next day, September 25, the nine Negro students were driven to school under armed guard and were admitted without difficulty. When one of Little Rock's protesting segregationists tangled with a paratrooper and was nicked slightly by the soldier's bayonet, Faubus declared on a television program that the administration's enforced "military occupation" of his state was spilling "the warm red blood of patriotic American citizens . . . [on] cold, naked, unsheathed knives." Georgia's Senator Richard Russell also censured Eisenhower for "applying tactics that must have been copied from the manual issued to the officers of Hitler's storm troopers." Led by North Carolina's Governor Luther Hodges, the chief executives of Maryland, Florida, and Tennessee tried to work out a compromise between Faubus and the President which would lead to the early removal of the federal paratroopers. But like the previous attempt to get Faubus to agree to a statement indicating his willingness to uphold the federal law, the efforts of these four moderate Southerners proved unsuccessful, and the Defense Department did not withdraw all of the soldiers until May, 1958, though the nine Negro students had been attending classes regularly without armed escorts since the previous December.

Much litigation followed before Little Rock accepted the principle of desegregation in its high schools. In June, 1958, the federal district court reversed its earlier ruling and extended the city another thirty-six months to complete integration of its high schools; but on September 12 the Supreme Court overruled this extension. A few days later Faubus closed Little Rock's four high schools. Virginia, which had also closed its schools, reopened them in February, 1959, but Little Rock held out until August, yielding to the inevitable only after a federal court had invalidated Faubus' school-closing law. From then on Arkansas, Virginia, and most of the other southern states followed a policy of slow "token desegregation." By the beginning of June, 1961, about 518,357 out of some

Rioting broke out in Little Rock, Arkansas, in September, 1957, when nine Negro students tried to secure admission to Central High School in accordance with court decisions ending segregation. This picture shows a group of white supremacists protesting integration. (Wide World Photos)

3 million Negro students in the District of Columbia and seventeen southern and border states were attending mixed classes.

The slow progress of integration and the sporadic outbursts of violence which followed the Supreme Court's 1954 decision detracted from the other substantial civil rights accomplishments achieved during the Eisenhower administration. Like Truman, Eisenhower ordered the armed forces to respect the principle of racial equality, and he insisted that civilian officials of the government also observe it in their employment policies. During Eisenhower's first term Negroes were appointed to several important posts, among the most notable being J. Ernest Wilkins, selected for the job of Assistant Secretary of Labor. In 1952, shortly after being nominated, Eisenhower had declared he was opposed to "every

460 THE U.S. & THE POSTWAR WORLD, 1945–1961

vestige of segregation in the District of Columbia," and after he became President he directed the head of the city's Board of Commissioners to begin enforcing desegregation in public places.

The Republican party had written strong civil rights planks in both 1952 and 1956, and after his reelection Eisenhower had called upon Congress to set up a federal commission to investigate reports "that in some localities Negro citizens are being deprived of their right to vote and are likewise being subjected to unwarranted economic pressures." Most of the President's cabinet and many of his other top advisers were opposed to introducing any kind of civil rights legislation, especially in view of the controversies and difficulties the administration was already facing in trying to enforce the Supreme Court's school desegregation ruling. For several months Eisenhower and his advisers debated the wisdom and need of introducing a civil rights bill, and Attorney General Brownell presented several proposals for their consideration. Finally, on April 9, 1956, after several members of the cabinet persuaded Brownell and the President to accept much less than either of them had originally hoped for, the administration asked Congress to enact a civil rights law, which it did, sixteen months later.

The Civil Rights Act which Eisenhower signed on September 9, 1957, was the first such law to be passed since the enactment of Senator Charles Sumner's bill in March, 1875. The act established a Civil Rights Division in the Department of Justice headed by an Assistant Attorney General whose duty it would be to enforce the federal civil rights statutes, investigate all charges involving alleged violations of these laws, recommend supplementary legislation when necessary, and provide individuals whose rights had been denied with advice and assistance in seeking relief. The administration's bill had originally called for a statute which would guarantee the Negro equal rights, but this was too much for the Southerners to accept, and the law as finally passed protected only his political rights, such as those designated in various federal election laws. Supporters of a more comprehensive statute disapproved of the limitations and other legal loopholes the Southerners had written into the law, but despite its obvious faults, the Civil Rights Act of 1957 made it considerably more difficult for state and local election boards to interfere with the Negro's right to vote.

Some progress was also made toward desegregating the South's public transportation system. On November 25, 1955, the Interstate Commerce Commission declared segregation illegal on all interstate carriers and in the station and terminal facilities that served them. The next year the Supreme Court, in the case of *Gayle v. Browder*, ruled that segregation on intrastate carriers deprived the Negro of his constitutional guarantees of equal protection and due process and was therefore illegal. This decision arose out of an incident on a Montgomery, Alabama, bus, in which a Negro woman was arrested and fined $14 for having refused to move from the white to the Negro section of the bus. Led by the Reverend Martin Luther King, a leading advocate of "nonviolent direct action," Negroes boycotted the Montgomery buses for eleven weeks. On February 21, 1956, the city retaliated by securing a grand jury indictment against 115 of them, including Dr. King, who was convicted but whose sentence was later suspended.

Elsewhere in the South, other anti-Negro die-hards also sought to circumvent the ICC and Supreme Court rulings against segregated transportation facilities. Several ugly instances of mob violence and rioting occurred, some of the worst of which took place in May, 1961, when a small group of Negro and white members of the Congress of Racial Equality (CORE) left Washington, D.C., by bus for a "Freedom Ride" through the South. The purpose of their trip was to investigate the extent to which the South had desegregated its transportation system. After minor skirmishes with segregationists in Virginia and North Carolina, the Freedom Riders, all of whom subscribed to Dr. King's principle of passive resistance, encountered increasing hostility as they moved into the deep South. In South Carolina two of them were assaulted and two others arrested, and in Anniston and Birmingham, Alabama, where the worst incidents occurred, several of them were badly beaten by a mob, which also firebombed the bus. At this point CORE appealed to the federal government for "guarantees of freedom on the public highways." After hesitating for four days and accusing the Freedom Riders of being a "bunch of rabble-rousers," Alabama's Governor John Patterson assured Washington that his state possessed "the will, the force, the men, and the equipment to fully protect everyone." The very next day, however, when the Freedom Riders reached Montgomery, their bus was mobbed, and in the riot which followed some twenty people were injured. President Kennedy, employing a law passed in 1871 to curb the violence of the Ku Klux Klan, ordered the Attorney General to restore order. Within a few hours 400 armed United States marshals arrived in the city, and Governor Patterson declared Montgomery under martial law. By the end of the month the worst was over: the government began

462   THE U.S. & THE POSTWAR WORLD, 1945–1961

withdrawing the federal marshals, the civilian authorities were once again running the city government, and the Freedom Riders continued on their way with an armed escort. In Jackson, Mississippi, they were arrested for sitting in the city's white bus terminal, but no violence occurred; and this instance of violation was left to the courts for settlement.

In the meantime, the federal government continued to press for peaceable integration by persuasion and to avoid the use of force insofar as possible. In November, 1961, by order of the Interstate Commerce Commission, all carriers crossing state lines and the terminals at which they stopped were forced to post signs declaring that their seating arrangements were "without regard to race, color, creed, or national origin." The South, as this and other federal actions indicated, still had far to go to achieve the goals set down by the Supreme Court's decision, but despite the opposition and resistance of the segregationists, much real progress had been made toward tearing down the barriers that separated the races.

Defense and the "Missile Gap"

Just at the time when the southern segregationists were challenging Eisenhower's determination to enforce the Supreme Court's school desegregation decision, a growing number of influential congressional and military leaders were questioning the wisdom and efficacy of the administration's defense policies. Shortly after Eisenhower first became President he told Congress that he intended "to achieve adequate military strength within the limits of an endurable strain on our economy. To amass military power without regard to our economic capacity would be to defend ourselves against one kind of disaster by inviting another." To secure what Eisenhower called "the most defense, at less cost with the least delay," the administration adopted a policy which called for a large build-up in nuclear weapons of mass destruction and a substantial reduction in the size and number of the country's conventional armaments and forces, both of which were cut in the first three Eisenhower budgets. The administration's defense policy, which came to be known as the New Look or the Radford Plan, named after Admiral Arthur W. Radford, Chairman of the Joint Chiefs of Staff, reflected the views of the President, Radford, and the three most influential members of the cabinet, Secretaries Wilson, Dulles, and Humphrey.

The decision to rely on massive nuclear retaliation as the primary basis of defense and the principal means to deter Soviet aggression was strongly criticized by some of the highest military leaders in the government as well as by civilian experts. The interests and security of the United States, these critics argued, required a balanced military establishment, one which would provide the country with the means to fight limited conventional conflicts as well as an all-out nuclear war. The necessity of maintaining strong, well-equipped conventional fighting forces was more important now than ever before since the postwar pattern of Communist aggression in Korea, Indochina, and elsewhere clearly indicated that the Soviet Union was seeking to achieve its objectives by means short of precipitating a total war. Moreover, as the progress of Soviet military science continued to reduce the margin of America's nuclear supremacy, the ability of each side to devastate the other would restrain both from employing nuclear weapons of massive destruction. In other words, since the approaching "balance of nuclear terror" upgraded the importance of conventional arms, the security of the United States required the establishment of two powerful defense systems. If America's military and strategic policies were to remain sufficiently flexible to counter the various kinds of challenges and indirect aggressions of which the Soviets were capable, the United States could not afford to reduce or neglect either its nuclear or its conventional strength.[5] "The problem of our military planners," wrote Hanson W. Baldwin, *The New York Times*'s military analyst, "is to organize and maintain armed forces capable of fighting any kind of war anywhere. . . . If we do not maintain these diverse capabilities we shall freeze, in a one-weapon, one-concept mold, not only tactics but strategy, and our foreign policy will be rigidly tied to an inflexible strategic concept that permits us no freedom of action. Yet the art of diplomacy, the art of politics, the art of strategy and war, is the art of choice." [6]

As the administration proceeded with its policy of cutting defense costs by reducing the country's nonnuclear capabilities and the size of the armed forces, the controversy over maintaining a dual capability grew increasingly pronounced. In a January, 1956, article in *The Saturday Evening Post*, Eisenhower's former Army Chief of Staff, General Matthew B. Ridgway, accused the administration of having allowed "political considerations" and "fiscal limits" rather than military requirements to

[5] Alvin J. Cottrell, "Military Security and the New Look, *Current History*, XXXVIII (April 1960), 220–27.
[6] Quoted in *ibid*, p. 227.

determine the size of its defense budgets. He believed that the improved military reserve program Eisenhower had fought for and won in the Reserve Forces Act of August 9, 1955, was no substitute for maintaining a strong standing army. The next month Washington's Democratic Senator Henry Jackson declared that the Soviet Union was far ahead of the United States in developing guided missiles, and two days later, almost as if to prove Senator Jackson's charges correct, Trevor Gardner, the Assistant Secretary of the Air Force, resigned because, as he wrote later, the "short-sighted limitations" of Defense Secretary Wilson were holding back the development of America's guided missile program.

For the next half-dozen years, through Eisenhower's second term, the election of 1960, and the first several months of President Kennedy's administration, the question of a "missile gap" between the United States and the Soviet Union remained a part of the public debate on defense policy. Early in February, 1956, Eisenhower tried to assure the public that the administration was not neglecting the missile program. "You get to the point where more expenditure of money in a field like this [missiles] does no good. We are about at our limit." This statement did not reassure those who believed that the administration was sacrificing national security by "pinching pennies." Missouri's Democratic Senator Stuart Symington, a former Secretary of the Air Force, asserted that Eisenhower was "badly informed if he believes that this country could not move faster in the missile field." The next month Defense Secretary Wilson announced the appointment of Eger V. Murphree, the chief of the Esso Research and Engineering Company, to assume responsibility for the country's missile program.

In the meantime, Senator Symington was chosen as chairman of a special armed forces subcommittee to investigate the strength and capabilities of America's defensive and retaliatory air power. Beginning on April 16, the five-man subcommittee listened to the testimony of a number of high-ranking military officers, all of whom warned of the danger of allowing the nation's defenses to fall behind those of the Soviet Union and of neglecting military research programs. General Curtis E. Le May, the head of the Strategic Air Command (SAC), claimed that if the administration adhered to its "present plans and programs" the Soviet Union "will have a greater striking power than we will have." By 1959, Le May said, Russia probably could, if it chose, launch a "complete surprise attack" of devastating proportions against the United States. Largely as a result of these hearings and despite the protests of the President

THE EISENHOWER YEARS 465

and Secretary Wilson, the Senate increased the air force's budget appropriation that year by $960 million.

Even though Eisenhower had been a soldier nearly all his life, he was, like President Truman before him, a staunch believer in the supremacy of civilian control over the nation's military establishment; and because of his World War II experiences and his knowledge of modern warfare, he was convinced of the necessity of a unified Defense Department capable of effectively coordinating the activities of the three services—army, navy, and air force.[7] Moreover, Eisenhower believed that by establishing a fully unified defense system, it would be possible to achieve greater security at less cost and prevent the kind of embarrassing interservice rivalries that, in his words, "find expression in Congressional and press activities which become particularly conspicuous in struggles over new weapons, funds, and publicity." Such a controversy had occurred in May, 1956, when the three services had become involved in a bitter public dispute over the relative merits of their weapons systems; the quarrel had ended only after Secretary Wilson had called a special press conference and, in the presence of the Joint Chiefs of Staff and the three service secretaries, sought to minimize the importance of the dispute and to restore harmony in the Pentagon.

As soon as Eisenhower proposed to integrate the services further, he quickly learned that despite a semblance of outward harmony, the army, navy, and air force were still as jealous and suspicious of each other and as determined to fight for their independence as they had been in 1947 and 1949, when President Truman had established the Defense Department and inaugurated the policy of unification. Undisturbed by the hostility of his service chiefs, Eisenhower, after studying the recommendations made by the second Hoover Commission and the report of a special Defense Department advisory group, submitted his reorganization proposal to Congress on April 3, 1958. The bill, largely written by the President himself, called for substantially increasing the authority of the Secretary of Defense by giving him full control over his Department's budget and thereby depriving the three service secretaries of their authority to appear before Congress and compete with each other for appropriations; centralizing all army, naval, and air research activities under

[7] On April 1, 1954, Eisenhower signed into law the bill creating the Air Force Academy at Colorado Springs, Colorado. Like the army and navy academies at West Point, New York, and Annapolis, Maryland, the Air Force Academy was to provide this branch of the service with its own professional training program.

a civilian officer directly responsible to the Secretary; and placing "full unified command over land, sea and air forces" in the hands of each theater commander. When certain congressional leaders, notably Carl Vinson, the Georgia Democrat, who headed the House Armed Services Committee, attempted to weaken his proposals with various amendments, Eisenhower expressed his disapproval through a statement to the press in which he said, "It just happens I have a little bit more experience in military organization and the directing of unified forces than anyone on the active list." He also wrote, by his own admission, "around 450 letters" to some of his influential friends, requesting them to ask their congressmen and senators to vote for his proposal. Finally, on July 24, both houses of Congress passed the reorganization bill. Two weeks later he signed it into law, observing, as Adams recalled later, that while it was "a major advance toward real unification . . . there was still much to be done in bringing centralized control to the armed forces."

The Dawn of the Space Age

The serious concern of many American with the Soviet Union's tremendous postwar achievements in military science and technology was heightened still further on October 4, 1957, when the Russians launched Sputnik I, the first man-made satellite to orbit the earth; and as if intent upon increasing the uneasiness of the American people by proving the superiority of Soviet scientists, technicians, and missiles, a month later they launched Sputnik II, a much larger satellite in which they enclosed a live dog. The impact of these accomplishments upon world opinion was immense: they boosted Soviet prestige to new heights, which the Kremlin exploited fully to advance its political and psychological cold war purposes, and dealt a heavy blow to the scientific reputation of the United States. Right or wrong, in the opinion of many people both in the United States and abroad, the undisputed lead in science and technology which had previously been granted to America was now accorded to Russia. What was perhaps even more important was the fact that a number of people, especially among America's friends abroad, interpreted this Soviet triumph not only as a Russian victory in space but as an indication that the United States was falling behind also in the other nonscientific areas in which it was competing with the Kremlin. And even though the Eisenhower administration announced that the United States was not engaged in a space race with the Soviet Union, the re-

THE EISENHOWER YEARS   467

action of the American people and the private remarks of some government leaders belied Washington's officially calm statement. Indeed, the President himself, as Adams reported later, while keeping "an official air of serenity . . . , was privately as concerned as everybody else . . . by the jump ahead that the Russians had made in scientific enterprise."

The success of Sputnik I and II immediately brought forth a widespread public demand, quickly taken up by Congress, to discover the reasons for Russia's accomplishment and to learn when the United States intended to match it. Though opinions varied, most observers seemed to agree that the Soviet Union had tackled the problem of penetrating space with a greater urgency, purpose, and concentration of effort than had the United States.[8] Russia's noteworthy strides in developing high-powered military rockets, which the United States at first had neglected in favor of heavy long-range bombers, also gave the Soviet Union an immense advantage which it continued to hold even after the United States launched its first space satellite. From the very beginning, probably the greatest technical problem to annoy and retard America's program involved the development of a rocket with sufficient thrust to place a heavy space craft, or "payload," into orbit. Sputnik I and II, for example, carried "scientific instrumentation payloads" of 184 and 1,120 pounds respectively, whereas the scientific equipment in America's first satellite, Explorer I, weighed only 18.13 pounds. Another and not the least of the reasons for America's slower space progress was the dual problem of money and administrative confusion, each of which presented numerous difficulties. Exploring space was and remains a very costly business. Partly because the Eisenhower administration was economy-minded and partly because some of its leaders and advisers believed that the space program should receive a lower priority than the development of new, complex defense systems, which were also very expensive, appropriations for probing space were either inadequate or, because of rivalry among the armed services and the overlapping interests of the bureaucratic and administrative agencies involved, poorly spent. Failure to integregate the various missile and rocket research programs effectively, for example, was often cited as having been both a costly and a damaging error.

Eisenhower tried to correct these shortcomings which were delaying the space program and injuring the nation's prestige by moderately in-

[8] Allan S. Nanes, "Challenge in Space," *Current History*, XXXVIII (April 1960), 194.

468   THE U.S. & THE POSTWAR WORLD, 1945-1961

creasing the sums appropriated for research and development and by appointing Dr. James R. Killian, Jr., president of the Massachusetts Institute of Technology, to a newly created White House post on November 7, 1957. As Special Assistant to the President for Science and Technology, Killian's job was to supervise the country's missile and space research as a whole. There then followed a series of Defense Department and other governmental reorganizations in which various special research bureaus and agencies were moved around, consolidated, or reconstituted; and finally, on July 17, 1958, Congress passed a bill, which Eisenhower signed into law twelve days later, creating the National Aeronautics and Space Administration (NASA), an independent agency charged with the responsibility of conducting "such activities as may be required for the exploration, scientific investigation, and utilizaton of space for peaceful purposes, and develop[ing] space vehicles for use in such activities." Except for depending upon the Defense Department to provide it with the missiles it needed to lift its payloads, the agency was designed to stress the nonmilitary aspects of America's space program.

In the meantime, regardless of official statements to the contrary, the United States and the Soviet Union continued to compete with each other in space. By maintaining their superiority in rocket thrust, the Russians were able to place heavy vehicles into orbit and thus score an impressive number of firsts. Among the more significant of these Soviet "space spectaculars" were the three *luniks*, the first of which orbited the sun on January 4, 1959, the second landed on the moon on September 13, 1959, and the third, after circling the moon, photographed its outer side on October 4, 1959. Then on April 12, 1961, the Soviets achieved an even greater feat when they launched Vostok I, a 10,460-pound space ship carrying the first man, Major Yuri Gagarin, on a 25,000-mile flight around the earth.

The United States suffered through the Soviet propaganda victories which accompanied these very real scientific accomplishments, and after numerous difficulties and delays started to make considerable progress and to narrow the Soviet lead. After it had launched Explorer I, its first space satellite, on January 31, 1958, the United States fired a series of other space probes which surpassed those of the Russians in number, if not in size, and which added significantly to man's scientific knowledge. Vanguard I, for example, launched on March 17, 1958, provided information that the earth was pear-shaped rather than spherical; others contributed data on cosmic rays, meteors, and radiation belts. Equally noteworthy results were achieved with communications and weather satellites. In the meantime, the United States continued to prepare to send an American into space. After President Kennedy entered the White House, space appropriations were greatly increased and a concerted effort was made to push Project Mercury, the so-called man-in-space program. On May 5, 1961, three weeks after Gagarin's earth-circling trip, the United States launched Freedom VII, which carried Navy Commander Alan B. Shepard, Jr., on a fifteen-minute, 302-mile suborbital flight. Compared to the Russian man-in-orbit shot, the American effort was far less significant and of minor technical and scientific value, but it lifted the people's morale and boosted the nation's prestige considerably. Shepard's flight, which was duplicated two months later, and the orbiting of a chimpanzee around the earth two times on November 29, 1961, were necessary preliminaries to matching the achievements of Gagarin and his successor, Major Gherman S. Titov, who on August 6, 1961, circled the globe seventeen times. Finally, on February 20, 1962, after three years of hard work beset by innumerable frustrations and delays and at a cost of some $400 million, the United States successfully rocketed Colonel John H. Glenn, Jr., into a triple orbit around the earth. Its impact upon the nation was electric. "The mood of the nation's millions," wrote *The New York Times*, "changed in an instant from frustration and suspense to exultation. The . . . [United States] had moved well into space and . . . had gone far toward overcoming the Russian lead." Except for Russia's continued superiority in rocket power, the success of Colonel Glenn's flight brought the United States space program very near the level of the Soviet Union's, and in terms of collecting scientific data and in the "miniaturization of equipment" it probably had surpassed Russia.

Recession and Politics

During the last six months of 1957, while the American people were being awed by Russia's "space spectaculars" and the Eisenhower administration was facing the crisis in Little Rock, the economy, which had started to show signs of weakness earlier in the year, began to move rapidly into a recession, the worst of the three post–World War II slumps up to that time. The descent from the heights of the Eisenhower prosperity of the previous two years was caused by a combination of factors: excess plant capacity, a decline in the demand for capital goods

470 THE U.S. & THE POSTWAR WORLD, 1945–1961

that caused their producers to cut expenditures, a 20 per cent drop in exports, a $600 million reduction in federal expenditures, and a considerable decrease in consumer purchases of certain durable goods. During this nine-month slump, which the administration labeled "moderate," industrial output dropped 14.3 per cent and unemployment increased by some 4.6 per cent. The decrease in personal income, however, was slight, about .3 per cent. As in the case of the two other postwar slumps, the "stabilizers" which had been previously legislated into the economy lessened the impact of the recession considerably. The Federal Reserve eased credit by reducing the discount rate, lowering reserve requirements, and buying government securities on the open market; the administration used its authority under the Housing Act of 1957 to stimulate the building industry by reducing the minimum down payment requirements on FHA housing, and took similar steps to encourage urban renewal projects as well as public and college residential construction and to expedite the interstate highway building program; the Defense Department increased its expenditures; and when state unemployment payments started to run out, Congress passed a Temporary Unemployment Compensation Act, which Eisenhower signed on June 4, 1958, authorizing the federal government to provide the states with additional funds. Since both the President and Treasury Secretary Humphrey were determined to avoid deficit financing if at all possible, they resisted all demands to stimulate recovery by cutting taxes, as had been done during the recession of 1953–54. Despite their intentions, additional expenditures and reduced tax receipts, largely brought about by nine months of recession, caused the administration to end fiscal 1958 on June 30 with a $2.8 billion deficit.

Even though by November the country was well over the recession, its occurrence undermined the people's confidence in the Republican party, which, as election results throughout the Eisenhower era had indicated, had never been strong. Doubts about the future vitality of the economy together with growing concern over the Soviet lead in space, the missile gap, and new tensions in Russian-American relations also proved heavy election-year burdens for the GOP. But what caused the administration its greatest embarrassment was the congressional investigation involving Sherman Adams, the President's closest adviser and the chief of the White House staff.

During the summer of 1958 the House Committee on Legislative Oversight was reviewing the business transactions between Bernard Goldfine, a wealthy Boston textile producer, and two government agencies, the

THE EISENHOWER YEARS 471

Securities and Exchange Commission and the Federal Trade Commission. The committee uncovered evidence apparently indicating that Adams, a long-time friend of the Goldfine family, had influenced these agencies to give the Bostonian preferential treatment. It disclosed numerous details of the friendship between the two men, listing the gifts they had exchanged and making much of an expensive vicuña overcoat Adams had accepted from Goldfine. On June 17 Adams went before the committee to explain his relations with Goldfine. In a prepared statement he declared that he had done no more for the Boston businessman than he had done for anyone else, and that his sole interest had been to satisfy a proper request for information. He concluded his remarks by saying, as he wrote later, that if he "had made mistakes in giving official attention to . . . [Goldfine's] request . . . the mistakes were those of judgment, not of intent." And though the committee found Adams guiltless of wrongdoing, the Democrats now raised the influence-peddling charge the Republicans had used against them in 1952. Eisenhower tried to save his White House aide by defending Adams' character and honesty. "I personally like Governor Adams," the President said; "I admire his abilities. I respect him because of his personal and official integrity. I need him." But because Goldfine's supposedly honest reputation became more and more suspect as the government discovered irregularities in his income tax returns (for which he was subsequently imprisoned), because Adams had alienated many of the GOP's Old Guard, who were insisting upon his resignation, and because many other Republicans were concerned about the forthcoming elections, Adams resigned on September 22.

Less than six weeks later, on November 4, the voters increased the Democratic majorities in both houses of Congress substantially—by fifteen in the Senate and forty-eight in the House. The gubernatorial races also indicated a strong Democratic trend, the only politically significant Republican victory being the election of Nelson A. Rockefeller to the New York governorship.

While the economy generally continued to prosper, many farmers were finding it increasingly difficult to make ends meet. Between 1950 and 1959, the number of farm families dropped by nearly 1.7 million, while total farm mortgage indebtedness during the same years increased from $5.5 to $11.2 billion. Except for the owners of large, mechanized farms, agriculture had ceased to be a profitable occupation. Urban workers, on the other hand, enjoyed considerable prosperity, though in certain parts of the country unemployment remained a chronic depressant.

472   THE U.S. & THE POSTWAR WORLD, 1945-1961

In July, 1958, out of a total civilian labor force of 70.4 million, nearly 5.3 million were jobless; a year later, before the beginning of a 116-day nationwide steel strike, the number of unemployed dropped to 3.7 million, but by January, 1960, it was up again to 4.1 million and it continued to climb, reaching nearly 5.4 million by the time President Kennedy was inaugurated on January 20, 1961. Not since 1940 had the number of jobless been so high.

Responsible labor leaders like George Meany, the president of the huge, consolidated AFL-CIO (these two previously separate organizations had merged on December 5, 1955), called upon the government to establish a public works program to create jobs, but neither the administration nor the conservative coalition in Congress was disposed to proceed in this direction. Balancing the budget or, if that goal was unattainable, keeping deficits as low as possible remained a basic objective of the President's economic policy. And even though some noted economists deplored this attitude, just as others asserted that inflation was a "lessening threat," the administration was as unwilling to test their theories as it was to follow the suggestions of labor leaders. Except for the jobless, most Americans were enjoying prosperous times.

Many of the public, moreover, had become indifferent if not hostile to organized labor, whose reputation had not recovered from the damaging disclosures of the special Senate committee headed by Arkansas' John L. McClellan which in 1957 had revealed the existence of widespread corruption and racketeering in certain unions, notably the Teamsters. Largely because of the information which had come out of the committee's hearings and which was subsequently publicized still further when its chief counsel, Robert F. Kennedy, turned many of these findings into a best-selling book, *The Enemy Within* (1959), Congress passed two bills in 1959 designed to prevent labor leaders from abusing their power and trust. On August 24, Congress passed the Labor Pension Reporting Act, which compelled unions to publish an accounting of the uses they made of the pension and welfare funds of their members. Three weeks later, on September 14, it passed by huge majorities (95 to 2 in the Senate and 352 to 52 in the House) the Landrum-Griffin Labor-Management Reporting and Disclosure Act. Designed to foster "the highest standards of responsibility and ethical conduct" in union practices and to "eliminate or prevent improper practices on the part of labor organizations, employers, labor relations consultants, and their officers and representatives," this lengthy, complex, and controversial statute included a "bill of rights" guaranteeing all union members the right to select their representatives without intimidation from officials, discuss issues and policies freely, and participate in other defined union activities. Besides trying to safeguard the principle of democracy in labor organizations, the law also sought to protect the financial interests of the membership by requiring union officers to report to the Secretary of Labor regularly and in considerable detail all moneys they managed and to submit other comprehensive information on the union's financial policies and practices. Other provisions limited the use of the secondary boycott and defined certain kinds of illegal picketing. The AFL-CIO, which had begun to clean its own house of corrupt leaders long before the committee's hearings and continued to do so after, saw in some of the provisions of the Landrum-Griffin law a disguised effort to strike at legitimate union activities.

Just as Congress and the administration refused to acknowledge the validity of labor's complaints about the Landrum-Griffin law, they also refused to make a serious effort to relieve unemployment, which grew increasingly worse during 1960 as the economy entered another slump. In February, 1960, Secretary of Commerce Frederick H. Mueller of Michigan, who had succeeded Lewis L. Strauss the previous year, declared that "1960 will be the best year of our lives." Thirty days after this optimistic assertion, the Federal Reserve Board declared that industrial production had dropped 1 per cent during March, and every month thereafter until the end of the year almost every economic indicator except personal income showed a decline. By the time Eisenhower retired from office, factory output was off 4.8 per cent, unemployment stood at more than 5.3 million, and steel production was at 50 per cent of capacity; but because not all regions or groups in the population were affected by this fourth postwar slump and because personal incomes remained high, 1960 was dubbed "the year of the hidden recession."

FOREIGN POLICY, 1956–1961

The Middle East

The two moderate recessions which marred the record of the Eisenhower prosperity and caused many Americans to wonder whether the United States was heading for a real depression occurred at a time of renewed and deepening international crises which quickly shattered the

474   THE U.S. & THE POSTWAR WORLD, 1945–1961

optimism and high hopes that had followed the Geneva summit conference of July, 1955. Shortly after Eisenhower's reelection, the American people, by now almost accustomed to periodic crises in Germany and the Far East, were forced to face a new and equally dangerous one in the oil-rich and strategic Middle East. During the fifteen years following World War II, the region's long-smouldering anticolonialism had been fanned into a powerful nationalistic flame which deprived a war-weakened Britain and France of their once dominant influence and authority over this part of the world. America's primary concern in the Middle East was to safeguard its own and the free world's access to the area's vital oil resources, which represented at least 75 per cent of the earth's proved reserves and from which Europe was then depending for more than 80 per cent of its needs.[9] The economic interests of the United States in the Middle East, which were exercised through various independent American oil companies, were complicated further by the nationalistic sensibilities of the newly emergent Arab world, which the Kremlin exploited for its own purposes; by historic, religious, ethnic, and social jealousies among the peoples of the region, which kept it in constant turmoil; by Washington's worldwide power rivalry with Moscow; by conflicts of interest and policy with and among the members of the Western alliance; and by the intense hatred that had long existed between the Arabs and the Jews in Palestine.

On November 29, 1947, much to the dissatisfaction of the Arabs, who claimed all of Palestine, the United Nations approved a resolution dividing this disputed land into an Arab and Jewish state, thereby satisfying the ancient hopes of many of the world's Jews for a national home in Palestine. Six months later, on May 15, 1948, while the Arabs and Jews were attacking each other, the provisional government of Israel proclaimed the birth of the new Zionist state. The disorganized but often violent fighting which had followed the United Nations resolution deepened into formal warfare which lasted until 1949, when Ralph J. Bunche, the American diplomat in the employ of the United Nations, arranged an armistice. But it proved impossible to negotiate a mutually acceptable peace: both sides often violated the truce terms, and border clashes and guerrilla raids remained an almost regular feature of Palestinian life.

The Arab-Israeli issue presented Washington with an exceptionally difficult diplomatic problem. The United States had long supported the rights

[9] George Lenczowski, "Oil in the Middle East," *Current History*, XXXVIII (May 1960), 262.

of the Jews to an independent and sovereign state of their own in Palestine, and the Truman administration had granted Israel recognition minutes after it had been proclaimed. At the same time, the economic, political, and strategic interests of the United States and its Western European allies also required the friendship of the Arab world, which, under the leadership of Egypt, refused to accept Israel as a permanent member of the new, postwar order in the Middle East. Once Israel had been established, the United States sought to enforce the armistice and to prevent Soviet penetration into that part of the world by cultivating the goodwill of Egypt and the other Arab states, with the hope that they would join the West in a collective defense system. While America's chief concern in the Middle East was to check the expansion of Soviet power, to which the Arabs were largely indifferent, Egypt's primary interest was to secure military assistance in crushing Israel, to which the West was firmly opposed. These pronounced differences were intensified further by the demands of Arab nationalists, who mistrusted the motives of the former imperial powers and sought to end the last vestiges of their influence in the Moslem world. In February, 1953, after years of tension and sporadic outbursts of violence, Britain decided to quit the Sudan, and agreed to allow the Sudanese to determine whether they wanted independence or union with Egypt; and less than eighteen months later, on July 27, 1954, Britain promised Gamel Abdel Nasser, the new Egyptian leader, that it would withdraw its forces from the Suez Canal early in 1956.

The success of these negotiations greatly strengthened Nasser's prestige among Arab nationalists, whose cause he repeatedly expressed with increasing stridency. "Prepare yourselves, O Israel . . . your destruction is near" and other similar declarations came out of Cairo wth alarming regularity. But despite these bellicose pronouncements, Nasser was sorely in need of both military aid to fight Israel and economic and financial assistance to develop his country's resources. The United States and Britain refused to supply him with arms, but they agreed to provide him with economic and technical aid in the hope of moderating Egypt's hatred toward Israel by diverting Nasser's energies to internal reform and development. By coming to Nasser's assistance, Britain and the United States also hoped to keep the Soviet Union out of the Middle East. But Nasser's hatred for Israel was not so easily diverted, and the Kremlin's ambitions in the Middle East proved just as difficult to thwart, a fact made abundantly apparent when, during the last days of September, 1955,

Russia and subsequently its Eastern European satellites and Red China agreed to accept large quantities of Egyptian cotton in payment for Soviet and Czechoslovakian arms and military equipment.

Secretary Dulles tried to counter the move by promising Nasser Anglo-American help in financing the billion-dollar Aswan Dam project, which the Egyptian leader had come to regard as an indispensable feature of his agricultural redevelopment program. During the nearly seven months while Nasser was studying the proposal, Soviet arms kept pouring into Egypt and its ally, Syria; Egyptian commando raids against Israel increased in both number and destructiveness; Cairo intensified its nationalist propaganda campaign throughout the Arab world, much to the annoyance of the French in Algeria; and Nasser denounced and tried to wreck the Baghdad Pact or Middle East Treaty Organization (METO) which Britain and four pro-Western states, (Turkey, Pakistan, Iraq, and Iran) had negotiated in November, 1955. While not a member of this alliance, the United States had promoted it, approved of its mutual cooperation and defensive provisions, which allowed for American and British military bases, and assigned an official observer to attend its sessions.

Nasser's anti-Western activities were strongly resented in the United States, and when, on July 17, 1956, he decided to accept the American offer for financial assistance to build the Aswan Dam, the United States withdrew it, declaring it was no longer "feasible in present circumstances." Since the contributions of Britain and the International Bank, which were also to participate in the loan, were contingent upon American participation, they too abandoned the project. A week later, after furiously denouncing the United States, Nasser retaliated by seizing the properties of the largely foreign-owned Suez Canal Company, declaring that Egypt would operate the canal itself and use the toll revenues to finance the dam. The next day, Britain and France froze all of Egypt's overseas assets, and the United States urged a meeting of the principal nations dependent on the canal to seek a peaceable and equitable solution.

For three months every effort to negotiate an agreement that would internationalize the canal while at the same time protecting "the sovereign rights of Egypt" failed. As these negotiations were going on, Britain and France, determined to defend their financial interests in the Suez Canal Company and to prevent Egypt from interfering with the operation of this vital waterway, consulted with each other about the possibility of intervention, and began strengthening their naval forces in the Eastern Mediterranean. The United States, occupied at home with the presidential election and reluctant to appear to be supporting colonialism, sought to restrain both sides by calling for more negotiations and preaching against the use of force. The crisis was intensified further by the growing violence between Israelis and Egyptians along the Gaza Strip and numerous skirmishes elsewhere along the Israeli frontier.

On October 29, ignoring previous American pleas against aggression, Israel, with the apparent support of Britain and France, invaded the Sinai Peninsula and forced the Egyptians into a major retreat. The next day Britain and France demanded a cease-fire, ordered both sides to withdraw their forces ten miles from the canal, and called upon Nasser to allow an Anglo-French occupation of certain principal points along the strategic waterway, declaring that unless these conditions were met within twelve hours the two powers would intervene by force. Israel, as was to be expected, agreed to the ultimatum, but Nasser refused. During the next few days, while Israeli troops were inflicting mortal defeats upon the Egyptians in the Sinai Peninsula and the Gaza Strip, British and French planes bombed Egyptian airfields, and on November 5 British and French troops began to land at Port Said. The Soviet Union threatened to intervene to "crush the aggressors and restore peace"; the United States censured Israel for resorting to force, disclaimed any prior knowledge of the invasion, and accused Britain and France of having acted precipitously and "in error"; and the United Nations appealed for a cease-fire, which all sides agreed to on November 7.

The last chapter of the Suez crisis was over in a week; its consequences, however, were long felt. The Anglo-French action, which failed to resolve the Arab-Israeli conflict, incurred ill will all over the world and revived Afro-Asian fears of Western colonialism, while diverting attention from the Soviet Union's suppression of the Hungarian uprising, which was going on at the same time. The weakness of Britain and France was revealed and their authority in the Middle East seriously damaged. The measure split the Western Allies and weakened the NATO alliance while it strengthened Nasser's position and prestige in the Arab world. Because of his wrecking activities in the canal zone, world trade was disrupted for at least six months, imposing considerable hardships on the European economy. The United States tried to repair the damage from what came to be known as the "Suez fiasco" by shipping oil to Europe and reaffirming the solidarity of the Western alliance. On No-

478   THE U.S. & THE POSTWAR WORLD, 1945–1961

vember 27, Eisenhower declared that the "difficulties" which had separated the United States from its two principal allies over this "particular international incident" should not be "construed as a weakening or disruption of the great bonds that have so long joined our nation with the United Kingdom and . . . France and our allies in assuring that peace, justice and freedom shall prevail."

Five weeks later, in an effort to prevent any further deterioration of the West's interests in the Middle East, Eisenhower went before Congress on January 5, 1957, and said that the United States could not afford to "leave a vacuum in the Middle East and prayerfully hope that Russia will stay out." Besides requesting $200 million in economic aid and development funds, Eisenhower asked for the authority to use American military forces "to secure and protect the territorial integrity and political independence of such nations requesting such aid against overt armed aggression from any nation controlled by International Communism." The Eisenhower Doctrine, as this statement of American policy came to be called, appeared not only to be very similar to the policy of containment but also to vindicate the assertions of those who had criticized the cutting of conventional forces and warned of the dangers of relying too heavily upon Dulles' massive deterrence. Partly because of the lingering effects of the Suez crisis and the role of American diplomacy in that debacle and partly because of growing criticism of Dulles, the Congress reacted slowly to the President's request, delaying its approval until the first week in March.

The Eisenhower Doctrine did not have such markedly successful results as had Truman's a decade earlier. It had little effect upon Egypt; Nasser continued to champion Arab nationalism, inflame Middle Eastern politics, and maintain friendly ties with Moscow, depending upon Soviet arms and the anticolonial feeling of the region's people to foster his own ambitions. After February, 1958, when Syria joined Egypt, Nasser became the president of the newly formed United Arab Republic, whose uneasy truce with Israel had to be maintained by a United Nations force. To counter the growing influence of Soviet aid and in the hope of keeping Nasser from going over entirely into the Kremlin's orbit, the United States, beginning in July, 1959, resumed its economic and technical assistance program.

Elsewhere in the Middle East, the effectiveness of the Eisenhower Doctrine in stemming the tide of Soviet penetration was mixed. During the summer of 1958, when pro-Nasser and Communist-inspired rebels tried to overthrow the Lebanese government, President Camille Chamoun called upon the United States for assistance. Washington responded by sending the Sixth Fleet and landing marines. By October order was restored. At the same time, the British were similarly successful in saving the government of Jordan's King Hussein. But in Iraq, King Faisal was assassinated in July, 1958, and a military clique led by General Obdul Karim Kassim overthrew the monarchy and established a republic, which Kassim declared to be "part of the Arab nation." The new government imitated Nasser's policies, accepted Soviet aid, chose a more neutralist course in foreign affairs, and in March, 1959, just after the United States had signed "bilateral agreements of cooperation" with Iran, Pakistan, and Turkey, withdrew from the Baghdad Pact, which was now called the Central Treaty Organization (CENTO). The political turbulence which marked the course of events in the Middle East and the growing influence of Soviet Russia in this region of the world, often called the "bridge of three continents," created potentially dangerous opportunities for war as the two superpowers sought to safeguard their interests there and competed for additional advantages.

From the Summit to U-2

The spirit of the Geneva summit meeting, widely hailed as providing a new and friendly basis for the two rival power blocs to resolve their differences, just outlasted the summer of 1955. Besides the Kremlin's efforts to subvert the nationalist aspirations of the underdeveloped and emerging nations of Africa and Asia, which engaged the United States in difficult negotiations with its allies and required the stationing of American forces all over the world, the two principal stumbling blocks to Soviet-American accord remained the unresolved German question and the accelerating tempo of the armaments race.

The inability of the United States and the Soviet Union to agree upon an effective and mutually satisfactory system of implementing the Eisenhower "open skies" proposal led both powers to improve their defenses against a massive surprise attack and to strengthen their retaliatory capabilities. The United States spent hundreds of millions of dollars on an extensive and complicated Arctic radar warning system, maintained the Strategic Air Command's bombers on a continuous alert, and, by negotiating with friendly governments for bases, stationed these planes around the world. The Defense Department developed a wide variety

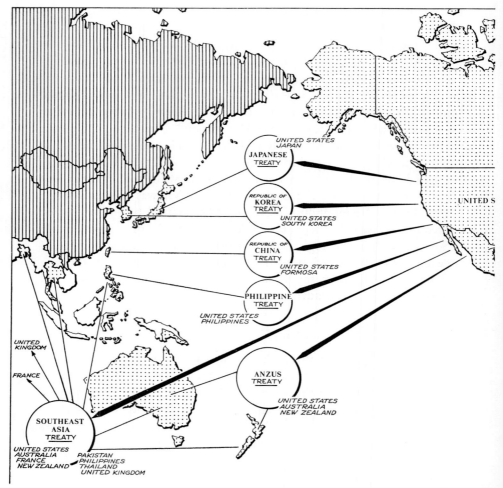

UNITED STATES COLLECTIVE DEFENSE AGREEMENTS, 1961

of atomic and thermonuclear weapons and rushed to narrow the Soviet lead in intercontinental ballistic missiles. The Soviets, according to supposedly reliable reports, were engaged in the same kinds of activities.

The stockpiling of these weapons, the continuous race to develop others of even greater destructivity, and the fact that they might be unleashed by mistake aroused the fears of many people. Others were concerned with their inevitable spread among the nonnuclear powers, augmenting greatly the opportunities for nuclear war; and still others were disturbed by the ill-effects of radioactive fallout from the testing of

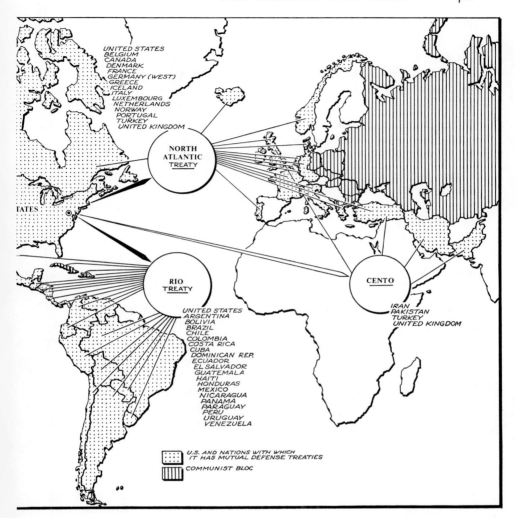

these weapons. All of these factors combined to create a strong worldwide demand for renewed efforts to achieve disarmament and a ban on nuclear testing.

After the Geneva summit meeting, a long series of multination conferences were held, all of which failed to produce a test-ban agreement, the principal reason being the inability of the United States and Russia to agree on such questions as the extent and form of inspection and the timing of the suspension. In July, 1957, after several months of discussion, these questions defeated the efforts of a United Nations subcommittee on disarmament. On March 31, 1958, four days after Nikita S. Khrushchev succeeded Bulganin as Soviet premier and after Russia had just completed a series of tests, the Kremlin's new leader declared a halt; and he called upon the United States and Britain, which had exploded its first nuclear bomb in October, 1952, to do likewise. The West, unwilling to grant the Soviets this advantage, continued their tests, but in August, 1958, after a meeting of nuclear scientists in Geneva disclosed that it was possible to develop an effective detection system, the West proposed a one-year moratorium on testing which the Soviets agreed to discuss, but only after they had carried on a new series of tests to equal those the West had completed earlier that year.

The next round of negotiations began at Geneva on October 31, 1958, and, except for an occasional adjournment, lasted for three years; but after more than 350 meetings, the talks produced no results. In the meantime, in February, 1960, France exploded an atomic bomb, thus becoming the fourth member of the nuclear club. The Geneva talks, despite some minor Soviet concessions, revealed once again the insurmountable difficulties blocking an East-West agreement. The Russians, for example, were willing to agree to a treaty outlawing large tests which both sides could detect without on-the-place inspection, but they stalled and shifted position on banning small blasts. The greatest difficulty, however, continued to be the question of inspection, with the United States insisting upon effective guarantees against cheating by means of annual on-site investigations. The question of who should determine the number of these annual inspections and who should police them also produced major deadlocks which contributed to defeating the chances for agreement.

These negotiations were adjourned in September, 1961, when the Soviet Union announced that it would soon start a major test series, including large atmospheric explosions. It did so the next month, despite appeals from President Kennedy and the United Nations to refrain from polluting the atmosphere with possibly dangerous amounts of radioactive fallout. The fear of and opposition to these tests among many people were reflected in the United Nations, which, despite American opposition, voted to ban the use of all nuclear weapons. In the meantime the United States, while continuing its small underground blasts, studied the problem of whether to resume its own atmospheric tests. On March 2, 1962, President Kennedy announced the decision in a nationwide television address: in view of the Soviet tests, the security and survival of the coun-

THE EISENHOWER YEARS 483

try required that the United States resume atmospheric testing. "In the absence of any major shift in Soviet policies," Kennedy declared, "no American President . . . could in good faith make any other decision." But before the United States would begin exploding nuclear weapons, it was disposed to try once again to achieve a test-ban treaty, and for this reason it was delaying its tests until after the opening of a new eighteen-power disarmament conference, scheduled to begin its work in Geneva on March 15, 1962. "If the Soviet Union should now be willing to accept . . . [a test-ban] treaty . . . there would be no need for our tests to begin," the President said. "Our real objective is to make our own tests unnecessary . . . . to prevent the nuclear arms race from mushrooming out of control. . . ."

The Soviet-American impasse which defeated the disarmament talks of the 1950's was duplicated in the two powers' search for a mutually satisfactory solution to the German and Berlin questions. The primary purposes of Soviet diplomacy were to get the United States to withdraw its forces from the continent and to disrupt the NATO alliance, thereby assuring the Kremlin European hegemony. The United States, however, could never permit the establishment of a balance of power so overwhelmingly unfavorable to its interests. The security of the United States required a strong, independent, and stable Europe as a counterweight to Russian power. So long as Germany remained divided, such an equilibrium of power was impossible, in Washington's opinion, especially since France's energies were being drained by its colonial troubles in Indochina and Algeria. As a result, American policy vis-à-vis Europe developed along two basic courses: the rearmament of West Germany and its full participation in NATO, and the strengthening of Western Europe, both militarily and economically.[10]

The understandable reluctance of the French and other victims of the Nazi occupation to welcome the West Germans as allies and the seemingly casual attitude of the Western European countries toward adopting policies to strengthen their defenses against Russia created considerable strain between the United States and its allies. In December, 1953, when the Western European nations were debating West Germany's admission into the European Defense Community (EDC), Secretary Dulles, in one of his more controversial statements, cautioned them that if the plan was not approved, the United States would be forced to undertake "an agonizing reappraisal" of its "basic policy." The warning

[10] Davids, *op. cit.*, pp. 468–70.

was intended especially for the French, who were hesitant to accept West Germany into an integrated European defense system. Prejudice against a long-time enemy and national pride and the aspiration to re-establish France as the *grande nation* of the continent, along with fear that once the EDC was established Britain and the United States would feel less compelled to maintain strong forces in Europe, combined to bring about the EDC's defeat in the French Assembly. This major blow to American policy was quickly softened by the able efforts of Foreign Secretary Eden, who within less than three months devised a new scheme whereby West Germany's forces could be added to those of France and the others in a common defense system. The Western European Union (WEU) agreements, which were signed in Paris on October 23, 1954, enlarged the membership of the five-power Brussels Treaty of 1948 to include Italy and West Germany, provided for the latter's membership in NATO, and established its contribution at twelve divisions. To allay French fears, the agreements pertaining to West Germany's military contribution were carefully defined and its military force was kept inferior to that of France.[11]

Despite these and other difficulties which separated the Western allies, NATO continued to function as the primary curb against Soviet power on the continent, and its strength was gradually increased, especially when the negotiations following the Geneva summit meeting indicated there was little likelihood that the two sides might find a more relaxed accommodation. Soviet insistence on a multination European security pact without American participation and the dissolution of the NATO and Warsaw alliances was as unacceptable to the West as the latter's demands—a unified Germany within NATO—were to Russia. The fact that the West was willing to reassure the Kremlin of its peaceful intentions by signing a mutual security treaty and imposing strict and carefully regulated limits on German armaments did not satisfy the Soviets. The cold war, which began in the Middle East and spread to Southeast Asia and Indonesia, erupted most dangerously in divided Berlin, where the thriving Western sector was becoming an increasingly traveled escape route for depressed and poverty-stricken East Germans seeking refuge from communism. Moreover, West Berlin's prosperity was also a source of considerable embarrassment to the East German Communists.

Partly because of this and partly because Khrushchev hoped that the Soviet Union's dramatic achievements in space and in missile technology

[11] Spanier, *op. cit.*, pp. 131–32.

THE EISENHOWER YEARS 485

might win him some concessions, he decided to reopen the German question. In a bold and surprising statement in November, 1958, he announced that in six months the Soviet Union would assign its rights in Berlin to the "sovereign German Democratic Republic." And he went on to say that after May, 1959, the three Western powers in the city would have to negotiate their continued status there with that government, which none of them recognized. The dangerous and unrealistic Berlin situation had to be "renegotiated," Khrushchev said; but the solution he proposed —uniting the four sectors into a single city government or creating a neutral "demilitarized free city" out of the three western ones—were rejected by the West, since either would leave West Berlin a defenseless enclave encircled by Soviet armed might and dependent upon the goodwill of the Communist East Germans for its continued existence.[12]

Since the Western Powers had repeatedly declared their determination to defend "their rights and responsibilities" in West Berlin, including the freedom of its people, Khrushchev's proposal to "abolish" the city's "occupation regime" by negotiating a German peace treaty with the Communist East German government presented the West with an exceedingly serious challenge. And while none of the Western Allies' leaders ever considered accepting the Kremlin's demands, there was considerable disagreement among some of them as to the response they should make to the Soviet proposal. West Germany's Chancellor Adenauer and France's President DeGaulle insisted upon standing firm. Any concession, they claimed, would lead to further demands. Britain's Prime Minister Harold Macmillan, on the other hand, favored a more conciliatory and flexible course, one which would allow for negotiation and minimize the risk of war. Macmillan's attitude reflected many of his people's fears of nuclear annihilation and their interest in what came to be known as disengagement, a policy designed to break the long East-West deadlock on Germany by establishing that divided country as a united neutralized sovereign state, a kind of buffer separating the two rival power blocs. This idea was first enunciated by Anthony Eden at the 1955 summit conference, subsequently elaborated with certain modifications by George Kennan, and in February, 1958, officially proposed as a permanent solution to the German problem by Adam Rapacki, Poland's foreign minister. France and West Germany opposed the idea strongly, now that they had decided to cooperate in building a new Europe under their joint leadership, and were greatly disturbed by what they considered to be signs of

[12] Davids, *op. cit.,* p. 530.

486   THE U.S. & THE POSTWAR WORLD, 1945-1961

British softness; and the United States discounted disengagement as potentially dangerous to its chief interest—the security of Western Europe.

Despite the doubts of his allies, Macmillan believed it was imperative to seek an honorable accommodation with the Russians over Berlin. He returned from a "reconnaissance trip" to the Kremlin in March, 1959, and flew to Washington the next month to persuade Eisenhower of the necessity for another meeting at the summit. The President, recalling the failure of the Geneva "big four" conference of July, 1955, and the disillusionment which followed it, was opposed to participating in another similar session. At the same time, unlike Adenauer and DeGaulle, he was unwilling to exclude any possibility which might provide a solution to the crisis, and with considerable reluctance he accepted Macmillan's proposal for a new meeting of the heads of state, provided, however, that the Soviets gave some prior indication of their willingness to negotiate in good faith. The test of Russian intentions came in May at a "big four" Foreign Ministers' Conference in Geneva. The results were completely unrewarding. After nine weeks of talk, no solution was found to compromise the differences which divided the East and the West on Berlin and German unification. As far as the West was concerned, the only beneficial result of the Geneva talks was the fact that Khrushchev did not fulfill his earlier threat to turn over the Soviet sector of Berlin to East Germany; and while this did not mean he had abandoned the project, it provided additional opportunities for further discussions.

During the last week of July, 1959, while the "big four" foreign ministers were concluding their fruitless talks, Vice President Nixon left for a two-week visit to Russia, where he opened the American Exhibition in Moscow. This display, like the earlier Soviet exhibition in New York City, was part of a cultural exchange program inaugurated by the two countries in the hope that if their peoples understood each other better, improved government relations would follow. The validity of this assumption was shaken somewhat when Nixon and Khrushchev, while walking through a model American kitchen, became involved in a heated, publicly televised debate on the benefits of capitalism and communism. The discussion, however, ended on a friendly note. Khrushchev then accepted Eisenhower's invitation to visit the United States, and arrived in Washington, D.C., on September 15. During his two-week stay, which included a cross-country tour and the usual official ceremonials, he conferred with Eisenhower on Berlin and Germany at Camp David, the President's secluded mountain retreat in Maryland. As a result of these

THE EISENHOWER YEARS 487

talks. Khrushchev retracted his previous threat to turn over the Soviet sector of Berlin to the East Germans, and Eisenhower admitted that a solution to the "abnormal" Berlin situation "should not be prolonged indefinitely." The President's statement frightened Adenauer and DeGaulle, who interpreted it as an indication of American weakness, but it was well received in Britain where it was taken as a sure sign that the United States was prepared to participate in a summit conference, a view confirmed at Paris in December, 1959, when Eisenhower met with Macmillan, DeGaulle, and Adenauer. After their discussions, they invited Khrushchev to a "meeting at the top" the following spring.

The prospects of reaching an East-West agreement on Berlin and Germany at the forthcoming summit meeting were never very good. Neither side had actually made any substantial concessions, and while both were willing to continue to negotiate, neither was prepared to yield much. The United States reasserted its determination to defend its rights in Berlin and moved to strengthen NATO's military capabilities; and Khrushchev, in a speech before the Supreme Soviet in January, 1960, declared, "If all our efforts to conclude a peace treaty with the two German states fail to be crowned with success . . . the Soviet Union and other willing states will sign a peace treaty with the [East] German Democratic Republic with all the consequences proceeding from this." [13] Statements like this cast grave doubts upon the likelihood of a successful summit conference, but what finally doomed the meeting two weeks before its scheduled opening was the events of the first week in May.

On May 5, 1960, the Soviet Union announced that it had shot down an American high-altitude U-2 reconnaissance plane near Sverdlovsk, some 1,200 miles inside Russia. For two days, while official Washington elaborated upon the loss of a National Aeronautics and Space Administration "weather research plane" and the State Department categorically denied any "attempt to violate . . . Soviet air space," Khrushchev kept his silence. Then on May 7, he demolished the American explanations by declaring that the plane's pilot was "alive and kicking" and that he had confessed to being engaged in an aerial espionage mission for the Central Intelligence Agency, using his plane's cameras to photograph Russia's defense installations. Caught in the embarrassing position of having Khrushchev expose the falsity of the original "cover story," Secretary of State Herter admitted the truth of the Soviet account on May 9. Fear of a "surprise attack," he said, had caused the government to engage in "ex-

[13] Quoted in Spanier, *op. cit.*, p. 164.

488   THE U.S. & THE POSTWAR WORLD, 1945–1961

tensive aerial surveillance [of the Soviet Union] by unarmed aircraft, normally of a peripheral character but on occasion by penetration." [14] Two days later, Eisenhower shocked the world by declaring that he had ordered the U-2 flights, thereby providing Khrushchev with the perfect opportunity to scuttle the summit meeting, which he proceeded to do as soon as he arrived in Paris.

The Soviet leader attacked the United States for its "aggressive acts" against Russia, threatened to destroy any nation which allowed American espionage planes to use its airfields, denounced Eisenhower, and demanded an apology. When the President would not go beyond saying that he had ordered all flights suspended, Khrushchev refused to meet with him and withdrew his earlier invitation for Eisenhower to visit Russia. Most observers believed that Khrushchev's rage over the U-2 incident was calculated to destroy the possibility of holding a "big four" meeting, either because of his own internal political difficulties or because of the opposition of Red China. Despite his bellicosity and threats, Khrushchev did not force a decision on Berlin, and by the end of the year he was again talking of a summit meeting with the next President. Thus, fifteen years after the end of World War II, Kennedy inherited the still-unresolved problem of a German peace treaty.

Latin America

Meanwhile the Latin American peoples continued to complain that the United States was showing little interest in or understanding of their political and economic problems. Regarding rapid industrialization as the only solution for mass poverty, which was now accentuated by a rapid growth of population, they hoped for substantial economic assistance. To an increasing extent the poorer classes were demanding social reforms and turning against the military dictatorships representing upper-class interests which had been the usual form of government in the more backward countries ever since they had become independent. Liberal and democratic spokesmen complained that the United States was too exclusively concerned with the Communist menace, giving approval to any government, however corrupt and reactionary, which would oppose communism and failing to recognize that there could be no stability in Latin America without substantial reforms. As Milton Eisenhower, the

[14] Quoted in Richard P. Stebbens, *The United States in World Affairs, 1960* (New York [1961]), p. 29.

THE EISENHOWER YEARS 489

President's brother, remarked after a fact-finding tour of Latin America in 1959, the United States might find it necessary to shake hands with dictators, but it ought not to embrace them.

These complaints had grown stronger after the Guatemalan incident of 1954. A left-wing government, including some Communists, took power in that country under the leadership of Jacobo Arbenz Guzmán, who became president in 1951. The government began to confiscate large plantations, including some belonging to the United Fruit Company, for distribution among the Indian peasants. The growth of Communist influence alarmed the United States, and at a Pan American Conference held at Caracas in March, 1954, Dulles secured passage of a resolution declaring international communism to be a threat to the security of the Americas, though he failed to secure any agreement for action against it. The Guatemalan government, increasingly controlled by Communists, now began to import arms from countries behind the iron curtain, and the United States retaliated by shipping arms to Honduras and Nicaragua. These were unofficially made available to conservative refugees from Guatemala. In June one of them, Colonel Carlos Castillo Armas, led an army into Guatemala and overthrew the government with little difficulty. He then assumed the presidency, abrogated the land reform program, and returned to conservative policies. No doubt the United States was justified in regarding the Arbenz Guzmán government as a threat to hemispheric security, but it was unfortunate that the only alternative seemed to be a right-wing military leader of the traditional type. Many Latin Americans accused the United States of being primarily concerned about the properties of the United Fruit Company rather than about the welfare of the Guatemalans.

That something was seriously wrong with hemispheric relations was brought home to the American people in 1958. On April 27 Vice President Nixon and his wife embarked on an eighteen-day goodwill tour of leading South American countries, which was not expected to be of any special importance. It quickly became apparent that Communists and other enemies of the United States were alarmingly successful in organizing popular demonstrations of hostility against these representatives of "Yankee imperialism." The worst of a series of unpleasant incidents occurred at Caracas, the capital of Venezuela, where a right-wing dictatorship which had received favors from the United States had recently been overthrown. During a tour of the city the Nixons were met by an angry mob which the local police authorities were incapable of controlling, and

490 THE U.S. & THE POSTWAR WORLD, 1945–1961

their lives were seriously endangered. Both Mr. and Mrs. Nixon displayed a physical courage which earned Latin American admiration, and the American government and people were shocked into the realization that a new approach to Latin America must be made.

In September, 1960, an Inter-American Development Bank was set up with an initial United States contribution of $500 million. The program of economic expansion was considerably enlarged by the Kennedy administration, which launched the Alliance for Progress and made plans to ensure that aid was combined with programs for social reform so that it would actually benefit the people who needed it most and not merely the upper classes. Meanwhile the Organization of American States, with the support of the United States, began to take a more positive stand against dictatorships. Diplomatic and economic pressure was applied against the thirty-one-year-old regime of Rafael Leonidas Trujillo in the Dominican Republic, which had intervened in the affairs of neighboring countries. The dictatorship ended in May, 1961, with the assassination of Trujillo, after which the Dominican Republic began to move in the direction of democracy.

These changes of policy were too late to prevent disaster in Cuba. Fulgencio Batista had ruled the island as a dictator since 1952, with the apparent support of the United States. In 1956 a young revolutionary, Fidel Castro, started a rebellion Batista was unable to suppress. After prolonged guerrilla warfare Castro won control of the country in January, 1959. American officials were not initially unsympathetic, but they grew increasingly alarmed as the Castro government shot more than 600 individuals associated with the Batista regime after farcical trials by military courts, embarked on an economic program of wholesale socialization, confiscated the properties of American corporations, engaged in intemperate denunciations of the United States, and cultivated friendly relations with the Soviet Union. It gradually became apparent that Cuba was being made into a Communist state. Thousands of Cubans fled to Florida and elsewhere. In January, 1961, the United States ended diplomatic relations and applied stringent economic pressures.

Worse was to come. Exiles from Cuba, including many who had originally supported Castro, planned to overthrow him by force, and were given secret help from the Central Intelligence Agency of the United States government, which arranged for them to receive arms and military training in Guatemala. It was felt that action must be taken quickly, since the Castro government was rapidly building up its military strength with arms supplied by Communist countries. When the Kennedy administration took office, it learned that an attack on Cuba was planned for the near future, and decided to proceed with it. On April 17, 1961, some 1,400 Cubans, armed and trained by the United States, made a landing in Cuba in the Bay of Pigs. Contrary to their hopes, they received no appreciable help from the Cuban population, and within three days the whole movement had collapsed, and all the participants were either killed or captured. Kennedy declared that the United States did not intend to abandon Cuba, and even hinted that it might violate its promises of non-intervention if this was necessary to destroy communism in the Americas. But it was obvious that the United States had suffered a severe blow, and there seemed to be no practicable way of preventing Cuba from becoming a full-fledged Communist state.

The six months preceding Eisenhower's retirement were probably the most difficult and frustrating of his entire Presidency. The three goals he had proclaimed so confidently in his 1952 inaugural address—peace, prosperity, and progress—seemed more unlikely of realization than ever before. Throughout the world the Communist challenge bore down upon the American people with a greater force than ever before. The old problems of disarmament and a German peace treaty were as far from resolution as they had been in Truman's days, and in Berlin the new cold war crisis posed as dangerous a threat to world peace as had the one of 1948. In addition to these almost chronic worries, the Eisenhower administration was forced to contend with the growing menace of Chinese communism in Asia and the increasing threat of Soviet penetration into Africa and Latin America. Sporadic outbreaks of violence endangered the precarious truce agreements which existed in Korea and Indochina; Chinese Communist infiltration of Laos created a new area of potential East-West conflict; and anti-American riots by neutralist and pro-Communist elements in Japan forced the President to cancel a ceremonial state visit to Tokyo. In June, 1960, after Belgium granted the Congo independence, a civil war broke out which required the United Nations to intervene in order to prevent that hapless country from becoming a pawn in the worldwide Soviet-American power rivalry. While most of these crises were far from American shores, the growing attachment of Fidel Castro's Cuba to the Soviet Union aroused considerable anxiety. During the fall and winter months of 1960, there was little on the international scene which seemed to indicate any relaxation in world tensions. Moreover, the progress of the Soviet Union in space, Khru-

492   THE U.S. & THE POSTWAR WORLD, 1945–1961

shchev's boasts about the superiority and range of his nuclear-armed rockets and missiles, and his continued threats about Berlin caused widespread concern among Americans over their individual safety and their country's defenses and its ability to match the Soviet Union in science and technology. These questions, along with a new economic slump, became the primary issues debated in the presidential campaign of 1960.

Suggested Readings

On the Eisenhower administration, Robert J. Donovan, *Eisenhower: The Inside Story* (New York, 1956) is reasonably complete on the first term. Merlo J. Pusey, *Eisenhower the President* (New York, 1956) is a favorable portrait, while Richard H. Rovere, *Affairs of State: The Eisenhower Years* (New York, 1956) is more critical, as is Marquis W. Childs, *Eisenhower: Captive Hero* (New York [1958]). Richard E. Neustadt, *Presidential Power: The Politics of Leadership* (New York, 1960) concerns itself largely with the Truman and Eisenhower administrations. The President's modern Republicanism is detailed in Arthur Larson, *A Republican Looks at His Party* (New York, 1956), but see also Samuel Lubell, *Revolt of the Moderates* (New York [1956]) for a perceptive analysis of the changes in American politics during the 1950's.

Sherman Adams, *Firsthand Report: The Story of the Eisenhower Administration* (New York [1961]) describes the events of these years as seen by the man in charge of the White House staff. See also the analysis of Adams' functions by Louis W. Koenig, *The Invisible Presidency* (New York [1960]).

Biographies of Nixon are mostly campaign tracts. See, for example, James Keogh, *This Is Nixon* (New York, [1956]); Earl Mazo, *Richard Nixon: A Political and Personal Portrait* (New York, 1960); and Stewart Alsop, *Nixon and Rockefeller: A Double Portrait* (New York, 1960). Ralph de Toledano, *Nixon* (New York, 1956) is heavily pro-Nixon; William Costello, *The Facts about Nixon* (New York, 1960) is more critical. Nixon guardedly describes some of his activities in his own *Six Crises* (New York, 1962).

On various domestic developments during the 1950's, see Arthur J. Goldberg, *The AFL-CIO United* (New York, 1957); Edward S. Mason, ed., *The Corporation in Modern Society* (Cambridge, Mass., 1960), a collection of essays on various phases of corporate activity; John K. Galbraith, *The Affluent Society* (Boston, 1958); Michael Straight, *Trial by Television* (Boston, 1954), the story of McCarthy's battle with the army; Charles P. Curtis, *The Oppenheimer Case* (New York, 1955), which details this famous investigation; William R. Willoughby, *The St. Lawrence Waterway: A Study in Politics and Diplomacy* (Madison, Wis., 1961), a detailed coverage of the history of this project; and Aaron Wildavsky, *Dixon-Yates: A Study in Power Politics* (New Haven, Conn., 1961).

A thoughtful and useful survey of American problems in the 1950's is John K. Jessup, *et al.*, *The National Purpose* (New York [1960]).

Desegregation is treated in Jack W. Peltason, *Fifty-eight Lonely Men: Southern Federal Judges and School Desegreation* (New York [1961]). On the legal aspects, consult Albert P. Blaustein and Clarence C. Ferguson, *Desegregation and the Law* (New Brunswick, N.J., 1957). William Peters, *The Southern Temper* (Garden City, N.Y., 1959) is a careful and perceptive analysis; Harry S. Ashmore, *The Negro and the Schools* (Chapel Hill, N.C., 1954) is detailed; and W. Hodding Carter, *The South Strikes Back* (Garden City, N.Y., 1959) covers the activities of Mississippi's White Citizen Councils.

On Dulles, see John R. Beal, *John Foster Dulles, 1888–1959* (New York, 1959); Roscoe Drummond and Gaston Coblentz, *Duel at the Brink* (Garden City, N.Y., 1960), an analysis of Dulles as Secretary of State; and Henry P. Van Dusen, ed., *The Spiritual Legacy of John Foster Dulles* (Philadelphia, 1960), a collection of Dulles' speeches and addresses. Dulles' own views before he became Secretary of State are expressed in his own, *War or Peace* (new ed., New York, 1957).

Eisenhower's foreign policy as he expressed it in some of his speeches is in Grayson Kirk, ed., *Peace With Justice* (New York, 1961). Richard P. Stebbins, *The United States in World Affairs* (New York, 1953–) are annual review volumes prepared under the auspices of the Council on Foreign Relations. A similar annual is published by the Brookings Institution, *Problems of United States Foreign Policy* (Washington, D.C., 1953–). Important interpretative accounts on developments during the 1950's include John H. Herz, *International Politics in the Atomic Age* (New York, 1959); Walt W. Rostow, *The United States in the World Arena: An Essay in Recent History* (New York, 1960), which emphasizes post-1939 developments; Norman A. Graebner, *The New Isolationism*, already cited; Edmund Stillman and William Pfaff, *The New Politics: America and the End of the Postwar Era* (New York, 1961), an important statement on the reaction of American foreign policy to developments arising out of the altered power equilibrium; George F. Kennan, *Russia, the Atom and the West* (New York, 1958) and the same author's *Realities of American Foreign Policy*, already cited; Kenneth W. Thompson, *Political Realism and the Crisis of World Politics: An American Approach to Foreign Policy Theory and Reality* (London [1960]); and the brief analysis by the English air marshal, Sir John C. Slesson, *What Price Coexistence? A Policy for the West* (New York [1961]). Harold K. Jacobson, ed., *America's Foreign Policy* (New York [1960]) is a collection of essays on various subjects by experts.

Bernard B. Fall, *Street Without Joy: Indochina at War, 1946–1954* (Harrisburg, Pa., 1961); Joseph W. Ballantine, *Formosa: A Problem for United States Foreign Policy* (Washington, D.C., 1952); Ephraim A. Speiser, *The United States and the Near East* (rev. ed., Cambridge, Mass., 1950); Erskine B. Childers, *Common Sense about the Arab World* (New York, 1960); Avrahm G. Mezerik, *Suez Canal: Nationalization, Invasion, International Action* (New York, 1956); John W. Campbell, *Defense of the Middle East*

494 THE U.S. & THE POSTWAR WORLD, 1945-1961

(New York [1958]); and Carol A. Fisher and Fred Krinsky, *Middle East in Crisis: Historical and Documentary Review* (Syracuse, N.Y., 1959) are all pertinent specialized works.

The arms and disarmament problem is covered in many works; see, for example, Donald G. Brennen, ed., *Arms Control, Disarmament and National Security* (New York, 1961), a collection of essays on the various problems that were discussed in the 1950's. Bernhard G. Bechhoefer, *Postwar Negotiations for Arms Control* (Washington, D.C., 1961) is a Brookings Institution study covering developments between 1946 and 1960. See also Thomas G. Schelling and Morton H. Halperin, *Strategy and Arms Control* (New York, 1961); Carnegie Endowment for International Peace, *Perspectives on Peace, 1910-1960* (New York [1960]); Anthony Nutting, *Disarmament* (London, 1959); Henry Kissinger, *Nuclear Weapons and Foreign Policy* (New York, 1957); and Hanson W. Baldwin, *The Great Arms Race: A Comparison of United States and Soviet Power Today* (New York, 1958).

II

Social and Cultural Developments

THE YEARS following the onset of the "great depression" forced Americans to face a series of tumultuous experiences, each more devastating than its predecessor, more threatening to American life, and more demanding of the nation's vision and courage. The depression brought not only material poverty to millions, but the demoralizing realization for great numbers of breadwinners that, despite the nation's long-vaunted tradition of free enterprise, they were powerless to find work to support their families. In consequence, the foundations of the social structure in which this powerlessness could occur came under close examination. During the 1930's, there was an extension, especially in intellectual circles, of interest in communism as a possible remedy for the ailments of the scapegrace capitalistic system. Alistair Cooke, in his *Generation on Trial* (1950), depicted with brilliance and compassion the characteristic attitude of intellectuals toward communism during this period; his analysis is particularly valuable because those of a later generation find it so difficult to reconstruct and understand these attitudes.

At the same time the mounting crises beyond American shores made increasing demands upon American attention and, as the months passed, forced Americans to an increasing recognition of their involvement in events that had hitherto been thought of as foreign. In Germany a vast

496 THE U.S. & THE POSTWAR WORLD, 1945–1961

and systematic campaign to control human thought was under way. Americans joined in a war against the Axis powers which President Roosevelt truly called "the War for Survival." The war was won by an unprecedented mobilization of the Allied nations' resources, but the relief felt at the defeat of the enemy in 1945 very shortly proved to be unjustified. A new Communist imperialism and a fantastic scientific advance, making weapons capable of destroying the human race at the pushing of a button, forced the Americans, in the postwar years, to act as leaders of the free world. The choice was very simple: find a means of preserving the peace, or perish. The only certainty was unending crisis. New devices of communication spared Americans no details of worldwide tension. A street riot in Iran, a famine in India, a Soviet mission to Cuba, each reverberated in Iowa and Maine. This was indeed "the Age of Anxiety."

At the same time the exact nature and depth of the reverberations were difficult to fathom, as America was extraordinarily rich, and its citizens were surrounded by every sort of physical comfort to block out oppressive realities. And, despite all change at home, and in contrast with most lands abroad, the United States remained faithful to a form of government that had flourished for more than a century and a half, and to ideals that had been established during the seventeenth and eighteenth centuries. Almost all Americans continued to believe in freedom and equality, even if some of them flinched at the process of realizing these ideals more fully. Americans were more sophisticated, more aware of their land's vulnerability to criticism; probably they were less moralistic. The whole foreign aid program, extended over twenty years, reflected a radical change in national attitude since the days of McKinley.

RELIGION

One strain of continuity in American civilization was offered by organized religion. Americans continued to believe in freedom for all faiths and in the separation of church and state, but at the same time they attended church in great numbers. Whereas early in the century, the churches seemed to be attracting fewer younger people, World War II produced, or coincided with, a remarkable revival of interest in religion —if church membership could be taken as an accurate gauge. By 1960 more than 110 million Americans were church members, distributed among 251 different denominations. This represented probably the highest proportion in American history—almost two-thirds of the total population, as contrasted with less than one-half thirty years earlier. Fifty-six per cent of all church members belonged to the various Protestant denominations, while thirty-six per cent were Roman Catholics.

Church membership and religious conviction were by no means necessarily one and the same. Current in popular thought was the idea, endorsed by many politicians, church spokesmen, and popular writers, that since Marxism was avowedly atheistic, adherence to one or another religious faith constituted loyalty to American ideals, and church-going was almost evidence of patriotism. Moreover, the churches were broadening their appeal—in particular they were taking on an increasingly social aspect—and for many lonely people, joining a church became a means of participating in community activities and assuming a recognizable identity.

But although some of the growth of church membership may have been due to nonreligious motivations, there was no doubt of the high quality of much of the religious thinking of the period. Particularly notable was the revived emphasis on the present-day applicability of the values of the traditional Protestant theology, as affirmed by the theologians Reinhold Niebuhr and Paul Tillich, both of whom taught at the Union Theological Seminary in New York. By this time, the optimism of much early twentieth-century religious thought seemed wholly unrealistic. Yet the pessimism of the new theology was by no means inconsistent with the hope of human improvement, and both Niebuhr and Tillich were militant supporters of political liberalism.

In other respects the trends that had developed in American Protestantism in the late nineteenth century remained dominant during the twentieth century. While some groups, mostly in rural areas, continued to preach strict fundamentalism, the more influential clergymen in most denominations no longer believed in the verbal inspiration of the Bible, and ethics and social service were emphasized more markedly than dogma. Theological differences became less important, and there was a strong tendency toward unification. Different groups of Lutherans, Congregationalists, and Methodists combined into single organizations, and in 1950 most of the Protestant churches came together to set up the National Council of Churches to coordinate their educational and welfare activities. And while many churches maintained a conservative attitude toward economic questions, the Federal Council of Churches, established in

1908, and other important bodies continued to preach a social gospel. In 1932, for example, the Federal Council adopted a revised social creed calling for extensive measures of social and economic planning along the lines afterward put into effect by the New Deal.

The Catholic Church in 1960 claimed a total membership of nearly 40 million as contrasted with 16 million in 1910. Thus, despite the decrease in immigration, its expansion was more than keeping pace with that of the population as a whole, rising from 17 per cent in 1910 to 23 per cent in 1960. There was a corresponding growth in its properties and institutional activities. By 1960 Catholic elementary and high schools numbered nearly 12,000 with about 5 million pupils, while there were 258 Catholic colleges and universities with a student enrollment of 290,000.

The fanatical anti-Catholicism that had flared up on several occasions in the nineteenth century now seemed to have subsided, and most Americans had accepted, if only abstractly, the principles of freedom and equality for all faiths. On the other hand, voting statistics in the 1960 presidential election suggested that many people in rural and small-town areas were still reluctant to support a candidate who, as John F. Kennedy put it, "happened to be a Catholic." Although there was remarkably little public expression of anti-Catholic attitudes during the campaign, Kennedy won less support in many rural and small-town areas than might have been expected if there had been no religious issue.

A number of disputes between Catholics and non-Catholics revealed disagreement about many aspects of church-state relations, and many non-Catholics feared an increase in Catholic strength. Especially difficult was the question of state support for religious education. While the Church was expanding its system of parochial schools and asking for state assistance, most non-Catholics insisted that a secular public school system for the instruction of children of all faiths was one of the essential foundations of American democracy. There were prolonged controversies as to whether public money might be used to provide free transportation for children going to parochial schools. This was allowed in a number of states and prohibited in others. In the Everson case, in 1947, the Supreme Court validated a New Jersey law to this effect by a five-to-four decision, but many non-Catholics continued to argue that such legislation was a violation, at least in spirit, of the first article of the Bill of Rights. Almost equally controversial was the problem of how far the state should seek to legislate moral standards, with reference to birth control, divorce, censorship of books and plays, and similar issues. While

SOCIAL & CULTURAL DEVELOPMENTS   499

Catholics believed it was the duty of the state to maintain morality, non-Catholic liberals feared the attempt to impose the principles of one group on the whole community.

From the eighteenth century to the days of Hitler, persecution of various forms had brought Jewish refugees from the Old World to American shores, so that by the middle of the twentieth century there were over 5 million Jews in the United States. The faith was divided into three streams: orthodox, reform, and conservative Judaism. Some Jews retained fidelity to the traditional faith, while many of the traditional forms were often discarded. American Jews were a resourceful people, as they had to overcome, as did all immigrants, the disadvantages of belonging to a minority group in a land in which anti-Semitism was never entirely absent. Their homogeneity was challenged increasingly through the years as the vital and demanding American culture about them tempted young Jews to break old ties and become merged in the main stream. The traditional Jewish respect for literature and learning endured, and they retained a predominantly urban character. The experience and culture of the Jews placed many of them in the vanguard of all movements against intolerance and discrimination.

EDUCATION

Another example of the continuity of the American heritage was the expansion of education on all levels. It remained an article of faith for most Americans that as much education as possible should be given to as many people as possible. After 1918, when all states had established compulsory education, the process of extending the years of attendance and increasing the number of public high schools went on steadily. By 1960 more than 33 million children were attending elementary schools, while high school attendance, which had amounted to only 700,000 in 1900, had risen to more than 9 million. Virtually all children below the age of fourteen, and 90 per cent of those between the ages of fourteen and seventeen, were now in school. An ever larger proportion of the American people went on to college. Attendance at accredited colleges, which had amounted to 250,000 in 1900 and 1 million in 1930, had risen by 1960 to 3.8 million, distributed among more than 1,000 different institutions. As the number of graduates expanded, a college degree, and in many instances some postgraduate training, became prerequisites for an increasing number of occupations, including virtually all professions.

School and college administrators were hard put to it to make adequate provision for this extraordinary expansion, which seemed likely to continue through the 1960's and 1970's because of the rise in the birth rate. Buildings and salaries remained generally inadequate, the result being over-crowded classrooms and a lack of qualified teachers. Educational facilities, moreover, varied sharply in different sections of the country. Whereas suburban areas in rich states like New York and California could afford to support good schools, education in most southern states was handicapped by acute poverty; yet most of these states devoted considerably larger proportions of their budgets to financing public schools than did most northern states. In rural areas throughout the country, moreover, there continued to be many thousands of one-teacher schools, most of them meagerly equipped. There was a growing belief that direct federal support for education was necessary, and during the 1950's the federal government did, in fact, contribute large sums to the colleges, mostly for scientific research. But many educators were afraid that federal support might bring with it too much federal control.

Even more important and controversial than the financial problems of American education was its qualitative level. By 1960 it was widely recognized that in most public schools intellectual standards were too low, discipline was lax, too much time was spent on nonacademic subjects, and —most important—children of superior ability were not receiving enough stimulation and encouragement. The abrupt realization during the later 1950's that Soviet scientists were in some ways ahead of their American counterparts and that this was in part due to the high standards of the Soviet school system had a healthily sobering effect. There was little dissent when James B. Conant, former president of Harvard, affirmed (after making a survey of American high schools) that "the academically talented student, as a rule, is not being sufficiently challenged, does not work hard enough, and his or her program of academic subjects is not of sufficient range." Assignment of the causes of this situation, however, remained highly controversial. Many people blamed the schools of education because of their emphasis on teaching methods rather than on knowledge of subject matter, declaring that teachers graduating from these schools were inadequately trained. They often went on to denounce the educational philosophy of John Dewey, with its inculcation of "learning by doing" in place of more old-fashioned disciplines, and its insistence that education should be closely linked with the student's concrete problems of daily living. So-called "progressive" educators continued to uphold Dewey's philosophy, maintaining that it was being inadequately understood and applied.

Debates about education on the college level were equally vigorous. Most college reformers were disturbed by the proliferation of different courses, many of which seemed to have little or no connection with a liberal arts education, by the excessive freedom permitted under the elective system, and by the distracting influence of athletics and other diversions. During the 1930's one extreme group, headed by Robert M. Hutchins, chancellor of the University of Chicago, argued that college education should be based on the "great tradition" of Western civilization as embodied in its great books, a program tried out in St. John's College, at Annapolis, Maryland. At the other extreme the advocates of progressivism declared that there were reactionary implications in this emphasis on tradition, that education should be oriented around the problems of the contemporary world, and that students should be free to work out their own programs in accordance with their own special interests. A number of small colleges, such as Bennington in Vermont, Sarah Lawrence in New York, and Reed in Oregon, provided good examples of this philosophy.

Most of the larger universities were influenced by both these extreme positions, retaining some of the freedom advocated by the progressives, but reaffirming the importance of the liberal arts, downgrading athletics, and placing increasing emphasis on some kind of core program which all students should be required to take. Probably the most influential statement of this central viewpoint was the report of a Harvard committee issued in 1945, *General Education in a Free Society*. The report emphasized the differences between "general education," meaning "that part of a student's whole education which looks first of all to his life as a responsible human being and citizen," and "special education," referring to "that part which looks to the student's competence in some occupation." The central trend in American colleges in the 1930's, 1940's, and 1950's was to reemphasize the importance of general education, with a recognition that their primary function was not to turn out skilled specialists but to produce men and women capable of enlightened citizenship. There was, indeed, a growing realization that specialists might perform their own functions more effectively if they had received the stimulus of a liberal arts education, and during the 1950's business corporations even began to organize college courses in literature and other cultural subjects for

502 THE U.S. & THE POSTWAR WORLD, 1945–1961

some of their younger executives. There was some fear lest competition with the Russians might lead to a narrow concentration on science and technology, but fortunately most of the responsible authorities seemed to be aware that this would defeat its own purposes. Scientific advance could not be effectively promoted by scientists who knew nothing except their own narrow areas of specialization.

THE PRESS

Americans continued to be a newspaper-reading people, though the function of informing and shaping public opinion was by this time shared by radio and television. During the twentieth century the press had continued to develop into a big business; however, the rise in circulation and the improvement in services were accompanied by a fall in the number of separate newspapers. By 1960 there were 1,750 dailies, having a total circulation of nearly 60 million, as contrasted with 2,226 dailies with a circulation of 15 million in 1900. Only 65 cities still retained competing dailies, while 1,385 cities had only one daily apiece.

A small number of responsible papers continued to flourish, most notably *The New York Times*, but the largest circulations were achieved by journals that relied largely on scandals and comic strips and inculcated ultranationalist and reactionary attitudes. Papers that championed liberal principles found it especially difficult to stay in business; the New York *World*, for example, an early depression casualty, was merged with the *Telegram* in 1930. Thus, there was reason for thinking that the press was catering to lower tastes and becoming less liberal, while outside a few large cities its inadequate coverage of world affairs left the American people dangerously uninformed. One ameliorating tendency, however, was the growth of syndicated columns by well-known commentators, some of whom displayed high degrees of skill, information, and responsibility. With the growth of radio, moreover, the press no longer had a monopoly on public information. Government regulation, exercised through the Federal Communications Commission (FCC), prohibited radio stations during election campaigns from giving the candidates of any one party exclusive access to the air. Owing partly to the radio speeches of Roosevelt, Truman, and their supporters, the opposition of a large proportion of the press did not prevent the Democrats from winning victories in the campaigns of 1936, 1940, 1944, and 1948.

Among magazines, similarly, increasingly high costs and the growth of mass-production methods meant some loss of quality. The depression years saw a high death rate among the more serious monthlies and quarterlies; apart from those that were subsidized by universities, the only survivors were *Harper's* and *The Atlantic Monthly*. Periodicals catering to a middle-class mass market, on the other hand, continued to flourish. *Time*, founded in 1923, presented busy Americans with spiced and predigested summaries of the weekly news. Its principal founder, Henry R. Luce, scored an even greater circulation triumph with *Life*, a new type of picture magazine founded in 1936, which combined news with superb photography. Though aimed at different audiences, *Time* and *Life* were akin in their self-assured tone; a *Life* editorial seemed unaware of the possibility of contradiction. The two magazines were spokesmen for a smoothly tailored conservatism, and they advocated a vigorous and emphatic foreign policy. The Luce editors saw no reason for unsettling their readers with complexities and ambiguities of interpretation, and they were gifted at presenting events in terms that were simple, single-minded, and, above all, amusing.

By 1960 six magazines enjoyed a circulation in excess of 6 million— two picture magazines, *Life* and *Look*, and three rivals of a more traditional type, *The Saturday Evening Post*, *The Ladies' Home Journal*, and *McCall's*. But the biggest circulation success of the period was scored by the *Reader's Digest*, founded by DeWitt Wallace in 1922, which by 1960 had a sale of 12 million at home and another 11 million in foreign editions. The *Digest* claimed to present summaries of the best articles in all current magazines, but its editorial policies reflected a strongly conservative viewpoint.

SOCIAL TRENDS

Although the postdepression decades brought no fundamental transformation of American ideals and institutions, they saw considerable changes in American society, some of which had significant intellectual and cultural implications. Partly because of general economic trends and partly because of the legislation of the New Deal period, up until 1944 there was both a leveling-up and a leveling-down of income levels, making the United States, even more than in the past, a predominantly middle-class nation. Although after 1944 the process of leveling seemed

504 THE U.S. & THE POSTWAR WORLD, 1945–1961

to have halted, the United States had made, wholly by peaceful methods, greater strides toward an equitable system of income distribution than other countries were able to achieve by violence and revolution.

Between 1929 and 1957 (the last year for which statistics are available), the share of the national income going to the richest 5 per cent of the total population dropped from 30 per cent to 22 per cent, and the share going to the richest 20 per cent dropped from 54 per cent to 45 per cent. During the same period the share going to the poorest 40 per cent rose from 27 per cent to 32 per cent. These figures, moreover, did not take account of income taxes, which made a further drastic reduction in the share going to families in the higher brackets. Yet the total national product had become so much larger that the richer groups were not absolutely poorer, in spite of the sharp relative decrease in their share of income. This change in income distribution was accompanied by a sharp rise in white-collar occupations and a decrease in jobs requiring manual labor. By 1960, 28 million Americans were employed as professional, managerial, clerical, and sales people, as contrasted with only 24 million Americans engaged as industrial workers, farmers, or other kinds of manual laborers. This big increase in white-collar workers was wholly among wage and salary earners, since the number of persons owning their own business was actually decreasing, amounting in 1960 to 6.3 million. Meanwhile the farm population continued to decrease, as it had done ever since World War I: by 1960 the number of farm families had dropped to less than 3.5 million.

This growth of the middle classes was accompanied by a movement to the suburbs, which was one of the most significant social trends of the period following World War II. The censuses of 1950 and 1960 showed a decline of population during the decade in rural regions (more than half the nation's counties lost population) and in the central sections of all but one of the nation's fifteen largest urban areas. Only in the suburbs was population expanding, and here the rapidity of growth was extraordinary. It was illustrated by the fact that in 1960 no less than one-quarter of all American homes had been built since 1950, the total mortgage debt for these homes amounting to no less than $116 billion.

In what ways did this suburban salary-earning American differ from his grandparents? Sociologists engaged in much gloomy speculation about his presumed loss of independence and his propensity to submit to social pressures making for conformity, but in areas of life that could be measured statistically, there seemed to be little reason for pessimistic verdicts.

SOCIAL & CULTURAL DEVELOPMENTS 505

Monogamy and the family unit continued to be the American norm, although apparently this was less rigidly the case than in the nineteenth century. If surface indications are any gauge, there was a revolution in American sexual mores after World War I. It is unwise to attempt to describe contemporary popular sexual behavior, and even more unwise to attempt comparisons of the sexual behavior of one generation with that of another; but certainly there was a new freedom of expression regarding sex. Subjects absolutely taboo in Victorian days, such as birth control and venereal disease, were freely discussed in conversation, in books, and in periodicals. The chaperone was a creature of the past, and supervision of young people was lighter and rarer. Beyond question, after World War I young people had more opportunity for sexual experimentation, abetted by the new availability of contraceptive devices and information, and endorsed, in a sense, by the new psychological research, which tended to dispel the old-fashioned religious concept of the equivalence of sex and sin; contemporary literature, as well as psychological and sociological studies, indicated that many of them took advantage of this opportunity.

The increase of divorce seemed at first to be an alarming phenomenon. This rose from 0.7 for every thousand people in 1900 to 2.9 in 1944. In 1946, a year that saw the dissolution of many hasty wartime marriages, it reached the record figure of 4.3. But by 1948 the figure was down to 2.8, and throughout the decade of the 1950's there continued to be a slow decline. Pessimistic prophets were similarly proved wrong by the movement of the birth rate. This had dropped fairly steadily ever since the eighteenth century, amounting to 27 per thousand in 1910 and to only 16.9 in 1935 (after several years of depression). Statisticians calculated that the population of the United States would soon show an absolute decrease. But after World War II the birth rate astonished all the experts by showing a rise, which was largely maintained through the 1950's. The rate amounted to 25.8 in 1946 and to 24.3 in 1958. Despite the insecurities of the postwar world and the apparent degree of relaxation of the family structure, it was obvious that most young American married couples still wanted children. Another shift in family patterns was a marked tendency toward earlier marriages and the consequent necessity that many wives helped to support their husbands until they had finished training for professional careers.

More disturbing was the apparent growth of emotional disorders. By 1948 there were 540,000 inmates of mental institutions, representing a ratio of 3.7 for every thousand people, as contrasted with only 1.1 per

506   THE U.S. & THE POSTWAR WORLD, 1945–1961

thousand in 1910. Among young men of draft age in World War II, 1,825,000 were rejected and 600,000 discharged because of psychoneurotic disturbances. This high figure was widely interpreted as an indication that modern living meant an increase in anxieties and insecurities. But possibly the increase was more apparent than real, and was due largely to a better understanding of what constituted emotional and mental disorders. Many people who in the nineteenth century would have been considered a little queer but in no need of medical attention were now diagnosed as having neurotic tendencies. The new science of psychiatry was one of the major intellectual influences of the twentieth century, and most educated Americans acquired some understanding of its basic concepts. The science was still in its infancy, the number of trained psychiatrists remained far less than the demand, and treatment was long, expensive, and uncertain. The profession, moreover, split into several different groups with different theoretical approaches, some practitioners following Freud in putting their main emphasis on the patient's early sexual development, others giving more attention to social factors and stressing the difficulties of adjustment to society during adolescence and maturity. The growth of psychiatry and of psychosomatic medicine, a complex matter not easily summed up, of necessity included considerable experimentation, much of which was purely theoretical, but nonetheless it represented one of the most significant scientific advances of the period.

The most widely expressed complaint against the modern middle-class American was that he was too often a conformist, lacking in the moral and intellectual independence displayed by earlier generations. Machine industry and mass production seemed to be leading to a cultural standardization on a relatively low level and to a decrease in individual initiative. The modern economy had relatively little room for the kind of aggressive individualist who could often rise to the top in the nineteenth century; it now set a higher premium on qualities making for group harmony and offered high rewards to persons with a talent for smooth handling of personal contacts. In spite of the continued emphasis on free enterprise and competition, most modern enterprises, however free from government control, were essentially cooperative. The central economic institution, the corporation, was a device for bringing together the labor and resources of different individuals and enabling them to work together for common objectives. There were similar tendencies toward teamwork in science and scholarship and in the popular arts. Except in the higher arts, it became increasingly unusual for one man working alone to accomplish anything of value.

SOCIAL & CULTURAL DEVELOPMENTS

The modern American—at least according to his critics—displayed a similar lack of initiative in his leisure hours. One of the most important developments of twentieth-century life was the astonishing growth of the mass media of entertainment—motion pictures, radio, and television. Appealing to nationwide popular audiences, these were dominated by commercial standards and made little attempt to discriminate between different intellectual levels. Good movies and radio and TV programs were admittedly rare, and many of them, particularly the soap operas that came over the air during the daytime hours for the edification of housewives, were beneath contempt. How far the blame belonged to the producers for underestimating their audiences and how far to the standards of popular taste remained a controversial question.

Sociologists often expressed alarm at this growth of mechanized entertainment. Unlike the recreational activities of earlier generations, it did not require the individual to participate but reduced him to the role of a passive spectator or auditor. It could not be considered an advance in civilization that the average American spent most of his evening hours watching a series of TV programs instead of engaging in some active form of recreation or reading a book. The same trend was exhibited in the continued popularity of professional athletics. In fact, the failure of many Americans to take enough physical exercise became a matter of public concern.

Yet the mere fact that so many Americans were disturbed by the apparent growth of social conformity and cultural standardization offered hope that the United States was far from becoming a nation of robots. And if Americans had more leisure and took more vacations than their ancestors, many of them found avocations that were not indolently passive or benumbingly gregarious but, instead, healthy and enriching. One of these was travel. In increasing numbers, Americans toured their own country and visited Canada, Latin America, and Europe. Just what they absorbed on their travels is not easy to determine, but certainly they had more opportunity to know what the world was like than ever before.

PROBLEMS OF INEQUALITY

The economic and social changes of the postdepression era brought about considerable advances toward the American ideal of equality. Particularly significant was the rapid integration into the American community of families belonging to recent immigrant groups. Although the

508   THE U.S. & THE POSTWAR WORLD, 1945–1961

Irish, Italians, and east European groups continued to be predominantly working class, an appreciable number of them had acquired middle-class status and shared in the move to the suburbs, and some were acquiring positions of leadership in business and federal politics. It was significant that the election of 1960 carried into the White House for the first time a descendant of nineteenth-century immigrants. It was also significant that Mr. Kennedy came from a family that had been thoroughly assimilated into American society and culture on the highest levels.

There were still, however, serious limitations to the equality in which most Americans professed to believe. It was restricted by barriers of both class and race; and though these barriers were notably less rigid than in earlier generations, it would plainly be a long time before they would become unimportant.

The strength of class differences in American urban communities was emphasized by many sociologists. Americans liked to believe that any individual, from any social background, could rise as high as his personal merits and abilities could carry him. But investigation showed that an individual's merit was a much less important factor in his occupation and social status than was popularly recognized. Most businessmen were the sons of businessmen; children born into working-class families mostly remained workers; and high social influence and prestige depended largely on birth into long-established upper-class families, rather than on money and achievement. These class lines added appreciably to the bitterness of political conflicts, particularly during the Roosevelt and Truman eras. Yet their importance should not be exaggerated. The upper class was very far from being a ruling class, its influence being mainly social rather than political; and class lines could be crossed, although not as easily as democratic idealists would have wished.

Much more serious were the barriers based on race. Although earlier immigrant groups had mostly been assimilated into the American community, the pattern of prejudice was repeated with the Puerto Ricans who came to the United States, mostly to New York, in the 1940's and 1950's. And one group whose ancestors, for the most part, had come to America during the Colonial period, the Negroes, were never permitted to move up the social ladder or become fully integrated into the American community. Most white Americans remained sharply aware of differences of color and were not yet willing to concede full equality to persons of Negro descent.

Appreciable advances toward the American ideal of equality were made, nevertheless. In fact, there was more progress during and after World War II than at any time since the abandonment of the post-Civil War Reconstruction experiment. A growing number of Americans were developing uneasy consciences about race discrimination and were beginning to realize its bad effects on American relations with other countries. As long as the United States practiced discrimination at home, its claim to be the champion of freedom abroad would be regarded as blatantly hypocritical. Another influential factor was the growing importance of the Negro vote in several large northern states; after the coming of the New Deal the Negroes largely abandoned their traditional support for the Republican party and were now willing to vote for whichever party seemed most likely to give them concrete assistance.

In 1941 Roosevelt set up a Fair Employment Practices Committee to end discrimination in industries working on government contracts, and some northern states subsequently passed legislation to promote the same objective. During the 1940's a series of Supreme Court decisions affirmed the right of Negroes in the South to vote in primary elections, sit on juries, and secure admission to white educational institutions when the facilities available for Negroes were plainly inadequate. A long list of items showed that real progress was being made, however slowly: the appointment during the war for the first time of a Negro brigadier general; the appointment of Ralph Bunche to several important positions in the United Nations; the increase in the number of Negro members of college faculties and of Negro employees in industries formerly restricted to white people; several successful battles against discrimination in housing; the admission of Negroes to professional baseball in 1948 (when Jackie Robinson joined the Brooklyn Dodgers). Although gains were most conspicuous in the North, there were visible changes in the South also. More than 1 million southern Negroes voted in the elections of 1952 and 1956. Another cause for satisfaction was the decrease in lynching. Although most southerners continued to advocate white supremacy, they were much less inclined to resort to violent methods of defending it.

During the 1950's Negro leaders, assured of support from the Executive and judicial branches of the federal government, made bolder moves to secure their civil rights, and there were some impressively orderly and well-organized protests against discrimination. There was growing resistance to the "Jim Crow" laws still enforced in the southern states, especially notable being a prolonged boycott of the local bus system by the Negro population of Montgomery, Alabama. In April, 1956, the

Supreme Court affirmed that enforced segregation on all public transportation, intrastate as well as interstate, was unconstitutional. The main storm center, however, was the maintenance of segregation in the public schools. Seventeen states, along with the District of Columbia, had established separate school systems, which theoretically offered equal educational opportunities, though in practice the Negro schools were much more poorly financed and equipped, and the enforcement of segregation branded Negro pupils as inferior, with obviously harmful emotional effects on their development. Under the guidance of the National Association for the Advancement of Colored People (NAACP), Negro parents in South Carolina initiated legal proceedings in the federal courts to secure adequate schooling for their children, and on May 27, 1954, the Supreme Court ruled by a unanimous vote that segregation in the public schools was a violation of the legal rights guaranteed to all citizens by the Fourteenth Amendment. The Court recognized that the abolition of segregation would necessarily be a long and difficult process, but declared that the southern states were legally obligated to begin moving in that direction.

There was much talk among white southerners of measures of resistance to the Court decision, some of them even proposing to abolish their public school systems. Negro students who attempted to secure admission to white institutions were sometimes in danger of mob attack, and during the first four years after the decision there were no less than 530 cases of arson, bombing, and other forms of violent protest. Yet there were only two occasions when the federal government found it necessary to resort to military intervention: at Little Rock, Arkansas, in September, 1957, when nine Negro students entered Central High School, and at Oxford, Mississippi, in September, 1962, when James Meredith entered the University of Mississippi. Otherwise, though progress in implementing the Court decision was slow, there were no serious setbacks. By the beginning of 1960 there were 762 integrated school districts out of a total of 2,880 which had maintained segregated schools; and 518,357 Negro children, approximately one-sixth of the total number, were attending integrated schools. By June, 1961, seventeen states, along with the District of Columbia, had begun to move toward integration, while only five—Alabama, Georgia, Louisiana, Mississippi, and South Carolina —had so far refused to take any action whatever.

Thus the United States was moving toward the solution of its most serious internal problem. Yet Americans could not afford to regard the

SOCIAL & CULTURAL DEVELOPMENTS 511

situation with complacency. Most Negroes still suffered from various forms of discrimination. They earned incomes far below the national average, they could find urban homes only in slums, and they were treated by most white people as members of an inferior race. It would be a long time before they could feel secure in the enjoyment of their constitutional rights.

THE ARTS AND THE SCIENCES

Periods of economic depression and political turmoil can be disrupting to artistic creation, and the thirty years following the onset of the depression were less productive than the 1920's. To a large extent the writers and artists who had emerged after World War I continued to dominate the cultural scene, and none of the younger men seemed to achieve a comparable magnitude. The one cultural activity that flourished was criticism. Never had American literary and artistic criticism been so varied, so complex, or so subtle.

During the 1930's economic problems absorbed attention, and most of the younger intellectuals were attracted to some form of radicalism. Communism never made any appreciable headway in the American working class, but it captured almost a whole generation of American writers and artists, though in most instances only for short periods. Impressed by the economic progress apparently being made in the Soviet Union, and feeling a sense of alienation from American institutions, young men and women became Communist fellow travelers and declared that literature and art should be regarded as instruments for promoting revolutionary attitudes. Most of them regarded communism as a method for achieving the traditional American ideals of freedom and equality, while the Soviet Union also gained credit because of its apparent opposition to Hitlerism and its support of the Loyalist side in the Spanish Civil War. Communism's appeal for American intellectuals was at a peak during the mid 1930's, after which its supporters became increasingly disillusioned by the discrepancies between Communist ideals and Communist practice, as demonstrated by Stalin's dictatorship, the Moscow trials, and the Nazi-Soviet pact of 1939. The whole movement produced little that seemed likely to have enduring value, and had tragic aftereffects a dozen years later when any record of support for communism, however brief, was considered grounds for public investigation.

Some former radicals, like John Dos Passos, swung from the extreme left to the extreme right, and after World War II there were some suggestions that extreme conservatism might have a vogue among young intellectuals comparable to that of communism during the 1930's. But the writings of the new conservatives were notable chiefly for their dullness and naïveté. Most of the better writers and artists of the 1940's and 1950's were nonpolitical, concentrating on personal emotions and experiences, often of an abnormal character, and turning away from the main currents of national life. World War I had produced an impressive literature of disillusionment, but Americans had entered World War II with a much clearer awareness of why they were fighting, hating it but at the same time recognizing its necessity and consequently not succumbing to disillusionment. World War II had relatively little effect on the arts. The main features of the postwar period were the continuing, and apparently insoluble, conflict with the Russians, and the widespread material prosperity at home, neither of which inspired young intellectuals either to enthusiasm or to condemnation. Many of them preferred to retreat into private worlds, an attitude which had had many precursors among earlier American writers since the time of Edgar Allan Poe and Herman Melville. The most extreme manifestation of this strategy of withdrawal was the so-called "beat" generation. The literature and art produced by the "beatniks" were not impressive, but in repudiating virtually all the standards and mores of traditional civilization and trying to find new values in personal experience, they were giving expression to a profound spiritual discontent which should not be too easily dismissed.

These generalizations can be applied to most of the different arts. In the novel, for example, none of the younger men achieved the breadth and stature of the major figures who had emerged in the 1920's, in particular Ernest Hemingway and William Faulkner. Both Hemingway and Faulkner won increasing international attention and, in time, became Nobel prize-winners. Few of the proletarian novelists of the 1930's continued to find readers, though exceptions should be made of John Steinbeck, whose *Grapes of Wrath* was perhaps the most moving of the novels of social protest, and of James T. Farrell, whose studies of middle-class Irish life in Chicago continued the naturalism of Theodore Dreiser with a more radical twist. Perhaps the most interesting novelist of this generation was Robert Penn Warren, whose politics were agrarian rather than Marxist and who combined a concern for metaphysical problems with

SOCIAL & CULTURAL DEVELOPMENTS 513

lively story-telling, but whose work was often dangerously close to melodrama. World War II produced many novels that were effective realistic reporting, the most admired being Norman Mailer's *The Naked and the Dead*, but none of them reached the levels achieved by Hemingway after World War I. As for the writers of the 1950's, some of them, like Saul Bellow and J. D. Salinger, seemed potentially important, but a large number seemed overly concerned with recondite and abnormal emotional subject matter.

In poetry, a leading influence continued to be that of T. S. Eliot, despite his long residence in England and his assumption of British citizenship, and despite the fact that since the early 1940's he had turned increasingly to playwriting. Other poets of his generation gained increasing recognition and critical attention and were still writing in the 1950's and even the 1960's—notably Marianne Moore, William Carlos Williams, Wallace Stevens, and E. E. Cummings. As Robert Frost entered old age, his concerns became more abstract and his metaphysics more prominent. He was in attendance at President Kennedy's inauguration in January, 1961, to recite his well-loved poem "The Gift Outright." Frost died in January, 1963, at the age of 88, active and alert to the end.

One career that had always been sensational became extraordinary. Since the 1920's the art of Ezra Pound had developed at the same pace as his obsessions. Pound was indicted for treason during World War II for broadcasting over the Rome radio, but he was declared insane and unfit to stand trial. In 1946 he was committed to St. Elizabeth's Hospital in Washington, where he stayed till 1958, continuing to write. His *Pisan Cantos*, based on his experiences in an American army prison camp in Pisa, brought him, in 1948, the Bollingen Award, sponsored by the Library of Congress. The judges' refusal to permit other considerations than that of poetic achievement to sway the decision created a furor in the literary world. Controversial though he is, Pound is acknowledged a great teacher.

Meanwhile most of the younger men and women who aspired to promote communism in verse during the 1930's were deservedly forgotten. The 1940's and 1950's produced a number of poets who seemed potentially important, Robert Lowell and Karl Shapiro being perhaps the most prominent, but none of them achieved major stature.

In painting, the radicalism of the 1930's produced interesting work by such men as Ben Shahn, William Gropper, and Philip Evergood, who devoted themselves to satirizing economic privilege. The 1930's also saw the federal government, for the first time in American history, becoming an art patron on a large scale. The WPA art project, launched in 1935 and wound up in 1940, gave employment to 5,000 artists in forty states, mostly in the painting of murals in public buildings. This was a valuable enterprise not only in enabling painters to continue painting but also in stimulating popular interest in art. During the 1940's and 1950's there was a marked improvement in the economic status of American painters, and it was estimated that during these two decades more money was paid to them than during the whole of previous history. There was also a vast increase in the number of amateurs who took up painting as a leisure-time recreation. But whether the new generation of American painters were equal to the best of their predecessors was a debatable question. Most of them seemed to be turning away from the life around them into a world of pure abstraction or adopting surrealist techniques which purported to reveal, often in terrifying forms, the emo-

The Marin County Civic Center in San Rafael, California, was one of the last buildings designed by architect Frank Lloyd Wright. It illustrates his originality of design, his preference for horizontal lines, and his belief that a building should be planned to harmonize with its environment. (Wide World Photos)

SOCIAL & CULTURAL DEVELOPMENTS

tional forces of the subconscious. Some of them, however, especially Jackson Pollock, were hailed by sympathetic critics as masters.

In architecture the record was more interesting, chiefly because the determining factor was the development of public taste, rather than that of the individual practitioners. American patrons, both official and private, now accepted the work of the functionalists and no longer insisted on the reproduction of earlier European styles. Frank Lloyd Wright, almost forgotten in the 1920's except by his European and Oriental admirers, was rediscovered in the 1930's, his Johnson Wax Company building at Racine, Wisconsin (completed in 1939), being widely recognized as a masterpiece. Younger modernist designers, like Mies Van Der Rohe, Philip Johnson, and Edward Stone found it increasingly easy to secure commissions, both for public and business buildings and for private homes. Thus there was a healthy experimentalism about American architecture, though unfortunately this did not prevent most of the new housing developments built after World War II from being oppressively monotonous. Meanwhile conservative critics, deploring the whole functionalist movement, insisted that the early twentieth century had been an age of great architecture, exemplified especially in the work of Stanford White.

None of the younger American dramatists reach the levels achieved in the 1920's by Eugene O'Neill. The proletarian theater of the 1930's produced one interesting figure in Clifford Odets, but he proved to have little staying power. After World War II, significant work was done by Tennessee Williams, Arthur Miller, and William Inge. Thematically, Williams set the tone for much of the drama of the period. Characteristic Williams motifs appeared in *Suddenly Last Summer*, which was centered on a possessive mother and her homosexual son; its action included a cannibalistic act, a threatened lobotomy, and the use of truth serum. His *Sweet Bird of Youth* balanced a hysterectomy at the beginning with a castration at the end. This aspect of Williams' drama had many imitators, and degeneracy, deterioration, decay, addiction, and perversion became prominent on the stage. However, Williams' finest plays, such as *The Glass Menagerie* and *A Streetcar Named Desire*, had true dramatic force and achieved a high degree of psychological penetration.

Arthur Miller was concerned with realistic criticism of American life. *Death of a Salesman* demonstrated his belief that tragedy is possible in the modern theater and that its proper hero is the common man; *The Crucible*, dealing with the Salem witchcraft trials, had parallels to the

McCarthyism prevalent in the early 1950's. William Inge, famous for *Come Back, Little Sheba, Bus Stop, Picnic,* and *The Dark at the Top of the Stairs,* explored the psychological depths of the "average" people of the Midwest.

Probably the most significant new development in the American theater was on a popular rather than an intellectual level. There was a marked rise in the aesthetic quality of Broadway musicals, as illustrated in such productions as *Oklahoma* and *South Pacific.* And yet the most successful musical comedy ever staged in the United States, the Lerner-Loewe *My Fair Lady,* which ran on Broadway for over five years, owed almost all its dialogue to Bernard Shaw's *Pygmalion,* half a century old.

In the field of music, the achievements of American composers were not recognized as having reached the heights that the greatest of the Europeans had reached, and many Americans worked within a framework that seemed to reflect only European initiatives. However, there were initiatives of an opposite kind. A tradition of private iconoclasm was developed by Charles E. Ives, whose courage in experimenting with polyharmonics and polyrhythms, powerful dissonances, atonality, and rhythmic intricacies gained him at first the admiration of only a few, but, in time, a substantial measure of recognition. One of the most important and most often performed composers was Aaron Copland, who early in his career seemed bent upon mastering the jazz idiom, but who moved on to many other media. Other significant composers included Roy Harris, whose work had great vitality but was obscure to many music lovers; Roger Sessions, who was influenced by Stravinsky, both spiritually and technically; and Walter Piston, who was perhaps easier to characterize than other contemporaries because he was so distinctly a neoclassicist.

There was a remarkable development of popular interest, aided by radio and the phonograph, and manifested in the proliferation of symphony orchestras and the high standards required of performances. Meanwhile America continued to lead the rest of the world in popular music and made its own special contribution in the form of jazz, which was regarded by its admirers as a serious art form as well as a source of popular entertainment.

In all the arts, the most notable feature of the postdepression epoch was that appreciation and understanding were moving forward faster than creation. In aesthetic history this was an age of criticism. The most influential critics of the 1920's (Van Wyck Brooks being perhaps the leading example) had believed that the function of the arts was to promote higher social values and combat materialism and injustice. This sociological emphasis had developed easily into the more explicit radicalism of the 1930's, a significant transitional figure being Vernon Louis Parrington, whose three-volume *Main Currents in American Thought* was published in 1927 and 1929. Parrington judged American writers in terms of social rather than aesthetic values and regarded economic and political progressivism as the central theme of American literature and thought. The proletarian criticism of the 1930's found it easy to reconcile the Parringtonian approach with the new Marxist view of social forces. While orthodox Communist criticism was narrowly dogmatic and intolerant, the study of literature through the analysis of its social background, as practiced by such writers as Newton Arvin and Granville Hicks, was sometimes decidedly illuminating.

Meanwhile a wholly different approach was represented by the so-called "New Critics," who were strongly influenced by the early writings of T. S. Eliot. The function of art, they declared, was to present human experience in its totality, not to propagate ethical or political values or to impel readers toward any kind of action. The "New Critics" analyzed content and construction in great detail and judged work by its internal organization. They were likely to admire writing in proportion to its complexity and to dislike almost anything romantic. While their standards were often narrowly intellectual, their evaluations of the literature of the past showed remarkable subtlety and discrimination. They included members of the group of southern agrarians, especially John Crowe Ransom and Allen Tate, and such other critics as R. P. Blackmur and Yvor Winters. Whereas the older critics had mostly been free-lance writers, with journalistic backgrounds, the "New Critics" usually held academic positions, and by the 1950's they were leading influences in many university departments of English.

The best critical work of the period, however, was done by writers who were able to combine alertness to the social and political implications of literature with sensitivity to aesthetic considerations. Two of the ablest intellects of the day were Edmund Wilson and Lionel Trilling, both with unlimited curiosity and range, as well as superb control of the English language. Both were concerned with the immediate background of twentieth-century thought; Trilling's work reflected a particular awareness of Freud, and Wilson's reflected an awareness of Marxism.

The advance of criticism showed that there was an increasingly large audience in America capable of appreciating creative work on the highest levels. It remained true that a considerable majority of the American people were not readers (except of newspapers) or museum-goers and were interested only in the arts of popular entertainment, such as the motion picture and television. While vast sums were spent on entertainment, the money available for the support of the fine arts seemed, by contrast, to be infinitesimal. But there was probably a larger audience for good work than had ever existed in the past. Particularly encouraging was the extraordinary increase of paperback reprints of serious books. In fact, it could probably be said in the 1950's that the reading public was capable of appreciating more works of high quality than were actually being produced, something that had not been true of any earlier period of American history. This seemed to justify a sober optimism about the future of the arts in America, and a hope that perhaps the 1960's would prove more productive than earlier periods.

Meanwhile the United States was making major contributions to every significant form of human knowledge. All leading American universities promoted research (sometimes, unfortunately, to the detriment of teaching), and large sums of money were made available by philanthropic foundations, by business corporations, and by the federal government. American intellectual progress was indirectly stimulated by the growth of European totalitarianism in the 1930's since many gifted scholars were compelled to take refuge in the United States. This was not an age that produced fundamentally new views of life: there was nothing comparable to the Darwinian theory or the theory of relativity in the sciences, or to pragmatism in philosophy. But the accumulation of significant new data in both the natural and the social sciences proceeded at a steadily accelerating speed. The growth of American preeminence in the sciences was indicated by the distribution of the Nobel prizes. Between 1930 and 1960 more than one-third went to American citizens, as contrasted with less than 6 per cent from 1901 to 1929. Britain and Germany together received another third, and the remainder were distributed over the rest of the world.

Science was international and knew no distinctions of ethnic or national origin. It would therefore be impossible to pick out any specifically American contributions or to write a history of science in America. But its advancement was unquestionably the most important development of modern times, and nowhere were its consequences more widespread or more fully understood than in the United States. From the viewpoint of the average citizen the most important results of scientific develop-

SOCIAL & CULTURAL DEVELOPMENTS 519

ment were in physics and medicine. Modern physics made possible the atomic bomb, and while physicists from half a dozen different countries contributed to the knowledge that made it possible, the United States contributed the money and resources, the practical know-how, and the capacity for organizing effective teamwork. But while science was thus making it easier to kill, it was also enabling human life to be prolonged. The growth of medical knowledge in the twentieth century and its application by doctors and public-health authorities caused remarkable changes in vital statistics. Between 1900 and 1957 the death rate dropped from 17.2 to 9.6 per thousand, male life expectancy (among the white population) increased from 48.23 to 67.3, and female life expectancy from 51.8 to 73.7. Thus, barring the outbreak of war, the white American of the 1950's could expect to live some twenty years longer than his nineteenth-century predecessor.

There was a similar activity in the social sciences, though the results may have been less spectacular. Scholars in increasing number explored every aspect of the past and present of American society; and as a result of the work of historians, political scientists, sociologists, and economists, it could safely be said that Americans knew more about themselves, both in the past and in the present, than any other people in history. While there were no new comprehensive generalizations comparable to the Turner thesis or the theory of economic determinism, accepted interpretations of the American past and present were subjected to constant revision in the light of new data. And while the main impetus in social studies continued to be scientific rather than literary, men like Samuel Eliot Morison of Harvard and Allan Nevins of Columbia, along with numerous younger men, showed that use of the apparatus of modern scholarship was not incompatible with high literary quality.

After being primarily concerned through most of their history with making a better life for themselves and their descendants, the American people in the twentieth century found themselves required to undertake the unwelcome tasks of leading the free world and conserving the heritage of Western civilization. No people in history had assumed such responsibilities with more hesitation or with more intense self-criticism. Yet the reluctance with which the United States accepted its great-power role offered some assurance that it would not seriously abuse its powers for its own advantage. And in spite of unsolved problems and various internal stresses and failings, a survey of American society seemed to justify a sober confidence. If the Americans remained true to their own traditional

520 THE U.S. & THE POSTWAR WORLD, 1945-1961

values, and if they learned how to make the most effective use of their intellectual and material resources, they could hope not only to preserve the civilization to which they belonged but to carry it to constantly higher levels of achievement.

Suggested Readings

For the general characteristics of American society, Robin M. Williams, *American Society* (2d rev. ed., New York, 1960) is an excellent survey. Max Lerner, *America as a Civilization* (New York, 1957) is more detailed. Robert S. and Helen M. Lynd, *Middletown* (New York [1929]) and *Middletown in Transition* (New York [1937]) are descriptions of a typical midwestern town. Frederick L. Allen, *The Big Change: America Transforms Itself, 1900–1950* (New York, 1952) is for the general reader. See also Dixon Wecter, *et al., Changing Patterns in American Civilization* (Philadelphia, 1949). David Riesman, *The Lonely Crowd* (New Haven, Conn., 1950) is a provocative analysis of changes in the American character.

For general religious development, see Herbert W. Schneider, *Religion in Twentieth Century America* (Cambridge, Mass., 1952) and Clifton E. Olmstead, *Religion in America* (Englewood Cliffs, N.J. [1961]). Will Herberg, *Protestant, Catholic, Jew: An Essay in Religious Sociology* (Garden City, N.Y., 1955) is a suggestive analysis. For theological changes, see Arnold S. Nash, *Protestant Thought in the Twentieth Century* (New York, 1951). The writings of Reinhold Niebuhr, especially *Moral Man and Immoral Society* (New York, 1932) and *The Nature and Destiny of Man* (2 vols., New York, 1941–43), illustrate the revived emphasis upon human sin. See also Henry N. Wieman, *et al., Religious Liberals Reply* (Boston, 1947). The books of Paul Blanshard, *American Freedom and Catholic Power* (2d rev. and enl. ed., Boston [1958]) and *Communism, Democracy and Catholic Power* (Boston, 1951) are militant examples of the liberal opposition to the Catholic Church. James M. O'Neill, *Catholicism and American Freedom* (New York [1952]) is a well-argued reply.

Different aspects of the controversy about public school education are presented in Arthur E. Bestor, *The Restoration of Learning* (New York, 1955) and *Educational Wastelands* (Urbana, Ill., 1953); James B. Conant, *Education in a Divided World* (Cambridge, Mass., 1948) and *Education and Liberty* (Cambridge, Mass., 1953); Benjamin Fine, *Our Children Are Cheated* (New York [1947]); Seymour Harris, *How Shall We Pay for Education?* (New York [1948]); Albert Lynd, *Quackery in the Public Schools* (Boston [1953]); and Robert Ulich, *Crisis and Hope in American Education* (Boston, 1951). The two most influential books dealing with college education have been Abraham Flexner, *Universities: American, German, English* (New York, 1930) and the Report of the Harvard Committee, *General Education in a Free Society*

SOCIAL & CULTURAL DEVELOPMENTS 521

(Cambridge, Mass., 1945). Jacques Barzun, *Teacher in America* (Boston [1945]) is a suggestive commentary.

A large number of books deal with the press and the other mass media. Among the more useful are Zechariah Chafee, *Government and Mass Communications* (Chicago [1947]); Morris L. Ernst, *The First Freedom* (New York, 1946); Gilbert Seldes, *The Great Audience* (New York, 1950); Charles A. Siepmann, *Radio, Television and Society* (New York, 1950); and William H. Whyte, *Is Anybody Listening?* (New York, 1952). Different aspects of the motion picture business are covered in Lewis Jacobs, *The Rise of the American Film* (New York [1939]); Hortense Powdermaker, *The Hollywood Dream Factory* (Boston, 1950); Leo C. Rosten, *Hollywood* (New York [1941]); and Martha Wolfenstein and Nathan Leites, *Movies* (Glencoe, Ill., 1950).

For class lines in American society, see Richard Centers, *The Psychology of Social Classes* (Princeton, N.J., 1949); W. Lloyd Warner, *et al.*, *Democracy in Jonesville* (New York [1949]) and *Social Class in America* (Chicago, 1949); and C. Wright Mills, *White Collar* (New York, 1951).

For the history of the Negro in America, standard works are John Hope Franklin, *From Slavery to Freedom* (2d rev. and enl. ed., New York, 1956) and E. Franklin Frazier, *The Negro in the United States* (New York, 1949). Gunnar Myrdal, *American Dilemma* (2 vols., New York, 1944) is an exhaustive analysis of race relationships. For more recent developments, see Richard Bardolph, *The Negro Vanguard* (New York [1959]) and Arnold M. Rose, *The Negro in America* (New York, [1948]). Oscar Handlin, *The Newcomers* (Cambridge, Mass., 1959) describes Negro and Puerto Rican problems in New York.

There are a large number of books dealing with different aspects of socioeconomic changes. Some of the more provocative are John K. Galbraith, *American Capitalism: The Concept of Countervailing Power* (rev. ed., Boston, 1956) and *The Affluent Society* (Boston, 1958); Samuel Lubell, *The Future of American Politics* (2d rev. ed., Garden City, N.Y., 1956) and *Revolt of the Moderates* (New York [1956]); Vance O. Packard, *The Hidden Persuaders* (New York [1957]); Harrison E. Salisbury, *The Shook-up Generation* (New York [1958]); and William H. Whyte, *The Organization Man* (New York, 1956). For family and sexual mores, see Alfred C. Kinsey, *et al.*, *Sexual Behavior in the Human Male* (Philadelphia, 1948) and *Sexual Behavior in the Human Female* (Philadelphia, 1953); Ferdinand Lundberg and Marynia F. Farnham, *Modern Woman: The Lost Sex* (New York [1947]); and the National Conference on Family Life, *The American Family* (Washington, D.C. [1949]).

For literary history, Robert E. Spiller, *et al.*, *Literary History of the United States* (2 vols., New York, 1948) is the standard work. Maxwell D. Geismar, *Writers in Crisis* (Boston, 1942) deals with the novelists of the 1930's, and John W. Aldridge, *After the Lost Generation* (New York [1951]) deals with those who emerged in the 1940's. Maxwell D. Geismar, *American Moderns* (New York, [1958]) is also useful. For criticism, see Stanley E. Hyman, *The Armed Vision* (New York, 1948) and Morton Dauwen Zabel, ed., *Literary*

522 THE U.S. & THE POSTWAR WORLD, 1945–1961

Opinion in America (rev. ed., New York [1951]). Outstanding specimens of American literary criticism are John Crowe Ransom, *The New Criticism* (Norfolk, Conn. [1941]); Lionel Trilling, *The Liberal Imagination* (New York, 1950); and various collections of writings by Edmund Wilson, especially *Classics and Commercials* (New York [1950]) and *The Shores of Light* (New York [1952]).

The standard work on American art and architecture is Oliver W. Larkin, *Art and Life in America* (rev. and enl. ed., New York [1960]). Modern painting is analyzed in John I. H. Baur, *Revolution and Tradition in Modern American Art* (Cambridge, Mass., 1951). Sam Hunter, *Modern American Painting and Sculpture* (New York [1959]) is also useful. For architecture, see Lewis Mumford, *Roots of Contemporary American Architecture* (New York [1952]).

12

The New Frontier
of John F. Kennedy

THE ELECTION OF 1960

On July 11, 1960, two months after the U-2 incident had disrupted the summit conference, the Democrats met in Los Angeles. Since the Twenty-second Amendment assured them that they would not have to run against the still very popular Eisenhower, the delegates convened with a greater hope of realizing victory than at any time since 1944. The principal contenders for the presidential nomination at Los Angeles were Adlai Stevenson, who still commanded the loyalty of a considerable and vociferous following; Lyndon B. Johnson of Texas, the Senate majority leader; Senator Stuart Symington of Missouri, the favorite of former President Truman; and Senator John F. Kennedy of Massachusetts, whose strenuous, well-organized, and effective primary campaigns had given him the largest number (600) of pledged delegates. Before the first ballot, the efficient Kennedy forces, realizing that the strategy of the other candidates was to prevent a decision on the first roll call, sought to capture the nomination for the Massachusetts senator by winning the remaining 161 votes required, which they did; and Kennedy received the nomination on the first ballot with 806 votes. His closest rival was Johnson with 409 votes, followed by Symington with 86 and Stevenson with

77½. The next day, before the convention chose the vice presidential nominee, Kennedy asked Johnson, his chief rival during the primaries and the man with whom he had exchanged many strong words, to be his running mate. Johnson accepted, and the convention duly ratified the Kennedy choice. With the nomination of Kennedy and Johnson, the leadership of the Democratic party passed to a new generation, born in the twentieth century and molded by the events of the "great depression" and World War II.

The Democratic platform criticized the Republicans for the economic slump with its attendant increase in unemployment, deplored the costly failure of the Benson farm policies, and blamed the administration for everything from the missile gap and the decline in America's defense capability to the loss of leadership in science, in the space race, and in world affairs. Besides accusing the GOP of having undermined the national interest both at home and abroad, the Democrats censured the administration for having neglected the welfare of the people, which they promised to remedy by granting "generous federal financial support" to education "within the traditional framework of local control," enacting a medical care insurance program for the aged which would be financed through the social security system, and increasing the minimum wage and extending additional assistance to the unemployed.

Since there were many Republicans, notably New York's Nelson A. Rockefeller, who supported a number of the programs which the Democrats were calling for and which the administration had opposed, the GOP was faced with a difficult task when it came to draft its platform. If this were not enough to dampen Republican spirits, the aftereffects of the humiliating U-2 incident and the disastrous events that followed it— the stillborn summit, the Tokyo riots which forced Eisenhower to cancel his visit to Japan, the crisis in the Congo, and the Russian attack upon an American RB-47 "reconnaissance plane" over the Barents Sea on July 1, just three weeks before the GOP convention met in Chicago—combined to embarrass the party's leaders still further. Moreover, on June 8, after having previously decided not to compete with Nixon for the nomination and having rejected every effort the Vice President made to get him second place on the GOP ticket, Nelson Rockefeller, in a shocking display of political candor, announced he was "deeply concerned that those now assuming control of the Republican Party have failed to make clear where this party is heading and where it proposes to lead the nation." He then called upon Nixon and the party leaders to "declare now, and not at some later date, precisely what they believe and what they propose, to meet the great matters before the nation. . . ." Rockefeller's own stand on what he considered to be the "great matters" of the day was spelled out in a nine-point program of action calling for energetic policies designed to stimulate the nation's rate of economic growth, provide better educational facilities for the young and medical care for the aged, expedite the civil rights and school desegregation programs, strengthen the national defenses to meet the emergency he believed to be critical, and improve the conduct of foreign affairs, including totally overhauling the country's Latin American policy. All in all, Rockefeller's statement was, as Theodore H. White has written, a declaration of "open warfare with the leadership of his own Party and [an] implicit denunciation of its conduct of national affairs," including "the entire policy of the Eisenhower administration." [1] As a final blow, Rockefeller concluded his assault by warning Nixon that "the path of great leadership does not lie along the top of a fence."

Whatever the New York governor's reason for issuing this declaration of principles, whether it was to make another bid for the nomination or to steer his party along a more progressive course, it struck Nixon and the GOP platform writers like a thunderbolt. To avert an open intraparty fight, which would provide the Democrats with deadly campaign ammunition, Rockefeller had to be mollified and his opinions incorporated into the platform in some acceptable way. This task Nixon assumed himself by asking for an appointment with Rockefeller, who graciously granted the Vice President's request for a meeting at his New York City apartment overlooking Central Park.

The revisions to the party platform which were made at this meeting were reached at a time when the platform committee in Chicago believed the final draft of the official document had already been agreed upon, and they were furious to learn of the extensive changes Nixon had accepted after his secret session with Rockefeller. "The Vice President and I met today at my home in New York City," the Rockefeller release on the conference read. "The meeting took place at the Vice President's request. The purpose of the meeting was to discuss the platform of the Republican Party. . . . The Vice President and I reached agreement on the following specific and basic positions on foreign policy and national defense. . . ." This introductory statement was followed

[1] Theodore H. White, *The Making of the President, 1960* (New York, 1961), pp. 184–85.

526   THE U.S. & THE POSTWAR WORLD, 1945–1961

by a detailed fourteen-point program reflecting Rockefeller's views on domestic and foreign policy, almost all of which were certain to infuriate the party's conservative wing, as they did Eisenhower, when he learned of them. The Fifth Avenue "surrender," the "Munich of the Republican Party," as Arizona's Senator Barry Goldwater, the GOP's new right-wing leader, called it, concluded with a promise that if the proposals were "embodied in the Republican Party platform, as adopted by the convention, they will constitute a platform that I [Rockefeller] can support with pride and vigor." The outcry from the platform committee made banner headlines. In a single evening, Rockefeller had forced Nixon to repudiate all the committee's work and expose its members "as clowns," as White stated it. The uproar at Chicago threatened to disrupt the entire convention, and as has rarely happened in the history of American politics, the adoption of the party platform attracted more public attention than the roll call for the presidential nomination. Nixon, whose own personal convictions were not offended by many of Rockefeller's proposals, finally succeeded in adjusting the platform so that the views expressed in it satisfied the New Yorker without causing the Old Guard to repudiate it publicly.

The rest of the Republican proceedings were anticlimactic. Nixon won the presidential nomination on the first ballot with 1,321 votes; his only opponent, Senator Goldwater, trailed far behind with 10. For Vice President, Nixon and the party leaders chose Henry Cabot Lodge, Jr., the Massachusetts-born ambassador to the United Nations, whom Kennedy had defeated in the Senate race of 1952.

Both candidates fought an energetic, hard-driving campaign. Nixon carried his battle to every state in the union, which now numbered fifty, Alaska and Hawaii having been admitted in July, 1958, and March, 1959, respectively. Nixon's principal theme was the need for continued experienced leadership, which he claimed to possess as a result of his eight-year apprenticeship under Eisenhower. "The major test to which the people of the country are putting the candidates," he said, "is which by experience, by background, by judgment, by record . . . can best continue the leadership of Dwight D. Eisenhower and keep the peace without surrender for America and extend freedom throughout the world." Kennedy fought the question of experience by indicating that both he and Nixon had entered national politics at the same time, in 1946, and that the Vice President's tour of the world did not make him better qualified to handle foreign affairs. "Peace takes more than talk . . . more

THE NEW FRONTIER OF JOHN F. KENNEDY   527

than 'experience,'" Kennedy declared, "particularly if that 'experience' is, in Oscar Wilde's words, 'the name everyone gives to their mistakes.' . . ." On most other issues, except to extol the Eisenhower record, Nixon was inclined to be vague and guarded, often giving the impression of straddling.

If Nixon's campaign tactics were circumscribed by the record of the previous administration and his party's conservative-liberal split, Kennedy also faced an exceedingly difficult problem of his own. As a Roman Catholic, he had to convince Protestant America that his religion would in no way interfere with his duties as President. And while there was less of the openly anti-Catholic feeling against his candidacy than had been manifested against Al Smith's in 1928, a number of Protestant ministers and laymen, among them the nationally famous Dr. Norman Vincent Peale, doubted any Roman Catholic's ability both to serve his church and to fulfill the presidential oath. On September 12, Kennedy appeared before a group of 300 Protestant leaders in Houston, Texas, to state his views on church and state and to answer any questions they chose to put to him. The Presidency, Kennedy said by way of introduction, "is a great office that must be neither humbled by making it the instrument of any religious group, nor tarnished by arbitrarily withholding its occupancy from the members of any religious group. I believe in a President whose views on religion are his own private affair, neither imposed upon him by the nation nor imposed upon him as a condition to holding that office. . . ." Kennedy's frank discussion of his religion, and his pledge that "if the time should ever come—and I do not concede any conflict to be remotely possible—when my office would require me to either violate my conscience or violate the national interest, then I would resign the office," won him widespread praise and applause. As Theodore White noted later, Kennedy had "more fully and explicitly than any other thinker of his faith defined the personal doctrine of a modern Catholic in a democratic society." [2] Nixon accepted Kennedy's statement and declared that his opponent's religion was not and should not be a campaign issue. Only the verdict of the people on election day, however, would tell whether this was to be the case or whether the question of Kennedy's religion would become the all-important concealed issue of the campaign.

While Nixon dwelt upon the need for experience, Kennedy hammered away at the economic slump, unemployment, and the decline in

[2] *Ibid.,* pp. 261–62.

President John F. Kennedy's effective performance in his television debates with Richard Nixon during the campaign of 1960 was a major factor in his election victory. (Culver Pictures, Inc.)

the nation's prestige abroad. "I have premised my campaign," he said, "on the single assumption that the American people are uneasy at the present drift in our vitality and prestige. . . . If I am wrong on this assumption, I fully expect to lose this election." These and other issues were given widespread coverage in a series of four television debates, watched by some estimated 80 to 100 million Americans, in which the two candidates answered questions posed them by a group of reporters and news analysts. The importance of these debates was not so much in what the candidates said but in the fact that they destroyed the image of an experienced Nixon and created in its place, as Theodore White reported, the "overwhelming impression that side by side the two [candidates] seemed evenly matched—and this even matching in the popular imagination was for Kennedy a major victory."[3]

Because of the difficulty of gauging the effect of the religious issue upon the voters, the pollsters predicted only that the race would be

[3] *Ibid.*, p. 288.

close, but few expected it to be as close as it was. Not since Woodrow Wilson had defeated Charles Evans Hughes in 1916 had the American people chosen a President by such a narrow margin. Kennedy won by the slight majority of 112,881 popular votes, representing 49.7 per cent of a total of 68,800,000 cast. The official count in the electoral college gave Kennedy 23 states with 303 electoral votes and credited Nixon with winning the 219 electoral votes of 26 states; the remaining state, Mississippi, cast its 8 electoral votes for Senator Harry Byrd of Virginia. The distribution of the popular vote indicated that Kennedy was elected by the nation's large cities, where his Catholicism and his appeal to labor and the Negro won him enough votes to carry such strategic states as New York, Illinois, Pennsylvania, Michigan, New Jersey, and his own state of Massachusetts. Of the states with large electoral votes, he lost only California and Ohio. The decision to ask Lyndon Johnson to be his running mate also added strength to the Democratic ticket in the South and the border states, where Kennedy's religion was a liability; his strong stand on civil rights had alienated Southerners further. But even with the able assistance of Johnson, he lost Florida, Virginia, Kentucky, Tennessee, and Oklahoma to the Republicans. The Democrats retained control of Congress but by slightly reduced majorities: they lost 2 seats in the Senate, giving them 64 and the Republicans 36, and the new line-up in the House was 259 to 178, indicating a Republican gain of 24. Of the 27 gubernatorial races, the Democrats won 15.

JOHN F. KENNEDY

The first Catholic and the youngest man ever to be elected President, forty-three-year-old John Fitzgerald Kennedy was descended from Irish immigrants, the first of whom arrived in the United States during the great migration of the 1840's. Like many of the other Irish immigrants of that time, the Kennedys and the Fitzgeralds remained in the port city where they first arrived rather than moving westward. Slowly they worked themselves out of poverty, each generation improving its economic status and acquiring greater influence in politics. The political tradition of the Kennedys began in Boston on the precinct level; it was the President's father, a self-made millionaire businessman and stock market operator, who extended it to the national level. In 1932 and 1936 he supported and campaigned vigorously for Franklin Roosevelt,

530   THE U.S. & THE POSTWAR WORLD, 1945–1961

who first rewarded him with the chairmanship of the newly created Securities and Exchange Commission, then made him head of the Maritime Commission, and in 1937 appointed him to the post of ambassador to Great Britain.

Joseph Kennedy's wealth and position allowed his children to enjoy all the privileges which went with economic security, from private schools to extensive travel abroad. John F. Kennedy, the second of his nine children, was graduated from the exclusive Choate School, studied a semester at the London School of Economics, and graduated *cum laude* from Harvard University in 1940. That same year he published his senior thesis, *Why England Slept,* a perceptive and well-written analysis of Britain's reaction to the growing threat of the Nazi war machine. This book made the then twenty-three-year-old Kennedy a best-selling non-fiction author. When the Japanese attacked Pearl Harbor, Kennedy was at a desk job in the navy; the next year he was assigned to motor torpedo boat training school, and in March, 1943, he was commanding his own PT boat off the Solomon Islands. When a Japanese destroyer crashed into his ship five months later, his successful and heroic efforts to save his men won him the Purple Heart and marine corps and navy medals. This difficult experience complicated a previous back injury, which terminated his naval career. After a long hospitalization, Kennedy decided upon a career in politics, and in 1946 he was elected to the House of Representatives, where he remained until 1952, when he won the seat of Henry Cabot Lodge, Jr., in the United States Senate. As a legislator, Kennedy supported most of the Truman policies. After 1952, when the Republicans captured the White House, he usually followed the Democratic leadership in Congress, voting for Eisenhower's foreign programs and some of his domestic ones, among them the soil bank bill and the Landrum-Griffin labor reform law, in which he was especially interested.

Young, energetic, ambitious, and an indefatigable worker, Kennedy brought to the White House a sophisticated understanding of the great currents of America's historical development, which he had displayed in his Pulitzer Prize–winning book, *Profiles in Courage* (1956), an analysis of the careers of various outstanding senators. His interest in politics, strengthened by study and deepened by careful observation, made him aware of the traditions, opportunities, and techniques of Executive leadership. Unlike Eisenhower, Kennedy believed that the Presidency required "a vigorous proponent of the national interest," capable of mold-ing and translating it into legislative action by his abilty to practice the art of politics effectively. "The facts of the matter are that legislative leadership is not possible," he said, "without party leadership, in the most political sense." The United States in January, 1960, he declared, required a President who would "be the head of a responsible party, not rise so far above politics as to be invisible; a man who will formulate and fight for legislative policies, not be a casual bystander to the legislative process." Like Wilson and the two Roosevelts, Kennedy rejected what he called "a restricted concept of the Presidency." The Chief Executive had to be much more than "a purely administrative officer," as Ulysses S. Grant had once defined the presidential job. The President, Kennedy asserted, "must be prepared to exercise the fullest powers of his office— all that are specified and some that are not." To Kennedy, the White House was "the vital center of action," and he gave every indication that he proposed to occupy that "center" fully, exercise its authority liberally, and, again like the two Roosevelts, derive a considerable amount of pleasure in doing so.

Cabinet and Advisers

To assist him in providing the political and moral leadership he believed the country and the times required, Kennedy selected an experienced and able cabinet and a group of personal advisers heavily oriented toward the academic. The latter, sometimes called the administration's "idea men," reflected the President's desire to have about him educated and experienced men in different fields of affairs, capable of satisfying his highly developed and disciplined intellectual curiosity. The most influential member of his official cabinet was his younger brother and campaign manager, Robert F. Kennedy, whom the President appointed Attorney General. All but one (Secretary of Commerce Luther H. Hodges) of the members of the Kennedy cabinet were born in the twentieth century; all classified themselves as moderately liberal and displayed for the most part a high level of qualification for the jobs to which they were appointed. The three top cabinet positions—State, Treasury, and Defense—were filled by Dean Rusk, C. Douglas Dillon, and Robert S. McNamara, respectively. Rusk, a one-time Rhodes scholar and political science professor, had studied at Davidson College, Woodrow Wilson's alma mater, and the universities of Oxford, Berlin, and California; he had served the government in the War and State depart-

532 THE U.S. & THE POSTWAR WORLD, 1945-1961

ments and, since 1952, had been president of the Rockefeller Foundation. Dillon was a prominent New York City investment banker who had served Eisenhower as ambassador to France and Under Secretary of State. McNamara, who headed Defense, the largest government department, was a former member of the Harvard Graduate School of Business faculty, who quit teaching in 1946 to join the Ford Motor Company, rising to become its president. The other posts were also filled by competent and energetic men: Arthur J. Goldberg, a distinguished labor lawyer and a special counsel to the AFL-CIO, became Secretary of Labor; J. Edward Day, the former Illinois commissioner of insurance, was named Postmaster General; Stewart L. Udall, a former Arizona congressman, took over the Department of the Interior; and former governors Abraham Ribicoff of Connecticut and Orville Freeman of Minnesota were appointed to the Health, Education, and Welfare and the Agriculture departments, respectively.

For his personal White House advisers, Kennedy collected a group of young men, most of them recruited from his previous staff, former government aides, and academic acquaintances; none, however, approached the influence exercised by Sherman Adams. Since Kennedy believed in being a strong Executive, his advisers filled many of the jobs for which Franklin Roosevelt had recruited his brain trust. The Kennedy "kitchen cabinet," as it was sometimes called, was designed to provide the President with expert advice in formulating long-term administration policy, resolving the many complex problems which crossed his desk daily, deciding upon the tactics to get administration bills through Congress, and exercising the authority of the White House throughout the many government departments. Theodore C. Sorensen, a long-time friend and adviser named Special Counsel to the President, was charged with the responsibility of keeping the White House "idea men" working smoothly and effectively with the other presidential assistants who occupied the various desks in the Executive Office of the President.

Launching the New Frontier

The temper and course of the new administration were revealed in President Kennedy's brief and beautifully phrased inaugural address. "Let the word go forth from this time and place, to friend and foe alike, that the torch has been passed to a new generation of Americans—born in this century, tempered by war, disciplined by a hard and bitter peace, proud of our ancient heritage—and unwilling to witness or permit the slow undoing of those human rights to which this nation has always been committed, and to which we are committed today at home and around the world." Pledging America's support to its allies and the United Nations, promising to extend the country's assistance to the underdeveloped nations of the world, and requesting "those nations who would make themselves our adversary" to make a renewed effort to establish a real peace, Kennedy exhorted both East and West to "explore what problems unite us instead of belaboring those . . . which divide us."

The President's address was widely applauded, both at home and abroad, for its content and felicity of expression; and the zest and energy with which he and his White House advisers tackled their jobs led some observers to liken the activity and excitement which accompanied the beginning of the new administration to that which had taken hold of the country when Franklin Roosevelt was first inaugurated. The similarities, however, were deceiving, for the problems that disturbed the American people in 1961 were far different from those that had worried them a generation earlier. In 1933 Roosevelt's primary concern was to revive the American economy; in 1961 Kennedy's first responsibility was to guarantee the nation's survival. Whereas Roosevelt had spoken largely of the obligations of the federal government to satisfy the needs of its citizens, Kennedy talked mostly of America's international responsibilities. And while both men inaugurated their administrations by calling for bold new action—one to fight a depression and the other to ensure world peace—the American people in 1961, unlike the generation of 1933, did not appear to share President Kennedy's sense of urgency or determination.

Because of many things—the continuing crises in Berlin, the Congo, and Laos; the aftereffects of the Cuban debacle, which interfered with the development and presentation of Kennedy's program; his narrow electoral victory, the generally complacent mood of the American people, the strength of the conservative bipartisan coalition on Capitol Hill —the reaction to the President's legislative program was mixed. Without much difficulty he secured additional funds for the unemployed and the depressed areas, an increase in the minimum wage, and several other antirecession laws. Similarly, Congress followed the President's recommendations and boosted the defense budget by $265.6 million and ap-

534 THE U.S. & THE POSTWAR WORLD, 1945–1961

propriated more money for space research. But important as these measures were, they did not represent the long-term objectives of the Kennedy administration. The goals the President had set for himself called for much more than extending and consolidating the Roosevelt and Truman domestic programs and continuing the uneasy truce in the cold war which had existed for the past sixteen years. During the campaign and throughout the first months of his administration, President Kennedy repeatedly emphasized the need for stimulating the rate of the nation's economic growth, not only to satisfy the enlarged needs of the American people or to sustain a strong and flexible defense system capable of countering effectively the Kremlin's power moves but also to provide the United States with enough energy to compete successfully with the Soviet Union in meeting the insistent demands of the world's underprivileged peoples. The great challenge of the 1960's, Kennedy declared, was to secure the victory of freedom over communism in the emerging nations. His efforts "to get the country going again" and his search for a solution to the arms race were essential steps to a single end—"a grand and global alliance . . . that can assure a more fruitful life for all mankind."

When measured against these proposals, the record of the Kennedy administration's first year was less than the President had hoped for but more than many observers had anticipated. The President was well aware that future generations would measure the success of his administration by his ability to arouse the American people to accept the grave responsibilities history had imposed upon them. This was the vitally important task to which he had dedicated himself, and as he told the Congress in his first State of the Union message, its fulfillment would require all the energies of the American people and challenge some of their most fundamental assumptions. "I speak today," he told the Congress, "in an hour of national peril and national opportunity. Before my term has ended, we shall have to test anew whether a nation organized and governed such as ours can endure. The outcome is by no means certain. The answers are by no means clear. All of us together—this Administration, this Congress, this Nation—must forge those answers."

Suggested Readings

The best account of the election of 1960 is Theodore H. White, *The Making of the President, 1960* (New York, 1961). Arthur M. Schlesinger, Jr., *Kennedy or Nixon: Does It Make a Difference?* (New York, 1960) contains the views of a liberal historian on the two men. Paul T. David, ed., *The Presidential Election and Transition, 1960–1961* (Washington, D.C., 1961) is a Brookings Institution study.

Many of Kennedy's views are expressed in John F. Kennedy, *The Strategy of Peace* (New York [1962]) and John W. Gardner, ed., *To Turn the Tide* (New York [1962]), a collection of excerpts from the President's 1961 messages and speeches. Richard L. Grossman, ed., *Let Us Begin: The First One Hundred Days of the Kennedy Administration* (New York [1961]) is a collection of essays and photographs on the men and programs of the new administration; Stan Opotowsky, *The Kennedy Government* (New York [1961]) and Lester Tanzer, ed., *The Kennedy Circle* (New York, 1961) analyze the personnel of the administration; and James T. Crown, *Kennedy in Power* (New York [1961]) appraises the accomplishments of the first year.

The "Foreign Policy of the Kennedy Administration" is discussed in eight essays in *Current History*, XLII (January 1962).

A first-rate campaign biography of the thirty-fifth President is James MacGregor Burns, *John Kennedy: A Political Profile* (New York [1959]). Robert J. Donovan, *PT 109: John F. Kennedy in World War II* (New York, 1961) details the President's naval career.

INDEX

Index

Acheson, Dean G., 323–24, 337, 438, 439
  China and, 367–68, 369
  Korea and, 371
  opinion of Alger Hiss, 389
  picture of, 368
  Secretary of State, 367, 371, 372, 377, 442, 445, 446, 448, 450
Act of Chapultepec, 249, 343
Adams, Sherman, 399, 410–13, 416, 418, 437, 441, 446, 447, 451, 466, 467, 532
  congressional investigation involving, 470–71
  picture of, 411
Adenauer, Konrad, 348, 485, 486, 487
Administrative Reorganization Act (1939), 120–21
Admiralty Islands, 214
adult education, 74
AFL-CIO, 472, 473
Africa, World War II and, 196–98
Afro-Asian Conference (Bandung), 448
Agar, Herbert, quoted, 390
Agricultural Adjustment Act (1933), 25–26, 37, 48, 49, 59
  declared unconstitutional, 93, 105–6, 111
Agricultural Adjustment Act (1938), 116–17, 127
Agricultural Adjustment Administration, 26–29, 389

Agricultural Trade Development and Assistance Act (1954), 415
agriculture
  Brannan Plan, 357–58
  during 1950's, 471
  Eisenhower administration and, 414–17
  mechanization of, 231
  New Deal and, 24–29, 116–17
  subsidies, 117
  Truman administration and, 357–58
  World War II and, 231
Agriculture Department, U. S., 25, 48, 118
aid (*see* federal aid; foreign aid)
Aiken, John W., 97
air force (*see* armed forces)
Air Force Academy, 465 n.
Akagi (aircraft carrier), 194
Alabama, University of, desegregation issue and, 457
Alaska, World War II and, 192, 214–15
Aleutian Islands, World War II and, 214–15
Alexander, Harold, 202
Algeria, 483
Alsop, John, quoted, 403–4
Altmark (German ship), 168
Amalgamated Clothing Workers Union, 77, 80
amendments, constitutional
  Fourteenth, 112, 510

540 INDEX

amendments (cont.)
  Eighteenth, 20
  Twentieth, 70, 104
  Twenty-first, 20
  Twenty-second, 313, 401, 523
America First Committee, 163, 164
American Agriculturalist, 11
American Bar Association, 436
American Farm Bureau Federation, 357
American Federation of Labor (AFL),
    76, 77, 78, 79, 80, 81, 82, 113, 119
  CIO versus, 82-83
  merger with CIO, 472
American Friends Service Committee,
    395
American Labor party, 64-65, 68
American Legion, 396, 436
American Liberty League, 60, 62, 69, 70
American Medical Association, 358
American Newspaper Guild, 82
American Telephone and Telegraph
    Company, 128-29
Americans for Democratic Action, 395
Anderson, Clinton P., 357
Anglo-American relations (see Great
    Britain)
anti-Catholicism, 498
antitrust laws, 116
ANZUS, 382
Arab-Israeli issue, 474-79
Arbenz Guzmán, Jacobo, 489
arbitration of labor disputes, 82, 94, 232
Arcadia Conference, 205
architecture, 515
Argentina
  isolationism, 248
  U. S. intervention in domestic affairs
    of, 362-63
  World War II and, 249, 361
Arías, Harmodio, 139
Arizona, U.S.S., 187
armaments, 234, 235, 462, 479
armed forces
  demobilization after World War II,
    288-90
  discrimination in, 242
  recruitment, 230-31
  unification of, 313-14, 315, 465-66
army-McCarthy hearings, 429-30
Arnold, Thurman, 116
arts, 511-18

Arvin, Newton, 517
Asia (see Far East; names of countries)
"Asia Firsters," 369, 374, 445
Aswan Dam project, 476
Atlantic Charter, 170, 186, 258, 259, 262,
    266, 269
Atlantic Monthly, The, 503
atomic bomb, 220-23, 268, 300, 301, 324,
    325, 370, 391, 394, 450, 482, 519
atomic energy, 422-23
  UN debates on international control of,
    323-25
Atomic Energy Act (1946), 300-302, 422;
    (1954), 422
Atomic Energy Commission
  United Nations, 323-25
  United States, 302, 324, 420, 421, 422,
    423, 432
Attlee, Clement
  picture of, 285
  Potsdam Conference, 283
Augusta, U.S.S., 170
Australia, 190, 191, 192, 194, 213
Austria, 255, 320-21
automobile industry, 78, 80, 81-82
Avery, Sewell, 234
Azerbaijan, 323

Badoglio, Pietro, 204
Baghdad Pact, 476, 479
balance of power system, 333, 483
Baldwin, Hanson W., 377, 463
Balkans, the, postwar plans for, 262
Bankhead, William B., 148
Bankhead Cotton Control Act (1934), 27,
    49
Bankhead-Jones Farm Tenant Act (1937),
    29
Banking Act (1935), 39, 88
banks
  Federal Reserve, 39
  Franklin D. Roosevelt and, 16-18
  Glass-Steagall Act and, 39
  see also Inter-American Development
    Bank; International Bank for Recon-
    struction and Development
Barkley, Alben W., 243, 351, 402
Baruch, Bernard M., 31, 324-25
Batista, Fulgencio, 139, 490
Bean, Louis, H., 25
"beatniks," 512

INDEX 541

Beer Act (1933), 19, 20
Bellow, Saul, 513
Bennett, Hugh, 46, 48
Benson, Elmer A., 63
Benson, Ezra T., 409, 414–17, 524
Bentley, Elizabeth, 388
Berle, Adolf A., Jr., 11
Berlin, Germany
  airlift, 347
  blockade, 346, 348
  crisis over, 345–48, 484–88
  postwar plans for, 267
Berlin Pact (1940), 161–62
Bevin, Ernest, 322
Bible, 497
Biddle, Francis, 304
Bikini Island, 325
Bill of Rights, Supreme Court's enforcement of, 433
birth rate, 505
Black, Hugo L., 30, 112
black market, 294
Blackmur, R. P., 517
Boa Dai, Emperor, 442
Bohlen, Charles E., 266, 269, 288, 427–28
Bonin Islands, 381
Bonneville Dam, 41
Borah, William E., 94–95, 96, 98
Borneo, 190
Bormann, Martin, 326
Boston Herald, 51
Bougainville, 214
Boulder Dam, 41
Bowles, Chester, 239, 294
boycott, secondary, 473
Boyle, William J., Jr., 397
Braden, Spruille, 362–63
Bradley, Omar N., 206, 208, 211, 212, 314 n., 377
  China policy, 368
  picture of, 203
Brandeis, Louis D., justice of the Supreme Court, 105, 109–10, 112
Brannan, Charles F., 357
Brannan Plan, 357–58
Brazil, World War II and, 248
Bretton Woods Conference, 260
Bricker, John W., 243, 244, 400, 436–37
Bricker Amendment, 436–37
Bridges, Henry Styles, 369
Brien, Charles O., 97

Brooks, Van Wyck, 516
Brophy, John, 77, 80
Browder, Earl, 69, 97, 100
Brown, Prentiss, 239
Brown v. Board of Education of Topeka, 455
Brownell, Herbert, Jr., 400, 409, 417, 451, 460
Brownlow Committee, 121
Brussels Pact, 342–43
Bryan, William Jennings, 38
budget, national
  Eisenhower and the, 413–14
  New Deal and the, 123–26
Bulganin, Nikolai, 482
  summit conference, 449, 450
Bulgaria, 262
  peace treaty, 285, 318–19
Bulge, Battle of the, 211
Bull Moose movement, 95
Bunche, Ralph J., 474, 509
Burke-Wadsworth Selective Training and Service Act (1940), 230
Burma, 189, 195, 218, 256
Burma Road, 195
Burns, James MacGregor, quoted, 71, 72, 107, 121–22
Bush, Vannevar, 152, 221
Butler, Pierce, 105, 112
Byrd, Harry, 244, 529
Byrnes, James F., 112, 238, 292
  opinion of Alger Hiss, 389
  quoted on foreign aid, 338
  quoted on Potsdam Conference, 288
  quoted on U. S.–Russian relations, 317
  Secretary of State, 284, 287, 304, 305, 306, 318, 319, 321, 322, 323, 327, 328, 345

Cairo Conference, 256, 370
Calhoun, John C., 308
Campos, Albizu, 364
capitalism, 63, 68
Cárdenas, Lázaro, 139
Cardozo, Benjamin, 105, 112
Carey, James, 80
Carmody, John, 121
Carnegie Endowment for International Peace, 389
Caroline Islands, 215
Carpenter, R. R. M., 60

542 INDEX

Casablanca Conference, 201–2, 204, 213, 251, 389
Case, Francis P., 418
Castillo Armas, Carlos, 489
Castro, Fidel, 490–91
Catholic Church (see Roman Catholic Church)
cattle, 45, 48
Caudle, T. Lamar, 398
Celebes, 190
Central Intelligence Agency (CIA), 315, 487, 490
Central Treaty Organization (CENTO), 479
Chamberlain, Neville, 160
Chambers, Whittaker, 389–91
Chamoun, Camille, 479
Chapultepec, Act of, 249, 343
Chiang Kai-shek, 144, 160, 189, 218, 256, 268–69, 364–69, 370, 374, 391, 440, 445–47
Chicago *Daily News*, 95
Chicago Tribune, 349, 400
child labor, 5, 31, 33, 118
Chile, World War II and, 248
China
  communism in, 364–70, 491
  Japanese imperialism and, 143–44
  Open Door policy in, 143
  People's Republic proclaimed, 367, 370
  U. S. aid to, 365, 367
Chou En-lai, 374, 445, 447, 448
Christian American Segregation Association, 456
churches, 496–99
Churchill, Winston S., 160
  Arcadia Conference, 205
  Atlantic Charter, 170
  atomic bombs and, 220–21
  Cairo Conference, 256, 370
  Casablanca Conference, 201, 204, 251
  Fulton, Missouri, speech, 328
  Moscow Conference, 206, 251, 255
  peace plans and, 258, 262–63
  picture of, 263
  Potsdam Conference, 283, 370
  Quebec Conference, 252
  quoted on Battle of El Alamein, 197
  quoted on Battle of Midway, 192
  quoted on Battle of the Atlantic, 201
  Roosevelt's relationship with, 250–52

Churchill, Winston S. (*cont.*)
  Russia and, 252–58
  Teheran Conference, 206, 256–57
  World War II and, 198, 201, 203, 206, 250–52
  Yalta Conference, 263–70
Civil and Defense Mobilization, Office of, 315 n.
civil rights
  Eisenhower and, 455–62
  Truman and, 242, 356–57, 360, 459
Civil Rights Act (1957), 460
Civil Service Commission, 388
Civil Works Administration, 21–22, 48
Civil Works Emergency Relief Act (1934), 22
Civilian Conservation Corps, 20–21, 48, 73
Civilian Conservation Corps Reforestation Relief Act (1933), 21
Civilian Production Administration (CPA), 292
Clark, Mark, 204, 205
Clark, Thomas C., 304
class differences, 508
Clay, Henry, 308
Clay, Lucius D., 347
Cleveland, Grover, 312
Clinton, Tennessee, desegregation issue, 457
closed (union) shop, 82, 232, 233, 379
coal, 91
Cohn, Roy M., 429
cold war, 341, 342, 352, 449, 484, 491, 534
collective bargaining, 14, 30, 32, 33, 78, 81, 82, 83, 85, 154, 155
collective security, 68, 134, 136, 141, 149, 342–45, 382
  Baghdad Pact and, 476
  Brussels Pact and, 342–43
  NATO and, 343–45
colleges, 499, 500, 501
Collier, John, 49
Colvin, D. Leigh, 97
Cominform, 340
Comintern, dissolution of the, 255
Committee for European Economic Cooperation (CEEC), 339
Committee for Industrial Organization (see Congress of Industrial Organizations)

INDEX 543

Committee for the Nation to Rebuild Prices and Purchasing Power, 37
Committee on Administrative Management, 121
Committee on Economic Security, 86, 87
Committee to Defend America by Aiding the Allies, 163
Commodity Credit Corporation, 27, 358, 417
Commonwealth and Southern Corporation, 43, 153
communism
　Chinese, 364–70, 491
　fight against, 341, 359, 387–96, 427–33, 435, 491, 534
　House Un-American Activities Committee and, 388
　interest in, 495, 511
　in Latin America, 362, 488–89
　McCarran Internal Security Act and, 395
Communist Control Act (1954), 432
Communist International, 68
Communist party, 68–69, 83, 97, 100, 159, 352, 393
　legally outlawed, 432
company unions, 31, 77
composers, 516
Compton, Arthur H., 221
Conant, James B., 500
Congo, 491
Congress, U. S.
　Eisenhower and, 412, 435–37
　Franklin D. Roosevelt and, 19, 71, 113, 114–15, 120, 121–23, 243
　Truman and, 297–98, 356–59
　Twentieth Amendment and, 70
Congress of Industrial Organizations (CIO), 79, 80–83
　merger with AFL, 472
　Political Action Committee, 245
Congress of Racial Equality (CORE), 461
congressional elections (see elections, congressional)
Connally, Tom, 259
conscription, 230
conservation
　Eisenhower administration and, 417
　forest, 5, 21, 44
　New Deal and, 14, 44–49

conservation (cont.)
　soil, 47–49
　Theodore Roosevelt and, 44
　Truman and, 357
conservatism, 512
Cooke, Alistair, 495
Cooke, Morris L., 47, 89
Coolidge, Calvin, elected President, 7
cooperatives, 5
Copland, Aaron, 516
Coplon, Judith, 393–94
Coral Sea, Battle of the, 191, 195, 215
Corcoran, Thomas G., 12, 121
Corporate Bankruptcy Act (1934), 34
Corregidor Island, 143, 190
corruption, in government, 397–98
cotton, 24, 27, 28
Coughlin, Father Charles E., 37, 65, 66, 67, 68, 69, 94, 97
Council of Economic Advisers, 299
Council of Foreign Ministers, 285–86, 317, 318–19, 323, 348, 440
crime, 396–97
Crimea Conference (see Yalta Conference)
Crop Loan Act (1934), 26–27
Cuba
　Castro regime, 490–91
　Platt Amendment and, 139
　revolution in (1933), 139
cultural exchange program, 486
Cummings, E. E., 513
Cummings, Homer, 10, 107
currency, New Deal and, 35–39
Current Tax Payment Act (1943), 237
Czechoslovakia, 149, 150, 156

Dairen, 268
Danaher, John A., 247
Daniels, Josephus C., 5, 6
Darlan, Jean François, 198, 251
Darrow, Clarence, 32
Davis, Chester C., 26
Davis, Elmer, 242
Davis, James J., 248
Davis, John W., 7, 60
Davis, Norman, 144
Davis, William H., 232, 233
Day, J. Edward, 532
Deane, John R., 254
death rate, 519

544 INDEX

debt, national, growth of, 125–26, 130
Declaration of Havana, 166
Declaration of Reciprocal Assistance and American Solidarity, 249
Declaration on Liberated Europe, 266, 284, 285, 317
defense
  hemispheric, 166
  national, 152
Defense Department, U. S., 314 n., 465
Defense Mobilization, Office of, 315 n., 378
Defense Production Act (1950), 378; (1951), 379
Defense Transportation, Office of, 293
de Gaulle, Charles, 198, 251, 485, 486, 487
democracy, 3, 135, 498
Democracy in America (Tocqueville), 342
Democratic party
  discord and disunity during Truman administration, 303 ff.
  platforms (*see* elections)
Dern, George H., 10
desegregation, 454–62
Dewey, John, 500
Dewey, Thomas E., 152, 349
  election of 1944 and, 243–47
  election of 1948 and, 349–55
  election of 1952 and, 399
DeWitt, John, 240
Dies, Martin, 388
Dillon, C. Douglas, 531, 532
direct primary, 5
Dirksen, Everett, 431
disarmament, 144–45, 449–50, 481–82, 483, 491
discrimination, Negroes and, 241–42, 508–11
Displaced Persons Act (1947), 355; (1950), 359
divorce, 505
Dixiecrats (*see* States' Rights Democratic party)
Dixon, Edgar H., 421
Dixon-Yates controversy, 420–22
Dodecanese Islands, 320
Doenitz, Karl, 212
Dominican Republic, 490
Doolittle, James H., 191
Dos Passos, John, 512
Douglas, William O., 112, 245, 350, 393

draft, World War II, 230
Dreiser, Theodore, 512
Dubinsky, David, 77
Dulles, John Foster, 438–48
  biographical sketch, 408
  Bricker Amendment opposed by, 436
  foreign aid and, 437
  foreign policy, 401, 408, 438–48, 478, 483
  Formosa crisis and, 445–48
  Indochina crisis and, 441–45
  Japanese peace treaty, 381
  Middle East crisis and, 476
  picture of, 439
  Secretary of State, 408, 410, 438–48, 451, 462, 483
Dumbarton Oaks Conference, 261, 282, 389
Du Pont family, 60
Durkin, Martin P., 410
Dust Bowl, 46, 47, 48

Earle, George H., 81
Earth as Modified by Human Action, The (Marsh), 44
East China Sea, Battle of the, 217
East Indies, 190
Eastman, Joseph B., 34
Eaton, Charles A., 340
Eccles, Marriner S., 88
Economic Charter of the Americas, 249
Economic Cooperation Act (1948), 340
Economic Cooperation Administration (ECA), 340, 341, 371
economic development, 128
Economic Stabilization, Office of (OES), 238
Economic Stabilization (Anti-inflation) Act (1942), 233
economic system
  New Deal and the, 126–30
  reconversion after World War II, 291–96
Economic Warfare, Office of, 234
Economy Act (1933), 19–20, 124
Eden, Anthony, 255, 262, 449, 484, 485
  summit conference, 449
education, 499–502
  adult, 74
  federal aid to, 358, 425, 426, 500
  National Defense Education Act, 427
  progressive, 500–501

Egypt, 475–78
Eighteenth Amendment, repeal of, 20
Einstein, Albert, 220
Eisenhower, Dwight D., 313
  advisers, 407, 408–12, 460
  agriculture and, 414–17
  atomic energy and, 422–23
  "atoms for peace" speech, 423
  Berlin crisis and, 487
  biographical sketch, 406–7
  Bricker Amendment opposed by, 436–37
  budget and, 413–14
  cabinet, 407, 408–10
  Casablanca Conference, 201
  civil rights and, 455–62
  Congress and, 412, 435–37
  conservation and, 417
  defense policies, 462–66
  domestic affairs and, 412–33
  election of 1948 and, 349, 350
  election of 1952 and, 399–406
  election of 1956 and, 451–55
  foreign aid and, 437
  foreign policy, 435–50, 473–92
  foreign trade and, 437
  Formosa crisis and, 445–48
  highway program, 424–25
  housing and, 424
  illness, 451–52
  Indochina crisis and, 441–45
  integration controversy and, 455–62
  Korean War and, 405, 454
  loyalty issue and, 427–32
  McCarthy and, 427–32
  Middle East crisis and, 473–79
  missile program and, 464
  "open skies" proposal, 450, 479
  picture of, 203, 399
  popularity of, 454, 523
  public power and, 418–23
  recession and, 469–73
  Sherman Adams defended by, 471
  social welfare and, 423–27
  space program and, 466–69
  summit conferences, 449–50, 486–88
  Supreme Commander of the Allied Powers in Europe, 345
  tariff and, 437
  taxes and, 414
  tidelands and, 417

Eisenhower, Dwight D. (*cont.*)
  U-2 incident, 487–88
  unification of armed forces, 465–66
  World War II and, 197, 204, 206–9, 211, 213, 407
Eisenhower, Milton, 488–89
Eisenhower Doctrine, 478
El Alamein, Battle of, 197
elections
  1916, 529
  1920, 6
  1924, 7
  1928, 7
  1932, 68
  1936, 69, 94–100, 406
  1940, 152–59
  1944, 242–48
  1948, 348–56
  1952, 398–406, 509
  1956, 451–55, 509
  1960, 464, 498, 508, 523–29
elections, congressional
  1934, 50–51
  1938, 121–23
  1942, 243
  1944, 247
  1946, 306, 349
  1948, 355, 356
  1950, 356
  1952, 406
  1954, 453
  1956, 455
  1958, 471
  1960, 529
Eliot, T. S., 513, 517
Elizabeth II, Queen, 420
Emergency Bank Act (1933), 17
Emergency Price Control Act (1942), 238
Emergency Railroad Transportation Act (1933), 34
Emergency Relief Appropriation Act (1935), 73
emotional disorders, growth of, 505
employment, full, 298–99
Employment Act (1946), 298–300
End Poverty in California plan, 64
Enemy Within, The (Kennedy), 472
Eniwetok, 215
Enterprise (aircraft carrier), 194
equality, ideal of, 507–11

546 INDEX

espionage, 83, 370, 387, 388, 390, 391, 393, 394, 487
Ethiopia, 146–47, 320
Eugene Dennis, et al. v. United States, 393
"Euratom" countries, 423
Europe
  Marshall Plan and, 336–42
  U. S. foreign policy and, 144–52
  see also names of countries
European Advisory Commission, 255, 267, 346
European Atomic Energy Community Act (1957), 423
European Defense Community (EDC), 345, 483–84
European Recovery Program (*see* Marshall Plan)
Evergood, Philip, 513
Everson case, 498
Exchange Stabilization Fund, 37
Executive Department
  changes in the, 311–15, 359
  loyalty probe, 387–88
Explorer I, 467, 468
Export-Import Bank, 141
exports, 138
Ezekiel, Mordecai, 25

Facts and Figures, Office of, 242
Fair Deal, 296–303, 356–64
Fair Employment Practices Committee (FEPC), 241, 297, 509
Fair Labor Standards Act (1936), 117–20
Fairless, Benjamin, 437
Faisal, King, 479
fallout, radioactive, 480, 482
Fansteel Metallurgical Corporation case, 85
Far East
  Truman administration and, 364–82
  U. S. policy in, 142–44, 167, 364–82, 441–48
  Yalta Conference decision about, 268–69
  see also names of countries
Farley, James A., 10, 11, 50, 99, 244
  election of 1940 and, 154, 155
  picture of, 99
Farm Credit Administration, 26

Farm Mortgage Foreclosure Act (1934), 27
Farm Security Administration, 29
Farrell, James T., 512
fascism, 134, 135, 141, 150, 164
Faubus, Orval M., 457–58
Faulkner, William, 512
Fechner, Robert, 21
federal aid, 418–19, 425, 426
  to education, 358, 425, 426, 500
federal budget (*see* budget, national)
Federal Bureau of Investigation, 239, 388, 392, 431, 433
Federal Communications Commission, 121, 502
Federal Council of Churches, 497–98
Federal Crop Insurance Corporation, 117
Federal Deposit Insurance Corporation, 39
Federal Emergency Relief Administration, 12, 21, 22–23, 48, 75
Federal Farm Board, 24
Federal Farm Mortgage Corporation, 26
Federal Housing Administration, 113, 424, 470
Federal Housing Authority, 35
Federal Loan Agency, 121
Federal Mortgage Refinancing Act (1934), 26
Federal Power Commission, 89, 417, 420
Federal Reserve banks, 39
Federal Reserve Board, 40, 88, 296, 473
Federal Reserve System, 18, 39, 237, 296, 413, 470
  Board of Governors, 88
Federal Securities Act (1933), 40
Federal Security Agency, 121
Federal Surplus Commodities Corporation, 117
Federal Theater, 74, 75
Federal Trade Commission, 78, 93, 121, 471
Federal Works Agency, 121
Fermi, Enrico, 221
financiers, 37, 40, 67
Finland, peace treaty, 285, 318–19
First Boston Corporation, 422
Fish, Hamilton, 248
Fiume, 320
"five percenters," 397
Flanagan, Hallie, 74

INDEX

Folsom, Marion B., 426
Food and Agriculture Organization (FAO), 260, 283
Food Stamp Plan (1939), 117
Ford, Henry, 31
Ford Motor Company, 82, 83–84, 532
Ford Service Men, 84
Foreign Affairs, 334
foreign aid
  Eisenhower administration and, 437
  Point Four program and, 360–61
  Russian, 340, 478, 479
  United States, 334–42, 344, 365, 367, 369, 371, 377, 444, 475, 476, 478, 490, 496
Foreign Aid Act (1947), 339
Foreign Ministers Conference
  Geneva (1959), 486
  Moscow (1943), 255
Foreign Operations Administration (FOA), 340 n.
foreign policy
  bipartisan, development of, 315–16
  Eisenhower administration and, 435–50, 473–92
  Franklin D. Roosevelt and, 133 ff.
  isolation vs. intervention, 134–36
  Truman administration and, 316–28, 333–48
foreign trade, Eisenhower administration and, 437
Formosa, 364, 367, 371, 372, 445–48
Forrestal, James V., 268, 290, 314
Fort Peck Dam, 42
Four Freedoms, 170
Fourteen Points, Wilson's, 170
Fourteenth Amendment, 112, 510
France
  atomic bomb exploded by, 482
  Indochina crisis, 441–45
  Middle East crisis and, 477
  World War II and, 150, 159, 165, 197–98
Franco, Francisco, 147
Frank, Jerome, 25
Frankfurter, Felix, 12, 112
Frazier-Lemke Bankruptcy Act, 27
Frazier-Lemke Farm Mortgage Moratorium Act (1935), 111
freedom, 496, 511
Freedom VII, 469
Freedom Riders, 461–62

Freeman, Orville, 532
Freud, Sigmund, 506, 517
Frost, Robert, 513
Fuchs, Klaus, 394
Fulbright, J. William, 259, 306, 397–98
full employment, 298–99
functionalism, 515
fundamentalism, 497

Gagarin, Yuri, 468, 469
Gallup, George, quoted, 355
Gardner, Trevor, 464
Garfield, James A., 312, 313
Garner, John Nance, 10, 50, 96
  election of 1940 and, 154, 155
Gayle v. Browder, 461
Gaza Strip, 477
General Electric Company, 30
General Motors Corporation, 60, 82, 83, 293, 294, 408, 409
General Theory of Employment, Interest and Money, The (Keynes), 125
Generation on Trial (Cooke), 495
George, Walter F., 122
Germany
  Democratic Republic of, 348
  division of, 286, 321
  East, uprising in (1953), 441
  Federal Republic of, 348
  invasion of Poland, 150–51
  NATO membership, 484
  peace treaty, 286, 320–22
  Potsdam Declaration and, 286, 321
  reparations, 286–87
  reunification of, 449
  war criminals, 287, 326–27
  withdrawal from League of Nations, 144
  World War II and, 150–51, 159 ff., 196 ff.
  Yalta Conference plans for, 266–67
  see also Berlin, Germany
GI Bill of Rights (*see* Servicemen's Readjustment Act)
Gilbert Islands, 215
Giraud, Henri, 198, 251
Girdler, Tom, 81
Glass-Steagall Banking Act (1933), 39
Glenn, John H., Jr., 469
Goering, Hermann, 207, 326
Gold, Harry, 394
Gold Repeal Joint Resolution, 35

548 INDEX

Gold Reserve Act (1934), 37, 49
gold standard, abandonment of, 35
Goldberg, Arthur J., 532
Goldfine, Bernard, 470–71
Goldsborough, T. Alan, 310
Goldwater, Barry, 526
Good Neighbor League, 99
Good Neighbor Policy, 138, 139, 140, 248
government, corruption in, 397–98
government regulation
  New Deal and, 29 ff.
  of stock exchanges, 14, 39–40
government reorganization, 120–21, 302–3, 311–15, 359, 465
Grace, Eugene, 81
Graf Spee (German ship), 168
Grand Coulee Dam, 41
Grant, Ulysses S., 531
Grapes of Wrath, The (Steinbeck), 47, 512
Great Britain
  Communist China recognized by, 367
  Iranian crisis and, 322–23
  Middle East crisis and, 477
  U. S. relations with, 170, 250–52
  World War II and, 150–51, 160, 166, 171, 189, 196 ff., 250–52
Great Depression, 3, 8, 495
  causes, 135
  labor and the, 76
Greece, 262, 320
  U. S. aid to, 334–36
Green, William, 30, 76, 119
Greenglass, David, 394
Greenland, 169
Greer (American destroyer), 169
Grew, Joseph C., 177, 178, 288
Gromyko, Andrei A., 325
Gropper, William, 513
Groves, Leslie R., 221
Guadalcanal, 194, 195, 213, 214
Guam, World War II and, 189, 215
Guatemala, 489, 490
Gubitchev, Valentine, 393
Guffey-Snyder Bituminous Coal Stabilization Act (1935), 91
Guffey-Vinson Act (1937), 91

Hagerty, James C., 451
Haiti, 139

Halsey, William F., 214, 215, 216
Hannegan, Robert E., 244
Harding, Warren G., 6
Harper's, 503
Harriman, Henry I., 30
Harriman, W. Averell, 206, 222, 251, 255, 263, 288, 305, 402, 453
Harris, Roy, 516
Hartley, Fred L., Jr., 310
Harvard University, 4
Hatch Act (1939), 75
Havana, Declaration of, 166
Hawes-Cutting Act (1933), 142
Hay-Bunau-Varilla Treaty, 139
Hearst, William Randolph, 62
Hell's Canyon, 420
Hemingway, Ernest, 512, 513
Henderson, Leon, 238, 239
Hendricks, Thomas A., 312
Henry, Patrick, 44
Herter, Christian A., 448, 452, 487
Hicks, Granville, 517
highways, 424–25, 470
Hill, Lister D., 421
Hillman, Sidney, 77, 80, 234
Hiroshima, atomic bomb attack on, 222–23
Hiss, Alger, 388–91
Hitler, Adolf, 68, 69, 144, 156, 159, 160, 164, 165, 167, 171, 172, 173, 187, 196, 199, 200, 203, 204, 205, 207, 208, 209, 211, 212, 253, 254, 255, 326
  Berlin Pact and, 161–62
  death of, 212
Ho Chi-minh, 442, 444
Hoare-Laval Pact, 146
Hobby, Mrs. Oveta Culp, 410, 425, 426
Hodges, Courtney H., 211
Hodges, Luther, 458, 531
Hoffman, Paul G., 340
holding companies, 40, 89, 153
Holmes, Oliver Wendell, 112, 389
Home Owners Loan Corporation, 34–35
Home Owners Refinancing Act (1933), 34–35
Homma, Masaharu, 189, 190
Honduras, 489
Hoover, Herbert
  election of 1936 and, 94, 98
  Latin America and, 138
  Philippines and, 142
Hoover Commission, 121, 359, 465

INDEX 549

Hopkins, Harry L., 12, 21, 22, 73, 75, 121, 266, 410
  mission to Moscow, 283, 284
  picture of, 22
Hornet (aircraft carrier), 191, 194
House, Edward M., 410
House Un-American Activities Committee, 388, 390
housing, 113–14, 358–59, 424, 470, 509
Howe, Louis McHenry, 6–7
Hughes, Charles Evans, 4, 5, 529
  Chief Justice, 105, 109–11, 112
Hull, Cordell, 10, 11, 36, 264
  election of 1940 and, 155
  foreign ministers conference (Moscow), (1943), 255
  foreign policy, 136 ff., 248, 256, 262
  Morgenthau plan for Germany opposed by, 266
  opinion of Alger Hiss, 389
  picture of, 253
  trade treaties, 137–38
  World War II and, 162, 167, 174–79
Humphrey, George M., 408, 413, 451, 462, 470
Humphrey, Hubert H., Jr., 351
Hungary, 262
  peace treaty, 285, 318–19
  uprising in (1956), 441, 477
Hussein, King, 479
Hutchins, Robert M., 501
hydroelectric plants, 41
hydrogen bomb, 432, 448, 454

Iceland, 169
Ickes, Harold L., 11, 23, 24, 107, 121, 233
  picture of, 23
  resignation of, 304
Idaho Power Company, 420
immigration, 395–96
imperialism, 135
  Japanese, 133, 142, 143, 160–61, 162
  Nazi, 170, 171
imports, 138
income, national, 127, 504
income taxes, 89–91, 125, 236–37
India, 191
Indian Reorganization Act (1934), 49
Indians, 49
Indochina, 441–45, 463, 483, 491
Indonesia, 484

industry
  discrimination in, 241–42
  Korean War and, 378
  New Deal and, 29–33
  reconversion to peacetime production, 291–92
  World War II and, 229–30, 234–35
inequality, problems of, 507–11
inflation
  demand for, 37
  prevention of, 230, 233, 235–39
  after World War II, 295–96
Inge, William, 515, 516
integration controversy, 455–62
intellectual trends, 495–503
Inter-American Conference (1940), 166
Inter-American Conference on Problems of War and Peace, 249
Inter-American Development Bank, 490
Inter-American Treaty of Reciprocal Assistance, 343, 362
Internal Revenue, Bureau of, corruption in, 397, 398
internal security, 387–96, 431–32
International Atomic Energy Agency (IAEA), 423
International Bank for Reconstruction and Development, 260, 476
International Court of Justice, 283
International Labor Organization (ILO), 283
International Ladies Garment Workers Union, 77, 80, 83
International Military Tribunal, 326–27
International Monetary Fund, 260–61
Interstate Commerce Commission, 91, 121, 460, 461, 462
interventionism, 134–36, 163–70
Iran, 257, 322–23
Iraq, 479
isolationism, 134–36, 145, 151, 153, 163, 164, 247, 258, 259, 316
Israel, 474–78
Istrian Peninsula, 320
Italy
  peace treaty, 218–19, 285, 320
  war with Ethiopia, 146–47
  World War II and, 159, 161, 165, 171, 201–5
Ives, Charles E., 516
Iwo Jima, 216–17

550 INDEX

Jackson, Andrew, 96
Jackson, Barbara Ward, quoted, 336, 341
Jackson, Henry, 464
Jackson, Mississippi, desegregation issue, 462
Jackson, Robert H., 112, 241, 326, 327
Japan
  anti-American riots in, 491
  Berlin Pact and, 161–62
  imperialism, 133, 142, 143, 160–61, 162
  peace treaty, 381
  Pearl Harbor attack, 179, 180, 187–88, 248
  reparations, 381–82
  U. S. occupation of, 380
  U. S. relations with, 142–44, 162, 165, 167–68, 174–81, 380–82
  war criminals, trial of, 326
  World War II and, 160–61, 172–81, 187–96, 213–24
Japanese-Americans, World War II and, 240–41
Java, 190
Jencks v. United States, 433
Jenner, William, 404
Jews, 474–75, 499
"Jim Crow" laws, 509
Jodl, Alfred, 213, 326
Johnson, Edwin C., 301
Johnson, Hugh S., 11, 30, 31, 32, 58
Johnson, Lyndon B., 523, 524, 529
Johnson, Philip, 515
Johnson, Walter, quoted, 8
Johnson Debt Default Act (1934), 145
Jones, Jesse, 33, 121
Jones-Connally Farm Relief Act (1934), 25
Jones-Costigan Sugar Act (1934), 25, 139
Jordan, 479
Judaism, 499
Judicial Reform Act (1937), 111
Justice Department, U. S., Civil Rights Division, 460

Kassim, Obdul Karim, 479
Kaufman, Irving R., 394
Kearny (American destroyer), 169
Kefauver, Estes, 397, 401–2, 453
Keitel, Wilhelm, 326
Kellogg-Briand Pact, 327
Kennan, George F., 254, 334, 485

Kennedy, John F.
  advisers, 531–32, 533
  Alliance for Progress plan, 490
  background, 508
  biographical sketch, 529–31
  cabinet, 531–32
  Cuban crisis of April, 1961, and, 491
  debates with Nixon, 448, 528
  desegregation issue and, 461
  election of 1956 and, 453
  election of 1960 and, 523–29
  Germany and, 488
  inaugural address, 532–33
  New Frontier, 532–34
  nuclear testing and, 482–83
  picture of, 528
  Profiles in Courage, 530
  religious issue and, 498, 527, 528, 529
  space program and, 469
  Why England Slept, 530
Kennedy, Joseph P., 40, 94, 529–30
Kennedy, Robert F., 531
  Enemy Within, The, 472
Kerr, Robert, 402
Kerr-Smith Tobacco Control Act, 27, 49
Kesselring, Albert, 204, 205
Keynes, John Maynard, 125, 298, 299
Khrushchev, Nikita S., 482, 492
  Berlin crisis and, 484–87
  summit meeting scuttled by, 488
  U-2 incident and, 487–88
  U. S. visit, 486
Killian, James R., Jr., 468
Kimmel, Husband E., 179, 188, 192
King, Martin Luther, 461
King, W. L. Mackenzie, 166
Kinkaid, Thomas C., 216
Knowland, William F., 369, 412, 431, 436, 426
Knox, Frank, 95, 153, 179, 188
Knudsen, William S., 167, 234
Knutson, Harold, 308
Koiso, Kuniaki, 216, 217
Konoye, Fumimaro, 173, 177, 178
Korean Mutual Defense Treaty (1954), 378
Korean War, 289 n., 364, 370–80, 405, 413, 445, 454
Korematsu v. United States, 241
Krock, Arthur, quoted, 51, 70, 100
Krug, Julius W., 305

INDEX

Ku Klux Klan, 112, 461
Kurile Islands, 268, 381
Kurusu, Saburu, 178
Kwajalein, 215

labor
  child, 5, 31, 33, 118
  disputes, arbitration of, 82, 94, 232
  Korean War and, 379
  New Deal and, 76–85, 117–20
  women and, 231
  World War II and, 231–34
  WPA and, 71, 73–76
Labor Department, U. S., 21
Labor Pension Reporting Act, 472
labor unions
  special Senate committee investigation
    of, 472
  see also trade unions; names of unions
Ladies' Home Journal, The, 503
La Follette, Philip, 64
La Follette, Robert M., 95, 97, 308
La Follette, Robert M., Jr., 63, 83, 247, 302
La Guardia, Fiorello, 64–65
laissez faire, doctrine of, 33, 106
Landon, Alfred M., 69
  election of 1936 and, 95–100
Landrum-Griffin Labor-Management Reporting and Disclosure Act, 472–73
Langer, William, 283
Laos, 491
Latin America
  communism in, 362, 488–89
  Hoover administration and, 138
  Roosevelt-Hull policy toward, 138–42
  Truman administration and, 361–64
  U. S. aid to, 361–62
  U. S. relations with, 248–50, 361–64, 488–92
  World War II and, 248–50
  see also names of countries
Lattre de Tassigny, Jean de, 208
Lawrence, Ernest O., 221
League of Nations, 6
  adoption of economic sanctions, 146–47
  Far East crisis and, 143
  German withdrawal from, 144
Leahy, William D., 167, 220, 221, 222
Lebanon, 479
Legislative Reference Service, 303

Legislative Reorganization Act (1946), 302–3
Lehman, Herbert H., 260
leisure, 507
Le May, Curtis E., 464
Lemke, William, 66, 67, 97, 100
lend-lease, 168, 253, 254, 255
Lewis, John L., 77, 80, 83, 159, 232, 233, 293, 309–10
Lexington (aircraft carrier), 192
Leyte Gulf, Battle of, 216
liberalism, 497
Life, 427, 447, 503
Lilienthal, David E., 42, 302, 324
Lima Declaration (1938), 249
Lincoln, Abraham, 243
Lindbergh, Charles A., picture of, 163
Lippmann, Walter, quoted, 342, 440
Literary Digest, The, 99
literature, 511–18
Little Rock, Arkansas, integration issue
  in, 457–59, 510
"Little Steel," 81, 233
"Little Steel formula," 233
Litvinov, Maxim, 142
  picture of, 253
Lodge, Henry Cabot, Jr., 399, 400, 441, 526, 530
London Economic Conference (1933), 137
London *Economist,* 442
Long, Huey P., 65–66, 67, 68, 70, 90, 97
Lovett, Robert A., 343
Lowell, Robert, 513
loyalty, 387–88
  Eisenhower administration and, 427–33
Loyalty Review Board, 388
Lubell, Samuel, 159
Lucas, John P., 204–5
Luce, Henry R., 503
Ludlow, Louis, 148
lumbering, 44–45
luniks, 468
lynching, 509

MacArthur, Douglas, 179, 243, 244, 268
  election of 1948 and, 349
  election of 1952 and, 400
  Korean War and, 372–78
  occupation of Japan, 380
  picture of, 193

INDEX

MacArthur, Douglas (*cont.*)
  relieved of command by Truman, 376
  World War II and, 190, 191, 195, 213, 214, 215, 216, 220, 223, 242
Macassar, 190
Macassar Straits, Battle of, 190
Machado, Gerardo, 139
machines, political, 10, 66
MacLeish, Archibald, 242
Macmillan, Harold, 487
  Berlin crisis and, 485–86
Madden, J. Warren, 79
magazines, 503
  see also names of magazines
Mailer, Norman, 513
Main Currents in American Thought (Parrington), 517
Makin, 215
Malaya, 189
Malenkov, Georgi M., 448, 449
Manchuria, 143, 162, 268, 365, 367, 374
Manila Pact, 444–45
Mansfield, Texas, desegregation issue, 457
Mao Tse-tung, 367, 370, 446–47
Marcantonio, Vito, 341
Mariana Islands, 215
Marine Corps, U. S.
  in Haiti, 139
  Korean War and, 373, 378
  Women's Reserve, 231
Maritime Commission, 93
Maritime Labor Board, 94
Marsh, George Perkins, 44
Marshall, George C., 179, 188, 201, 220, 254
  mission to China, 366
  picture of, 337
  Secretary of State, 322, 328, 335, 362
Marshall Islands, 215, 325
Marshall Plan, 336–42, 352, 360, 371
Martin, Homer, 81, 82
Martin, Joseph W., Jr., 375, 376, 400
Marxism, 497, 517
massive retaliation, doctrine of, 440, 442, 462
Matsu, 446–47
Matsuoka, Yosuke, 172, 173, 174
May, Andrew J., 301
McCarran Internal Security Act (1950), 395

McCarran-Walter Immigration and Nationality Act (1952), 395–96
McCarthy, Joseph R., 391–93, 404, 435
  fall of, 427–32
  picture of, 430
McClellan, George B., 243
McClellan, John L., 472
McCormick, Anne O'Hare, quoted on Franklin D. Roosevelt, 270–71
McCormick, Robert, 349
McGranery, James P., 398
McGrath, J. Howard, 398
McKay, Douglas, 409, 418
McMahon, Brien, 301
McNamara, Robert S., 531, 532
McNary, Charles L., 153
McNutt, Paul V., 121, 232
McReynolds, James C., 105, 108, 112
Means, Gardiner C., 25
Meany, George, 472
mechanization, 128, 231
medical care, 425–26
Medical Care Act (1960), 426
medicine, progress in, 223, 519
Medina, Harold R., 393
Merchant Marine Act (1936), 93
Meredith, James, 510
Merriam, Frank, 64
Mexico
  U. S. relations with, 139–40
  World War II and, 248
Middle East crisis, 473–79
Middle East Treaty Organization (METO), 476
Middle South Utilities, Inc., 421
Middleton, Troy H., 211
Midway Island, World War II and, 192, 194, 213, 215
Mikolajczyk, Stanislaw, 262
Miller, Arthur, 515
Miller, Nathan L., 60
minimum wages, 117–20, 358, 423, 533
Mink Ranchers' Association, 397
Minnesota Farmer-Labor party, 63
missile program, 464, 480
Mississippi, University of, integration issue at, 510
Missouri (battleship), 223
Mitchell, James P., 410, 454
Mitscher, Marc A., 217
"Mohawk Valley Formula," 85

INDEX 553

Moley, Raymond, 11, 36, 58
Molotov, Vyacheslav M., 255, 256, 318, 319, 320, 321, 322, 328, 339
  San Francisco Conference and, 284
Molotov Plan, 340
Mongolian People's Republic, 268
monopolies, attitude of federal government toward, 116
Monroe Doctrine, 135, 138–39, 149, 362
Monroney, Mike, 302
Montgomery, Alabama, desegregation issue, 461–62, 509
Montgomery, Bernard, 197, 202, 204, 206, 209, 211
Moore, Marianne, 513
Morgan, Arthur E., 11, 42, 43
Morgan, Harcourt, 42
Morgenthau, Henry, Jr., 11, 24, 266, 304
Morison, Samuel Eliot, 519
Morris, Newbold, 398
Moscow Conference, 206, 251, 255
Motor Carrier Act (1935), 91
Mountbatten, Louis, 218
Mueller, Frederick H., 473
Mundt, Karl, 404
Munich conference, 149, 156
Municipal Bankruptcy Act (1934), 34
Muñoz Marín, Luis, 363–64
Murphree, Eger V., 464
Murphy, Frank, 82, 112, 241
Murray, Philip, 80, 81, 379
Muscle Shoals, 42
music, 516
Mussolini, Benito, 156, 159, 161, 171, 202, 203–4, 320
Mutual Defense Assistance Act (1949), 344
Mutual Security Administration (MSA), 340 n., 402

Nagasaki, atomic bomb attack on, 223
Nagumo, Chuichi, 180, 194
Naked and the Dead, The (Mailer), 513
Nasser, Gamel Abdel, 475–79
National Aeronautics and Space Administration (NASA), 468, 487
National Association for the Advancement of Colored People (NAACP), 510
National Association of Manufacturers, 85, 295

National Bituminous Coal Commission, 91
national budget (*see* budget, national)
National Citizens Political Action Committee, 245
National Council of Churches, 497
national debt (*see* debt, national)
National Defense Education Act (1958), 427
National Defense Mediation Board (NDMB), 232
National Defense Research Committee, 152
National Housing Act (1934), 35; (1949), 358
national income, 127, 504
National Industrial Recovery Act (1933), 23, 30–33, 76, 78
  declared unconstitutional, 32, 71, 72, 78, 105
National Labor-Management Conference, 293
National Labor Relations Board (NLRB), 78–79, 81, 83, 85, 234, 310, 311
National Military Establishment, 314, 315
National Progressives of America, 64
National Recovery Administration, 30–33, 59, 71, 72, 119, 127
National Recovery Plan, Townsend's, 67
National Recovery Review Board, 32
National Resources Board, 47
National Security Act (1947), 312, 313–15
National Security Council (NSC), 315
National Security Resources Board (NSRB), 315
National War Labor Board (NWLB), 233, 238
National Youth Administration, 71, 74
Natural Gas Act (1938), 417
Navy, U. S.
  strength of, 135
  World War II and, 195, 196
  see also armed forces
Nazis, 133, 135, 144, 150–51, 159, 164, 170–72, 204, 253
  war criminals, trials of, 326–27
Nazi-Soviet Nonaggression Pact (1939), 69
Nebbia v. New York, 105
Negroes
  civil rights and, 455–62, 509
  discrimination against, 241–42, 508–11

554 INDEX

Negroes (cont.)
Fair Employment Practices Committee and, 241
integration controversy, 455–62
status of, 508
voting by, 99, 509
Nelson, Donald, 234
neutrality, Franklin D. Roosevelt and, 145–48, 150–51
neutrality acts, 145–47, 151
Nevins, Allan, 519
New Britain, 190, 194, 213, 214
"New Critics," 517
New Deal, 3–132, 297, 498, 503
agriculture and, 24–29, 116–17
banking and utility legislation, 88–89
beginning of, 18–50
conservation and, 44–49
credit, currency, and finance and, 33–40
decline of, 120–21
economic system and, 126–30
federal budget and, 123–26
industrial recovery under, 29–33
labor and, 76–85, 117–20
opposition to, 59–70, 96, 105, 230
personnel of, 10–12
power industry and, 40–44
purposes of, 12–16
regulation of security markets, 39–40
shipping and, 93–94
social security, 85–88
Supreme Court and, 105–12
tax revision, 89–91
unemployment relief, 20–24
New Frontier, 532–34
New Georgia, 214
New Guinea, 190, 195, 213, 214
New York City, political corruption in, 64
New York Factory Investigation Commission, 5
New York Post, 405
New York State Power Authority, 418, 419–20
New York Times, The, 62, 70, 108, 310, 327, 341, 353, 392, 406, 408, 440, 456, 463, 469, 502
New York World-Telegram, 502
newspapers, 45, 239, 502, 518
see also press; names of papers
Ngo Dinh Diem, 444

Niagara Power Act (1957), 418
Nicaragua, 489
Niebuhr, Reinhold, 497
Nimitz, Chester W., 192, 214–16
picture of, 193
nisei, 240
Nixon, Richard M.
debates with Kennedy, 448, 528
election of 1956 and, 452, 454
election of 1960 and, 524–29
Hiss case and, 388, 390
nomination for Vice President, 400, 405
South American tour, 489
Vice President, 451
visit to Russia, 486
Nixon, Mrs. Richard, 489–90
NLRB v. Friedman-Harry Marks Clothing Company, 79
NLRB v. Jones and Laughlin Steel Corporation, 79, 111
Nomura, Kichisaburo, 174–78
Nonpartisan League (Labor's), 99
Norris, George W., 41, 42
Norris-La Guardia Act, 310
North Atlantic Treaty Organization (NATO), 343–45, 380, 449, 477, 483, 484, 487
nuclear power, 422–23
nuclear testing, 481–83
Nuremberg trials, 326–27
Nye, Gerald P., 145, 247
Nye Committee, 145

O'Connor, John J., 122
Odets, Clifford, 515
oil, 140
Middle East and, 474
offshore, 417
Okinawa Island, 217, 218
Oliphant, Charles, 398
Olson, Floyd B., 63
One World (Willkie), 260
O'Neill, Eugene, 515
Open Door policy, 143
Operation Husky, 201–2
Operation Overlord, 206
Operation Torch, 197–98
Oppenheimer, J. Robert, 221, 432
Organization of American States (OAS), 343, 362, 490

INDEX 555

Outer Mongolia (*see* Mongolian People's Republic)
outer space, 426, 466–69
Oxford, Mississippi, integration issue, 510

pacifism, 145
Padilla, Ezequiel, 248
Pahlevi, Mohammed Reza Shah, 322
painting, 513–15
Palau, 216
Palestine, 474–75
Panama, 139
Pan-American conferences, 140–41, 249, 343, 362, 489
Pan-Americanism, 140, 250, 362
Panay (gunboat), 143
Paris Peace Conference (1946), 319, 328
Parrington, Vernon Louis, 517
Patch, Alexander M., 208
patronage, 19
Patterson, John, 461
Patton, George S., Jr., 202, 206, 208, 211
picture of, 203
Pauley, Edwin W., 304
"peace amendment," 148
peace treaties, World War II, 285, 318–20
"peaceful coexistence," 448
Peale, Norman Vincent, 527
Pearl Harbor, 179, 180, 187–88, 248, 316
Peek, George N., 26, 31
Pendergast, Tom, 280
Peress, Irving, 429
Perkins, Frances, 11, 30
Perón, Juan Domingo, 362–63
Persia (*see* Iran)
Persons, Wilton B. ("Jerry"), 451
Pescadores, 381, 446, 447
Pétain, Henri Philippe, 159, 160, 165, 167
Philippine Military Assistance Act (1946), 382
Philippine Sea, Battle of the, 215
Philippine Trade Act (1946), 382 n.
Philippines
Franklin D. Roosevelt administration and, 142–43
independence proclaimed, 371
Japanese threat to, 143
U. S. mutual assistance treaty with, 382
World War II and, 189–90, 216
picketing, 83, 85, 473
Pine, David A., 379

Pisan Cantos (Pound), 513
Piston, Walter, 516
Pittman Resolution, 165
Platt Amendment, repeal of, 139
Plessy v. Ferguson, 455
poetry, 513
Point Four program, 360–61
Poland
German invasion of, 150–51
postwar plans for, 262–63
Potsdam Conference and, 287
Russian occupation of, 261, 266
Yalta Conference and, 264–66
Political Action Committee, 245
political parties (*see* elections; names of parties)
Pollock, Jackson, 515
Pope, James P., 43
Port Moresby, New Guinea, 195
Potsdam Conference, 200, 283, 284–88, 370
Pound, Ezra, 513
power industry
Eisenhower administration and, 418–23
New Deal and, 40–44
presidential elections (*see* elections)
Presidential Succession Act (1947), 311–13
President's Commission on Immigration and Naturalization, 396
President's Committee on Civil Rights, 356
press, the, 502–3
Franklin D. Roosevelt and, 19
Price Administration, Office of (OPA), 238, 239, 295
price controls, 238
Prince of Wales, H.M.S., 170, 189
Princeton (light carrier), 216
Pritchett, C. Herman, 379
production, World War II and, 229–30, 234–35
Production Management, Office of, 167, 234
Profiles in Courage (Kennedy), 530
Progressive Citizens of America, 352
Progressive National Committee, 99
Progressive party, 63, 351, 352–53
progressivism, Franklin D. Roosevelt and, 5
prohibition, 159
repeal of, 20

556 INDEX

Prohibition party, 97, 100, 247
Project Mercury, 469
Protestantism, 497
psychiatry, 506
public opinion, shaping of, 502
public power (see power industry)
public utilities, 40
  government regulation of, 14
public works, 72–76
Public Works Administration (PWA),
  23–24, 113–14, 89
Puerto Ricans, 508
Puerto Rico, 363–64
Pure Food and Drug Act (1906), 120
Pusey, Merlo J., quoted, 107, 111

Quantico Panel, 450
Quebec Conference, 218, 252
Quemoy, 446–47
Quezon, Manuel, 143

Rabaul, New Britain, 194, 213–14
Radford, Arthur W., 443, 462
radicalism, 511, 513
radio, 502, 507, 516
radioactive fallout, 480, 482
Railroad Pension Act (1934), 92
Railroad Retirement Board v. Alton Railroad Company, 92
railroads, Emergency Railroad Transportation Act and, 34
Rand, James H., 84–85
Rankin, Jeannette, 181
Ransom, John Crowe, 517
Rapacki, Adam, plan for Germany, 485
Raskob, John J., 60
rationing, 239
  end of, 294
Rauch, Basil, quoted, 72
Reader's Digest, 503
recession
  during Eisenhower administration, 469–73
  of 1937–38, 115–16
Reciprocal Trade Act, 437
Reclamation Bureau, 357
Reconstruction Finance Corporation, 12,
  15, 17, 33–34, 126, 397–98
Reed, Stanley, 112
reforestation, 44, 45

refugees
  Hungarian, 441
  Jewish, 499
regulation, government (see government regulation)
religion, 496–99
Rendova, 214
reorganization, government, 120–21, 302–3, 311–15, 359, 465
Reorganization Act (1949), 359
reparations (World War II), 286–87, 319, 321, 345, 381–82
Republican party platforms (see elections)
Repulse, H.M.S., 189
research, 518
Reserve Forces Act (1955), 464
Resettlement Administration, 28, 29, 48, 71
Reston, James, quoted, 270
Reuben James (American destroyer), 169
Reuther, Walter, 294, 310
Rhee, Syngman, 370–73, 377–78
Ribbentrop, Joachim von, 326
Ribicoff, Abraham, 532
Richberg, Donald, 32
Ridgway, Matthew B., 374, 376, 377, 446, 463–64
Rio de Janeiro Treaty (see Inter-American Treaty of Reciprocal Assistance)
Road to Serfdom, The (von Hayek), 299
Roberts, Owen J., 105, 106, 110, 111, 241
Robinson, Jackie, 509
Robinson, Joseph T., 111
Robinson-Patman Federal Anti-Price Discrimination Act (1936), 93
Rockefeller, Nelson A., 450, 471
  election of 1960 and, 524–26
Rodell, Fred, quoted on Alger Hiss case, 391
Roman Catholic Church, 497, 498–99
Rommel, Erwin, 171, 197, 198, 204, 206
Roosevelt, Anna Eleanor, 4, 6, 7
Roosevelt, Franklin Delano
  administration of, 8 ff.
  advisers, 11–12, 15, 16, 17, 19, 23, 115, 133, 259, 297
  antiinflation program, 238
  Arcadia Conference, 205
  Assistant Secretary of the Navy, 5–6
  Atlantic Charter, 170
  atomic bomb and, 220–21

INDEX 557

Roosevelt, Franklin Delano (*cont.*)
bank crisis and, 16–18
biographical sketch, 4–8
cabinet, 10–11, 153
Cairo Conference, 256, 370
Casablanca Conference, 201, 204, 251
Churchill's relationship with, 250–52
Congress and, 19, 71, 113, 114–15, 120, 121–23, 243
congressional elections (1938) and, 121–23
death of, 12, 270–71
"economic Bill of Rights," 298
election of 1936 and, 94–100, 406, 455, 529
election of 1940 and, 152–59
election of 1944 and, 243–47
Fair Employment Practices Committee and, 241, 509
federal budget and, 123–26
fireside chats, 8, 18, 50, 109, 114, 115, 119, 122, 257
first inaugural address, 138
foreign policy, 133 ff.
Four Freedoms, 170
Good Neighbor Policy, 138, 139, 140
governor of New York, 7
health, 246, 247, 270
inaugural address, 3–4
Japanese-Americans and, 240
Latin America and, 138–42
National War Labor Board established, 233
neutrality and, 146–48, 150–51
New Deal, 3–132
Patman bonus bill vetoed by, 92–93
peace plans, 258–63
personality, 8, 51, 271
picture of, 193, 263
popularity, 115, 120, 247
press and, 19
progressivism and, 5
Quebec Conference, 252
recession (1937–1938) and, 115–16
reelection (1936), 99; (1940), 158–59; (1944), 242–48
Russia and, 252–58
second inaugural address, 104–5, 113, 121
second term, 100, 104 ff.
Stilwell recalled by, 218

Roosevelt, Franklin Delano (*cont.*)
Supreme Court and, 105–13
Teheran Conference, 206, 229, 256–57
third nomination, 154–55
United Nations and, 261, 270
victim of infantile paralysis, 6
War Manpower Commission created by, 232
World War II and, 198, 203, 206, 496
Yalta Conference, 263–70
Roosevelt, Theodore, 4, 5, 95, 400, 443
conservation and, 44
Roper, Daniel C., 10
Rosenberg, Ethel, 394
Rosenberg, Julius, 394
Rosenman, Samuel I., 12, 158, 297
Rovere, Richard H., quoted on McCarthy, 392
Rubber Administration, 234
rubber industry, 78
Rumania, 262, 284
peace treaty, 285, 318–19
Rundstedt, Karl von, 211
Rural Electrification Administration, 71, 89, 357
Rusk, Dean, 531–32
Rusk, Howard A., 223
Russell, George William, 25
Russell, Richard, 402, 458
Russia
Anglo-American relations with, 252–58, 316–28
atom bomb exploded by, 370
Berlin crisis and, 345–48
"containment" of, 334, 382
expansionism, 322, 333, 334, 340, 341, 382, 391
Far East and, 364–82
Iranian crisis and, 322–23
Korean War, 370–80
lend-lease and, 253, 254
nuclear testing, 481–82
outer space program, 426, 466–69, 484, 491
Stalin's death, 441, 448
U-2 incident, 487–88
U. S. recognition of, 142
World War II and, 171–72, 198 ff., 205–6, 212, 223, 252–58, 261–63, 267–70
Russo-Finnish War (1940–1941), 167

558 INDEX

Rutledge, Wiley, 112
Ryukyu Islands, 381

St. Lawrence–Great Lakes Seaway project, 357, 419–20
Saipan, 215
Sakhalin, 268, 381
Salinger, J. D., 513
Salk, Jonas, 426
San Francisco, general strike (1934), 77
San Francisco Conference, 249, 282–83, 389
San Martin, Grau, 139
satellites, space, 426, 466–68
Saturday Evening Post, The, 463, 503
savings, 238–39, 294
Savo Island, Battle of, 195
Schechter Poultry Corporation v. the United States, 32, 105
Schine, G. David, 429
schools
  Catholic, 498
  desegregation issue and, 454, 455–59, 510
  see also colleges; education; universities
science, 518–20
Seabury, Samuel, 64
secondary boycott, 473
Securities Act (1933), 49
Securities and Exchange Act (1934), 40, 49
Securities and Exchange Commission, 40, 89, 422, 471
security (*see* collective security; internal security)
security risks, 431
segregation (*see* desegregation; integration controversy)
Selective Service System, 230, 232
  extension of, 289
  Korean War and, 378
Semper Paratus Always Ready Service (SPARS), 231
Senate Subcommittee to Investigate Interstate Crime, 396–97
senators, direct election of, 5
Servicemen's Readjustment Act (1944), 290
Sessions, Roger, 516
sexual mores, 505
Shahn, Ben, 513

Shapiro, Karl, 513
Shaw, Bernard, 516
Shepard, Alan B., Jr., 469
shipping, New Deal and, 93–94
Shipstead, Henrik, 63, 283
Short, Walter, 188
Shouse, Jouett, 60
Sicily, invasion of, during World War II, 201–3, 251, 252
Silver Purchase Act (1934), 38, 49
Sinai peninsula, 477
Sinclair, Upton, 64
Sinclair Oil Company, 140
Sino-Soviet treaty (1945), 269, 381
sit-down strikes, 82, 85
slum clearance projects, 358
Smith, Alfred E., 7, 60, 527
Smith, Ellison D. ("Cotton Ed"), 122
Smith, Gerald L. K., 66, 67, 70, 94
Smith, Walter Bedell, 347
Smith Act (1940), 393, 433
Smith Alien Registration Act (1940), 152, 240
Smith-Connally War Labor Disputes Act (1943), 234, 309
Snyder, John W., 304
social gospel, 498
social justice, 5
Social Justice (magazine), 67
social legislation, 5, 72, 117–20, 423–27
social sciences, 519
social security, 72, 85–88, 297, 358, 423–24
Social Security Act (1935), 86–87; (1950), 358
  amendments, 123
Social Security Board, 123
social trends, 503–7
socialism, 63
Socialist party, 68, 97, 100, 159, 247
  disintegration of, 68
Socialist-Labor party, 97, 100, 159, 247
"socialized medicine," 87, 358, 425
soil conservation, 47–49
Soil Conservation Act (1934), 48, 71
Soil Conservation and Domestic Allotment Act (1936), 93
Soil Conservation Service, 46, 48
soil erosion, 44–48
Soil Erosion Service, 48
Solomon Islands, 194, 214
Sorensen, Theodore C., 532

INDEX

559

South, the, desegregation issue and, 455–62

South America (*see* names of countries)

Southeast Asia Treaty Organization (SEATO), 444–45

Southern Company, 421

Soviet Union (*see* Russia)

space (*see* outer space)

Spain, civil war in, 147

Spanish-American War, 95

Sparkman, John J., 403

speculation, 40

spies, 393–96

Sprague, O. M. W., 11

Spruance, Raymond A., 215

Sputnik I, 426, 466, 467

Sputnik II, 466, 467

Stabilization of the Cost of Living Act (1942), 238

Stalin, Joseph, 171, 198, 206, 212, 223, 252–55, 261–63, 283, 284, 286, 320, 323, 511

  Berlin crisis and, 347

  death of, 441, 448

  Moscow Conference, 206, 251, 255

  picture of, 263, 285

  Potsdam Conference, 283–88

  Teheran Conference, 206, 229, 256–57

  Yalta Conference, 263–70

Stalingrad, Battle of, 199

Stark, Harold R., 179

Stassen, Harold E., 243, 349, 399, 452, 454

State Department, U. S.

  China and, 368, 369, 370

  Japanese peace treaty, 381

  McCarthy's attack on, 428–29

  opposition to postwar plans for Germany, 266

  Point Four program and, 361

states' rights, 106

  integration controversy and, 456

States' Rights Democratic party (Dixiecrats), 351–52, 355

Steagall, Henry B., 17

steel, 78, 80–81

steel mills, Truman's seizure of, 379

Steel Workers Organizing Committee, 81

Steinbeck, John, 47, 517

Stettinius, Edward R., Jr., 264, 266, 284, 304, 389

Stevens, Robert T., 429

Stevens, Wallace, 513

Stevenson, Adlai E.

  election of 1952 and, 401–6

  election of 1956 and, 453–55

  election of 1960 and, 523

  quoted, 379

Stilwell, Joseph W., 189, 195, 218

Stimson, Henry L., 153, 179, 188, 222, 266

  Far East policy and, 179–80

stock exchanges, government regulation of, 14, 39–40

Stone, Edward, 515

Stone, Harlan F., 105, 106, 110, 112

Straus, Nathan, 114

Strauss, Lewis L., 432, 473

strikebreaking, technique of, 84–85

strikes

  after World War II, 293–94

  automobile, 82

  coal, 232, 233, 293, 309–10

  during 1930's, 77, 81–82, 83, 84–85

  General Motors, 293, 294

  Korean War and, 379

  National Defense Mediation Board and, 232

  railroad, 293

  sit-down, 82, 85

  steel, 81, 293, 294, 379

  World War II and, 232–34

subsidies, agricultural, 117

Subsistence Homesteads, Division of, 28

suburbs, 504

Sudan, 475

Suez Canal, 475, 476–77

suffrage, woman, 5

sugar, 25

  Cuban, 139

  Puerto Rican, 363

Sumatra, 190

Summerfield, Arthur E., 409

Sumner, Charles, 460

Sunshine Anthracite Coal Company v. Adkins, 91

Supreme Court, U. S.

  AAA declared unconstitutional, 93, 105–6, 111

  Bill of Rights enforced by, 433

  civil rights decisions, 509

  Communist leaders and, 393

  conservatism and, 105, 113

  desegregation decisions, 454, 455–62, 510

560 INDEX

Supreme Court, U. S. (*cont.*)
  Everson case, 498
  Franklin D. Roosevelt and the, 105–13
  Guffey-Vinson Act upheld by, 91
  Korematsu v. United States, 241
  liberal tendencies, 105, 112–13
  "little NRA" declared unconstitutional, 91
  minimum wage legislation and, 110
  Nebbia v. New York, 105
  New Deal legislation and, 105–12
  NLRB decision upheld by, 81
  NRA declared unconstitutional by, 32, 71, 72, 78, 105
  sit-down strike technique declared illegal, 85
  Wagner Act upheld by, 79, 111, 112
Sutherland, George, 105, 112
Suzuki, Kantaro, 217, 222
Swanson, Claude A., 10
Sweezy v. New Hampshire, 433
Swope, Gerard, 30
Symington, Stuart, 464, 523
Syria, 476, 478

Taber, John, 85
Tachens, 446
Taft, Robert A., 153, 296, 306–7, 310, 336, 341, 358, 369, 372, 409, 412, 413, 428, 440
  death of, 412
  election of 1948 and, 349–50, 355
  election of 1952 and, 398–99, 400, 404
  McCarthyism supported by, 392
  NATO opposed by, 344
  picture of, 307
Taft, William H., 400
Taft-Hartley Labor-Management Relations Act (1947), 309–11, 350, 351, 352, 356, 357, 401, 403, 453
Tamborini, José, 362
Tammany machine, 4–5, 64
Tarawa Island, 215
tariff
  Eisenhower administration and, 437
  Franklin D. Roosevelt administration and, 136, 137
Tate, Allen, 517
taxes
  Eisenhower administration and, 414
  income, 89–91, 125, 236–37, 308–9

taxes (*cont.*)
  Korean War and, 378
  revision of, 89–91, 414
  Truman administration and, 308–9
  withholding of, 237
Taylor, Glen H., 352
Taylor, Myron C., 81
Taylor Grazing Act (1934), 48
Teamsters Union, 472
technical assistance, Point Four program and, 360–61
Teheran Conference, 206, 229, 256–57, 322
Teichert, Edward A., 247
television, 502, 507, 518
Teller, Edward, 432
Temporary Commission on Employee Loyalty, 387
Temporary National Economic Committee, 116
Temporary Unemployment Compensation Act (1958), 470
Tennessee River, 42
Tennessee Valley Authority (TVA), 42–43, 48, 58, 420–22
Thailand, 189
theater, 74, 515–16
Thomas, Norman, 68, 97, 100, 247
Thomas, R. J., 82
Thurmond, James Strom, 352
Tillich, Paul, 497
Time, 71, 389, 503
Tinian, 215
Tito, Marshal, 257, 320
Titov, Gherman S., 469
tobacco, 27
Tocqueville, Alexis de, 342
Togo, Shigenori, 220
Tojo, Hideki, 173, 178, 187, 215, 326 n.
Tokyo, Doolittle's raid on, 191
Townsend, Francis E., 65, 66–67, 68, 70, 86, 94, 97
Townsend plan, 66–67, 86
Toyoda, Teijuro, 174
trade (*see* foreign trade)
Trade Agreements Act (1934), 137
Trade Agreements Extension Act (1958), 437
trade associations, 31
Trade Union Unity League, 69
trade unions
  decline in membership during 1930's, 76

INDEX 561

trade unions (*cont.*)
  growth of, 31
  New Deal and, 76–85
  opposition to, 83–85
  see also labor unions
Trading with the Enemy Act (1917), 17
treaties
  Bricker Amendment and, 436–37
  see also peace treaties; names of treaties
Trieste, 320
Trilling, Lionel, 517
Tripartite Alliance (1940), 161–62
Trujillo, Rafael Leonidas, 490
Truk, 215
Truman, Harry S.
  administration, 281 ff.
  advisers, 281
  agriculture and, 357–58
  assassination attempt, 364
  Berlin crisis and, 347
  biographical sketch, 279–80
  cabinet and, 304–6
  civil rights and, 242, 356–57, 360, 459
  Congress and, 297–98, 356–59
  conservation and, 357
  corruption during administration of, 397–98
  displaced persons, 355–56, 359
  election of 1948 and, 350–56
  election of 1952 and, 401, 402, 403
  election of 1956 and, 453
  election of 1960 and, 523
  Fair Deal, 296–303, 356–64
  Far East and, 364–82
  foreign aid and, 334–42, 344, 355
  foreign policy, 316–28, 333–48, 446
  Germany and, 322
  Hiss case and, 388–91
  Iranian crisis, 323
  Israel recognized by, 475
  Korean War, 364, 370–80
  lend-lease terminated by, 168, 284
  loyalty probe and, 387–88
  MacArthur affair, 374–78
  McCarran Internal Security Act vetoed by, 395
  NATO and, 344
  nomination for Vice President, 244–45
  personality, 281
  picture of, 285, 354
  Point Four program, 360–61

Truman, Harry S. (*cont.*)
  Potsdam Conference, 283–88, 370
  San Francisco Conference, 282–83
  seizure of steel mills, 379
  selective service and, 287–90
  succeeds Franklin D. Roosevelt, 271, 279
  tidelands issue and, 417
  United Nations and, 282–83
Truman Doctrine, 334–36, 342, 352
Tugwell, Rexford G., 11, 18, 25, 28, 30, 58
Tulagi, 194
Tunisia, World War II and, 198
Turkey, U. S. aid to, 334–36
Twentieth Amendment, 70, 104
Twenty-first Amendment, 20
Twenty-second Amendment, 313, 401, 523
Tydings, Millard F., 122, 155
Tydings-McDuffie Act (1934), 142

U-2 incident, 487–88
Udall, Stewart L., 532
unemployment, 3, 14, 28, 59, 72, 86, 94, 115, 130, 470, 471–72, 473
  after World War II, 292
  relief, New Deal and, 20–24, 71, 72–76
unemployment compensation, 123
unemployment insurance, 14, 86
Union of Soviet Socialist Republics (*see* Russia)
Union party, 66, 97, 100
union shop (*see* closed [union] shop)
United Arab Republic, 478
United Automobile Workers, 81–82, 294
United Fruit Company, 489
United Mine Workers, 31, 77, 78, 80, 99, 233, 293, 309–10
United Nations, 260, 352, 360, 401, 402, 436, 452, 454, 533
  Atomic Energy Commission, 324
  atomic energy control, 323–25
  Berlin crisis and, 347
  Charter, 282–83, 284, 343, 344, 349, 371
  Commission on Conventional Armaments, 325
  Congo crisis and, 491
  disarmament subcommittee, 481–82
  Dumbarton Oaks Conference and, 261
  General Assembly, 282, 283, 373, 401
  Hungarian uprising and, 441

562   INDEX

United Nations (*cont.*)
  International Court of Justice, 283
  Iranian crisis and, 322–23
  Korean War and, 364, 370–80
  Middle East crisis and, 477, 478
  nuclear testing ban favored by, 482
  Palestine and, 474
  San Francisco Conference, 249, 282–83
  Secretariat, 283
  Secretary-General, 283
  Security Council, 261, 264, 282, 283, 320, 324, 365, 371–72
  Social and Economic Council, 283
  specialized agencies, 283
  Trieste and, 320
  Truman Doctrine and, 336
  Trusteeship Council, 283
  War Crimes Commission, 326
  World War II peace treaties and, 286
  Yalta Conference and, 264
United Nations Educational, Scientific, and Cultural Organization (UNESCO), 283
United Nations Relief and Rehabilitation Administration (UNRRA), 260, 338
United States Chamber of Commerce, 30, 70
United States Housing Authority, 114
United States Steel Corporation, 60, 81
United States v. Butler, 106
United Steel Workers, 379
universities, 501, 518
urban renewal, 470
Urey, Harold C., 221

Vandenberg, Arthur H., 94, 95, 153, 301–2, 304, 305, 306, 322, 336, 340, 343, 372, 408
  election of 1948 and, 349, 350
  foreign policy and, 315–16
  opinion of Alger Hiss, 389
Vandenberg Resolution, 343, 344
Vanderlip, Frank A., 37
Van Der Rohe, Mies, 515
Van Devanter, Willis, 105, 110, 111–12
Vanguard I, 468
Vargas, Getulio, 248
Vaughan, Harry, 397
Venezia Giulia, 320

Versailles Treaty, 133, 134
veterans (*see* war veterans)
Veterans' Administration, 290
Veterans' Placement Service, 290
Victor Emmanuel III, 203
Vietminh, 444
Vietnam, 444
vigilantes, 84
Vinson, Carl, 466
Vinson, Fred M., 304, 401
"Voice of America" radio broadcasts, 428
Von Hayek, Friedrich A., 299
Vostok I, 468

Wadsworth, James W., Jr., 60
Wage Stabilization Board, 379
wages
  Fair Labor Standards Act and, 117–20
  minimum, 117–20, 358, 423, 533
  World War II and, 233, 238
Wages and Hours Law (*see* Fair Labor Standards Act)
Wagner, Robert F., 78
Wagner Act (1935), 68, 72, 78–80, 85, 111, 112, 123, 154, 309, 310
Wagner-Crosser Railroad Retirement Act (1935), 91–92
Wagner-Steagall National Housing Act (1937), 113, 114
Wake Island, 189, 374
Walker, Frank C., 174
Walker, Walton H., 373
Wallace, DeWitt, 503
Wallace, Henry A., 11, 25, 26, 28, 116, 244, 245, 258, 328, 341
  election of 1948 and, 352, 355
  nomination for Vice President, 155
  resignation as Secretary of Commerce, 304, 305
Walsh-Healy Public Contracts Act (1936), 119
war criminals, trials of, 287, 326–27
War Information, Office of, 242
War Manpower Commission (WMC), 232, 241
War Mobilization and Reconversion, Office of, 291–92
War Mobilization, Office of, 292
War Production Board (WPB), 234, 235, 241, 291, 292

INDEX   563

war veterans
benefits, 290–91
Patman bonus bill vetoed by Franklin D. Roosevelt, 92–93
Warren, Earl, 240, 349, 350, 399, 400
Chief Justice, 432–33
Warren, George F., 37
Warren, Robert Penn, 512
Warsaw Pact, 449, 484
Washington, George, 44
Watkins, Arthur V., 431
Watkins v. United States, 433
Watson, Claude A., 247
Wavell, Sir Archibald, 191, 195
Wealth Tax Act (1935), 89–91
Webster, Daniel, 308
Wedemeyer, Albert C., 218, 369
Weeks, Sinclair, 409
Weir, Ernest T., 31
Welles, Sumner, 151, 248, 258, 261
Wenzell, Adolphe H., 422
West Coast Hotel Company v. Parrish, 110
Western European Union, 484
Wheeler, Burton K., 108, 109, 110
Wheeler-Lea Food, Drug, and Cosmetic Act (1938), 119–20
Wheeler-Rayburn Public Utility Holding Company Act (1935), 72, 88
White, Paul Dudley, 451
White, Stanford, 515
White, Theodore H., 525, 526, 527, 528
White, William Allen, 163, 164
White America, Inc., 456
White Citizens' Councils, 456
White House Office for Emergency Management, 152
Why England Slept (Kennedy), 530
Wiley-Dondero Act (1954), 419
Wilkins, J. Ernest, 459
Williams, Aubrey, 74
Williams, S. Clay, 32
Williams, Tennessee, 515
Williams, William Carlos, 513
Willkie, Wendell L., 43, 243
death of, 245
election of 1940 and, 153–59
One World, 260
Wilson, Charles E. (General Electric Company), 378

Wilson, Charles E. (General Motors Corporation), 408–9, 413, 462, 464, 465
Wilson, Edmund, 517
Wilson, Milburn L., 25
Wilson, Woodrow, 5, 6, 313, 529
Brandeis appointed to Supreme Court by, 105
Fourteen Points, 170
Winters, Yvor, 517
Wisconsin Progressive party, 63–64
Witte, Edwin E., 310
women
armed forces and, 231
labor force and, 231
suffrage, 5
Women Appointed for Voluntary Emergency Service (WAVES), 231
Women's Auxiliary Army Corps (WAAC), 231
Wood, Robert E., 37, 164
Woodin, William H., 11, 17
workmen's compensation, 5
Works Progress Administration, 12, 71, 73–76, 514
Works Projects Administration, 73
World Court (*see* International Court of Justice)
World Monetary and Economic Conference, 36
World War I, economic results of, 135
World War II
agriculture and, 231
Atlantic Charter and, 170
Battle of Britain, 160
beginning of, 150
Berlin Pact, 161
civil liberties and, 239–42
conscription, 230
cost of, 223–24, 259
end of, 223, 288
expansion of Axis power, 170 ff.
financing of, 236–38
Germany's unconditional surrender, 213
industry and, 229–30, 234–35
labor and, 231–34
lend-lease and, 168, 253, 254, 255
peace treaties, 285, 318–20
Pearl Harbor attack, 179, 180, 187–88
price controls, 238

564 INDEX

World War II (*cont.*)
  rationing, 239
  reparations, 286–87, 319, 321, 345, 381–82
  U. S. entry into, 181, 186
  U. S. participation in, 186 ff.
Wright, Fielding Lewis, 352
Wright, Frank Lloyd, 514, 515

Yalta Conference, 263–70, 284, 389, 435, 439

Yamamoto, Isoroku, 192
Yamato (battleship), 217
Yates, Eugene A., 421
Yates v. United States, 433
yellow-dog contracts, 77
Yorktown (aircraft carrier), 194
Youngstown Sheet and Tube Company v. Charles Sawyer, 379
Yugoslavia, 257, 262, 320, 321

Zwicker, Ralph, 429